2021

Guidebook to
ILLINOIS
TAXES

Wolters Kluwer

Wolters Kluwer Editorial Staff Publication

Editors . . . . Timothy Bjur, Brian Nudelman

Production Coordinator . . . . Govardhan. L

Production Editors . . . . Shashikant G, Ravikishore. M

This publication is designed to provide accurate and authoritative information in regard to the subject matter covered. It is sold with the understanding that the publisher is not engaged in rendering legal, accounting or other professional service. If legal advice or other expert assistance is required, the services of a competent professional person should be sought. All views expressed in this publication are those of the author and not necessarily those of the publisher or any other person.

ISBN: 978-0-8080-5477-1

No claim is made to original government works; however, within this publication, the following are subject to CCH Incorporated's copyright: (1) the gathering, compilation, and arrangement of such government materials; (2) the magnetic translation and digital conversion of data, if applicable; (3) the historical, statutory and other notes and references; and (4) the commentary and other materials.

Do not send returns to the above address. If for any reason you are not satisfied with your book purchase, it can easily be returned within 30 days of shipment. Please go to *support.cch.com/returns* to initiate your return. If you require further assistance with your return, please call: (800) 344-3734 M-F, 8 a.m. – 6 p.m. CT.

Printed in the United States of America

PREFACE

This *Guidebook* gives a general picture of the taxes imposed by the state of Illinois and the general property tax levied by the local governments. All 2020 legislative amendments received as of press time are reflected, and references to Illinois and federal laws are to the laws as of the date of publication of this book.

The emphasis is on the law applicable to the filing of income tax returns in 2021 for the 2020 tax year. However, if legislation has made changes effective after 2020, we have tried to note this also, with an indication of the effective date to avoid confusion.

The taxes of major interest—income and sales and use—are discussed in detail. Other Illinois taxes are summarized, with particular emphasis on application, exemptions, returns, and payment.

Throughout the *Guidebook,* tax tips are highlighted to help practitioners avoid pitfalls and use the tax laws to their best advantage.

The *Guidebook* is designed as a quick reference work, describing the general provisions of the various tax laws, regulations, and administrative practices. It is useful to tax practitioners, businesspersons, and others who prepare or file Illinois returns or who are required to deal with Illinois taxes.

The *Guidebook* is not designed to eliminate the necessity of referring to the law and regulations for answers to complicated problems, nor is it intended to take the place of detailed reference works such as the CCH ILLINOIS TAX REPORTS. With this in mind, specific references to the publisher's Illinois and federal tax products are inserted in most paragraphs. By assuming some knowledge of federal taxes, the *Guidebook* is able to provide a concise, readable treatment of Illinois taxes that will supply a complete answer to most questions and will serve as a time-saving aid where it does not provide the complete answer.

SCOPE OF THE BOOK

This *Guidebook* is designed to do three things:

1. Give a general picture of the impact and pattern of all taxes levied by the state of Illinois and the general property tax levied by local governmental units.

2. Provide a readable quick-reference work for the personal income tax and the tax on corporate income. As such, it explains briefly what the Illinois law provides and indicates whether the Illinois provision is the same as federal law.

3. Analyze and explain the differences, in most cases, between Illinois and federal law.

HIGHLIGHTS OF 2020 ILLINOIS TAX CHANGES

The most important 2020 Illinois tax changes received by press time are noted in the "Highlights of 2020 Illinois Tax Changes" section of the *Guidebook*, beginning on page 7. This useful reference gives the practitioner up-to-the-minute information on changes in tax legislation.

FINDERS

The practitioner may find the information wanted by consulting the general Table of Contents at the beginning of the *Guidebook*.

October 2020

CONTENTS

HIGHLIGHTS OF 2020 ILLINOIS TAX CHANGES

The most important 2020 tax changes and new developments are noted below.

Sales and Use Taxes

- *Economic nexus for marketplace facilitators*

Marketplace facilitators may find themselves liable for Illinois use and service use tax beginning in 2020. Illinois omnibus tax legislation includes the economic nexus thresholds and rules that will apply to marketplace facilitators. A marketplace facilitator that meets one of two economic thresholds for nexus in Illinois will be a retailer under sales and use tax law, effective January 1, 2020. The thresholds are similar to existing thresholds for out-of-state sellers:

- the total revenues from sales by the marketplace facilitator and marketplace sellers are $100,000 or more; or

- the marketplace facilitator and marketplace sellers enter into 200 or more sales transactions.

(P.A. 101-09 (S.B. 689), Laws 2019, effective as noted) (¶60-025)

- *Economic Nexus to Apply to Retailers' Occupation Tax*

Illinois has enacted economic nexus for retailers' occupation tax purposes effective July 1, 2020. Economic nexus already applies to remote retailers and marketplace facilitators with respect to Illinois use and service use tax. (S.B. 690, Laws 2019, effective as noted) (¶60-025)

- *Sourcing and Additional Nexus Changes Enacted*

Illinois enacts sourcing and additional use tax changes concerning the $100,000/200-transaction economic nexus thresholds. (P.A. 101-0031 (S.B. 690), Laws 2019, effective June 28, 2019 and applicable as noted) (¶60-025)

Sourcing changes. On July 1, 2020, Illinois requires remote retailers that satisfy an economic nexus threshold to use destination sourcing rather than origin sourcing for local retailers' occupation tax rate purposes.

Nexus changes. For remote retailers, satisfying an economic nexus threshold beginning July 1, 2020, no longer triggers a use tax collection obligation, but triggers the new retailers' occupation tax collection obligation. For marketplace facilitators, satisfying an economic nexus threshold beginning January 1, 2020, triggers a use and service use tax collection obligation.

- *Second Budget Implementation Act Enacted*

Enacted Illinois legislation creates the Second FY2020 Budget Implementation Act that, among other things, does the following:

- requires both remote retailers and marketplace facilitators to collect and remit the state and locally imposed retailers' occupation tax for the jurisdictions where the product is delivered starting Jan. 1, 2021;

- makes changes to aviation fuel tax returns;

- removes the requirement that a sales and use tax exemption certificate is required for each transaction qualifying for the manufacturing and assembly exemption;

- provides that the municipal motor fuel tax will be imposed as a retailers' occupation tax on the occupation of selling motor fuel and providing for its collection;

- makes changes to the data center sales and use tax exemption; and

- adds a yearly Consumer Price Index (CPI) increase to motor fuel taxes imposed by county boards in DuPage, Kane, Lake, Will, and McHenry counties.

(P.A. 101-0604 (S.B. 119), Laws 2019, effective December 13, 2019, except as noted)

• *Illinois Legalizes Recreational Marijuana, Taxing its Distribution and Sale*

Illinois legalizes growing and selling cannabis as of June 25, 2019, and taxes cannabis sales as well, as of September 1, 2019. The state imposes:

- a cannabis purchaser excise tax, varying from 10% to 25%;
- a 7% privilege tax on cannabis cultivation centers;
- a 7% privilege tax on craft growers of cannabis; and
- a 7% "cannabis cultivation privilege tax" on both cultivation centers and craft growers.

Purchaser excise tax on cannabis. The "sales tax" rate on recreational marijuana depends on the level of delta-9-tetrahydrocannabinol (THC) in the cannabis. A retail sale of cannabis with a level of THC at or below 35% is subject to a 10% tax rate. If the level of THC exceeds 35%, the tax rate is 25%. Retail sales of cannabis-infused products are subject to a 20% tax rate. The cannabis purchaser excise tax is imposed in addition to all other state and local sales and use taxes in Illinois.

Privilege taxes on cultivation and craft growers. Illinois imposes general privilege taxes based on the gross receipts either a cultivator or craft grower receives from selling cannabis to a dispensing organization.

Cannabis cultivation privilege tax. The "cannabis cultivation privilege tax" is imposed on the first sale of cannabis as of September 1, 2019. This tax ensures that sales between affiliated persons are taxed, such as a sale from a craft grower to the craft grower's dispensing organization.

Returns and payments. All returns and tax payments for cannabis tax: are due monthly; and must be filed electronically.

Municipalities and counties. Beginning September 1, 2020, all municipalities and counties may impose a local cannabis retailers' occupation tax upon all persons engaged in the business of selling cannabis, other than medical cannabis, at retail in the municipality or county on the gross receipts from cannabis sales. Municipalities may impose a tax at a rate that may not exceed 3%, imposed in 1/4% increments. Counties may impose a tax (also in 1/4% increments) at the following rates: (1) in unincorporated areas of the county, the rate may not exceed 3.75%; and (2) in a municipality located in the county, the rate may not exceed 3%. (H.B. 1438 and S.B. 2023, Laws 2019, effective as noted) (¶60-520)

• *State Parking Tax Enacted*

Illinois has enacted a state-level parking tax that takes effect January 1, 2020. The tax is imposed at these rates:

- 6% of the purchase price for a parking space paid for on an hourly, daily, or weekly basis; and
- 9% of the purchase price for a parking space paid for on a monthly or annual basis.

The tax will apply to charges for parking spaces in parking areas and garages used to park one or more: motor vehicles, recreational vehicles, or other self-propelled vehicles. The operator must collect the tax from the purchaser. (P.A. 101-0031 (S.B. 690), Laws 2019, effective June 28, 2019, and applicable as noted) (¶60-570)

• *Manufacturing exemption expanded*

Supplies and consumables used in manufacturing are exempt from Illinois sales and use tax beginning July 1, 2019. A manufacturer's use of the item also must meet existing requirements for its purchase to qualify for the exemption. For example, the property must be primarily used in manufacturing and assembly. Further, product or good manufactured or assembled must be for wholesale or retail sale or lease. (P.A. 101-09 (S.B. 689), Laws 2019, effective as noted) (¶60-510)

- *Trade-In Exemption Changed to Apply to Vehicles and Capped*

Enacted Illinois legislation makes changes to sales tax exemptions on trade-ins. Specifically, effective January 1, 2020, the legislation eliminates the sales tax exemption for the value of or credit given for traded-in personal property where the item that is traded-in is of like kind and character as that being sold. Also, a partial sales tax exemption for certain traded-in vehicles is enacted. Specifically, the taxable "selling price" will only include the part of the value or credit given for the vehicle of like kind and character as that being sold that exceeds $10,000. The vehicles to which this change applies are those designed to carry up to 10 persons. (S.B. 690, Laws 2019, effective as noted)

- *Incentives for Data Centers Enacted*

Illinois has enacted retailers' occupation, use, service use, service occupation, and electricity excise tax incentives for data centers. The exemption is available through June 30, 2019. To document the exemption, the retailer must obtain from the purchaser a copy of the certificate of eligibility issued by the DOR. (S.B. 690, Laws 2019, effective June 28, 2019, and applicable as noted) (¶ 60-360)

- *Tax on Aviation Fuel Reported on New Return*

Retailers that sell aviation fuel will file an aviation fuel tax return for sales tax collected on fuel sold for aircraft as of January 1, 2020. The aviation fuel tax return is due, with payment, on or before the 20th day of each month. The Department of Revenue may require electronic filing of the returns. (P.A. 101-09 (S.B. 1814), Laws 2019, effective as noted) (¶ 60-560)

Income Taxes

- *Illinois extends student-assistance contributions credit sunset date*

Illinois extended a corporate and personal tax credit for employers that match employee contributions to Illinois college savings programs. It extended the sunset date from December 31, 2020 to December 31, 2021. (P.A. 101-645 (S.B. 1857), Laws 2020, effective June 26, 2020) (¶¶ 12-001, 16-805)

- *Illinois amends related-party addback regulations*

Illinois amended corporate and personal income tax regulations that reflect, among other changes, elimination of the related-party expense addback requirement for noncombination rule companies. The regulations also provide guidance on computing the IRC Sec. 163(j) interest expense deduction limits for related-party interest paid. (86 Ill. Adm. Code Secs. 100.2430) (¶¶ 10-620, 16-125)

- *Illinois releases COVID-19 withholding guidance*

Illinois released personal income tax withholding guidance for employers due to the COVID-19, or coronavirus, outbreak. The guidance applies to out-of-state employers who employ Illinois residents working from home during the pandemic. (*Informational Bulletin FY 2020-29*, Illinois Department of Revenue, May 19, 2020) (¶ 16-615)

- *Illinois adopts combined reporting apportionment rules*

Illinois adopted final rules on how unitary groups compute tax liability if the group includes members who use different apportionment formulas. (86 Ill. Adm. Code Secs. 100.3600) (¶ 11-550)

Miscellaneous Taxes

- *Motor Fuel Rates Increased*

Effective July 1, 2019, the following state motor fuel rates apply:
  - Gasoline/Gasohol - $0.38 per gallon (previously, $0.19 per gallon)
  - Diesel - $45.5 per gallon (previously, $21.5 per gallon)
  - CNG - $0.38 per gallon (previously, $0.19 per gallon)
  - LNG - $0.455 per gallon (previously, $0.215 per gallon)
  - LPG - $0.455 per gallon (previously, $0.215 per gallon)

In addition, municipalities in Cook County are authorized to levy a motor fuel tax at a rate of up to $0.03 per gallon. (P.A. 101-32 (S.B. 1939), Laws 2019, effective June 28, 2019, and applicable as noted; Notice, Illinois Department of Revenue, June 28, 2019, ¶ 403-436; Motor Fuel Tax Rates and Fees, Illinois Department of Revenue, July 1, 2019) (¶ 40-001, ¶ 40-003, and ¶ 40-007)

- *Cigarette Rate Hike Enacted*

Effective July 1, 2019, Illinois cigarette tax rates are as follows:

- 149 mills per cigarette or $2.98 per pack of 20 (previously, 99 mills per cigarette or $1.98 per pack of 20)

- 149 mills (previously, 99 mills) per cigarette made or fabricated in a cigarette machine owned by a licensed cigarette machine operator.

(P.A. 101-0031 (S.B. 690), Laws 2019, effective June 28, 2019, and applicable as noted; Excise Tax Rates and Fees, Illinois Department of Revenue, July 1, 2019) (¶ 55-001)

- *E-Cigarette Tax Enacted*

Effective July 1, 2019, a state-level tobacco products tax is imposed on electronic cigarettes at the rate of 15%. The tax is imposed on the wholesale price of e-cigarettes sold or disposed of to Illinois retailers or consumers. It is imposed in addition to other state and local occupation or privilege taxes. (P.A. 101-0031 (S.B. 690), Laws 2019, effective June 28, 2019 and applicable as noted) (¶ 55-001)

- *Tax on Sports Betting Enacted*

Illinois has enacted state taxes on sports betting. Under the new Sports Wagering Act, a sports wagering tax is imposed on:

- 15% of a master sports wagering licensee's adjusted gross sports wagering receipts from sports wagering. The accrual method of accounting must be used to calculate the tax owed. The tax is due to the Illinois Gaming Board by the last day of the month following the calendar month when the receipts were received; and

- an additional 2% of adjusted gross sports wagering receipts from wagers placed within a home rule county with a population over 3 million.

(P.A. 101-0031 (S.B. 690), Laws 2019, effective June 28, 2019 and applicable as noted) (¶ 35-001)

- *Video Gaming Tax Increased*

The tax on video gaming net terminal income increases:

- from 30% to 33% on July 1, 2019; and

- from 33% to 34% on July 1, 2020.

(P.A. 101-0031 (S.B. 690), Laws 2019, effective June 28, 2019 and applicable as noted) (¶ 35-001)

All Taxes

- *Amnesty in 2019*

Illinois offered a tax amnesty program for all state taxes from October 1, 2019, to November 15, 2019. The program applies to unreported or unpaid tax liabilities for the tax periods ending after June 30, 2011, and before July 1, 2018. Penalties and interest are waived on a qualifying delinquency if the delinquency is paid and the return is filed during the amnesty program's duration. The taxpayer must pay all delinquent taxes that were due to qualify for amnesty. (P.A. 101-09 (S.B. 689), Laws 2019, effective as noted)

CORPORATE INCOME

[¶10-050]

FEDERAL/MULTISTATE ISSUES

[¶10-055] Comparison of Federal/State Key Features

The following is a comparison of key features of federal income tax laws that have been enacted as of March 27, 2020, and the Illinois corporate income tax law. The starting point for computing Illinois corporation income and replacement tax liability is federal taxable income after the net operating loss and special deductions. Federal taxable income is modified by Illinois addition and subtraction adjustments. Federal conformity for purposes of computing the Illinois corporation income tax is based on the Internal Revenue Code as amended to date.

• *Foreign Tax Credit (IRC Sec. 27)*

Illinois has no equivalent to the federal foreign tax credit (IRC Sec. 27). It also does not allow a subtraction from federal taxable income for foreign income, franchise, or capital stock taxes if the federal foreign tax credit is taken (see ¶ 10-510).

• *Alcohol Fuels Credit (IRC Sec. 40)*

Illinois has no equivalent to the federal alcohol fuels credit (IRC Sec. 40). It allows a subtraction from federal taxable income for amount of the credit that taxpayers must include in federal gross income if the federal credit is taken (see ¶ 10-855).

• *Incremental Research Expenditures Credit (IRC Sec. 41)*

Illinois provides a credit for research and development expenses in the state that qualify for the federal credit (IRC Sec. 41) (see ¶ 12-001). It also allows a subtraction from federal taxable income for expenses disallowed as deductions under IRC Sec. 280C if the federal credit is taken (see ¶ 10-855).

• *Low-Income Housing Credit (IRC Sec. 42)*

Illinois has no equivalent to the federal low-income housing credit. (IRC Sec. 42) It provides a credit for donations to sponsors of affordable housing projects (see ¶ 12-001).

• *Disabled Access Credit (IRC Sec. 44)*

Illinois has no equivalent to the federal disabled access credit (IRC Sec. 44).

• *Indian Employment Credit (IRC Sec. 45A)*

Illinois has no equivalent to the federal Indian employment credit (IRC Sec. 45A). It allows a subtraction from federal taxable income for wages or salaries disallowed as a deduction IRC Sec. 280C if the federal credit is taken (see ¶ 10-855).

• *Employer Social Security Credit (IRC Sec. 45B)*

Illinois has no equivalent to the federal employer social security credit (IRC Sec. 45B).

• *Orphan Drug Credit (IRC Sec. 45C)*

Illinois has no equivalent to the federal orphan drug credit (IRC Sec. 45C). It allows a deduction for expenses disallowed as deductions under IRC Sec. 280C if the federal credit is taken (see ¶ 10-855).

• *New Markets Credit (IRC Sec. 45D)*

Illinois provides a credit for investments in a qualified community development entities (CDEs) that participate in the federal new markets tax credit program (IRC Sec. 45D) and provide financing to businesses in Illinois low-income communities (see ¶ 12-001).

• *Small Employer Pension Plan Start-Up Costs (IRC Sec. 45E)*

Illinois has no equivalent to the federal small employer pension plan start-up costs credit (IRC Sec. 45E).

• *Employer-Provided Child Care Credit (IRC Sec. 45F)*

Illinois has no equivalent to the federal employer-provided child care credit (IRC Sec. 45F). It provides a credit to employers for the start-up and operating costs for Illinois employee child care facilities (see ¶ 12-001).

• *Fuel from Nonconventional Source Credit (IRC Sec. 45K)*

Illinois has no equivalent to the federal fuel from nonconventional source credit (IRC Sec. 45K).

• *New Energy Efficient Homes Credit (IRC Sec. 45L)*

Illinois has no equivalent to the federal new energy efficient homes credit (IRC Sec. 45L).

• *Energy Efficient Appliances Credit for Manufacturers (IRC Sec. 45M)*

Illinois has no equivalent to the federal energy efficient appliances credit for manufacturers (IRC Sec. 45M).

• *Investment Credit (Former Law) (IRC Sec. 46 — IRC Sec. 49)*

Illinois has no equivalent to the former federal investment or reforestation credits (IRC Sec. 48). Illinois also has no equivalent to the federal energy credit (IRC Sec. 48) or the federal advanced energy project credit (IRC Sec. 48C). It provides a credit for historic structure rehabilitation expenses (see ¶ 12-001) that qualify for the federal rehabilitation credit (IRC Sec. 47). It also provides credits similar to federal investment credits (IRC Sec. 48A and 48B) for investments in gasification and coal based energy generating facilities (see ¶ 12-001).

• *Wage Credits (IRC Secs. 51 — 52 and IRC Sec. 1396))*

Illinois has no equivalent to the federal work opportunity credit (IRC Sec. 51— IRC Sec. 52) or the empowerment zone employment credit (IRC Sec. 1396). It allows a subtraction from federal taxable income for wages disallowed under IRC Sec. 280C if the federal credit is taken (see ¶ 10-855). It also allows a credit for hiring ex-felons (see ¶ 12-001).

• *Alternative Minimum Tax (IRC Sec. 55 — IRC Sec. 59)*

Illinois has no equivalent to the federal alternative minimum tax on tax preference items (IRC Sec. 55—IRC Sec. 59).

• *Base Erosion and Anti-Abuse Tax (IRC Sec. 59A)*

Illinois has no equivalent to the base erosion and anti-abuse tax (BEAT) (IRC Sec. 59A).

• *Deemed Dividends (IRC Sec. 78)*

Illinois allows a subtraction from federal taxable income (see ¶ 10-810) for foreign dividend gross-up income (IRC Sec. 78).

¶10-055

• *Interest on Federal Obligations*

Illinois allows a subtraction from federal taxable income for interest on federal obligations that is exempt from state taxation. It also allows a subtraction for mutual fund distributions from federal obligations (see ¶10-815).

• *Interest on State Obligations (IRC Sec. 103)*

Illinois requires an addition to federal taxable income (see ¶10-610) for interest income received from state or local obligations (IRC Sec. 103), including Illinois and its localities.

• *Discharge of Indebtedness (IRC Sec. 108)*

The same as federal (IRC Sec. 108) because the starting point for computing Illinois corporation income and replacement tax liability is federal taxable income (see ¶10-510). Illinois requires a reduction to any net operating loss (NOL) for income from the discharge of indebtedness that a taxpayer excluded from federal taxable income (see ¶10-805).

• *Contributions to the Capital of a Corporation (IRC Sec. 118)*

The same as federal (IRC Sec. 118), because the starting point for determining Illinois corporation income and replacement tax liability is federal taxable income (see ¶10-510).

• *Certain Excessive Employee Remuneration (IRC Sec. 162(m))*

The same as federal (IRC Sec. 162(m)), because the starting point for determining Illinois corporation income and replacement tax liability is federal taxable income (see ¶10-510).

• *Interest on Indebtedness (IRC Sec. 163)*

The same as federal (IRC Sec. 163, including IRC Sec. 163(j)) because the starting point for computing Illinois corporation income and replacement tax liability is federal taxable income (see ¶10-510).

• *Income and Franchise Tax Deductions (IRC Sec. 164)*

Illinois requires an addition to federal taxable income if the taxpayer deducted Illinois income or replacement tax on its federal return (see ¶10-615).

• *Losses (IRC Sec. 165)*

The same as federal (IRC Sec. 165) because the starting point for computing Illinois corporation income and replacement tax liability is federal taxable income (see ¶10-510).

• *Bad Debts (IRC Sec. 166)*

The same as federal (IRC Sec. 166) because the starting point for computing Illinois corporation income and replacement tax liability is federal taxable income (see ¶10-510).

• *Depreciation (IRC Secs. 167, 168, and 1400N)*

Generally the same as federal (IRC Sec. 167, IRC Sec. 168, and IRC Sec. 1400N) because the starting point for computing Illinois corporation income and replacement tax liability is federal taxable income (see ¶10-510). Illinois requires an addition to federal taxable income for IRC Sec. 168(k) bonus depreciation (see ¶10-670). The addition modification does not apply to 100% bonus depreciation. Illinois allows a subtraction from taxable income in the last year of regular depreciation for some or all bonus depreciation. (see ¶10-900).

• *Safe Harbor Leasing (Pre-1984 Leases) (IRC Sec. 168(f))*

Illinois recognizes safe harbor leases under former IRC Sec. 168(f)(8) (see ¶10-670).

• *Pollution Control Facilities Amortization (IRC Sec. 169)*

The same as federal (IRC Sec. 169) because the starting point for computing Illinois corporation income and replacement tax liability is federal taxable income (see ¶10-510).

• *Charitable Contributions (IRC Secs. 170 and 1400S))*

Generally the same as federal (IRC Sec. 170 and IRC Sec. 1400S) because the starting point for computing Illinois corporation income and replacement tax liability is federal taxable income (see ¶10-510). Illinois allows a subtraction from federal taxable income for certain charitable contributions to designated enterprise zone organizations (see ¶10-845).

• *Amortizable Bond Premium (IRC Sec. 171)*

Generally, the same as federal (IRC Sec. 171) because the starting point for computing Illinois corporation income and replacement tax liability is federal taxable income (see ¶10-510). Illinois allows a subtraction from federal taxable income (see ¶10-815) for amortizable bond premiums from tax-exempt bonds disallowed as a deduction under IRC Sec. 171(a)(2).

• *Net Operating Loss (IRC Secs. 172 and 1400N))*

The starting point for computing Illinois corporation income and replacement tax liability is federal taxable income after the net operating loss (NOL) deduction. Illinois requires an addition to federal taxable income (see ¶10-605) for a taxpayer's NOL deduction (IRC Sec. 172). It allows a subtraction from Illinois adjusted and apportioned base income for NOL carryforward from a loss year return. Taxpayers compute the subtraction adjustment based on the federal deduction. Illinois has its own NOL carryforward period and does not allow carrybacks (see ¶10-805).

• *Research and Experimental Expenditures (IRC Sec. 174)*

The same as federal (IRC Sec. 174) because the starting point for computing Illinois corporation income and replacement tax liability is federal taxable income (see ¶10-510).

• *Asset Expense Election (IRC Secs. 179 and 1400N)*

The same as federal (IRC Sec. 179) because the starting point for computing Illinois corporation income and replacement tax liability is federal taxable income (see ¶10-510).

• *Energy Efficient Commercial Building Deduction (IRC Sec. 179D)*

The same as federal (IRC Sec. 179A) because the starting point for computing Illinois corporation income and replacement tax liability is federal taxable income (see ¶10-510).

• *Deduction for Barriers Removal (IRC Sec. 190)*

The same as federal (IRC Sec. 190) because the starting point for computing Illinois corporation income and replacement tax liability is federal taxable income (see ¶10-510).

• *Start-Up Expenditures (IRC Sec. 195)*

The same as federal (IRC Sec. 195) because the starting point for computing Illinois corporation income and replacement tax liability is federal taxable income (see ¶10-510).

¶10-055

• *Amortization of Intangibles (IRC Sec. 197)*

The same as federal (IRC Sec. 197) because the starting point for computing Illinois corporation income and replacement tax liability is federal taxable income (see ¶10-510).

• *Domestic Production Activities (IRC Sec. 199)*

Illinois required an addition to federal taxable income (see ¶10-660) for the domestic production activities deduction (DPAD) (IRC Sec. 199). The addition applied only for the 2017 tax year. The federal DPAD was repealed for tax years beginning after 2017.

• *Pass-Through Deduction (IRC Sec. 199A)*

Illinois has no equivalent to the qualified business income deduction (pass-through deduction) (IRC Sec. 199A). So, it also does not have any pass-through entity reporting requirement for the deduction.

• *Dividends Received Deduction (IRC Sec. 243 — IRC Sec. 245)*

The same as federal (IRC Sec. 243—IRC Sec. 245) because the starting point for computing Illinois corporation and replacement tax liability is federal taxable income after the special dividends deductions (see ¶10-510). Illinois allows a subtraction from federal taxable income for a portion of dividends received from foreign corporations, including both actual and deemed dividends under the IRC (see ¶10-810).

• *Participation Dividends Received Deduction (IRC Sec. 245A)*

The same as federal (IRC Sec. 245A) because the starting point for computing Illinois corporation and replacement tax liability is federal taxable income after the special dividends deductions (see ¶10-510).

• *Organizational Expenditures (IRC Sec. 248)*

The same as federal (IRC Sec. 248) because the starting point for computing Illinois corporation income and replacement tax liability is federal taxable income (see ¶10-510).

• *Foreign-Derived Intangible Income and Global Intangible Low-Taxed Income (IRC Sec. 250)*

Illinois requires an addition to federal taxable income (see ¶10-630) for the deduction allowed in computing global intangible low-taxed income (GILTI) and foreign-derived intangible income (FDII) (IRC Sec. 250).

• *Corporate Distributions and Adjustments (IRC Sec. 301 — IRC Sec. 385)*

The same as federal (IRC Sec. 301—IRC Sec. 385) because the starting point for computing Illinois corporation income and replacement tax liability is federal taxable income (see ¶10-630).

• *Accounting Periods and Methods (IRC Sec. 441 —IRC Sec. 483)*

The same as federal (IRC Sec. 441—IRC Sec. 483) because Illinois adopts federal income tax accounting periods and methods. Illinois also has a provision similar to IRC Sec. 482 that gives the state tax agency the authority to allocate income and deductions among related taxpayers.

• *Exempt Organization (IRC Sec. 501 — IRC Sec. 530)*

Organizations that are exempt from the federal income tax (IRC Sec. 501(a)) are also exempt from the Illinois corporation income and replacement taxes. Exempt organizations must pay tax on unrelated business income to the same extent as under federal law (IRC Sec. 512). This includes the federal rule that exempt organizations with more than one unrelated business must calculate unrelated business taxable income separately for each unrelated trade or business (see ¶ 10-245).

• *Corporations Used to Avoid Shareholder Taxation (IRC Sec. 531 — IRC Sec. 547)*

Illinois has no provisions regarding corporations used to avoid shareholder taxation (IRC Sec. 531—IRC Sec. 547). Illinois also does not impose a tax on accumulated earnings or an additional tax on the undistributed income of personal holding companies (IRC Sec. 541).

• *Banking Institutions (IRC Sec. 581 — IRC Sec. 597)*

Illinois has no equivalent to the federal provisions on financial institutions (IRC Sec. 581—IRC Sec. 597). All banks, investment companies, and savings and loan associations must pay Illinois corporation income and replacement tax to the same extent as corporations (see ¶ 10-340).

• *Natural Resources (IRC Sec. 611 — IRC Sec. 638)*

The same as federal (IRC Sec. 611—IRC Sec. 638) because the starting point for computing Illinois corporation income and replacement tax liability is federal taxable income (see ¶ 10-510).

• *Insurance Companies (IRC Sec. 801 — IRC Sec. 848)*

Illinois does not follow the federal income tax treatment of insurance companies (IRC Sec. 801—IRC Sec. 848). Insurance companies must pay Illinois corporation and replacement taxes in the same manner as other corporations, (see ¶ 10-335) except special apportionment rules apply (see ¶ 11-540). Insurance companies doing business in Illinois must also pay a privilege tax on net premiums (see ¶ 88-001).

• *RICs, REITs, REMICs, and FASITs (IRC Sec. 851 — IRC Sec. 860L)*

In general, Illinois follows the federal treatment (IRC Sec. 611—IRC Sec. 638) of RICs, REITs, and REMICs. Illinois requires an addition to federal taxable income for dividends paid by captive REITs. RICs must include undistributed capital gains in Illinois taxable income (see ¶ 10-525).

Federal provisions on the tax treatment of FASITs (IRC Sec. 860H—IRC Sec. 860L), were generally repealed after 2004.

• *Foreign Source Income (IRC Sec. 861 — IRC Sec. 865)*

Illinois does not follow the foreign sourcing rules (IRC Sec. 861—IRC Sec. 865). Multistate and international businesses that conduct business both in and outside Illinois use the state's allocation (see ¶ 11-515) and apportionment rules (see ¶ 11-520) for determining whether income is from state sources.

• *Foreign Tax Credit (IRC Sec. 901 — IRC Sec. 908)*

Illinois has no equivalent to the federal foreign tax credit (IRC Sec. 901—IRC Sec. 908). It also does not allow a subtraction from federal taxable income for foreign income, franchise, or capital stock taxes if the federal foreign tax credit is taken (see ¶ 10-510).

• *Global Intangible Low-Taxed Income (GILTI) (IRC Sec. 951A)*

The same as federal (IRC Sec. 951A) because the starting point for computing Illinois corporation income and replacement tax liability is federal taxable income after special dividends deductions. Illinois allows a subtraction for part of GILTI under its foreign dividends received deduction (see ¶ 10-810).

• *Transition (Repatriation) Tax (IRC Sec. 965)*

Illinois requires an addition to federal taxable income (see ¶ 10-615) for the foreign income (repatriation) transition tax (IRC Sec. 965). Taxpayers can include part of the IRC Sec. 965 net income in their foreign dividends received subtraction adjustment (see ¶ 10-810).

¶10-055

• *Gain or Loss on Disposition of Property (IRC Sec. 1001 — IRC Sec. 1092)*

Generally, the same as federal (IRC Sec. 1001—IRC Sec. 1092) because the starting point for computing Illinois corporation income and replacement tax liability is federal taxable income (see ¶ 10-510).

• *Alternative Capital Gains Tax (IRC Sec. 1201)*

Illinois does not provide for an alternative tax on capital gains (IRC Sec. 1201).

• *Capital Losses (IRC Secs. 1211 and 1212)*

The same as federal (IRC Sec. 1211 and IRC Sec. 1212) because the starting point for computing Illinois corporation income and replacement tax liability is federal taxable income (see ¶ 10-510).

• *Determining Capital Gains and Losses (IRC Sec. 1221 — IRC Sec. 1260)*

The same as federal (IRC Sec. 1221—IRC Sec. 1260) because the starting point for computing Illinois corporation income and replacement tax liability is federal taxable income (see ¶ 10-510).

• *S Corporations (IRC Sec. 1361 — IRC Sec. 1379)*

Generally, Illinois adopts the federal income tax treatment of S corporations (IRC Sec. 1361—IRC Sec. 1379). S corporations are subject to the Illinois personal property replacement tax (see ¶ 10-215).

• *Empowerment Zones and Renewal Communities (IRC Secs. 1391 — 1397F and IRC Secs. 1400E — 1400J)*

Illinois has no equivalent to the federal provisions regarding empowerment zones and renewal communities (IRC Sec. 1391—IRC Sec. 1400J). It allows a credit for investments in qualified property placed in service in designated enterprise zones (see ¶ 12-001).

• *Consolidated Returns (IRC Sec. 1501 — IRC Sec. 1504)*

Illinois does not allow the filing of consolidated returns. Corporations that are members of the same unitary group must file a combined return (see ¶ 11-550).

[¶ 10-075] Nexus--P.L. 86-272--Doing Business in State

What is the Illinois nexus standard?

Illinois' income tax nexus standard is not based on the physical or factor presence of a nonresident taxpayer in the state. Illinois also has not adopted an "economic presence" standard by statute, regulation, or administrative guidance. Illinois imposes the corporation income tax (35 ILCS 5/201(a); 86 Ill. Adm. Code 100.9720(a)) and personal property replacement income tax (replacement tax) (35 ILCS 5/201(c); 86 Ill. Adm. Code 100.9720(a)) on nonresident taxpayers for the privilege of "earning or receiving income" in the state. The Illinois standards for determining sufficient tax nexus are based on federal statutes regulating interstate commerce and Illinois tax law. (86 Ill. Adm. Code 100.9720(b)) The fact that Illinois tax law requires a nonresident taxpayer to allocate (see ¶ 11-515) or apportion (see ¶ 11-520) income to the state does not create a presumption that the taxpayer has nexus with the state. (86 Ill. Adm. Code 100.9720(a))

Illinois accepts controlling decisions that assert protections in the U.S. Constitution by the Interstate Commerce Clause, the Foreign Commerce Clause, and the Due Process Clause as limitations on the reach of its income and replacement tax.

However, nothing prevents Illinois from challenging taxpayer assertions of U.S. Constitutional protection. (86 Ill. Adm. Code 100.9720(e))

P.L. 86-272 provisions in general. Illinois is prohibited by federal Public Law 86-272 (P.L. 86-272) from imposing a net income tax on nonresident taxpayers if:

— the sole activity in Illinois is the solicitation by the taxpayer or its representatives of orders for the sale of tangible personal property;

— the orders are sent outside Illinois for approval or rejection; and

— the orders are filled by shipment or delivery from a point outside Illinois. (86 Ill. Adm. Code 100.9720(c)(1))

If a nonresident taxpayer's activities in Illinois exceed "mere solicitation," it then does not qualify for immunity from income tax under P.L. 86-272. The taxpayer is subject to Illinois income and replacement tax for the entire taxable year and its business income is subject to apportionment. Whether a nonresident taxpayer's conduct exceeds "mere solicitation" depends upon the facts in each particular case. (86 Ill. Adm. Code 100.9720(c)(2))

P.L. 86-272 applies to solicitation in Illinois only for the sale of tangible personal property and does not provide immunity from income taxation for solicitation regarding:

— the sale of intangibles, like services, franchises, patents, copyrights, trade-marks and service marks;

— leasing, renting or licensing of tangible personal property; or

— the sale or delivery of any type of service that is not either ancillary to solicitation, or that is not sufficient to create nexus in Illinois. (86 Ill. Adm. Code 100.9720(c)(2))

Ancillary activities. "Solicitation of orders" in Illinois means speech or conduct that explicitly or implicitly invites an order and activity ancillary to invitations for an order. An activity is considered ancillary if it serves no independent business function for the seller apart from its connection to the solicitation of orders. (86 Ill. Adm. Code 100.9720(c)(2)(C)) The following activity is not ancillary to the solicitation of orders:

— activity that a seller would engage in apart from soliciting orders;

— assignment of an activity to a salesperson; and

— activity that attempts to promote sales. (86 Ill. Adm. Code 100.9720(c)(2)(C))

De minimis activities. De minimis activities in Illinois are those that, when taken together, establish only a trivial additional connection with the state. Normally, an activity is not trivial if it is conducted in Illinois on a regular or systematic basis or in connection with a company policy, regardless of whether the policy is in writing. Whether an activity consists of a trivial or non-trivial additional connection with Illinois is measured on both a qualitative and quantitative basis. If the activity either qualitatively or quantitatively creates a non-trivial connection with Illinois, then the activity exceeds the protection of P.L. 86–272. The determination of whether an unprotected activity creates a non-trivial connection with Illinois is made on the basis of the taxpayer's entire business activity, not merely its activities conducted in the state. The ratio of the amount of unprotected activities to the amount of protected activities conducted in Illinois is not determinative of whether the unprotected activities are de minimus. An unprotected activity that would not be de minimus if it were the only business activity of the taxpayer conducted in Illinois will not be de minimus merely because the taxpayer also conducts a substantial amount of protected activities in Illinois. Likewise, an unprotected activity that would be de minimus if conducted in conjunction with a substantial amount of protected activities does not fail to be de minimus merely because the taxpayer does not conduct protected activities in Illinois. (86 Ill. Adm. Code 100.9720(c)(2)(C))

Activities of independent contractors. Independent contractors may engage in the following limited activities in Illinois without the taxpayer's loss of protection under P.L. 86-272:

— soliciting sales;

— making sales; and

— maintaining an office. (86 Ill. Adm. Code 100.9720(c)(6))

Sales representatives who represent a single business are not considered to be independent contractors. In addition, an independent contractor's maintenance of an inventory of goods in Illinois under consignment or any other type of arrangement with the taxpayer, except for purposes of display and solicitation, is not protected activity. (86 Ill. Adm. Code 100.9720(c)(6))

Activities in foreign commerce. Whether business activities are conducted by a taxpayer selling property from Illinois into a foreign country or by a taxpayer selling property into Illinois from a foreign country, the principles of P.L. 86-272 will apply equally to determine whether the sales transactions are protected and the nonresident is immune from taxation in either Illinois or in the foreign country. (86 Ill. Adm. Code 100.9720(c)(8))

Unprotected activities during part of tax year. The protection under P.L. 86-272 is determined on a tax year by tax year basis. So, if at any time during a tax year a taxpayer conducts activities in Illinois that are not protected under P.L. 86–272, none of the income that the taxpayer earns or receives in the state during any part of that tax year is protected from taxation under P.L. 86–272. (86 Ill. Adm. Code 100.9720(c)(11))

Application of the Joyce Rule. Illinois follows the "Joyce Rule" for determining whether the activity of a nonresident taxpayer in Illinois is sufficient to create income and replacement tax nexus. Under the Joyce Rule, only activity conducted by or for the nonresident taxpayer is considered for purposes of establishing nexus. Activity conducted by any business entity or other person, whether or not affiliated with the nonresident taxpayer, is not considered to be attributable to the taxpayer, unless the business entity or person was acting in a representative capacity on behalf of the taxpayer. Since the income of any partnership, S corporation or other pass–through entity is treated as income of its owners, activity of a pass–through entity is conducted on behalf of its owners. (86 Ill. Adm. Code 100.9720(f))

Nexus creating activities. Activities in Illinois that create income and replacement tax nexus and are not protected by P.L. 86-272 include:

— selling intangibles, like services, franchises, patents, copyrights, trademarks and service marks;

— leasing, renting or licensing tangible personal property; (86 Ill. Adm. Code 100.9720(c)(2)(B))

— owning interests in a partnership or limited liability company (LLC) classified as a partnership for income tax purposes; (86 Ill. Adm. Code 100.9720(f))

— making repairs or providing maintenance or service to property sold or to be sold in Illinois;

— collecting current or delinquent accounts in Illinois directly or by third parties, whether by assignment or other means;

— investigating credit worthiness in Illinois;

— installation or supervision of installation in Illinois at or after shipment or delivery;

— conducting training courses, seminars or lectures for personnel in Illinois, other than personnel involved only in solicitation of sales of tangible personal property;

— providing technical assistance or services, including engineering assistance or design service, in Illinois other than facilitating the solicitation of orders;

— investigating, handling, or assisting in resolving customer complaints in Illinois;

— approving or accepting orders in Illinois;

— repossessing property in Illinois;

— securing deposits on sales in Illinois;

— picking up or replacing damaged or returned property in Illinois;

— hiring, training, or supervising personnel in Illinois, other than personnel involved only in solicitation;

— maintaining a sample or display room for more than 14 days at any one location in Illinois during the tax year;

— carrying samples into Illinois for sale, exchange or distribution in any manner for consideration;

— consigning for sale an inventory of goods or other tangible personal property to a person in Illinois, including an independent contractor;

— entering into franchising or licensing agreements, selling or otherwise disposing of franchises and licenses, or selling or otherwise transferring tangible personal property to a franchisee or licensee in Illinois; and

— conducting any activity that is not on the list of protected activities under P.L. 86-272 and that is not entirely ancillary to requests for orders, even if the activity helps to increase purchases. (86 Ill. Adm. Code 100.9720(c)(4))

In addition, owning, leasing, or maintaining any of the following in Illinois creates income tax nexus:

— repair shop;

— parts department;

— an office or other place of business that does not strictly qualify as an "in–home" office;

— warehouse;

— meeting place for directors, officers, or employees;

— inventory of goods, other than samples for sales personnel or that are used entirely ancillary to solicitation;

— telephone listing or answering service, advertising, or business literature that is publicly attributed to the taxpayer or to an employee or agent representing the taxpayer;

— mobile stores (i.e., vehicles with drivers who are sales representatives that make sales from the vehicles); and

— real property or fixtures. (86 Ill. Adm. Code 100.9720(c)(4))

Activities not sufficient to create nexus. Activities in Illinois that are protected under P.L. 86-272 and that are not sufficient to create income and replacement tax nexus include:

— soliciting orders for sales in Illinois by any type of advertising;

— soliciting orders for sales in Illinois by an employee or representative who does not maintain or use any office or place of business in the state besides an "in–home" office;

— carrying samples and promotional materials into Illinois for display or distribution only without charge or other consideration;

— furnishing and setting up display racks in Illinois and advising customers on the display of products without charge or other consideration;

— providing automobiles to sales personnel for their use in conducting protected activities in Illinois;

— passing orders, inquiries and complaints from Illinois to the taxpayer's home office;

— solicitation of indirect customers for taxpayer's goods, otherwise known as missionary sales (e.g., solicitation of retailers to buy the manufacturer's goods from the manufacturer's wholesale customers);

— coordinating shipment or delivery to Illinois without payment or other consideration and providing information relating to shipment or delivery either before or after the placement of an order;

— checking customer inventories in Illinois without charge for reorder, except for other purposes like quality control;

— maintaining a sample or display room for 14 days or fewer at any one location in Illinois during the tax year;

— recruiting, training or evaluating sales representatives in Illinois, including occasionally using homes, hotels or similar places for meetings with sales personnel;

— mediating direct customer complaints if the purpose is solely for ingratiating the sales representative with the customer and facilitating requests for orders;

— owning, leasing, using or maintaining personal property in Illinois for use in an employee's or representative's residential home office (e.g., cellular telephone, fax or copy machine, personal computer, and computer software, etc.), if the office is not publicly attributed to the taxpayer or to the employee or other representative and use of the property is limited to the conducting of protected activities;

— shipping or delivering goods into Illinois using a private carrier or using vehicles that the taxpayer owns or leases (e.g., motor vehicles, rail, water, air or other modes of transportation), regardless of whether a direct or indirect fee or charge is imposed on the purchaser; (86 Ill. Adm. Code 100.9720(c)(5)) and

— registering or qualifying to conduct business in Illinois. (86 Ill. Adm. Code 100.9720(c)(10))

An out-of-state business that has contracted for printing in Illinois does not create income and replacement tax nexus merely on the basis of:

— ownership of tangible personal property at the premises of a printer in Illinois; or

— activities of employees or agents located solely at a printer's premises that are related to quality control, distribution, or printing services performed by a printer in Illinois. (86 Ill. Adm. Code 100.9720(d))

[¶10-200]

BUSINESS ENTITIES

[¶10-210] C Corporations

Illinois follows the federal income tax treatment of C corporations, as set out in IRC Secs. 301 through 385. The definition of corporation in IRC Sec. 7701(a)(3) is identical to the definition in Sec. 1501(a)(4) of the Illinois Income Tax Act except that the Illinois definition includes cooperatives. Accordingly, any entity treated as a corporation for federal income tax purposes is treated as a corporation for Illinois income tax purposes, and no entity (other than a cooperative) that is not treated as a corporation for federal income tax purposes may be treated as a corporation for Illinois purposes. (35 ILCS 5/1501(a)(4); 35 ILCS 5/1501(b)(2); 86 Ill. Adm. Code 100.9750)

The Illinois income tax is imposed on corporations for the privilege of earning or receiving income in Illinois. An additional income tax, known as the personal property replacement income tax, is also applicable to all corporations subject to the regular income tax. (35 ILCS 5/201(a))

• *Federal income tax provisions*

Every corporation that is taxed under subchapter C of the tax code is called a C corporation. A C corporation is a separate taxpaying entity independent from its shareholders. It is organized under state law by filing a corporate charter with the competent state authorities. The corporation must also comply with other state law formalities such as the holding of an organizational meeting and issuance of stock. Individuals, corporations or non-corporate business entities may become shareholders in a corporation by contributing money or other property to the corporation's capital in exchange for its stock. There is no limitation on the number of shareholders, and any changes in the type or the number of shareholders do not affect the existence of the corporation. The liability of the shareholders for the corporation's debts is limited to their investment in the corporation's capital.

Federal tax law rather than state law determines if a corporation exists for tax purposes. State law determines if relationships essential to the federal tax concept of a corporation exist. An entity that qualifies as a corporation under state law is usually taxed as a corporation, unless it is a sham, inactive or organized solely for tax avoidance purposes. On the other hand, a business entity that fails to comply with some of the corporate organization formalities under state law may be treated as a corporation for federal tax purposes.

A C corporation pays a corporate income tax on its annual taxable income at specified corporate tax rates. The shareholders are taxed if and when the corporation's earned income is distributed in the form of dividends. Thus, the distributed corporate income of a C corporation may be subject to double taxation, first at a corporate level and then at a shareholder level. The corporation may also be subject to additional taxes, such as the accumulated earnings tax and the personal holding company tax.

[¶10-215] S Corporations (IRC Sec. 1361--IRC Sec. 1379)

Since Illinois adopts the federal income tax treatment of S corporations, as set out in IRC Secs. 1361 through 1379, income and losses, including net losses, of the S corporation flows to its shareholders. (86 Ill. Adm. Code 100.9750) S corporations are exempt from the Illinois corporate income tax but are subject to the personal property replacement income tax equal to 1.5%. (35 ILCS 5/201(c); 35 ILCS 5/205(c))

• *Interaction of federal and state provisions*

"S corporations" are defined to include not only corporations having an election in effect under IRC Sec. 1362, but also certain corporations producing oil and gas that elect federally to "opt out" of the provisions of the Subchapter S Revision Act of 1982. These latter corporations may, for state purposes, apply the prior Subchapter S rules as they were in effect on July 1, 1982, under former IRC Secs. 1371 *et seq.* Illinois Department of Revenue regulations provide guidance as to when the transfer of ownership of an S corporation causes the entity to ceaseto exist or continue as the same entity for Illinois income tax purposes. (35 ILCS 5/1501; 86 Ill. Adm. Code 100.4500; 86 Ill. Adm. Code 100.9750)

Base income and taxable income.—S corporations that do business entirely within Illinois compute a hypothetical federal base income, "unmodified base income," from information reported on federal Form 1120-S. Illinois addition and subtraction modifications are then made to arrive at "base income." Taxable income is then determined by deducting a standard exemption of $1,000. (35 ILCS 5/204(b))

Modifications to base income.—Multistate S corporations subtract nonbusiness income from the modified hypothetical federal base income figure. After the remainder is apportioned, nonbusiness income allocable to Illinois is added to arrive at "base income allocable to Illinois." A standard exemption, computed by dividing the base income allocable to Illinois by the total base income and multiplying the result by $1,000, is then subtracted to arrive at taxable income. (35 ILCS 5/204(a))

Regulations effective December 11, 2000, provide special carryover periods allowed under IRC Sec. 172(b) for specific kinds of losses or taxpayers. (86 Ill. Adm. Code 100.2330) For example, "specified liability losses" may be carried back to each of the ten taxable years preceding the taxable year in which the loss was incurred. (86 Ill. Adm. Code 100.2330(b)(2)(C)(i)) Similarly, bad debt losses of commercial banks may be carried back to each of the ten taxable years preceding the taxable year in which the loss was incurred, and to each of the five taxable years following the taxable year in which the loss was incurred. (86 Ill. Adm. Code 100.2330(b)(2)(C)(ii))

The treatment of net operating loss carryover is covered in the discussion of subtractions from taxable income for NOLs that may be claimed when computing Illinois corporate income tax income tax liability. (see ¶ 10-805)

CCH COMMENT: *S corporation income computation modified.*—Public Act 91-913 (House Bill 4431) provides that an S corporation is entitled to a subtraction modification for Illinois income allocable to shareholders who are themselves subject to the Illinois Personal Property Replacement Income Tax. The legislation applies to tax years ending on or after December 31, 1997. Previously, both the S corporation and an Electing Small Business Trust (ESBT) shareholder were required to pay the replacement tax on the same income. This legislation provides a subtraction modification to an S corporation for income allocable to shareholders subject to the replacement tax (such as ESBTs) or that are exempt from federal income tax under IRC 501(a). Though technically effective January 1, 2001, the Illinois Department of Revenue has indicated that taxpayers may file amended returns and request a refund earlier. [See IITA Sec. 203(b)(2)(S)]

Valuation elimination deduction.—Although individuals, estates, and trusts are permitted to deduct the appreciation to capital assets that occurred prior to the 1969 enactment of the income tax in determining income, corporations—including S corporations—are not entitled to do so. (35 ILCS 5/203(f)(1); *Brown v. Department of Revenue* (1980, App Ct) 89 IllApp3d 238, 411 NE2d 882)

• *Nonresident withholding requirements*

Effective for taxable years ending on or after December 31, 2008, S corporations are subject to withholding requirements for each nonresident individual shareholder. (35 ILCS 5/709.5; 35 ILCS 5/201)

• *Federal income tax provisions*

An S corporation is a small business corporation that satisfies the requirements of Subchapter S of the tax code and has elected to be taxed under those rules. In order to qualify as a small business corporation, the corporation must be a domestic corporation and is restricted on the number and types of shareholders it can have and on the type of stock that it can issue.

The difference between an S corporation and a regular corporation is that the S corporation has elected to be taxed similarly to a partnership for federal tax purposes. After making the S election, the income, losses, tax credits, and other tax items of the corporation flow through the corporation to the shareholders. Thus, income is only taxed once, at the shareholder level. However, an S corporation that was formerly a C corporation may be subject to taxes at the corporate level for LIFO recapture, excessive net passive income, and built-in gains.

[¶10-220] General Partnerships

Since Illinois generally follows the federal income tax treatment of general partnerships and their partners, as set out in IRC Secs. 701 through 761, income and losses, including net losses, of the partnership flow to its partners. (86 Ill. Adm. Code 100.9750) Partnerships are not subject to corporate income tax but are subject to the personal property replacement income tax at the entity level. (35 ILCS 5/201(c); 35 ILCS 5/205(b); 35 ILCS 5/1501(16))

A partnership must file an Illinois partnership replacement tax return if it has base income or loss allocable to the state. Effective for tax years before 2014, partnerships were allowed to file an Illinois composite income and replacement tax return for participating nonresident partners.

Investment partnerships: For tax years ending on or after December 31, 2004, investment partnerships are not subject to personal property replacement income tax. (35 ILCS 5/205(b))

The term "investment partnership" means any entity treated as a partnership for federal income tax purposes and that meets the following requirements:

(1) no less than 90% of the investment partnership's cost of its total assets consists of qualifying investment securities, deposits at banks or other financial institutions, and office space and equipment reasonably necessary to carry on its activities as an investment partnership;

(2) no less than 90% of its gross income consists of interest, dividends, and gains from the sale or exchange of qualifying investment securities; and

(3) the partnership is not a dealer in qualifying investment securities. (35 ILCS 5/1501(a))

The term "investment securities" means:

— common and preferred stock;

— bonds, debentures, and other debt securities;

— foreign and domestic currency deposits;

— mortgage or asset-backed securities;

— repurchase agreements and loan participation;

— forward currency exchange contracts and forward and futures contracts on foreign currencies;

— stock and bond index securities and futures contracts and other similar financial securities and futures contracts on those securities;

— options for the purchase or sale of the foregoing securities, currencies, or contracts;

— regulated futures contracts;

— commodities or futures, forwards, or options with respect to such commodities;

— derivatives; and

— a partnership interest in another partnership that is an investment partnership. (35 ILCS 5/1501(a))

• *Interaction of federal and state provisions*

The Illinois definition of "partnership," which includes limited liability companies that are classified as partnerships for federal income tax purposes, syndicates, groups, or other unincorporated organizations, parallels the federal definition found in IRC Sec. 761. However, the term "partnership" does not include a syndicate, group, pool, joint venture, or other unincorporated organization that is established for the sole purpose of playing the Illinois lottery. Illinois regulations provide guidance as to when a partnership ceases to be a partnership for Illinois income tax purposes and how reorganization or transfer of shares of the partnership will effect taxation. (35 ILCS 5/1501(a)(16); 86 Ill. Adm. Code 100.4500; 86 Ill. Adm. Code 100.9750)

CCH COMMENT: *No constitutional violation imposing replacement tax on limited partner's income.*—In *Borden Chemicals and Plastics, L.P. v. Zehnder*, decided February 14, 2000, the Illinois Appellate Court, First District, in a case of first impression, held that the imposition of Illinois personal property replacement income tax on the distributable income received by a Delaware limited partner of a limited partnership that operated in Illinois was not in violation of the Due Process and Commerce Clauses of the U.S. Constitution. Although the limited partner asserted that it could not be taxed because it had no connection with Illinois other than the investment in a partnership that operated in Illinois, the limited partnership availed itself of the laws of Illinois and the limited partner received distributable income earned in Illinois and, thus, imposition of the tax did not violate the Due Process Clause of the U.S. Constitution.

Further, the Commerce Clause of the U.S. Constitution was not violated because the limited partnership had substantial nexus with Illinois. The limited partner agreed that there was substantial nexus between Illinois and the limited partnership but argued that substantial nexus had to exist between it and Illinois. The limited partner asserted that because it had no physical presence in Illinois, substantial nexus did not exist and it could not be taxed. However, physical presence was not required to establish substantial nexus between the limited partner and Illinois because the limited partnership was physically present in Illinois and operated in Illinois and served only as a conduit to shift the incidence of the tax to the partners.

• *Computation of Illinois base income*

Computation of Illinois base income for purposes of the determining the partnership's personal property replacement tax liability and for determining the partnership income passing through to partners begins with the partnership's federal taxable income, except that items of income, loss, or deductions separately stated for the partners for federal purposes on federal Form 1065, Schedule K are taken into account for purposes of computing Illinois "unmodified base income." (35 ILCS 5/203(e)(2)(H))

The following income, loss, and deduction items that are required to be separately stated for federal purposes on federal *Form 1065, Schedule K* are added to or subtracted from ordinary income or loss for replacement tax purposes:

— net income or loss from rental real estate activities;

— net income or loss from other rental activities;

— portfolio income or loss;

— net IRC Sec. 1231 gain or loss from involuntary conversions;

— net gain or loss from sale or exchange of property used in trade or business;

— other items of income or loss not included on page 1 of federal Form 1065 or 1065-B;

— charitable contribution deduction;

— expense deduction under IRC Sec. 179;

— payments for partners for IRA, Keogh, or SEP;

— oil and gas depletion;

— interest on investment indebtedness; or

— any other items of expense not deducted on page 1 of federal Form 1065 or 1065-B.

The resulting "unmodified base income" is then adjusted by Illinois addition and subtraction modifications to determine Illinois base income. Effective for tax years ending after September 11, 2001, Illinois has decoupled from the federal bonus depreciation legislation. As a result, Illinois additions and subtractions must be adjusted on *Form IL-4562 (Special Depreciation)* to reverse the effects of federal bonus depreciation. If the partnership derives all of its income from Illinois sources, the standard exemption is subtracted, and the resulting net income is subject tax. Partnerships that derive income from inside and outside Illinois allocate and apportion base income to determine base income allocable to Illinois. Then, the standard exemption is subtracted to determine net replacement tax income.

• *Additions and subtractions*

The Illinois additions and subtractions for replacement tax purposes are:

— interest;

— dividends;

— constitutionally exempt obligations;

— modifications from other entities;

— partnership acquisitions;

— capital gains deduction;

— partnership income distributed to other entities;

— bond premiums;

— contributions to job training projects;

— guaranteed payments;

— repayment to another of items previously included in income;

— replacement tax;

— personal service income;

— net loss deduction; and

— standard exemption.

Interest.—In computing the replacement tax, interest excluded on the federal return is added to income. (35 ILCS 5/203(d)(2)(A))

Interest on federal obligations and other constitutionally exempt obligations is subtracted from federal taxable income. (35 ILCS 5/203(d)(2)(A))

Dividends.—In computing income subject to the replacement tax, dividends excluded on the federal return (in pre-1987 tax years) are added back to income. (35 ILCS 5/203(d)(2)(A))

Prior to August 7, 2012, dividends included on the federal return from corporations that conduct substantially all of their operations in enterprise zones were subtracted from federal taxable income. (35 ILCS 5/203(d)(2)(K)) Dividends included federally from high impact businesses located in Illinois that conduct business operations in federally designated Foreign Trade Zones or Sub Zones are still subtracted. (35 ILCS 5/203(d)(2)(M))

Constitutionally exempt income.—In computing the replacement tax, items exempted by the Illinois Constitution or federal law are subtracted from federal taxable income. (35 ILCS 5/203(d)(2)(G))

Distributable income.—In the case of a partner subject to replacement tax, the share of distributable income should be reflected in Line 5d. Multiply each line referenced in the worksheet by the percentage of total ownership in the partnership attributable to these partners, and any share of distributable loss should be reported on Line 2e. Form IL-2569 must be attached to Form IL-1065. (*Instructions, Form IL-1065, Illinois Partnership Replacement Tax Form*)

Partnership acquisitions.—An acquiring partnership may claim the state income tax credits and net operating losses of a partnership that is acquired in an IRC Sec. 708 continuation of a partnership, applicable retroactively to all acquisitions occurring in taxable years ending after December 30, 1986. However, transitional rules apply concerning a taxpayer's eligibility for refunds and assessment reductions for pre-1999 tax liabilities. (35 ILCS 5/405)

Capital gains.—In computing the replacement tax, the federal capital gains deduction for pre-1987 tax years and beginning on September 1, 1989, is added back to income. (35 ILCS 5/203(d)(2)(D))

The portion of capital gain attributable to pre-August 1, 1969, asset appreciation is subtracted from federal adjusted gross income. (35 ILCS 5/203(d)(2)(E)) This appreciation is called the "valuation limitation amount." The valuation limitation amount is equal to the pre-August 1, 1969, appreciation recaptured under IRC Sec. 1245 and IRC Sec.1250 for the taxable year, plus the lesser of (1) the portion of federal capital gain for the tax year attributable to pre-August 1, 1969, appreciation amounts, or (2) the net capital gain for the tax year reduced by capital gains recognized federally from distributions from public retirement plans, individual retirement accounts, retirement bonds and payments to retired partners. (35 ILCS 5/203(f)(1)(A), (B), (2)(A), (B))

If the fair market value of property was readily ascertainable on August 1, 1969, the "pre-August 1, 1969, appreciation amount," is the lesser of (1) the excess of the August 1, 1969, value over the federal basis of the property on that date; or (2) the total gain reportable federally with respect to the property. (35 ILCS 5/203(f)(1)(A), (B), (2)(A), (B), (B), (2)(A), (B))

If the fair market value of property was not readily ascertainable on August 1, 1969, the "pre-August 1, 1969, appreciation amount" is that portion of the federal gain as the number of full calendar months in the holding period of the property ending July 31, 1969, bears to the number of full calendar months in the entire holding period. (35 ILCS 5/203(f)(1)(A), (B), (2)(A), (B))

The valuation limitation subtraction is computed and reported on Schedule F, Gains from Sales or Exchanges of Property Acquired Before August 1, 1969. (Instructions, Form IL-1065, Illinois Partnership Replacement Tax Form, Schedule F)

Income distributed to other entities.—In computing the replacement tax, partnership income distributable to another partnership, trust, or estate subject to the Personal Property Replacement Income Tax, including amounts distributable to charitable, religious, and educational organizations that are exempt from federal income tax under IRC Sec. 501(a), is subtracted from income. (35 ILCS 5/203(d)(2)(I))

Bond premiums.—In computing the replacement tax, the following items are subtracted from federal taxable income: (1) amortizable bond premium not deducted federally under IRC Sec. 171(a)(2), because attributable to tax-free bonds and (2) interest not deducted federally under IRC Sec. 265, because incurred or continued to purchase or carry tax-free obligations. In addition, effective for taxable years ending after August 12, 1999, taxpayers may deduct from federal adjusted income expenses associated with federal employment credits, the credit for qualified clinical testing expenses, and the credit for increasing research activities that are disallowed as federal deductions under IRC Sec. 280C. (35 ILCS 5/203(d)(2)(J))

Job training project contributions.—In computing the replacement tax, contributions to a job training project established pursuant to the "Real Property Tax Increment Allocation Redevelopment Act" are subtracted from federal taxable income. (35 ILCS 5/203(d)(2)(L))

Guaranteed payments.—In computing the replacement tax, amounts deducted on the federal return as guaranteed payments under IRC Sec. 707(c) are added to income. "Guaranteed payments" are fixed amounts paid for services or the use of capital without regard to the income of the partnership. (35 ILCS 5/203(d)(2)(C))

Repayment of items previously included in gross income.—Partnerships that take the federal income tax credit under IRC Sec. 1341 for repayment to another of income items previously included in gross income as being held under a claim of right may subtract from federal taxable income, for Illinois income tax purposes, an amount equal to the deduction used to compute the federal income tax credit. (35 ILCS 5/203(d)(2)(N))

Replacement tax expenses.—In computing the replacement tax, the amount of personal property replacement income tax deducted for federal purposes is added to income. (35 ILCS 5/203(d)(2)(B))

The amount of replacement tax refunds that were included in the partnership's federal taxable income is subtracted. (35 ILCS 5/203(d)(2)(F))

Personal service income.—In computing the replacement tax, partnership income that constitutes personal service income is subtracted from income. The amount of the subtraction is the greater of (1) the amount of "personal service income" under IRC Sec. 1348(b)(1) as in effect December 31, 1981; or (2) a reasonable allowance for compensation paid or accrued for service rendered by the partners to the partnership. (35 ILCS 5/203(d)(2)(H))

Standard exemption.—The standard exemption is subtracted from partnership base income to arrive at replacement tax net income. The applicable amount is multiplied by the percentage the portion of partnership base income allocable to Illinois bears to total partnership base income. (35 ILCS 5/204(a)) (Instructions, Form IL-1065 Illinois Partnership Replacement Tax Return)

Net loss deduction.—If Illinois net income results in a loss, it may generally be carried back or forward. For tax years ending on or after December 31, 2003, a net loss may be carried forward 12 years and may not be carried back. For tax years ending on or after December 31, 1999 and prior to December 31, 2003, a net loss may be carried back two years or carried forward 20 years. (35 ILCS 5/207)

Nonresident withholding requirements.—Partnerships are subject to withholding requirements for each nonresident partner.

• *Allocation and apportionment rules*

Partnerships that derive business income from within and without the state allocate and apportion such income. (35 ILCS 5/301(c))

Partnership business income is allocated to Illinois if derived solely from the state. (35 ILCS 5/304(a))

If the partnership business income is derived from Illinois and one or more other states it is apportioned. (35 ILCS 5/304(f)) Illinois uses a single-factor apportionment formula that consists of the sales factor. (see ¶11-520)

The distinction between business income and nonbusiness income is discussed at ¶11-510 Income Subject to Allocation and Apportionment.

Interest.—In computing the replacement tax, partnership nonbusiness interest income is allocated to Illinois if the partnership has its commercial domicile in the state at the time the interest is paid, incurred, or accrued. (35 ILCS 5/301(c)(2)(B))

Dividends.—In computing the replacement tax, partnership nonbusiness dividend income is allocated to Illinois if the partnership has its commercial domicile in the state at the time the dividend is paid, incurred, or accrued. (35 ILCS 5/301(c)(2)(B))

Royalty income.—In computing the replacement tax, partnership nonbusiness royalty income from real property is allocable to Illinois if the property is located in Illinois. (35 ILCS 5/303(c)(1)) Economic interests in minerals in place are considered real property for allocation purposes. (86 Ill. Adm. Code 100.3220(c)) Such interests include, among other interests, royalties, overriding royalties, participating interests, production payments, and working interests.

Partnership nonbusiness income from royalties from tangible personal property is allocable to Illinois (1) to the extent that the property is used in Illinois; or (2) entirely, if the partnership has its commercial domicile in Illinois at the time the royalty is paid, incurred, or accrued and the partnership was not organized or taxable in the state where the property is used. (35 ILCS 5/303(c)(2)) The extent to which property is used in Illinois is determined according to the ratio of days the property was in Illinois during the royalty period to the total number of days in the royalty period. (35 ILCS 5/303(c)(1)) If the location of the property during the royalty period is unascertainable by the partnership, tangible personal property is considered to be used in the state in which the property was located at the time the rental payor obtained possession.

Partnership nonbusiness income from patent and copyright royalties is allocable to Illinois in the same manner as are royalties from personal property: (1) to the extent the patent or copyright is used by the payor in Illinois; or (2) entirely, if the partnership has its commercial domicile in Illinois at the time the royalty is paid, incurred, or accrued and the taxpayer is not taxable in the state where the patent or copyright is used. A patent is used in Illinois to the extent that it is employed in production or other processing in Illinois or to the extent that a patented product is produced in the state. A copyright is used in Illinois to the extent that publication originates in Illinois. (35 ILCS 5/303(d))

CCH COMMENT: Reporting royalty income.—Effective for tax years ending on or after December 31, 1999, income from royalties from intangibles must be included in a nonresident partner's business income subject to formula apportionment if gross receipts from the royalties comprise more than 50% of the taxpayer's total gross receipts during the tax year and each of the two immediately preceding tax years. If a taxpayer is a member of a unitary business group, this determination is made on the basis of the entire group's gross receipts. Taxpayers may make an irrevocable election to apply formula apportionment to royalty income for prior tax years; however, a refund of taxes assessed prior to 1999 will not be issued as a result of the election.

Gross receipts from the licensing, sale, or other disposition of a patent, copyright, trademark, or similar item of intangible property are required to be included in the numerator of the Illinois apportionment formula's sales factor to the extent that the item is utilized in Illinois during the year the gross receipts are included in gross income.

— A patent is utilized in Illinois to the extent that it is employed in production, fabrication, manufacturing, or other processing in Illinois or to the extent that a patented product is produced in Illinois.

— A copyright is utilized in Illinois to the extent that publication originates in Illinois.

— Trademarks and other items of intangible property are utilized in Illinois if the commercial domicile of the licensee or purchaser is located in Illinois.

If the state of utilization cannot be determined from the taxpayer's books and records or from books and records of a related person, the gross receipts attributable to that item must be excluded from both the numerator and denominator of the sales factor. (35 ILCS 5/304(a))

Gains and losses on property.—Computation of the Illinois partnership replacement tax for nonbusiness capital gains and losses, allocable to Illinois, is calculated based on whether the property is real property, tangible personal property, or intangible personal property.

In computing the replacement tax, nonbusiness capital gains and losses from real property are allocated to Illinois if the property is located in the state. (35 ILCS 5/303(b)(1), (2), (3))

Economic interests in minerals in place are considered real property for allocation purposes. (86 Ill. Adm. Code 100.3220(b)) Such interests include, among other interests, royalties, overriding royalties, participating interests, production payments, and working interests.

In computing the replacement tax, nonbusiness capital gains and losses from tangible personal property are allocable to Illinois if, at the time of the sale or exchange, (1) the property had its situs in Illinois; or (2) the partnership had its commercial domicile in Illinois and was not taxable in the state in which the property had its situs.

In computing the replacement tax, nonbusiness capital gains and losses from intangible property are allocable to Illinois if Illinois was the state of partnership's commercial domicile at the time of the sale or exchange.

Rental income.—In computing the replacement tax, partnership nonbusiness rental income from real property is allocable to Illinois if the property is located in Illinois. (35 ILCS 5/303(c)(1), (2)) Economic interests in minerals in place are considered real property for allocation purposes. Such interests include, among other interests, royalties, overriding royalties, participating interests, production payments, and working interests. (86 Ill. Adm. Code 100.3220(c))

Nonbusiness rental income from partnership tangible personal property is allocable to Illinois to the extent the property is used in the state. The extent that property is used in Illinois is determined according to the ratio of days the property was in Illinois during the rental period to the total number of days in the rental period. If the location of the property during the rental period is unascertainable by the partnership, tangible personal property is considered used in the state in which the property was located at the time the rental payer obtained possession. (35 ILCS 5/303(c)(1), (2))

Annuity income.—In computing the replacement tax, partnership nonbusiness income from annuities is allocable to Illinois if the partnership's commercial domicile is in Illinois. (35 ILCS 5/301(c)(2))

• *Computation of partner income*

Computation of Illinois base income for purposes of partnership income passing through to nonresident partners begins with federal taxable income of the partnership, except that items of income, loss, or deductions individually stated by the partners for federal purposes (entered on federal U.S. Form 1065, Schedule K) are taken into account for purposes of computing Illinois "unmodified base income." Certain of the Illinois addition and subtraction modifications used to determine Illinois base income for purposes of the personal property replacement income tax are then applied, resulting in modified partnership income to be passed through to nonresident partners. (35 ILCS 5/203(e)(2)(H))

The Illinois modifications are:

— interest;

— repayment of items previously included in income; and

— modifications from other entities.

Interest.—For nonresident partners' income tax purposes, all interest excluded federally is added to income. (35 ILCS 5/203(d)(2)(A))

Repayment of items previously included in income.—For nonresident partners' income tax purposes, an amount equal to the deduction used to compute the federal income tax credit under IRC Sec. 1341 for repayment to another of income items previously included in gross income as being held under a claim of right is subtracted from "unmodified base income." (35 ILCS 5/203(d)(2)(N))

Partnership's share of other entities.—For income tax purposes, a partnership or an S corporation is required to send an Illinois Schedule K-1-P and the trust or the estate is required to send an Illinois Schedule K-1-T, specifically identifying the share of income. Illinois addition and subtraction modifications from other partnerships, trusts, or estates of which the partnership is a partner or beneficiary must be taken into account. (Instructions, Form IL-1065, Illinois Partnership Replacement Tax Form)

• *Income attributable to nonresident partners*

Although partnerships are subject to the replacement tax and not the income tax, they compute an income tax base for the purpose of the Illinois income tax imposed on the partners as individuals. The computation of the partnership income tax base attributable to Illinois begins with ordinary income or loss from the federal partnership return. Income, loss, and deduction items that are required to be separately stated for federal purposes (Form 1065, Schedule K) are taken into account for Illinois income tax purposes, resulting in "unmodified base income." For purposes of the income tax, unmodified base income is then subject to Illinois addition and subtraction modifications to determine Illinois base income. "Unmodified base income" is equivalent to the aggregate federal taxable income reported by the partners on their federal return.

Illinois base income (as computed above) passing through to nonresident partners is allocated and apportioned to determine the amount each partner reports on his individual Illinois income tax return.

Resident partners report their pro rata share of Illinois addition and subtraction modifications on their individual Illinois returns. Nonresident partners report to Illinois their share of partnership income attributable to Illinois, as well as their share of Illinois addition and subtraction modifications to such income.

The entire portion of partnership base income passing through to partners who are Illinois residents is attributed to Illinois. (35 ILCS 5/301(a))

Nonresident partners are taxed only on their distributive share of income allocated and apportioned to Illinois. (35 ILCS 5/305(a)) A nonresident partner's share of partnership items of nonbusiness income is attributed to the partner as if such items had been paid, incurred, or accrued directly to the partners in their separate capacities. (35 ILCS 5/305(b))

Partnership business income.—If the business income of a partnership is derived solely from Illinois sources, a nonresident partner is taxed on his or her entire distributive share. However, if partnership business income is derived from inside and outside the state, the business income of the partnership is subject to formula apportionment. Partnerships use the same apportionment factor and formula for purposes of the income tax (and the replacement tax base) as do nonresident individuals. (35 ILCS 5/305(a); 35 ILCS 5/305(c); 35 ILCS 5/304(a))

Interest.—A nonresident partner's share of partnership nonbusiness interest is attributed to the partner as if such items had been paid, incurred, or accrued directly to the partner in his or her individual capacity. (35 ILCS 5/305(b))

Dividends.—A nonresident partner's share of partnership nonbusiness dividends is attributed to the partner as if such items had been paid, incurred, or accrued directly to the partner in his or her individual capacity. (35 ILCS 5/305(b))

Royalties.—A nonresident partner's share of partnership nonbusiness royalty is attributed to the partner as if such items had been paid, incurred, or accrued directly to the partner in his or her individual capacity. (35 ILCS 5/305(b))

Nonbusiness rental income.—A nonresident partner's share of partnership nonbusiness rental income is attributed to the partner as if such items had been paid, incurred, or accrued directly to the partner in his or her individual capacity. (35 ILCS 5/305(b))

Gains and losses from disposition of partnership.—A nonresident partner's share of partnership nonbusiness gains and losses from dispositions is attributed to the partner as if such items had been paid, incurred, or accrued directly to the partner in his or her individual capacity. (35 ILCS 5/305(b))

• *Federal income tax provisions*

A partnership is a pass-through entity that does not pay tax on its income. Instead, the partnership passes along its income or loss, gains, deductions, and credits to the partners. Each partner reports a percentage of the partnership income and other items on the partner's own tax return.

A partnership does not pay tax, but it does compute income, deductions and credits on an annual basis. Information about the business is reported to the IRS on Form 1065 and to the individual partners on separate Schedules K-1. The partners report the partnership income on their own returns and pay any taxes due based on their own tax rates.

[¶10-225] Limited Partnerships; Limited Liability Partnerships

Since Illinois adopts the federal income tax treatment of limited partnerships and limited liability partnerships (LLPs) and their partners, as set out in IRC Secs. 701 through 761, income and losses, including net losses, of the limited partnerships and LLPs flow to their partners. In order to form a limited partnership, a partnership must file a certificate of limited partnership with the Illinois Secretary of State. (805 ILCS 210/201) A partnership may convert to an LLP by filing an application with the Secretary of State. The application must be executed by a majority in interest of the partners or by one or more partners authorized to execute an application. (805 ILCS 205/8.1)

An LLP is not subject to corporate income tax, but is subject to personal property replacement income tax at the entity level equal to 1.5%. For details, see ¶10-220 General Partnerships.

Nonresident withholding requirements.—Effective for taxable years ending on or after December 31, 2008, LLPs are subject to withholding requirementsfor each nonresident partner. (35 ILCS 5/709.5; 35 ILCS 5/201)

• *Federal income tax provisions*

The state laws regulating limited liability partnerships (LLPs) vary widely. Accordingly, it is difficult to generalize about the requirements and state law consequences of obtaining LLP status.

LLPs are general partnerships in which each individual partner is liable for the partnership's general contractual obligations, his or her own individual business liability, and the tort liabilities deriving from the acts of those over whom the partner had supervisory duties. By complying with a prescribed registration requirement, the partner is otherwise insulated from the malpractice, negligence and similar liabilities of the other partners in excess of the value of the partner's interest in the partnership. The classification and tax treatment of LLPs is not affected by the check-the-box entity selection rules. The federal income tax status of an LLP depends on the provisions of the state law under which the partnership is formed.

[¶10-240] Limited Liability Companies (LLCs)

Since Illinois adopts the federal income tax treatment of limited liability companies (LLCs) and their members, as set out in the federal "check-the-box" regulations, income and losses, including net losses, of the LLC flow to its members. An LLC that is treated as a partnership for federal income tax purposes is also treated as a partnership for Illinois tax purposes. (35 ILCS 5/1501(a)(4) and (16))

An LLC that is treated as a partnership is not subject to corporate income tax but is subject to the personal property replacement income tax at the entity level (see ¶10-220 General Partnerships). (35 ILCS 5/201(c))

LLC organizational provisions are found in the Limited Liability Company Act, located at 805 ILCS 180/1-1 *et seq.*

• *Nonresident withholding requirements*

Effective for taxable years ending on or after December 31, 2008, LLCs are subject to withholding requirementsfor each nonresident member. (35 ILCS 5/709.5; 35 ILCS 5/201)

• *Federal income tax provisions*

A limited liability company (LLC) is a business entity created under state law. Every state and the District of Columbia have LLC statutes that govern the formation and operation of LLCs. An LLC has the characteristics of both a corporation and a partnership. Like a corporation, the owners (referred to as members) are usually not personally liable for the debts and other obligations of the LLC. Like a partnership or sole proprietorship, an LLC has great flexibility in the way it operates and does not need to follow corporate formalities, such as holding special and annual meetings with shareholders and directors.

An LLC has the flexibility to decide whether to be taxed as a partnership, S corporation, C corporation. A single-member LLC, is a disregarded entity, unless it elects to be taxed as a corporation for federal tax purposes. If an LLC chooses to be taxed as a partnership or S corporation, or if a single-member LLC is disregarded as an entity, the LLC profits and losses are reported on the member's personal federal income tax return.

[¶10-245] Exempt Organizations

Since Illinois generally conforms to federal income tax law, (see ¶10-515) the state's corporate income tax provisions governing exempt organizations are generally the same as federal income tax provisions, IRC Sec. 501—IRC Sec. 530.

• *Interaction of federal and state provisions*

Certain exempt organizations must file annual Illinois income and replacement tax returns. (see ¶89-102)

Unrelated business income.—An exempt organization any Illinois unrelated business income (UBI) that is determined under IRC Sec. 512 is subject to income and replacement taxes and must file an Illinois return. The Illinois standard income tax exemption is not allowed in determining the Illinois net income of an exempt organization. (35 ILCS 5/205(a)) If the organization deducted any Illinois income and replacement taxes on the organization's federal return, it must make an addition adjustment for the amount of the federal deduction in determining taxable Illinois UBI. (35 ILCS 5/205(a)) (Instructions, Form IL-990-T, Exempt Organization Income and Replacement Tax Return)

Political organizations and homeowners' associations.—Exempt political organizations under IRC Sec. 527 that report taxable income on federal Form 1120-POL and exempt homeowners' associations under IRC Sec. 528 that report taxable income on federal Form 1120-H are also subject to Illinois income and replacement taxes and must file an Illinois corporate income and replacement tax return. (Instructions, Form IL-1120, Corporation Income and Replacement Tax Return)

• *Federal income tax provisions*

Organizations may qualify for tax-exempt status if they are organized and operated exclusively for religious, charitable, scientific, testing for public safety, literary, or educational purposes, promotion of amateur sports, or the prevention of cruelty to animals or children (Section 501(c)(3) organizations). Any corporation, community chest, fund, trust, or foundation may qualify for this exemption. Private foundations and organizations that are not public charities are exempt from tax if they are not organized for profit and their earnings do not benefit any individual. Each type of organization must meet specific requirements for exemption. Organizations that are granted exemption will still be taxed on their unrelated business income. In general, an organization must apply for exemption.

[¶10-325]

REGULATED INDUSTRIES

[¶10-335] Insurance Companies

Illinois generally follows the federal income tax treatment of insurance companies, as set out in IRC Secs. 801 through 848. Insurance companies are included in the

¶10-245

definition of "corporation" and as such are subject to income and replacement taxes. Foreign insurance companies and domestic insurance companies that are controlled or owned by foreign taxpayers also pay a privilege tax, based on gross premiums, toward which they receive a credit for any income tax paid to the state. (35 ILCS 5/1501(a)(4); 35 ILCS 5/201(a); 215 ILCS 5/409)

Provisions relating to the taxable income computation of insurance companies are discussed at ¶10-525 Special Industries or Entities.

•*Federal income tax provisions*

Insurance companies are generally subject to income tax computed at the normal corporate tax rates. However, the taxable income of insurance companies is determined under special rules. A company qualifies as an insurance company if more than half of its business during the tax year is the issuing of insurance or annuity contracts, or the reinsuring of risks underwritten by insurance companies. If an insurance company's net written premiums or direct written premiums (whichever is greater) for the tax year do not exceed a specified amount, the company may elect to be taxed only on its taxable investment income. Very small property and casualty (non-life) insurance companies may be exempt from tax if they meet certain requirements.

[¶10-340] Banks--Financial Corporations

Illinois follows the federal income tax treatment of banks, as set out in IRC Secs. 581 through 597. (*Illinois Response to CCH Corporate Income Tax Multistate Survey*, Illinois Department of Revenue, June 27, 2003)

Financial organizations determine taxable income from federal taxable income as do other corporations and make the same modifications. (see ¶10-510) In addition, financial organizations are entitled to certain interest-related subtractions. (see ¶10-815)

Special apportionment rules applicable to multistate financial organizations are discussed at ¶11-540 Apportionment Factors for Specific Industries.

•*Interaction of federal and state provisions*

Financial organizations are broadly defined by statute to include any bank, bank holding company, trust company, savings bank, industrial bank, land bank, safe deposit company, private banker, savings and loan association, building and loan association, credit union, currency exchange, cooperative bank, small loan company, sales finance company, investment company, or any person owned by a bank or bank holding company under provisions of the federal 1956 Bank Holding Company Act. Also, examples are provided explain when an entity engaged in activities other than a that of a financial institution can still be considered a financial institution. (35 ILCS 5/1501(a)(8); 86 Ill. Adm. Code 100.9710)

The term "bank" as used in the definition of "financial organization," includes any entity regulated by the Comptroller of the Currency under the National Bank Act, by the Federal Reserve Board or by the Federal Deposit Insurance Corporation. It also includes a federal or state chartered bank that operates as a credit card bank. The term "sales financing company" means a person who is primarily engaged in the business of purchasing or obtaining loans based upon the security of a retail installment contract, retail charge agreement or the outstanding balance on a retail installment contract or charge agreement. (35 ILCS 5/1501(a)(8); 86 Ill. Adm. Code 100.9710)

•*Federal income tax provisions*

A "bank" for federal tax purposes is a corporation that receives deposits and makes loans or that exercises fiduciary powers as a trust company, and that is subject to banking regulatory supervision by a state or federal government. Banks are subject to the same federal income tax rates that apply to other corporations. Banking institutions are categorized as either commercial or non-commercial institutions. Non-commercial banking institutions include mutual savings banks, savings and loan associations, and credit unions. While similar in many respects to commercial banks, they are controlled by different sets of organizational, operational and regulatory rules, as well as by different sections of the Internal Revenue Code (IRC). Special tax treatment applies to insolvent banks and common trust funds. The definition of "bank" applies specifically under the IRC to bad debts, losses and securities gains, common trust funds, and bad debt reserves.

[¶10-375]
RATES

[¶10-380] Rates of Tax

What is the Illinois corporate income tax rate?

The Illinois corporation income tax rate is 7% of a corporation's net income. (35 ILCS 5/201(b)(13) and (14); *Informational Bulletin FY 2018-02*, Illinois Department of Revenue, July 2017) The tax was imposed at rate of:

- 5.25% for taxable years beginning on or after January 1, 2015 and before July 1, 2017 (35 ILCS 5/201(b)(12) and (13); *Informational Bulletin FY 2015-09*, Illinois Department of Revenue, January 2015); and

- 7% for taxable years before 2015. (35 ILCS 5/201(b)(10))

Planning Note: The tax rate may increase to 7.99% beginning January 1, 2021. The increase will take effect only if voters approve an amendment to the Illinois Constitution authorizing graduated personal income tax rates. (35 ILCS 5/201(b)(15))

If income tax rates change, fiscal year taxpayers must divide total net income between the periods subject to different rates. The apportionment or blended rate method taxes net income as though it was received evenly throughout a single taxable year based on the total number of days in one accounting period and the total number of days in the second accounting period. (35 ILCS 5/202.5(a); *Informational Bulletin FY 2018-14*, Illinois Department of Revenue, November 2017) Taxpayers may make an irrevocable election to use the specific accounting method to treat net income or loss and modifications as though those items were earned in two different taxable years and calculate tax liability at the appropriate rate for each period. (35 ILCS 5/202.5(b); *Informational Bulletin FY 2018-14*, Illinois Department of Revenue, November 2017)

Personal property replacement tax. The Illinois personal property replacement tax rate, which corporations, partnerships, and trusts must pay in addition to the state income tax, is equal to:

- 2.5% of a corporation's net income; and

- 1.5% of a partnership's, trust's, or S corporation's net income. (35 ILCS 5/201(d))

Rate reduction for foreign insurers. An insurer whose state or country of domicile imposes a retaliatory tax on insurers domiciled in Illinois may reduce its Illinois corporate income and personal property replacement tax liability. The insurer may reduce rates to the point that total Illinois tax imposed equals the tax the state or country of domicile would impose on the amount of the insurer's Illinois net income.

The reduction in tax rates cannot reduce the insurer's total liability for Illinois income and replacement, insurance privilege, and fire marshal taxes below 1.75% of the insurer's privilege tax on gross premiums. The rate reduction must be applied first against the corporate income tax rate, minus all credits. Once income tax is reduced to zero, the rate reduction is applied against the insurer's replacement tax. The rate reduction does not apply if 50% or more of an insurer's total insurance premiums for the tax year is from reinsurance, excluding premiums from interaffiliate reinsurance arrangements. (35 ILCS 5/201(d-1)) (Instructions, Schedule INS, Tax for Foreign Insurers; Instructions, Schedule UB/INS, Tax for a Unitary Business Group with Foreign Insurer Members)

The rate reduction is determined by completing Schedule INS and attaching it to the insurer's Illinois corporation income and replacement tax return. If the insurer is a member of a unitary business group, Schedule UB/INS must be completed and attached to the insurer's Illinois income and replacement tax return. A pro forma return from the insurer's state or country of domicile must be attached to the schedule showing the amount of tax the insurer would owe to that state or country on Illinois net income. (Instructions, Schedule INS, Tax for Foreign Insurers; Instructions, Schedule UB/INS, Tax for a Unitary Business Group with Foreign Insurer Members)

Medical cannabis surcharge. Illinois imposes a surcharge on the federal income tax liability of all taxpayers from the sale or exchange of capital assets, depreciable business property, real property used in the trade or business, and Section 197 intangibles of any registrant organization under the Compassionate Use of Medical Cannabis Program. (35 ILCS 5/201(o); 86 Ill. Adm. Code 100.2060) The surcharge does not apply to S corporations, partnerships, or other pass-through entities, but it must be paid by the shareholders, partners, or pass-through entity owners. (86 Ill. Adm. Code 100.2060(c))

The federal income tax liability from transactions triggering the surcharge means the taxpayer's federal income tax liability for the taxable year, minus the taxpayer's federal income tax liability for the taxable year computed as if the transactions had not been made by the registrant organization. If a taxpayer is a member of an affiliated group of corporations that files a federal consolidated income tax return, the resulting amount is multiplied by a fraction equal to the separate taxable income of the member that is subject to the surcharge divided by the sum of the separate taxable incomes of all members of the affiliated group. (86 Ill. Adm. Code 100.2060(d)) The taxpayer's surcharge liability for a taxable year is included in the tax liability for which estimated tax payments must be made for that taxable year. (86 Ill. Adm. Code 100.2060(f)(1))

The surcharge does not apply if the medical cannabis registrant's property is transferred because of:

- bankruptcy, a receivership, or a debt adjustment initiated by or against the initial registrant or the initial registrant's owners;

- cancellation, revocation, or termination of any registration by the Illinois Department of Public Health;

- a determination by the Department of Public Health that transfer is in the best interests of Illinois qualifying patients as defined by the Medical Cannabis Pilot Program Act;

- the death of a registrant's equity owner;

- the acquisition of a controlling interest in the stock or substantially all of the assets of a registrant that is a publicly traded company;

- a transfer by a parent company to a wholly owned subsidiary; or

- the transfer or sale to or by one person to another person who were both initial registrant owners. (35 ILCS 5/201(o)(1); 86 Ill. Adm. Code 100.2060(e)(1))

In addition, the surcharge does not apply if the medical cannabis registrant's property, or the controlling interest in a registrant's property, is transferred to:

- lineal descendants in which no gain or loss is recognized; or

- a controlled corporation in which no gain or loss is recognized. (35 ILCS 5/201(o)(2); 86 Ill. Adm. Code 100.2060(e)(2))

Gaming license surcharge. Effective for tax years 2019 through 2027, Illinois imposes an income tax surcharge on the sale or exchange by gaming licensees of:

- capital assets;

- depreciable business property;

- real property used in the trade or business; and

- IRC Sec. 197 intangibles. (35 ILCS 5/201(b-5))

The surcharge equals the amount of the federal income tax liability for the tax year from the sale or exchange. (35 ILCS 5/201(b-5))

The surcharge does not apply if the sale or exchange results from:

- bankruptcy, a receivership, or a debt adjustment by or against the initial licensee or the owners of the initial licensee;

- cancellation, revocation, or termination of the license by Illinois;

- a determination by Illinois that the transfer is in the best interests of state gaming;

- the death of an equity owner in a licensee;

- the acquisition by a public company of a controlling interest in the licensee's stock or assets;

- a transfer by a parent company to a wholly owned subsidiary; or

- the transfer by one person to another person where both were initial license owners. (35 ILCS 5/201(b-5))

It also does not apply to:

- a transfer to lineal descendants in which there is no recognition of gain or loss;

- a transfer under IRC Sec. 351 to a controlled corporation in which there is no recognition of gain or loss; or

- a transfer by a person other than the initial licensee.

[¶10-500]
TAXABLE INCOME COMPUTATION

[¶10-505] Overview of Taxable Income Computation

A taxpayer computes Illinois corporation income tax liability by:

- starting with federal taxable income;

- making Illinois addition and subtraction adjustments;

- multiplying base income by the taxpayer's apportionment fraction;

- subtracting any net operating loss (NOL) carryover;

- multiplying net income by the income tax rate; and

- applying any income tax credits.

For related information on determining corporation income tax liability, see:

- federal conformity;
- accounting methods and periods; and
- rules for special industries and entities.

[¶10-510] Starting Point for Computation

What is the starting point for computation of the Illinois corporate income tax?

The starting point for the computation of Illinois corporate income tax is the taxpayer's federal taxable income reported on Line 30 of its federal income tax return. This amount reflects the taxpayer's federal taxable income after federal net operating loss and special deductions. (35 ILCS 5/203(e); Instructions, Form IL-1120, Corporation Income and Replacement Tax Return)

The Illinois taxable income base is determined differently for certain special industries and entities, including:

— life insurance companies;

— nonlife mutual or nonlife stock insurance companies;

— regulated investment companies (RICs);

— real estate investment trusts (REITs);

— cooperatives or associations;

— non-U.S. corporations.

[¶10-515] Federal Conformity

Illinois incorporates by reference the Internal Revenue Code of 1986, as amended, and other federal provisions relating to federal income tax laws applicable for the taxable year. (35 ILCS 5/102)

An overview of taxable income computation is located at ¶10-505.

[¶10-525] Special Industries or Entities

Illinois taxable income/base income is determined differently for certain types of corporations.

•*Insurance companies*

Life insurance companies compute their income tax liability in the same manner as other corporations except that "Gross income", for tax years after 2011, means all amounts included in life insurance gross income under IRC §803(a)(3). For prior periods, it was defined as the life insurance company's gross investment income for the taxable year. (35 ILCS 5/203(b)(3); 35 ILCS 5/203(b)(1) and (2)(A); 35 ILCS 5/203(b)(2))

In addition, life insurance companies subject to the federal income tax imposed by IRC Sec. 801(a) add the amount of distribution from pre-1984 policyholder surplus accounts as calculated under IRC Sec. 815(c). Mutual insurance companies subject to the tax imposed by IRC Sec. 803 begin computation of Illinois net income with federal insurance company taxable income. (35 ILCS 5/203(e)(2)(A); 35 ILCS 5/203(e)(2)(B)) (*Instructions, Form IL-1120, Illinois Corporation Income and Replacement Tax Return*)

Additionally, in the case of an attorney-in-fact with respect to whom an interinsurer or reciprocal insurer has made the election under IRC Sec. 835, a subtraction modification may be taken in an amount equal to the excess of the amounts paid or incurred by that interinsurer or reciprocal insurer in the taxable year to the attorney-in-fact over the deduction allowed to that interinsurer or reciprocal insurer with respect to the attorney-in-fact. (35 ILCS 5/203(b)(2)(R))

Additional discussion of insurance companies is located at ¶10-335 and a discussion of the addition of insurance premium expenses and costs is located at ¶10-620.

• *Interinsurers and reciprocal underwriters*

If a mutual insurance company that is an interinsurer or reciprocal insurer has made an election under IRC Sec. 835 to take into account the income of an attorney-in-fact that results from the interinsurer's or reciprocal insurer's payment of commissions to the attorney-in-fact, the interinsurer or reciprocal insurer may take an adjustment for that income in calculating its base income for Illinois corporate income tax purposes. An interinsurer or reciprocal insurer makes the adjustment in calculating base income by adding to federal taxable income the excess, if any, of the amounts the interinsurer or reciprocal insurer paid to the attorney-in-fact during the taxable year over the deduction allowed to the interinsurer or reciprocal insurer under IRC Sec. 835(b) for the attorney-in-fact's deductions allocable to the income received from the insurer. (35 ILCS 5/203(b)(2))

• *Nonlife mutual/nonlife stock insurance companies*

For nonlife mutual or nonlife stock insurance companies subject to the tax imposed by IRC Sec. 831, taxable income is the insurance company taxable income. (*Instructions, Form IL-1120, Illinois Corporation Income and Replacement Tax Return*)

• *Regulated investment companies*

A regulated investment company's Illinois base income starts with taxable income under IRC Sec. 852. (35 ILCS 5/203(e)(2)(C); Instructions, Form IL-1120, Corporation Income and Replacement Tax Return) Regulated investment companies (RICs) must include the excess of the net long-term capital gain for the tax year over the amount of:

- capital gain dividends under IRC Sec. 852(b)(3)(C); and

- undistributed capital gains designated under IRC Sec. 852(b)(3)(D). (35 ILCS 5/203(b)(2)(C); Instructions, Form IL-1120, Corporation Income and Replacement Tax Return)

A RIC can subtract from federal taxable income the amount of exempt interest dividends paid to shareholders under IRC Sec. 852(b)(5). (35 ILCS 5/203(b)(2)(H)) The deduction is entered on Schedule M. (Instructions, Schedule M, Schedule M, Other Additions and Subtractions (for businesses))

• *Real estate investment trusts*

The starting point for computing Illinois corporate income tax liability for real estate investment trusts (REITs) subject to tax under IRC Sec. 857 is the REIT's federal taxable income. (35 ILCS 5/203(e)(2)(D))

Illinois requires an addition to federal taxable income for the federal dividends paid deduction allowed to captive REITs under IRC Sec. 857(b)(2)(B). (35 ILCS 5/203(E-15))

The term "captive real estate investment trust" is a corporation, trust, or association of which more than 50% of the voting power or value is owned or controlled by a single corporation. (35 ILCS 5/1501(a)(1.5)(A)) The constructive ownership rules under IRC Sec. 318 apply in determining the ownership of stock, assets, or net profits. (35 ILCS 5/1501(a)(1.5)(B))

A captive REIT does not include:

- a corporation exempt from tax under IRC Sec. 501 and that is not required to treat the dividends as unrelated taxable business income;

• a listed Australian property trust that does not meet the definition of a captive REIT; or

• a business organized outside the U.S. that does not meet the definition of a captive REIT. (35 ILCS 5/1501(a)(1.5)(B))

• *Cooperatives or associations*

Cooperatives or associations determine taxable income in accordance with the provisions of IRC Secs. 1381 through 1388. (*Instructions, Form IL-1120, Illinois Corporation Income and Replacement Tax Return*)

• *S corporations and partnerships*

The computation of Illinois personal property replacement tax liability (replacement tax) for a partnership or S corporation generally starts with a taxpayer's federal taxable income. (35 ILCS 5/203(d)(1) and (e)(1)) However, taxable income must take into account that must be separately stated under:

• IRC Sec. 703(a)(1) for partnerships; (35 ILCS 5/203(e)(2)(H)) or

• IRC Sec. 1363(b)(1) for S corporations. (35 ILCS 5/203(e)(2)(G))

Partners in a partnership or beneficiaries of a trust or an estate must add their distributive share of additions received from the partnership, trust, or estate on Form IL-1120 Illinois Corporation Income and Replacement Tax Return. (*Instructions, Form IL-1120, Illinois Corporation Income and Replacement Tax Return*)

Partners in a partnership or beneficiaries of a trust or an estate subtract their distributive share of subtractions received from the partnership, trust, or estate on Form IL-1120 Illinois Corporation Income and Replacement Tax Return. (*Instructions, Form IL-1120, Illinois Corporation Income and Replacement Tax Return*)

Ordinary income or loss. Illinois ordinary income or loss corresponds to a partner's distributive, or shareholder's pro rata, share of federal income from:

• Form 1120S, Schedule K, lines 1-8a and 9; (Instructions, Form IL-1120-ST, Small Business Corporation Replacement Tax Return) or

• Form 1065, Schedule K, lines 1-9a and 10. (Instructions, Form IL-1065, Partnership Replacement Tax Return)

Compliance Alert: A partnership's or S corporation's ordinary income or loss for the 2017 tax year must include the amount from line 1 of the IRC Sec. 965 Transition Tax Statement. Taxpayers must attach a copy of the federal transition tax statement to their Illinois replacement tax return. Electronic filers may submit the statement by email to rev.BitSupplemental@illinois.gov as a PDF file. The filename and email subject line should be "965 Tax." (Instructions, Form IL-1120-ST, Small Business Corporation Replacement Tax Return; Instructions, Form IL-1065, Partnership Replacement Tax Return)

Taxpayers that already filed a 2017 Illinois replacement tax return and did not include IRC Sec. 965 net income must amend their return to report that income. (*Informational Bulletin FY 2018-23*, Illinois Department of Revenue, March 21, 2018)

Unmodified bases income or loss. Illinois "unmodified base income" corresponds to a partner's distributive, or shareholder's pro rata share, of federal deductions from:

• Form 1120S, Schedule K, lines 11, 12a, and 12b; (Instructions, Form IL-1120-ST, Small Business Corporation Replacement Tax Return) or

• Form 1065, Schedule K, lines 12, 13a, and 13b. (Instructions, Form IL-1065, Partnership Replacement Tax Return)

Compliance Alert: Illinois unmodified base for the 2017 tax year must include the IRC Sec. 965 deduction from line 3 of the Transition Tax Statement. Taxpayers must attach a copy of the federal transition tax statement to their Illinois replacement tax return. Electronic filers may submit the statement by email to rev.BitSupplemental@illinois.gov as a PDF file. The filename and email subject line should be "965 Tax." (Instructions, Form IL-1120-ST, Small Business Corporation Replacement Tax Return; Instructions, Form IL-1065, Partnership Replacement Tax Return)

Unmodified base income or loss may not include:

- net operating loss (NOL) carryovers;

- IRC Sec. 199 domestic production activities deduction (DPAD); or

- oil and gas depletion deduction. (Instructions, Form IL-1120-ST, Small Business Corporation Replacement Tax Return; Instructions, Form IL-1065, Partnership Replacement Tax Return)

Although S corporations and partnerships may not claim a DPAD, they may calculate and pass through the deduction to their partners and shareholders. (*Informational Bulletin FY 2006-07*, Illinois Department of Revenue, February 2006; Instructions, Form IL-1120-ST, Small Business Corporation Replacement Tax Return; Instructions, Form IL-1065, Partnership Replacement Tax Return)

Additions to base income. S corporations and partnerships computing Illinois replacement tax liability must add to base income:

- federally exempt interest from state, municipal, or other government obligations excluded from federal taxable income; (35 ILCS 5/203(d)(2)(A))

- Illinois replacement tax deducted from federal taxable income; (35 ILCS 5/203(d)(2)(B))

- guaranteed payments deducted from federal taxable income under IRC Sec. 707(c) (partnerships only);

- bonus depreciation under IRC Sec. 168(k), other than 100% bonus depreciation; (35 ILCS 5/203(d)(2)(D-5))

- related party expenses (i.e., interest, intangibles, or insurance premiums); (35 ILCS 5/203(d)(2)(D-7), (D-8), and (D-9))

- distributive share of additions received from a partnership, S corporation, trust or estate as reported on Schedules K-1-P or K-1-T.

Prior to August 7, 2012, dividends included on the federal return from corporations that conduct substantially all of their operations in enterprise zones were subtracted from federal taxable income. (35 ILCS 5/203(d)(2)(K)) Dividends included federally from high impact businesses located in Illinois that conduct business operations in federally designated Foreign Trade Zones or Sub Zones are still subtracted. (35 ILCS 5/203(d)(2)(M))

Constitutionally exempt income.—In computing the replacement tax, items exempted by the Illinois Constitution or federal law are subtracted from federal taxable income. (35 ILCS 5/203(d)(2)(G))

Distributable income.—In the case of a partner subject to replacement tax, the share of distributable income should be reflected in Line 5d. Multiply each line referenced in the worksheet by the percentage of total ownership in the partnership attributable to these partners, and any share of distributable loss should be reported on Line 2e. Form IL-2569 must be attached to Form IL-1065. (*Instructions, Form IL-1065, Illinois Partnership Replacement Tax Form*)

¶10-525

Partnership acquisitions.—An acquiring partnership may claim the state income tax credits and net operating losses of a partnership that is acquired in an IRC Sec. 708 continuation of a partnership, applicable retroactively to all acquisitions occurring in taxable years ending after December 30, 1986. However, transitional rules apply concerning a taxpayer's eligibility for refunds and assessment reductions for pre-1999 tax liabilities. (35 ILCS 5/405)

The portion of capital gain attributable to pre-August 1, 1969, asset appreciation is subtracted from federal adjusted gross income. (35 ILCS 5/203(d)(2)(E)) This appreciation is called the "valuation limitation amount." The valuation limitation amount is equal to the pre-August 1, 1969, appreciation recaptured under IRC Sec. 1245 and IRC Sec. 1250 for the taxable year, plus the lesser of (1) the portion of federal capital gain for the tax year attributable to pre-August 1, 1969, appreciation amounts, or (2) the net capital gain for the tax year reduced by capital gains recognized federally from distributions from public retirement plans, individual retirement accounts, retirement bonds and payments to retired partners. (35 ILCS 5/203(f)(1)(A), (B), (2)(A), (B))

If the fair market value of property was readily ascertainable on August 1, 1969, the "pre-August 1, 1969, appreciation amount," is the lesser of (1) the excess of the August 1, 1969, value over the federal basis of the property on that date; or (2) the total gain reportable federally with respect to the property. (35 ILCS 5/203(f)(1)(A), (B), (2)(A), (B), (B), (2)(A), (B))

If the fair market value of property was not readily ascertainable on August 1, 1969, the "pre-August 1, 1969, appreciation amount" is that portion of the federal gain as the number of full calendar months in the holding period of the property ending July 31, 1969, bears to the number of full calendar months in the entire holding period. (35 ILCS 5/203(f)(1)(A), (B), (2)(A), (B))

The valuation limitation subtraction is computed and reported on Schedule F, Gains from Sales or Exchanges of Property Acquired Before August 1, 1969. (Instructions, Form IL-1065, Illinois Partnership Replacement Tax Form, Schedule F)

Income distributed to other entities.—In computing the replacement tax, partnership income distributable to another partnership, trust, or estate subject to the Personal Property Replacement Income Tax, including amounts distributable to charitable, religious, and educational organizations that are exempt from federal income tax under IRC Sec. 501(a), is subtracted from income. (35 ILCS 5/203(d)(2)(I))

Bond premiums.—In computing the replacement tax, the following items are subtracted from federal taxable income: (1) amortizable bond premium not deducted federally under IRC Sec. 171(a)(2), because attributable to tax-free bonds and (2) interest not deducted federally under IRC Sec. 265, because incurred or continued to purchase or carry tax-free obligations. In addition, effective for taxable years ending after August 12, 1999, taxpayers may deduct from federal adjusted income expenses associated with federal employment credits, the credit for qualified clinical testing expenses, and the credit for increasing research activities that are disallowed as federal deductions under IRC Sec. 280C. (35 ILCS 5/203(d)(2)(J))

Job training project contributions.—In computing the replacement tax, contributions to a job training project established pursuant to the "Real Property Tax Increment Allocation Redevelopment Act" are subtracted from federal taxable income. (35 ILCS 5/203(d)(2)(L))

Repayment of items previously included in gross income.—Partnerships that take the federal income tax credit under IRC Sec. 1341 for repayment to another of income items previously included in gross income as being held under a claim of right may subtract from federal taxable income, for Illinois income tax purposes, an amount equal to the deduction used to compute the federal income tax credit. (35 ILCS 5/203(d)(2)(N))

The amount of replacement tax refunds that were included in the partnership's federal taxable income is subtracted. (35 ILCS 5/203(d)(2)(F))

Personal service income.—In computing the replacement tax, partnership income that constitutes personal service income is subtracted from income. The amount of the subtraction is the greater of (1) the amount of "personal service income" under IRC Sec. 1348(b)(1) as in effect December 31, 1981; or (2) a reasonable allowance for compensation paid or accrued for service rendered by the partners to the partnership. (35 ILCS 5/203(d)(2)(H))

Standard exemption.—The standard exemption is subtracted from partnership base income to arrive at replacement tax net income. The applicable amount is multiplied by the percentage the portion of partnership base income allocable to Illinois bears to total partnership base income. (35 ILCS 5/204(a)) (Instructions, Form IL-1065 Illinois Partnership Replacement Tax Return)

Net loss deduction.—If Illinois net income results in a loss, it may generally be carried back or forward. For tax years ending on or after December 31, 2003, a net loss may be carried forward 12 years and may not be carried back. For tax years ending on or after December 31, 1999 and prior to December 31, 2003, a net loss may be carried back two years or carried forward 20 years. (35 ILCS 5/207)

Nonresident withholding requirements.—Partnerships are subject to withholding requirements for each nonresident partner.

Partnership's share of other entities.—For income tax purposes, a partnership or an S corporation is required to send an Illinois Schedule K-1-P and the trust or the estate is required to send an Illinois Schedule K-1-T, specifically identifying the share of income. Illinois addition and subtraction modifications from other partnerships, trusts, or estates of which the partnership is a partner or beneficiary must be taken into account. (Instructions, Form IL-1065, Illinois Partnership Replacement Tax Form)

• *S corporation shareholder income*

S corporations may subtract an amount equal to all income allocable to a shareholder subject to the personal property replacement income tax, including amounts allocable to organizations exempt under IRC 501(a). (35 ILCS 5/203(b)(2)(S))

S corporations are discussed at ¶ 10-215.

• *Foreign corporations*

Foreign corporations determine taxable income in accordance with the provisions of IRC Secs. 881 through 885. (*Instructions, Form IL-1120, Illinois Corporation Income and Replacement Tax Return*)

An overview of taxable income computation is located at ¶ 10-505.

[¶ 10-530] Alternate Taxable Income Computation Methods

The personal property replacement income tax (which was enacted to replace the corporate personal property tax) is an additional income tax that is imposed on corporations, partnerships, S corporations, and limited liability companies (LLCs). The required additions and subtractions for replacement tax purposes are the same as the corporate income tax additions (see ¶ 10-600) and subtractions (see ¶ 10-800). The replacement tax is calculated on Form IL-1120, Illinois Corporation Income and Replacement Tax Return.

[¶10-600] Additions to Taxable Income Base

Taxpayers computing Illinois corporate income and replacement tax liability must add to the federal taxable income starting point:

- net operating losses;
- federally exempt interest;
- taxes;
- IRC Sec. 965 transition income;
- related party expenses;
- the GILTI and FDII deduction;
- business expense recapture;
- student assistance contributions; and
- bonus depreciation. (see ¶10-670)

For a list of Illinois subtraction adjustments, see Subtractions from Taxable Income Base.

[¶10-605] Additions--Net Operating Loss

Does Illinois require an addback for the NOL deduction?

The starting point for computing Illinois corporate income tax liability is federal taxable income after net operating losses (NOLs). Illinois requires an addition to federal taxable income for a taxpayer's NOL deduction. (35 ILCS 5/203(b)(2)(D); 86 Ill. Adm. Code 100.2320; 86 Ill. Adm. Code 100.2410) It allows a NOL deduction from adjusted and apportioned Illinois income.

For a list of other Illinois addition adjustments, see Additions to Taxable Income Base.

[¶10-610] Additions--Federally Exempt Interest

Interest on state and local obligations, including those of Illinois and its political subdivisions, is exempt from federal income taxation but is generally subject to Illinois corporate income tax. Such interest, as well as distributions received from regulated business companies investing in such obligations, must be added back to taxable income on Form IL-1120Corporation Income and Replacement Tax Return, to the extent excluded from gross income in computing federal taxable income. (35 ILCS 5/203(b)(2)(A); *Publication 101, Income Exempt from Tax*, Illinois Department of Revenue) See ¶10-525 for a discussion of gross income for insurance company purposes.

Certain interest income is also exempt from Illinois corporate income tax but is not included in federal taxable income. (*Publication 101, Income Exempt from Tax*, Illinois Department of Revenue, December 2004) Income from the following must be added to federal taxable income for Illinois purposes but then can be claimed as subtractions when figuring Illinois base income:

— Government of Guam; (86 Ill. Adm. 100.2470(c)(12))

— Government of Puerto Rico; (86 Ill. Adm. 100.2470(c)(16))

— Government of the Virgin Islands; (86 Ill. Adm. 100.2470(c)(24)); and

— Mutual Mortgage Insurance Fund (income from such is issued in exchange for property covered by mortgages insured after February 3, 1988). (86 Ill. Adm. 100.2470(c)(13))

The subtractions from federal taxable income for interest income that is exempt from Illinois corporate income tax are discussed at ¶10-815.

Other additions to the taxable income base are listed at ¶10-600.

[¶10-615] Additions--Taxes

Illinois requires an addition adjustment by taxpayers computing corporate income and replacement tax liability for:

- Illinois income and replacement tax deducted from federal taxable income; and
- the IRC Sec. 965 foreign income repatriation transition tax.

- *Illinois income and replacement tax*

Taxpayers that claimed a federal income tax deduction for Illinois income and replacement taxes must add the amount back to federal taxable income for Illinois tax purposes. (35 ILCS 5/203(b)(2)(B)) The addition adjustment must be reported on Schedule M The schedule must be attached to the taxpayer's Illinois corporate income and replacement tax return. (Instructions, Schedule M, Other Additions and Subtractions (for businesses))

- *Foreign income repatriation transition tax*

IRC Sec. 965 requires taxpayers with untaxed foreign earnings and profits to pay a tax as if those earnings and profits had been repatriated to the U.S. A deduction is allowed that reduces the tax rate on those earnings. Taxpayers with IRC Sec. 965 income must include a transition tax statement with their return. This statement is separate from the federal income tax return. Due to the separate nature of the IRC Sec. 965 transition tax statement, the income is not included in federal taxable income. However, Illinois taxpayers must include the tax when determining base income for state tax purposes. (*Informational Bulletin FY 2018-23*, Illinois Department of Revenue, March 21, 2018)

Reporting requirements. Illinois corporate income and replacement taxpayers must report IRC Sec. 965 net income (i.e., IRC Sec. 965 income minus the allowable deduction) as an addition adjustment on Schedule M. Taxpayers that already filed a 2017 Illinois income tax return and did not include IRC Sec. 965 net income must amend their return to report that income. (*Informational Bulletin FY 2018-23*, Illinois Department of Revenue, March 21, 2018; Instructions, Schedule M, Other Additions and Subtractions (for businesses))

Taxpayers must attach a copy of the federal transition tax statement to their Illinois returns and computation schedules as a PDF file. Electronic filers may submit the statement by email to rev.BitSupplemental@illinois.gov as a PDF file. The filename and email subject line should be "965 Tax." Taxpayers should also include their business name and FEIN. (Instructions, Schedule M, Other Additions and Subtractions (for businesses))

Installment payment election. Illinois does not follow the election under IRC Sec. 965 to pay the tax liability in installments over eight years. (*Informational Bulletin FY 2018-23*, Illinois Department of Revenue, March 21, 2018)

For a list of other Illinois addition adjustments, see Additions to Taxable Income Base.

[¶10-620] Additions--Corporate Transactions

Does Illinois require an addback for related party expenses?

Illinois requires an addition to federal taxable income for certain expenses paid to affiliated:

- 80/20 companies; and
- effective for tax years before 2017, noncombination rule companies. (35 ILCS 5/203(b)(2)(E-12), (E-13), and (E)(14); 86 Ill. Adm. Code Sec. 100.2430(a))

To avoid double taxation, Illinois allows a corresponding subtraction adjustment for the income received from the affiliated company.

An 80/20 company is any company that a unitary business group cannot include in an Illinois combined report because it conducts 80% or more of its business activities outside the U.S. (35 ILCS 5/203(b)(2)(E-12) and (E-13); 86 Ill. Adm. Code Sec. 100.2430(b)(2))

Does Illinois require an addback for related party interest expenses? Every taxpayer must add back to its base income any federal deduction for interest paid to:

- an 80/20 company; and

- effective for tax years before 2017, a noncombination rule company. (35 ILCS 5/203(b)(2)(E-12); 86 Ill. Adm. Code Sec. 100.2430(c)(1))

Interest includes the amortization of any discount at which an obligation is purchased and is net of the amortization of any premium at which an obligation is purchased. (86 Ill. Adm. Code Sec. 100.2430(b)(3))

A taxpayer can reduce the addition adjustment by dividends received from each affiliated company, plus:

- IRC Sec. 78 gross-up income; and

- Subpart F income. (35 ILCS 5/203(b)(2)(E-12); Instructions, Schedule 80/20, Related Party Expenses)

If a taxpayer's business interest deduction is subject to limitation under IRC Sec. 163(j), the taxpayer must use a formula to determine the amount of interest paid to an affiliated company and deducted in computing base income for the tax year. The formula is equal to the business interest paid to that affiliate for the tax year, including any business interest carryforward from a previous tax year, multiplied by a fraction. The fraction is equal to the business interest deduction allowed under IRC Sec. 163(j) divided by the total business interest paid for the tax year. (86 Ill. Adm. Code Sec. 100.2430(b)(10))

Example: In Year 1, Taxpayer paid $100 in business interest to an 80/20 affiliate and $1,000 in total business interest. There is no carryforward under IRC Sec. 163(j)(2) from the previous year. Under IRC Sec. 163(j), Taxpayer's federal income tax deduction for business interest in Year 1 is limited to $800. In Year 2, Taxpayer paid $130 in business interest to an 80/20 affiliate and $1,800 in total business interest. Taxpayer's federal income tax deduction for business interest in Year 2 is limited under IRC Sec. 163(j) to $1,200.

The federal income tax deduction allowed to Taxpayer for interest paid equals $80: the $100 actually paid multiplied by 80% (the $800 federal income tax deduction allowed for business interest divided by the $1,000 in total business interest paid). The carryforward of interest paid in Year 1 to Year 2 equals $20: the $100 actually paid multiplied by 20% (the $200 carryforward to Year 2 divided by the $1,000 in total business interest paid in Year 1).

The federal income tax deduction for interest paid in Year 2 equals $90: the $130 in interest actually paid plus the $20 paid in Year 1 and carried forward to Year 2, or $150, multiplied by 60% (the $1,200 federal income tax deduction allowed for business interest divided by the $2,000 in total business interest for Year 2, which equals the $1,800 actually paid plus the $200 carryover from Year 1). The carryforward of interest paid in Year 2 to Year 3 equals $60: the $150 paid in Year 2 or carried forward from Year 1, multiplied by 40% (the $800 carryforward to Year 3 divided by the $2,000 in total business interest paid in Year 2 or carried forward from Year 1).

The interest addback does not apply if:

- the affiliated company is subject to income tax on that interest in a foreign country or another state that does not require mandatory unitary reporting;

- the taxpayer can establish by clear and convincing evidence that the addback is unreasonable; or

- the taxpayer received written permission to use an alternative apportionment method. (35 ILCS 5/203(b)(2)(E-12); 86 Ill. Adm. Code Sec. 100.2430(c)(1))

The addback also does not apply if the taxpayer can establish by a preponderance of evidence that:

- the transaction did not have a principal purpose of avoiding federal or Illinois income tax;

- it paid the interest at arm's-length rates and terms; and

- the affiliated company paid interest to an unrelated party during the same tax year. (35 ILCS 5/203(b)(2)(E-12); 86 Ill. Adm. Code Sec. 100.2430(c)(1))

Does Illinois require an addback for related party intangible expenses? Every taxpayer must add back to its base income intangible expenses paid to a:

- an 80/20 company; and

- effective for tax years before 2017, a noncombination rule company. (35 ILCS 5/203(b)(2)(E-13); 86 Ill. Adm. Code Sec. 100.2430(c)(2))

Intangible expenses include:

- expenses for the acquisition, use, management, ownership, or sale or other disposition of intangible assets;

- losses from sales or other dispositions of intangible assets to an 80/20 company;

- losses on factoring or discounting transactions with an 80/20 company; and

- royalty, patent, technical, and copyright fees;

- licensing fees; and

- other similar expenses and costs. (86 Ill. Adm. Code Sec. 100.2430(b)(4); Instructions, Schedule 80/20, Related Party Expenses)

Intangible assets include:

- patents and patent applications;

- trade names, trademarks, and service marks;

- copyrights;

- mask works;

- trade secrets; and

- similar intangible property. (35 ILCS 5/203(b)(2)(E-13); 86 Ill. Adm. Code Sec. 100.2430(b)(6))

A taxpayer can reduce the addition adjustment by dividends received from each affiliated company, plus:

- IRC Sec. 78 gross-up income; and

- Subpart F income. (35 ILCS 5/203(b)(2)(E-13); Instructions, Schedule 80/20, Related Party Expenses)

The addback does not apply if:

- the affiliated company is subject to tax on the intangible income in a foreign country or another state that does not require mandatory unitary reporting;

- the taxpayer can establish by clear and convincing evidence that the addback is unreasonable; or

- the taxpayer received written permission to use an alternative apportionment method. (35 ILCS 5/203(b)(2)(E-13); 86 Ill. Adm. Code Sec. 100.2430(c)(2))

The addback also does not apply if the taxpayer can establish by a preponderance of evidence that:

- the transaction did not have a principal purpose of avoiding federal or Illinois income tax;

- it paid the intangible expenses at arm's-length rates and terms; and

- the affiliated company incurred intangible expenses in a transaction with an unrelated party during the same tax year. (35 ILCS 5/203(b)(2)(E-12); 86 Ill. Adm. Code Sec. 100.2430(c)(2))

Does Illinois require an addback for other related party expenses? Effective for tax years before 2017, Illinois required an addback for insurance premiums paid to noncombination rule companies. (35 ILCS 5/203(b)(2)(E-14); 86 Ill. Adm. Code Sec. 100.2430(c)(3))

How do taxpayers report the related party expense addbacks?

Taxpayers compute and report the related party interest and intangible expenses addbacks on Schedule 80/20. (Instructions, Schedule 80/20, Related Party Expenses)

For a list of other Illinois addition adjustments, see Additions to Taxable Income Base.

[¶10-630] Additions--Dividends

Does Illinois require an addback for the GILTI and FDII deduction?

Yes, Illinois requires an addback for the federal deduction allowed under IRC Sec. 250 in computing:

- global intangible low-taxed income (GILTI); and

- foreign-derived intangible income (FDII). (35 ILCS 5/203(b)(E-18))

The Tax Cuts and Jobs Act (TCJA) added IRC Sec. 951A to tax U.S. corporations on GILTI and FDII. IRC Sec. 250 allows a corporation with GILTI and FDII to deduct part of that income on its federal return. The deduction reduces the rate of U.S. tax on GILTI and FDII.

The Illinois addback applies to tax years beginning after 2018. (35 ILCS 5/203(b)(E-18))

For a list of other Illinois addition adjustments, see Additions to Taxable Income Base.

[¶10-650] Additions--Charitable Contributions

If a taxpayer has made contributions to the student assistance contributions credit, the taxpayer must add an amount equal to the credit under 35 ILCS 5/218(a), determined without regard to 35 ILCS 5/218(c). (35 ILCS 5/203(b)(2)(E-16))

[¶10-660] Additions--Items Related to Federal Deductions or Credits

Effective for the 2017 tax year, Illinois required an addition to federal taxable income by taxpayers for the amount of any IRC Sec. 199 domestic production activity deduction (DPAD). (35 ILCS 5/203(b)(2)(E-17)) The federal DPAD was repealed for tax years after 2017.

[¶10-670] Additions--Depreciation

Does Illinois require an addback of federal bonus depreciation deductions?

Yes, Illinois requires an addback of federal bonus depreciation deductions under Internal Revenue Code (IRC) Sec. 168(k). (35 ILCS 5/203(b)(2)(E-10))

Compliance Alert: Illinois allows the 100% bonus depreciation deduction enacted by the Tax Cuts and Jobs Act (TCJA). The 100% bonus depreciation deduction applies to qualified property acquired and placed in service after September 27, 2017. (Instructions, Form IL-4562, Special Depreciation) The amount of bonus depreciation allowed under the TCJA for property acquired before September 28, 2017, is:

- 50% if the placed in service in 2017;
- 40% if placed in service in 2018; and
- 30% if placed in service in 2019.

The Illinois addition adjustment applies to taxpayers claiming the 40% federal bonus depreciation deduction. (Instructions, Form IL-4562, Special Depreciation)

A corporation that claims a federal bonus depreciation deduction must enter the addition adjustment on Form IL-4562. The corporation must attach the depreciation form to its Illinois corporation income and replacement tax return. (Instructions, Form IL-4562, Special Depreciation)

Illinois allows a subtraction adjustment for a portion of bonus depreciation a corporation claimed on its federal income tax return. If the taxpayer sells, transfers, abandons, or otherwise disposes of property for which it claimed an Illinois depreciation deduction, an addition adjustment is required for the amount of the state depreciation deductions taken in all tax years for that property. If the corporation continues to own property through the last day of the last tax year for which it may claim a federal depreciation deduction and for which it was allowed an Illinois subtraction adjustment, an addition must be made for the amount of that subtraction adjustment. (35 ILCS 5/203(b)(2)(E-11))

Does Illinois require an addback of federal deductions taken for depreciation other than bonus depreciation?

No, Illinois does not require an addback of federal deductions taken for depreciation other than bonus depreciation. (35 ILCS 5/203(b)(2); Instructions, Form IL-1120, Corporation Income and Replacement Tax Return; Instructions, Schedule M, Other Additions and Subtractions)

Does Illinois require an addback of Sec. 179 asset expense deduction amounts?

No, Illinois does not require an addback of Sec. 179 asset expense deduction amounts. (35 ILCS 5/203(b)(2); Instructions, Form IL-1120, Corporation Income and Replacement Tax Return; Instructions, Schedule M, Other Additions and Subtractions)

[¶10-800] Subtractions from Taxable Income Base

Taxpayers computing Illinois corporate income and replacement tax liability can subtract from the federal taxable income starting point:

- net operating losses;
- dividends;
- GILTI;

- IRC Sec. 965 transition income;
- Subpart F income;
- interest;
- taxes;
- income from targeted business activity and zones;
- job training project contributions; and
- bonus depreciation

For a list of Illinois addition adjustments, see Additions to Taxable Income Base.

[¶10-805] Subtractions--Net Operating Loss

Does Illinois allow a net operating loss (NOL) deduction?

Yes, Illinois allows a net operation loss deduction (NOLD) based on IRC Sec. 172. (35 ILCS 5/207; 86 Ill. Adm. Code 100.2300(a))

Comment: The Tax Cuts and Jobs Act (TCJA) (P.L. 115-97) added an 80% taxable income on NOLs from tax years after 2017. Illinois has a rolling IRC conformity tie-in provision. So, it automatically adopted the 80% limit. (*Press Release: Impact of Federal Tax Cuts and Jobs Act,* Illinois Department of Revenue, March 1, 2018) The Coronavirus Aid, Relief, and Economic Security (CARES) Act (P.L. 116-136) suspended the limit until tax years beginning after 2020. Illinois has not issued guidance on the CARES Act change. Taxpayers can contact the Illinois Department of Revenue about its treatment of the CARES Act change or request a private letter ruling.

A taxpayer can claim a NOL carryforward deduction after it:

- applies all Illinois addition and subtraction modifications; and
- allocates and apportions income to Illinois. (35 ILCS 5/207; 86 Ill. Adm. Code 100.2300(a); 86 Ill. Adm. Code 100.2320(b))

A taxpayer's NOLD for any tax year equals the sum of the Illinois net loss carryforwards to that tax year. (86 Ill. Adm. Code 100.2310(a))

Example: Corporation A has federal taxable income of $200, less a $100 federal NOLD relating to a NOL incurred in 2015. In 2016, Corporation A also has $300 of Illinois addition modifications relating to income from state obligations, $200 of subtraction modifications for income from U.S. obligations, $400 of nonbusiness loss allocable to Illinois, and a 50% apportionment factor in Illinois. Corporation A would compute its 2016 Illinois net loss as follows:

Line 1	taxable income	$100
Plus	addition modification for	$100 federal NOLD relating to 1986 loss
Plus	other addition modification	$300
Minus	subtraction modification	($200)
Equals	base income	$300
Minus	nonbusiness loss	($400)
Equals	business income	$700
Times	50% apportionment factor	$350
Plus	nonbusiness loss allocable to Illinois	($400)
Equals	Illinois net loss	($50)

A taxpayer claiming an Illinois NOL must:

- complete Schedule NLD;
- enter the resulting NOL on its annual Illinois income tax return; and
- attach the computation schedule to the return. (Instructions, Schedule NLD, Illinois Net Loss Deduction)

Schedule NLD shows:

- the total amount of Illinois net loss available;
- the amount deductible for the tax year; and
- the remaining NOLD available for use in later tax years. (Instructions, Schedule NLD, Illinois Net Loss Deduction)

Does Illinois require NOL adjustments for debt cancellation income? A corporation that reduced its federal NOL carryforward by the amount of debt cancellation income excluded under IRC Sec. 108(a) must also reduce its Illinois NOL carryforward. The reduction applies to the year of the debt cancellation. Taxpayers calculate the amount by dividing:

- the debt cancellation income that would have been allocated or apportioned to Illinois if it was not excluded from federal gross income for the tax year by
- the debt cancellation income excluded from gross income. (35 ILCS 5/207(c); 86 Ill. Adm. Code 100.2310(c))

If all debt cancellation income would have been business income, the taxpayer must use the apportionment factor for the tax year of the debt cancellation. (Instructions, Schedule NLD, Illinois Net Loss Deduction)

A taxpayer must apply the reduction to the NOL carryforward beginning with the earliest loss year and continue in order until:

- it has applied the entire NOL carryforward reduction; or
- it has reduced carryforwards to zero. (86 Ill. Adm. Code 100.2310(c)) (Instructions, Schedule NLD, Illinois Net Loss Deduction)

Example 1: For its taxable year ending December 31, 2016, Taxpayer has $50,000 of debt cancellation income excluded from gross income under IRC section 108(a). The entire $50,000 would have been included in the Taxpayer's Illinois business income and a total of $10,000 of the income would have been apportioned to Illinois. Taxpayer has a federal NOL of $40,000 for its December 31, 2016 taxable year, and an Illinois net loss of $8,000. Taxpayer is required to reduce its federal net operating loss from $40,000 to $0 and is required to reduce its Illinois net loss from $8,000 to $0 ($8,000 - [$40,000 × ($10,000/$50,000)]).

Example 2: Same facts as Example 1, except that Taxpayer makes a federal election to reduce its basis in depreciable property, with the result that no reduction is made to Taxpayer's federal NOL. No reduction is required to Taxpayer's Illinois net loss.

Example 3: For its taxable year ending December 31, 2016, Taxpayer has $200,000 of debt cancellation income excluded from federal gross income. The entire $200,000 would have been included in Taxpayer's Illinois business income and a total of $100,000 of that income would have been apportioned to Illinois. Taxpayer has $50,000 of federal taxable income for its December 31, 2016 taxable year before application of a federal NOL carryover of $75,000 from its December 31, 2013 taxable year, leaving $25,000 of that loss to carry forward to 2017. In addition, Taxpayer has an Illinois net loss for its December 31, 2016 taxable year of $10,000, but no Illinois net loss carryovers to that year. Taxpayer is required to reduce its 2013 federal NOL remaining to carry forward to 2017 from $25,000 to $0. Since no reduction is made to a federal NOL incurred in 2016, no reduction is required to be made to Taxpayer's 2016 Illinois net loss deduction.

Example 4: Same facts as in Example 3, except that Taxpayer has $25,000 of Illinois net income for its December 31, 2016 taxable year and has Illinois net loss carryovers of $20,000 from its December 31, 2014 taxable year and $20,000 from its December 31, 2015 taxable year. The $20,000 Illinois net loss carryover from 2014 and $5,000 of the 2015 Illinois net loss carryover are first applied to reduce

Taxpayer's Illinois net income to $0 for its December 31, 2016 taxable year. The remaining $15,000 Illinois net loss carryover from 2015 is reduced to $2,500 ($15,000 - [$25,000 × ($100,000/$200,000)]). Reduction is required even though the Taxpayer's federal net operating loss carryover relates to its December 31, 2013 taxable year while the Illinois net loss carryover is from Taxpayer's December 31, 2015 taxable year.

Example 5: For its taxable year ending December 31, 2016, Taxpayer has $200,000 of debt cancellation income excluded from federal gross income. The entire $200,000 would have been included in Taxpayer's Illinois business income and a total of $100,000 of that income would have been apportioned to Illinois. Taxpayer has a $50,000 federal NOL for the 2016 taxable year and federal NOL carryovers of $25,000 from its December 31, 2013 taxable year and $75,000 from its December 31, 2014 taxable year. Taxpayer has an Illinois net loss of $25,000 for its December 31, 2016 taxable year, and Illinois net loss carryovers of $6,000 from its December 31, 2013 taxable year and $30,000 from its December 31, 2014 taxable year. Taxpayer's $50,000 federal NOL for 2016 and $25,000 net operating loss carryover from 2013 are each reduced to $0. In addition, the $75,000 net operating loss carryover from 2014 is reduced to $50,000. Taxpayer's Illinois net loss from 2016 is reduced to $0 ($25,000 - [$50,000 × ($100,000/$200,000)]). In addition, Taxpayer's Illinois net loss carryover from 2013 is reduced to $0, and its Illinois net loss carryover from 2014 is reduced to $11,000. The $25,000 reduction to Taxpayer's Illinois net loss carryover is first applied to reduce the carryover from 2013 from $6,000 to $0, and the remaining reduction is applied to reduce the carryover from 2014 from $30,000 to $11,000.

How does Illinois treat NOLs following mergers and acquisitions? A corporation that acquires the assets of another corporation in an IRC Sec. 381(a) transaction takes into account all the target corporation's net losses at the close of the distribution or transfer day. (35 ILCS 5/405(a); 86 Ill. Adm. Code 100.4500(b)) This includes the right to carry forward NOLs incurred by the target corporation. (86 Ill. Adm. Code 100.4500(b))

Illinois does not follow:

• IRC Sec. 382 loss limitation rules; or

• IRC Sec. 1502 separate return limitation year (SRLY) rules. (35 ILCS 5/405(b-5); 86 Ill. Adm. Code 100.4500(d))

Illinois also has no equivalent to:

• IRC Sec. 269 anti-abuse rules; or

• IRC Sec. 384 built-in loss limitation rules. (35 ILCS 5/405; 86 Ill. Adm. Code 100.4500; *Unofficial Guidance*, Illinois Department of Revenue, April 2011)

How does Illinois treat farm losses? Illinois has no special provisions covering NOLs from farming trade or business. Taxpayers cannot carryback NOLs. So, the change in the IRC Sec. 172 carryback period for those losses does not impact Illinois corporation income tax liability. (35 ILCS 5/207; 86 Ill. Adm. Code 100.2310)

How does Illinois treat S corporation losses? Illinois allows S corporations to claim an NOLD against personal property replacement tax liability. S corporations compute the NOLD in the same way as C corporations. (86 Ill. Adm. Code 100.2300(a); 86 Ill. Adm. Code 100.2330(f)(4))

IRC Sec. 1371(b), which prohibits S corporations from using NOL carryback or carryforward amounts from C corporation years, does not apply for Illinois income tax purposes. So, an S corporation that incurs a NOL in a tax year can carryforward and deduct the loss in any year in which it is a C corporation. Likewise, a C corporation that incurs a NOL in a tax year can carryforward and deduct the loss in any year in which it is an S corporation. (86 Ill. Adm. Code 100.2330(f)(4))

Does Illinois allow NOL carryback and/or carryforward adjustments?

Illinois no longer follows the IRC Sec. 172 NOL carryback or carryforward periods. It does not allow NOL carrybacks. (35 ILCS 5/207(a); 86 Ill. Adm. Code 100.2330(b)) Taxpayers can carryforward NOLs for up to:

- 12 tax years for tax years ending on or after December 31, 2003; and

- 20 tax years for tax years ending before December 31, 2003. (35 ILCS 5/207(a); 86 Ill. Adm. Code 100.2330(b))

Illinois suspended the NOL carryforward deduction for the 2011 tax year. It limited the deduction to $100,000 for tax years ending on or after December 31, 2012 and before December 31, 2014. (35 ILCS 5/207(d); *Informational Bulletin FY 2015-09*, Illinois Department of Revenue, January 2015) The tax years during the NOL suspension and limitation do not count toward the Illinois NOL carryforward period. (35 ILCS 5/207(d))

For a list of other Illinois subtraction adjustments, see Subtractions from Taxable Income Base.

[¶10-810] Subtractions--Dividends

A taxpayer's starting point for computing Illinois corporate income and replacement tax liability includes the federal special dividends received deduction.

Does Illinois allow a dividends received deduction?

Yes, Illinois allows a deduction from federal taxable income for dividends received from foreign corporations. The Illinois foreign dividends received deduction follows the percentages allowed under IRC Sec. 243. (35 ILCS 5/203(b)(2)(O)) Those percentages equal:

- 100% of dividends received from 80% or greater owned foreign corporations;

- 65% of dividends received from 20% or greater owned foreign corporations; and

- 50% of dividends received from less than 20% owned foreign corporations. (Schedule J, Foreign Dividends)

Effective for tax years beginning before 2018, the percentages were equal to:

- 100% of dividends received from 80% or greater owned foreign corporations;

- 80% of dividends received from 20% or greater owned foreign corporations; and

- 70% of dividends received from less than 20% owned foreign corporations or captive REITs. (Schedule J, Foreign Dividends)

Taxpayers compute the foreign dividends received deduction on Schedule J. Taxpayers must attach a copy of federal:

- Form 1120, 1120F, or 1120-PC, Schedule C;

- Form 1120-L, Schedule A;

- Form 1120-FSC, Schedule F; or

- Form 1120-H or 1120-POL, page 1. (Instructions, Schedule J, Foreign Dividends)

Does Illinois allow a deduction for foreign gross-up dividends?

Yes, Illinois allows a deduction on Schedule J for IRC Sec. 78 gross-up dividends included in federal taxable income. (35 ILCS 5/203(b)(2)(G))

Does Illinois allow a deduction for Subpart F and IRC Sec. 965 income?

Yes, Illinois allows a deduction on Schedule J for dividends received or deemed received or paid under IRC Sec. 951 through IRC Sec. 965. Taxpayers compute the deduction for Subpart F income and IRC Sec. 965 repatriation income using the same percentages allowed under the Illinois foreign dividends received deduction. (35 ILCS 5/203(b)(2)(O)) The deduction for IRC 965 income excludes the federal deduction allowed under IRC Sec. 965(c). (Instructions, Schedule J, Foreign Dividends)

Does Illinois allow a deduction for global intangible low-taxed income?

Yes, Illinois allows a deduction for IRC Sec. 951A global intangible low-taxed income (GILTI). (35 ILCS 5/203(b)(2)(O)) Taxpayers compute the GILTI deduction on Schedule J using the same percentages allowed under the Illinois foreign dividends received deduction. (Schedule J, Foreign Dividends) The deduction excludes the federal IRC Sec. 250 deduction that is allowed in computing GILTI. (Instructions, Schedule J, Foreign Dividends)

Does Illinois allow a deduction for real estate investment trust dividends?

Yes, Illinois allows a deduction on Schedule J for dividends received from captive real estate investment trusts (REITs). Taxpayers compute the deduction using the same percentages allowed under the Illinois foreign dividends received deduction. (35 ILCS 5/203(b)(2)(O))

For a list of other Illinois subtractions adjustments, see Subtractions from Taxable Income Base.

[¶10-815] Subtractions--Interest

Corporations may subtract interest amounts that are exempt for Illinois corporate income tax purposes under Illinois law, the Illinois or U.S. Constitutions, or U.S. treaties or statutes. The exempt amount of income derived from bonds or other obligations is the interest net of bond premium amortization. (35 ILCS 5/203(b)(2)(J); Ill. Adm. Code 100.2470(a))

The subtraction for interest income derived from federal obligations that are exempt from Illinois taxation is entered on Form IL-1120. The subtraction for interest income derived from state and local obligations that are exempt from Illinois taxation is entered on Form IL-1120, Schedule M. (Instructions, Form IL-1120, Illinois Corporation Income and Replacement Tax Return)

• *Federal obligations*

"Obligations of the United States," means obligations issued "to secure credit to carry on the necessary functions of government." (86 Ill. Adm. 100.2470(b)(1)) (*Publication 101, Income Exempt from Tax,* Illinois Department of Revenue) A governmental obligation that is secondary, indirect, or contingent (e.g., a guaranty of a nongovernmental obligor's primary obligation to pay the principal amount and interest on a note), is not exempt from Illinois corporate income tax. (86 Ill. Adm. 100.2470(b)(1)(B))

Interest income from the following federal obligations are exempt from state taxation (Ill. Adm. Code 100.2470(b), (c)) (*Publication 101, Income Exempt from Tax,* Illinois Department of Revenue) and may be subtracted from federal taxable income for Illinois purposes:

— Banks for Cooperatives;

— Commodity Credit Corporation;

— Farm Credit System Financial Assistance Corporation;

— Federal Deposit Insurance Corporation;

— Federal Farm Credit Banks;

— Federal Home Loan Banks;

— Federal Intermediate Credit Banks;

— Federal Land Banks and Federal Land Bank Association;

— Federal Savings and Loan Insurance Corporation;

— Financing Corporation (FICO);

— General Insurance Fund (including debentures issued under the War Housing Insurance Law; General Insurance Fund to acquire rental housing projects; and Armed Services Housing Mortgage Insurance Debentures);

— National Credit Union Administration Central Liquidity Facility;

— Production Credit Association;

— Railroad Retirement Act (including annuity and supplemental annuity payments as qualified under the Railroad Retirement Act of 1974);

— Railroad Unemployment Insurance Act;

— Resolution Funding Corporation;

— Special Food Service Program;

— Student Loan Marketing Association;

— Tennessee Valley Authority; and

— United States Postal Service.

• *State and local obligations*

Interest income from the following state and local obligations is exempt from Illinois corporate income tax (86 Ill. Adm. 100.2470) (*Publication 101, Income Exempt from Tax*, Illinois Department of Revenue) and may be subtracted from federal taxable income:

— Illinois Housing Development Authority bonds and notes, except housing-related commercial facilities bonds and notes (20 ILCS 3805/31);

— Export Development Act bonds (20 ILCS 3505/7.61);

— Illinois Development Finance Authority bonds, notes, and other evidence of obligation (venture fund and infrastructure bonds) (20 ILCS 3505/7.61);

— Quad Cities Regional Economic Development Authority bonds and notes (70 ILCS 515/11);

— Illlinois Sports Facilities Authority bonds (70 ILCS 3205/15);

— Illinois Development Finance Authority bonds issued under the Asbestos Abatement Finance Act (20 ILCS 3510/8);

— Rural Bond Bank Act bonds and notes (30 ILCS 360/3-12);

— Illinois Development Finance Authority bonds issued pursuant to the Illinois Development Finance Authority Act (20 ILCS 3505/7.86);

— Quad Cities Interstate Metropolitan Authority bonds (45 ILCS 35/110); and

— Southwestern Illinois Development Authority bonds. (70 ILCS 520/7.5)

• *Other exempt obligations*

Certain interest income from obligations is also exempt from Illinois corporate income tax but is not included in federal taxable income. (*Publication 101, Income Exempt from Tax*, Illinois Department of Revenue, December 2004) Income from the following must be added to federal taxable income for Illinois purposes (see ¶ 10-610) and then can be claimed as subtractions when computing Illinois base income:

— Government of Guam; (86 Ill. Adm. 100.2470(c)(12))

— Government of Puerto Rico; (86 Ill. Adm. 100.2470(c)(16))

— Government of the Virgin Islands (86 Ill. Adm. 100.2470(c)(24)); and

— Mutual Mortgage Insurance Fund (income from such is issued in exchange for property covered by mortgages insured after February 3, 1988). (86 Ill. Adm. 100.2470(c)(13))

• *Mutual fund distributions*

Illinois allows a from federal taxable income for distributions received from mutual funds investing exclusively in U.S. obligations. In addition, a percentage exemption is allowed in situations where a mutual fund invests in both exempt and nonexempt federal obligations. (*Publication 101, Income Exempt from Tax*, Illinois Department of Revenue)

• *Expense related income*

Corporations may deduct expenses and interest related to federally tax-exempt income that is taxable in Illinois and is added back on the Illinois return. "Deductible expenses" are defined as those amounts disallowed under IRC Sec. 171(a)(2), amortizable bond premiums attributable to tax-exempt bonds, and IRC Sec. 265 interest incurred to carry tax-exempt obligations. (35 ILCS 5/203(b)(2)(I))

Other subtractions from the taxable income base are listed at ¶ 10-800.

[¶ 10-835] Subtractions--Corporate Transactions

Does Illinois allow subtraction adjustments for income from related parties?

Illinois requires an addition to federal taxable for interest, intangible expenses, and insurance premiums paid to affiliated:

• 80/20 companies; and

• effective for tax years before 2017, noncombination rule companies.

It provides corresponding subtraction adjustments to ensure that the addition adjustments do not result in double taxation. (86 Ill. Adm. Code Sec. 100.2430(a)) A taxpayer can subtract from federal taxable income:

• interest income received from each affiliated company; (35 ILCS 5/203(b)(2)(W); 86 Ill. Adm. Code Sec. 100.2430(d)(3))

• intangible income received from each affiliated company; (35 ILCS 5/203(b)(2)(X); 86 Ill. Adm. Code Sec. 100.2430(d)(4)) and

• effective for tax years before 2017, insurance reimbursements received from each affiliated insurance company. (35 ILCS 5/203(b)(2)(Y); 86 Ill. Adm. Code Sec. 100.2430(d)(6))

The 80/20 company or, effective for tax years before 2017, noncombination company can subtract from federal taxable income:

• interest income received from the taxpayer;

• intangible income received from the taxpayer;

• insurance premiums received from the taxpayer. (35 ILCS 5/203(b)(2)(V); 86 Ill. Adm. Code Sec. 100.2430(d)(1), (3), and (5))

Illinois limits the subtraction adjustment to the amount of the taxpayer's addition adjustment for interest, intangible expenses, and insurance premiums paid to the affiliated company. It is also net of any deduction for related expenses. (35 ILCS 5/203(b)(2)(V)-(Y); 86 Ill. Adm. Code Sec. 100.2430(d))

Taxpayers compute and report the subtraction adjustments on Schedule 80/20. (Instructions, Schedule 80/20, Related Party Expenses)

For a list of other Illinois subtraction adjustments, see Subtractions from Taxable Income Base.

[¶10-840] Subtractions--Taxes

The amount of any Illinois corporate income tax that was refunded to a corporation and was, therefore, included in federal taxable income is subtracted for Illinois purposes because it has previously been included in the measure of tax. (35 ILCS 5/203(b)(2)(F))

The tax is subtracted on Form IL-1120 Corporation Income and Replacement Tax Return. (*Instructions, Form IL-1120, Illinois Corporation Income and Replacement Tax Return*)

Other subtractions from the taxable income base are listed at ¶10-800.

[¶10-845] Subtractions--Targeted Business Activity or Zones

Taxpayers computing Illinois corporation income and replacement tax liability are allowed the following subtractions from federal taxable income:

— river edge redevelopment zone dividends;

— foreign trade zone or sub-zone dividends;

— charitable contributions to zone organizations; and

— interest income from river edge redevelopment zone or high impact business property.

The subtraction adjustments may be claimed by completing Schedule 1299-B and attaching it to the taxpayer's annual Illinois corporation income tax return. (Instructions, Schedule 1299-B, River Edge Redevelopment Zone or Foreign Trade Zone (or sub-zone) Subtractions)

Effective for tax years before August 7, 2012, a subtraction from federal taxable income was also allowed for dividends (86 Ill. Adm. Code Sec. 100.2480(a)(2)) and interest received from Illinois enterprise zones. (86 Ill. Adm. Code Sec. 100.2655(a))

• *River edge redevelopment zone dividends*

Taxpayers computing Illinois corporation income and replacement tax liability may subtract from federal taxable income an amount equal to dividends received from a corporation that conducts substantially all of its operations in a river edge redevelopment zone or zones. (35 ILCS 5/203(b)(2)(K); 86 Ill. Adm. Code Sec. 100.2480(a)(1)) Taxpayers are allowed to subtract distributions from a corporation only to the extent:

— such distributions are characterized as dividends;

— such dividends are included in federal taxable income of the taxpayer; and

— the taxpayer has not subtracted such dividends from federal taxable income. (86 Ill. Adm. Code Sec. 100.2480(d)(1))

Example: A taxpayer receives a dividend from another corporation that qualifies for the 70% dividends received deduction under IRC §243(a)(1). Because only 30% of the dividend is included in taxpayer's federal taxable income, Illinois allows the taxpayer to subtract only 30% of the dividend from its federal taxable income. (86 Ill. Adm. Code Sec. 100.2480(d)(2))

A corporation conducts substantially all of its business within a river edge redevelopment zone when 95% or more of its total business activity during a taxable year is operated within the zone. Business activity within a river edge redevelopment zone is measured by means of the property (see ¶11-530) and payroll (see ¶11-535) factors for apportioning the business income of a corporation. (86 Ill. Adm. Code Sec. 100.2480(b)) The corporation's property and payroll within the river edge redevelopment zone must be compared to the corporation's property and payroll everywhere. If the amount is 95% or greater, the dividends paid by the corporation will qualify for the subtraction. (86 Ill. Adm. Code Sec. 100.2480(b)(1))

In the case of insurance companies, financial organizations, and transportation companies, which are required to use a one-factor special industry apportionment formula, (see ¶11-540) business activity conducted within a river edge redevelopment zone is measured by comparing business income from sources within the zone and everywhere else. A corporation using an alternative method of apportionment (see ¶11-520) must petition the Illinois Department of Revenue for approval of an appropriate method of determining its qualification for the subtraction adjustment. (86 Ill. Adm. Code Sec. 100.2480(b)(2))

In measuring the business activity of a corporation within a river edge redevelopment zone, the apportionment factors of that corporation must be determined without regard to the factors or business activity of any other corporation. In the case of a corporation engaged in a unitary business with any other person, the apportionment factors of that corporation must be determined as if it were not engaged in a unitary business. (86 Ill. Adm. Code Sec. 100.2480(b))

• *Foreign trade zone or sub-zone dividends*

Taxpayers computing Illinois corporation income and replacement tax liability may subtract from federal taxable income an amount equal to dividends paid by a corporation that is qualified as a "high impact business" and that conducts business within a federally designated foreign trade zone or sub-zone. (35 ILCS 5/203(b)(2)(L); 86 Ill. Adm. Code Sec. 100.2490(a)) Taxpayers are allowed to subtract distributions from a corporation only to the extent:

— the distributions are characterized as dividends;

— the dividends are included in federal taxable income of the taxpayer;

— the dividends are not eligible for the river edge redevelopment zone subtraction adjustment; and

— the taxpayer has not subtracted such dividends from federal taxable income. (86 Ill. Adm. Code Sec. 100.2490(e)(1))

Example: A taxpayer receives a dividend from another corporation that qualifies for the 70% dividends received deduction under IRC § 243(a)(1). Because only 30% of the dividend is included in taxpayer's federal taxable income, Illinois allows the taxpayer to subtract only 30% of the dividend from its federal taxable income. (86 Ill. Adm. Code Sec. 100.2490(e)(2))

A corporation conducts business operations in a federally designated foreign trade zone or sub-zone when any portion of its total business activity during a taxable year is operated within such a zone. Business activity within a federally designated foreign trade zone or sub-zone is measured by means of the property (see ¶11-530) and payroll (see ¶11-535) factors for apportioning the business income of a corporation. (86 Ill. Adm. Code Sec. 100.2490(b)) The corporation's ratio of property and payroll within the zone must be compared to the corporation's property and payroll everywhere. If the amount greater than 0%, the dividends paid by the corporation will qualify for the subtraction. (86 Ill. Adm. Code Sec. 100.2490(b)(1))

In the case of insurance companies, financial organizations, and transportation companies, which are required to use a one-factor special industry apportionment formula, (see ¶11-540) business activity conducted within a federally designated foreign trade zone or sub-zone is measured by comparing business income from sources within the zone and everywhere else. A corporation using an alternative method of apportionment (see ¶ 11-520) must petition the Illinois Department of Revenue for approval of an appropriate method of determining its qualification for the subtraction adjustment. (86 Ill. Adm. Code Sec. 100.2490(b)(2))

In measuring the business activity of a corporation within a federally designated foreign trade zone or sub-zone, the apportionment factors of that corporation must be determined without regard to the factors or business activity of any other corporation. In the case of a corporation engaged in a unitary business with any other person, the apportionment factors of that corporation must be determined as if it were not engaged in a unitary business. (86 Ill. Adm. Code Sec. 100.2490(b))

• *Charitable contributions to zone organizations*

Taxpayers computing Illinois corporation income and replacement tax liability may subtract from federal taxable income two times the amount of charitable contributions made to a designated zone organization that are used for an enterprise zone or river edge redevelopment zone project approved by the Illinois Department of Commerce and Economic Opportunity (DCEO), provided the contribution qualifies as a charitable contribution under IRC § 170(c). (35 ILCS 5/203(b)(2)(N); 20 ILCS 655/11) The total of all contributions approved by the DCEO for deductions is capped at $15,400,000 in any one calendar year. (20 ILCS 655/11)

• *Interest income from river edge redevelopment zone or high impact business property*

Taxpayers computing Illinois corporation income and replacement tax liability that are financial organizations may subtract interest income from a loan made to a borrower to the extent that the loan is secured by property eligible for the river edge redevelopment zone investment credit (35 ILCS 5/203(b)(2)(M); 86 Ill. Adm. Code Sec. 100.2655(a)) or high impact business investment credit. (35 ILCS 5/203(b)(2)(M-1); 86 Ill. Adm. Code Sec. 100.2657(a)) To determine the portion of a loan that is secured by property eligible for either the river edge redevelopment zone investment credit (35 ILCS 5/203(b)(2)(M); 86 Ill. Adm. Code Sec. 100.2655(c)) or the high impact business investment credit, (35 ILCS 5/203(b)(2)(M-1); 86 Ill. Adm. Code Sec. 100.2657(c)) the entire principal amount of the loans between the financial organization and the borrower should be divided into the basis of the property securing the loans. The original basis of the property on the date that it was placed into the river edge redevelopment zone (35 ILCS 5/203(b)(2)(M); 86 Ill. Adm. Code Sec. 100.2655(c)) or a federally-designated foreign trade zone or sub-zone located in Illinois (35 ILCS 5/203(b)(2)(M-1); 86 Ill. Adm. Code Sec. 100.2657(c)) is used for purposes of the determination. The basis of eligible property is its borrower's basis in the eligible property for federal income tax purposes, including the costs of any improvements or repairs included in that basis, but without adjustment for depreciation or IRC § 179 deductions claimed with respect to the property. (86 Ill. Adm. Code Sec. 100.2655(e); 86 Ill. Adm. Code Sec. 100.2657(e))

> *Example 1:* Bank lends $1,000 to Borrower, secured by eligible property with a basis of $900. The portion of the loan secured by eligible property is the $900 basis of the borrower in eligible property divided by the $1,000 principal amount of the loan, or 90%. (86 Ill. Adm. Code Sec. 100.2657(f)(1))

> *Example 2:* Bank lends $1,000 to Borrower, secured by eligible property with a basis of $1,000 and by other property with a basis of $2,000. The portion of the loan secured by eligible property is the $1,000 basis of the borrower in eligible property divided by the $1,000 principal amount of the loan, or 100%. The existence of other property securing the loan is irrelevant. (86 Ill. Adm. Code Sec. 100.2657(f)(2))

> *Example 3:* In 2008, DCEO designated ABC Company a high impact business. In 2009, ABC Company built a new warehouse at the cost of $1,000,000 and

is able to claim the high impact business investment credit under IITA Section 201(h) with respect to the warehouse. ABC takes out a $2,000,000 loan at Bank A, which then places a lien on the property. In 2010, when the warehouse had an adjusted basis (after depreciation) of $900,000 and a fair market value of $1,300,000, ABC refinanced the loan for the same principal amount, but at a lower interest rate. For both loans, the portion of the loan secured by eligible property is the $1,000,000 original basis in the warehouse divided by the $2,000,000 principal. Neither the adjusted basis after depreciation nor the fair market value is relevant to the computation for the refinanced amount. (86 Ill. Adm. Code Sec. 100.2657(f)(3))

Example 4: Assume the facts are the same as in Example 3, except that, in 2011, ABC Company again refinanced the loan, this time at Bank B (unrelated to Bank A). There was no change in the principal amount. Bank B takes a lien on the warehouse to secure the new loan. The portion of the Bank B loan that qualifies for the subtraction modification is 50% because the principal amount of the loan and ABC Company's original basis in the property remain unchanged. (86 Ill. Adm. Code Sec. 100.2657(f)(4))

Example 5: The facts are the same as in Example 4, except that Bank B purchased the refinanced loan from Bank A. The loan is not refinanced. ABC continues to pay the same amount, but now pays Bank B rather than Bank A. Bank B does not qualify for the subtraction modification, which is allowed only with respect to a loan "made by such taxpayer to a borrower" and Bank B did not make the loan. (86 Ill. Adm. Code Sec. 100.2657(f)(5))

Example 6: X Corp., headquartered outside the river edge redevelopment zone, builds a $100,000,000 warehouse in a river edge redevelopment zone in 2007 and claims the river edge redevelopment zone credit. X takes out a 20-year loan at Bank A in the principal amount of $1,000,000. In 2017, X takes out a new $1,750,000 loan at the same bank and uses $1,000,000 of the proceeds to pay off the old loan and spends the remaining $750,000 to renovate its corporate headquarters located outside the zone. Bank A takes a lien on the warehouse as security for each loan. Because X Corp.'s $100,000,000 basis in the warehouse exceeds the principal amount of each loan, Bank A is entitled to subtract the entire amount of interest received from each loan. The portion of the loan whose interest may be subtracted need not be reduced by the $750,000 portion not spent inside the river edge redevelopment zone because use of the borrowed funds is not relevant to the subtraction. (86 Ill. Adm. Code Sec. 100.2655(e)(6))

A taxpayer may not claim a subtraction adjustment interest income from high impact business property for any taxable year in which the taxpayer is allowed to claim the subtraction adjustment for interest on a loan secured by property eligible for the river edge redevelopment zone investment credit. (86 Ill. Adm. Code Sec. 100.2657(b))

Illinois allows other subtractions from the federal taxable income base. (see ¶ 10-800)

[¶10-855] Subtractions--Items Related to Federal Deductions or Credits

Illinois corporate income taxpayers may deduct an amount equal to the sum of all amounts disallowed as deductions by the following sections of the Internal Revenue Code:

— 45G (railroad track maintenance credit);

— 87 (alcohol and biodiesel fuel credit);

— 171 (a)(2) (amortizable bond premium);

— 265 (expenses and interest related to tax-exempt income);

— 280C (expenses associated with federal employment credits, the credit for qualified clinical testing expenses, and the credit for increasing research activities);

— 291(a)(3) (certain financial institution preference items);

— 807(a)(2)(B) or (b)(1)(B) (reserves included in gross income); and

— 832(b)(5)(B)(i) (reduction of the deduction in computing insurance company taxable income).

(35 ILCS 5/203(b)(2)(I))

In addition, corporations that take the federal income tax credit under IRC Sec. 1341 for repayment to another of income items previously included in gross income as being held under a claim of right may subtract from federal taxable income an amount equal to the deduction used to compute the federal income tax credit. (35 ILCS 5/203(b)(2)(Q))

The allowable deductions are subtracted on Schedule M, Form IL-1120 Corporation Income and Replacement Tax Return. (*Instructions, Form IL-1120, Illinois Corporation Income and Replacement Tax Return*)

Other subtractions from the taxable income base are listed at ¶ 10-800.

[¶ 10-890] Subtractions--Job Programs or Employee Benefits

Corporations may subtract amounts contributed to job training projects established under the Tax Increment Allocation Redevelopment Act on Form IL-1120 Corporation Income and Replacement Tax Return. These projects, funded by municipalities so that contributing corporations may have employees vocationally trained, do not qualify for the federal IRC Sec. 170 charitable deduction. (35 ILCS 5/203(b)(2)(P); *Instructions, Form IL-1120, Illinois Corporation Income and Replacement Tax Return*)

Other subtractions from the taxable income base are listed at ¶ 10-800.

[¶ 10-900] Subtractions--Depreciation

Taxpayers computing Illinois corporate income and replacement tax liability may subtract a portion of federal bonus depreciation under IRC Sec. 168(k). (35 ILCS 5/203(b)(2)(T)) However, the Illinois bonus depreciation subtraction adjustment may not be claimed until:

• the last tax year that the taxpayer claims federal regular depreciation on the property; or

• the taxpayer sells, transfers, abandons, or otherwise disposes of the property. (35 ILCS 5/203(b)(2)(U); Instructions, Form IL-4562 Special Depreciation)

The subtraction is computed on Form IL-4562 and it is equal to:

• 42.9% of the depreciation on property for which 30% or 50% federal bonus depreciation was claimed in tax years beginning after 2001 and ending on or before December 31, 2005; and

• 100% of the depreciation on property for which 50% federal bonus depreciation was claimed in tax years beginning after December 31, 2005. (35 ILCS 5/203(b)(2)(T); Instructions, Form IL-4562 Special Depreciation)

Taxpayers claiming a bonus depreciation subtraction adjustment must:

• check the box on the taxpayers' Illinois corporate income and replacement return; and

• attach Form IL-4562. (Instructions, Form IL-1120, Corporation Income and Replacement Tax Return)

Illinois requires an addition adjustment for bonus depreciation (see ¶ 10-670).

For a list of other Illinois subtractions adjustments, see Subtractions from Taxable Income Base.

[¶11-500]

ALLOCATION AND APPORTIONMENT

[¶11-505] Allocation and Apportionment

To prevent excessive taxation of the same income when a corporation does business in more than one state, the Federal Constitution limits each state to taxing that portion of a corporation's income that is fairly representative of the corporation's in-state activities. (see ¶10-105)Assigning the income of a multijurisdictional corporation among various taxing states is generally accomplished by a process known as allocation and apportionment.

• *Allocation and apportionment distinguished*

Allocation.—Allocation (see ¶11-515) refers to directly assigning certain types of income, which are usually designated nonbusiness income, (see ¶11-510) to a state on the basis of rules varying according to the type of property that gave rise to the income. Rental income from real property, for instance, is commonly assigned to the state in which the property is located. Allocation rules purport to assign income to the state that is its source. However, when the source of the income is intangible property (e.g., patents or investments), the location of which may be difficult to ascertain, allocation rules may adopt such an objective criterion for assignment as the taxpayer's commercial domicile. (see ¶11-515)

Apportionment.—Apportionment (see ¶11-515) refers to assigning a portion of multistate business income (see ¶11-510) to a state by means of a formula based on such objective factors as sales, (see ¶11-525) property, (see ¶11-530) or payroll. (see ¶11-535) Formula apportionment (see ¶11-520) is an attempt to measure, if imprecisely, the taxing state's contribution to the environment that permitted the corporation to earn its income.

• *Taxable in another state*

Illinois has adopted tests for determining if a taxpayer is taxable in another state and, therefore, subject to Illinois allocation and apportionment provisions. (35 ILCS 5/303(f); 86 Ill. Adm. Code Sec. 100.3200) A taxpayer is taxable in another state if:

— the taxpayer is subject to a net income tax, a franchise tax measured by net income, a franchise tax for the privilege of doing business, or a corporate stock tax in that state; or

— that state has jurisdiction to subject the taxpayer to a net income tax regardless of whether, in fact, the state does or does not subject the taxpayer to such a tax. (35 ILCS 5/303(f); 86 Ill. Adm. Code Sec. 100.3200(a)(1))

Subject to tax test.—Illinois provides additional guidance on when a taxpayer is subject to tax in another state and satisfies the first test for determining if a taxpayer is taxable in another state. A taxpayer is subject to the specified taxes in a particular state only if the taxpayer is subject to the tax by reason of income-producing activities in that state. For example, a corporation that pays a minimum franchise tax in order to qualify for the privilege of doing business in a state is not subject to tax by that state if the amount of that minimum tax bears no relation to the corporation's activities within that state. Further, a taxpayer claiming to be taxable in another state must establish not only that under the laws of that state the taxpayer is subject to one of the specified taxes, but that the taxpayer, in fact, pays the tax. If a taxpayer is subject to one of the specified taxes but does not, in fact, pay the tax, the taxpayer may not claim to be taxable in the state imposing the tax. (86 Ill. Adm. Code Sec. 100.3200(a)(2))

Example: A corporation, although subject to the provisions of the net income tax statute imposed by X state, has never filed income tax returns in that jurisdiction and has never paid income tax to X. For purposes of allocation and apportionment of A's income, A is not taxable in X state because it does not meet the subject to tax test. (86 Ill. Adm. Code Sec. 100.3200(b)(1))

Jurisdiction to tax test.—Illinois also has a provision for determining when a state has jurisdiction to impose an income tax on the taxpayer. If the taxpayer establishes that its activities in that state are such as to give the state jurisdiction to impose a net income tax on the taxpayer, then the taxpayer is taxable in that state, notwithstanding the fact that state has not enacted legislation subjecting the taxpayer to the tax. (86 Ill. Adm. Code Sec. 100.3200(a)(2)) A net income tax is a tax for which the taxpayer may claim a federal deduction for income taxes paid under IRC § 164(a)(3) or for which a foreign tax credit may be claimed under IRC § 901. (86 Ill. Adm. Code Sec. 100.3200(a)(2)(A))

In the case of any state, other than a foreign country or political subdivision of a foreign country, the determination of whether a state has jurisdiction to subject the taxpayer to a net income tax will be determined under the Constitution, statutes and treaties of the United States. Such a state does not have jurisdiction to subject the taxpayer to a net income tax if it is prohibited from imposing that tax by reason of Illinois nexus standards (see ¶ 10-075) and the provisions of Public Law 86-272. (86 Ill. Adm. Code Sec. 100.3200(a)(2)(C))

A taxpayer is not subject to tax in another state or in a foreign country if that state or country imposes a tax on net income, unless the taxpayer can show a specific provision of that state's or country's constitution, statutes or regulations, or a holding of that state's or country's courts or taxing authorities, that exempts the person from taxation even though that person could be subject to a net income tax under the Constitution, statutes and treaties of the United States. (86 Ill. Adm. Code Sec. 100.3200(a)(2)(D))

Example: B corporation, an Illinois corporation, is actively engaged in manufacturing farm equipment in Y foreign country. Y does not impose a franchise tax measured by net income or a corporate stock tax. It does impose a franchise tax for the privilege of doing business, but B corporation is not subject to that tax because it applies only to corporations incorporated under Y's laws. Y also imposes a net income tax upon foreign corporations doing business within its boundaries, but B is not subject to that tax because the income tax statute grants a tax exemption to corporations manufacturing farm equipment. For purposes of allocation and apportionment of B's income, B is taxable in Y country. B does not meet the subject to tax test, but does meet the jurisdiction to tax test, since Y has jurisdiction to impose a net income tax on B. (86 Ill. Adm. Code Sec. 100.3200(b)(2))

• *Unitary business principle and combined reporting*

Illinois follows the unitary business principle. Where 2 or more corporations are engaged in a unitary business a part of which is conducted in Illinois by one or more members of the group, the business income attributable to Illinois by any such member or members must be apportioned by means of the combined apportionment method (35 ILCS 304(a)) and the group is required to file a combined unitary return. (see ¶ 11-550)

¶ 11-505

• *Special industry apportionment rules*

Illinois has special apportionment rules with respect to the following industries:

— airlines; (see ¶ 11-540)

— broadcasting; (see ¶ 11-540)

— financial organizations; (see ¶ 11-540)

— insurance companies; (see ¶ 11-540)

— federally regulated exchanges; (see ¶ 11-540)

— pipeline transportation services; (see ¶ 11-540)

— publishing services; (see ¶ 11-540)

— telecommunication services; (see ¶ 11-540) and

— trucking, railroads, and similar transportation services. (see ¶ 11-540)

• *Conformity with uniformity provisions*

The Uniform Division of Income Tax for Tax Purposes Act (UDITPA) was drafted in 1957 to create a uniform method for the allocation and apportionment of a multistate corporation's income among states and to address the many variations in methods of apportionment employed by the states. UDITPA incorporated the business and nonbusiness income concepts, an equally weighted three-factor apportionment formula, and an alternative apportionment mechanism.

Unfortunately, very few states adopted UDITPA at first. In addition, by the 1960s, Congress was threatening to impose its own set of uniform standards for taxing the income of multistate corporations. As a result, in 1966, the Multistate Tax Compact (Compact) was drafted with the stated purpose of facilitating the "proper determination of state and local tax liability of multistate taxpayers, including the equitable apportionment of tax bases and settlement of apportionment disputes." Article IV of the Compact incorporated UDITPA almost word-for-word.

The Compact also established the Multistate Tax Commission (MTC) to administer the Compact and promote uniformity among state tax laws. In 1973, the MTC drafted a set of model allocation and apportionment regulations. These regulations added much needed detail to the UDIPTA provisions in the Compact, introduced the unitary business principle, and stimulated more movement towards uniformity among the states.

While complete uniformity never materialized, enough states adopted all or parts of UDITPA, the Compact, and/or the MTC regulations to create a basic apportionment process that the majority of states follow today.

CCH Comment: In July 30, 2014, the MTC approved several amendments to the Compact's UDITPA provisions. The Compact amendments replace the traditional income-producing activity/cost-of-performance sourcing rule for sales with market-based sourcing rules. The amendments must be specifically adopted by a state in order to become the law of that state. In addition, the MTC is expected to amend existing regulations or draft new ones in light of the Compact changes.

Although Illinois allocation and apportionment provisions are substantially similar to UDITPA and the MTC regulations, (*General Information Letter, IT 00-0096-GIL,* Illinois Department of Revenue, December 28, 2000) one significant difference is Illinois utilizes a single sales factor apportionment formula (see ¶ 11-520) rather than a three-factor formula. (see ¶ 11-520) However, taxpayers may be permitted or required to use an alternative apportionment formula (see ¶ 11-520) that includes or excludes one or more additional factors. In addition, unitary business groups that file a combined report (see ¶ 11-550)must use a special apportionment formula consisting of property (see ¶ 11-530) and payroll. (see ¶ 11-535) to determine whether members meet the 80/20 U.S. business activity test and are eligible for inclusion in the combined report.

Illinois also uses different sales factor sourcing rules for business income from transactions and activities (i.e., intangible property, services) other than the sales of tangible personal property. (see ¶ 11-525)

UDITPA.—The following table shows differences, if any, between the Illinois apportionment and allocation provisions and corresponding sections of UDITPA:

Subject	UDITPA (Sec. No.)	Illinois Income Tax Act (Sec. No.)
Definitions	1.	
"Business income"	1(a)	1501(a)(1), except extends definition to the limits of U.S. Constitution.
"Commercial domicile"	1(b)	1501(a)(2).
"Compensation"	1(c)	1501(a)(3).
"Financial organization"	1(d)	1501(a)(8), except adds the following entities to the definition: bank holding company, building and loan association, currency exchange, small loan company, sales finance company, any "person" that is owned by a bank or bank holding company, finance leasing company, and affiliated unitary groups.
"Nonbusiness income"	1(e)	1501(a)(13) all income other than business income or compensation.
"Public utility"	1(f)	None
"Sales"	1(g)	1501(a)(21).
"State"	1(h).	1501(a)(22).
Applicability	2.	304(a), except does not preclude the activity of a financial organization or public utility from coverage of the allocation and apportionment provisions.
Taxable in another state	3.	303(f), except refers only to allocation of nonbusiness income.
Allocation of nonbusiness income	4.	303(a), except adds a provision for allocation of Illinois lottery prizes and deductions directly allocable to nonbusiness income.
Rents and royalties	5.	303(c), except omits the term "net."
Capital gains and losses	6.	303(b), except adds the term "exchanges."
Interest and dividends	7.	303(g), 301(c)(2)(B).
Patent and copyright royalties	8.	303(d).
Apportionment of business income	9.	304(a), (h)(3), except single-factor formula based on sales.
Property factor	10.	304(a)(1)(A), not applicable except in the case of alternative apportionment methods or 80/20 determinations.
Property valuation	11.	304(a)(1)(B), not applicable except in the case of alternative apportionment methods or 80/20 determinations.
Average property value	12.	304(a)(1)(C), not applicable except in the case of alternative apportionment methods or 80/20 determinations.
Payroll factor	13.	304(a)(2)(A), not applicable except in the case of alternative apportionment methods or 80/20 determinations.
Compensation "in this state"	14.	304(a)(2)(B), not applicable except in the case of alternative apportionment methods or 80/20 determinations.
Sales factor	15.	304(a)(3)(A).
Sales "in this state"	16.	304(a)(3)(B), except adds special throwback rules for property shipped from premises owned or leased by a person who has independently contracted with the seller for the printing of newspapers, periodicals or books and for sales by members of a unitary business group that do not satisfy the 80/20 rules.
Numerator for other receipts	17.	304(a)(3)(C), except sourcing based on income producing activity applies only to certain interest and net gains.
Other allocation and apportionment methods	18.	304(f).

MTC regulations.—The following table shows differences, if any, between the Illinois apportionment and allocation provisions and corresponding MTC regulations:

¶11-505

Title	MTC Reg. No.	IL Reg. or Statute No.
Business and nonbusiness income defined	IV.1.(a)	86 Ill. Adm. Code 100.3010(a)(2) and (3), except extends definition of business income to the limits of U.S. Constitution and does not follow functional and transactional tests.
Unitary business principle and tests	IV.1.(b)	86 Ill. Adm. Code 100.3010(b), 100.9700, except omits certain details (e.g., economies of scale), requires 80/20 business activity test, and notes that existence of centralized management and exercise of such authority over any function is not determinative of strong centralized management.
Rents from real and tangible personal property as business income:	IV.1.(c)(1)	86 Ill. Adm. Code 100.3010(c)(2).
Gains or losses from sales of assets as business income:	IV.1.(c)(2)	86 Ill. Adm. Code 100.3010(c)(3).
Interest as business income:	IV.1.(c)(3)	86 Ill. Adm. Code 100.3010(c)(4).
Interest as business income:	IV.1.(c)(4)	86 Ill. Adm. Code 100.3010(c)(5).
Patent and copyright royalties as business income:	IV.1.(c)(5)	86 Ill. Adm. Code 100.3010(c)(6).
Proration of deductions	IV.1.(d)	86 Ill. Adm. Code 100.3010(d).
Definitions	IV.2.(a)	86 Ill. Adm. Code 100.3010(e), except omits definition of "gross receipts."
Application of Article IV: Apportionment	IV.2.(b)(1)	86 Ill. Adm. Code 100.3330.
Application of Article IV: combined report	IV.2.(b)(2)	35 ILCS 5/304(e).
Application of Article IV: allocation	IV.2.(b)(3)	86 Ill. Adm. Code 100.3330.
Consistency and uniformity in reporting	IV.2.(c)	86 Ill. Adm. Code 100.3340.
Taxable in another state	IV.3.(a)	86 Ill. Adm. Code 100.3200(a)(1).
Taxable in another state: when a corporation is "subject to" a tax under Article IV.3.(1)	IV.3.(b)	86 Ill. Adm. Code 100.3200(a)(2).
Taxable in another state: when a state has jurisdiction to subject a taxpayer to a net income tax	IV.3.(c)	86 Ill. Adm. Code 100.3200(a)(2).
Apportionment formula	IV.9	35 ILCS 5/304(a).
Property factor: in general	IV.10.(a)	86 Ill. Adm. Code 100.3350(a), not applicable except in the case of alternative apportionment methods or 80/20 determinations.
Property factor: property used for the production of business income	IV.10.(b)	86 Ill. Adm. Code 100.3350(b), not applicable except in the case of alternative apportionment methods or 80/20 determinations.
Property factor: consistency in reporting	IV.10.(c)	86 Ill. Adm. Code 100.3350(c), not applicable except in the case of alternative apportionment methods or 80/20 determinations.
Property factor: numerator	IV.10.(d)	86 Ill. Adm. Code 100.3350(d), not applicable except in the case of alternative apportionment methods or 80/20 determinations.
Property factor: valuation of owned property	IV.11.(a)	86 Ill. Adm. Code 100.3350(e), not applicable except in the case of alternative apportionment methods or 80/20 determinations.
Property factor: valuation of rented property	IV.11.(b)	86 Ill. Adm. Code 100.3350(f), not applicable except in the case of alternative apportionment methods or 80/20 determinations.
Property factor: averaging property values	IV.12	86 Ill. Adm. Code 100.3350(g), not applicable except in the case of alternative apportionment methods or 80/20 determinations.
Payroll factor: in general	IV.13.(a)	86 Ill. Adm. Code 100.3360(a), not applicable except in the case of alternative apportionment methods or 80/20 determinations.
Payroll factor: denominator	IV.13.(b)	86 Ill. Adm. Code 100.3360(b), not applicable except in the case of alternative apportionment methods or 80/20 determinations.
Payroll factor: numerator	IV.13.(c)	86 Ill. Adm. Code 100.3360(c), except omits the presumption that equates the compensation reported to the state for unemployment compensation purposes with the numerator of the payroll factor. Provision is not applicable except in the case of alternative apportionment methods or 80/20 determinations.

Title	MTC Reg. No.	IL Reg. or Statute No.
Payroll factor: compensation paid in this state	IV.14	86 Ill. Adm. Code 100.3120(a)(1), not applicable except in the case of alternative apportionment methods or 80/20 determinations.
Sales factor: in general	IV.15.(a)	86 Ill. Adm. Code 100.3370(a).
Sales factor: denominator	IV.15.(b)	86 Ill. Adm. Code 100.3370(b).
Sales factor: numerator	IV.15.(c)	86 Ill. Adm. Code 100.3370(c).
Sales factor: sales of tangible personal property	IV.16.(a)	86 Ill. Adm. Code 100.3370(c)(1).
Sales factor: sales of tangible personal property to United States government	IV.16.(b)	86 Ill. Adm. Code 100.3370(c)(2).
Sales factor: sales other than sales of tangible personal property	IV.17	86 Ill. Adm. Code 100.3370(c)(3), except sourcing based on income producing activity applies only to certain interest and net gains.
Special rules: in general	IV.18.(a)	86 Ill. Adm. Code 100.3380(a)(1).
Special rules: property factor	IV.18.(b)	86 Ill. Adm. Code 100.3380(b), not applicable except in the case of alternative apportionment methods or 80/20 determinations.
Special rules: sales factor	IV.18.(b)	86 Ill. Adm. Code 100.3380(c), except sourcing based on income producing activity applies only to certain interest and net gains.
Special regulation: construction contractors	IV.18.(d).	None
Special rules: airlines	IV.18.(e)	35 ILCS 5/304(d), except single-factor formula based on revenue miles.
Special rules: railroads	IV.18.(f)	35 ILCS 5/304(d), except single-factor formula based on ratio of miles traveled in state over total miles from point of origin to point of destination.
Special rules: trucking	IV.18.(g)	35 ILCS 5/304(d), except single-factor formula based on ratio of miles traveled in state over total miles from point of origin to point of destination.
Special rules: Television and radio	IV.18.(h)	35 ILCS 5/304(B-7), except single-factor formula based on sales and special sourcing rules.
Special rules: telecommunications and ancillary service providers	IV.18.(i)	86 Ill. Adm. Code 100.3371, except single-factor formula based on sales and special rules for sourcing sales.
Special rules: publishing	IV.18.(j)	86 Ill. Adm. Code 100.3373, except single-factor formula based on sales and special rules for computing and sourcing sales.

[¶11-510] Income Subject to Allocation and Apportionment

Illinois has adopted provisions similar to the UDITPA (see ¶11-505) provisions that divide income into business income, which is subject to formula apportionment, (see ¶11-520) and nonbusiness income, which is subject to allocation. (see ¶11-515)

• *Business income*

"Business income" is broadly defined for Illinois income tax purposes as all income that may be treated as apportionable business income under the U.S. Constitution. Business income is net of deductions attributable to that income and does not include compensation. (35 ILCS 5/1501(a)(1); 86 Ill. Adm. Code 100.3010(a)(2))

In *MeadWestvaco Corp. v. Illinois Department of Revenue* 553 U.S. 16 (2008) a unanimous U.S. Supreme Court ruled that the operational function concept is not a separate ground for apportionment in the absence of a unitary business. According to the Court, the Illinois courts misinterpreted references to "operational function" in previous Court deisions, and erred in considering whether a business division served an operation function in its out-of-state parent's business without first finding that the two were unitary. The Illinois trial court in this case ruled that Mead and Lexis were not a unitary business because they were not functionally integrated or centrally managed and enjoyed no economies of scale. Nevertheless, the court held that Illinois could tax an apportioned share of the capital gain because Lexis had served an operational purpose in Mead's business. The court based its conclusion on a finding that Mead considered Lexis in its strategic planning, including the allocation of resources. The Illinois Appellate Court affirmed. It cited as evidence that Lexis served an operational function that it was wholly owned by Mead, Mead had exercised control over Lexis in various ways, and Mead had described itself in filings as engaged in electronic publishing and information retrieval. The appellate court did not address the question whether the two formed a unitary business.

Elective treatment.—A taxpayer may make an irrevocable election to treat all income other than compensation as business income. (35 ILCS 5/1501(a)(1); 86 Ill. Adm. Code 100.3015; *Information Bulletin FY 2004-21*, Illinois Department of Revenue, December 2003) The election must be made on the original return for the taxable year to which the election applies or on a corrected return filed prior to the extended return due date. An election made on an original return may also be revoked on a timely-filed corrected return. After the extended due date for filing the return has passed, the election may still be made on an original return, but an election that has been made on the original or corrected return may no longer be revoked. (86 Ill. Adm. Code 100.3015(b))

In the case of a combined group of corporations filing a combined return, (see ¶11-550) the election must be made each year by the designated agent of the group and applies to all income of the unitary business group required to be shown on the combined return, including income of members who do not join in the filing of the combined return. (86 Ill. Adm. Code 100.3015(d))

Transactional test.—Illinois no longer follows the UDITPA transactional test for determining business income. (35 ILCS 5/1501(a)(1); 86 Ill. Adm. Code 100.3010)

Functional test.—Illinois no longer follows the UDITPA functional test for determining business income. (35 ILCS 5/1501(a)(1); 86 Ill. Adm. Code 100.3010)

• *Nonbusiness income*

"Nonbusiness income" is all income other than business income or compensation. (35 ILCS 5/1501(a)(14); 86 Ill. Adm. Code 100.3010(a)(3)(B))

• *Specific types of income or activities*

Rents.—Rental income from real and tangible property is business income if the property with respect to which the rental income was received is used in the taxpayer's trade or business or is attendant to it. (86 Ill. Adm. Code 100.3010(c)(2))

Gains or losses.—Gain or loss from the sale, exchange or other disposition of real or tangible personal property constitutes business income if the property, while owned by the person, was used in its trade or business. However, if such property was utilized for the production of nonbusiness income or otherwise was removed from the property factor before its sale, exchange or other disposition, the gain or loss will constitute nonbusiness income. (86 Ill. Adm. Code 100.3010(c)(3))

By adopting a constitutional standard for the scope and definition of "business income", the statutory provision effectively nullified a series of Illinois court cases that had ruled that gain from the disposition of an entire business, including a deemed sale of assets under IRC Sec. 338(h)(10), or from property that previously had been used in a business was not business income. (Instructions, 2004 Form 1120, Corporation Income and Replacement Tax Return)

Interest.—Interest income is business income where the intangible with respect to which the interest was received, is held or was created in the regular course of the person's trade or business operations or where the purpose for acquiring or holding the intangible is related or attendant to such trade or business operations. (86 Ill. Adm. Code 100.3010(c)(4))

Dividends.—Dividends are business income where the stock with respect to which the dividends are received, is held or was acquired in the regular course of the person's trade or business operations or where the purpose for acquiring or holding the stock is related or attendant to such trade or business operations. (86 Ill. Adm. Code 100.3010(c)(5))

Royalties.—Patent and copyright royalties are business income where the patent or copyright with respect to which the royalties were received, is held or was created in the regular course of the person's trade or business operations or where the purpose for acquiring or holding the patent or copyright is related or attendant to such trade or business operations. (86 Ill. Adm. Code 100.3010(c)(6))

Distributive S corporation or partnership income.—All income of a partnership or S corporation is business income, unless it is clearly attributable to only one state and is earned or received through activities totally unrelated to any business the partnership is conducting in more than one state. (Instructions, Schedule K-1-P, Partner's or Shareholder's Share of Income, Deductions, Credits, and Recapture)

An election made by the partnership or S corporation to treat all of its income as business income is binding on its partners and shareholders. An election by a partner or shareholder to treat all income as business income causes the nonbusiness income received from the pass-through entity to be treated as business income received directly by the partner or shareholder. (86 Ill. Adm. Code 100.3015(c))

Taxable income of an investment partnership that is distributable to a nonresident partner is treated as nonbusiness income and allocated to the partner's state of residence, unless the partner has made an election to treat all such income as business income or the income is from investment activity:

— that is directly related to any other business activity conducted in Illinois by the nonresident partner;

— that serves an operational function to any other business activity of the nonresident partner; or

— where assets of the investment partnership were acquired with working capital from a trade or business in Illinois in which the nonresident partner owns an interest. (35 ILCS 5/305)

[¶11-515] Allocation

Illinois provides rules for the allocation of capital gains or losses, property rents or royalties, interest and dividends, patent or copyright royalties, and Illinois lottery prizes that a taxpayer reports as nonbusiness income. (35 ILCS 5/303(a); 86 Ill. Adm. Code 100.3220(a))

Nonbusiness income or loss is reported on Illinois Schedule NB, which must be attached to the taxpayer's annual return. (Instructions, Schedule NB, Nonbusiness Income)

• *Capital gains and losses*

Capital gains and losses resulting from the sale or exchange of property are allocated to Illinois if:

• real property is located in Illinois;

• tangible personal property had its situs in Illinois at the time of the sale or exchange;

• the taxpayer had its commercial domicile in Illinois at the time of the sale or exchange and the taxpayer was not taxable in the state in which the tangible personal property had its situs; or

• the taxpayer had its commercial domicile in Illinois at the time of the sale or exchange of intangible property. (35 ILCS 5/303(b); 86 Ill. Adm. Code 100.3220(a))

Economic interests in minerals in place are considered real property for alloca-tion purposes. (86 Ill. Adm. Code 100.3220(b)) These interests include:

- royalties and overriding royalties;
- participating interests;
- production payments; and
- working interests. (86 Ill. Adm. Code 100.3220(b))

● *Property rents and royalties*

Rents and royalties from real property are allocated to Illinois if the property is located in Illinois. (35 ILCS 5/303(c)(1); 86 Ill. Adm. Code 100.3220(c)) Rents and royalties from tangible personal property are allocated to Illinois:

— if the property is used in Illinois; or

— if the taxpayer had its commercial domicile in Illinois at the time the rents or royalties were paid or accrued and the taxpayer was not organized under the laws of, or taxable with respect to the rents or royalties in, the state in which the property was used. (35 ILCS 5/303(c)(2); 86 Ill. Adm. Code 100.3220(c))

The extent of use of tangible personal property in Illinois is determined by multiplying the rents or royalties derived from the property by a fraction:

— the numerator of which is the number of days of physical location of the property in the state during the rental or royalty period in the taxable year; and

— the denominator of which is the number of days of physical location of the property everywhere during all rental or royalty periods in the taxable year. (35 ILCS 5/303(c)(2)(B); 86 Ill. Adm. Code 100.3220(c))

If the physical location of the property during the rental or royalty period is unknown or unascertainable, tangible personal property is used in the state in which the property was located at the time the rental or royalty payer obtained possession. (35 ILCS 5/303(c)(2)(B); 86 Ill. Adm. Code 100.3220(c))

● *Patent and copyright royalties*

Patent and copyright royalties are allocated to Illinois if and to the extent:

— the patent or copyright is used by the payer in Illinois; or

— the patent or copyright is used by the payer in a state in the taxpayer is not taxable with respect to the royalties and the taxpayer had its commercial domicile in Illinois at the time the royalties were paid or accrued. (35 ILCS 5/303(d)(1); 86 Ill. Adm. Code 100.3220(d))

A patent is used in Illinois:

— if it is employed in production, fabrication, manufacturing, or other processing in the state;

— if a patented product is produced in the state; or

— if the taxpayer had its commercial domicile and the basis of receipts from patent royalties do not permit allocation to states or the accounting procedures do not reflect states of use. (35 ILCS 5/303(d)(2)(A); 86 Ill. Adm. Code 100.3220(d))

A copyright is used in Illinois:

— if printing or other publication originates in the state; or

— if the taxpayer had its commercial domicile and the basis of receipts from copyright royalties do not permit allocation to states or the accounting proce-dures do not reflect states of use. (35 ILCS 5/303(d)(2)(B); 86 Ill. Adm. Code 100.3220(d))

• *Lottery prizes*

Prizes awarded under the Illinois Lottery Law are allocated to Illinois. Payments received in taxable years ending on or after December 31, 2013, from the assignment of a prize are also allocated to Illinois. (35 ILCS 5/303(e); 86 Ill. Adm. Code 100.3220(g))

• *Interest and dividends*

Interest and dividends that constitute nonbusiness income must be allocated to Illinois if the taxpayer had its commercial domicile in Illinois at the time such item was paid, incurred or accrued. (35 ILCS 5/301(c)(2)(B); 35 ILCS 5/303(g)(1))

[¶11-520] Apportionment

What is the standard Illinois apportionment formula?

Corporations must assign income from business activity both in and outside Illinois using a single sales factor apportionment formula. (35 ILCS 5/304(h))

Illinois also applies special apportionment factors to specific industries, including:

- insurance companies;
- financial organizations;
- federally regulated exchanges; and
- transportation companies.

How do pass-throughs apportion income to Illinois? Pass-through entities doing business in Illinois must use the same single sales factor apportionment as C corporations. This includes:

- S corporations; (Instructions, Form IL-1120-ST, Small Business Corporation Replacement Tax Return)

- partnerships; (35 ILCS 5/305(c); 86 Ill. Adm. Code 100.3500(b)(2); Instructions, Form IL-1065, Illinois Partnership Replacement Tax Return) and

- limited liability companies (LLCs) classified as partnerships for income tax purposes. (35 ILCS 5/305(c); 35 ILCS 5/1501(a)(16); 86 Ill. Adm. Code 100.3500(b)(2))

How do corporate partners apportion distributive income to Illinois? A corporate partner must apportion to Illinois its distributive share of the partnership's business income apportioned to the state. (35 ILCS 5/305(c); 86 Ill. Adm. Code 100.3500(b); Instructions, Form IL-1120, Corporation Income and Replacement Tax Return; Instructions, Schedule K-1-P, Partner's or Shareholder's Share of Income, Deductions, Credits, and Recapture)

What if the corporate partner is engaged in a unitary business with the partnership? A corporate partner engaged in a unitary business with a partnership must combine its distributive share of the partnership's business income and sales factor with its own business income and sales factor. (86 Ill. Adm. Code 100.3380(d); Instructions, Schedule K-1-P, Partner's or Shareholder's Share of Income, Deductions, Credits, and Recapture) The unitary business group cannot eliminate transactions between its members and the partnership in determining the partnership's business income. However, the group must eliminate all transactions between the unitary business group and the partnership in computing the unitary partners's and any other member's sales factor. (86 Ill. Adm. Code 100.3380(d)(2)(A))

Example: Partner and Partnership are engaged in a unitary business. Partner owns a 20% interest in Partnership. Partnership has $10,000,000 in sales everywhere, $3,000,000 of which are to Partner, and $4,000,000 in Illinois sales, $1,000,000 of which are to Partner. In computing its apportionment factor, Partner will include $1,400,000 from Partnership in its everywhere sales (20% of Partnership's $10,000,000 in everywhere sales, after eliminating the $3,000,000 in sales to Partner) and $600,000 from Partnership in its Illinois sales (20% of Partnership's $4,000,000 in Illinois sales, after eliminating the $1,000,000 in sales to Partner). Also, Partner must eliminate any sales it made to Partnership.

An exception to the unitary rules applies if the group cannot include the partnership because:

— the partner and the partnership must use different Illinois apportionment formulas and cannot be members of a unitary group; or

— the partner or the partnership conducts 80% or more of its total worldwide business activities outside the U.S. (86 Ill. Adm. Code 100.3380(d)(3))

A taxpayer determining the 80/20 business activity test cannot include any apportionment factors from a unitary partnership or partner. (86 Ill. Adm. Code 100.3380(d)(3))

This exception does not apply if:

• the partnership is itself a partner in a second partnership;

• one of its partners is engaged in a unitary business with the second partnership; and

• that partner is not prohibited from being a member in a unitary business group that includes the second partnership. (86 Ill. Adm. Code 100.3380(d)(3))

The unitary partner must combine its business income and sales factor with its share of the partnership's share of the second partnership's business income and apportionment factors. (86 Ill. Adm. Code 100.3380(d)(3))

How do individual owners apportion distributive income to Illinois? Nonresident shareholders, partners, or members must apportion to Illinois their distributive share of the pass-through entity's business income apportioned to the state. (35 ILCS 5/305(c); 86 Ill. Adm. Code 100.3500(b)) The nonresident shareholder, partner, or member must report this amount on Schedule NR to compute income tax liability from Illinois sources. (Instructions, Schedule NR, Nonresident and Part-Year Resident Computation of Illinois Tax; Instructions, Schedule K-1-P, Partner's or Shareholder's Share of Income, Deductions, Credits, and Recapture)

How do lower-tier partnerships apportion distributive income to Illinois? A lower-tier partnership must include its distributive share of the upper-tier partnership's business income apportioned to Illinois. An upper tier partnership that is itself a partner in a third partnership must include its distributive share of the third partnership's business income that the third partnership apportions to Illinois. The tiered partnership rule applies to all partnerships that are themselves partners in other partnerships. (86 Ill. Adm. Code 100.3500(b)(3))

A unitary partner cannot include the sales factor and business income of a second partnership that the unitary partnership is itself a partner. Instead, the partner must include its share of the unitary partnership's share of the second partnership's base income apportioned to Illinois. However, a partner engaged in a unitary business with the second partnership must combine its business income and sales factor with its share of the first partnership's share of the second partnership's business income and sales factor. (86 Ill. Adm. Code 100.3380(d)(2)(B))

How do foreign taxpayers apportion income to Illinois? Under IRC Sec. 882, a foreign corporation includes only income effectively-connected to the U.S. in its federal taxable income. Foreign taxpayers can exclude other items of income from their federal taxable income if authorized by treaty. (86 Ill. Adm. Code 100.3380(e))

A foreign taxpayer cannot use its worldwide apportionment factors to apportion its domestic business income to Illinois. Worldwide apportionment factors would not fairly represent that taxpayer's business activities in Illinois. Therefore, a foreign taxpayer must use only the apportionment factors from its domestic business income when apportioning its business income to Illinois. (86 Ill. Adm. Code 100.3380(e))

Does Illinois allow alternative apportionment methods?

Illinois allows or requires an alternative apportionment method if the standard allocation and apportionment provisions do not fairly represent the market for:

- the taxpayer's goods;
- the taxpayer's services; or
- other sources of the taxpayer's business income in the state. (35 ILCS 5/304(f); 86 Ill. Adm. Code 100.3380(a)(1); 86 Ill. Adm. Code 100.3390(a))

Neither the taxpayer nor the Illinois Department of Revenue (DOR) can seek an alternative apportionment method merely because it reaches a different result than the standard formula. (86 Ill. Adm. Code 100.3390(c))

What alternative apportionment methods does Illinois allow? Illinois alternative apportionment methods include:

- separate accounting;
- the exclusion of any one or more factors;
- the inclusion of one or more additional factors that will fairly represent the taxpayer's market in Illinois; or
- the employment of any other method that will result in an equitable allocation and apportionment of the taxpayer's business income. (35 ILCS 5/304(f); 86 Ill. Adm. Code 100.3380(a)(1); 86 Ill. Adm. Code 100.3390(a))

Who carries the burden of proof? The party seeking to use an alternative apportionment method carries the burden of proof. That party must show by clear and convincing evidence that the standard apportionment formula:

- results in the taxation of extraterritorial values; or
- operates unreasonably and arbitrarily to apportion income to Illinois out of all proportion to the taxpayer's market in the state. (86 Ill. Adm. Code § 100.3390(c))

Evidence must also prove that the proposed alternative apportionment method fairly and accurately apportions income to Illinois based on the taxpayer's market in the state. (86 Ill. Adm. Code § 100.3390(c))

How does a taxpayer apply for alternative apportionment? A taxpayer must file a clearly labeled petition for alternative apportionment:

- 120 days before the original or extended due date of the tax return in question;
- as an attachment to an amended return that used the standard allocation and apportionment rules; or
- as part of a protest to a deficiency notice resulting from an audit of the taxpayer's return and supporting books and records. (86 Ill. Adm. Code § 100.3390(e))

The explanations section of the taxpayer's amended return must state that the return includes a petition for alternative apportionment. (86 Ill. Adm. Code § 100.3390(e)) A protest to a deficiency notice cannot raise alternative apportionment unless:

• the taxpayer submitted a written request to use alternative apportionment and the auditor denied the request; or

• the audit rejects an alternative apportionment method the taxpayer used on its return. (86 Ill. Adm. Code § 100.3390(e))

The DOR will issue a private letter ruling advising the taxpayer that it accepts, partially accepts, or rejects the petition. (86 Ill. Adm. Code § 100.3390(f))

What if the DOR denies an alternative apportionment request? A taxpayer can protest the DOR's decision to deny the taxpayer's petition to use an alternative apportionment method. (86 Ill. Adm. Code § 100.3390(g))

If the DOR denies the petition before the taxpayer files its original or extended return, the taxpayer must file and pay tax using the standard apportionment formula. A taxpayer that files using the standard formula after the DOR denies its petitions can file an amended return and claim a refund based on the original petition. (86 Ill. Adm. Code § 100.3390(g)) If the DOR denies the taxpayer's refund claim, the taxpayer can:

• file a protest and request an administrative hearing; or

• file a petition with the Illinois Independent Tax Tribunal. (86 Ill. Adm. Code § 100.3390(g))

[¶ 11-525] Sales Factor

What is the Illinois sales factor?

The Illinois apportionment formula sales factor measures the ratio of a taxpayer's total sales in Illinois to its total sales everywhere during the tax year. (35 ILCS 5/304(a)(3)(A))

What sales or receipts must taxpayers include in the Illinois sales factor? Illinois generally defines "sales" as all gross receipts that a taxpayer does not allocate to the state. This means all the taxpayer's gross receipts from transactions and activity in the regular course of its trade or business. (35 ILCS 5/1501(a)(21); 86 Ill. Adm. Code Sec. 100.3370(a)(1))

Compliance Tip: The taxpayer may request an alternative apportionment method if the determination of "sales" does not clearly reflect the market for the taxpayer's goods, services or other sources of income in Illinois. (86 Ill. Adm. Code Sec. 100.3370(a)(1))

Sales includes gross receipts from:

• sales of manufactured goods or products, less returns and allowances;

• contract fees and expense reimbursements relating to cost-plus-fee contracts, like a fee for operating a government-owned plant;

• performance of services, including service fees, commissions, and similar items;

• rental, leasing, and licensing of real or tangible property; and

• sales of business assets. (86 Ill. Adm. Code Sec. 100.3370(a)(1))

Gross receipts from sales of manufactured goods or products includes:

• interest income;

• service and carrying charges; and

• time-price differential charges. (86 Ill. Adm. Code Sec. 100.3370(a)(1))

Does the Illinois sales factor include receipts a taxpayer excludes or deducts from federal taxable income? A taxpayer's Illinois sales factor must include gross receipts the taxpayer excludes or deducts from its federal taxable income if those receipts:

- are added back to Illinois base income;

- are not subtracted from Illinois base income; or

- are not eliminated from the Illinois unitary group's combined income. (86 Ill. Adm. Code Sec. 100.3370(a)(2)(D))

Examples include:

- interest from federally exempt state or local bonds and obligations; and

- intercompany transactions that a federal consolidated group defers for federal income tax purposes. (86 Ill. Adm. Code Sec. 100.3370(a)(2)(D))

Does the Illinois sales factor include receipts from lottery winnings? Effective for tax years beginning after 2013, a taxpayer's Illinois sales factor must include gross receipts from the assignment of Illinois lottery winnings. (35 ILCS 5/304(a)(3)(B-8); *Informational Bulletin FY 2014-08*, Illinois Department of Revenue, January 2014)

Does the Illinois sales factor include gains or losses from foreign currency transactions? Illinois treats foreign currency gain or loss from IRC Sec. 988 transactions as an adjustment to the income, expense, gain or loss. (86 Ill. Adm. Code 100.3380(c)(7)) This applies to accrued interest income or expense, gain or loss payable in foreign currency on:

- debt instruments;

- receivables; and

- forward contracts. (86 Ill. Adm. Code 100.3380(c)(7))

A taxpayer's Illinois sales factor must include its gain or loss from a foreign currency transaction only if the taxpayer also includes the income from the transaction. However, a taxpayer must exclude gains and losses relating to foreign currency expenses. (86 Ill. Adm. Code 100.3380(c)(7))

A taxpayer excludes IRC Sec. 986 foreign exchange gain or loss on distributions if it was previously taxed as:

- Subpart F income; or

- qualified electing fund earnings. (86 Ill. Adm. Code 100.3380(c)(7))

A taxpayer excludes those distributions from federal gross income and, therefore, excludes them from the Illinois sales factor. (86 Ill. Adm. Code 100.3380(c)(7))

Does the Illinois sales factor include gross receipts from intangible property? A taxpayer's Illinois sales factor must include gross receipts from intangible personal property if it makes up more than 50% of the taxpayer's total gross income during the current and previous 2 tax years. (35 ILCS 5/304(a)(3)(B-2); 86 Ill. Adm. Code Sec. 100.3370(a)(2)(F))

Unitary business group members must determine the gross receipts threshold using the entire group's gross receipts. (35 ILCS 5/304(a)(3)(B-2); 86 Ill. Adm. Code Sec. 100.3370(a)(2)(F)) A taxpayer in existence less than 3 tax years must determine the gross receipts threshold using each tax year of its existence. (86 Ill. Adm. Code Sec. 100.3370(a)(2)(F))

A taxpayer's gross receipts from intangible property includes receipts from the licensing, sale, or transfer of:

- patents issued under federal law;
- copyrights registered or eligible for registration under federal law;
- trademarks registered or eligible for registration under federal law;
- intellectual property registered or enforceable under another country's equivalent patent, copyright, or trademark laws. (86 Ill. Adm. Code Sec. 100.3370(a)(2)(F))

It also includes amounts received as damages or settlements from claims of infringement. (86 Ill. Adm. Code Sec. 100.3370(a)(2)(F))

A taxpayer's gross receipts from a patent includes only receipts from:

- using the patent in the production, fabrication, manufacturing, or other processing of a product; or
- producing, fabricating or manufacturing a product subject to the patent. (86 Ill. Adm. Code 100.3380(a)(2)(F))

A taxpayer's gross receipts from a copyright includes only receipts from printing or publishing material protected by the copyright. (86 Ill. Adm. Code Sec. 100.3370(a)(2)(F)) It does not include receipts from:

- broadcasting; or
- publishing or advertising services. (86 Ill. Adm. Code Sec. 100.3370(a)(2)(F))

The 50% total gross receipts threshold for a unitary combined reporting group includes gross receipts from all taxpayers who are group members at some time during the tax year. It does not matter whether those taxpayers were group members in the previous tax year. (86 Ill. Adm. Code Sec. 100.3370(a)(2)(F))

Does the Illinois sales factor exclude any sales or receipts? A taxpayer's Illinois sales factor must exclude:

- dividends, foreign IRC Sec. 78 gross-up dividends and Subpart F income; (35 ILCS 5/304(a)(3)(D); 86 Ill. Adm. Code Sec. 100.3370(a)(2))
- gross receipts the taxpayer excludes or deducts from its federal taxable income that it does not addback to Illinois base income;
- gross receipts the taxpayer subtracts from federal taxable income in computing Illinois base income (e.g., interest and dividends); and
- intercompany transactions that a unitary business group eliminates from combined income. (86 Ill. Adm. Code Sec. 100.3370(a)(2))

A sales factor throwout rule also applies under certain circumstances to receipts from intellectual property and services.

Does the Illinois sales factor exclude income from hedging transactions? In general, a taxpayer's Illinois sales factor must exclude any income, gain or loss from hedging transactions as defined under:

- IRC Sec. 475;
- IRC Sec. 1221; or
- IRC Sec. 1256. (86 Ill. Adm. Code 100.3380(c)(6))

A special rule applies if:

- the taxpayer's books and records clearly identify the transaction as managing risk relating to a particular or anticipated gross receipt item or items; and
- the taxpayer includes the gross receipts from the hedged item. (86 Ill. Adm. Code 100.3380(c)(6))

If the transaction relates to a group of hedged items, the taxpayer's sales factor includes the income, gain or loss in the same proportion that it includes the gross receipts from the hedged items. (86 Ill. Adm. Code 100.3380(c)(6))

Does the Illinois sales factor include incidental or occasional sales? A taxpayer's Illinois sales factor must exclude gross receipts from incidental or occasional sales. (86 Ill. Adm. Code 100.3380(c)(2)) This applies to incidental or occasional:

- sales of assets used in the regular course of trade or business (e.g., gross receipts from the sale of a factory or plant); and

- sales of stock in a subsidiary. (86 Ill. Adm. Code 100.3380(c)(2))

What are the Illinois sourcing rules for sales of tangible property?

Illinois follows the destination test for the sourcing of income from the sales of tangible personal property. Taxpayers must source sales of tangible personal property to Illinois if the taxpayer delivers or ships the property to a purchaser in the state. This applies to sales of tangible personal property, regardless of the F.O.B. point or other conditions of sale. (35 ILCS 5/304(a)(3)(B)(i); 86 Ill. Adm. Code Sec. 100.3370(c)(1)(A))

A taxpayer delivers or ships property to a purchaser in Illinois, if:

- the purchaser is located in Illinois, even though the purchaser ordered the property from outside the state; (86 Ill. Adm. Code Sec. 100.3370(c)(1)(B))

- the shipment ends in Illinois, even though the purchaser transfers the property afterward to another state; (86 Ill. Adm. Code Sec. 100.3370(c)(1)(C)) or

- the seller ships the property from the state of origin to a consignee in another state and it is diverted while on the way to a purchaser in Illinois. (86 Ill. Adm. Code Sec. 100.3370(c)(1)(E))

Example 1: A corporation, with inventory in State A, sold $100,000 of its products to a purchaser having branch stores in several states including Illinois. The order for the purchase was placed by the purchaser's central purchasing department located in State B. $25,000 of the purchase order was shipped directly to purchaser's branch store in Illinois. The branch store in Illinois is the purchaser with respect to $25,000 of the corporation's sales.

Example 2: A corporation makes a sale to a purchaser who maintains a central warehouse in Illinois where all merchandise purchases are received. The purchaser reships the goods to its branch stores in other states for sale. All of the corporation's products shipped to the purchaser's warehouse in Illinois is property delivered or shipped to a purchaser within Illinois.

Example 3: Corporation X, a produce grower in State A, begins shipment of perishable produce to the purchaser's place of business in State B. While en route the produce is diverted to the purchaser's place of business in Illinois where Corporation X is subject to tax. The sale by the corporation is attributed to Illinois.

A purchaser in Illinois includes the ultimate recipient of the property in the state. If an out-of-state purchaser instructs the taxpayer to direct an out-of-state manufacturer or supplier to deliver or ship the property to the purchaser's Illinois customers, the sale is in Illinois.

Sales of tangible personal property are not in Illinois if the seller and purchaser would be unitary business group members, except that:

- either the seller or purchaser conducts 80% or more of its total business activity outside the U.S.; and

- the purchaser acquires the property for resale. (35 ILCS 5/304(a)(3)(B)(ii))

What are the sourcing rules in Illinois for sales of other than tangible property?

Illinois generally follows market-based sourcing rules for most sales of other than tangible property, including gross receipts from:

- the licensing, sale, or transfer of intellectual property; and

- services.

What are the Illinois sales factor sourcing rules for the sale or lease of real property? Taxpayers must source receipts to Illinois from the sale or lease of real property located in the state. (35 ILCS 5/304(a)(3)(C-5)(i); 86 Ill. Adm. Code Sec. 100.3370(c)(6)(A))

What are the Illinois sales factor sourcing rules for the lease or rental of tangible personal property? Taxpayers must source receipts to Illinois from the lease or rental of tangible personal property located in the state during the rental period. (35 ILCS 5/304(a)(3)(C-5)(ii); 86 Ill. Adm. Code Sec. 100.3370(c)(6)(B))

Taxpayers must also source receipts to Illinois from the lease or rental of moving property used in the state. (35 ILCS 5/304(a)(3)(C-5)(ii); 86 Ill. Adm. Code Sec. 100.3370(c)(6)(B)) Moving property includes:

- motor vehicles;

- trains and trucks;

- aircraft;

- ships and boats; and

- mobile equipment. (35 ILCS 5/304(a)(3)(C-5)(ii); 86 Ill. Adm. Code Sec. 100.3370(c)(6)(B))

What are the Illinois sales factor sourcing rules for interest, net gains, and other intangible property income? Taxpayers must source interest, net gains, and other intangible personal property income to Illinois if:

- the taxpayer performed the income-producing activity in Illinois; or

- the taxpayer performed the income-producing activity both in and outside Illinois, but performed a greater proportion of the activity in the state based on costs of performance. (35 ILCS 5/304(a)(3)(C-5)(iii)(b); 86 Ill. Adm. Code Sec. 100.3370(c)(6)(C))

Intangible property dealers, including securities dealers within the meaning of IRC Sec. 475, must source interest, net gains, and other income to Illinois if the dealer receives that income from a customer:

- who is a resident individual, trust or estate; or

- who has a commercial domicile in the state. (35 ILCS 5/304(a)(3)(C-5)(iii)(a); 86 Ill. Adm. Code Sec. 100.3370(c)(6)(C))

A dealer must source the interest, gain, or other income to Illinois if its records show an Illinois billing address for the customer. The customer billing address applies unless the dealer possess actual knowledge of a customer's residence or commercial domicile. (35 ILCS 5/304(a)(3)(C-5)(iii)(a); 86 Ill. Adm. Code Sec. 100.3370(c)(6)(C))

"Intangible personal property" includes only an item that the customer or holder can resell or transfer after acquiring it from the taxpayer. (86 Ill. Adm. Code Sec. 100.3370(c)(6)(C)) It does not include a taxpayer's obligation to:

- make any payment;
- perform any act; or
- otherwise provide anything of value to another person. (86 Ill. Adm. Code Sec. 100.3370(c)(6)(C))

Example 1: A sports ticket is not intangible personal property for the stadium owner who issues the ticket and must grant admission to the ticket holder. Rather, the ticket sale is prepayment for a service. However, the ticket is intangible personal property in the hands of the original purchaser and any later purchaser of the ticket. A ticket broker buying and reselling tickets is an intangible dealer with respect to the ticket.

Example 2: A taxpayer selling canned computer software is selling intangible personal property. If the taxpayer sells software to customers in the ordinary course of its business, it is an intangible property dealer for those sales. In contrast, a taxpayer providing programming or maintenance services to its customers is selling services rather than intangible personal property.

Example 3: A taxpayer administers a rewards program for a group of unrelated businesses. Under the program, a customer of one business can earn discounts or rebates on products and services provided by any of the businesses. As each customer earns rewards, measured in units, from one of the businesses, that business pays a specified amount for each unit to the taxpayer. When a customer uses units earned in the program to purchase products or services at a discount from a participating business, the taxpayer pays that business a specified amount for each unit used by the customer. Rebates may be paid to the customer directly by the taxpayer or by one of the businesses, which is then reimbursed by the taxpayer. If payments made to the taxpayer by businesses awarding units exceed the payments the taxpayer must make for discounts and rebates, the excess is payment for operating the program. The units awarded are the taxpayer's obligations to make payments to the business providing products or services at a discount or to pay rebates. Payments received by the taxpayer from the participating businesses for units awarded are not income from sales of intangible personal property by the taxpayer.

What are the Illinois sales factor sourcing rules for the licensing, sale, or transfer of intellectual property?

Taxpayers must source receipts to Illinois from the licensing, sale, or transfer during the tax year of:

- patents used in the state;
- copyrights used in the state;
- trademarks used in the state; and
- similar intellectual property used in the state. (35 ILCS 5/304(a)(3)(B-1); 86 Ill. Adm. Code Sec. 100.3370(c)(3))

When is a patent used in Illinois? A licensee, purchaser, or transferee uses a patent in Illinois if it:

- employs the patent in production, fabrication, manufacturing, or other processing in the state; or
- produces a patented product in the state. (35 ILCS 5/304(a)(3)(B-1); 86 Ill. Adm. Code Sec. 100.3370(c)(3))

If the licensee, purchaser, or transferee uses a patent both in Illinois and other states, taxpayers must divide the gross receipts from its use in Illinois by the total gross receipts from its use in all states. (35 ILCS 5/304(a)(3)(B-1); 86 Ill. Adm. Code Sec. 100.3370(c)(3))

¶11-525

When is a copyright used in Illinois? A licensee, purchaser, or transferee uses a copyright in Illinois if printing of publishing originates in the state. (35 ILCS 5/304(a)(3)(B-1); 86 Ill. Adm. Code Sec. 100.3370(c)(3)) Printing or publishing originates in Illinois if it is the state where:

- the licensee, purchaser, or transferee incorporates the copyrighted material into a physical medium for delivery to purchasers; or

- if there is no physical delivery medium, the licensee, purchaser, or transferee delivers the copyrighted material to purchasers. (35 ILCS 5/304(a)(3)(B-1); 86 Ill. Adm. Code Sec. 100.3370(c)(3))

If a licensee, purchaser, or transferee uses a copyright both in Illinois and other states, taxpayers must divide the gross receipts from its use in Illinois by the total gross receipts from its use in all states. (35 ILCS 5/304(a)(3)(B-1); 86 Ill. Adm. Code Sec. 100.3370(c)(3))

When is a trademark and other intellectual property used in Illinois? A licensee, purchaser, or transferee uses trademarks and other intellectual property in Illinois if its commercial domicile is located in the state. (35 ILCS 5/304(a)(3)(B-1); 86 Ill. Adm. Code Sec. 100.3370(c)(3))

What are the Illinois sourcing rules for services?

Taxpayers must source sales of services to Illinois if a customer received the service in the state. (35 ILCS 5/304(a)(3)(C-5)(iv); 86 Ill. Adm. Code Sec. 100.3370(c)(6)(D))

What if a service contract involves use of service provider's property? If a service contract also involves use of the service provider's property, Illinois generally treats the arrangement as a sale of services. (86 Ill. Adm. Code Sec. 100.3370(c)(6)(D)) However, if the service contract treats the property as a lease under IRC Sec. 7701(e)(1), Illinois considers other factors including whether:

- the customer physically possesses the property;

- the customer controls the property;

- the customer has a significant economic or possessory interest in the property;

- the taxpayer bears no risk of substantially diminished receipts or increased expenditures for nonperformance under the contract;

- the taxpayer does not use the property simultaneously to provide significant services to other unrelated customers; and

- the total contract price does not substantially exceed the property's rental value for the contract period. (86 Ill. Adm. Code Sec. 100.3370(c)(6)(D))

What if a service involves tangible personal property? If a taxpayer's service involves tangible personal property, the taxpayer must apply the sourcing rules for the sale of tangible personal property. The customer receives the service in Illinois if the taxpayer restores possession of the property to the customer. (86 Ill. Adm. Code Sec. 100.3370(c)(6)(D))

Example 1: A customer returns a computer to the manufacturer for repair. The manufacturer performs the repairs in Indiana and ships the computer to the customer's Illinois address. The customer receives the service in Illinois.

Example 2: An individual purchases clothing from an Illinois retail store. The individual uses a credit card issued by a bank under a licensing agreement with a credit card company. The credit card company is not a financial organization required to apportion its business income to Illinois using special apportionment rules. The bank remits the purchase price to the credit card company, which deposits the purchase price with the retail store's bank, minus a fee or discount. All fees and discounts earned by the credit card company for this purchase are for services received in Illinois.

What if a service involves real property? If the taxpayer's service involves real property located in Illinois, the customer receives the service in the state. (86 Ill. Adm. Code Sec. 100.3370(c)(6)(D))

Example 3: An individual purchases a piece of land in Illinois and constructs a house on it. Services performed at an architect's Wisconsin office for the design and construction of the house are received in Illinois.

What if a service involves a personal service? If the taxpayer performs a personal service on or for an individual located in Illinois at the time of the service (e.g., medical treatment services), the individual receives the service in the state. (86 Ill. Adm. Code Sec. 100.3370(c)(6)(D))

What if a service involves connected or support services? If the taxpayer performs services directly connected to or in support of services received in Illinois, those services are also received in the state. (86 Ill. Adm. Code Sec. 100.3370(c)(6)(D))

Example 4: An individual purchases automobile repair services from an automobile dealership at its Illinois facility. The individual uses a credit card issued by a bank under a licensing agreement with a credit card company. The bank remits the purchase price to the credit card company, which deposits the purchase price with the automobile dealership's bank, minus a fee or discount. All fees and discounts earned by the credit card company in connection with this purchase are for services received in Illinois.

Example 5: A taxpayer's investment fund performs services for individual investors who reside in Illinois and other investors who have an ordering or billing address in the state. The taxpayer's services directly connected with services provided to those investors, like preparing communications and statements to investors, and providing earnings and distributions to investors, are also received in Illinois.

What if a service provider cannot determine if a customer received a service in Illinois? Special sourcing rules apply when a service provider cannot determine if a customer received the service in Illinois. (86 Ill. Adm. Code Sec. 100.3370(c)(6)(D))

A business customer received the service in Illinois if:

(1) the customer ordered the service in the regular course of its trade or business at its Illinois office address; or

(2) the taxpayer cannot determine (1) and it billed the customer for the services at an Illinois office address. (86 Ill. Adm. Code Sec. 100.3370(c)(6)(D))

The same rules apply in the same order for individual customers. An individual customer received the service in Illinois if the customer's residential address in the state was the place of ordering or billing the service. (86 Ill. Adm. Code Sec. 100.3370(c)(6)(D))

The special sourcing rules apply if:

• the taxpayer's or related party's books and records do not show that the customer received the service in Illinois; or

• reasonable parties would reach different determinations about the state where the customer received the service. (86 Ill. Adm. Code Sec. 100.3370(c)(6)(D))

What if a service provider is a subcontractor or agent? Special sourcing rules also apply if a subcontractor or agent provides the services. A customer received the services in Illinois if:

- the contractor or principal owns or operates a fixed place of business in the state;

- the contractor's or principal's customer owns or operates a fixed place of business in the state; or

- the contractor's or principal's customer is an individual. (86 Ill. Adm. Code Sec. 100.3370(c)(6)(D))

Does Illinois have a throwback or throwout rule?

Yes, Illinois applies sales factor throwback and throwout rules.

When does the Illinois sales factor throwback rule apply? A taxpayer must source or throwback sales of tangible personal property to Illinois if:

- the purchaser's state does not tax the income from the sale (35 ILCS 5/304(a)(3)(B)(ii); 86 Ill. Adm. Code Sec. 100.3370(c)(1)(F)) or the purchaser is the U.S. government; (35 ILCS 5/304(a)(3)(B)(ii); 86 Ill. Adm. Code Sec. 100.3370(c)(2)) and

- the taxpayer ships the property from an office, store, warehouse, factory, or other place of storage in Illinois.

Example 1: A corporation has its head office and factory in State A. It maintains a branch office and inventory in Illinois. The corporation's only activity in State B is the solicitation of orders by a resident salesperson. All orders by the State B salesperson are sent to the branch office in Illinois for approval and are filled by shipment from the inventory in Illinois. Since the corporation is immune under Public Law 86-272 from tax in State B, all sales of merchandise to purchasers in State B are attributed to Illinois, the state from which the merchandise was shipped.

Example 2: A corporation contracts with General Services Administration to deliver trucks paid for by the U.S. Government. The corporation ships the trucks from its factory in Illinois. The sale is a sale to the United States Government. The corporation must source the sales to Illinois.

Example 3: A corporation as a subcontractor to a prime contractor with the National Aeronautics and Space Administration (NASA) contracts to build a component of a rocket for $1 million. The sale by the subcontractor to the prime contractor is not a sale to the United States Government.

An office, store, warehouse, factory, or place of storage does not include property owned or leased by an independent contractor for printing newspapers, periodicals, or books. (35 ILCS 5/304(a)(3)(B)(ii); 86 Ill. Adm. Code Sec. 100.3370(c)(1)(A))

Illinois no longer applies a "double throwback rule" to certain "drop shipments." The rule does not fairly represent the market for the taxpayer's goods, services, or other sources of business income in Illinois. (86 Ill. Adm. Code 100.3380(c)(1))

When does the Illinois sales factor throwout rule apply? Illinois applies a sales factor throwout rule under certain circumstances. A taxpayer must exclude or throwout gross receipts from a patent, copyright, trademark, or similar item of intangible property if it cannot determine the property's place of use from:

- the taxpayer's books and records; or

- any affiliate's books and records. (35 ILCS 5/304(a)(3)(B-1)(iii); 86 Ill. Adm. Code Sec. 100.3370(c)(3)(D))

Similarly, a taxpayer must exclude or throwout gross receipts from services if the state where a customer receives the services does not tax the taxpayer. (35 ILCS 5/304(a)(3)(C-5)(iv); 86 Ill. Adm. Code Sec. 100.3370(c)(6)(D))

[¶11-530] Property Factor

Although the Illinois apportionment formula (see ¶ 11-520) for general business corporations consists of a single sales factor, (see ¶ 11-525) taxpayers may be permitted or required to use an alternative apportionment formula (see ¶ 11-520) that includes or excludes one or more additional factors. In addition, unitary business groups that file a combined report (see ¶ 11-550) must use a special apportionment formula consisting of property and payroll factors to determine whether members meet the 80/20 U.S. business activity test and are eligible for inclusion in the combined report. (35 ILCS 5/1501(a)(27)(A); 86 Ill. Adm. Code 100.9700(c))

The Illinois property factor is a fraction, the numerator of which is the average value of the taxpayer's real and tangible personal property owned or rented and used in trade or business in Illinois during the tax period and the denominator of which is the average value of all the taxpayer's real and tangible personal property owned or rented and used during the tax period. (35 ILCS 5/304(a)(1)(A))

• *Definition of real and tangible personal property*

The term "real and tangible personal property" is generally defined by Illinois income tax law to include land, buildings, machinery, stocks of goods, equipment, and other real and tangible personal property, but does not include coin or currency. (86 Ill. Adm. Code 100.3350(a))

• *Items included or excluded and valuation*

Property must be included in the Illinois property factor if it is actually used or is available for or capable of being used during the tax period in the regular course of the trade or business of the taxpayer. (86 Ill. Adm. Code 100.3350(b)) Property used both in the regular course of taxpayer's trade or business and in the production of nonbusiness income must be included in the factor only to the extent the property is used in the regular course of taxpayer's trade or business. The method of determining that portion of the value to be included in the factor will depend upon the facts of each case. (86 Ill. Adm. Code 100.3350(a))

Owned property.—The numerator of the Illinois property factor must include the average value of the real and tangible personal property owned by the taxpayer and used in Illinois during the tax period in the regular course of the trade or business of the taxpayer. (86 Ill. Adm. Code 100.3350(d)) Property owned by the taxpayer must be valued at its original cost, (35 ILCS 5/304(a)(1)(B); 86 Ill. Adm. Code 100.3350(e)) representing the basis of the property for federal income tax purposes at the time of acquisition by the taxpayer. (86 Ill. Adm. Code 100.3350(e)) Original cost does not include any federal adjustments for depreciation, depletion, or amortization, (86 Ill. Adm. Code 100.3350(e)) but does include the original cost, at acquisition, of any capital improvement as well as partial dispositions of any portion by reason of sale, exchange, or abandonment. (86 Ill. Adm. Code 100.3350(e)(1))

> *Example 1:* Corporation W acquired a factory building in Illinois at a cost of $500,000 and 18 months later expended $100,000 for major remodeling of the building. The corporation files its return for the current taxable year on the calendar-year basis. A depreciation deduction in the amount of $22,000 was claimed on the building for its return for the current taxable year. The value of the building includable in the numerator and denominator of the property factor is $600,000 as the depreciation deduction is not taken into account in determining the value of the building for purposes of the factor. (86 Ill. Adm. Code 100.3350(e)(3))

Example 2: During the current taxable year, X Corporation merges into Y Corporation in a tax-free reorganization under the Internal Revenue Code. At the time of the merger, X Corporation owns a factory which X built five years earlier at a cost of $1,000,000. X has been depreciating the factory at the rate of two percent per year, and its basis in X's hands at the time of the merger is $900,000. Since the property is acquired by Y in a transaction in which, under the Internal Revenue Code, its basis in Y's hands is the same as its basis in X's, Y includes the property in Y's property factor at X's original cost, without adjustment for depreciation, i.e., $1,000,000. (86 Ill. Adm. Code 100.3350(e)(4))

If the original cost of property is unascertainable, the property must be included in the factor at its fair market value as of the date of acquisition by the taxpayer. (86 Ill. Adm. Code 100.3350(e)(5)(A))

Capitalized intangible drilling and development costs must be included in the Illinois property factor whether or not they have been expensed for either federal or state tax purposes. Intangible drilling and development costs include such elements as wages, fuel, repairs, hauling, draining, roadbuilding, surveying, geological works, construction of derricks, tanks, pipelines, and other physical structures necessary for the drilling of wells and preparation for the production of oil and gas, plus supplies incident to and necessary for the drilling of wells and clearing of ground. (86 Ill. Adm. Code 100.3350(e)(2))

Rented property.—The numerator of the Illinois property factor must include the average value of the real and tangible personal property rented by the taxpayer and used in Illinois during the tax period in the regular course of the trade or business of the taxpayer. (86 Ill. Adm. Code 100.3350(d)) Property rented by the taxpayer is valued at eight times the net annual rental rate. The net annual rental rate for any item of rented property is the annual rental rate paid by the taxpayer for that property, less the aggregate annual subrental rates paid by subtenants of the taxpayer. (35 ILCS 5/304(a)(1)(B); 86 Ill. Adm. Code 100.3350(f)(1)) Subrents are not deducted when the subrents constitute business income because the property which produces the subrents is used in the regular course of a trade or business of the taxpayer when it is producing that income. Accordingly, there is no reduction in its value. (86 Ill. Adm. Code 100.3350(f)(1))

Example A: Corporation A receives subrents from a bakery concession in a food market operated by it. Since the subrents are business income they are not deducted from the rent paid by Corporation A for the food market. (86 Ill. Adm. Code 100.3350(f)(1)(A))

Example B: Corporation B rents a 5-story office building primarily for use in its multistate business, uses three floors for its offices and subleases two floors to various other businesses and persons such as professional people, shops and the like. The rental of the two floors is attendant to the operation of the corporation's trade or business. Since the subrents are business income they are not deducted from the rent paid by the corporation. (86 Ill. Adm. Code 100.3350(f)(1)(B))

Example C: Corporation C rents a 20-story office building and uses the lower two stories for its general corporation headquarters. The remaining 18 floors are subleased to others. The rental of the eighteen floors is not attendant to but rather is separate from the operation of the corporation's trade or business. Since the subrents are nonbusiness income they are to be deducted from the rent paid by the corporation. (86 Ill. Adm. Code 100.3350(f)(1)(C))

If subrents produce a negative or clearly inaccurate value for any item of property, another method which will properly reflect the value of rented property may be required by the Illinois Director of Revenue or requested by the taxpayer. The value may not be less than an amount which bears the same ratio to the annual rental rate paid by the taxpayer for such property as the fair market value of that portion of the property used by the taxpayer bears to the total fair market value of the rented property. (86 Ill. Adm. Code 100.3380(b)(1))

> *Example:* A corporation rents a 10-story building at an annual rental rate of $1,000,000. The corporation occupies two stories and sublets eight stories for $1,000,000 a year. The net annual rental rate of the taxpayer must not be less than two-tenths of the corporation annual rental rate for the entire year, or $200,000.

If property owned by others is used by the taxpayer at no charge or rented by the taxpayer for a nominal rate, the net annual rental rate for that property must be determined on the basis of a reasonable market rental rate for that property. (86 Ill. Adm. Code 100.3380(b)(2))

Annual rental rate: The "annual rental rate" is the amount paid as rental for property for a 12-month period. Where property is rented for less than a 12-month period, the rent paid for the actual period of rental constitutes the annual rental rate for the tax period. However, where a taxpayer has rented property for a term of 12 or more months and the current tax period covers a period of less than 12 months (e.g., reorganization or change of accounting period), the rent paid for the short tax period must be annualized. If the rental term is for less than 12 months, the rent cannot be annualized beyond its term. Rent cannot be annualized because of the uncertain duration when the rental term is on a month-to-month basis. (86 Ill. Adm. Code 100.3350(f)(2))

> *Example A:* Corporation A which ordinarily files its returns based on a calendar year is merged into Corporation B on April 30. The net rent paid under a lease with 5 years remaining is $2,500 a month. The rent for the tax period January 1 to April 30 is $10,000. After the rent is annualized the net rent is $30,000 ($2,500 × 12). (86 Ill. Adm. Code 100.3350(f)(2)(A))

> *Example B:* Same facts as in Example A except that the lease would have terminated August 31. In this case the annualized net rent is $20,000 ($2,500 × 8). (86 Ill. Adm. Code 100.3350(f)(2)(B))

Annual rent is the actual sum of money or other consideration payable, directly or indirectly, by the taxpayer or for its benefit for the use of the property and includes:

— any amount payable for the use of real or tangible personal property, or any part of it whether designated as a fixed sum of money or as a percentage of sales, profits, or otherwise; (86 Ill. Adm. Code 100.3350(f)(3)(A)) and

— any amount payable as additional rent or in lieu of rents, such as interest, taxes, insurance, repairs or any other items which are required to be paid by the terms of the lease or other arrangement. (86 Ill. Adm. Code 100.3350(f)(3)(B))

If a payment includes rent and other charges unsegregated, the amount of rent must be determined by consideration of the relative values of the rent and the other items. (86 Ill. Adm. Code 100.3350(f)(3)(B))

> *Example i:* A corporation pursuant to the terms of a lease, pays a lessor $1,000 per month as a base rental and at the end of the year pays the lessor one percent of its gross sales of $400,000. The annual rent is $16,000 ($12,000 plus one percent of $400,000 or $4,000). (86 Ill. Adm. Code 100.3350(f)(3)(A))

> *Example ii:* A corporation, pursuant to the terms of a lease, pays the lessor $12,000 a year rent plus taxes in the amount of $2,000 and interest on a mortgage in the amount of $1,000. The annual rent is $15,000. (86 Ill. Adm. Code 100.3350(f)(3)(B)(i))

Service charges and incidental expenses: Annual rent does not include amounts paid as service charges, such as utilities and janitor services. (86 Ill. Adm. Code 100.3350(f)(3)(B))

Example: A corporation stores part of its inventory in a public warehouse. The total charge for the year was $1,000 of which $700 was for the use of storage space and $300 for inventory insurance, handling and shipping charges, and C.O.D. collections. The annual rent is $700. (86 Ill. Adm. Code 100.3350(f)(3)(B)(ii))

Annual rent also does not include incidental day-to-day expenses, such as hotel or motel accommodations and daily rental of automobiles. (86 Ill. Adm. Code 100.3350(f)(3)(C))

Royalties: Annual rent includes royalties based on extraction of natural resources, whether represented by delivery or purchase. A royalty for this purpose includes any consideration conveyed or credited to a holder of an interest in property that constitutes a sharing of current or future production of natural resources from such property, irrespective of the method of payment or how such consideration may be characterized, whether as a royalty, advance royalty, rental or otherwise. (86 Ill. Adm. Code 100.3350(f)(3)(C))

Construction in progress.—Property or equipment under construction during the tax period, except inventoriable goods in process, must be excluded from the factor until that property is actually used in the regular course of the trade or business of the taxpayer. If the property is partially used in the regular course of the trade or business of the taxpayer while under construction, the value of the property to the extent used must be included in the property factor. (86 Ill. Adm. Code 100.3350(b))

Standyby or Idle Property.—Property held as reserves or standby facilities or property held as a reserve source of materials must be included in the Illinois property factor. For example, a plant temporarily idle or raw material reserves not currently being processed are includable in the factor. (86 Ill. Adm. Code 100.3350(b))

Property used in the regular course of the trade or business of the taxpayer must remain in the property factor until its permanent withdrawal is established by an identifiable event such as its conversion to the production of nonbusiness income, its sale, or the lapse of an extended period of time (normally, five years), during which the property is held for sale. (86 Ill. Adm. Code 100.3350(b))

Example 1: Corporation A closed its manufacturing plant in State X and held such property for sale. The property remained vacant until its sale one year later. The value of the manufacturing plant is included in the property factor until the plant is sold. (86 Ill. Adm. Code 100.3350(b)(1))

Example 2: Same as above except that the property was rented until the plant was sold. The plant is included in the property factor until the plant is sold. (86 Ill. Adm. Code 100.3350(b)(2))

Example 3: Corporation A operates a chain of retail grocery stores. The corporation closed Store A, which was then remodeled into three small retail stores, such as a dress shop, dry cleaning, and barber shop, which were leased to unrelated parties. The property is removed from the property factor on the date the remodeling of Store A commenced. (86 Ill. Adm. Code 100.3350(b)(3))

Property in transit.—Property in transit between locations of the taxpayer to which it belongs is considered to be at the destination for purposes of the Illinois property factor. Property in transit between a buyer and seller which is included by a taxpayer in the denominator of its property factor in accordance with its regular accounting practices must be included in the numerator of its property factor if Illinois is the state of destination. (86 Ill. Adm. Code 100.3350(d))

Mobile or movable property.—The value of mobile or movable property, such as construction equipment, trucks or leased electronic equipment, which is located in Illinois and outside of the state during the tax period must be determined for purposes of the numerator of the Illinois property factor on the basis of total time within the state during the tax period. (86 Ill. Adm. Code 100.3350(d))

An automobile assigned to a traveling employee must be included in the numerator of the taxpayer's property factor if the employee's compensation is assigned under the payroll factor to Illinois or if the automobile is licensed in Illinois. (86 Ill. Adm. Code 100.3350(d))

Inventory.—Inventory of stock of goods must be included in the Illinois property factor in accordance with the valuation method used for federal income tax purposes. (86 Ill. Adm. Code 100.3350(e)(5)(B))

Leasehold improvements.—Leasehold improvements are treated as property owned by the taxpayer for the purposes of the Illinois property factor, regardless of whether the taxpayer is entitled to remove the improvements or the improvements revert to the lessor upon expiration of the lease. Hence, the original cost of leasehold improvements must be included in the factor. (86 Ill. Adm. Code 100.3350(f)(4))

Method of averaging property values.—The average value of the property is determined by averaging the values at the beginning and ending of the tax period. However, the Illinois Director of Revenue may require or allow the averaging by monthly values if such method is required to properly reflect the average value of the taxpayer's property during the tax period. (35 ILCS 5/304(a)(1)(C); 86 Ill. Adm. Code 100.3350(g)) Averaging by monthly values will generally be applied if substantial fluctuations in the values of property exist during the tax period or where property is acquired after the beginning of the tax period or disposed of before the end of the tax period. (86 Ill. Adm. Code 100.3350(g))

Averaging with respect to rented property is achieved automatically by the method of determining the net annual rental rate of that property. (86 Ill. Adm. Code 100.3350(g))

[¶11-535] Payroll Factor

Does the Illinois apportionment formula include a payroll factor?

The standard Illinois apportionment formula does not include a payroll factor and consists only of a single sales factor. But, Illinois allows and can require an alternative apportionment formula that includes or excludes one or more additional factors. In addition, unitary combined reporting groups must use a special apportionment formula consisting of property and payroll factors to determine whether to include members that meet the 80/20 U.S. business activity test and are eligible for inclusion in the combined report. (35 ILCS 5/1501(a)(27); 86 Ill. Adm. Code 100.9700(c))

What is the Illinois payroll factor?

The Illinois payroll factor measures the ratio of a taxpayer's total compensation paid in Illinois (35 ILCS 5/304(a)(2)(A); 86 Ill. Adm. Code 100.3360(c)) to its total compensation paid everywhere during the tax year. (35 ILCS 5/304(a)(2)(A); 86 Ill. Adm. Code 100.3360(b))

The payroll factor must include the total amount of compensation paid by the taxpayer in the regular course of its trade or business. (86 Ill. Adm. Code 100.3360(a)(1))

> *Example A:* A corporation uses some of its employees in the construction of a storage building that, after completion, it uses in the regular course of its trade or business. The corporation treats the wages paid to those employees as a capital expenditure. It must include the wages in its payroll factor.

> *Example B:* A corporation owns various securities that it holds as an investment separate and apart from its trade or business. The management of

the corporation's investment portfolio is the only duty of Mr. X, an employee. The corporation must exclude the salary paid to Mr. X from its payroll factor.

A taxpayer determines the total amount paid to employees based on its accounting method. If the taxpayer uses the accrual method of accounting, all compensation accrued is considered to have been paid. (86 Ill. Adm. Code 100.3360(a)(2))

"Compensation" means:

- wages;
- salaries;
- commissions; and
- any other form of remuneration paid to employees for personal services. (86 Ill. Adm. Code 100.3100(a))

Illinois adopts the definition of "wages" under IRC Sec. 3401(a), but it does not follow the exceptions set forth in the federal definition. (86 Ill. Adm. Code 100.3100(a)) Thus, salaries, fees, bonuses, commissions on sales or on insurance premiums, and pensions and retired pay are compensation. (86 Ill. Adm. Code 100.3100(c))

The name used to designate remuneration for services is immaterial. (86 Ill. Adm. Code 100.3100(c)) So, compensation, if paid for services performed by an employee, includes:

- fees;
- bonuses;
- pensions and retirement pay; and
- commissions on sales or insurance premiums. (86 Ill. Adm. Code 100.3100(c))

The term "employee" includes every individual performing services if the legal relationship between the individual and the taxpayer is that of employer and employee. The term has the same meaning as the definition under IRC Sec. 3401(c) and 26 CFR 31.3401(c)-1. If the employer-employee relationship does not exist, remuneration for services performed does not represent compensation. (86 Ill. Adm. Code 100.3100(b)) But, remuneration for personal services is compensation so long as the employer-employee relationship existed when the employee rendered the services. (86 Ill. Adm. Code 100.3100(d))

What are the Illinois sourcing rules for payroll?

Effective for tax years before 2020, taxpayers must source or assign compensation to Illinois if:

- the employee performs services entirely in Illinois;
- the services performed by the employee in Illinois are not incidental to services performed outside the state;
- the employee performs some services for the employer in Illinois and the employee's base of operations is in the state;
- the employee performs some services in Illinois and the place from which the services is directed or controlled is in the state; or
- the employee is an Illinois resident. (35 ILCS 5/304(a)(2)(B); 86 Ill. Adm. Code 100.3120(a))

Effective for tax years ending on or after December 31, 2020, taxpayers must source or assign compensation to Illinois if:

- the employee performs some services in Illinois;
- the services performed in Illinois are not incidental to services performed outside the state; and
- the employee performs the services in Illinois for more than 30 working days during the tax year. (35 ILCS 5/304(a)(2)(B))

A taxpayer determines the amount of compensation paid in Illinois based on a ratio that compares the number of working days spent in the state to the total number of working days spent both in and outside the state during the tax year. (35 ILCS 5/304(a)(2)(B))

A working day covers all days during the tax year in which employees perform duties for their employer. (35 ILCS 5/304(a)(2)(B)) It does not include:

- weekends;

- vacation days;

- sick days;

- holidays; or

- other days in which employees perform no duties for their employer. (35 ILCS 5/304(a)(2)(B))

Employees spend a working day in Illinois if:

- they spend a greater amount of time that day performing services for their employer in the state than outside the state; or

- the only service they perform for their employer on that day is traveling to a destination in the state and they arrive on that day. (35 ILCS 5/304(a)(2)(B))

Working days spent in Illinois do not include any days that employees spend performing services in the state during a disaster period. (35 ILCS 5/304(a)(2)(B)) The exception applies only to a disaster or emergency relief request made to an employer by:

- Illinois state and local government agencies or officials; or

- businesses in the state. (35 ILCS 5/304(a)(2)(B))

The exception covers the period that:

- begins 10 days before the date of the state's proclamation or federal declaration of a disaster, whichever is earlier; and

- extends for 60 calendar days after the end of the declared disaster or emergency. (35 ILCS 5/304(a)(2)(B))

Disaster services consist of activities that relate to infrastructure that has been damaged or destroyed by the disaster or emergency. (35 ILCS 5/304(a)(2)(B))

[¶11-540] Apportionment Factors for Specific Industries

What special industry apportionment formulas does Illinois use?

Illinois uses special apportionment formulas or rules for transportation services, banks and financial institutions, insurance companies, and federally regulated exchanges. Illinois also has special sourcing rules for broadcasting, telecommunications, and publishing services.

Transportation services. Taxpayers providing transportation services in Illinois, other than airline services, including any movement or shipment of people, goods, mail, oil, gas, or any other substance, must apportion business income to the state using a special apportionment formula based on miles traveled in the state. The formula numerator is the sum of:

— all gross receipts from transportation that both originates and terminates in Illinois; and

— gross receipts from interstate transportation, multiplied by a fraction equal to the miles traveled in Illinois on all interstate trips divided by miles traveled everywhere on all interstate trips. (35 ILCS 5/304(d)(3); 86 Ill. Adm. Code 100.3450(a)(2))

The formula denominator is the amount of all gross receipts from transportation services. (35 ILCS 5/304(d)(3); 86 Ill. Adm. Code 100.3450(a)(2))

Companies providing airline transportation services in Illinois also must apportion business income to the state using a special apportionment formula based on revenue miles. The formula numerator is revenue miles in the state and the denominator is revenue miles everywhere. (35 ILCS 5/304(d)(4); 86 Ill. Adm. Code 100.3450(a)(2)(B))

Mixed transportation services. A company that is engaged in the transportation of both passengers and freight or transportation by airline and other means must apportion its income by computing a separate apportionment fraction for the company's air and surface transportation services and for its passenger and freight transportation services. The average of the fractions is then weighted by the gross receipts from the transportation services related to each separate fraction. (86 Ill. Adm. Code 100.3450(d)) If transportation is by railroad, the average is weighted by the transportation company's operating income from transportation of passengers and from transportation of freight, as reported to federal regulators. (86 Ill. Adm. Code 100.3450(d))

A transportation company may use any other reasonable method supported by its books and records for allocating gross receipts from the transaction between airline transportation and other means of transportation. If the miles traveled by airline is more than 95% of the total miles traveled, the entire transaction is considered to be transportation by airline. (86 Ill. Adm. Code 100.3450(b)(4))

Determination of miles transported or traveled. If transportation is by land or water, the miles transported or traveled is the standard distance in miles between the points of pickup and delivery, unless the taxpayer maintains specific records of miles or routes actually traveled by a vehicle or vessel in a particular trip. If transportation is by air, the miles transported in a flight is the air distance in miles on the most common route between airports. Distances may be rounded to the nearest mile in all cases, except transportation by air may also be rounded to the nearest tens of miles. (86 Ill. Adm. Code 100.3450(b)(1))

Determination of revenue miles. A "revenue mile" is the:

— transportation of one net ton of freight, or one passenger the distance of one mile for consideration; (35 ILCS 5/304(d)(4); 86 Ill. Adm. Code 100.3450(b)(2)) or

— transportation by pipeline of one barrel of oil, 1,000 cubic feet of gas, or any other substance the distance of one mile for consideration. (86 Ill. Adm. Code 100.3450(b)(2))

Transportation in Illinois. A revenue mile or a mile traveled is in Illinois if the transportation occurs in the geographic boundaries of the state. If interstate transportation is by land, the revenue miles or miles traveled in Illinois are the miles between the point or points where the route used in determining those miles intersects the Illinois border and the point, if any, in Illinois where the route begins or ends. In the absence of other evidence, the number of transportation miles in Illinois by a vessel operating on water that is not wholly in or outside the state must be 50% of the total number of transportation miles on that water. If interstate transportation is by airline, the revenue miles in Illinois are the miles between the point where the route used in determining those miles intersects the Illinois border and the Illinois airport where the flight begins or terminates. Revenue miles in a flight that neither begins nor terminates in Illinois ("flyover miles") may not be included in the numerator. (86 Ill. Adm. Code 100.3450(b)(3))

Banks and financial institutions. Banks and financial organizations must apportion business income to Illinois using a special apportionment formula based on gross receipts. The formula numerator is the bank's or financial organization's gross receipts from sources in Illinois or attributable to the state's marketplace. The denominator is the bank's or financial organization's gross receipts from everywhere during the taxable year. (35 ILCS 5/304(c)(3); 86 Ill. Adm. Code 100.3405(a))

Items included or excluded from gross receipts. A bank's or financial organization's "gross receipts" means gross income, including net taxable gain on disposition of assets, securities, and money market instruments, from transactions and activities in the regular course of the bank's or financial organization's trade or business. (35 ILCS 5/304(c)(3); 86 Ill. Adm. Code 100.3405(b)(2)) Any gross receipt that is deducted in computing a bank's or financial organization's federal taxable income or subtracted in computing Illinois base income, like dividends received, must be excluded from the receipts factor. (86 Ill. Adm. Code 100.3405(a))

Interest, dividends, net gains (but not less than zero) and other income from investment assets and activities from trading assets and activities must be included in the receipts factor. Investment assets and activities and trading assets and activities include:

— investment securities;

— trading account assets;

— federal funds;

— securities purchased and sold under agreements to resell or repurchase;

— options;

— futures contracts, forward contracts, and notional principal contracts like swaps;

— equities; and

— foreign currency transactions. (35 ILCS 5/304(c); 86 Ill. Adm. Code 100.3405(c))

The receipts factor must include the amount by which interest from federal funds sold and securities purchased under resale agreements exceeds interest expense on federal funds purchased and securities sold under repurchase agreements. In addition, the receipts factor must include the amount by which interest, dividends, gains and other income from trading assets and activities, including but not limited to assets and activities in the matched book, in the arbitrage book, and foreign currency transactions, exceed amounts paid instead of interest, amounts paid instead of dividends, and losses from those assets and activities. (35 ILCS 5/304(c); 86 Ill. Adm. Code 100.3405(c))

Sourcing rules. A bank's or financial organization's gross receipts from Illinois sources or attributable to the state's marketplace is the sum of:

— sales, leases, or rental of real or tangible personal property located in Illinois;

— interest income, commissions, fees, gains on disposition, and other receipts from loans secured by real or tangible personal property located in Illinois;

— interest income, commissions, fees, gains on disposition, and other receipts from unsecured consumer loans to Illinois residents;

— credit card receivables regularly billed to a customer in Illinois;

— fiduciary, advisory, and brokerage services received in Illinois;

— travelers checks and money orders issued at a location in Illinois; and

— any other receipts that would be included in a general business corporation's Illinois sales factor. (35 ILCS 5/304(c); 86 Ill. Adm. Code 100.3405(c))

Caution Note: Unlike general business corporations, Illinois does not allow banks and financial organizations to exclude gross receipts from the licensing, sale or other disposition of patents, copyrights, trademarks and similar items from the receipts factor, if those items do not exceed more than 50% of the taxpayer's gross receipts. (86 Ill. Adm. Code 100.3405(c))

Interest income, commissions, fees, gains on disposition, and other receipts from unsecured commercial loans and installment obligations must be sourced to Illinois if:

— the proceeds of the loan are to be applied in Illinois; or

— the borrower's office from which the loan was negotiated is located in Illinois. (35 ILCS 5/304(c); 86 Ill. Adm. Code 100.3405(c))

If the location of the borrower's office cannot be determined, the receipts must be excluded from the bank's or financial organization's receipts factor. (35 ILCS 5/304(c); 86 Ill. Adm. Code 100.3405(c))

Interest, dividends, net gains, and other income from investment and trading assets and activities must be sourced to Illinois if:

— the asset or activity is assigned to a bank's or financial organization's fixed place of business in Illinois that has the majority of contacts with the asset or activity; or

— the bank's or financial organization's commercial domicile is located in Illinois. (35 ILCS 5/304(c); 86 Ill. Adm. Code 100.3405(c))

If a bank or financial organization assigns an asset or activity on its books and records to a fixed place of business consistent with federal or state regulatory requirements, there is a rebuttable presumption the assignment is correct. There is also a rebuttable presumption that a bank's or financial organization's commercial domicile is in the state where the greatest number of employees are regularly connected with the management of the investment or trading income or out of which they are working on the last day of the taxable year, regardless of where the services are performed by those employees. (35 ILCS 5/304(c); 86 Ill. Adm. Code 100.3405(c))

Insurance companies. An insurance company must apportion its business income to Illinois using a special apportionment formula based on premiums written. The formula numerator is the sum of the direct premiums written for insurance on property or risk in Illinois. The denominator is direct premiums written everywhere. (35 ILCS 5/304(b)(1); 86 Ill. Adm. Code 100.3420(a))

Direct premiums. "Direct premiums" means the total amount of direct premiums written, assessments, and annuity considerations as reported for the taxable year on the annual statement the insurance company files with the Illinois Department of Insurance. (35 ILCS 5/304(b)(1); 86 Ill. Adm. Code 100.3420(c)) The apportionment factor may take into account only those receipts that are included in an insurance company's federal taxable income and that are not subtracted in computing Illinois base income. (86 Ill. Adm. Code 100.3420(c)) Examples of receipts that must be excluded from the apportionment factor include:

— interest, dividends and other income from investments;

— gains or losses from the adjustment of reserves, salvage or subrogation;

— deposit-type funds because those funds involve no insurance risk and are reported separately from premiums, assessments and annuity considerations on the annual report; and

— premiums on which state income taxes are prohibited by federal law. (86 Ill. Adm. Code 100.3420(c))

Premiums rebated or repaid to policyholders and reported as negative amounts on the annual statement are treated as negative amounts in computing the apportionment factor. However, neither the numerator nor the denominator may be reduced below zero. (86 Ill. Adm. Code 100.3420(c))

If an insurance company does not file an annual statement with the Department of Insurance or if any direct premiums written by an insurance company are not allocated to a specific state on its annual statement, that insurance company must include in its apportionment factor the direct premiums written for insurance on property or risk in Illinois, determined in the same way as the determination of the company's gross taxable premium. (86 Ill. Adm. Code 100.3420(d)) However, the determination must be made without allowing the exceptions for:

— premiums on annuities;

— premiums on which Illinois premium taxes are prohibited by federal law;

— premiums paid by Illinois for health care coverage for Medicaid eligible insureds;

— premiums paid for health care services included as an element of tuition charges at any university or college owned and operated by the state of Illinois;

— premiums on group insurance for state employees; and

— premiums on deferred compensation plans for state and local government or school district employees. (86 Ill. Adm. Code 100.3420(d))

Reinsurance premiums. If more than 50% of an insurance company's premiums are from reinsurance, business income must be apportioned to Illinois using a special apportionment formula based on direct premiums written and reinsurance premiums accepted. The formula numerator is the sum of the direct premiums written for insurance on property or risk in Illinois, plus premiums for reinsurance accepted for property or risk in Illinois. The formula denominator is the sum of direct and reinsurance premiums written everywhere by the company. (35 ILCS 5/304(b)(2); 86 Ill. Adm. Code 100.3420(e)) (Instructions, Form IL-1120, Corporation Income and Replacement Tax Return)

An insurance company may elect to determine reinsurance premiums from Illinois sources using one of the following methods:

— reinsurance premiums assumed on property or risk located in Illinois;

— the ratio of each ceding insurance company's direct premiums on property or risk located in Illinois compared to its total direct premiums; or

— the amount of reinsurance premiums assumed, or accepted, from insurance companies commercially domiciled in Illinois. (35 ILCS

5/304(b)(2); 86 Ill. Adm. Code 100.3420(e)) (Instructions, Form IL-1120, Corporation Income and Replacement Tax Return)

The company's election for determining reinsurance premiums from Illinois sources is binding for its first taxable year and all later taxable years, unless written permission to change methods is received from the Illinois Department of Revenue. (35 ILCS 5/304(b)(2))

Federally regulated exchanges. A federally regulated exchange, as defined for federal regulatory purposes, may elect to use a special apportionment formula to apportion business income to Illinois based on the sum of receipts from:

— transactions executed on a physical trading floor located in Illinois;

— all other matching, execution, or clearing transactions, including without limitation receipts from the provision of matching, execution, or clearing services to another entity, multiplied by 27.54%;

— all other sales in Illinois. (35 ILCS 5/304(c-1))

The apportionment formula numerator is the exchange's business income from sources in Illinois. The denominator is the exchange's business income from all sources. (35 ILCS 5/304(c-1))

The apportionment rule applies to all taxpayers who are members of the same unitary business group as a federally regulated exchange, determined regardless of the Illinois prohibition against including in a unitary business group taxpayers who are ordinarily required to apportion business income using different rules. However, 50% or more of the unitary group's business receipts for the taxable year must be related to the matching, execution, or clearing of transactions conducted by the federally regulated exchange. (35 ILCS 5/304(c-1))

Broadcasting services. Taxpayers providing broadcasting services in Illinois, including television, radio, cable, and satellite broadcasting, must apportion business income to the state using the same standard apportionment formula as general business corporations. Receipts from the sale of broadcasting services must be sourced to Illinois if the broadcasting services are received in Illinois. (35 ILCS 5/304(a)(3)(B-7)) Other receipts from broadcasting services that must be sourced to Illinois include:

— advertising revenue received from an advertiser whose commercial domicile is in Illinois;

— fees or other charges received by a broadcaster from its viewers or listeners in Illinois;

— fees or other charges received by a broadcaster for programming from a producer or content owner based on the portion of the broadcast's viewing or listening audience located in Illinois; and

— fees received by a broadcaster for programming from a content owner if the broadcaster is located in Illinois. (35 ILCS 5/304(a)(3)(B-7)) (Instructions, Form IL-1120, Corporation Income and Replacement Tax Return)

Telecommunication services. Taxpayers providing telecommunication services in Illinois must apportion business income to the state using the same standard apportionment formula as general business corporations. However, special rules apply to the sourcing of receipts from telecommunication services. (35 ILCS 5/304(a)(3)(B-5))

"Telecommunications service" means the electronic transmission, conveyance, or routing of voice, data, audio, video, or any other information or signals to a point, or between or among points, including:

— transmission, conveyance, or routing in which computer processing applications are used to act on the form, code or protocol of the content for purposes of transmission; and

— conveyance or routing regardless of whether the service is referred to as voice over internet protocol services (VOIP) or is classified by the Federal Communications Commission as enhanced or value added. (35 ILCS 5/304(a)(3)(B-5))

"Telecommunications service" does not include:

— data processing and information services that allow data to be generated, acquired, stored, processed, or retrieved and delivered by an electronic transmission to a purchaser when the purchaser's primary purpose for the underlying transaction is the processed data or information;

— installation or maintenance of wiring or equipment on a customer's premises;

— tangible personal property;

— advertising, including but not limited to directory advertising;

— billing and collection services provided to third parties;

— internet access service;

— radio and television audio and video programming services, including cable services and audio and video programming services delivered by commercial mobile radio service providers, regardless of the medium, including the furnishing of transmission, conveyance and routing of those services by the programming service provider;

— ancillary services, including detailed telecommunications billing, directory assistance, vertical service, and voice mail services; and

— Digital products delivered electronically, including software, music, video, reading materials or ring tones. (35 ILCS 5/304(a)(3)(B-5))

Receipts from the sale of telecommunications services or mobile telecommunications service must be sourced to Illinois if the customer's service address is in the state. (35 ILCS 5/304(a)(3)(B-5); 86 Ill. Adm. Code 100.3371) Other receipts from telecommunication services that must be sourced to Illinois include:

— sales of telecommunications service sold on a call-by-call basis, if the call both originates and terminates in Illinois, or the call either originates or terminates in Illinois and the customer's service address is in Illinois; (35 ILCS 5/304(a)(3)(B-5); 86 Ill. Adm. Code 100.3371(c))

— retail sales of postpaid telecommunications service if the point of origination of the signal, as first identified by the service provider's telecommunication system or as identified by information received by the seller from its service provider, is located in Illinois; (35 ILCS 5/304(a)(3)(B-5); 86 Ill. Adm. Code 100.3371(d)) (Instructions, Form IL-1120, Corporation Income and Replacement Tax Return)

— retail sales of prepaid telecommunications or mobile telecommunications service if the purchaser receives the prepaid card or similar means of transfer at an Illinois location; (35 ILCS 5/304(a)(3)(B-5); 86 Ill. Adm. Code 100.3371(e)) (Instructions, Form IL-1120, Corporation Income and Replacement Tax Return)

— recharging a prepaid telecommunications or mobile telecommunication service if the purchaser's billing address is in Illinois; (35 ILCS 5/304(a)(3)(B-5); 86 Ill. Adm. Code 100.3371(e)) (Instructions, Form IL-1120, Corporation Income and Replacement Tax Return)

— charges imposed at a channel termination point in Illinois; (35 ILCS 5/304(a)(3)(B-5); 86 Ill. Adm. Code 100.3371(f)) (Instructions, Form IL-1120, Corporation Income and Replacement Tax Return)

— charges for channel mileage between two channel termination points in Illinois; (35 ILCS 5/304(a)(3)(B-5); 86 Ill. Adm. Code 100.3371(f)) (Instructions, Form IL-1120, Corporation Income and Replacement Tax Return)

— charges for channel mileage between one or more channel termination points in Illinois and one or more channel termination points outside Illinois, times the number of channel termination points in Illinois divided by total termination channels; (86 Ill. Adm. Code 100.3371(f)) (Instructions, Form IL-1120, Corporation Income and Replacement Tax Return)

— charges for services ancillary to sales of services in Illinois if the customer's primary place of use of telecommunications services associated with those ancillary services is in Illinois or the customer is in Illinois; (35 ILCS 5/304(a)(3)(B-5); 86 Ill. Adm. Code 100.3371(g)) (Instructions, Form IL-1120, Corporation Income and Replacement Tax Return)

— access fees charged to a reseller of telecommunication for a call that both originates and terminates in Illinois; (86 Ill. Adm. Code 100.3371(h)) (Instructions, Form IL-1120, Corporation Income and Replacement Tax Return)

— 50% of access fees charged to a reseller of telecommunications services for an interstate call that originates or terminates in Illinois; (86 Ill. Adm. Code 100.3371(h)) (Instructions, Form IL-1120, Corporation Income and Replacement Tax Return) and

— end user access line charges, if the customer's service address is in Illinois. (86 Ill. Adm. Code 100.3371(h)) (Instructions, Form IL-1120, Corporation Income and Replacement Tax Return)

Gross receipts from sales of telecommunication services or from ancillary services for telecommunications services sold to other telecommunication service providers for resale must be sourced to Illinois using the apportionment rules used for non-resale receipts of telecommunications services if the information is readily available. If information for non-resale receipts is not readily available, then the taxpayer may use any other reasonable and consistent method. (86 Ill. Adm. Code 100.3371(h))

Publishing services. Taxpayers providing publishing services in Illinois, including publishing, selling, licensing or distributing newspapers, magazines, periodicals, trade journals or other published material, must apportion business income to the state using the same standard apportionment formula as general business corporations. (86 Ill. Adm. Code 100.3373(a)) Gross receipts from the sale of published materials in the form of tangible property must be sourced to Illinois using the sales factor sourcing rules for sales of tangible personal property. The portion of gross receipts from sales of published materials in a form other than tangible personal property, from advertising and from the sale, rental or other use of the taxpayer's customer lists for a particular publication must be sourced to Illinois using the taxpayer's circulation factor for that publication during the tax period. (86 Ill. Adm. Code 100.3373(c))

The circulation factor for each individual publication containing advertising is based on the ratio that the taxpayer's in-state circulation to purchasers and subscribers of the published material bears to its total circulation of the published material to purchasers and subscribers everywhere. If the geographic location of purchasers and subscribers of a publication is determined by the taxpayer for a business purpose, the circulation factor must be determined for that publication using the same geographic information. Otherwise, the circulation factor must be determined from the taxpayer's books and records. If the taxpayer's books and records are inadequate to determinate the circulation factor, the circulation factor for a publication must be determined, or the taxpayer may elect to determine the circulation factor, by reference to the rating statistics as reflected in sources like Audit Bureau of Circulations, Internet World Stats, or other comparable sources. The taxpayer must use the sourcing method selected consistently from year to year for determining its circulation factor. (86 Ill. Adm. Code 100.3373(b))

> *Example:* Company A publishes advertising on the Internet for its customers. In order to calculate its circulation factor, Company A elects to use Internet World Stats. Company A determines its circulation factor by multiplying Illinois' population by the Internet penetration percentage of the U.S., as reported on Internet World Stats, divided by the combined populations of the jurisdictions in which Company A does business multiplied by their respective Internet penetration percentages as reported on Internet World Stats. Company A must use this method consistently from year to year to compute its circulation factor.

"Publication" or "published material" means the physical embodiment or printed version of any thought or expression, including a play, story, article, column or other literary, commercial, educational, artistic or other written or printed work. The determination of whether an item is or consists of published material must be made without regard to its content. Published material may take the form of a book, newspaper, magazine, periodical, trade journal or any other form of printed matter and may be contained on any property or medium, including any electronic medium, like the internet. Published material does not include any broadcasting medium. (86 Ill. Adm. Code 100.3373(b))

"Purchaser" and "subscriber" means the individual, residence, business or other outlet that is the ultimate or final recipient of the published material. The term does not include a wholesaler, retailer or other distributor of published material. (86 Ill. Adm. Code 100.3373(b))

Gross receipts from the performance of publishing services provided to a corporation, partnership, or trust must be sourced to Illinois if that corporation, partnership, or trust has a fixed place of business in the state. If the state where the publishing services are received is not readily determinable or is a state where the corporation, partnership, or trust receiving the services does not have a fixed place of business, the services are considered to be received at the location of the customer's office from which the services were ordered in the regular course of the customer's trade or business. If the ordering office cannot be determined, the publishing services are considered to be received at the customer's office to which the services are billed. These sourcing rules do not apply if circulation factor is determined by a method other than the taxpayer's own books and records. The sale must be excluded from sales factor if the taxpayer is not taxable in the state in which the publishing services are received. (86 Ill. Adm. Code 100.3373(d))

[¶11-550] Combined Reports

Does Illinois allow elective combined reporting?

Corporations that are members of the same unitary business group do not have an option to elect to report income on a worldwide or water's-edge combined basis. (35 ILCS 5/502(e); 86 Ill. Adm. Code Sec. 100.5205; 86 Ill. Adm. Code Sec. 100.5210(a))

Does Illinois require combined reporting for unitary business groups?

The water's edge combined reporting method is mandatory for two or more corporations engaged in a unitary business conducted in and outside Illinois. (35 ILCS 5/502(e); 86 Ill. Adm. Code Sec. 100.5200; 86 Ill. Adm. Code Sec. 100.5210(b); 86 Ill. Adm. Code 100.9700(b))

Unitary business groups composed exclusively of members whose business income is solely from Illinois are required to file as a unitary group. (Instructions, Schedule UB, Combined Apportionment for Unitary Business Group)

Unitary business group and eligible group members. "Unitary business group" means a group of taxpayers related through common ownership whose business activities are integrated with, dependent upon, and contribute to each other. (35 ILCS 5/1501(a)(27)(A))

An "eligible member" is any corporation that is a unitary business group member and that has taxable presence in Illinois. S corporations, partnerships, and limited liability companies (LLCs) classified as partnerships for income tax purposes, are not eligible members. Unitary business group members are eligible members even though the unitary business group includes noncorporate members or S corporations that are not eligible to join in the filing of a combined return. (86 Ill. Adm. Code Sec. 100.5201(i))

Part-year unitary business group members are eligible members. (86 Ill. Adm. Code Sec. 100.5201(i)) All part-year members are required to file as part of the unitary business group for the portion of the year the taxpayer is a member. For the remainder of the year, the member is required to file a separate nonunitary return. However, if the member belongs to another unitary business group during the remainder of the year, that member is required to file as part of that group. (Instructions, Schedule UB, Combined Apportionment for Unitary Business Group)

Combined group members are jointly and severally liable for Illinois income tax liability, penalties, and interest. (86 Ill. Adm. Code Sec. 100.5250(a))

Common ownership test. "Common ownership" means the direct or indirect control or ownership of more than 50% of a corporation's outstanding voting stock. (35 ILCS 5/1501(a)(27)(A); 86 Ill. Adm. Code 100.9700(e)) One corporation has direct ownership of another corporation's outstanding voting stock if it owns the stock. It has indirect control if it owns the voting stock of a third corporation that itself owns the stock. Any combination of direct and indirect control or ownership totaling more than 50% will make the corporation whose stock is owned eligible for unitary business group membership if other tests unrelated to ownership are met. (86 Ill. Adm. Code 100.9700(e))

Example 1: Corporation A owns 60% of Corporation B's outstanding voting stock. Corporation B owns 60% of Corporation C's outstanding voting stock. There is common ownership of Corporations A, B, and C because of Corporation A's direct ownership of more than 50% of Corporation B's outstanding voting stock and indirect control of more than 50% of Corporation C's outstanding voting stock.

Example 2: Corporation A owns 60% of Corporation B's outstanding voting stock and 60% of Corporation C's outstanding voting stock. Corporations B and C each own 30% of Corporation D's outstanding voting stock. Corporations A, B, C, and D are all under common ownership because of Corporation A's direct ownership of more than 50% of Corporations B's and C's outstanding voting stock and because of Corporation A's indirect control of more than 50% of Corporation D's outstanding voting stock.

Example 3: Corporation A owns 60% of Corporation B's outstanding voting stock and 40% of Corporation C's outstanding voting stock. Corporations B and C each own 30% of Corporation D's outstanding voting stock. Corporations A and B are under common ownership because of Corporation A's direct ownership of more than 50% of Corporation B's outstanding voting stock, but neither Corporations C nor D are under common ownership with Corporations A and B because neither Corporation A nor Corporation B has direct or indirect control or ownership of more than 50% of Corporations C's or D's outstanding voting stock.

Example 4: Corporation A owns 60% of Corporation B's outstanding voting stock and 40% of Corporation C's outstanding voting. Corporation B owns 30% of Corporation D's outstanding voting stock and Corporation C owns 60% of Corporation D's outstanding voting stock. Corporations A and B are under common ownership because Corporation A owns more than 50% of Corporation B's outstanding voting stock, and Corporations C and D are under separate common ownership because Corporation C owns more than 50% of Corporation D's outstanding voting stock.

Common ownership of any other entity means direct or indirect ownership of an interest sufficient to exercise control over the activities of the entity. For example, ownership of a general partnership interest gives the partner the authority to act for the partnership and bind the partnership, regardless of actual ownership share. So, a general partner in any partnership has an interest in the partnership sufficient to establish common ownership. (86 Ill. Adm. Code 100.9700(e))

Indirect ownership of an interest includes constructive ownership under Internal Revenue Code (IRC) § 318 of an interest that is owned by a related party, whether the related party is itself a member of the combined group. (86 Ill. Adm. Code Sec. 100.5201(f); 86 Ill. Adm. Code 100.9700(e))

Example: Mr. and Mrs. X each individually own 30% of Corporation A's outstanding voting stock and 30% of Corporation B's outstanding voting stock. Corporations A and B are under common ownership, and assuming that they meet other unitary requirements, they will be members of the same unitary business group. The common ownership exists because Mr. X's stock ownership is imputed to Mrs. X and vice versa. It is not necessary that the common owner also be a unitary business group member.

80/20 business activity test. A unitary business group cannot include any member whose business activity outside the U.S. is 80% or more of its total business activity. (35 ILCS 5/1501(a)(27)(A)) The phrase "United States" means only the 50 states, the District of Columbia, but does not include any U.S. territory or possession. Effective for taxable years ending on or after December 31, 2017, the definition also includes any area over which the U.S. has asserted jurisdiction or claimed exclusive rights over natural resource exploration or exploitation. (35 ILCS 5/1501(a)(27)(B))

A two-factor apportionment formula must be used to determine what percentage of business activity is conducted outside the U.S. (35 ILCS 5/1501(a)(27)(A); 86 Ill. Adm. Code 100.9700(c)) The numerators of the formula represent:

— U.S. property and payroll for any group member required to apportion business income to Illinois using a single sales factor apportionment formula;

— premiums on property or risk in the U.S. for any group member that is an insurance company;

— business income from sources in the U.S. for any group member that is a financial organization; or

— U.S. revenue miles for any group member that is a transportation company. (35 ILCS 5/1501(a)(27)(A); 86 Ill. Adm. Code 100.9700(c))

The denominators of the formula represent the worldwide figures for these items. (35 ILCS 5/1501(a)(27)(A); 86 Ill. Adm. Code 100.9700(c))

The factors used in determining whether 80% or more of a group member's business activity is conducted outside the U.S. must be based on gross amounts without intercompany eliminations and must relate to the unitary business group's common taxable year. The 80/20 business activity test must be applied only to that part of the prospective member's taxable year for which that member otherwise qualifies for unitary business group membership. If that member is a corporation and is a prospective unitary business group member, the test must be applied only to that part of the combined group's common taxable year for which that corporation otherwise qualifies for group membership. (86 Ill. Adm. Code 100.9700(c))

In determining whether 80% or more of a foreign taxpayer's total business activity is conducted outside the U.S. that taxpayer must use only the apportionment factors related to the business income included in its federal taxable income (plus addition modifications), rather than use of its worldwide factors. A foreign corporation that is a unitary business group member can only include in the combined group's income the amount of federal taxable income that is effectively connected with U.S. trade or business, rather than its worldwide federal taxable income. A foreign sales corporation (FSC) that is a unitary business group member must use its worldwide apportionment factors in determining whether 80% or more of its business activity is conducted outside the U.S. because certain foreign trade income of a FSC is exempt from federal gross income under IRC § 921. (86 Ill. Adm. Code 100.3380(e)) (Instructions, Schedule UB, Combined Apportionment for Unitary Business Group)

Common apportionment formula test. In 2017, Illinois repealed its "noncombination rule." The rule prohibited unitary groups from including members that used different apportionment formulas. The change took effect for tax years ending on or after December 31, 2017. A unitary group can now include all taxpayers regardless of the apportionment formula used by each taxpayer. (35 ILCS 5/1501(a)(27)(B); 86 Ill. Adm. Code 100.9700(d))

Vertical and horizontal integration test. Business activity is ordinarily unitary if activities of the members are:

— in the same general line (e.g., manufacturing, wholesaling, retailing, insurance, transportation, or finance); or

— steps in a vertically structured enterprise or process (e.g., steps involved in the production of natural resources, including exploration, mining, refining, and marketing). (35 ILCS 5/1501(a)(27)(A); 86 Ill. Adm. Code 100.9700(h))

There is no requirement that the activities of unitary group members relate to the same product or product line in order for the members to be in the same general line of business. In addition, two members are steps in a vertically structured enterprise or process even though others who are also steps in that enterprise or process are not members of the same unitary business group because of the 80/20 business activity or common apportionment formula tests. (86 Ill. Adm. Code 100.9700(h))

Example 1: Corporation A manufactures furniture. Corporation C retails the furniture manufactured by Corporation A. Corporation B is a furniture finisher and wholesaler operating exclusively in Mexico that purchases Corporation A's unfinished furniture, applies the appropriate finishing materials in its Mexican plants, and sells the finished furniture to Corporation C. Corporations A and C are steps in a vertically structured enterprise and can be members of the same unitary business group. They do not lose their status as steps in a vertically structured enterprise because of the fact that they never directly deal with one another, since they both deal with Corporation B which is also a step in the vertically structured enterprise. Also, Corporation B would be a member of the unitary business group were it not for the 80/20 business activity test.

A member will not be a step in a vertically structured enterprise or process unless it is connected to one or more members that are steps in the vertically structured enterprise or process by a flow of goods or services. This includes management services, to itself or from itself. However, if the flow of goods or service is present with respect to a particular member, that member's status as a step in the vertically structured enterprise or process does not depend on the relationship between the price at which this flow exists and the fair market price at which this flow would exist in an arm's length transaction.

Example 2: Same facts as in the Example 1, except that Corporation A can establish that it sells its unfinished furniture to Corporation B at a fair market arm's length price and Corporation C can establish that it purchases the finished furniture from Corporation B at a fair market arm's length price. Even with their respective showing that the flow of furniture connecting them to Corporation B existed at an arm's length price, Corporations A and C are still steps in a vertically structured enterprise and can still be members of the same unitary business group.

Strong centralized management test. A unitary business group does not exist unless the group is functionally integrated through the exercise of strong centralized management. (35 ILCS 5/1501(a)(27)(A); 86 Ill. Adm. Code 100.9700(g)) The exercise of strong centralized management is the main indicator of mutual dependency, mutual contribution and mutual integration between members of the same unitary business group. The exercise of strong centralized management will exist if authority over matters like purchasing, financing, tax compliance, product line, personnel, marketing and capital investment is not left to each member. So, a group is considered a unitary business group if the executive officers of one of the members are normally involved in the operations of the other group members and there are centralized units that perform for some or all of the members functions that they would perform for themselves. (86 Ill. Adm. Code 100.9700(g))

Compliance Note: Neither the existence of central management authority, nor the exercise of that authority over any one function through centralized operations, is determinative by itself. The entire operations of the group must be examined in order to determine whether strong centralized management exists.

Strong centralized management cannot be supported merely by showing that the required ownership percentage exists or that there is some incidental economic benefit accruing to a group because the ownership improves its financial position. Both elements of strong centralized management (i.e., strong central management authority and the exercise of that authority through centralized operations) must be present for there to be a unitary business group. Finally, strong centralized management can be supported even though the authority resides in someone that is not a member of the group, as long as that authority is actually exercised by the nonmember. (86 Ill. Adm. Code 100.9700(g))

Designated agent. The combined group members must choose which Illinois taxpayer member will be the designated agent. If the group has a controlling corporation that is a member of the combined group and an Illinois taxpayer, the combined group members must designate the controlling corporation as the agent. (86 Ill. Adm. Code Sec. 100.5220(a)) The combined group's controlling corporation is the corporation that directly or indirectly owns a controlling interest (i.e., more than 50% of a member's outstanding voting stock) in all of the other eligible combined group members. (86 Ill. Adm. Code Sec. 100.5201(f)) Designation of the agent is made on Illinois Schedule UB. (Instructions, Schedule UB, Combined Apportionment for Unitary Business Group)

A controlling corporation cannot be a combined group's designated agent if:

— the combined group is wholly owned by an individual in which case there is no controlling corporation; or

— the controlling corporation does not have nexus with Illinois. (86 Ill. Adm. Code Sec. 100.5220(a))

A designated combined group agent may be appointed solely to contest the Illinois Department of Revenue's determination that:

— one or more corporations that did not file a combined return are combined group members; or

— one or more corporations that did file a combined return are not combined group members. (86 Ill. Adm. Code Sec. 100.5220(f))

The appointment of a designated agent for disputes over combined group membership is not considered a concession by either the members or the department regarding the combined group's composition. The designated agent has all the rights and duties of a regularly appointed agent and represents all corporations that filed a combined return or that the department asserts are combined group members. The department may allow any corporation that it asserts should be added to or eliminated from the combined group to represent itself after receipt of a written request from the corporation. However, the corporation is bound by any action taken by the designated agent (e.g., extensions of the statute of limitations, settlements, stipulations or concessions of fact) before the department accepts the request to represent itself. (86 Ill. Adm. Code Sec. 100.5220(f))

Duties. The designated agent is the sole agent for each combined group member and is authorized to act in all matters for each member relating to the tax liability for the combined return year, including:

— corresponding with the Illinois Department of Revenue;

— filing the combined return and all extensions of time;

— handling notices of deficiency and demand for tax payments;

— paying all taxes, including estimated taxes;

— participating in investigations and hearings;

— claiming refunds and credits; and

— executing powers of attorney, waivers, closing agreements, and all other documents. (86 Ill. Adm. Code Sec. 100.5220(b))

If the department deals in good faith with a member representing itself as the combined group's designated agent, any action of that member or the department in the course of that dealing will have the same effect as if that member were the designated agent. (86 Ill. Adm. Code Sec. 100.5220(b)) If the designated agent is unable or unwilling to satisfy the combined group's tax liability or is unresponsive, the Department may, after notifying the designated agent, deal directly with any combined group member concerning its liability, in which case each member will have full authority to act for itself. (86 Ill. Adm. Code Sec. 100.5220(d)(2)(B))

The failure of the department to list all combined group members in any notice of deficiency will not affect the validity of the notice for any combined group member. (86 Ill. Adm. Code Sec. 100.5220(c)) A corporation that has ceased to be a combined group member and that files a written notice to that effect with the department may request a copy of any notice of deficiency and demand for tax payment for a combined return year in which it was a combined group member. A corporation's filing of the written notification and request does not have the effect of limiting the scope of the designated agent's duties for those tax years in which the corporation was a combined group member. In addition, failure by the department to comply with the written request does not have the effect of limiting the corporation's liability. (86 Ill. Adm. Code Sec. 100.5220(e))

Continuity. Once a combined group member is appointed the group's designated agent, it must remain the designated agent for all future tax years, unless:

— the designated agent ceases to be an eligible combined group member;

— the unitary business group's controlling corporation either becomes an eligible member or is replaced as the controlling corporation by an eligible member;

— the designated agent is being dissolved; or

— a new designated agent has been appointed for the combined group. (86 Ill. Adm. Code Sec. 100.5220(d))

If a new designated agent is named for the group for a later tax year, the old designated agent may act as the member responsible for the earlier tax years, or the designated agent for the earlier years may be changed to the group's new designated agent or to any other group member. (Instructions, Schedule UB, Combined Apportionment for Unitary Business Group) The Illinois Department of Revenue must be notified in writing of a new designated agent. (86 Ill. Adm. Code Sec. 100.5220(d)) (Instructions, Schedule UB, Combined Apportionment for Unitary Business Group) The notice must include the name, FEIN, and address of the member that will replace the old designated agent, and the name and telephone number of the contact person. (Instructions, Schedule UB, Combined Apportionment for Unitary Business Group)

Accounting periods. The combined group's common taxable year is the designated agent's taxable year. (86 Ill. Adm. Code Sec. 100.5265(a)) If a member has a taxable year that differs from the combined group's common taxable year, the taxable income of that member must be determined using one of three possible methods.

Method 1: the member may compute its pro-forma taxable income from its books and records for the common taxable year.

Method 2: the member may determine its income based on the number of months of its tax year that are within the common accounting period, but only if the group's return may be timely filed after the member's taxable year ends.

Method 3: the group may include in its taxable income all of the taxable income of a member whose tax year ends within the group's tax year. (86 Ill. Adm. Code Sec. 100.5265(b)) (Instructions, Schedule UB, Combined Apportionment for Unitary Business Group)

Example: Corporation A is a calendar-year combined group member having a common taxable year ending July 31. If Corporation A uses Method 2, its taxable income for the taxable year ending July 31, 2016 would be five-twelfths of its 2015 taxable income and seven-twelfths of its 2016 taxable income. Rather than using months to pro-rate its income, Corporation A may use the number of days in its taxable year or (in the case of a corporation using a 52/53 week taxable year) the number of weeks in the taxable year. The combined return for the common taxable year ending July 31, 2016, may not be filed until after December 31, 2016, the close of Corporation A's taxable year which begins during that common taxable year.

Each member having a taxable year different from the combined group's common taxable year may separately elect which of the methods it will use for the first combined return in which the taxpayer is a combined group member. Once a member uses one of these methods, that member must continue to use that method for all later combined group returns. (86 Ill. Adm. Code Sec. 100.5265(c)) (Instructions, Schedule UB, Combined Apportionment for Unitary Business Group)

A corporation that joins a unitary business group member after the beginning of the combined return year must use either Method 1 or Method 2 to determine its separate company items for the portion of the year before it became a member and the portion of the year after it became a member. (86 Ill. Adm. Code Sec. 100.5270(f)) A corporation that is ineligible because it has a different taxable year must use either method of accounting available to part-year members. If two or more corporations are ineligible because they have an accounting period that is different from other members, they may elect to file their own combined return if they have the same taxable year. This rule also applies to a member that is erroneously included in a group otherwise required to file a combined return. (86 Ill. Adm. Code Sec. 100.5270(e))

Change in method or common taxable year. A change in accounting method for any member must be disclosed in an attachment that shows for each year in which the new method is used:

— the combined group's net income computed with that member using its old method;

— the combined group's net income computed with that member using its new method; and

— the totals of the combined net incomes computed using each method. (86 Ill. Adm. Code Sec. 100.5265(c))

In addition, any excess of the total amounts of combined net income computed using the new method over the total amounts computed using the old method must be added to (or any deficiency be subtracted from) the combined group's net income for the year in which the new method is first used. (86 Ill. Adm. Code Sec. 100.5265(c))

If a combined group's common taxable year is changed, and the new common taxable year ends before the end of the old common taxable year during which the change occurs, each member's separate company items arising after the end of the old common taxable year must be taken into account on the combined return for the new common taxable year. Any separate company item reported on a combined return for the old common taxable year must be excluded from the combined return for the new common taxable year. (86 Ill. Adm. Code Sec. 100.5265(d))

Example: Combined group ABC uses a common taxable year ending on December 31, the taxable year of all three corporations. Corporation D is the controlling corporation of ABC, but is not an eligible member because it has no taxable presence in Illinois. On January 1, 2016, Corporation D establishes a taxable presence in Illinois, and becomes the designated agent of the combined group. The group is required to use Corporation D's taxable year, which ends on June 30. If Corporation A, B, or C elect to use either Method 1 or Method 2, the group's combined return for the common taxable year ending June 30, 2016 must include the separate company items of that corporation only for the period from January 1, 2016 through June 30, 2016 as determined under the elected method. If one of the corporations elects to use Method 3, it must determine its separate company items for the period from January 1, 2016 through June 30, 2016 using either Method 1 or Method 2 and include the items in the group's combined return for the common taxable year ending June 30, 2016. The remainder of the corporation's income for its taxable year ending December 31, 2016 will then be included in the combined return for the common year ending June 30, 2017.

If a combined group's common taxable year is changed, and the new common taxable year ends after the end of the old common taxable year during which the change occurs, the combined group must file a combined return for the period ending with the date the common taxable year is changed and a combined return for the period from the date of change to the end of the new common taxable year. (86 Ill. Adm. Code Sec. 100.5265(e))

Effect of entering or departing members. If a corporation was not a member of another combined group immediately before it joins a combined group, the corporation must file a separate return for the short taxable year ending on the day before the date it joins the combined group. The net income reported on that separate return must be determined using the method the corporation elected for determining the portion of its separate taxable income that will be included in the combined group's net income for the common taxable year. The separate return is due by the original or extended due date of the combined group's return for the common taxable year. (86 Ill. Adm. Code Sec. 100.5265(f))

Example 1: Corporation A uses a calendar taxable year. On April 1, 2016, a member of unitary business group BCD acquires 51% of Corporation A's stock and Corporation A immediately becomes a unitary business group member. Group BCD has a common taxable year ending June 30, which remains the combined group's common taxable year. If Corporation A elects to use Method 1, it must:

— report pro-forma taxable income for the period from January 1 through March 31, 2016 on a separate return;

— include pro-forma taxable income for the period from April 1 through June 30, 2016 in the group's combined return for the common taxable year ending June 30, 2016; and

— include pro-forma taxable income for the period from July 1 through December 31, 2016 and for the period from January 1 through June 30, 2017 in the group's combined return for the common taxable year ending June 30, 2017.

The separate return for the period ending March 31, 2016 will be due on the due date of the group's combined return for June 30, 2016. If Corporation A elects to use Method 2, it must report its income for 2016 in the same manner, except that it will pro-rate its income among the four different periods in proportion to the length of each period. If Corporation A elects to use Method 3, it must use either Method 1 or Method 2 to determine its taxable income for its separate return for the period ending March 31, 2016, and will include the remainder of its income in the group's combined return for the common taxable year ending June 30, 2017.

A corporation that was a member of another combined group before it joins a new combined group must include in the new group's combined net income for the common taxable year all of its separate company taxable income for its taxable year that was not included in the old combined group's net income for the common taxable year. The corporation must use either Method 1 or Method 2 to determine the separate company items to include in each combined return that includes the date it leaves the old combined group and joins the new combined group. If its taxable year is not the common taxable year of the new combined group, it may elect any of the three methods. (86 Ill. Adm. Code Sec. 100.5265(f))

Example 2: Assume the same facts in Example 1, except that Corporation A is a combined group member of AXYZ before the date its stock was acquired by a member of combined group BCD. Corporation A must use either Method 1 or Method 2 to determine the portion of its 2016 separate company taxable income for the period from January 1 through March 31, 2016, that will be included in AXYZ's combined group net income. If Corporation A was using either Method 1 or Method 2 while a member of group AXYZ, it must use the same method. Corporation A may then elect any of the three methods for use in computing ABCD's combined group net income, as long as its separate company taxable income for the period from April 1 through December 31, 2016 is equal to its separate company taxable income for 2016 minus the amount of its separate company taxable income for January 1 through March 31, 2016 that is included in AXYZ's combined group net income.

If a corporation ceases to be a member of a combined group, the corporation's taxable income that was included in the group's combined net income cannot be included in net income on any separate company return or any combined return of another combined group. (86 Ill. Adm. Code Sec. 100.5265(f))

Computation of taxable income. The combined base income is determined by first computing the combined group's combined net income and then modifying that amount by the combined group's combined Illinois addition and subtraction modifications. Combined base income is determined by treating all unitary business group members, including ineligible members, as if they were a federal consolidated group. The federal treasury regulations for determining consolidated taxable income apply, except the separate return limitation year provisions and the limitations on consolidation of life and non-life companies. (86 Ill. Adm. Code 100.5270(a)) Federal taxable income or loss is separate taxable income that each member would compute for purposes of a federal consolidated return. (35 ILCS 5/203(e)(2)(E)) (Instructions, Schedule UB, Combined Apportionment for Unitary Business Group) In computing federal taxable income, each member is required to follow all federal income tax elections it made, or which were made for it. (Instructions, Schedule UB, Combined Apportionment for Unitary Business Group)

The combined base income allocable to Illinois is the sum of the combined business income or loss apportioned to Illinois, plus the combined nonbusiness income or loss allocated to Illinois, plus the combined nonunitary partnership income or loss allocated to Illinois, less the combined net loss deduction. (86 Ill. Adm. Code 100.5270(b))

The combined return for a member that either became a unitary business group member or ceased to be a member the during the taxable year must include that member's separate company items for the part of the year it was a unitary business group member. (86 Ill. Adm. Code Sec. 100.5270(f)) A part-year member's separate company items for any portion of its taxable year before the date it joined or after the date it left the unitary business group must be:

— reported in a short-year separate return filed by the part-year member, if it was subject to Illinois income tax during that period; or

— included in any combined return filed by the unitary business group to which it belonged during that portion of the year. (86 Ill. Adm. Code Sec. 100.5270(f))

Each member of a unitary business group who is subject to Illinois income tax and who does not join in the filing of a combined return must separately determine the amount of its nonbusiness income allocable to Illinois, the amount of the non-member's Illinois personal income tax exemption, the amounts of net loss carryovers, and the amounts of any credits and credit carryforwards to which it is entitled, without regard to the income, deductions, credits and other tax items of other members of the unitary business group, except to the extent those items must be included the computation of business income of the member apportioned to Illinois. (86 Ill. Adm. Code Sec. 100.5215(c))

Intercompany transactions. Items of income and deduction from transactions between unitary business group members must be eliminated if necessary to avoid distortion of the denominators used by the unitary business group for calculating apportionment factors, or of the numerators used by the combined group or by ineligible members for calculating apportionment factors. (86 Ill. Adm. Code Sec. 100.5270(b)(1))

Treatment of net operating losses. A unitary business group's Illinois net operating loss (NOL) and NOL deduction is determined as if the group were one taxpayer. The rules for determining a combined unitary group's Illinois NOL deduction apply in the same manner as separate returns. (Ill. Adm. Code Sec. 100.2340(a); 86 Ill. Adm. Code 100.5270(b)(3))

A net operating loss that a combined group member incurs may be shared and used to offset other group member's taxable income for the taxable year. (86 Ill. Adm. Code 100.2220; Ill. Adm. Code Sec. 100.2340(c); 86 Ill. Adm. Code 100.5270(b)(3))

Example: Corporations A, B, C, and D are unitary business group members. Corporations A, B, and C had Illinois taxable income for the 2016 year of $100,000, $200,000, and $300,000, respectively. Corporation D had an Illinois NOL for the 2016 tax year of $150,000. The group's 2016 combined federal taxable income is $450,000.

The separate return limitation year (SRLY) provisions for federal consolidated returns do not apply to any Illinois NOL carryover. If a member joins the group, any unused state NOL that member incurs before joining the group may be used by the group in the year the member joined and in following years, up to the maximum number of carryforward years allowed under Illinois law. If a member leaves the group after the group incurred a state NOL, any loss of that member that was not used before the member left may be used only by the departing member or by any unitary business group that it joins later. (Ill. Adm. Code Sec. 100.2350(c)) (Instructions, Schedule UB/NLD, Unitary Illinois Net Loss Deduction)

Schedule UB/NLD must be completed to claim an Illinois NOL carryforward deduction on a unitary business group's original or amended combined Illinois return. The schedule must be attached to the original or amended Illinois return. (Instructions, Schedule UB/NLD, Unitary Illinois Net Loss Deduction)

If a member acquires another taxpayer's Illinois NOL under IRC §381, regardless of whether the other taxpayer was a combined group member, that member is entitled to carry forward any unused loss to the year of the acquisition and to following years, up to the maximum number of carryforward years allowed under Illinois law. (Instructions, Schedule UB/NLD, Unitary Illinois Net Loss Deduction) A separate schedule must be attached to the combined Illinois corporation income tax return showing:

— the name and taxpayer identification number of the group member that acquired the loss;

— the name and taxpayer identification number from whom the loss was acquired;

— the year of the acquisition;

— the tax year in which the loss was incurred; and

— the amount of unused loss acquired. (Instructions, Schedule UB/NLD, Unitary Illinois Net Loss Deduction)

Apportionment. The numerators and denominators of the Illinois single factor sales apportionment formula are computed on an individual basis for each water's edge return member and the resulting amount combined. A unitary business groups must complete Schedule UB to determine the amount of its unitary business income from Illinois sources. The group must attach the schedule to its combined Illinois income tax return. (86 Ill. Adm. Code 100.5270(b)(1)) (Instructions, Schedule UB, Combined Apportionment for Unitary Business Group)

The combined reporting group is not required to include an out-of-state member's Illinois sales in the numerator of the sales factor if the member does not have nexus with Illinois (i.e., Joyce rule). (86 Ill. Adm. Code 100.5270(b)(1); 86 Ill. Adm. Code 100.9720(f))

Example 1: Corporations A, B, and C are a unitary business group, except Corporation C is not taxable in Illinois under Public Law 86-272. The combined Illinois sales factor must be determined by dividing the combined group's total combined Illinois sales, excluding any sales of Corporation C shipped to purchasers in Illinois, by the total combined sales of the unitary business group everywhere.

Example 2: Same facts as in Example 1, except Corporations B and C are taxable in South Carolina, but Corporation A is not. The combined Illinois sales factor must be determined by dividing the combined group's total combined Illinois sales, including any sales of Corporation A shipped to purchasers in South Carolina from any place of storage in Illinois (i.e., throwback sales), by the total sales of the unitary business group everywhere.

If a unitary business group contains one or more ineligible members (e.g., an S Corporation), the ineligible member must file a separate unitary return. In the separate unitary return, the ineligible member's apportionment percentage must be determined by dividing that member's Illinois factor or factors by the combined everywhere factor or factors of all the unitary group's members. The apportionment percentage must then be multiplied by the unitary group's combined business income to determine the ineligible member's business income that is apportionable to Illinois. (86 Ill. Adm. Code 100.5270(e))

All S corporations that are unitary business group members must file Schedule UB to enable the unitary business group to determine the amount of its unitary business income from Illinois sources. Schedule UB also must be filed by partnerships that are engaged in a unitary business with one or more of its partners if the unitary partners own more than 90% of all the interest in the partnership. The schedule must be attached to the S corporation's or partnership's Illinois return. (Instructions, Schedule UB, Combined Apportionment for Unitary Business Group)

Each member of a unitary business group who is subject to Illinois income tax and who does not join in the filing of a combined return must file a separate return, and compute its business income apportionable to Illinois by computing the base income of the unitary business group and by multiplying the business income included in the nonmember's base income the Illinois apportionment factor or factors and the everywhere factor or factors of the entire unitary business group. (86 Ill. Adm. Code 100.5215(b))

Example 1: Individual A is a nonresident and is the sole shareholder of Corporation S, an S corporation, and Corporation C, a C corporation. Corporation S and Corporation C are engaged in a unitary business. Corporation S' taxable year is the calendar year. Corporation C's taxable year is the fiscal year ending June 30. For its taxable year ending December 31, 2014, Corporation S has business income of $125,000, Illinois sales of $750,000, and total sales of

$1,000,000. For its taxable year ending June 30, 2014, Corporation C has business income of $75,000, Illinois sales of $40,000, and total sales of $500,000. Corporation S must file a separate return using the combined apportionment method to determine its business income apportionable to Illinois. Combined apportionment must be computed on the basis of Corporation S' taxable year. Because Corporation C's taxable year differs, Corporation S may elect to apply any of the accounting methods available under 86 Ill. Adm. Code 100.5265 by treating S' taxable year as the common taxable year. Assume S elects to use method 3 to determine combined business income for the common taxable year ending December 31, 2014. S' business income apportionable to Illinois is computed as follows: $200,000 × ($750,000/$1,500,000) = $100,000. Corporation C must also file a separate return computing its business income apportionable to Illinois by applying the combined apportionment method. Corporation C may elect to apply any of the accounting methods available under Section 100.5265 to determine the amount of business income and apportionment factors of Corporation S to be used in computing Corporation C's business income apportioned to Illinois.

Example 2: Assume that Corporation A owns a 91% interest, Corporation B a 4% interest and nonresident Individual Y a 5% interest, in P, a partnership. Corporation A and P are engaged in a unitary business. Because Corporation A owns more than 90% of P, the alternative apportionment provisions for unitary partners and partnerships in 86 Ill. Adm. Code 100.3380(d) do not apply and P must be treated as a member of Corporation A's unitary business group for all purposes. Corporation A, Corporation B, Individual Y, and P all use the calendar year as their taxable year. For taxable year December 31, 2014, Corporation A has business income of $300,000 (not including any business income from P), Illinois sales of $450,000, and total sales of $600,000. P has business income of $100,000, Illinois sales of $30,000, and total sales of $400,000. There are no intercompany sales. Substantially all of the interests in P are owned or controlled by members of the same unitary business group, so that P is treated as a member of the unitary business group for all purposes. Because Corporation A's share of the business income of P will be eliminated in combination, combined business income is $400,000. Corporation A and P are required to file separate returns in which business income apportionable to Illinois is computed by applying the combined apportionment method. Under the combined apportionment method, P's business income apportionable to Illinois is computed by combining its business income and total sales everywhere with the business income and total sales everywhere of A. P's business income apportioned to Illinois is thus $12,000, computed as follows: $400,000 in combined business income × ($30,000 of P's Illinois sales/$1,000,000 of combined total sales) = $12,000. Corporation A's business income apportionable to Illinois is $180,000, computed as follows: $400,000 in combined business income × ($450,000 of Corporation A's Illinois sales/$1,000,000 of combined total sales) = $180,000. In addition, Corporation A must include its $10,920 distributive share (i.e., 91% × $12,000) of the business income of P apportioned to Illinois in its Illinois net income. Also, Individual Y must include her $600 distributable share of the business income of P apportioned to Illinois in her Illinois net income (i.e., 5% × $12,000), and Corporation B must include its $480 distributable share of the business income of P apportioned to Illinois in its Illinois net income (i.e., 4% of $12,000). Finally, P computes Illinois personal property tax replacement income tax on net income of $600, computed as follows: $400,000 - $380,000 (95% of its base income distributable to partners subject to replacement tax) = $20,000, and $20,000 × ($30,000/$1,000,000) = $600.

Example 3: Assume the same facts as Example 2, except that P's business income is a loss of ($100,000). Under the combined apportionment method, P's business income apportionable to Illinois is computed by combining its business loss and total sales everywhere with the business income and total sales everywhere of A. P's business income apportioned to Illinois is thus $6,000, computed as follows: $200,000 × ($30,000/$1,000,000) = $6,000. Corporation A's business income apportionable to Illinois is $90,000, computed as follows: $200,000 × ($450,000/$1,000,000) = $90,000. In addition, Corporation A must include its $5,460 distributive share of the business income of P apportioned to Illinois in its Illinois net income. Individual Y must include her $300 distributable share of the business income of P apportioned to Illinois in her Illinois net income (i.e., 5% × $6,000), and Corporation B must include its $240 distributable share. P computes Illinois personal property tax replacement income tax of $300, computed as follows: $200,000 - $190,000 = $10,000, and $10,000 × ($30,000/$1,000,000) = $300.

Effective for tax years ending on or after December 31, 2017, a unitary group must use a subgroup method of apportionment if the group includes members that use different apportionment formulas. A subgroup consists of members of the group that use the same formula to apportion business income. (86 Ill. Adm. Code 100.3600) For example, a subgroup can include:

— a sales factor subgroup;

— an insurance company subgroup;

— a financial organization subgroup; and

— a transportation company subgroup. (86 Ill. Adm. Code 100.3600(c))

Each subgroup member must determine its apportionment percentage based on a formula that consists of:

— the member's apportioned Illinois income (e.g., sales, insurance company's premiums, financial organization's gross receipts, transportation company's gross receipts, etc);

— the subgroup's everywhere income; and

— the total everywhere income of all group members. (86 Ill. Adm. Code 100.3600(b))

The apportionment fraction of the unitary group is the sum of the apportionment percentages for each subgroup member. (86 Ill. Adm. Code 100.3600(c))

The formula must also include a member's distributive share of the:

— Illinois sales of any unitary partnership; and

— the everywhere sales of that partnership. (86 Ill. Adm. Code 100.3380(d))

If the partner and partnership use a different formula, the partner's apportionment percentage is equal to:

— the partner's subgroup apportionment percentage plus

— the partnership's subgroup apportionment percentage. (86 Ill. Adm. Code 100.3380(d))

Credits. Any Illinois credit must be based on the combined activities of the unitary business group's members and must be applied against the group's combined tax liability. (86 Ill. Adm. Code 100.5270(d))

Example 1: Corporations A, B and C are unitary business group members that filed a combined return for 2015. Corporation D was not a member of the ABC combined group in 2015, but became a member of ABCD's combined group in 2016. During 2015, Corporations A, B, and C employed a total of 150 persons in Illinois and Corporation D employed 50 people in Illinois, for a total of 200. During 2016, Corporations A, B and C employed 100 persons in Illinois and Corporation D employed 100 persons in Illinois, again for a total of 200. A replacement tax investment credit is allowed for investments in qualified property the taxpayer placed in service during the year and an additional 0.5% credit for the property is allowed to a taxpayer whose Illinois employment has increased by at least 1% over its Illinois employment in the previous year. ABCD's combined group cannot qualify for the additional 0.5% credit during 2016 because the combined Illinois employment of Corporations A, B, C and D remained unchanged between 2015 and 2016. Because eligibility is determined at the combined group level, no additional credit can be allowed for qualified property placed in service by Corporation D in 2016, even though Corporation D's Illinois employment doubled between 2015 and 2016.

Example 2: Corporations P, Q, R and S filed a combined Illinois return for calendar year 2015. On January 1, 2016, Corporation S was sold to an unrelated purchaser. Corporations P, Q and R filed a combined Illinois return for calendar year 2016. PQRS's combined group employed 400 people in Illinois during 2015, 100 of whom were Corporation P's employees of and 100 of whom were Corporation S's employees. PQR's combined group employed 350 people in Illinois during 2016, 50 of whom were Corporation P's employees. PQR's combined group can qualify for the additional 0.5% replacement tax investment credit for qualified property placed in service during 2015 because the combined group's Illinois employment increased from 300 in 2015 to 400 in 2016. Because the eligibility is determined at the combined group level, property placed in service by Corporation P during 2015 may qualify for the additional 0.5% credit even though Corporation P's Illinois employment actually decreased.

Eligibility for the Illinois research and development (R&D) credit during a combined-return year must be determined by the increase in research activities conducted by all combined group members in Illinois and not an individual member's research activities. (86 Ill. Admin. Code 100.5270(d)(5))

Carryforward provisions. Any credit carryforward is available to the combined group for the next combined-return year. If a member is no longer eligible to join, or is no longer part of, a combined group, the credit carryforward for the Illinois replacement tax investment credit, high impact business investment credit, and enterprise zone investment credit is available to the remaining members if they continue to both own and use the property for which the credit was claimed for 48 months after the placed-in-service date. The credit carryforward is available to the former member if that former member both owns and uses the property for which the credit was claimed for the remainder of the 48-month period after the placed-in-service date. The amount of a former member's carryforward is equal to the combined unused credit multiplied by a fraction. The numerator of the fraction is the credit attributable to the former member's qualified property for the unused credit year, and the denominator is the credit attributable to the combined group's qualified property for the unused credit year. (86 Ill. Admin. Code 100.5270(d)(6))

Example: In 2013, Corporation A purchased $300,000 of property eligible for the Illinois replacement tax investment credit, $200,000 of which was used by A and $100,000 of which was transferred to and used by Corporation B. A and B filed a combined return for that year which showed an income tax liability of $1,000 and an investment credit of $1,500. The group's unused credit was $500. In 2015, B left the group, and during that year it owned and continued to use the $100,000 of eligible property. Its credit carryforward would be: $500 x [$100,000 ÷ $300,000] = $166.67.

Recapture provisions. Combined unitary business group members are responsible for any increase in corporation income or replacement tax liability resulting from the recapture of credits. (86 Ill. Admin. Code 100.5270(d)(7))

Example: In 2013, Corporation A purchased property eligible for the Illinois replacement tax investment credit. A and B filed a combined return for that year which showed an income tax liability of $1,000 and an investment credit of $1,500. In 2015 Corporation A transferred its eligible property to Corporation B. Corporation B was acquired by Corporation C in 2015 and, immediately afterward, B sold all the eligible property to an unrelated third party. B and C file a combined return for that year and they must increase their tax liability by $1,000 due to the credit that was claimed on A's and B's combined return in 2013.

Estimated tax payments. If a combined return is filed for two consecutive taxable years, payments of estimated tax must be made on a combined basis for each following taxable year until separate returns are filed. The combined group must be treated as one taxpayer for the taxable years in which combined estimated payments are required. If separate returns are filed in a year after a combined return year, the amount of any estimated tax payments made on a combined basis for that year must be credited against the separate tax liabilities of the combined group's former members in a manner determined by the designated agent and that is satisfactory to the Illinois Department of Revenue. (86 Ill. Adm. Code Sec. 100.5230(a))

For the first two years in which a combined return is filed, estimated tax payments may be made on either a combined or separate basis. The amounts of any separate estimated tax payments made by a combined group member are credited against the combined tax liability. (86 Ill. Adm. Code Sec. 100.5230(b))

Estimated tax thresholds, installment amounts, and payment due dates are discussed under Practice and Procedure.

Underpayment penalty. If a combined return is filed, the amount of any estimated tax underpayment penalty must be computed as if the combined group were one taxpayer. In the first combined return year, the determination of any underpayment penalty must be made using the total of the tax and income shown on the returns filed by the combined group members for the previous year. If combined estimated tax payments are made, but separate returns are filed for a tax year following a combined return year, the determination of any underpayment penalty for any combined group members making the estimated payments, must be made using each former member's separate company items from the combined return for the previous year and the member's share of the combined estimated payments for the current year. If combined estimated payments are made for a tax year but no combined return is filed for that year and no combined return was filed in the previous year, the estimated tax will be a credit only for the members that made the payment. (86 Ill. Adm. Code Sec. 100.5230(c))

Entering members. If a corporation becomes a member of a new or existing combined group during a common taxable year, estimated tax is determined for the combined group by combining the entering member's separate company items shown on its return for its taxable year before the entry year with the corresponding items of the combined group members for the common taxable year before the entry year. If the corporation is not a member of the combined group for the entire entry year, the corporation's separate company items for that portion of the entry year must be included with the corresponding items of the combined group for that taxable year. If a corporation was a member of another combined group during any portion of the entry year or during any portion of the taxable year before the entry year, the corporation's separate company items must include the items attributed to the corporation by the designated agent of the first combined group. (86 Ill. Adm. Code Sec. 100.5230(d)(1))

Departing members. If a corporation leaves a combined group during a common taxable year, estimated tax for the combined group is determined by excluding the separate company items attributed to that corporation for the common taxable year before the departure year from the corresponding items of the combined group as if that corporation had not been a member of the combined group during the common taxable year before the departure year. If a corporation is departing a combined group after the beginning of the departure year, separate company items attributed to that corporation for the portion of the year before its departure must be excluded from the corresponding items of the combined group as if that corporation had not been a member of the group during that portion of the departure year. If a corporation leaves a group before the end of that corporation's taxable year, for the portion of its separate taxable year remaining after the date of departure, the corporation must take into account the separate company items attributed to it by the designated agent. (86 Ill. Adm. Code Sec. 100.5230(d)(2))

Does Illinois allow or require affiliated group combined reporting?

Taxpayers are not allowed or required to report Illinois corporate income tax on an affiliated combined basis that includes the same members as a federal affiliated group regardless of whether the members are engaged in a unitary business. (35 ILCS 5/502(e); 86 Ill. Adm. Code Sec. 100.5205; 86 Ill. Adm. Code Sec. 100.5210(a))

[¶12-000]

CREDITS

[¶12-001] Overview of Credits

Illinois allows taxpayers to claim credits against corporate income tax liability for variety of investment, job creation and other business activities.

• *Education credits*

    Student-assistance contribution credit

    Invest in Kids credit

• *Film, entertainment, and media production credits*

    Film production services credit

    Live theater production credit

• *Investment credits*

    High impact business program

    Replacement tax investment credit

• *Enterprise zone credits*

    Enterprise zone program

    River edge redevelopment zone construction jobs credit

• *Research credits*

    Research and development credit

• *Job creation/hiring credits*

    Small business job creation tax credit

    Ex-felons jobs credit

    Data center construction jobs credit

- *Worker training/Basic skills credits*

  Apprenticeship education expense credit

- *Economic development credits*

  Economic development for a growing economy (EDGE) program credit

- *Historic Property*

  Historic preservation credit

  River edge historic preservation credit

- *Venture capital, equity, and other investment financing credits*

  New markets credit

  Angel investment credit

- *Housing credits*

  Affordable housing donation credit

- *Family credits*

  Dependent care assistance program credit

  Employee child care credit

- *Youth credits*

  Tech-prep youth vocational program credit

- *Other credits*

  Hospital credit

  Natural disaster credit

  Minimum wage withholding tax credit

- *General credit provisions*

  Carryforward period.—Although most credits that may be claimed against Illinois corporate income tax liability provide that unused credits may be carried forward for five tax years, the state does not have a general carryforward provision applicable to credits.

  Filing requirements.—Most Illinois income tax credits are computed and claimed by completing and attaching the following schedule to the taxpayers's annual Illinois tax return:

  — Schedule 1299-A for S corporations, partnerships, and LLCs; (Instructions, Schedule 1299-A, Tax Subtractions and Credits for Partnerships and S Corporations) or

  — Schedule 1299-D for C corporations. (Instructions, Schedule 1299-D, Income Tax Credits for Corporations and Fiduciaries)

Sunset date.—If a law creating a credit does not specify a sunset date, the credit will sunset or expire 5 years after the effective date of the law. (35 ILCS 5/250(a)) Illinois extended the automatic sunset date for credits scheduled to expire in 2011, 2012, or 2013 for an additional 5 years. (35 ILCS 5/250(b))

Accountability disclosure and recapture provisions.—The Illinois Corporate Accountability for Tax Expenditures Act (CAA) requires reporting of firm-level tax exemptions or credits authorized by the Department of Commerce and Economic Opportunity (DCEO), (20 ILCS 715/5) including the following credits:

  — High impact business investment credit;

  — Enterprise zone investment credit;

— River edge redevelopment zone investment credit; and

— Economic development for a growing economy (EDGE) credit.

Disclosure provisions: Each recipient of assistance from the DCEO must submit an annual progress report disclosing the following information

— an application tracking number;

— the office mailing address, telephone number, and the name of the chief officer of the granting body;

— the office mailing address, telephone number, four-digit SIC number or successor number, and the name of the chief officer of the applicant or authorized designee for the specific project site for which development assistance is requested;

— the type of development assistance program and value of assistance that was approved by the state granting body;

— the applicant's total number of employees at the specific project site on the date the application is submitted to the granting agency, including the number of full-time permanent jobs, the number of part-time jobs, and the number of temporary jobs;

— the number of new employees and retained employees the applicant stated in its development assistance agreement, if any, if not, then in its application, would be created by the development assistance broken down by full-time, permanent, part-time, and temporary;

— a declaration of whether the recipient is in compliance with each development assistance agreement;

— a detailed list of the occupation or job classifications and number of new or retained employees to be hired in full-time permanent jobs, a schedule of anticipated starting dates of the new hires, the anticipated average wage by occupation or job classification, and the total payroll to be created as a result of the development assistance;

— a narrative, if necessary, describing why the development assistance is needed and how the applicant's use of the development assistance may reduce unemployment at any site in Illinois; and

— a certification by the chief officer of the applicant, or by a authorized designee, that the information contained in the application submitted to the granting body contains no knowing misrepresentation of material fact upon which eligibility for development assistance is based. (20 ILCS 715/20(b))

Recapture provisions: The CCA requires that all development assistance agreements for credits and other forms of development assistance must contain recapture provisions. At a minimum, incentives recipients must:

— make the level of capital investment in the economic development project specified in the development assistance agreement; and

— create and/or retain the requisite number of jobs, paying at least the wages specified for the jobs, for the duration of time specified in the authorizing legislation or the implementing administrative rules. (20 ILCS 715/25(a)(1))

If the recipient fails to create or retain the requisite number of jobs within and for the time period specified, in the legislation authorizing, or the administrative rules implementing, the development assistance programs and the development assistance agreement, the recipient is deemed to no longer qualify for the state economic assistance and the applicable recapture provisions take effect. (20 ILCS 715/25(a)(2))

¶12-001

PERSONAL INCOME

[¶15-050]

FEDERAL/MULTISTATE ISSUES

[¶15-055] Comparison of Federal/State Key Features

The following is a comparison of key features of federal income tax laws that have been enacted as of March 27, 2020, and the Illinois personal income tax laws. The starting point for computing Illinois personal income tax liability is federal adjusted gross income (AGI). Federal AGI is subject to Illinois addition and subtraction adjustments. Federal conformity for computing the Illinois personal income tax liability is based on the Internal Revenue Code as amended to date.

Nonresidents must pay tax only on income from Illinois sources. Part-year residents must pay tax on all income received while a resident and income from Illinois sources while a nonresident.

• *Alternative Minimum Tax (IRC Sec. 55 — IRC Sec. 59)*

Illinois has no equivalent to the federal alternative minimum tax on tax preference items (IRC Sec. 55—IRC Sec. 59).

• *Asset Expense Election (IRC Secs. 179 and 1400N)*

The same as federal (IRC Sec. 179) because the starting point for computing Illinois personal income liability is federal adjusted gross income (see ¶15-510).

• *Bad Debts (IRC Sec. 166)*

The same as federal (IRC Sec. 166) because the starting point for computing Illinois personal income liability is federal adjusted gross income (see ¶15-510).

• *Capital Gains and Capital Losses (IRC Secs. 1(h), 1202, 1211, 1212, and 1221)*

Generally, the same as federal (IRC Sec. 1(h), IRC Sec. 1211, IRC Sec. 1212, and IRC Sec. 1221) because the starting point for computing Illinois personal income liability is federal adjusted gross income (see ¶15-510). Illinois allows a subtraction from federal adjusted gross income for capital gains on employer securities received from a qualified employee benefit plan. It also allows a subtraction adjustment for capital gains from appreciation of certain property acquired before August 1, 1969 (see ¶16-270).

• *Charitable Contributions (IRC Sec. 170)*

Illinois does not allow itemized deductions (see ¶15-545) for charitable contributions (IRC Sec. 170 and IRC Sec. 1400S). It also does not allow a subtraction from federal adjusted gross income for charitable contributions (see ¶16-205).

• *Child Care Credit (IRC Sec. 45F)*

Illinois has no equivalent to the federal employer-provided child care credit (IRC Sec. 45F).

• *Civil Rights Deductions (IRC Sec. 62)*

The same as federal (IRC Sec. 62) because the starting point for computing Illinois personal income liability is federal adjusted gross income (see ¶15-510).

• *Dependents (IRC Sec. 152)*

Illinois adopts the federal definition of "dependent" (IRC Sec. 152). Any term used under Illinois income tax law has the same meaning as used under federal income tax law (see ¶15-515). Illinois allows a standard exemption for each dependent (see ¶15-535).

- *Depreciation (IRC Secs. 167, 168 and 1400N)*

Generally the same as federal (IRC Sec. 167 and IRC Sec. 168) because federal adjusted gross income is the starting point for computing Illinois personal income tax liability (see ¶15-510). Illinois requires an addition to federal adjusted gross income for IRC Sec. 168(k) bonus depreciation (see ¶16-040). The addition modification does not apply to 100% bonus depreciation. Illinois allows a subtraction from federal adjusted gross income for some or all bonus depreciation in the last year of federal regular depreciation or when the taxpayer disposes of the property (see ¶16-245).

- *Earned Income Credit (IRC Sec. 32)*

Illinois provides an earned income tax credit (EITC) (see ¶16-805 that is a percentage of the federal credit (IRC Sec. 32)).

- *Educational Benefits and Deductions (IRC Secs. 62(a)(2)(D), 127, 221, 222, and 529)*

The same as federal (IRC Sec. 62(a)(2)(D), IRC Sec. 127, IRC Sec. 221, IRC Sec. 222, IRC Sec. 529) because the starting point for computing Illinois personal income tax liability is federal adjusted gross income (see ¶15-510). Illinois allows a subtraction from federal adjusted gross income for contributions to the state's IRC Sec. 529 plans. (see ¶16-255) It requires an addition to federal adjusted gross income if the taxpayer uses a distribution for nonqualified expenses. (see ¶16-050) The Illinois definition of "qualified higher education expenses" does not include expenses for tuition at an elementary or secondary public, private, or religious school.

- *Excess Business Loss Limitation (IRC Sec. 461(l))*

The same as federal (IRC Sec. 461(l)) because the starting point for computing Illinois personal income liability is federal adjusted gross income (see ¶15-510).

- *Foreign Earned Income (IRC Secs. 911 and 912)*

The same as federal (IRC Sec. 911 and IRC Sec. 912) because the starting point for computing Illinois personal income liability is federal adjusted gross income (see ¶15-510).

- *Health Insurance and Health Savings Accounts (HSAs) (IRC Secs. 105(b), 106(e), 139C, 139D, 162(l), and 223)*

The same as federal (IRC Sec. 105(b), IRC Sec. 106(e), IRC Sec. 139C, IRC Sec. 139D, IRC Sec. 162(l), IRC Sec. 223) because the starting point for computing Illinois personal income liability is federal adjusted gross income (see ¶15-510). Illinois does not allow an itemized deduction for unreimbursed medical expenses (see ¶15-545).

- *Indebtedness (IRC Secs. 108 and 163)*

The same as federal (IRC Sec. 108 and IRC Sec. 163) because the starting point for computing Illinois personal income liability is federal adjusted gross income (see ¶15-510).

- *Interest on Federal Obligations (IRC Sec. 61)*

Illinois allows a subtraction from federal adjusted gross income for interest on tax-exempt federal obligations (IRC Sec. 61) and distributions from mutual funds investing exclusively in U.S. government obligations (see ¶16-280).

- *Interest on State and Local Obligations (IRC Sec. 103)*

Illinois requires an addition to federal adjusted gross income (see ¶16-075) for interest on state and local obligations (IRC Sec. 103). It allows a subtraction from federal adjusted gross income for interest from exempt Illinois and local government obligations (see ¶16-280).

¶15-055

• *Losses Not Otherwise Compensated (IRC Secs. 165 and 1400S)*

The same as federal (IRC Sec. 165 and IRC Sec. 1400S) because the starting point for computing Illinois personal income tax liability is federal adjusted gross income (see ¶15-510). Illinois does not allow an itemized deduction for casualty and theft losses (see ¶15-545).

• *Net Operating Loss (IRC Secs. 172 and 1400N)*

The same as federal (IRC Sec. 172 and IRC Sec. 1400N) because the starting point for computing Illinois personal income tax liability is federal adjusted gross income. Illinois does not require any adjustment by personal income taxpayers for the federal net operating loss deduction. (see ¶16-005).

• *Pass-Through Deduction (IRC Sec. 199A)*

Illinois has no equivalent to the qualified business income deduction (pass-through deduction) (see IRC Sec. 199A).

• *Personal Residence (IRC Secs. 121, 132(n), 163, and 1033)*

The same as federal (IRC Sec. 121 and IRC Sec. 1033) because the starting point for computing Illinois personal income liability is federal adjusted gross income (see ¶15-510). Illinois does not allow an itemized deduction for home mortgage interest (see ¶15-545).

• *Retirement Plans (IRC Secs. 401 — 424 andIRC Secs. 457A and 1400Q)*

The same as federal (IRC Sec. 401—IRC Sec. 424, IRC Sec. 457A, and IRC Sec. 1400Q) because the starting point for computing Illinois personal income liability is federal adjusted gross income (see ¶15-510). Illinois allows a subtraction from federal adjusted gross income for retirement, pension, and Social Security benefits included in the taxpayer's federal return (see ¶16-345).

• *Start-Up Expenses (IRC Sec. 195)*

The same as federal (IRC Sec. 195) because the starting point for computing Illinois personal income liability is federal adjusted gross income (see ¶15-510).

• *Taxes Paid (IRC Sec. 164)*

Illinois does not allow itemized deductions for state and local taxes (see ¶15-545). It has a credit for real property taxes paid on a principal residence located in Illinois. Taxpayers who have adjusted gross income exceeding a certain threshold cannot claim the credit (see ¶16-805). Illinois also provides residents and part-year residents a credit income tax paid to another state (see ¶16-805).

• *Unemployment Compensation (IRC Sec. 85)*

The same as federal (IRC Sec. 85) because the starting point for computing Illinois personal income liability is federal adjusted gross income (see ¶15-510).

[¶15-100]
TAXPAYERS

[¶15-105] Taxation of Part-Year Residents and Nonresidents

Nonresidents are subject to Illinois personal income tax only on income from state sources. Part-year residents are taxable on all income received during the period of residency and income received as a nonresident from state sources.

[¶15-110] Residents

A resident must pay Illinois tax on all income taken into account in the computation of base income. (35 ILCS 5/301(a)) The starting point for computing Illinois base income is federal adjusted gross income (AGI). Federal AGI is subject to Illinois addition and subtraction adjustments.

[¶15-115] Nonresidents

Nonresidents must pay Illinois tax on income from Illinois sources. (35 ILCS 5/301(b); Instructions, Schedule NR, Nonresident and Part-Year Resident Computation of Illinois Tax) The starting point for computing Illinois income tax liability is the part of federal adjusted gross income (AGI) from state sources. Federal AGI is subject to the part of Illinois addition and subtraction adjustments from state sources. (Instructions, Schedule NR, Nonresident and Part-Year Resident Computation of Illinois Tax)

A nonresident then determines tax liability by:

• dividing adjusted Illinois source income by the amount of adjusted Illinois base income determined as if the nonresident was a resident;

• subtracting the part of the nonresident's standard exemption allowance from Illinois sources; and

• applying the Illinois tax rate. (Instructions, Schedule NR, Nonresident and Part-Year Resident Computation of Illinois Tax)

Illinois has nonresident sourcing rules that apply to:

• business income;

• income from intangibles;

• beneficiary income;

• retirement and pension income;

• property-related income;

• gains and losses;

• pass-through entity income and deductions;

• compensation for personal services; and

• Illinois lottery prizes.

[¶15-120] Part-Year Residents

Part-year residents must pay tax on:

• all income earned or received while a resident of Illinois; and

• income earned or received from Illinois sources while a nonresident. (35 ILCS 5/301(c)(1); Instructions, Schedule NR, Nonresident and Part-Year Resident Computation of Illinois Tax)

[¶15-150]

SPECIAL TAXPAYERS

[¶15-175] Military Personnel

Military personnel who are Illinois residents or part-year residents must file a return if:

• the individual must file a federal return; or

• the individual's Illinois base income is greater than the individual's standard exemption allowance. (Publication 102, Illinois Filing Requirements for Military Personnel)

Individuals who are nonresidents must file if the individual's taxable income from Illinois sources is greater than the individual's standard exemption allowance. (Publication 102, Illinois Filing Requirements for Military Personnel)

A resident's federal adjusted gross income (AGI) includes military pay. A part-year resident must complete Schedule NR to report the Illinois portion of military pay included in federal AGI. A nonresident is not required to report military pay to Illinois. (Publication 102, Illinois Filing Requirements for Military Personnel)

Illinois allows a subtraction from federal AGI for military pay received for active duty.

[¶15-185] Owners of Pass-Through Entities

Partners and shareholders must pay Illinois income tax on their distributive share of income received from:

- S corporations;
- partnerships; and
- limited liability companies (LLCs) classified as a partnership for income tax purposes. (35 ILCS 5/205(b); 86 Ill. Adm. Code 100.2405(c)(7) and (8); *Publication 129, Pass-Through Entity Income*, Illinois Department of Revenue, May 2018; Instructions, Schedule K-1-P, Partner's or Shareholder's Share of Income, Deductions, Credits, and Recapture)

Beneficiaries of Illinois trusts and estates must also pay income tax on their distributive share of income. (Instructions, Schedule K-1-T, Beneficiary's Share of Income and Deductions)

[¶15-200]

ESTATES AND TRUSTS

[¶15-205] Estates and Trusts--Residency

Illinois law does not provide specific definitions of the terms "estates" and "trusts." Therefore, the federal definition of the terms is adopted for Illinois purposes. (35 ILCS 5/102)

Both estates and trusts are liable for the Illinois income tax; however, only trusts are also liable for the Illinois personal property replacement income tax. (see ¶15-215) Because the computation of Illinois base income begins with federal taxable income, federal deductions, such as the deduction for distributions to beneficiaries under IRC Sec. 661, are incorporated into Illinois law, subject to Illinois modifications.

Estates and trusts may be either residents or nonresidents. Resident estates and trusts are taxed on federal taxable income modified by Illinois additions and subtractions. Nonresident estates and trusts allocate and apportion modified fiduciary income and are taxed on the amount attributable to Illinois. (see ¶15-215)

• *Beneficiaries*

Beneficiaries of estates and trusts are taxed for Illinois income tax purposes on their pro rata share, if any, of fiduciary income that is deemed to have been paid, credited, or distributed by the entity. The trust or estate furnishes a schedule detailing information reportable by the beneficiaries on their individual income tax returns. A resident beneficiary's entire pro rata share of fiduciary base income is attributed to Illinois. Nonresident beneficiaries take into account their share of estate and trust income allocated and apportioned to Illinois. (see ¶15-235)

The following estates and trusts are treated as residents for purposes of the Illinois income tax (35 ILCS 5/1501(a)(20)): (1) the estate of a decedent who was domiciled in Illinois at the date of death; (2) a trust created by the will of a decedent who at death was domiciled in the state; (3) an irrevocable trust, if the grantor was domiciled in Illinois at the time the trust became irrevocable. A trust is considered irrevocable to the extent that the grantor is not considered the owner of the trust under the grantor trust provisions of IRC Secs. 671—678.

The fiduciary of an estate or trust must file an Illinois fiduciary return if

(1) the trust or estate has Illinois net income without regard to any deductions for distributions to beneficiaries; or

(2) the trust or estate is a resident of the state and is required to file a federal fiduciary income tax return.

[¶15-215] Estates and Trusts--Computation of Income

What is the starting point for computing personal income tax liability for estates and trusts?

Fiduciaries must compute Illinois personal income tax liability for estates and trusts starting with federal taxable income. (35 ILCS 5/203(e))

Does Illinois require addition modifications to federal taxable income for trusts or estates?

Illinois requires addition modifications to the federal taxable income of a trust or estate for:

- any net operating loss (NOL) deduction; (35 ILCS 5/203(c)(2)(D))

- the $600 estate, the $300 trust, or $100 disability trust exemption; (35 ILCS 5/203(c)(2)(B))

- any Illinois income or replacement tax deduction; (35 ILCS 5/203(c)(2)(C))

- interest income excluded from the federal fiduciary return; (35 ILCS 5/203(c)(2)(A))

- taxes paid to another state if the estate or trust is claiming an Illinois credit for those taxes; (35 ILCS 5/203(c)(2)(F))

- any capital gain deduction; (35 ILCS 5/203(c)(2)(G))

- any bonus depreciation deduction; (35 ILCS 5/203(c)(2)(G-10))

- interest, (35 ILCS 5/203(c)(2)(G-12)) intangible, (35 ILCS 5/203(c)(2)(G-13)) or insurance premium expenses paid to a related party; (35 ILCS 5/203(c)(2)(G-14)) and

- the amount of any Illinois student-assistance contribution credit taken. (35 ILCS 5/203(c)(2)(G-15))

Illinois allows a downward adjustment to any addition modification for the amount permanently set aside for charitable purposes under IRC Sec. 642(c). (86 Ill. Adm. Code Sec. 100.2680; Instructions, Form IL-1041, Fiduciary Income and Replacement Tax Return)

> *Example:* Estate A has $100 of capital gain income which it permanently sets aside for ultimate distribution to the University of Illinois. Estate A can claim a charitable deduction of $100 under IRC Sec. 642(c)(2) and a capital gain deduction of $60. Estate A must adjust its federal charitable deduction to reflect the $60 capital gain deduction. It can claim a charitable deduction of $40. Thus, Estate A's taxable income is reduced by the full amount of the $100 of capital gain income permanently set aside for the University. Estate A's Illinois base income is identical to its taxable income. The base income takes into account the $40 federal charitable deduction and the $60 capital gain deduction. Estate A can reduce its Illinois addition modification for the capital gain deduction to zero since it relates entirely to capital gain income for which it claimed IRC Sec. 642(c) deduction.

Does Illinois allow subtraction modifications to federal taxable income for trusts or estates?

Illinois allows subtraction modifications to federal taxable income of a trust or estate for:

- retirement and pension income distributions; (35 ILCS 5/203(c)(2)(H))

- the valuation limitation amount on gain from the sale or exchange of property acquired before August 1, 1969; (35 ILCS 5/203(c)(2)(I))

- the amount of any Illinois income tax refund included in taxable income for the tax year; (35 ILCS 5/203(c)(2)(J))

- interest income from exempt federal obligations; (35 ILCS 5/203(c)(2)(K))

- amounts disallowed as federal deductions or interest expenses under IRC Secs. 171(a)(2), 265, or 280C; (35 ILCS 5/203(c)(2)(L))

- River Edge Redevelopment Zone (35 ILCS 5/203(c)(2)(M)) and High Impact Business dividends; (35 ILCS 5/203(c)(2)(O))

- contributions made to a job training project under the Tax Increment Allocation Redevelopment Act; (35 ILCS 5/203(c)(2)(N))

- the amount of the deduction under IRC Sec. 1341 for restoration of substantial amounts held under a claim of right; (35 ILCS 5/203(c)(2)(P))

- reparations or other amounts received as a victim of persecution for racial or religious reasons by Nazi Germany or any other Axis regime; (35 ILCS 5/203(c)(2)(Q))

- bonus depreciation; (35 ILCS 5/203(c)(2)(R))

- interest or intangible income received from a related party required to addback interest or intangible expenses paid; (35 ILCS 5/203(c)(2)(T))

- amounts recovered by the decedent of an estate under the IRC Sec. 111 tax benefit rule; (35 ILCS 5/203(c)(2)(W)) and

- for tax years beginning after 2018 and before 2026, excess business losses disallowed under IRC Sec. 461(l)(1)(B). (35 ILCS 5/203(c)(2)(Z))

Does Illinois require the allocation and apportionment of income for nonresident estates and trusts?

Illinois requires the allocation and apportionment of base income or net loss for nonresident estates and trusts. (35 ILCS 5/306) Fiduciaries must follow the same rules that apply to nonresident individuals and multistate corporations.

Can estates and trusts claim a net operating loss deduction?

Illinois allows a net operation loss deduction (NOLD) by estates and trusts based on IRC Sec. 172. (35 ILCS 5/207; 86 Ill. Adm. Code 100.2300(a); 86 Ill. Adm. Code 100.2320(b)) This includes the 80% taxable income limitation on NOLs arising in tax years beginning after 2017. (*Press Release: Impact of Federal Tax Cuts and Jobs Act,* Illinois Department of Revenue, March 1, 2018)

A fiduciary can claim a NOL carryforward deduction after it:

- applies all Illinois addition and subtraction modifications; and

- allocates and apportions income to Illinois. (35 ILCS 5/207; 86 Ill. Adm. Code 100.2300(a); 86 Ill. Adm. Code 100.2320(b))

The NOLD for any tax year equals the sum of the Illinois net loss carryforwards to that tax year. (86 Ill. Adm. Code 100.2310(a))

A fiduciary claiming an Illinois NOLD must:

- complete Schedule NLD;

- enter the resulting NOLD on the income tax return; and

- attach the computation schedule to the return. (Instructions, Schedule NLD, Illinois Net Loss Deduction)

Schedule NLD shows:

- the total amount of Illinois net loss available;

- the amount deductible for the tax year; and

- the remaining NOLD available for use in later tax years. (Instructions, Schedule NLD, Illinois Net Loss Deduction)

The fiduciary must reduce the NOLD by the amount of debt cancellation income excluded under IRC Sec. 108(a). (35 ILCS 5/207(c); 86 Ill. Adm. Code 100.2310(c))

[¶15-220]　Estates and Trusts--Exemptions

Illinois provides estates and trusts a standard exemption from adjusted taxable income of $1,000. (35 ILCS 5/204(a)) Estates or trusts cannot claim the exemption if adjusted gross income for the tax year is $250,000 or more. (35 ILCS 5/204(g))

Nonresidents must multiply the standard exemption by a fraction. The numerator of the fraction is base income allocated and apportioned allocable to Illinois for the tax year. The denominator is total base income for the tax year. (Instructions, Schedule NR, Nonresident Computation of Fiduciary Income)

[¶15-225]　Estates and Trusts--Rates of Tax

What is the Illinois income tax rate on estates and trusts?

The Illinois income tax rate on estates and trusts is 4.95%. (35 ILCS 5/201(b)(5.4); *Informational Bulletin FY 2018-02*, Illinois Department of Revenue, July 2017)

The tax was imposed at a rate of:

- 3.75% for taxable years beginning on or after January 1, 2015 and before July 1, 2017 (35 ILCS 5/201(b)(5.2) and (5.3)); and

- 5% for tax years 2011-2014. (35 ILCS 5/201(b)(5))

Trusts must also pay Illinois personal property replacement tax on taxable income (35 ILCS 5/201(c)) at a rate of 1.5%. (35 ILCS 5/201(d))

Planning Note: Illinois may adopt graduated income tax rates beginning January 1, 2021. Those rates will take effect only if voters approve an amendment to the Illinois Constitution authorizing graduated rates.

Estates and trusts will pay income tax at the rate of:

- 4.75% on net income of $10,000 or less;

- 4.9% on net income between $10,001 and $100,000;

- 4.95% on net income between $100,001 and $250,000;

- 7.75% on net income between $250,001 and $350,000;

- 7.85% on net income between $350,001 and $750,000; (35 ILCS 201.1(1)) and

- 7.99% on net income over $750,000. (35 ILCS 201.1(2))

[¶15-235]　Estates and Trusts--Beneficiaries

Beneficiaries must compute and pay tax on the income and modifications reported by a trust or estate on Schedule K-1-T. (35 ILCS 5/307; Instructions, Schedule K-1-T, Beneficiary's Share of Income and Deductions) A beneficiary computes and pays tax based on the distributive share of:

- the income and modifications apportioned to Illinois by the estate or trust; (35 ILCS 5/307(a)) and

- the nonbusiness income allocated to Illinois by the estate or trust. (35 ILCS 5/307(b))

[¶15-250]
FILING THRESHOLDS

[¶15-255] Residency and Filing Thresholds

A "resident" is an individual who:

- is in Illinois for other than a temporary or transitory purpose during the tax year; or

- is domiciled in Illinois but is absent for a temporary or transitory purpose during the tax year. (35 ILCS 5/1501(a)(20); 86 Ill. Adm. Code 100.3020(a))

The purpose of the definition is to:

- include in the category all individuals who are physically present in Illinois and enjoy the benefit of its government; and

- exclude from the category all individuals who are outside Illinois for other than temporary and transitory purposes and do not enjoy the benefit of its government. (86 Ill. Adm. Code 100.3020(b))

A "nonresident" is a person who is not a resident. (35 ILCS 5/1501(a)(14)) An individual who begins or ends Illinois residency during the taxable year is a "part-year resident". (35 ILCS 5/1501(a)(17))

Individuals who are physically present in Illinois for other than temporary or transitory purposes remain a resident even though temporarily absent from the state. An individual who leaves Illinois for other than temporary or transitory purposes is no longer a resident. An individual who has an Illinois domicile remains a resident unless he or she is outside Illinois for other than temporary or transitory purposes. (86 Ill. Adm. Code 100.3020(b))

What is a temporary or transitory presence?

Whether an individual is in Illinois for a temporary or transitory purpose will depend on the facts and circumstances. An individual is in Illinois for temporary or transitory purposes and does not establish residency if the individual:

- is simply passing through Illinois on his or her way to another state;

- is in Illinois for a brief rest or vacation; or

- is in Illinois to complete, perform, or fulfill a particular transaction, contract, or engagement for a short period of time. (86 Ill. Adm. Code 100.3020(c))

An individual is in Illinois for more than a temporary or transitory purposes and establishes residency if the individual:

- is in Illinois for medical purposes that require a long or indefinite period to recuperate;

- is in Illinois for business purposes that require a long or indefinite period to accomplish;

- is employed in Illinois for a position that may last permanently or indefinitely; or

- has retired from business and moved to Illinois with no definite intention of leaving. (86 Ill. Adm. Code 100.3020(c))

The individual establishes Illinois residency under these circumstances even though he or she may also maintain a residence in some other state. (86 Ill. Adm. Code 100.3020(c))

Example 1: X is domiciled in Fairbanks, Alaska, where he had lived for 50 years and had accumulated a large fortune. For medical reasons, X moves to Illinois where he now spends his entire time, except for yearly summer trips of about 3 or 4 months to Fairbanks. X maintains a residence in Illinois and still maintains, and occupies on visits there, his old residence in Fairbanks. Since his yearly presence in Illinois is not temporary or transitory, he is a resident of Illinois, and is taxable on his entire net income.

Example 2: Until the summer of 2019, Y lived in Illinois. At that time, however, to avoid the Illinois income tax, Y declared himself a resident of Nevada, where he had a summer home. Y moved his bank accounts to banks in Nevada, and each year spent about 3 or 4 months in Nevada. He continued to spend 6 or 7 months of each year at his estate in Illinois, which he continued to maintain. He also continued his social club and business connections in Illinois. The other months he spent traveling in other states. Since his yearly presence in Illinois is not temporary or transitory, he is a resident of Illinois, and is taxable on his entire net income.

Example 3: B and C, husband and wife, live in Minnesota where they maintain their family home. They come to Illinois each November and stay here until the middle of March. Originally, they rented an apartment or house for their stay in Illinois, but 3 years ago they purchased a house. The house is either rented or put in the charge of a caretaker from March to November. B has retired from active control of his Minnesota business but still keeps office space and nominal authority in it. He belongs to clubs in Minnesota, but to none in Illinois. He has no business interests in Illinois. C has little social life in Illinois, more in Minnesota, and has no relatives in Illinois. Neither B nor C is a resident of Illinois. The connection of each to Minnesota in each year is closer than it is to Illinois. Their presence here is for temporary or transitory purposes.

How does Illinois define "domicile"?

"Domicile" is:

• the place where an individual has a fixed, permanent home and principal establishment; and

• the place to which the individual intends to return whenever absent. (86 Ill. Adm. Code 100.3020(d))

It is the place an individual has voluntarily fixed a residence with the intention of making a permanent home, until some unexpected event occurs resulting in the adoption of some other permanent home. (86 Ill. Adm. Code 100.3020(d))

Another definition of "domicile" is the place where an individual has a fixed and permanent residence without any intention of permanently moving. (86 Ill. Adm. Code 100.3020(d))

An individual can only have one domicile at a time. An individual who has a domicile at one place retains that domicile until he or she acquires another elsewhere. For example, if an individual who has a domicile in California and visits Illinois for rest, vacation, business or some other purpose, but intends to return to California, he or she does not acquire domicile in Illinois. Likewise, an individual who has an Illinois domicile and leaves the state retains Illinois domicile as long as he or she has the definite intention of returning to Illinois. (86 Ill. Adm. Code 100.3020(d))

An individual who has a California domicile loses that domicile and acquires an Illinois domicile the moment he or she enters the state if he or she comes to Illinois with:

- the intention of remaining indefinitely; and

- no fixed intention of returning to California. (86 Ill. Adm. Code 100.3020(d))

Similarly, an individual domiciled in Illinois loses that domicile by:

- locating elsewhere with the intention of establishing the new location as his or her domicile, and

- abandoning any intention of returning to Illinois. (86 Ill. Adm. Code 100.3020(d))

What is the standard of proof for residency?

There is a rebuttable presumption that an individual is an Illinois resident if:

- the individual claims a homestead exemption for Illinois property; or

- the individual is present in Illinois for more days than in any other state. (86 Ill. Adm. Code 100.3020(f))

These presumptions are not conclusive. A taxpayer can overcome the presumption by clear and convincing evidence. (86 Ill. Adm. Code 100.3020(f))

The type and amount of proof to establish residency or nonresidency depends largely on facts and circumstances. (86 Ill. Adm. Code 100.3020(f)) The evidence can include affidavits and evidence of:

- the location of a spouse and dependents;

- voter registration;

- automobile registration or driver's license;

- filing an income tax return as a resident of another state;

- home ownership or rental agreements;

- the permanent or temporary nature of work assignments in a state;

- location of professional licenses;

- location of medical professionals, other healthcare providers, accountants and attorneys;

- club and organizational memberships and participation; and

- telephone and other utility usage over a duration of time. (86 Ill. Adm. Code 100.3020(g))

Charitable contributions to IRC Sec. 503(c)(3) tax exempt corporations or organizations in a state is not evidence of domicile or residence in that state. (86 Ill. Adm. Code 100.3020(g); *Informational Bulletin FY 2014-13*, Illinois Department of Revenue, April 2014)

Individuals should file a protective return if a presumption of residency applies for the tax year. (86 Ill. Adm. Code 100.3020(g)) An individual should file as a:

- resident if the individual believes he or she is a nonresident and does not have income from Illinois sources; or

- nonresident if the individual has income tax liability from Illinois sources. (86 Ill. Adm. Code 100.3020(g))

The return enables the individual to avoid failure to file penalties (86 Ill. Adm. Code 100.3020(g))

A protective return should include a signed statement:

  • indicating which presumption of residence the individual is subject to; and

  • setting forth in detail the reasons why the individual believes he or she is a nonresident for the tax year. (86 Ill. Adm. Code 100.3020(g))

The return should also include any evidence showing that the individual is a nonresident for the tax year. (86 Ill. Adm. Code 100.3020(g))

If the return and evidence does not clearly show that the individual is a nonresident, he or she can submit additional supporting information. Illinois will issue a notice of deficiency if:

  • the individual fails to submit additional information; or

  • the additional information submitted does not, when considered with the information from the return, overcome the presumption that the individual is a resident for the tax year. (86 Ill. Adm. Code 100.3020(g))

How does Illinois treat minors and military personnel?

The domicile of a minor is ordinarily the same as the domicile of his or her parents or guardians. If either parent is deceased, the domicile of a minor is ordinarily the same as the surviving parent. If the minor's parents are divorced, the domicile of the minor is the same as the domicile of the parent who has custody. (86 Ill. Adm. Code100.3020(e))

Military personnel do not lose Illinois resident status solely because of long periods of active military duty in other states. (86 Ill. Adm. Code100.3020(h); Publication 102, Illinois Filing Requirements for Military Personnel) Likewise, nonresidents do not become Illinois residents solely by active military duty in Illinois. (86 Ill. Adm. Code100.3020(h); Publication 102, Illinois Filing Requirements for Military Personnel)

Military spouses are not a resident of Illinois if they:

  • are a resident of the same state as their spouse; and

  • are present in Illinois only to accompany their spouse on his or her military assignment. (Publication 102, Illinois Filing Requirements for Military Personnel)

A military spouse can elect to use the same residence for tax purposes as the service member even if the spouse is not present in the same state as the service member. This election is effective for the entire tax year regardless of the date of marriage. (Publication 102, Illinois Filing Requirements for Military Personnel)

[¶15-260] Filing Thresholds--Residents

Illinois residents must file a return if:

  • they had to file a federal income tax return; or

  • their Illinois base income is greater than their standard exemption allowance. (35 ILCS 5/502(a))

[¶15-265] Filing Thresholds--Nonresidents and Part-Year Residents

Nonresidents must file an Illinois income tax return and Schedule NR if:

  • the nonresident earned enough taxable income from state sources to have tax liability; or

  • the nonresident can a claim refund of Illinois income tax that was withheld in error. (Instructions, Form IL-1040, Illinois Individual Income Tax Return; Instructions, Schedule NR, Nonresident and Part-Year Resident Computation of Illinois Tax)

A nonresident of a reciprocal state who worked in Illinois must file an Illinois income tax return if:

- the nonresident received income in Illinois from sources other than wages, salaries, tips, and commissions; or

- the nonresident wants a refund of any Illinois income tax withheld. (Instructions, Form IL-1040, Illinois Individual Income Tax Return)

Nonresident aliens must file an Illinois income tax return if the nonresident alien's income is subject to federal income tax law. (Instructions, Form IL-1040, Illinois Individual Income Tax Return)

Part-year residents must file an Illinois income tax return and Schedule NR if:

- the part-year resident earned income from any source while a resident;

- the part-year resident earned income from state sources while a nonresident; or

- the part-year resident wants a refund of any Illinois income tax withheld. (Instructions, Form IL-1040, Illinois Individual Income Tax Return; Instructions, Schedule NR, Nonresident and Part-Year Resident Computation of Illinois Tax)

[¶15-300]
FILING STATUS

[¶15-305] Filing Status

Taxpayers, including taxpayers in a civil union, generally must use the same filing status for Illinois personal income tax returns as they used for their federal return:

- married filing jointly;
- married filing separately;
- head of household;
- widowed; or
- single. (Instructions, Form IL-1040, Individual Income Tax Return)

[¶15-310] Joint Filers
Joint Filers

Spouses who file a joint federal income tax return must file a joint Illinois income tax return for:

- tax years ending on or after December 31, 2009 and before December 31, 2021, if they do not elect to file separately; and

- tax years ending before December 31, 2009 and on or after December 31, 2021. (35 ILCS 5/502(c))

If neither spouse has to file a federal income tax return, they can elect to file separate or joint Illinois returns. (35 ILCS 5/502(c))

If one spouse is an Illinois resident and the other is a part-year resident or nonresident, they can file a separate or joint Illinois return. If they elect to file jointly, they must treat both spouses as residents. (Instructions, Form IL-1040, Individual Income Tax Return)

[¶15-315] Married, Filing Separately

If spouses file a joint federal income tax return for a tax year ending on or after December 31, 2009 and ending before December 31, 2021, they can elect to file separate Illinois returns. They must make the election by the original or extended due date of the return. The election is irrevocable. (35 ILCS 5/502(c))

If neither spouse has to file a federal income tax return, they can elect to file separate or joint Illinois returns. (35 ILCS 5/502(c))

If one spouse is an Illinois resident and the other is a part-year resident or nonresident, they can file a separate or joint Illinois return. If they file separate Illinois returns, they must divide each federal item of income and deduction between their separate Illinois returns. (Instructions, Form IL-1040, Individual Income Tax Return)

[¶15-320] Head of Household

Taxpayers who file as head of household for federal income tax purposes should use the same filing status on their Form IL-1040. (Instructions, Form IL-1040, Individual Income Tax Return)

[¶15-325] Qualifying Widow(er) with Dependent Child

Taxpayers who file as a qualifying widow or widower for federal income tax purposes should use the widowed filing status on their Form IL-1040. (Instructions, Form IL-1040, Individual Income Tax Return)

[¶15-330] Single

Taxpayers who file as a single taxpayer or widower for federal income tax purposes should use the same filing status on their Form IL-1040. (Instructions, Form IL-1040, Individual Income Tax Return)

[¶15-350]
RATES

[¶15-355] Rates of Tax

What is the Illinois personal income tax rate?

The Illinois personal income tax rate on individuals is 4.95%. (35 ILCS 5/201(b)(5.4); *Informational Bulletin FY 2018-02*, Illinois Department of Revenue, July 2017)

The tax was imposed at a rate of:

- 3.75% for taxable years beginning on or after January 1, 2015 and before July 1, 2017 (35 ILCS 5/201(b)(5.2) and (5.3)); and

- 5% for tax years 2011-2014. (35 ILCS 5/201(b)(5))

Planning Note: Illinois may adopt graduated income tax rates beginning January 1, 2021. Those rates will take effect only if voters approve an amendment to the Illinois Constitution authorizing graduated rates.

Taxpayers who do not file a joint return will pay tax at the rate of:

- 4.75% on net income of $10,000 or less;

- 4.9% on net income between $10,001 and $100,000;

- 4.95% on net income between $100,001 and $250,000;

- 7.75% on net income between $250,001 and $350,000;

- 7.85% on net income between $350,001 and $750,000; (35 ILCS 201.1(1)) and

- 7.99% on net income over $750,000. (35 ILCS 201.1(2))

Taxpayers who file a joint return will pay tax at the rate of:
- 4.75% on net income of $10,000 or less;
- 4.9% on net income between $10,001 and $100,000;
- 4.95% on net income between $100,001 and $250,000;
- 7.75% on net income between $250,001 and $500,000;
- 7.85% on net income between $500,001 and $1 million; (35 ILCS 201.1(3)) and
- 7.99% on net income over $1 million. (35 ILCS 201.1(4))

If income tax rates change, fiscal year taxpayers must divide total net income between the periods subject to different rates. The apportionment or blended rate method taxes net income as though it was received evenly throughout a single taxable year based on the total number of days in one accounting period and the total number of days in the second accounting period. (35 ILCS 5/202.5(a); *Informational Bulletin FY 2018-14*, Illinois Department of Revenue, November 2017) Taxpayers can make an irrevocable election to use the specific accounting method to treat net income or loss and modifications as though those items were earned in two different taxable years and calculate tax liability at the appropriate rate for each period. (35 ILCS 5/202.5(b); *Informational Bulletin FY 2018-14*, Illinois Department of Revenue, November 2017)

Personal property replacement tax. For the personal property replacement tax rate on the net income of partnerships, trusts, and S corporations, see the Corporate Income Tax Division.

Medical cannabis surcharge. Illinois imposes a surcharge on the federal income tax liability of all taxpayers from the sale or exchange of:
- capital assets;
- depreciable business property;
- real property used in the trade or business; and
- IRC Sec. 197 intangibles of any registrant organization under the Compassionate Use of Medical Cannabis Program. (35 ILCS 5/201(o); 86 Ill. Adm. Code 100.2060)

The surcharge does not apply to S corporations, partnerships, or other pass-through entities. But, the shareholders, partners, or pass-through entity owners must pay the surcharge. (86 Ill. Adm. Code 100.2060(c))

The federal income tax liability from transactions triggering the surcharge means the taxpayer's federal income tax liability for the taxable year, minus the taxpayer's federal income tax liability for the taxable year computed as if the transactions had not been made by the registrant organization. (86 Ill. Adm. Code 100.2060(d)) The taxpayer's surcharge liability for a taxable year is included in the tax liability for which estimated tax payments must be made for that taxable year. (86 Ill. Adm. Code 100.2060(f)(1))

The surcharge does not apply if the medical cannabis registrant's property is transferred because of:
- bankruptcy, a receivership, or a debt adjustment initiated by or against the initial registrant or the initial registrant's owners;
- cancellation, revocation, or termination of any registration by the Illinois Department of Public Health;
- a determination by the Department of Public Health that transfer is in the best interests of Illinois qualifying patients as defined by the Medical Cannabis Pilot Program Act;

- the death of a registrant's equity owner;
- the acquisition of a controlling interest in the stock or substantially all of the assets of a registrant that is a publicly traded company;
- a transfer by a parent company to a wholly owned subsidiary; or
- the transfer or sale to or by one person to another person who were both initial registrant owners. (35 ILCS 5/201(o)(1); 86 Ill. Adm. Code 100.2060(e)(1))

In addition, the surcharge does not apply if the medical cannabis registrant's property, or the controlling interest in a registrant's property, is transferred to:

- lineal descendants in which no gain or loss is recognized; or
- a controlled corporation in which no gain or loss is recognized. (35 ILCS 5/201(o)(2); 86 Ill. Adm. Code 100.2060(e)(2))

Gaming license surcharge. Effective for tax years 2019 through 2027, Illinois imposes an income tax surcharge on the sale or exchange by gaming licensees of:

- capital assets;
- depreciable business property;
- real property used in the trade or business; and
- IRC Sec. 197 intangibles. (35 ILCS 5/201(b-5))

The surcharge equals the amount of the federal income tax liability for the tax year from the sale or exchange. (35 ILCS 5/201(b-5))

The surcharge does not apply if the sale or exchange results from:

- bankruptcy, a receivership, or a debt adjustment by or against the initial licensee or the owners of the initial licensee;
- cancellation, revocation, or termination of the license by Illinois;
- a determination by Illinois that the transfer is in the best interests of state gaming;
- the death of an equity owner in a licensee;
- the acquisition by a public company of a controlling interest in the licensee's stock or assets;
- a transfer by a parent company to a wholly owned subsidiary; or
- the transfer by one person to another person where both were initial license owners. (35 ILCS 5/201(b-5))

It also does not apply to:

- a transfer to lineal descendants in which there is no recognition of gain or loss;
- a transfer under IRC Sec. 351 to a controlled corporation in which there is no recognition of gain or loss; or
- a transfer by a person other than the initial licensee.

[¶15-500]
TAXABLE INCOME COMPUTATION

[¶15-505] Determination of Income

Illinois personal income tax for resident individuals, nonresident individuals, and part-year residents is determined using a federal income tax return starting point, which is modified by Illinois:

— addition adjustments;
— subtraction adjustments; and
— personal exemptions.

The resulting net income of resident taxpayers is multiplied by the Illinois personal income tax rate. Nonresident and part-year resident taxpayers must determine the portion of their net income attributable to Illinois sources before multiplying the amount by the personal income tax rate.

The taxable amount is then adjusted by:

— nonrefundable Illinois credits the taxpayer may claim;

— Illinois household employment tax, use tax on internet, mail order, or other out-of-state purchases, and the medical cannabis surcharge the taxpayer may owe;

— withholding tax and estimated tax payments;

— the refundable Illinois earned income tax credit if the taxpayer is eligible;

— any estimated tax underpayment penalty the taxpayer may owe; and

— any voluntary charitable donations by the taxpayer.

[¶15-510] Starting Point for Computation

The starting point for computing Illinois personal income tax liability for residents, nonresidents, and part-year residents is federal adjusted gross income (AGI) from line 37 of the taxpayer's federal income tax return. (35 ILCS 5/203(a)(1); Instructions, Form IL-1040, Illinois Individual Income Tax Return) Illinois personal income taxpayers must make certain Illinois additions to federal AGI resulting in total base income. Illinois allows certain subtractions from total base income.

[¶15-515] Federal Conformity

Illinois incorporates by reference the Internal Revenue Code of 1986, as amended, and other federal provisions relating to federal income tax laws applicable for the taxable year. (35 ILCS 5/102)

A comparison of key federal and state provisions is located at ¶15-055.

[¶15-535] Personal Exemptions

Does Illinois allow personal exemptions?

Illinois allows a standard income tax exemption for each taxpayer and each individual who qualifies as a taxpayer's dependent. (35 ILCS 5/204(b)(5)) It provides an annual cost-of-living adjustment based on the Consumer Price Index. (35 ILCS 5/204(d-5))

The standard exemption equals:

• $2,275 for the 2019 tax year; (Instructions, Form IL-1040, Individual Income Tax Return)

• $2,225 for the 2018 tax year; (*Informational Bulletin FY 2019-04*, Illinois Department of Revenue, August 2018)

• $2,175 for the 2017 and 2016 tax years; (*Informational Bulletin FY 2016-08*, Illinois Department of Revenue, January 2016; Instructions, Form IL-1040, Illinois Individual Income Tax Return)

• $2,150 for the 2015 tax year; (*Informational Bulletin FY 2016-08*, Illinois Department of Revenue, January 2016) and

• $2,125 for the 2014 tax year. (*Informational Bulletin FY 2014-10*, Illinois Department of Revenue, January 2014)

An additional $1,000 exemption can be claimed by each taxpayer who is:

• 65 or older; and

• blind. (35 ILCS 5/204(d))

Taxpayers cannot claim the personal exemptions if adjusted gross for the tax year is more than:

- $500,000 for taxpayers filing a joint federal return; or
- $250,000 for all other taxpayers. (35 ILCS 5/204(g))

[¶15-540] Standard Deduction

Individuals are not allowed a standard deduction in computing the Illinois income tax.

[¶15-545] Itemized Deductions

Individuals are not allowed the itemized deductions allowed under federal law (e.g., medical expenses, taxes, mortgage interest payments, charitable contributions) in computing the Illinois income tax.

[¶16-000]

TAXABLE INCOME COMPUTATION--ADDITIONS

[¶16-005] Additions to Taxable Income Base

The determination of Illinois personal income tax liability requires addition adjustments to the federal adjusted gross income starting point. The Illinois addition adjustments include:

- bonus depreciation;
- dividend income;
- ABLE savings account distributions and withdrawals;
- education savings account distributions and withdrawals;
- interest income;
- pass-through entity adjustments;
- recovery of tax benefit items;
- related party expenses; and
- taxes.

For a list of Illinois subtraction adjustments, see Subtractions from Taxable Income Base.

[¶16-040] Additions--Depreciation

Does Illinois require an addback of federal bonus depreciation deductions?

Yes, Illinois requires an addback of federal bonus depreciation deductions under IRC Sec. 168(k). (35 ILCS 5/203(a)(2)(D-15))

> *Compliance Alert:* Illinois allows the 100% bonus depreciation deduction enacted by the Tax Cuts and Jobs Act (TCJA). The 100% bonus depreciation deduction applies to qualified property acquired and placed in service after September 27, 2017. (Instructions, Form IL-4562, Special Depreciation) The amount of bonus depreciation allowed under the TCJA for property acquired before September 28, 2017, is:
>
> - 50% if the placed in service in 2017;
> - 40% if placed in service in 2018; and
> - 30% if placed in service in 2019.

The Illinois addition adjustment applies to taxpayers claiming the 40% federal bonus depreciation deduction. (Instructions, Form IL-4562, Special Depreciation)

Individuals who claim a federal bonus depreciation deduction must enter the addition adjustment on Form IL-4562. The depreciation form must be attached to the taxpayers Illinois personal income tax return. (Instructions, Form IL-4562, Special Depreciation)

Illinois allows a subtraction adjustment for a portion of bonus depreciation claimed on a taxpayer's federal income tax return.

Does Illinois require an addback of federal deductions taken for depreciation other than bonus depreciation?

No, Illinois does not require an addback of federal deductions taken for depreciation other than bonus depreciation. (35 ILCS 5/203(a)(2); Instructions, Individual Income Tax Return; Instructions, Schedule M, Other Additions and Subtractions)

Does Illinois require an addback of Sec. 179 asset expense deduction amounts?

No, Illinois does not require an addback of Sec. 179 asset expense deduction amounts. (35 ILCS 5/203(a)(2); Instructions, Individual Income Tax Return; Instructions, Schedule M, Other Additions and Subtractions)

For a list of other Illinois addition adjustments, see Additions to Taxable Income Base.

[¶16-043] Additions--Disability Expenses and Savings Accounts

IRC Sec. 529A established the Achieving a Better Life Experience (ABLE) program. Taxpayers must use ABLE funds for a designated beneficiary's blindness or disability expenses. These include expenses for:

- education, housing, and transportation;
- employment training and support;
- assistive technology and personal support services;
- health, prevention and wellness;
- legal fees;
- oversight and monitoring; and
- funeral and burial.

Illinois allows a subtraction from federal adjusted gross income (AGI) for personal income taxpayers who make contributions to an Illinois ABLE account. It requires addition adjustments to federal AGI for:

- earnings distributed from an ABLE account if the taxpayer excluded those earnings from federal AGI; (35 ILCS 5/203(a)(2)(D-20.5))
- recapture of deductions for Illinois ABLE account contributions if the taxpayer transferred those contributions to an out-of-state plan; (35 ILCS 5/203(a)(2)(D-21.5)) and
- recapture of deductions for Illinois ABLE account contributions if the taxpayer made a nonqualified withdrawal. (35 ILCS 5/203(a)(2)(D-22))

Taxpayers must make the addition adjustments on Schedule M and attach it to their annual Illinois personal income tax return. (Instructions, Schedule M, Other Additions and Subtractions for Individuals)

For a list of other Illinois addition adjustments, see Additions to Taxable Income Base.

[¶16-045] Additions--Dividends

Dividends received by individuals during the taxable year are added back to federal adjusted gross income to the extent they were excluded on the federal return. (35 ILCS 5/203(a)(2)(J); 86 Ill. Adm. Code 100.2480)

Other additions to the taxable income base are listed at ¶16-005.

[¶16-050] Additions--Education Expenses

Applicable to taxable years beginning with 2009, an Illinois addition modification is required in an amount equal to the contribution component of any nonqualified withdrawal or refund from a tuition savings program that was previously deducted from base income and was not used for qualified education expenses at an eligible education institution, if it did not result from the death or disability of the beneficiary. (35 ILCS 5/203(a)(2)(D-22)) More information about Illinois education programs can be found at ¶16-255.

Effective August 10, 2009, taxpayers must add to their adjusted gross income an amount equal to the student assistance contribution credit allowable to the taxpayer under 35 ILCS 5/218(a), determined without regard to 35 ILCS 5/218(c). (35 ILCS 5/203(a)(2)(D-22)) More information about student assistance credit can be found at ¶12-055c

Other additions to the taxable income base are listed at ¶16-005.

[¶16-075] Additions--Interest

Does Illinois require an addback for interest income?

Illinois requires an addback to federal adjusted gross income for interest income. (35 ILCS 5/203(a)(2)(A)) Income from state and local obligations is not exempt from Illinois income tax, except where authorizing legislation specifically provides for an exemption. Income from state and local bonds is not exempt even if the taxpayer owns the bonds indirectly through a mutual fund. (Ill. Adm. Code 100.2470(f); *Publication 101: Income Exempt from Tax*, Illinois Department of Revenue)

Illinois allows a subtraction for exempt interest income.

For a list of other Illinois addition adjustments, see Additions to Taxable Income Base.

[¶16-113] Additions--Pass-Through Entity Adjustments

Illinois requires an addition to federal adjusted gross income for a taxpayer's distributive share of additions from a:

- partnership;

- limited liability company (LLC); and

- S corporation. (Instructions, Schedule M, Other Additions and Subtractions for Individuals)

The taxpayer's Illinois income tax return must include a copy of:

- Illinois Schedule K-1-P that identifies the taxpayer as a partner, shareholder, or member and lists the taxpayer's Social Security number; or

- the notification that specifically details the amount of the taxpayer's distributive share of the pass-through entity's Illinois additions. (Instructions, Schedule M, Other Additions and Subtractions for Individuals)

For a list of other Illinois addition adjustments, see Additions to Taxable Income Base.

[¶16-120] Additions--Recovery of Tax Benefit Items

Illinois an addition adjustment by personal income taxpayers for the amount of recovery of items, including refunds of any state and local income taxes, other than Illinois, deducted under IRC Sec. 111 from federal adjusted gross income. (35 ILCS 5/203(a)(2)(I))

Illinois requires other additions to federal adjusted gross income. (see ¶16-005)

[¶16-125] Additions--Related Party Transactions

Does Illinois require an addback for related party expenses?

Illinois requires an addback to federal adjusted gross income (AGI) for expenses paid to certain related parties. (35 ILCS 5/203(a)(2)(D-17), (D-18), and (D-19); 86 Ill. Adm. Code Sec. 100.2430(a)) The addback applies to:

- interest expenses; (35 ILCS 5/203(a)(2)(D-17); 86 Ill. Adm. Code Sec. 100.2430(a))

- intangible expenses; (35 ILCS 5/203(a)(2)(D-18); 86 Ill. Adm. Code Sec. 100.2430(a)) and

- effective for tax years before 2017, insurance premium expenses. (35 ILCS 5/203(a)(2)(D-19); 86 Ill. Adm. Code Sec. 100.2430(a))

To avoid double taxation, Illinois allows a corresponding subtraction adjustment for the income received from the related party.

Comment: The related party transaction adjustments impact pass-through income reported to individuals by S corporations, partnerships, and limited liability companies (LLCs). The adjustments are made on the pass-through entity's Illinois tax return. The pass-through must report the shareholder's, partner's, or member's distributive share of the adjustments on Schedule K-1-P. If the shareholder, partner, or member is a nonresident, the adjustments apply to the amount of tax that is subject to pass-through entity withholding.

If a taxpayer's business interest deduction is subject to limitation under IRC Sec. 163(j), the taxpayer must use a formula to determine the amount of interest paid to a related party and deducted in computing base income for the tax year. The formula is equal to the business interest paid for the tax year, including any business interest carryforward from a previous tax year, multiplied by a fraction. The fraction is equal to the business interest deduction allowed under IRC Sec. 163(j) divided by the total business interest paid for the tax year. (86 Ill. Adm. Code Sec. 100.2430(b)(10))

Does Illinois provide exceptions to the related party addback?

The interest or intangible expense addback does not apply if:

- the related party is subject to tax in a foreign country or another state on the income received from the taxpayer ;

- the taxpayer can establish by clear and convincing evidence that the addback is unreasonable; or

- the taxpayer received written permission to use an alternative apportionment method. (35 ILCS 5/203(a)(2)(D-17) and (D-18); 86 Ill. Adm. Code Sec. 100.2430(c))

The addback also does not apply if the taxpayer can establish by a preponderance of evidence that:

- the transaction did not have a principal purpose of avoiding federal or Illinois income tax;

- it paid the interest at arm's-length rates and terms; and
- the related party paid interest or intangible expenses to an unrelated party during the same tax year. (35 ILCS 5/203(a)(2)(D-17) and (D-18); 86 Ill. Adm. Code Sec. 100.2430(c))

For a list of other Illinois addition adjustments, see Additions to Taxable Income Base.

[¶16-145] Additions--Taxes

Any Illinois income tax deducted from gross income in the computation of federal adjusted gross income must be added back in computing Illinois base income. However, for individuals, generally, no adjustment will be necessary, since under the federal law, deductions for state personal income taxes are allowed from adjusted gross income, as itemized deductions, rather than from gross income in the computation of adjusted gross income. Illinois income tax refunds included in adjusted gross income for the taxable year are subtracted. There is no modification for tax imposed by other states. (35 ILCS 5/203(a)(2)(B); 35 ILCS 5/203(a)(2)(H))

Other additions to the taxable income base are listed at ¶16-005.

[¶16-200]
TAXABLE INCOME COMPUTATION--SUBTRACTIONS

[¶16-205] Subtractions from Taxable Income Base

Individuals computing Illinois personal income tax liability can subtract from the federal adjusted gross income (AGI) starting point:

- ABLE account contributions;
- claim of right payments;
- college savings account contributions;
- depreciation;
- dividends from high impact and river edge development zone businesses;
- gains on the sale of certain property and securities;
- Illinois tax refunds included in federal adjusted gross income;
- exempt interest income;
- job training program contributions;
- military pay;
- net operating losses (NOLs);
- pass-through entity adjustments;
- reparation payments;
- ridesharing money and benefits; and
- retirement, pension, and Social Security income;

For a list of Illinois addition adjustments, see Additions to Taxable Income Base.

[¶16-225] Subtractions--Claim of Right Adjustment

Taxpayers computing Illinois personal income tax liability can subtract from federal adjusted gross income:

- the deduction used to compute the federal tax credit for restoration of claim of right payments under IRC Sec. 1341; (35 ILCS 5/203(a)(2)(P)) or
- any itemized deduction taken for restoration of amounts held under a claim of right for the tax year. (35 ILCS 5/203(a)(2)(I))

For a list of other Illinois subtractions adjustments, see Subtractions from Taxable Income Base.

[¶16-245] Subtractions--Depreciation

Taxpayers computing Illinois personal income tax liability may subtract a portion of federal bonus depreciation under IRC Sec. 168(k). (35 ILCS 5/203(a)(2)(Z)) However, the Illinois bonus depreciation subtraction adjustment may not be claimed until:

- the last tax year that the taxpayer claims federal regular depreciation on the property; or
- the taxpayer sells, transfers, abandons, or otherwise disposes of the property. (Instructions, Form IL-4562 Special Depreciation)

The subtraction is computed on Form IL-4562 and it is equal to:

- 42.9% of the depreciation on property for which 30% or 50% federal bonus depreciation was claimed in tax years beginning after 2001 and ending on or before December 31, 2005; and
- 100% of the depreciation on property for which 50% federal bonus depreciation was claimed in tax years beginning after December 31, 2005. (35 ILCS 5/203(a)(2)(Z); Instructions, Form IL-4562 Special Depreciation)

Taxpayers claiming a bonus depreciation subtraction adjustment must attach Form IL-4562 and any supporting documents.

Illinois requires an addition adjustment for bonus depreciation (see ¶16-040)

For a list of other Illinois subtractions adjustments, see Subtractions from Taxable Income Base.

[¶16-247] Subtractions--Disability Income

IRC Sec. 529A established the Achieving a Better Life Experience (ABLE) program. Taxpayers computing personal income tax liability can subtract from federal adjusted gross income up to $10,000 of their contribution to an Illinois ABLE account. (35 ILCS 5/203(a)(2)(HH)) A taxpayer can claim the deduction for contributions each tax year:

- beginning on or after January 1, 2018; and
- before January 1, 2023. (35 ILCS 5/203(a)(2)(HH))

Illinois treats employer contributions and employee matching contributions as made by the employee. (35 ILCS 5/203(a)(2)(HH))

IRC Sec. 529 and IRC Sec. 529A permit taxpayers to exclude from their federal gross income:

- rollover distributions from a 529 education savings account to an ABLE account; and
- rollover distributions from one ABLE account to another ABLE account.

Illinois taxpayers cannot include the rollover amounts in calculating their deductible ABLE contribution. (35 ILCS 5/203(a)(2)(HH))

Taxpayers can claim the ABLE deduction by completing Schedule M and attaching it to their annual Illinois personal income tax return. (Instructions, Schedule M, Other Additions and Subtractions for Individuals)

Illinois requires addition adjustments for:

- rollovers to out-of-state ABLE accounts;
- distributions from out-of-state accounts; and
- nonqualfied withdrawals.

For a list of other Illinois subtractions adjustments, see Subtractions from Taxable Income Base.

[¶16-255] Subtractions--Education Expenses

States offer state tax incentives to pay for college in two forms: prepaid tuition programs and college savings plans. Illinois authorizes a prepaid tuition program, *College Illinois!, and* a college savings plan, Bright Start. Under IRC Sec. 529, college savings plans, such as Bright Start, are exempt from federal income tax under the Economic Growth and Tax Relief Reconciliation Act of 2001 (The law allowing federal tax-free qualified withdrawals is set to expire on December 31, 2010).

Participants in these programs receive federal tax exemption on the investment earnings of the accounts when the funds are used to pay for qualified higher education expenses including tuition, room and board, books and fees, and any other expenses that students are required to pay to attend any accredited college or university in the United States.

A taxpayer must include amounts excluded from his or her federal gross income for *distributions* received from qualified federal tuition programs other than the Illinois Prepaid Tuition Trust Fund, *College Illinois!,* or the Illinois College Savings Pool. The taxpayer's Illinois adjusted gross income must be increased by these amounts. In addition, amounts *contributed* to a College Savings Pool, except amounts excluded from federal adjusted gross income, may be deducted from Illinois adjusted gross income. (35 ILCS 5/203(a)(2)(D-15))

For taxable years beginning on or after January 1, 2005, a maximum of $10,000 per taxable year may be deducted from a taxpayer's adjusted gross income for amounts contributed to a College Savings Pool or the Illinois Prepaid Tuition Trust Fund. For purposes of this deduction, contributions made by an employer on behalf of an employee, or matching contributions made by an employee, must be treated as made by the employee. (35 ILCS 5/203(a)(2)(Y)) However, amounts excluded from federal gross income under IRC Sec. 529 will not be considered moneys contributed for purposes of the deduction.

For taxable years beginning on or after January 1, 2007, distributions from qualified tuition programs under the IRC administered by other states are exempt from the requirement that a distribution from an IRC qualified tuition program be included when determining adjusted gross income for purposes of determining base income. Taxpayers must add an amount equal to the amount previously deducted for deposits into a qualified tuition program to their base income, provided the moneys are transferred from a qualified tuition program that is administered by Illinois to an out-of-state program. (35 ILCS 5/203(a)(2)(D-21))

• *College Illinois prepaid tuition program*

Tax treatment.—Under *College Illinois!,* the accrued earnings of an Illinois pre-paid tuition contract are exempt from personal income and all other taxation pro-vided that disbursements are used for educational purposes in accordance with the prepaid tuition contract. (110 ILCS 979/55) A prepaid tuition plan is available for attendance at a public university, public community college, and a combination of two years at a community college and two years at a public university. Relatives and non-relatives of the beneficiary may contribute under the contract. The amount contributed under the prepaid tuition contract will vary depending on its terms. (110 ILCS 979/45)

A "qualified beneficiary" is anyone who has been a resident of Illinois for at least 12 months prior to the date of the contract; a nonresident of Illinois, as long as the purchaser has been a resident of Illinois for at least 12 months; or any person less than a year old whose parent or legal guardian has been a resident of Illinois for at least 12 months. (110 ILCS 979/10)

A "prepaid tuition contract" is entered into between the state and a purchaser to provide for the higher education expenses of a beneficiary. The contract can be purchased by lump sum or by installments. The terms of the contract will vary, but must contain provisions for (1) refunds or withdrawals; (2) conversion of the contract from distributions from one type of eligible institution to another; (3) portability of the accrued value for use at an out-of-state institution; (4) transferability of contract benefits to a beneficiary's immediate family member; and, (5) a specified benefit period during which the contract can be redeemed. (110 ILCS 979/45; 110 ILCS 979/10)

The prepaid tuition contract must also contain (110 ILCS 979/45):

— the amount of payment and number of payments required from a purchaser on behalf of a beneficiary;

— the terms and conditions under which the purchasers shall remit payments, including the date that the payments are due;

— provisions for late payment;

— the name, birthday, and social security number of the qualified beneficiary;

— the name and social security number of any person who can terminate the contract, and the terms and conditions under which the contract can be terminated; and

— the time limitations the qualified beneficiary must claim the benefits.

Contract purchases are limited to 135 hours at an Illinois public university and 60 5B8 credit hours for an Illinois community college. (110 ILCS 979/45)

Withdrawals.—Non-qualified withdrawals are subject to a 10% penalty tax withheld on earnings. In addition, personal income tax will be assessed against the purchaser at the purchaser's tax rate.

Monies paid out of the plan are exempt from all claims of creditors of the purchaser or beneficiary, so long as the contract has not been terminated. (110 ILCS 979/45)

Nonresidents.—Nonresidents can be beneficiaries of a prepaid tuition contract, provided that the contract purchaser has been an Illinois resident for at least 12 months prior to the date of the contract. (110 ILCS 979/10)

Penalties.—Generally, no refund shall exceed the amount paid for the prepaid tuition contract. However, in the event that the qualified beneficiary dies or becomes totally disabled, the amount contributed under the prepaid tuition contract will be refunded to the purchaser together with all accrued earnings. In addition, no refund will be provided for any semester partially attended but not completed. (110 ILCS 979/45)

Transferability.—The prepaid tuition plan may be converted from a public university plan to a community college plan, or vice versa. (110 ILCS 979/45)

In addition, the contract terms may specify the condition under which the prepaid tuition contract can be transferred to a family member of the qualified beneficiary. (110 ILCS 979/45)

Portability.—The qualified beneficiary may apply the benefits of the prepaid tuition contract toward an out-of-state college or university. However, the benefits of the prepaid tuition contract cannot be used at any postsecondary institution operated for profit and located outside Illinois. If the qualified beneficiary transfers to an eligible out-of-state institution, the contract will be converted for use by referencing the current average mean-weighted credit hour value of registration fees purchased under the contract. (110 ILCS 979/45)

• *Bright Start college savings plan (IRC Sec. 529)*

The Illinois *Bright Start* college savings pool plan is administered by the Illinois State Treasurer. The funds can be used for qualified post-secondary education expenses, including tuition, fees, and the costs of books. Certain room and board expenses qualify. The funds are paid into the College Savings Pool to supplement and enhance investment.

Contributions.—Contributions to an Illinois *Bright Start* savings plan can be deducted from Illinois personal income tax. The minimum contribution to open a *Bright Start* account is $25; however there is no minimum on contributions made pursuant to employee payroll deductions. The maximum yearly contribution to a savings plan is $55,000 per beneficiary ($110,000 for married couples) in the first year of a five year period to avoid estate and/or gift tax consequences. In addition, contributions may be limited based on the actuarial estimate of the cost of tuition, fees, and room and board for a five years of undergraduate study. In addition, the contributions made on behalf of a beneficiary who is also a beneficiary under the prepaid college tuition program will be restricted to ensure that the combined contributions do not exceed the limit established by the College Savings Pool. Contributions can be made by relatives and non-relatives

---

CCH COMMENT: The "Bright Start" College Savings Pool is the only IRC Sec. 529 college savings plan for which Illinois taxpayers may deduct contributions made during the tax year. However, if contributions were made by rolling over funds from another college savings program into a "Bright Start" account, the taxpayer must exclude (from the deduction) any income that was earned in the other savings program. (*Instructions, Form IL-1040, Illiniois Individual Income Tax Return*) The "Bright Star" College Savings Pool deduction is claimed on Schedule M, line 10a.

Monies from the savings plan can be used at any accredited college or university in the U.S., including graduate schools, community colleges, and accredited vocational and technical schools. (15 ILCS 505/16.5)

Beginning on or after January 1, 2005, contributions to the Bright Start Program may be counted against the financial aid awarded by the Illinois Student Assistance Commission, Illinois, or any agency of Illinois. (15 ILCS 505/16.5)

Earnings.—Earnings are free from Illinois personal and federal income tax. (15 ILCS 505/16.5)

Withdrawals.—Qualified distributions from the savings plan for qualified expenses will be paid directly to the eligible educational institution. (15 ILCS 505/16.5)

Nonresidents.—There are no residency restrictions on who can participate and/or be a designated beneficiary of a *Bright Start* account. (15 ILCS 505/16.5)

Penalties.—Any distribution made from the college savings plan used for expenses other than qualified expenses will be subject to a 10% penalty of the earnings, unless the beneficiary dies, becomes disabled, or receives a scholarship. Penalties will be withheld at the time the distribution is made. (15 ILCS 505/16.5)

Transferability.—If you are the custodian for the beneficiary, you may elect to place part or all of the UTMA/UGMA assets into a Bright Start Account. When transferring UGMA/UTMA assets they must be liquidated since only cash contributions are permitted into a college savings account. www.brightstartsavings.com

¶16-255

Bright Start.—Allows the participant to change the beneficiary at any time, provided that your new beneficiary is a family member of the original beneficiary. (15 ILCS 505/16.5)

Portability.—Monies from the *Bright Start* account can be used at any "eligible educational institution" as defined by the federal Higher Education Act of 1965, 20 U.S.C. 1088, and are eligible to participate in Department of Education student aid programs. (15 ILCS 505/16.5)

•Nursing Home Grant Assistance Act deduction was allowed for one taxable year beginning after January 1, 1994, for recipients of grants under the Nursing Home Grant Assistance Act during taxable years 1992 and 1993. (35 ILCS 5/203(a)(2)(U)) The amount of the deduction equaled the amount of income tax paid on the grant amount.

Caution Note: The Illinois Supreme Court has determined that Public Act 88-669 (effective November 29, 1994), which enacted 35 ILCS 5/203(a)(2)(U), was enacted in violation of the single-subject requirement of the Illinois Constitution and, therefore, is void in its entirety. *People of the State of Illinois v. Olender*, Illinois Supreme Court, December 15, 2005. That section was reenacted by P.A. 1074 (S.B. 3088), Laws 2006, effective December 26, 2006.

Other subtractions from the taxable income base are listed at ¶ 16-205.

[¶ 16-270] Subtractions--Gains

In computing base income for Illinois purposes, certain capital gains on employer securities received in a lump-sum distribution and capital gains resulting from appreciation of certain property acquired before August 1, 1969 may be subtracted from federal adjusted gross income.

• *Sales of employer's securities*

Capital gains on employer securities received in a lump-sum distribution from a qualified employee pension, profit-sharing, or stock bonus plan, to the extent the gains are due to net unrealized appreciation on the securities at the time of distribution and included in federal adjusted gross income may be subtracted from federal adjusted gross income for Illinois net income tax purposes. The subtraction is entered on Form IL-1040, Step 3, line 5. (Instructions, Form IL-1040, Illinois Individual Income Tax Return)

• *Sale of Pre-August 1, 1969 acquired property*

The portion of capital gain attributable to appreciation on pre-August 1, 1969 acquired property may be subtracted from federal adjusted gross income in computing the income base for Illinois purposes. (35 ILCS 5/203(a)(2)(G))

The capital gain attributable to pre-August 1, 1969, appreciation (the "valuation limitation amount") is equal to:

(1) the pre-August 1, 1969, appreciation recaptured federally for the taxable year (35 ILCS 5/203(f)(1)(A)); plus

(2) the lesser of:

— the federal capital gain for the tax year attributable to pre-August 1, 1969, appreciation; or

— the net capital gain for the tax year reduced by capital gains recognized federally from distributions from public retirement plans, individual retirement accounts, retirement bonds, and payments to retired partners. (35 ILCS 5/203(f)(1)(B))

If the fair market value of property was readily ascertainable on August 1, 1969, the "pre-August 1, 1969, appreciation amount" is the lesser of:

(1) the excess of the August 1, 1969, value over the federal basis of the property on that date; or

(2) the total gain reportable federally with respect to the property. (35 ILCS 5/203(f)(2)(A))

If the fair market value of property was not readily ascertainable on August 1, 1969, the "pre-August 1, 1969, appreciation amount" is computed by multiplying the federal gain by the ratio of:

(1) the number of full calendar months in the holding period of the property ending July 31, 1969, to

(2) the number of full calendar months in the entire holding period. (35 ILCS 5/203(f)(2)(B))

The subtraction for capital gain attributable to appreciation on pre-August 1, 1969 acquired property is entered on Form IL-1040, Schedule M, line 19. Illinois Schedule F, which is used to compute the amount of the subtraction, must be attached to the Illinois return along with copies of federal Form 1040, Schedule D and, if filed, federal Forms 4797 and 6252. (Instructions, Form IL-1040, Illinois Individual Income Tax Return)

Other subtractions from the taxable income base are listed at ¶ 16-205.

[¶16-280] Subtractions--Interest

Does Illinois allow a subtraction for interest income?

Illinois allows a subtraction from federal adjusted gross income for interest income from:

- tax exempt federal obligations; and
- tax exempt Illinois obligations. (35 ILCS 5/203(a)(2)(N); Ill. Adm. Code 100.2470(a))

The subtraction is net of bond premium amortization. (35 ILCS 5/203(a)(2)(N); Ill. Adm. Code 100.2470(a))

What federal obligations are exempt from taxation?

The subtraction for interest income from tax exempt federal obligations applies to:

- U.S. Treasury bonds, notes, bills, certificates, and savings bonds; and
- GSA Public Building Trust Participation Certificates: First Series, Series A through E; Second Series, Series F; Third Series, Series G; Fourth Series H and I. (Ill. Adm. Code 100.2470(b); *Publication 101, Income Exempt from Tax*, Illinois Department of Revenue)

It also applies to interest income from notes, bonds, debentures, and other obligations issued by:

- Banks for Cooperatives;
- the Commodity Credit Corporation;
- the Farm Credit System Financial Assistance Corporation;
- the Federal Deposit Insurance Corporation;
- Federal Farm Credit Banks;
- Federal Home Loan Banks;
- Federal Intermediate Credit Banks;

- the Federal Land Banks and Federal Land Bank Association;
- the Federal Savings and Loan Insurance Corporation;
- the Financing Corporation (FICO);
- the General Insurance Fund;
- the Mutual Mortgage Insurance Fund;
- the National Credit Union Administration Central Liquidity Facility;
- the Production Credit Association;
- the Railroad Retirement Act;
- the Railroad Unemployment Insurance Act;
- the Resolution Funding Corporation;
- the Special Food Service Program;
- the Student Loan Marketing Association;
- the Tennessee Valley Authority;
- the U.S. Postal Service;
- American Samoa, Guam, the Northern Mariana Islands, Puerto Rico, and the Virgin Islands. (Ill. Adm. Code 100.2470(c); *Publication 101, Income Exempt from Tax*, Illinois Department of Revenue)

Illinois does not have a provision that exempts interest income from all federal obligations. (Ill. Adm. Code 100.2470(h); *Publication 101, Income Exempt from Tax*, Illinois Department of Revenue) The subtraction does not apply to interest income from:

- the Government National Mortgage Association (GNMA);
- the Federal National Mortgage Association (FNMA);
- the Federal Home Loan Mortgage Corporation (FHLMC); and
- Federal Home Loan Banks. (Ill. Adm. Code 100.2470(h); *Publication 101, Income Exempt from Tax*, Illinois Department of Revenue)

It also does not apply to income from U.S. securities acquired by a taxpayer under a repurchase agreement with a bank or similar financial organization. Illinois treats the agreement as a loan. (Ill. Adm. Code 100.2470(h); *Publication 101, Income Exempt from Tax*, Illinois Department of Revenue)

What Illinois obligations are exempt from taxation?

The subtraction for interest income from tax exempt Illinois obligations applies to:

- Illinois Housing Development Authority notes and bonds, except those for housing-related commercial facilities;
- Export Development Act bonds;
- certain Illinois Development Finance Authority bonds;
- Quad Cities Regional Economic Development Authority bonds and notes that it determines are exempt;
- College Savings bonds;
- Illinois Sports Facilities Authority bonds;
- Higher Education Student Assistance Act bonds and notes;
- Rural Bond Bank Act bonds and notes;
- Quad Cities Interstate Metropolitan Authority bonds;
- Southwestern Illinois Development Authority bonds;

- certain Illinois Finance Authority bonds;

- Illinois Power Agency bonds;

- Central Illinois Economic Development Authority bonds;

- Eastern Illinois Economic Development Authority bonds;

- Southeastern Illinois Economic Development Authority bonds;

- Southern Illinois Economic Development Authority bonds;

- Upper Illinois River Valley Development Authority bonds;

- Illinois Urban Development Authority bonds;

- Western Illinois Economic Development Authority bonds;

- Downstate Illinois Sports Facilities Authority bonds;

- Will-Kankakee Regional Development Authority bonds;

- Tri-County River Valley Development Authority bonds; (Ill. Adm. Code 100.2470(f); *Publication 101, Income Exempt from Tax*, Illinois Department of Revenue)

- New Harmony Bridge Authority bonds; and

- New Harmony Bridge Bi-State Commission bonds. (*Publication 101, Income Exempt from Tax*, Illinois Department of Revenue)

Does Illinois allow a subtraction for mutual fund distributions?

Illinois allows a subtraction for distributions from mutual funds that invest exclusively in tax exempt federal obligations. If the mutual fund invests in both exempt and nonexempt federal obligations, the subtraction applies to the distribution that the mutual fund identifies as exempt. (Ill. Adm. Code 100.2470(d); *Publication 101, Income Exempt from Tax*, Illinois Department of Revenue)

If the fund does not identify an exempt amount, a taxpayer can figure the subtraction by using a fraction. The numerator of the fraction is the amount invested by the fund in state-exempt U.S. obligations. The denominator is the fund's total investment. (Ill. Adm. Code 100.2470(d); *Publication 101, Income Exempt from Tax*, Illinois Department of Revenue)

A taxpayer can use the year-end amounts to figure the fraction if the percentage ratio remained constant throughout the year. If the percentage ratio has not remained constant, the taxpayer can use the average of the ratios from the fund's quarterly financial reports. (Ill. Adm. Code 100.2470(d); *Publication 101, Income Exempt from Tax*, Illinois Department of Revenue)

Does Illinois exempt other investment income?

Illinois allows a subtraction from federal AGI for investment income from the Home Ownership Made Easy (HOME) Program. (310 ILCS 55/5.1(f))

How do taxpayers determine and report the subtraction adjustments?

Taxpayers must determine and report the subtraction adjustments for exempt interest and investment income on:

- the specified lines of their Illinois income tax return; and

- Schedule M. (*Publication 101, Income Exempt from Tax*, Illinois Department of Revenue; Instructions, Schedule M, Other Additions and Subtractions for Individuals)

For a list of other Illinois subtractions adjustments, see Subtractions from Taxable Income Base.

[¶16-295] Subtractions--Job Programs or Employee Benefits

Taxpayers computing Illinois personal income tax liability can subtract from federal adjusted gross income (AGI) contributions made under the "Tax Increment Allocation Redevelopment Act" to a job training project. (35 ILCS 5/203(a)(2)(O)) Illinois also allows a subtraction from federal AGI for ridesharing money and benefits received by a driver in a motor vehicle ridesharing arrangement. (35 ILCS 5/203(a)(2)(BB))

For a list of other Illinois subtractions adjustments, see Subtractions from Taxable Income Base.

[¶16-308] Subtractions--Military Pay

Pay received for active duty in the U.S. Armed Forces or for annual training in the Illinois National Guard (or, beginning with taxable years ending on or after December 31, 2007, the National Guard of any state). (35 ILCS 5/203(a)(2)(E)) is exempt from Illinois income tax and is subtracted from federal adjusted gross income. Effective August 3, 2001, for taxable years ending on or after December 31, 2001, any compensation paid to a member of the Illinois National Guard (or, beginning with taxable years ending on or after December 31, 2007, the National Guard of any state) may be deducted from adjusted gross income. (35 ILCS 5/203(a)(2)(E)) The exemption also applies to pay received for full-time active duty for serving in the U.S. Armed Forces Reserves or a National Guard Unit, including the ROTC, and to income received for full-time duty as a cadet at the U.S. Military, Air Force, and Coast Guard academies or as a midshipman at the U.S. Naval Academy. Pay earned at weekly or monthly training meetings of the Reserves or National Guard is not exempt and may not be subtracted. The following income is also subject to taxation: (1) pay for duty as an officer in the Public Health Service; (2) pay received under the Voluntary Separation Incentive Program; (3) payments made under the Ready Reserve Mobilization Income Insurance Program, and (4) pay received from the military as a civilian. (35 ILCS 5/203(a)(2)(E); *Publication 102*, Illinois Department of Revenue, January 2009)

The tax treatment of military personnel is discussed at ¶15-175.

•*Military personnel serving in Bosnia*

All military income of personnel serving in Operation Joint Endeavor in Bosnia-Herzegovinia, Croatia, and Macedonia, that is exempted from taxation under the Internal Revenue Code by congressional action will be exempt from Illinois taxation under the Illinois Income Tax Act. (*Executive Order No. 2 (1996)*, Governor Jim Edgar, filed in the Office of the Secretary of State, March 27, 1996)

•*Bonuses paid to Gulf War veterans*

Federal and state bonuses paid to Persian Gulf war veterans are subtractable from federal adjusted gross income. (35 ILCS 5/203(a)(2)(R))

Other subtractions from the taxable income base are listed at ¶16-205.

[¶16-310] Subtractions--Net Operating Loss

In general, Illinois allows taxpayers to take the same net operating loss carryback or carryforward deduction allowed under IRC Sec. 172. (Instructions, Form IL-1040-X, Illinois Amended Individual Income Tax Return) Taxpayers can include their federal NOL deduction in the starting point for computing Illinois personal income tax liability. However, a taxpayer must reduce that amount by any carryback to an earlier tax year. (Instructions, Form IL-1040, Individual Income Tax Return)

Illinois does not allow taxpayers to deduct the same NOL twice. (35 ILCS 5/203(g)) Thus, it limits the deduction to the federal NOL deduction allowed for that tax year minus any carryforward that remains for later tax years. (86 Ill. Adm. Code 100.2410(a)(1); Instructions, Form IL-1040-X, Illinois Amended Individual Income Tax Return)

Finally, the NOL deduction cannot reduce Illinois adjusted gross income to less than zero for the tax year. Taxpayers can use negative income to offset net addition modifications for the tax year, but only if the taxpayer has not carried back and deducted it as a loss or deduction in an earlier tax year. The sum of carryover deductions for all years, plus the offset, also cannot exceed the amount of the loss. Illinois requires an addback for the amount that exceeds the loss. (86 Ill. Adm. Code 100.2410(c)(1))

> *Example:* Taxpayer's adjusted gross income for 2017 results in a loss of $10,000. The taxpayer carries back $5,000 to prior years as federal net operating loss deductions. The taxpayer's 2017 addition modifications exceed subtraction modifications by $7,000. The taxpayer's base income for 2017 equals $2,000 (-$10,000 minus $5,000 plus $7,000). The taxpayer used up the loss for Illinois income tax purposes and cannot carry any of the loss forward. The taxpayer must addback any carryforward deduction claimed for the 2017 loss in a later tax year.

[¶16-317] Subtractions--Pass-Through Entity Adjustments

Illinois allows a subtraction from federal adjusted gross income for a taxpayer's distributive share of subtractions from a:

- partnership;
- limited liability company (LLC); and
- S corporation. (Instructions, Schedule M, Other Additions and Subtractions for Individuals)

The taxpayer's Illinois income tax return must include a copy of:

- Illinois Schedule K-1-P that identifies the taxpayer as a partner, shareholder, or member and lists the taxpayer's Social Security number; or
- the notification that specifically details the amount of the taxpayer's distributive share of the pass-through entity's Illinois subtractions. (Instructions, Schedule M, Other Additions and Subtractions for Individuals)

For a list of other Illinois subtraction adjustments, see Subtractions from Taxable Income Base.

[¶16-330] Subtractions--Related Party Transactions

Does Illinois allow subtraction adjustments for income from related parties?

Illinois requires an addition to federal adjusted gross (AGI) for expenses paid to certain related parties. It provides corresponding subtraction adjustments to ensure that the addition adjustments do not result in double taxation. (86 Ill. Adm. Code Sec. 100.2430(a))

> *Comment:* The related party transaction adjustments impact pass-through income reported to individuals by S corporations, partnerships, and limited liability companies (LLCs). The adjustments are made on the pass-through entity's Illinois tax return. The pass-through must report the shareholder's, partner's, or member's distributive share of the adjustments on Schedule K-1-P. If the shareholder, partner, or member is a nonresident, the adjustments apply to the amount of tax that is subject to pass-through entity withholding.

The subtraction from federal AGI applies to:

- interest income received from each related party; (35 ILCS 5/203(a)(2)(DD); 86 Ill. Adm. Code Sec. 100.2430(d)(3))

- intangible income received from each related party; (35 ILCS 5/203(a)(2)(EE); 86 Ill. Adm. Code Sec. 100.2430(d)(4)) and

- effective for tax years before 2017, insurance reimbursements received from each related party. (35 ILCS 5/203(a)(2)(GG); 86 Ill. Adm. Code Sec. 100.2430(d)(6))

Illinois limits the subtraction adjustment to the amount of addition adjustment for interest, intangible expenses, and insurance premiums paid to the related party. It is also net of any deduction for related expenses. (35 ILCS 5/203(a)(2)(DD) and (EE); 86 Ill. Adm. Code Sec. 100.2430(d))

For a list of other Illinois subtraction adjustments, see Subtractions from Taxable Income Base.

[¶16-335] Subtractions--Reparation Payments

*Settlement Payments to Holocaust Victims*For tax years beginning in 1999, Holocaust victims may deduct settlement payments from their income to the extent such amounts are includible in their federal adjusted gross income. The deduction applies to distributions or income received by individuals, trusts, and estates as a result of the their status as a victim or descendant of a victim of Nazi persecution. A victim of Nazi persecution is defined as an individual persecuted for racial or religious reasons by Nazi Germany or any other Axis regime. (35 ILCS 5/203(a)(2)(X))

A taxpayer who is a victim or a descendant of a victim of racial or religious persecution by Nazi Germany or any of its World War II allies is eligible to take this subtraction if they received compensation for persecution or for resulting losses, and that compensation is included in their federal adjusted gross income. (*Informational Bulletin FY 2000-15*, Department of Revenue, January 2000)

Taxpayers may include:

(1) compensation received by the taxpayer because of racial or religious persecution;

(2) any payments and items of income received by the taxpayer for property stolen, taken, or lost as a result of persecution; and

(3) interest received from the taxpayer's insurance policies covering losses incurred as the result of persecution. (*Informational Bulletin FY 2000-15*, Department of Revenue, January 2000)

This subtraction does not apply to gains from assets acquired with the compensation or proceeds from the sale of the original assets, and is only allowed to the taxpayer who was the first recipient of the compensation and was a victim of persecution.

The subtraction for Holocaust reparations is entered on Form IL-1040, Schedule M, line 28. (*Instructions, Form IL-1040, Schedule M, Other Additions and Subtractions*)

Awards for Time Unjustly Served in Prison Illinois allows a deduction in an amount equal to any amount awarded to the taxpayer during the taxable year by the Court of Claims for time unjustly served in a state prison (35 ILCS 5/203(a)(2)(FF))

Other subtractions from the taxable income base are listed at ¶16-205.

[¶16-345] Subtractions--Retirement Plans and Benefits

Conversions From Regular IRAs to Roth IRAs.—For tax years beginning after 1997, the amount included in an individual's federal gross income from a conversion of a regular IRA to a Roth IRA is subtracted from the individual's federal adjusted gross income in computing base income for purposes of the Illinois personal income tax. Sunset date provisions do not apply to this subtraction modification. (35 ILCS 5/203(a)(2)(W))

• *Social Security and Railroad Retirement Benefits*

Social security and railroad retirement benefits included in federal adjusted income that are paid to individuals are subtracted from federal adjusted gross income. (35 ILCS 5/203(a)(2)(L))

• *Pension, Profit-Sharing, Retirement, and Accelerated Payments of Life, Endowment, or Annuity Benefits Used to Indemnify Terminal Illnesses*

Income received by individuals from the following sources is subtracted, to the extent that it has been included in federal adjusted gross income (and excluded in computing net earnings from self-employment under IRC Sec. 1402):

—qualified employee benefit plan ("qualified" is defined in IRC Secs. 402-408 or Sec. 457) and retirement plans (however, ordinary income from a qualified retirement plan that has been elected under the "Special 10-Year Averaging Method" or "Special 5-Year Averaging Method" on U.S. Form 4972, *Tax on Lump-Sum Distributions* may not be subtracted),

—distributions from individual retirement accounts (IRAs), including Roth IRAs,

—a self-employed retirement (H.R. 10/Keogh) plan,

—or a 401(k) plan,

—a lump-sum distribution of appreciated employer securities,

—retirement payments to retired partners,

—railroad retirement income,

—the redemption of U.S. retirement bonds,

—a government retirement or government disability plan, including military plans,

—payments received from life insurance proceeds to the extent they are included in federal adjusted gross income policy,

—an endowment,

—or an annuity that are used as an indemnity for a terminal illness. (35 ILCS 5/203(a)(2)(F); 35 ILCS 5/203(a)(2)(Q))

Ordinary income from a qualified retirement plan for which the special federal ten-year averaging method is elected on the federal return is not subtracted on the Illinois return. (Instructions, Form IL-1040, Illinois Individual Income Tax Return)

The following forms or schedules must be attached to the Illinois return to substantiate the subtraction of retirement payments (Instructions, Form IL-1040, Illinois Individual Income Tax Return):

For pension and annuity payments, redemption of U.S. retirement bonds, government disability income, Social Security, railroad retirement payment, IRA distribution, and retirement to retired partners, attach federal U.S. Form 1040 or U.S. 1040A, page 1;

¶16-345

For lump-sum distributions (cash or property), such as employer securities, retirement income, endowment or life insurance contracts, be sure to attach federal Form 1040, page 1, and Schedule D, including both ordinary income and capital gains income included on U.S. 1040, page 1; and

For gain on sale or exchange of employer's securities, attach federal U.S. Form 1040, Schedule D, and Illinois Form IL-4644.

Any W-2 and 1099–R forms must also be attached.

• *IRC Sec. 457 plans*

Although IRC Sec. 457 relates to deferred compensation plans of state and local government agencies and tax-exempt organizations, the Illinois subtraction applies only to government agencies and does not apply to payments under employee benefit plans of tax-exempt organizations.

CCH COMMENT: U.S. 1040 or U.S. 1040A, page 1, and Form W-2 showing the amount of state and local governmental deferred compensation paid under IRC Sec. 457 must be attached to the Illinois return to show that the income is subtractable. (Instructions, Form IL-1040, Illinois Individual Income Tax Return)

• *Federally-taxed income that may not be subtracted*

Income received as third-party sick pay, nongovernment disability plans, or nongovernment deferred compensation plans, which are not qualified employee benefit plans, may not be included in the subtraction. (Instructions, Form IL-1040, Illinois Individual Income Tax Return)

Other subtractions from the taxable income base are listed at ¶ 16-205.

[¶16-350] Subtractions--Targeted Business Activity or Zones

Individuals computing Illinois personal income tax liability can subtract from the federal adjusted gross income (AGI) dividends received from:

 • corporations that conduct substantially all of its business operations in an Illinois river edge redevelopment zone; (35 ILCS 5/203(a)(2)(I); 86 Ill. Adm. Code Sec. 100.2480) and

 • corporations designated as a "High Impact Business"" that conduct business operations in a federally designated foreign trade zone or sub-zone located in Illinois. (35 ILCS 5/203(a)(2)(K); 86 Ill. Adm. Code Sec. 100.2490)

Taxpayers can claim the subtraction adjustments by completing Schedule 1299-C and attaching it to their annual Illinois personal income tax return. (Instructions, Schedule 1299-C, Income Tax Subtractions and Credits for Individuals)

For a list of other Illinois subtractions adjustments, see Subtractions from Taxable Income Base.

[¶16-360] Subtractions--Taxes

Taxpayers computing personal income tax liability can subtract Illinois income tax refunds included in federal adjusted gross income for the tax year. (35 ILCS 5/203(a)(2)(H))

Illinois allows a credit for taxes paid to other states.

For a list of other Illinois subtractions adjustments, see Subtractions from Taxable Income Base.

[¶16-500]
SOURCING RULES

[¶16-505] Income Attributable to State Sources

Nonresidents (35 ILCS 5/301(c)) and part-year residents (35 ILCS 5/301(c)) must determine the portion of income and deductions from Illinois sources using allocation and apportionment rules. Illinois sourcing rules apply to:

- business income;
- income from intangibles;
- beneficiary income;
- retirement and pension income;
- property-related income;
- gains and losses;
- pass-through entity income and deductions;
- compensation for personal services; and
- Illinois lottery prizes.

[¶16-515] Sourcing of Business Income

Nonresidents who receive income from business conducted entirely in Illinois must source or allocate that income to the state. A nonresident who receives income from business conducted in and outside Illinois must source that income to the state using an apportionment formula. (35 ILCS 5/304(a); 86 Ill. Adm. Code 100.3310)

What is business income?

Business income is all income that is apportionable among the states in which the taxpayer is doing business without violating the U.S. Constitution. (35 ILCS 5/1501(a)(1); 86 Ill. Adm. Code 100.3010(a)(2)) It does not include:

- deductions related to business income; or
- wages or other compensation. (35 ILCS 5/1501(a)(1); 86 Ill. Adm. Code 100.3010(a)(3))

Nonbusiness income is all income other than business income or compensation. (35 ILCS 5/1501(a)(14); 86 Ill. Adm. Code 100.3010(a)(3)(B)) A nonresident's income from trade or business is business income unless clearly classifiable as nonbusiness income. (86 Ill. Adm. Code 100.3010(a)(3))

A nonresident who changes the classification of either business or nonbusiness income must disclose the change. (86 Ill. Adm. Code 100.3340)

Can nonresidents treat all income as business income?

Nonresidents can make a binding election to treat all income, other than compensation, as business income. (35 ILCS 5/1501(a)(1); 86 Ill. Adm. Code 100.3015(a)) A nonresident can make the election on:

- the original return for the tax year to which the election applies; or
- an amended return before the original or extended due date for the return. (86 Ill. Adm. Code 100.3015(b))

A nonresident can also file an amended return to revoke an election on the original return. But, a nonresident cannot revoke an election made on an original return after the extended due date for the return. (86 Ill. Adm. Code 100.3015(b))

[¶16-515a] Sourcing of Business Income--Apportionment Formula

Nonresidents must source income from business conducted both in and outside Illinois using a single sales factor apportionment formula. (35 ILCS 5/304(h))

[¶16-515d] Sourcing of Business Income--Sales Factor

The Illinois sales factor measures the ratio of a nonresident's total sales in Illinois to total sales everywhere during the tax year. (35 ILCS 5/304(a)(3)(A)) Illinois generally follows market-based sourcing rules for business income from most sales of other than tangible property.

What sales or receipts do nonresidents include in the sales factor?

"Sales" means as all gross receipts that a nonresident does not allocate to the state. This includes the nonresident's gross receipts from transactions and activity in the regular course of its trade or business. (35 ILCS 5/1501(a)(21); 86 Ill. Adm. Code Sec. 100.3370(a)(1))

Compliance Tip: A nonresident may request an alternative apportionment method if the determination of "sales" does not clearly reflect the market for the goods, services or other sources of income in Illinois. (86 Ill. Adm. Code Sec. 100.3370(a)(1))

Sales includes gross receipts from:
- sales of manufactured goods or products, less returns and allowances;
- performance of services, including service fees, commissions, and similar items;
- rental, leasing, and licensing of real or tangible property; and
- sales of business assets. (86 Ill. Adm. Code Sec. 100.3370(a)(1))

Do nonresidents include receipts they exclude or deduct from federal taxable income? The sales factor must include gross receipts the nonresident excludes or deducts from its federal taxable income if those receipts:
- are added back to Illinois base income;
- are not subtracted from Illinois base income. (86 Ill. Adm. Code Sec. 100.3370(a)(2)(D))

Do nonresidents include gains or losses from foreign currency transactions? Illinois treats foreign currency gain or loss from IRC Sec. 988 transactions as an adjustment to the income, expense, gain or loss. (86 Ill. Adm. Code 100.3380(c)(7)) The sales factor must include gain or loss from a foreign currency transaction only if the nonresident also includes the income from the transaction. However, a nonresident must exclude gains and losses from foreign currency expenses. (86 Ill. Adm. Code 100.3380(c)(7))

Do nonresidents include gross receipts from intangible property? The sales factor must include gross receipts from intangible personal property if it makes up more than 50% of the nonresident's total gross income during the current and previous 2 tax years. (35 ILCS 5/304(a)(3)(B-2); 86 Ill. Adm. Code 100.3380(a)(2)(F))

Gross receipts from intangible property include receipts from the licensing, sale, or transfer of:
- patents issued under federal law;
- copyrights registered or eligible for registration under federal law;

- trademarks registered or eligible for registration under federal law;

- intellectual property registered or enforceable under another country's equivalent patent, copyright, or trademark laws. (86 Ill. Adm. Code 100.3380(a)(2)(F))

It also includes amounts received as damages or settlements from claims of infringement. (86 Ill. Adm. Code 100.3380(a)(2)(F))

Do nonresidents include income from hedging transactions? Nonresidents generally must exclude any income, gain or loss from hedging transactions from the sales factor. This applies to hedging transactions under:

- IRC Sec. 475;

- IRC Sec. 1221; or

- IRC Sec. 1256. (86 Ill. Adm. Code 100.3380(c)(6))

Do nonresidents include incidental or occasional sales? Nonresidents must exclude gross receipts from incidental or occasional sales from the sales factor. This applies to incidental or occasional sales of assets used in the regular course of trade or business. (86 Ill. Adm. Code 100.3380(c)(2))

[¶16-515e] Sourcing of Business Income--Alternative Methods

Illinois allows or requires an alternative apportionment method if the standard allocation and apportionment provisions do not fairly represent the market for:

- the taxpayer's goods;

- the taxpayer's services; or

- other sources of the taxpayer's business income in the state. (35 ILCS 5/304(f); 86 Ill. Adm. Code 100.3380(a)(1); 86 Ill. Adm. Code 100.3390(a))

Neither the taxpayer nor the Illinois Department of Revenue (DOR) can seek an alternative apportionment method merely because it reaches a different result than the standard formula. (86 Ill. Adm. Code 100.3390(c))

What alternative apportionment methods does Illinois allow?

Illinois alternative apportionment methods include:

- separate accounting;

- the exclusion of any one or more apportionment factors;

- the inclusion of one or more additional apportionment factors that will fairly represent the taxpayer's market in Illinois; or

- the employment of any other method that will result in an equitable allocation and apportionment of the taxpayer's business income. (35 ILCS 5/304(f); 86 Ill. Adm. Code 100.3380(a)(1); 86 Ill. Adm. Code 100.3390(a))

Who carries the burden of proof?

The party seeking to use an alternative apportionment method carries the burden of proof. That party must show by clear and convincing evidence that the standard apportionment formula:

- results in the taxation of extraterritorial values; or

- operates unreasonably and arbitrarily to apportion income to Illinois out of all proportion to the taxpayer's market in the state. (86 Ill. Adm. Code § 100.3390(c))

Evidence must also prove that the proposed alternative apportionment method fairly and accurately apportions income to Illinois based on the taxpayer's market in the state. (86 Ill. Adm. Code § 100.3390(c))

How does a taxpayer apply for alternative apportionment?

A taxpayer must file a clearly labeled petition for alternative apportionment:

- 120 days before the original or extended due date of the tax return in question;

- as an attachment to an amended return that used the standard allocation and apportionment rules; or

- as part of a protest to a deficiency notice resulting from an audit of the taxpayer's return and supporting books and records. (86 Ill. Adm. Code § 100.3390(e))

The explanations section of the taxpayer's amended return must state that the return includes a petition for alternative apportionment. (86 Ill. Adm. Code § 100.3390(e)) A protest to a deficiency notice cannot raise alternative apportionment unless:

- the taxpayer submitted a written request to use alternative apportionment and the auditor denied the request; or

- the audit rejects an alternative apportionment method the taxpayer used on its return. (86 Ill. Adm. Code § 100.3390(e))

The DOR will issue a private letter ruling advising the taxpayer that it accepts, partially accepts, or rejects the petition. (86 Ill. Adm. Code § 100.3390(f))

What if the DOR denies an alternative apportionment request?

A taxpayer can protest the DOR's decision to deny the taxpayer's petition to use an alternative apportionment method. (86 Ill. Adm. Code § 100.3390(g))

If the DOR denies the petition before the taxpayer files its original or extended return, the taxpayer must file and pay tax using the standard apportionment formula. A taxpayer that files using the standard formula after the DOR denies its petitions can file an amended return and claim a refund based on the original petition. (86 Ill. Adm. Code § 100.3390(g)) If the DOR denies the taxpayer's refund claim, the taxpayer can:

- file a protest and request an administrative hearing; or

- file a petition with the Illinois Independent Tax Tribunal. (86 Ill. Adm. Code § 100.3390(g))

[¶16-530] Sourcing of Income from Intangibles

How do nonresidents source interest from nonbusiness income?

Illinois does not tax interest or dividends from nonbusiness income. So, it does not require allocation of that income by nonresidents. (35 ILCS 5/301(c)(2))

How do nonresidents source interest from business income?

Nonresidents must source interest from business income to Illinois if:

- the nonresident performed the income-producing activity in Illinois; or

- the nonresident performed the income-producing activity both in and outside Illinois, but performed a greater proportion of the activity in the state based on costs of performance. (35 ILCS 5/304(a)(3)(C-5)(iii)(b); 86 Ill. Adm. Code 100.3380(c)(6)(C))

Interest income is business income if:

- the intangible generating the interest was received, held or created in the regular course of the nonresident's trade or business operation; or

• the purpose for acquiring or holding the intangible is related to the nonresident's trade or business operations. (86 Ill. Adm. Code 100.3010(c)(4))

How do nonresidents source nonbusiness patent and copyright royalty income?

Nonresidents must allocate nonbusiness patent and copyright royalty income to Illinois if the payer used the patent or copyright in the state. (35 ILCS 5/303(d); 86 Ill. Adm. Code 100.3220(d))

How do nonresidents source patent, copyright, and trademark royalties from trade or business operations?

Illinois treats patent and copyright royalties as business income if:

• the patent or copyright was received, held or created in the regular course of the nonresident's trade or business operations; or

• the purpose for acquiring or holding the patent or copyright is related to the nonresident's trade or business operations. (86 Ill. Adm. Code 100.3010(c)(6))

Nonresidents must source business income to Illinois from the licensing, sale, or transfer during the tax year of:

• patents used in the state;

• copyrights used in the state;

• trademarks used in the state; and

• similar intellectual property used in the state. (35 ILCS 5/304(a)(3)(B-1); 86 Ill. Adm. Code 100.3380(c)(3))

When is a patent used in Illinois? A licensee, purchaser, or transferee uses a patent in Illinois if it:

• employs the patent in production, fabrication, manufacturing, or other processing in the state; or

• produces a patented product in the state. (35 ILCS 5/304(a)(3)(B-1); 86 Ill. Adm. Code 100.3380(c)(3))

If the licensee, purchaser, or transferee uses a patent both in Illinois and other states, nonresidents must divide the gross receipts from its use in Illinois by the total gross receipts from its use in all states. (35 ILCS 5/304(a)(3)(B-1); 86 Ill. Adm. Code 100.3380(c)(3))

When is a copyright used in Illinois? A licensee, purchaser, or transferee uses a copyright in Illinois if printing of publishing originates in the state. (35 ILCS 5/304(a)(3)(B-1); 86 Ill. Adm. Code 100.3380(c)(3)) Printing or publishing originates in Illinois if it is the state where:

• the licensee, purchaser, or transferee incorporates the copyrighted material into a physical medium for delivery to purchasers; or

• if there is no physical delivery medium, the licensee, purchaser, or transferee delivers the copyrighted material to purchasers. (35 ILCS 5/304(a)(3)(B-1); 86 Ill. Adm. Code 100.3380(c)(3))

If a licensee, purchaser, or transferee uses a copyright both in Illinois and other states, nonresidents must divide the gross receipts from its use in Illinois by the total gross receipts from its use in all states. (35 ILCS 5/304(a)(3)(B-1); 86 Ill. Adm. Code 100.3380(c)(3))

How do nonresidents source business income from services?

Nonresidents must source business income from the sales of services to Illinois if a customer received the service in the state. (35 ILCS 5/304(a)(3)(C-5)(iv); 86 Ill. Adm. Code 100.3380(c)(6)(D)) A business customer receives a service in Illinois if:

(1) the customer ordered the service in the regular course of its trade or business at its Illinois office address; or

(2) the taxpayer cannot determine (1) and it billed the customer for the services at an Illinois office address. (86 Ill. Adm. Code 100.3380(c)(6)(D))

The same rules apply in the same order for individual customers. An individual customer receives the service in Illinois if the customer's residential address in the state was the place of ordering or billing the service. (86 Ill. Adm. Code 100.3380(c)(6)(D))

Does Illinois have a sales factor throwout rule for intangibles?

Illinois applies a sales factor throwout rule under certain circumstances. A nonresident must exclude or throwout business income from:

- a patent, copyright, trademark, or similar item of intangible property if the nonresident cannot determine the property's place of use; (35 ILCS 5/304(a)(3)(B-1)(iii); 86 Ill. Adm. Code Sec. 100.3370(c)(3)(D)) or

- services if the state where a customer receives the services does not tax the nonresident. (35 ILCS 5/304(a)(3)(C-5)(iv); 86 Ill. Adm. Code Sec. 100.3370(c)(6)(D))

[¶16-540] Sourcing of Nonresident Beneficiary Income

Nonresident beneficiaries must allocate or apportion income received from a trust or estate. (35 ILCS 5/307) A nonresident beneficiary allocates or apportions the income based on the distributive share of:

- the business income apportioned to Illinois by the estate or trust; (35 ILCS 5/307(a)) and

- the nonbusiness income allocated to Illinois by the estate or trust. (35 ILCS 5/307(b))

Illinois treats all income of a trust or estate as business income, unless:

- it is clearly from one state; and

- it is earned or received through activities totally unrelated to any business conducted in more than one state. (Instructions, Schedule NR, Nonresident Computation of Fiduciary Income)

A trust or estate can elect to treat all of its income as business income. This election is binding on its beneficiaries. A beneficiary can also make the election. If this occurs, nonbusiness income received from the trust or estate gets treated as business income received directly by the beneficiary. (86 Ill. Adm. Code 100.3015(c))

Illinois does not require beneficiaries to source income to Illinois from:

- retirement or pension plans; or

- supplemental unemployment benefit trusts. (35 ILCS 5/301(c)(2))

Illinois provides special rules for trusts that make an accumulation or capital gain distribution as defined under IRC Sec. 665. Each nonresident and part-year resident must allocate that income to Illinois if it was allocable to the state before the distribution. (35 ILCS 5/307(c))

[¶16-545] Sourcing of Retirement Income

Illinois does not tax retirement, pension, or Social Security income included in federal taxable income. So, it does not require allocation of that income by nonresidents. (35 ILCS 5/301(c)(2))

[¶16-550] Sourcing of Property-Related Income

How do nonresidents source nonbusiness rental and royalty income?

Nonresidents must allocate nonbusiness rental and royalty income to Illinois from:

- real property located in Illinois; and
- tangible personal property used in the state. (35 ILCS 5/303(c); 86 Ill. Adm. Code 100.3220(c))

A nonresident measures the use of tangible personal property in Illinois by multiplying the net rents or royalties by a fraction. (35 ILCS 5/303(c); 86 Ill. Adm. Code 100.3220(c)) The fraction is computed by dividing:

- the number of days the property was in the state during the rental or royalty period by
- the number of days the property was everywhere during all rental or royalty periods in the tax year. (35 ILCS 5/303(c); 86 Ill. Adm. Code 100.3220(c))

How do nonresidents source business income from the sale, lease, or rental of real or tangible personal property?

Illinois follows the destination test for the sourcing of business income from the sales of tangible personal property. Nonresidents must source sales of tangible personal property to Illinois if the nonresident delivers or ships the property to a purchaser in the state. This applies to sales of tangible personal property, regardless of the F.O.B. point or other conditions of sale. (35 ILCS 5/304(a)(3)(B); 86 Ill. Adm. Code Sec. 100.3370(c)(1))

Rental income from real and tangible property is business income if the property was received or used in the taxpayer's trade or business. (86 Ill. Adm. Code 100.3010(c)(2)) Nonresidents must source business receipts to Illinois from the lease or rental of tangible personal property located in the state during the rental period. (35 ILCS 5/304(a)(3)(C-5)(ii); 86 Ill. Adm. Code 100.3370(c)(6)(B))

Nonresidents must source business income to Illinois from the sale or lease of real property located in the state. (35 ILCS 5/304(a)(3)(C-5)(i); 86 Ill. Adm. Code 100.3370(c)(6)(A))

Does Illinois have a throwback rule?

A nonresident must source or throwback business income from sales of tangible personal property to Illinois if:

- the purchaser's state does not tax the income from the sale (35 ILCS 5/304(a)(3)(B)(ii); 86 Ill. Adm. Code Sec. 100.3370(c)(1)(F)) or the purchaser is the U.S. government; (35 ILCS 5/304(a)(3)(B)(ii); 86 Ill. Adm. Code Sec. 100.3370(c)(2)) and
- the taxpayer ships the property from an office, store, warehouse, factory, or other place of storage in Illinois.

[¶16-555] Sourcing of Gains and Losses

How do nonresidents source gains or losses from nonbusiness income?

Nonresidents must allocate nonbusiness capital gains and losses from the sale or exchange of real or personal property located in Illinois. (35 ILCS 5/303(b); 86 Ill. Adm. Code 100.3220(b))

Illinois treats economic interests in minerals in place as real property for allocation purposes. (86 Ill. Adm. Code 100.3220(b)) These interests include:

- royalties and overriding royalties;
- participating interests;
- production payments; and
- working interests. (86 Ill. Adm. Code 100.3220(b))

Illinois does not tax a nonresident's nonbusiness gains or losses from intangibles. So, it does not require allocation of that income by nonresidents. (Instructions, Schedule NR, Nonresident and Part-Year Resident Computation of Illinois Tax)

How do nonresidents source gains or losses from business income?

Gain or loss from the sale or exchange of real or tangible personal property is business income if the property was used in a nonresident's (86 Ill. Adm. Code 100.3010(c)(3)) Nonresidents must source net business gains to Illinois if:

- the nonresident performed the income-producing activity in Illinois; or

- the nonresident performed the income-producing activity both in and outside Illinois, but performed a greater proportion of the activity in the state based on costs of performance. (35 ILCS 5/304(a)(3)(C-5)(iii)(b); 86 Ill. Adm. Code 100.3370(c)(6)(C))

[¶16-565] Sourcing of Pass-Through Entity Income and Deductions

Nonresident partners or shareholders must allocate or apportion income and deductions received from a partnership or S corporation. (35 ILCS 5/305; 35 ILCS 5/308; 86 Ill. Adm. Code 100.3500) A nonresident partner or shareholder allocates or apportions the income based on the distributive share of:

- the business income apportioned to Illinois by the S corporation or partnership; (35 ILCS 5/305(a); 35 ILCS 5/308(a); 86 Ill. Adm. Code 100.3500(b)) and

- the nonbusiness income allocated to Illinois by the S corporation or partnership. (35 ILCS 5/305(b); 35 ILCS 5/308(b); 86 Ill. Adm. Code 100.3500(c))

Illinois treats all income of a partnership or S corporation as business income, unless:

- it is clearly from one state; and

- it is earned or received through activities totally unrelated to any business conducted in more than one state. (Instructions, Schedule K-1-P, Partner's or Shareholder's Share of Income, Deductions, Credits, and Recapture)

A partnership or S corporation can elect to treat all of its income as business income. This election is binding on its partners or shareholders. A partner or shareholder can also make the election. If this occurs, nonbusiness income received from the pass-through entity gets treated as business income received directly by the partner or shareholder. (86 Ill. Adm. Code 100.3015(c))

Illinois treats distributive income from investment partnerships as nonbusiness income. Nonresident partners must allocate that income to their state of residence. A nonresident partner must treat the income as apportionable business income if:

- it is directly related or serves an operational function to the partner's other business activities in Illinois; or

- the partner's contribution to the partnership was made from the partner's trade or business in Illinois. (35 ILCS 5/305(c-5); 86 Ill. Adm. Code 100.3500(d))

[¶16-570] Sourcing of Compensation for Personal Services

How do nonresidents source compensation from personal services?

Nonresidents must source or allocate to Illinois all wages or other compensation paid in the state. (35 ILCS 5/302(a)) Effective for tax years before 2020, compensation is paid in Illinois if the nonresident:

- performed services entirely in Illinois or performed only incidental services outside the state;

- performed services in Illinois and the nonresident's base of operations is in the state;

- performed services directed or controlled in Illinois; or

- performed services in Illinois and is a resident of the state. (35 ILCS 5/304(a)(2)(B)); 86 Ill. Adm. Code 100.3120(a)

Effective for tax years ending on or after December 31, 2020, compensation is paid in Illinois if the nonresident:

- performed some services in Illinois;

- performed services in Illinois that are not incidental to services performed outside the state; and

- performed services in Illinois for more than 30 working days during the tax year. (35 ILCS 5/304(a)(2)(B))

A nonresident determines the amount of compensation paid in Illinois based on a ratio that compares the number of working days spent in the state to the total number of working days spent both in and outside the state during the tax year. (35 ILCS 5/304(a)(2)(B))

A working day covers all days during the tax year in which nonresidents performed duties for their employer. (35 ILCS 5/304(a)(2)(B)) It does not include:

- weekends;

- vacation days;

- sick days;

- holidays; or

- other days in which nonresidents performed no duties for their employer. (35 ILCS 5/304(a)(2)(B))

Nonresidents spend a working day in Illinois if:

- they spend a greater amount of time that day performing services for their employer in the state than outside the state; or

- the only service they perform for their employer on that day is traveling to a destination in the state and they arrive on that day. (35 ILCS 5/304(a)(2)(B))

Working days spent in Illinois do not include any days that nonresidents spend performing services in the state during a disaster period. (35 ILCS 5/304(a)(2)(B)) The exception applies only to a disaster or emergency relief request made to an employer by:

- Illinois state and local government agencies or officials; or

- businesses in the state. (35 ILCS 5/304(a)(2)(B))

The exception covers the period that:

- begins 10 days before the date of the state's proclamation or federal declaration of a disaster, whichever is earlier; and

- extends for 60 calendar days after the end of the declared disaster or emergency. (35 ILCS 5/304(a)(2)(B))

Disaster services consist of activities that relate to infrastructure that has been damaged or destroyed by the disaster or emergency. (35 ILCS 5/304(a)(2)(B))

A nonresident must allocate to Illinois unemployment benefits paid by the state. (35 ILCS 5/303(e-5); 86 Ill. Adm. Code 100.3220(h))

How does Illinois treat deferred compensation paid to nonresidents?

The standard allocation rules for determining if compensation is paid in Illinois applies to deferred compensation paid to nonresidents. (86 Ill. Adm. Code 100.3120(b)) Illinois presumes that the nonresident earned the deferred compensation ratably over the last 5 years of service with the employer, unless clear and convincing evidence shows that:

- the compensation relates to a different employment period; or
- it was not earned ratably over the employment period. (86 Ill. Adm. Code 100.3120(b))

How does Illinois treat compensation paid to nonresidents for military service?

Compensation paid in Illinois does not include compensation paid to a nonresident for military service. (86 Ill. Adm. Code 100.3120(a))

How does Illinois treat compensation paid to nonresident members of sports teams?

Illinois treats services performed by nonresidents under a contract at a sporting event in the state as performed entirely in the state. Nonresident members of sports teams must allocate compensation paid in Illinois using a formula based on duty days. (86 Ill. Adm. Code 100.3100(e); 86 Ill. Adm. Code 100.3120(a)) The formula is the number of duty days spent in Illinois divided by the total number of duty days spent performing services for the team. (35 ILCS 5/304(a)(2)(B)(iv); 86 Ill. Adm. Code 100.3120(a))

Total duty days for managers, coaches, and players, including players on the disabled list, include all days from the beginning of the official pre-season training period through:

- the last game in which the player competes; or
- the last post-season or playoff game in which the player participates. (35 ILCS 5/304(a)(2)(B)(iv); 86 Ill. Adm. Code 100.3100(e))

Post-season games include any all star game in which the player is chosen to participate. (35 ILCS 5/304(a)(2)(B)(iv); 86 Ill. Adm. Code 100.3100(e)) Performing a service for a team includes conducting training and rehabilitation activities at team facilities. (35 ILCS 5/304(a)(2)(B)(iv))

Duty days include:

- off days;
- practice days; and
- travel days. (86 Ill. Adm. Code 100.3100(e))

Duty days spent in Illinois do not include travel days that do not involve either a game, practice, team meeting, or other similar team event. (35 ILCS 5/304(a)(2)(B)(iv))

For trainers and other full time traveling employees, total duty days include all days in the calendar year. (86 Ill. Adm. Code 100.3100(e))

Duty days for any person who joins a team during a season begin on the day that person joins the team. Duty days for any person who leaves a team during this period end on the day that person leaves the team. (35 ILCS 5/304(a)(2)(B)(iv))

[¶16-600]
WITHHOLDING

[¶16-605] Withholding Introduction

Illinois requires withholding of personal income tax on the following:

— wages; (see ¶16-615)

— lottery winnings; (see ¶16-655) and

— gambling winnings. (see ¶16-655)

The frequency of payroll withholding tax returns and payments is determined by reference to a 12-month look-period. Employers generally must deduct and withhold tax on semi-weekly, monthly, or annual payment schedule. (see ¶89-102)

[¶16-610] Withholding Administration

The Department of Revenue is the state taxing authority that administers Illinois personal income withholding tax. (see ¶89-060)

[¶16-615] Withholding on Wages

Who must withhold Illinois income tax on wages?

Every employer maintaining an office or transacting business in Illinois must withhold income tax on compensation paid in the state if the employer must withhold federal income tax. (35 ILCS 5/701(a); 86 Ill. Adm. Code 100.7000; 86 Ill. Adm. Code 100.7030; *Publication 130*, Who is Required to Withhold Illinois Income Tax, Illinois Department of Revenue) The employer must deduct and withhold the amount by which the compensation exceeds the employee's withholding exemption for the payroll period multiplied by the Illinois personal income tax rate. (35 ILCS 5/701(a)) Employers can determine the withholding amount using tax tables or the automated payroll method.

An employer is liable for withholding tax and subject to penalties or interest for the failure to withhold. (35 ILCS 5/705; 35 ILCS 5/706) Employers and employees can enter agreements for additional (86 Ill. Adm. Code 100.7060) or voluntary withholding. (86 Ill. Adm. Code 100.7070)

Who is an employer?

An employer is any person or organization who:

- must withhold and pay federal income taxes;

- transacts business in Illinois and has a worker who performs services as an employee;

- has control of the payment of wages for employee services. (86 Ill. Adm. Code 100.7030(a)(1); 86 Ill. Adm. Code 100.7360(d); *Publication 130*, Who is Required to Withhold Illinois Income Tax, Illinois Department of Revenue)

An employer is transacting business in Illinois if it, or any subsidiary, has or maintains in the state:

- an office;

- a distribution or sales facility;

- a warehouse; or

- other place of business. (86 Ill. Adm. Code 100.7020)

Transacting business in Illinois can include any agent or other representative, including any independent contractor, operating in the state under the authority of the employer or its subsidiary. (86 Ill. Adm. Code 100.7020) It does not matter whether:

- the employer's place of business, agent or other representative is permanently or temporarily in Illinois; or

- the employer or subsidiary is licensed to do business in the state. (86 Ill. Adm. Code 100.7020)

Who is an employee?

An employee is either:

- an individual who performs services under the legal control and direction of an employer; (86 Ill. Adm. Code 100.3100(b); *Publication 130*, Who is Required to Withhold Illinois Income Tax, Illinois Department of Revenue) or

- an individual or Illinois resident who receives payments on which the employer must withhold federal income tax. (86 Ill. Adm. Code 100.7030(a)(2); 86 Ill. Adm. Code 100.7360(d); *Publication 130*, Who is Required to Withhold Illinois Income Tax, Illinois Department of Revenue)

The term "employee" includes every individual performing services if the legal relationship between the individual and the taxpayer is that of employer and employee. The term has the same meaning as the definition under IRC Sec. 3401(c) and 26 CFR 31.3401(c)-1. If the employer-employee relationship does not exist, payment for services performed does not represent compensation. (86 Ill. Adm. Code 100.3100(b)) But, payment for personal services is compensation, so long as the employer-employee relationship existed when the employee rendered the services. (86 Ill. Adm. Code 100.3100(d))

What is compensation?

"Compensation" means:

- wages;

- salaries;

- commissions; and

- any other form of payment to employees for personal services. (86 Ill. Adm. Code 100.3100(a))

Illinois adopts the definition of "wages" under IRC Sec. 3401(a), but it does not follow the exceptions set forth in the federal definition. (86 Ill. Adm. Code 100.3100(a))

The name used to designate payment for services is immaterial. (86 Ill. Adm. Code 100.3100(c)) So, compensation, if paid for services performed by an employee, includes:

- fees;

- bonuses;

- pensions and retirement pay; and

- commissions on sales or insurance premiums. (86 Ill. Adm. Code 100.3100(c))

Compensation subject to Illinois withholding includes supplemental wages, including bonuses, commissions, and overtime pay, when paid. (86 Ill. Adm. Code 100.7050(c)) Employers can determine the amount of tax to withhold using:

- the methods provided under the IRC and federal regulations; or

- the Illinois personal income tax rate in effect on the date the compensation is paid. (86 Ill. Adm. Code 100.7050(c)

Employers must withhold from vacation pay for the period covered by the vacation. If vacation pay is in addition to the regular wage payment for the payroll period, the employer must treat it like a supplemental wage payment. (86 Ill. Adm. Code 100.7050(d))

When is compensation paid in Illinois?

Compensation is paid in Illinois if the employee:

- performed some services in Illinois;

- performed services in Illinois that are not incidental to services performed outside the state; and

- performed services in Illinois for more than 30 working days during the tax year. (35 ILCS 5/304(a)(2)(B))

An employer determines the amount of compensation paid in Illinois based on a ratio that compares the number of working days spent in the state to the total number of working days spent both in and outside the state during the tax year. (35 ILCS 5/304(a)(2)(B))

A working day covers all days during the tax year in which employees performed duties for their employer. (35 ILCS 5/304(a)(2)(B)) It does not include:

- weekends;

- vacation days;

- sick days;

- holidays; or

- other days in which nonresidents performed no duties for their employer. (35 ILCS 5/304(a)(2)(B))

Employees spend a working day in Illinois if:

- they spend a greater amount of time that day performing services for their employer in the state than outside the state; or

- the only service they perform for their employer on that day is traveling to a destination in the state and they arrive on that day. (35 ILCS 5/304(a)(2)(B))

Effective for tax years before 2020, compensation is paid in Illinois if the employee:

- performed services entirely in Illinois;

- performed services in and outside Illinois, but the services outside the state are incidental to the services performed in the state;

- performed some services in Illinois and the employee's base of operations is in the state;

- performed some services in Illinois and the place from which the services is directed or controlled is in the state; or

- performed services in Illinois and is a resident of the state. (86 Ill. Adm. Code 100.7010(a)(1); *Publication 130*, Who is Required to Withhold Illinois Income Tax, Illinois Department of Revenue)

Compliance Alert: Illinois issued withholding guidance for employers due to the COVID-19, or coronavirus, outbreak. The guidance applies to out-of-state employers who employ Illinois residents working from home during the pandemic. Illinois will waive penalties and interest for out-of-state employers who fail to withhold if employees are working at home in the state solely due to the pandemic. Employees who do not have Illinois income tax withheld may owe income tax. Estimated tax requirements may also apply. (*Informational Bulletin FY 2020-29*, Illinois Department of Revenue, May 19, 2020)

Incidental services are temporary, transitory, or isolated transactions that support the employee's primary service. (86 Ill. Adm. Code 100.7010(c)(3); *Publication 130*, Who is Required to Withhold Illinois Income Tax, Illinois Department of Revenue) Employment contracts commonly provide a territorial assignment that provides strong evidence a service is localized in that territory. But, the presence or absence of an employment contract is only one factor to consider. (86 Ill. Adm. Code 100.7010(c)(3)) The ultimate determination is whether:

• the individual's service was intended to be and was in fact principally performed in Illinois; and

• any service that was performed in another state was temporary, transitory, infrequent, or arose out of special circumstances.

The amount of time spent or the amount of service performed outside of Illinois is not decisive by itself. (86 Ill. Adm. Code 100.7010(c)(3))

Example 1: A is a resident of State X and a sales representative for the B Corporation, located in State X. A's territory covers the northern part of Illinois. A is requested by B corporation to call on particular customers who are located in State X. The compensation for service which A performs in Illinois and State X is subject to withholding because the service performed in State X is incidental to the service performed in Illinois, since it consists of isolated transactions.

Example 2: The same facts as example 1, except that A's regular territory covers several counties in Illinois and one or two towns in State X. A goes to the State X towns on a regular basis even though more than 95% of his time and sales are to A's Illinois Territory. The compensation for service which A performs in Illinois and State X is not localized in Illinois because the service performed in State X is regular and permanent in nature and is not necessary to or supportive of sales made in Illinois. Withholding is required in this example, if the base of operations is in Illinois or the place from which the service is directed or controlled is in Illinois.

Example 3: A works for B construction company in Chicago. Occasionally the company obtains a construction job in State X which may last from one to several weeks. A is sent by the company to supervise the construction jobs in State X. The compensation for the service A performs in Illinois and State X is subject to withholding because the service performed in State X, being temporary in nature, is incidental to the service which A performs in Illinois.

Example 4: A is a resident of Illinois and a buyer for a department store located in State X. Regular buying trips by A to Illinois are incidental to the service performed in State X because they are necessary to and supportive of A's primary duties which are localized in State X and not in Illinois. Unless compensation for the services A performs in Illinois and State X is deemed compensation paid in the state, compensation for the services A performs in Illinois and State X is not subject to withholding, notwithstanding that A being a resident, is taxable in Illinois on such compensation.

Does Illinois provide any exceptions to wage withholding requirements?

Illinois withholding requirements do not apply to:

• railroad employees, truck and bus drivers, or other employees who work under the jurisdiction of the Surface Transportation Board (STB) and perform regularly assigned duties in more than 1 state;

• airline employees who perform regularly assigned duties in more than 1 state and do not earn more than 50% of their compensation in Illinois based on Illinois flight miles versus all flight miles;

• marine vessel employees who perform regularly assigned duties in more than 1 state. (86 Ill. Adm. Code 100.2590 86 Ill. Adm. Code 100.7010(b))

• Illinois unemployment insurance benefit payments; (35 ILCS 5/701(b))

• compensation paid to residents of states that have reciprocal collection agreements with Illinois; (86 Ill. Adm. Code 100.7010(a)(1))

• compensation paid to a non-military employee whose spouse is stationed in Illinois by the military; and

• compensation paid to an employee whose compensation is exempt from federal withholding requirements, like wages paid to certain types of ministers. (*Publication 130*, Who is Required to Withhold Illinois Income Tax, Illinois Department of Revenue)

Example: An airline company employs a Missouri resident to fly to various destinations in the U.S. The employee reports to and flies out of a terminal in Illinois. According to company records, 58% of the employee's compensation (flight time in Illinois versus flight time to other destinations) is earned in Illinois. Therefore, the company must withhold Illinois income tax because more than 50% of the employee's compensation was earned in Illinois. Illinois flight miles do not include miles flown over Illinois without taking off or landing.

Compensation paid to household employees is not subject to Illinois withholding unless:

• the employer is withholding for federal purposes; or

• the employer and household employee have entered into a voluntary withholding agreement. (*Publication 121*, Income Tax Withholding for Household Employees, Illinois Department of Revenue; *Publication 130*, Who is Required to Withhold Illinois Income Tax, Illinois Department of Revenue)

Effective for tax years ending on or after December 31, 2020, working days spent in Illinois do not include any days that nonresidents spend performing services in the state during a disaster period. (35 ILCS 5/304(a)(2)(B)) The exception applies only to a disaster or emergency relief request made to an employer by:

• Illinois state and local government agencies or officials; or

• businesses in the state. (35 ILCS 5/304(a)(2)(B))

The exception covers the period that:

• begins 10 days before the date of the state's proclamation or federal declaration of a disaster, whichever is earlier; and

• extends for 60 calendar days after the end of the declared disaster or emergency. (35 ILCS 5/304(a)(2)(B))

Disaster services consist of activities that relate to infrastructure that has been damaged or destroyed by the disaster or emergency. (35 ILCS 5/304(a)(2)(B))

Does Illinois have any recordkeeping requirements for wage withholding?

Effective for tax years beginning after 2020, employers who maintain a time and attendance system that tracks where employees perform services on a daily basis must use the system to determine compensation paid in Illinois to nonresident employees. (35 ILCS 5/701(a-5)) A time and attendance tracking system is a tool that:

• requires employees to record their work location for every day worked outside the state where the employment duties are primarily performed; and

• allows the employer to divide the employee's wages among all states in which the employee performs services. (35 ILCS 5/701(a-5))

Otherwise, employers must get a written statement from nonresident employees of the number of days that the employee expects to spend performing services in Illinois during the tax year. (35 ILCS 5/701(a-5))

Does Illinois require employers to register for withholding?

Every employer required to deduct and withhold Illinois income tax must register with the Illinois Department of Revenue (DOR) (86 Ill. Adm. Code 100.7040) by:

• completing an online business registration application at https://mytax.illinois.gov/_/#1;

- completing and mailing Form REG-1; or
- visiting a regional DOR office. (*Publication 130*, Who is Required to Withhold Illinois Income Tax, Illinois Department of Revenue)

The DOR will assign a temporary tax account number unless the employer already has a federal employer identification number (FEIN). (86 Ill. Adm. Code 100.7040; *Publication 130*, Who is Required to Withhold Illinois Income Tax, Illinois Department of Revenue)

[¶16-620] Withholding Tables and Schedules

Illinois provides withholding tax tables each tax year for determining the amount to withhold from wages and other compensation. The withholding tables appear in Booklet IL-700-T on the Illinois Department Revenue's website at https://www2.illinois.gov/rev/forms/withholding/Pages/default.aspx.

[¶16-635] Withholding from Nonresident Personal Service Income

Illinois no longer requires withholding from payments made to nonresident individuals on contracts for personal services. (*General Information Letter IT 10-0012-GIL*, Illinois Department of Revenue, May 28, 2010; Publication 130, Who is Required to Withhold Illinois Income Tax, Illinois Department of Revenue) However, any person maintaining an office or transacting business in Illinois must maintain a record of all payments made under contracts for personal services that is available for review by the Illinois Department of Revenue. Information reporting is not required if there is certification on Form IL-W5 that the individual is an Illinois resident. (35 ILCS 5/1405.2)

[¶16-645] Withholding from Pensions, Annuities, and Other Deferred Compensation

Illinois does not require withholding from pension, annuity or other deferred compensation that is not included in Illinois base income. (35 ILCS 5/701(e); Publication 130, Who is Required to Withhold Illinois Income Tax, Illinois Department of Revenue)

[¶16-650] Withholding from Rents and Royalties Paid to Nonresidents

Illinois does not require withholding for income from rents and royalties paid to nonresidents. (35 ILCS 5/1405.1; *Informational Bulletin, FY 88-17*, Department of Revenue, April 1988) However, copies of federal information returns must be maintained by the taxpayer for review by the Department of Revenue that include a payment of $1,000 or more which is, in whole or part, for one or more of the following:

— rents and royalties for real property located in Illinois;

— rents and royalties for tangible personal property if the tangible personal property was physically located in Illinois at any time during the rental period;

— royalties paid on a patent which was employed in production, fabrication, manufacturing, or other processing in Illinois;

— royalties paid on a patented product which was produced in Illinois; and

— royalties paid on a copyright to compensate the holder of the copyright for printing or other publication which originates in Illinois. (35 ILCS 5/1405.1(a))

[¶16-655] Withholding at Source from Nonwage Income

Illinois imposes the special withholding tax requirements on lottery winnings, gambling winnings, and sales outside the ordinary course of business (bulk sales). (35 ILCS 5/902(d))

Taxpayers who receive payment of Illinois lottery or gambling winnings over $1,000 must complete Form IL-5754. This form provides a record of who received winnings and to whom the winnings are taxable. (Instructions, Form IL-5754, Statement by Person Receiving Gambling Winnings)

• *Lottery winnings*

Withholding of Illinois income tax is required for any single payment of Illinois lottery winnings of $1,000 or more to a resident or nonresident. (35 ILCS 5/710(a); Publication 130, Who is Required to Withhold Illinois Income Tax, Illinois Department of Revenue) It does not matter that several individuals may jointly hold the winning ticket and each person's "share" is less than $1,000. (Publication 130, Who is Required to Withhold Illinois Income Tax, Illinois Department of Revenue)

Payors of lottery winnings must file withholding tax returns and pay the tax in the same manner as employers withholding on wages. (35 ILCS 5/711)

Every payor who is required to withhold Illinois income tax on Illinois lottery winnings is liable for the tax. (35 ILCS 5/712) If the payor fails to deduct and withhold the required amount and the tax is paid by the payee directly, the payor is not relieved of liability for penalties or interest for failure to withhold the tax. (35 ILCS 5/713)

A purchaser of rights to future payments of Illinois lottery winnings after December 31, 2013 must withhold Illinois income tax equal to the applicable individual income tax rate (see ¶15-355) from the seller's payment at the time of the transaction. (35 ILCS 5/710(a)(2)) The amount withheld must be paid to the Illinois Department of Revenue with a payment coupon by the 15th day of the month following the purchase. The purchaser must file a withholding income tax return by the last day of January following the year in which the rights are purchased. The purchaser must also report the income and withholding to the seller at the end of the year. Lottery purchase withholding must be reported separately from employee wage withholding with the special account ID assigned by the department, which is different from employee withholding account numbers. (*Informational Bulletin FY 2014-08*, Illinois Department of Revenue, January 2014)

Any person who receives a payment of lottery winnings may claim a credit against Illinois income tax liability for the amount of the tax withheld. (see ¶16-826)

• *Gambling winnings*

Illinois follows federal law and requires withholding on gambling winnings that are paid to a resident of Illinois if the proceeds are equal to $5,000 or more in a single payment and at least 300 times greater than the wager in a:

— sweepstakes;

— wagering pool or transactions;

— lottery, other than a state-conducted lottery; or

— pari-mutuel pool with respect to horse races, dog races, or jai alai. (86 Ill. Adm. Code Sec. 100.7030(b)(2)(C); Publication 130, Who is Required to Withhold Illinois Income Tax, Illinois Department of Revenue)

Bingo and slot machine winnings are subject to withholding requirements for amounts of $1,200 or more. Winnings from keno of $1,500 or more are also subject to withholding requirements. (Publication 130, Who is Required to Withhold Illinois Income Tax, Illinois Department of Revenue)

Nonresidents are not taxed by Illinois on gambling winnings unless they are professional gamblers. (Publication 130, Who is Required to Withhold Illinois Income Tax, Illinois Department of Revenue)

[¶16-656] Withholding Provisions for Farmers

Agricultural employers are required to withhold Illinois income tax from cash wages paid to farm workers in the same manner as required under the provisions of the Internal Revenue Code. (35 ILCS 5/701(a); 86 Ill. Adm. Code 100.7030(a); *Informational Bulletin, FY 90-16*, Department of Revenue, February 1990; *Taxation Today*, Department of Revenue, Spring 1990) Agricultural employers must have each farm worker complete a state Form IL W-4. If farm workers do not have a social security number, they are required to get one. If a farmer hires a crew leader as an independent contractor to provide farm workers, the workers are considered employees of the crew leader, who is responsible for withholding income taxes from the farm worker's pay. Farmers who have never withheld state taxes must register with Illinois as withholding agents. (*Taxation Today*, Department of Revenue, Spring 1990)

[¶16-660] Withholding Exemptions

Employees must complete Form IL-W-4 and submit it to their employer on or before the date employment begins, so the correct amount of Illinois income tax is withheld by the employer. The amount withheld depends, in part, on the number of personal exemption allowances (see ¶15-535) the employee claims on the form. An employee is entitled to receive one personal exemption allowance, unless the employee is claimed as a dependent on another individual's tax return. Employees who are married may claim additional personal exemption allowances for their spouse and any dependents that they are entitled to claim for federal income tax purposes. Finally, additional personal exemption allowances may be claimed if the employee or the employee's spouse is 65 or older or legally blind. (35 ILCS 5/702; 86 Ill. Adm. Code 100.7110)

Employees must complete and sign a statement of nonresidence in Illinois, Form IL-W-5-NR, if the employee's wages are exempt from Illinois income tax withholding under a reciprocal agreement (see ¶89-184) between Illinois and another state. (86 Ill. Adm. Code 100.7120)

[¶16-800]

CREDITS

[¶16-805] Credits Against Tax

Illinois allows taxpayers to claim the following personal income tax credits:

- earned income credit;
- credit for taxes paid;
- trust accumulation and capital gains distribution credit;
- property tax credit;
- withholding tax credit;
- estimated tax credit;
- high impact business credit;
- new markets credit;
- angel investment credit;
- enterprise zone credit;
- river edge redevelopment zone construction jobs credit;

- research and development credit;
- small business job creation tax credit;
- data center construction jobs credit;
- ex-felons jobs credit;
- apprenticeship education expense credit;
- Economic Development for a Growing Economy (EDGE) credit;
- river edge historic preservation credit;
- historic preservation credit;
- affordable housing donation credit;
- dependent care assistance program credit;
- adoption credit;
- education expense credit;
- student-assistance contribution credit;
- school instructional materials and supplies credit;
- Invest in Kids credit;
- TECH-PREP youth vocational programs credit;
- film production services credit;
- live theater production credit;
- hospital credit;
- natural disaster credit; and
- minimum wage withholding tax credit.

Does Illinois have any general credit provisions?

Carryforward period. Although most credits that may be claimed against Illinois personal income tax liability provide that unused credits may be carried forward for five tax years, the state does not have a general carryforward provision applicable to credits.

Filing requirements. Most Illinois personal income tax credits are computed and claimed by completing and attaching Schedule 1299-C to the taxpayer's annual Illinois income tax return. (Instructions, Schedule 1299-C, Income Tax Subtractions and Credits for Individuals)

Sunset date. Illinois income tax law provides that if the sunset date is not specified in the law that creates a credit, a taxpayer is not entitled to the credit for tax years beginning on or after 5 years from the effective date of the law creating the credit. (35 ILCS 5/250(a)) However, the automatic sunset date for credits scheduled to expire in 2011, 2012, or 2013 was extended for an additional 5 years. (35 ILCS 5/250(a))

Accountability disclosure and recapture provisions. The Illinois Corporate Accountability for Tax Expenditures Act (CAA) requires reporting of firm-level tax exemptions or credits authorized by the Department of Commerce and Economic Opportunity (DCEO), (20 ILCS 715/5) including the following credits:

- economic development for a growing economy (EDGE) credit;
- enterprise zone investment credit;and
- high impact business investment credit.

¶16-805

Disclosure provisions: Each recipient of assistance from the DCEO must submit an annual progress report disclosing the following information

- an application tracking number;

- the office mailing address, telephone number, and the name of the chief officer of the granting body;

- the office mailing address, telephone number, four-digit SIC number or successor number, and the name of the chief officer of the applicant or authorized designee for the specific project site for which development assistance is requested;

- the type of development assistance program and value of assistance that was approved by the state granting body;

- the applicant's total number of employees at the specific project site on the date the application is submitted to the granting agency, including the number of full-time permanent jobs, the number of part-time jobs, and the number of temporary jobs;

- the number of new employees and retained employees the applicant stated in its development assistance agreement, if any, if not, then in its application, would be created by the development assistance broken down by full-time, permanent, part-time, and temporary;

- a declaration of whether the recipient is in compliance with each development assistance agreement;

- a detailed list of the occupation or job classifications and number of new or retained employees to be hired in full-time permanent jobs, a schedule of anticipated starting dates of the new hires, the anticipated average wage by occupation or job classification, and the total payroll to be created as a result of the development assistance;

- a narrative, if necessary, describing why the development assistance is needed and how the applicant's use of the development assistance may reduce unemployment at any site in Illinois; and

- a certification by the chief officer of the applicant, or by a authorized designee, that the information contained in the application submitted to the granting body contains no knowing misrepresentation of material fact upon which eligibility for development assistance is based. (20 ILCS 715/20(b))

Recapture provisions: The CCA requires that all development assistance agreements for credits and other forms of development assistance must contain recapture provisions. At a minimum, incentives recipients must:

- make the level of capital investment in the economic development project specified in the development assistance agreement; and

- create and/or retain the requisite number of jobs, paying at least the wages specified for the jobs, for the duration of time specified in the authorizing legislation or the implementing administrative rules. (20 ILCS 715/25(a)(1))

If the recipient fails to create or retain the requisite number of jobs within and for the time period specified, in the legislation authorizing, or the administrative rules implementing, the development assistance programs and the development assistance agreement, the recipient is deemed to no longer qualify for the state economic assistance and the applicable recapture provisions take effect. (20 ILCS 715/25(a)(2))

PROPERTY

[¶20-100]

TAXABILITY OF PROPERTY AND PERSONS

[¶20-105] Classification of Property

Illinois law provides a single rate of assessment for all property with the exception that the Illinois Constitution authorizes counties with a population of 200,000 or more to classify real property for purposes of taxation. (Ill. Const., Art. IX, Sec. 4(b)) The classifications must be reasonable and the assessments uniform within each class. The state supreme court held that the constitutional provision was not unreasonable or arbitrary. The Property Tax Code requires such classifications to be established by ordinance of the county board. (Property Tax Code, Sec. 9-150 [35 ILCS 200/9-150])

For property subject to classification, the level of assessment or rate of tax of the highest class of property cannot exceed $2^1/_2$ times the rate of the lowest class. (Ill. Const., Art. IX, Sec. 4(b)) In addition, farm property cannot be assessed at a higher level of assessment than single family residential property. (see ¶20-115 Agriculture)

For single parcels of property that are partially includable in two or more classes, each portion is assessed at the assessment level prescribed for that class. (Cook County Real Property Taxation, Sec. 74-66)

•*Cook County*

Cook County is the only county that has classified real property. The classification ordinance divides real estate in Cook County into 15 classes and provides for varying assessment levels according to the property's uses. Tax incentives in the form of reduced assessment levels are available to qualifying industrial and commercial property in order to encourage preservation, rehabilitation and new development in certain designated areas. (Cook County Real Property Taxation, Sec. 74-63; Cook County Real Property Taxation, Sec. 74-64; Cook County Real Property Taxation, Sec. 74-70)

The classes are as follows:

Class 1 property.—This classification relates to unimproved real estate.

Class 2 property.—Included in this class are the following types of real estate:

(1) real estate used as a farm;

(2) real estate used for residential purposes when improved with a house;

(3) an apartment building of not more than six living units;

(4) a residential condominium or cooperative; and

(5) a government-subsidized housing project if required by statute to be assessed in the lowest assessment category.

Also included is real estate improved with a single room occupancy building provided the following are true:

— at least $1/_3$ of the units are leased at no more than 80% of the current fair market rent schedule (FMR schedule) for existing housing for single room occupancy units as set by the U.S. Department of Housing and Urban Development;

— no single room units are leased at rents in excess of 100% of the current FMR schedule;

— the overall maximum average rent per unit for all the units does not exceed 90% of the current FMR schedule;

— the property is in compliance with all local building, safety, and health codes and requirements.

Class 3 property.—Includes all improved real estate used for residential purposes that is not included in Class 2 or Class 9, including a single room occupancy building.

Class 4 property.—Real estate owned and used by a nonprofit corporation in furtherance of the purposes set forth in its charter, unless used for residential purposes, in which case it is classified in the appropriate residential class.

Class 5a property.—All real estate not included in Classes 1, 2, 3, 4, 6b, C, 7a, 7b, 8, 9, S, or L.

Class 5b property.—All real estate used for industrial purposes and not included in any other class.

Class 6b property.—Included in this class is the following:

(1) real estate used primarily for industrial purposes, consisting of newly constructed buildings or other structures, including land on which situated;

(2) abandoned property, including land on which property is situated; and

(3) all buildings and other structures which were substantially rehabilitated to the extent such rehabilitation has added to their value.

This classification is designed to encourage industrial development by offering a tax incentive for the development of new facilities, rehabilitation of existing structures, and the reutilization of abandoned buildings. Qualifying real estate is eligible for a reduced level of assessment from the date that new construction or substantial rehabilitation is completed, or the date of substantial reoccupancy in the case of abandoned property.

The classification will continue for 12 years from the date of new construction or assessed substantial rehabilitation or, in the case of abandoned property, the date of substantial reoccupancy. The number of renewal period requests is not limited for Class 6b treatment as long as the property continues to qualify for the classification.

Class C property.—Real estate which is used for industrial and commercial purposes, including qualifying abandoned property and the land on which the property is situated or vacant land and real estate that has undergone environmental testing and remediation due to contamination and has received a No Further Remediation letter from the Site Remediation program.

To be eligible for this classification, the applicant must have received a No Further Remediation letter confirming achievement of the remediation objectives based on the industrial or commercial use. However, property owners who previously owned or operated the site, or have business partners or family members who owned or operated the site and caused the contamination are ineligible.

An eligibility application, along with a certified copy of an ordinance or resolution adopted by the municipality in which the property is located stating that it supports and consents to the filing and finds the incentive necessary for development to occur on the property, must be filed with the Office of the Assessor within one year of the receipt of the No Further Remediation letter. In addition, the estimated remediation costs must total at least $100,000, or 25% of the property's market value prior to the remediation, whichever is less.

For industrial property, this classification may be renewed after the 9th year by filing a renewal application, along with a certified copy of an ordinance or resolution by the municipality stating that it supports and consents to the renewal and determines that the industrial use of the property is necessary and beneficial to the local economy. The number of renewal period requests is not limited as long as the property continues to qualify for the classification. For commercial property, this classification may not be renewed.

Class 7a property.—Real estate used primarily for commercial purposes and comprised of a qualified commercial development project located in an area in need of commercial development, consisting of newly constructed or substantially rehabilitated buildings or abandoned property, including land on which the property is located where total development costs excluding land does not exceed $2 million.

This incentive is intended to encourage, in areas determined to be in need of commercial development, commercial projects that would not be economically feasible without the incentive. The classification continues for a period of 12 years from the date of the new construction, substantial rehabilitation, or substantial reoccupancy in the case of abandoned property. This classification may not be renewed.

The essential part of a Class 7a application is the satisfaction of five eligibility requirements that all must be present for a project to qualify. The five factors are:

(1) *Designation of area:* the project is located in an area designated within the last 10 years as one in need of commercial development by a federal, state, or local government or agency;

(2) *Real estate tax analysis:* real estate taxes have declined or remained stagnant due to the depressed condition of the area;

(3) *Viability and timeliness:* a reasonable expectation that the development is viable and will move forward on a timely basis. Evidence of economic viability and timely completion include the following: (a) Development plan: a specific development plan is submitted, (b) Economic feasibility: the application includes pro forma financial statements which demonstrate that the proposed development is economically viable and able to sustain itself beyond the incentive period, (c) Financing: sources and terms of proposed debt and equity financing for all aspects of the project are identified, (d) Owners, developers, prime tenants, and other interested parties: detailed financial information about the project participants must be disclosed, and (e) Development schedule: a schedule that includes the construction start date, projected time to completion, and projected date of occupancy must be provided;

(4) *Assistance and necessity:* certification of the project will materially assist development of the area and it would not go forward without the incentive; and

(5) *Increased tax revenue and employment:* a statistical analysis projecting the added tax revenue and employment that will result from the development, with and without the incentive, is supplied.

An eligibility application, along with a certified copy of an ordinance or resolution adopted by the municipality in which the property is located stating that the five eligibility factors which demonstrate that the area is in need of commercial development are satisfied, must be filed with the Office of the Assessor. In addition, during the incentive period, property owners are required to file a triennial affidavit verifying the use of the property and number of employees at the site. Failure to timely file the affidavit will result in the loss of the incentive for the period relating to the nonfiling.

Class 7b property.—Real estate used primarily for commercial purposes and comprised of a qualified commercial development project located in an area in need of commercial development and used primarily for commercial purposes, consisting of newly constructed or substantially rehabilitated buildings or abandoned property, including land on which the property is located where total development costs excluding land exceeds $2 million.

This nonrenewable incentive is intended to encourage, in areas determined to be in need of commercial development, commercial projects that would not be economically feasible without the incentive. The classification continues for a period of 12 years from the date of the new construction, substantial rehabilitation, or substantial reoccupancy in the case of abandoned property.

The essential part of a Class 7b application is the satisfaction of five eligibility requirements stated for a Class 7a application and all must be present for a project to qualify. An eligibility application, along with a certified copy of an ordinance or resolution adopted by the municipality in which the property is located stating that the five eligibility factors which demonstrate that the area is in need of commercial development are satisfied, must be filed with the Office of the Assessor. In addition, during the incentive period, property owners are required to file a triennial affidavit verifying the use of the property and number of employees at the site. Failure to timely file the affidavit will result in the loss of the incentive for the period relating to the nonfiling.

Class 8 property.—Includes real estate used primarily for industrial or commercial purposes consisting of newly constructed or substantially rehabilitated buildings or abandoned property in areas certified as in need of substantial revitalization, within an enterprise community, in an empowerment zone, or in one of the townships targeted by the South Suburban Tax Reactivation Program.

This incentive is designed to encourage industrial and commercial development in areas experiencing severe economic stagnation. Qualifying real estate is assessed at reduced levels for a period of 12 years from the date that new construction or substantial rehabilitation is completed, or the date of substantial reoccupancy in the case of abandoned property. For industrial property, an application may be filed during the 10th year for a renewal of the incentive for an additional 10 year period.

An eligibility application, along with a certified copy of an ordinance or resolution adopted by the municipality in which the property is located stating that the subject area is in need of revitalization and, without public assistance, development of the area cannot be accomplished, must be filed with the Office of the Assessor. Property developed through the South Suburban Tax Reactivation Program automatically qualifies for the incentive without need for Class 8 area certification, resolution, or ordinance.

Class 9 property.—Real estate entitled to Class 3 classification must consist of multifamily residential real estate, that has undergone major rehabilitation or is new construction, is located in a targeted area, empowerment zone, or enterprise community, has at least 35% of the units leased at rents affordable to low to moderate income persons or, and is in substantial compliance with all local building, safety, and health requirements.

The goal of Class 9 is to encourage the rehabilitation and new construction of multifamily rental housing as to increase and improve the number of decent, safe, and affordable housing for low and moderate income households. Qualifying real estate is assessed at the reduced level of 16% for 10 years from the date of completion of major rehabilitation and is eligible for extensions for up to two additional 10 year terms. No real estate will be eligible for more than three 10-year periods of this designation. After the expiration of this incentive, the property will be assessed at 33% of market value.

To qualify for this classification, the applicant must:

(1) file an eligibility application prior to the commencement of rehabilitation or new construction;

(2) undertake and complete the rehabilitation or construction;

(3) maintain the property in substantial compliance with all local building, safety, and health requirements;

(4) lease at least 35% of the property dwelling units to tenants with low or moderate incomes;

(5) make a current listing of tenants and their income available to the Assessor; and

(6) annually provide the tenants with a list of permissible Class 9 rents.

Class S property.—Real estate entitled to Class 3 classification consisting of land and existing buildings and structures subject to a Section 8 contract renewed under the "Mark Up To Market" option. The portion of the land and building eligible for this incentive will be in proportion to the number of Section 8 units used for residential purposes.

Class L property.—Real estate used for commercial or industrial purposes and which:

(1) is a landmark; and

(2) has undergone substantial rehabilitation which constitutes an investment of at least 50% of the building's full market value.

The incentive will apply to the building only unless, the building has been vacant and unused for at least 24 continuous months prior to filing the eligibility application in which case the land on which the building is situated would also be eligible for the incentive.

The goal of this classification is to encourage the preservation and rehabilitation of historically and architecturally significant commercial and industrial buildings.

An eligibility application, along with a certified copy of an ordinance or resolution adopted by the municipality in which the property is located that it supports and consents to the incentive and it has reviewed and accepted its Preservation Commission's recommendation for the incentive, must be filed with the Office of the Assessor. In addition, the application must be made within one year prior to the commencement of substantial rehabilitation.

During the incentive period, property owners are required to file a triennial affidavit verifying the use of the property and number of employees at the site. Failure to timely file the affidavit will result in the loss of the incentive for the period relating to the nonfiling.

For industrial property, the incentive may be renewed during year 8 by filing a renewal application, along with a copy of an ordinance or resolution adopted by the municipality stating that it supports and consents to the renewal and the industrial use of the property is necessary and beneficial to the local economy. The number of renewal periods is not limited as long as the property continues to qualify for Class L. For commercial properties, the classification is not subject to renewal.

• *Definitions*

"Real estate" is the land and all buildings, structures, and improvements contained therein, and includes any vehicle or portable structures used as a dwelling if such structure rests on a permanent foundation.

"Market value" is the value estimated at the price it would bring at a fair voluntary sale.

"Real estate used for residential purposes" means any improvement or portion thereof occupied solely as a dwelling unit.

"Real estate used for industrial purposes" is any real estate used primarily in manufacturing, in the extraction or processing of raw materials to create new physical products, in the processing of materials for recycling, or in the transportation or storage of raw materials or finished goods in the wholesale distribution of such items for sale or leasing.

"Real estate used for commercial purposes" means any real estate used primarily for buying, selling, or providing of goods and services, including hotels and motels.

"Landmark" is a building which is specifically designated as a historic or landmark structure by local ordinance and approved by local government using criteria that have been certified by the Illinois Historic Preservation Agency.

"In need of substantial revitalization" is an area no less than ten contiguous acres or more than one contiguous square mile in size which is in a state of extreme economic depression evidenced by:

— substantial unemployment;

— low level of median family income;

— aggravated abandonment, deterioration, and underutilization of properties;

— lack of viable industrial and commercial buildings whose absence significantly contributes to the depressed economic and unemployment conditions in the area;

— a clear pattern of stagnation or decline of real estate taxes in the area as a result of its depressed condition;

— a manifest lack of economic feasibility for private enterprise to accomplish necessary development of the area without public assistance; and

— other factors which evidence an imminent threat to public health, welfare, and safety.

"Major rehabilitation" means (for Class 9 only) the extensive renovation or replacement of primary building components or systems. (Cook County Real Property Taxation, Sec. 74-62)

[¶20-115] Agriculture

There are three components in the assessment of farm real estate, and each component is separately assessed and valued in a different manner. (Property Tax Code, Sec. 10-125—Sec. 10-145 [35 ILCS 200/10-125])—(Property Tax Code, Sec. 10-145 [35 ILCS 200/10-145]) These components—farmland, farm dwellings, and farm buildings—are discussed below.

The Illinois Department of Revenue has issued instructions for assessing farmland that are updated periodically. (Publication 122, Instructions for Farmland Assessments, Illinois Department of Revenue)

Farm property assessed under these special provisions is excluded from the quadrant quadrennial assessment authorized in some larger Illinois counties. (Property Tax Code, Sec. 9-225 [35 ILCS 200/9-225]) Farmland is assessed annually.

• *Farmland*

A parcel of land used for agricultural purposes for two years is eligible for assessment as a farm. (Property Tax Code, Sec. 10-110 [35 ILCS 200/10-110])

"Farm" is defined as any tract of land used for one or more of the following uses:

— for the growing and harvesting of crops;

— for the feeding, breeding and management of livestock;

— for dairying; or

— for any other agricultural or horticultural use or combination thereof; including, but not limited to, hay, grain, fruit, truck or vegetable crops; floriculture, mushroom growing, plant or tree nurseries, orchards, forestry, sod farming and greenhouses; the keeping, raising, and feeding of livestock or poultry, including dairying, poultry, swine, sheep, beef cattle, ponies or horses, fur farming, bees, fish and wildlife farming.

(Property Tax Code, Sec. 1-60 [35 ILCS 200/1-60])

A farm does not include property that is primarily used as a residence even though some farm products are produced on the property incidental to its primary use. Farmland subject to the ongoing removal of oil, gas, coal, or any other mineral will not lose its status as farmland.

The value of farmland for assessment purposes is based on the productivity of the soil. Each soil type in the state is rated by the University of Illinois College of Agriculture according to its capability of producing crops. This rating is known as the "soil productivity index." For each of these soil ratings, there is calculated a five-year average net income, derived by taking the average gross income per acre less the average production costs per acre. The net income for each soil productivity index is then divided by the five-year moving average of the Federal Land Bank farmland mortgage interest rate to yield the soil's "agricultural economic value per acre." The equalized assessed value per acre of farmland for that soil productivity index is $33^1/_3$% of its agricultural economic value. Any increase or decrease in the equalized assessed value cannot exceed 10% of the preceding year's value, except that the limitation will be reduced by $5 per acre in tax year 2015. (Property Tax Code, Sec. 10-115 [35 ILCS 200/10-115]; *Informational Bulletin FY 2014-06*, Illinois Department of Revenue, June 2014)

This figure forms the basis for valuation of three types of farmland—cropland, permanent pasture, and "other farmland." County assessing officials value all farmland in the county on the basis of this figure, making current adjustments on individual parcels for such factors as slope, erosion, flooding, and drainage. (Property Tax Code, Sec. 10-125 [35 ILCS 200/10-125])

Other means of assessment include:

— Cropland acreage is assessed at the equalized assessed value of its soil productivity index.

— Permanent pasture is assessed at $1/_3$ of the equalized assessed value of cropland.

— Other farmland, which is neither cropland nor pasture, is assessed at $1/_6$ of the equalized assessed value of cropland.

— Wasteland is assessed on its contributory value to the farm.

The term "other farmland" includes land that is covered by an approved forestry management plan accepted by the Department of Natural Resources. (Property Tax Code, Sec. 10-150 [35 ILCS 200/10-150])

The equalized assessed value per acre of all farmland in Cook County is the lesser of either 16% of the fair cash value as measured by the price the land would bring at a fair, voluntary sale for use by the buyer for farming, or 90% of the actual 1983 average equalized assessed value per acre certified by the Department. (Property Tax Code, Sec. 10-130 [35 ILCS 200/10-130])

Farmland assessments are not subject to state or local equalization as are other residential real property assessments. (Property Tax Code, Sec. 10-135 [35 ILCS 200/10-135])

• *Farm dwellings*

Farm dwellings and the land on which they are immediately situated are assessed as part of the farm. (Property Tax Code, Sec. 10-145 [35 ILCS 200/10-145]) Farm dwellings are assessed at 33^1/3% of fair cash value; in counties that classify real property for purposes of taxation (Cook County), they are assessed at the percentage required by the county ordinance. The equalization factors of the normal assessment procedure are applied to the assessed value of farm dwellings.

• *Farm buildings*

Roadside stands and buildings used for storing and protecting farm machinery and equipment, housing livestock or poultry, or storing feed or grain are assessed at 33^1/3% of their value on the basis of their current use and contribution to the productivity of the farm. (Property Tax Code, Sec. 10-140 [35 ILCS 200/10-140])

• *Administration of farmland assessment law*

A five-person Farmland Assessment Technical Advisory Board assists the Department in calculating the assessments for each productivity index. (Property Tax Code, Sec. 10-115 [35 ILCS 200/10-115]) By May 1 prior to the assessment date, the Department of Revenue must make a certification of use-value assessment data and county-average assessments to all local county assessing officials.

Local assessing officials are responsible for applying the certified values for the various soil types to individual parcels. County Farmland Assessment Review Committees are established in each county to advise the chief county assessing official with regard to the Department's recommendation and application of the values certified. (Property Tax Code, Sec. 10-120 [35 ILCS 200/10-120]) A department rule details the receipt and processing requirements for farmland reviews. (86 Ill. Admin. Code Sec. 110.165) This committee may also propose alternate recommendations to the Department if the committee disagrees with the state-certified values. The State Property Tax Appeal Board makes the final decision as to the appropriate values and procedures to be used in a county. Decisions of the Board on the use-values are not subject to administrative review by the courts.

The Department of Revenue is further responsible for reviewing the assessments to determine compliance with the law. (Property Tax Code, Sec. 16-200 [35 ILCS 200/16-200]) The Department may also order reassessments.

• *Vegetative filter strips*

Through December 31, 2026, land located between a farm field and an area to be protected, including surface water, streams, rivers, or sinkholes, is considered a vegetative filter strip. The land must be at least 66 feet in width and contain vegetation that has a dense top growth, forms a uniform ground cover, has a heavy fibrous root system, and tolerates pesticides used in the farm field. (Property Tax Code, Sec. 10-152 [35 ILCS 200/10-152])

In counties with fewer than 3 million inhabitants, vegetative filter strips will be valued at one-sixth of their productivity index equalized assessed value as cropland. In counties with 3 million or more inhabitants, the land will be valued at the lesser of:

(1) 16% of the fair cash value of the farmland estimated at the price it would bring at a fair, voluntary sale for use by the buyer as a farm; or

(2) 90% of the 1983 average equalized assessed value per acre certified by the Department of Revenue.

(Property Tax Code, Sec. 10-152 [35 ILCS 200/10-152])

CCH COMMENT: *Disparate treatment between farms and nurseries valid.—* Crops growing on a farm are assessed as personal property that is not subject to property tax. However, stock growing at a nursery is assessed as real estate subject to property tax. This differing tax treatment was found to be constitutional because nursery stock has the characteristics of growing trees permanently located on realty. In addition, the importance of nursery stock cannot compare to that of food crops. (*Knupper et al. v. Board* (IL App Ct 1978) 61 IllApp3d 884, 378 NE2d 340)

• *Agricultural societies*

The General Assembly is authorized by the Illinois Constitution to enact provisions exempting property used exclusively for agricultural and horticultural societies. (Ill. Const., Art. IX, Sec. 6) The legislative enactment statute repeats the constitutional exemption with the added requirement that the property not be used with a view to profit. (Property Tax Code, Sec. 15-85 [35 ILCS 200/15-85])

[¶20-135] Computer Hardware and Software

Illinois has no specific statutory or regulatory provisions regarding computer hardware and software.

[¶20-145] Construction Work in Progress

The construction of new or added buildings, structures, or other improvements on property after January 1 causes the property owner to be liable for increased taxes on a proportionate basis from the date on which the occupancy permit was issued or on which the improvement was inhabitable and fit for occupancy or for intended customary use. The owner must notify the assessor within 30 days of completion of the issuance of an occupancy permit or within 30 days of completion of the improvement and must request reassessment. (Property Tax Code, Sec. 9-180 [35 ILCS 200/9-180])

Illinois also has provisions addressing the taxability of repair and maintenance work done on residential property (see ¶20-640 Real Property Valuation) and for the construction of model homes built for display or demonstration purposes only. The law also allows the valuation to stay the same after subdividing property, adding streets and utilities, etc.

[¶20-165] Energy Systems or Facilities

Illinois has special assessment provisions for low sulfur dioxide emission coal-fueled devices, solar heating and cooling systems, and wind energy devices.

• *Low-sulphur dioxide emission coal-fueled devices*

Low sulfur dioxide emission coal-fueled devices certified as such by the Illinois Pollution Control Board are assessed at $33^1/3\%$ of fair cash value. (Property Tax Code, Sec. 11-35 [35 ILCS 200/11-35]) Fair cash value is the net value realized by the owner after removal and sale of the device at a fair, voluntary sale, giving consideration to the expense of removal, site restoration, and transportation. (Property Tax Code, Sec. 11-45 [35 ILCS 200/11-45]; 86 Ill. Admin. Code Sec. 110.110)

Any device used or intended to burn or convert locally available coal in a manner that eliminates or significantly reduces the need for additional sulfur abatement qualifies as a low sulfur dioxide emission coal-fueled device. All machinery, equipment, structures, and related apparatus of a coal gasification facility qualify, including coal feeding equipment, for conversion of coal into low sulfur gaseous fuel and management of wastes. (Property Tax Code, Sec. 11-40 [35 ILCS 200/11-40])

Proceedings for the assessment of certified devices are in accordance with the procedural regulations of the Department of Revenue. (Property Tax Code, Sec. 11-65 [35 ILCS 200/11-65])

Certification process.—Low sulfur dioxide emission coal-fueled devices certified by the Pollution Control Board are assessed by the Department of Revenue. (Property Tax Code, Sec. 11-50 [35 ILCS 200/11-50]; 86 Ill. Admin. Code Sec. 110.110) In order to be eligible for the special assessment, an application for certification must be filed with the Illinois Pollution Control Board. (Property Tax Code, Sec. 11-55 [35 ILCS 200/11-55]; 86 Ill. Admin. Code Sec. 110.110) The effective date of certification is the January 1 preceding the date of construction of the device or the date of application, whichever is later. Once certified, the Department assesses the property and notifies the local county assessor to remove the property from the local property tax rolls. (86 Ill. Admin. Code Sec. 110.110)

Before denying any certificate, notice and an opportunity for hearing must be given in writing to the applicant. The Pollution Control Board may on its own initiative revoke or modify a sulfur dioxide emission coal fueled device certificate when the certificate was obtained by fraud or misrepresentation and the holder of the certificate has failed substantially to proceed with the construction or installation of the device. (Property Tax Code, Sec. 11-30 [35 ILCS 200/11-30]) Appeal from a decision of the Pollution Control Board may be sought under the Administrative Review Law. (see ¶20-906) (Property Tax Code, Sec. 11-60 [35 ILCS 200/11-60])

• *Solar heating and cooling systems*

When a solar energy system is installed as an improvement on any property, the property may be assessed, on application to the chief county assessment officer, as though a conventional heating or cooling system were installed if it provides a lower valuation. This valuation remains in effect as long as the solar energy equipment is used. When the equipment ceases to be used, the owner must notify the chief county assessment officer by certified mail within 30 days. (Property Tax Code, Sec. 10-10 [35 ILCS 200/10-10])

The law defines "solar energy," "solar collector," "solar storage mechanism" and "solar energy system". (Property Tax Code, Sec. 10-5 [35 ILCS 200/10-5])

• *Wind energy property assessment*

The fair cash value of wind energy devices is determined by subtracting the allowance for physical depreciation from the trended real property cost basis. Functional obsolescence and external obsolescence may further reduce the fair cash value of the device, to the extent they are proved. (Property Tax Code, Sec. 200/10-605 35 ILCS 200/10-605]) These assessment provisions apply for assessment years through 2021 and do not apply to wind energy devices owned by any person or entity that is otherwise exempt from property taxation. (Property Tax Code, Sec. 200/10-610 [35 ILCS 200/10-610])

A "wind energy device" is any device with a nameplate capacity of at least 0.5 megawatts, that is used in the process of converting kinetic energy from the wind to generate electric power for commercial use. (Property Tax Code, Sec. 200/10-600 [35 ILCS 200/10-600])

Wind energy assessable property is not subject to equalization or equalization factors applied by the Department of Revenue or any board of review, assessor, or chief county assessment officer. (Property Tax Code, Sec. 200/10-615 [35 ILCS 200/10-615]) A wind energy device owner must, at the owner's own expense, use an Illinois registered land surveyor to prepare a plat showing the metes and bounds description, including access routes, of the area immediately surrounding the device. The owner also is responsible for recording the plat and delivering a copy to the chief county assessment officer and the owner of the land surrounding the platted area. (Property Tax Code, Sec. 200/10-620 [35 ILCS 200/10-620])

¶20-165

[¶20-170] Enterprise Zones and Other Redevelopment Areas

Local property tax abatement is authorized for real property, or any class thereof, located within an enterprise zone created under the Illinois Enterprise Zone Act. The amount of taxes that may be abated cannot exceed the amount attributable to new construction, renovation, or rehabilitation. In the case of property within a redevelopment area created under the Real Property Tax Increment Allocation Redevelopment Act, or the County Economic Development Project Area Property Tax Allocation Act, abatement cannot exceed the amount of taxes allocable to the taxing district. (Property Tax Code, Sec. 18-170 [35 ILCS 200/18-170]; Real Property Tax Increment Allocation Redevelopment Act, Sec. 11-74.4-1 [65 ILCS 5/11-74.4-1]; County Economic Development Project Area Property Tax Allocation Act, Sec. 7.80 [20 ILCS 3505/7.80])

The authority of a taxing district to abate taxes of enterprise zone property is neither expressly nor by implication made subject to the limitations contained in the abatement provisions for industrial firms.

[¶20-195] Health Care Facilities and Equipment

Illinois has no specific statutory or regulatory provisions regarding health care facilities and equipment. However, see ¶20-285 Nonprofit, Religious, Charitable, Scientific, and Educational Organizations regarding the property of health service plans.

[¶20-205] Homestead

The Illinois Constitution authorizes homestead exemptions or rent credits. (Ill. Const., Art. IX, Sec. 6) Pursuant to this authorization, the legislature has established several types of homesteads exemptions, some of which are discussed below.

• *General homestead exemption*

A general homestead exemption is given to residential property occupied by the owner as a principal residence unless an alternative general homestead exemption has been adopted by the county where the residence is located. The maximum exemption is $10,000 in Cook County and $6,000 in all other counties.

If a county has elected to subject itself to the alternative general homestead exemption (see below), then for the first taxable year only after the provisions of that exemption no longer apply, for owners who, for the taxable year, have not been granted a senior citizens assessment freeze homestead exemption, or a long-time occupant homestead exemption (see below), there shall be an additional exemption of $5,000 for owners with a maximum household income of $30,000. (Property Tax Code, Sec. 15-175 [35 ILCS 200/15-175])

A leasehold interest in a single-family dwelling that is occupied as a residence by a person who is liable for the payment of property taxes and who has an ownership interest in the residence qualifies for the exemption. (Property Tax Code, Sec. 15-175 [35 ILCS 200/15-175])

In counties with populations of less than 3 million, in the event of a sale of homestead property, the homestead exemption will remain in effect for the rest of the assessment year. The county assessment officer may require that the new owner apply for the homestead exemption for the following year. If the current equalized assessed value of the homestead property is greater than the equalized value of the property for 1977, the owner will automatically receive the exemption in an amount equal to the increase over the 1977 assessment up to the maximum allowed. (Property Tax Code, Sec. 15-175 [35 ILCS 200/15-175])

In the event of a sale of homestead property in counties with populations of more than 3 million, the homestead exemption shall remain in effect for the remainder of the assessment year of the sale. Upon receipt of an appropriate transfer declaration transmitted by the recorder, the assessor must mail a notice and forms to the new owner of the property providing information pertaining to filing periods for applying or reapplying for homestead exemptions. If the new owner fails to timely apply or reapply for a homestead exemption or the property no longer qualifies for an existing homestead exemption, the assessor shall cancel such exemption for any ensuing assessment year. (Property Tax Code, Sec. 15-175 [35 ILCS 200/15-175])

Certain "life care facilities" are cooperatives eligible for the homestead exemption when the applicant for the homestead exemption has a life care contract requiring the applicant to pay real property taxes. The exemption will be based on the number of apartments or units occupied by persons 65 years or older, irrespective of any legal, equitable, or leasehold interest in the facility. (Property Tax Code, Sec. 15-170 [35 ILCS 200/15-170]; Property Tax Code, Sec. 15-175 [35 ILCS 200/15-175])

Married persons living in separate qualifying residences each receive 50% of the exemption. (Property Tax Code, Sec. 15-175 [35 ILCS 200/15-175])

The assessor or chief county assessment officer may determine the eligibility of residential property to receive the exemption by application, visual inspection, questionnaire, or other reasonable methods. (Property Tax Code, Sec. 15-175 [35 ILCS 200/15-175])

• *Alternative general homestead exemption*

In lieu of the general homestead exemption, a county may adopt ordinances to establish an annual homestead exemption equal to a reduction in the property's equalized assessed value up to pre-set maximum values. (Property Tax Code, Sec. 15-176(a) [35 ILCS 200/15-176(a)])

• *Longtime occupant homestead exemption*

If a county has elected to be subject to the alternative general homestead exemption, regardless of whether that exemption applies, qualified homestead property is entitled to an annual homestead exemption for homeowners who generally have occupied a homestead property as a principal residence for 10 years (five years for persons receiving qualifying government assistance) and who have a household income of less than $100,000. (Property Tax Code, Sec. 15-177 [35 ILCS 200/15-177]) The amount of the exemption is the greater of:

(1) the equalized assessed value of the homestead property for the current tax year minus the adjusted homestead value; or

(2) the general homestead deduction.

(Property Tax Code, Sec. 15-177(d) [35 ILCS 200/15-177(d)])

For married persons who maintain separate residences, this exemption may be claimed by only one person and for only one residence. Anyone who receives the long-time occupant homestead exemption cannot also receive a senior citizen assessment freeze homestead exemption, a general homestead exemption, or an alternative general homestead exemption. (Property Tax Code, Sec. 15-177(f) [35 ILCS 200/15-177(f)])

If a qualified homestead property is sold or the ownership is transferred between spouses or between a parent and a child, the exemption will remain in effect if the new owner has a household income of less than $100,000. (Property Tax Code, Sec. 15-177(g) [35 ILCS 200/15-177(g)]) For all other sales or transfers, the exemption will remain in effect for the remainder of the tax year and be calculated using the same base homestead value in which the sale or transfer occurs. (Property Tax Code, Sec. 15-177(h) [35 ILCS 200/15-177(h)])

• *Longtime owner-occupant exemption or deferral*

Longtime owner-occupants may be granted an exemption or deferral, or a combination of the two, by counties for that portion of an increase in real property taxes that is due to an increase in the market value of the real property as a consequence of the refurbishing or renovating of other residences or the construction of new residences in long-established residential areas or areas of deteriorated, vacant, or abandoned homes and properties. The exemption or deferral may be effective until the longtime owner-occupant transfers title to the property. (Longtime Owner-Occupant Property Tax Relief Act, Sec. 15 [35 ILCS 250/15])

Eligibility notifications must be mailed to the address of the record owner on file with the county. If the notification is mailed to a mortgagee as the only address of the record owner on file, then the mortgagee is required to forward a copy of the notice to each mortgagor within 30 days of receipt. However, the mortgagee will have no liability for failure to forward such notice. (Longtime Owner-Occupant Property Tax Relief Act, Sec. 15 [35 ILCS 250/15])

The corporate authority of a county may impose additional criteria for qualifying for an exemption or deferral including age and income limitations, and a requirement that an applicant own or occupy the property as a principal residence for 10 or more years. A deferral or exemption may not exceed $20,000 in equalized assessed value per tax year. (Longtime Owner-Occupant Property Tax Relief Act, Sec. 20 [35 ILCS 250/20])

A "longtime owner-occupant" is defined as a person who, for at least 10 continuous years, has owned and occupied the same dwelling as a principal residence and domicile, or any person who for at least five years has owned and occupied the same dwelling as a principal residence and domicile if that person received assistance in the acquisition of the property as part of a government or nonprofit housing program. (Longtime Owner-Occupant Property Tax Relief Act, Sec. 10 [35 ILCS 250/10])

• *Erroneous grants of exemption—Cook County*

In Cook County, when the chief county assessment officer determines that one or more erroneous homestead exemptions was applied to the property, the erroneous exemption principal amount, together with all applicable interest and penalties, will constitute a lien on the property receiving the erroneous homestead exemption. A lien will not be filed if the property owner pays the erroneous exemption principal amount, plus penalties and interest, within 30 days of service of the notice of intent to record a lien. (35 ILCS 200/9-275) "Erroneous exemption principal amount" means the total amount of property tax principal that would have been billed to a property index number but for the erroneous homestead exemption or exemptions a taxpayer received. (35 ILCS 200/9-275)

The chief assessment officer of Cook County, Illinois, can record liens against certain property in the county that has received one or more erroneous homestead exemptions from property tax. (35 ILCS 200/9-275)

The law is applicable to nine homestead exemptions that respectively apply to disabled veterans, returning veterans, disabled persons, disabled veterans standard homestead, senior citizens, senior citizens assessment freeze, general homestead, alternative general homestead, or long-time occupant. (35 ILCS 200/9-275) The chief county assessment officer is required to include in each assessment notice during any general assessment year information on homestead exemptions, including penalties and interest that may be incurred for erroneous exemptions received in earlier years. The notice also must inform owners of a 60-day grace period in which to pay the tax and avoid penalties. (35 ILCS 200/9-275)

Penalties and limitations periods, as well as access to amnesty provisions, depend, in part, on the number of erroneous exemptions granted. A lien can be recorded against property in the county if the property owner received:

(1) one or two erroneous homestead exemptions for real property, including at least one erroneous exemption granted for the property against which the lien is sought, during any of the three assessment years immediately prior to the assessment year in which the notice of intent to record a lien is served; or

(2) three or more erroneous exemptions for real property, including at least one erroneous exemption granted for the property against which the lien is sought, during any of the six assessment years immediately prior to the assessment year in which the notice of intent to record a lien is served.

(35 ILCS 200/9-275)

If a person received an erroneous homestead exemption, the person is not liable for penalties for any year(s) during which the chief county assessment officer did not require a renewal application for a multi-year exemption if: (1) the person was the spouse, child, grandchild, brother, sister, niece, or nephew of the previous taxpayer; and (2) the person received the property by bequest or inheritance. (35 ILCS 200/9-275)

Aside from identifying the specific property, specific erroneous homestead exemption granted, and the erroneous principal amount due and the interest amount and any penalty, a notice of intent to record a tax lien must inform the owner of the right to request a hearing and appeal a hearing officer's ruling, as well as inform the owner that the amount due, plus interest and penalties, must be paid within 30 days. A lien will not be filed if the property owner pays the erroneous exemption principal amount, plus penalties and interest, within 30 days of service of the notice. (35 ILCS 200/9-275)

For taxable years 2019 through 2023, if the chief county assessment officer in Cook County learns that a taxpayer who has been granted a senior citizens homestead exemption has died during the exemption period, the officer must send notice to the address on record for the property owner of record notifying them the exemption will be terminated unless they provide within 90 days a basis to continue the exemption. (35 ILCS 200/9-275)

Penalties.—A lien may not be filed sooner than 60 days after:

(1) notice is delivered to the owner if no hearing is requested or

(2) the conclusion of the hearing and appeals, if requested.

For owners of property that received one or two erroneous exemptions in the immediately preceding three assessment years, the erroneous exemption principal amount plus 10% annual interest or portion thereof from the date the erroneous exemption principal amount would have become due if properly included in the tax bill will be charged against the property. For owners of property that receive three or more erroneous exemptions in the immediately preceding six assessment years, the arrearage, a penalty of 50% of the total amount of arrearage for each year, and 10% annual interest will be charged against the property. (35 ILCS 200/9-275)

[¶20-215] Housing

A common area in a residential development, not including condominiums, is assessed proportionately among the owners in the development that have the beneficial use and enjoyment of such area. For assessment purposes, common areas used for recreational or similar residential purposes and separately assessed to an owner listed on separately identified parcels are valued at $1 per year. In Cook County, application to reestablish an assessment of $1 for any parcel on grounds of common area status must be submitted to the assessor. (Property Tax Code, Sec. 10-35 [35 ILCS 200/10-35])

• *Platted and subdivided land*

In counties with fewer than 3 million inhabitants, the improvement of platted and subdivided property into separate lots with streets, sidewalks, curbs, gutters, sewer, water, and utility lines does not increase its valuation until a habitable structure is completed on the lot, the property is used for any business, commercial, or residential purpose, or the lot is sold.

The land must be:

— platted and subdivided in accordance with the Plat Act (765 ILCS 205/0.01, *et seq.*);

— platted after January 1, 1978;

— in excess of ten acres at the time of platting; and

— vacant land or be used as a farm at the time of platting.

Generally, until a subdivided lot has a completed habitable structure, the property is assessed yearly based on the estimated price it would bring at a fair voluntary sale for use by the buyer for the same purpose for which it was used before platting. (Property Tax Code, Sec. 10-30 [35 ILCS 200/10-30]) However, the annual assessment requirement does not apply to property in a special service area for which the ad valorem taxes are extended solely upon the equalized assessed value of the land without regard to improvements. (Property Tax Code, Sec. 27-75 [35 ILCS 200/27-75])

• *Old people's homes and facilities for developmentally disabled*

A charitable exemption for an old people's home or facility for the developmentally disabled is discussed at ¶ 20-155 Disabled Persons.

[¶ 20-230] Intangible Property

Illinois has no statutory or regulatory provisions regarding intangible property.

[¶ 20-245] Leased Property

Although some land within the state may itself be exempt from taxation, leases of that same property are taxable to the lessee. (Property Tax Code, Sec. 9-195 [35 ILCS 200/9-195])

With the exception of Cook County, taxable leasehold estates are assessed at 33¹/₃% of fair cash value. (Property Tax Code, Sec. 9-145 [35 ILCS 200/9-145]) In Cook County, leaseholds are assessed under the county's classification ordinance. Buildings and structures located on the right-of-way of any canal, railroad, or other company that are leased or granted to another company for a term of years are also subject to the general 33¹/₃% assessment rule.

The leasehold estate and the improvements thereon are listed as the property of the lessee or assignee. (Property Tax Code, Sec. 9-195 [35 ILCS 200/9-195])

The proper basis for computing fair cash value of a leasehold is the current market rental of the property over the unexpired term of the lease. Since rent is paid in future installments, not in a lump sum, the value of the future installments is determined by multiplying the current market rental of the entire property by the present value of an annual payment of $1 for the unexpired term of the lease. Incremental or potential profit value have been rejected as methods for valuing leaseholds.

When a lease covers only unimproved land, and the lessee constructs improvements on the leasehold, the fair cash value of the leasehold is computed by the market rental for the land as improved, rather than the contractual rent or the market rental for an unimproved lot. This result obtains whether the improvements are owned by the lessor or by the lessee, even though they revert to the lessor upon termination of the lease.

• *License v. lease*

The distinction between a "license" or a "lease" arising from an interest in tax-exempt land has been the issue of several Illinois court decisions. A license differs from a lease in that the former gives the licensee a right to enter on the licensor's land and use it for a specific purpose. The licensor has legal possession and control over the property. In a lease, the lessee possesses an estate and controls the property against the lessor. Unlike leases, licenses for the use of exempt property are not a taxable interest under. (Property Tax Code, Sec. 9-195 [35 ILCS 200/9-195])

• *Other tax-exempt property*

There are several provisions throughout the Illinois Compiled Statutes authorizing a leasehold tax on exempt property (*i.e.,* property owned by a port district Property Tax Code, Sec. 15-155 [35 ILCS 200/15-155]), property of the Illinois State Toll Highway Authority (Illinois Toll Highways Act, Sec. 22 [605 ILCS 10/22]), and property of the Industrial Project Revenue Bond Act. (Illinois Industrial Project Revenue Bond Act, Sec. 11-74-4 [65 ILCS 5/11-74-4]) Generally, the statutes state that property acquired by the municipality under the terms of the Act is exempt from taxation while owned by the governmental entity, but a tax to be paid by the lessee is levied on any lease of such property for uses not exempt under. (Property Tax Code, Sec. 15-10—Sec. 15-20 [35 ILCS 200/15-10]—[35 ILCS 200/15-20]) This does not include a leasehold created pursuant to a transaction set out in (Property Tax Code, Sec. 15-100 [35 ILCS 200/15-100])

For a municipality with a population over 100,000, an exemption applies to property the municipality owns (or property interests or rights the municipality holds) that is used for toll road or toll bridge purposes and that is leased or licensed for these purposes to another entity whose property, property interests, or rights, are not exempt. The exemption applies regardless of whether such property, interests or rights are wholly or partially inside or outside the corporate limits. The exemption does not apply to any leasehold interest in such property, interest, or rights. (Property Tax Code, Sec. 15-60 [35 ILCS 200/15-60])

There is an exemption for leasehold interests in government-owned property leased by either municipalities of over 500,000 inhabitants, units of local governments at least partially within those municipalities, or any municipality with home rule powers that is contiguous to a municipality with a population of over 500,000 inhabitants, that, effective January 1, 2020, is used by the lessee for the purpose of parking and is leased for continued use for the same purpose to another entity whose property is not exempt. (Property Tax Code, Sec. 15-185(b) [35 ILCS 200/15-185(b)]) Effective January 1, 2020, the exemption is also amended to stipulate that property located in a municipality with a population of over 500,000 is exempt due to its use for parking. Any part of the property used for other purposes is subject to tax for the time that it is used for a non-exempt purpose. However, the use of a part of the property for a non-exempt purpose has no effect on:

• the exemption of the remaining part of the property that continues to be used for parking, or

• the future exemption of that same part of the property if it stops being used for a non-exempt purpose and returned to use for parking. No taxes will be assessed on any part of the property before January 1, 2020.

(Property Tax Code, Sec. 15-185(b) [35 ILCS 200/15-185(b)])

Leaseback of government property.—If the state of Illinois sells the James R. Thompson Center or the Elgin Mental Health Center in Elgin, Illinois, to another entity and immediately thereafter enters into a leaseback agreement that gives the state a right to use, control, and possess the property, that portion of the property will remain exempt from taxation. (Property Tax Code, Sec. 15-155 [35 ILCS 200/15-55]) Also, property owned by either a municipality with a population of over 500,000 inhabitants, a unit of local governments at least partially within those municipalities, or any municipality with home rule powers that is contiguous to a municipality with a population of over 500,000 inhabitants, will remain exempt if the property is leased, sold, or transferred to another entity and immediately thereafter is the subject of a leaseback agreement that gives the municipality a right to:

> (1) use, control, and possess the property or

> (2) require the other entity to use the property in the performance of services for the municipality.

(Property Tax Code, Sec. 15-185(a) [35 ILCS 200/15-185(a)])

• *PPV leases*

Illinois property tax valuation provisions have been adopted for leasehold interests in U.S. military public/private residential developments (PPV lease). Unless otherwise agreed pursuant to a qualifying separate agreement, PPV leases must be classified and valued during the period beginning January 1, 2006, and ending December 31, 2055. (Property Tax Code, Sec. 10-365 [35 ILCS 200/10-365]) A PPV lease is a leasehold interest in exempt U.S. property of a non-exempt party for the purpose of designing, financing, constructing, renovating, managing, operating, and maintaining rental housing units and associated improvements at military training facilities, military bases, and related military support facilities in Illinois. (Property Tax Code, Sec. 10-370 [35 ILCS 200/10-370])

Counties must use certain PPV-related provisions in assessing and valuing any PPV lease for taxable years 2006 through 2055. (Property Tax Code, Sec. 10-380 [35 ILCS 200/10-380]) A PPV lease must be valued at its fair cash value, which must be determined by using an income capitalization approach. The fair cash value of a PPV lease is determined by dividing the net operating income by a rate of 12% plus the actual or most recently ascertainable tax load factor for the year. Financial information is to be reported to the appropriate chief county assessment officer by April 15 of each year. (Property Tax Code, Sec. 10-375 [35 ILCS 200/10-375])

For naval training facilities, naval bases, and naval support facilities, in assessing and determining the value of any PPV leases for property tax purposes "net operating income" all revenues received minus actual expenses before interest, taxes, depreciation, and amortization. (Property Tax Code, Sec. 10-370 [35 ILCS 200/10-370])

For all other military training facilities, military bases, and related military "net operating income" means all revenues received minus the lesser of:

The definition of "new property" under the Property Tax Extension Limitation Law includes, upon final stabilization of occupancy after new construction, any real property located within the boundaries of an otherwise or previously exempt military reservation that is intended for residential use and owned by or leased to a private corporation or other entity. (Property Tax Code, Sec. 18-185 [35 ILCS 200/18-185])

[¶20-260] Manufactured and Mobile Homes

Whether a manufactured or mobile home is assessed and taxed as chattel or as real property depends upon when and where it was installed. Manufactured and mobile homes will be assessed and taxed under either the Property Tax Act, the Mobile Home Local Services Tax Act, and/or the Manufactured Home Installation Act. Primarily, the difference relates to whether the manufactured or mobile home is located within a mobile home park or on private property outside a mobile home park and when it was installed. Whether a mobile or manufactured home is affixed to a permanent foundation generally will not bear on its taxability.

• *Mobile homes located in mobile home parks (Mobile Home Local Services Tax Act)*

Mobile homes and manufactured homes in mobile home parks must be assessed and taxed as chattel under the terms of the Mobile Home Local Services Tax Act. For purposes of the act, the terms "mobile home" and "manufactured home" are synonymous. (Mobile Home Local Services Tax Act, Sec. 1 [35 ILCS 515/1(a)])

There is an exemption from the Mobile Home Local Services Tax Act for, among others, disabled veterans.

"Manufactured home" means a factory-assembled, completely integrated structure designed for permanent habitation, with a permanent chassis, and so constructed as to permit its transport, on wheels temporarily or permanently attached to its frame, and is a movable or portable unit that is:

  (i) 8 body feet or more in width;

  (ii) 40 body feet or more in length; and

  (iii) 320 or more square feet.

It is constructed to be towed on its own chassis from the place of its construction to the location, or subsequent locations, at which it is installed and set up and connected to utilities for year-round occupancy for use as a permanent habitation, and designed and situated so as to permit its occupancy as a dwelling place for one or more persons. The term includes units containing parts that may be folded, collapsed, or telescoped when being towed and that may be expected to provide additional cubic capacity, and that are designed to be joined into one integral unit capable of being separated again into the components for repeated towing. The term excludes campers and recreational vehicles. ([35 ILCS 515/1])

The tax assessed under the act is in lieu of property tax and is assessed at a rate/ per square feet that changes based on how old the mobile home is, as follows:

Tax year following model year	Tax per square foot
model year - second year	15 cents
third - fifth years	13.5 cents
sixth - eighth	12 cents
ninth - eleventh	10.5 cents
twelfth - fourteenth	9 cents
fifteenth and subsequent	7.5 cents

(Mobile Home Local Services Tax Act, Sec. 3 [35 ILCS 515/3])

Penalties.—Failure to pay the tax will result in a penalty of $25 for each month the tax is delinquent up to a maximum of $100. In counties with a population over 700,000 and less than 900,000, if any local services tax (or part thereof) imposed under the Mobile Home Local Services Tax Act is not paid by the due date for the tax, the taxpayer must pay a penalty of $25 per month (or any part thereof) not to exceed the lesser of: (1) $100, or (2) 50% of the original tax imposed. In all counties, if the failure to pay is due to fraud, an additional penalty of 50% of the deficiency will be assessed. ([35 ILCS 515/9])

In Illinois counties designated as disaster areas that enact qualified ordinances, taxpayers whose mobile homes were substantially or adversely damaged during the disaster may pay delinquent mobile home local services taxes without penalty until the last working day before a court enters an order for sale of the property. In addition, the date on which the taxes become delinquent may be postponed. The ordinance also may direct the county to refund tax payments under certain circumstances. ([35 ILCS 515/9.3])

• *Mobile homes located outside mobile home parks*

Mobile homes and manufactured homes (homes) that are installed on private property that is not a mobile home park will be assessed and subject to Illinois property tax as real property. ([35 ILCS 200/1-130]; [35 ILCS 517/10])

Any home that is located outside of a mobile home park and taxed under the Mobile Home Local Services Tax Act prior to 2011 will continue to be taxed under that act and will not be classified, assessed, and taxed as real property until the mobile home is sold, transferred, or relocated to a different parcel of land outside of a mobile home park. However, the owner of a mobile home located outside of a mobile home park can ask the Department of Revenue to have the home classified, assessed, and taxed as real property. ([35 ILCS 200/1-130(b)]; [35 ILCS 517/10])

• *Permanent foundations*

Mobile homes and manufactured homes that are sold and transferred from a mobile home park to private property, or that are already located on private property, are subject to property tax, whether or not the mobile home or manufactured home is affixed to, or installed on, a permanent foundation or is considered real property under other Illinois law. Such homes located outside of a mobile home park also are taxable whether or not they are affixed to a permanent foundation or are considered real property under other Illinois law. ([35 ILCS 200/1-130(b)])

For mobile home local services tax purposes, mobile homes and manufactured homes located outside a mobile home park are assessed as real property whether or not they are affixed to a permanent foundation or are considered real property under other Illinois law. Such homes that are sold and transferred from a mobile home park to private property are taxable, whether or not the mobile home or manufactured home is affixed to a permanent foundation or is considered real property under other Illinois law. Such homes that are already located on private property when they are sold are taxable whether or not the mobile home or manufactured home is affixed to, or installed on, a permanent foundation or is considered real property under other Illinois law. Both mobile homes and manufactured homes located on a dealer's lot for resale purposes or as a temporary office are not subject to the tax. ([35 ILCS 517/10])

[¶20-265] Manufacturing and Industrial Property

Land used for industrial purposes is assessed as other land in Illinois because there is a single rate of assessment for real property in Illinois, except in Cook County. (Property Tax Code, Sec. 24-5 [35 ILCS 200/24-5]) Cook County divides real estate into 15 classes and provides varying assessment levels according to the property's uses. Cook County classes relating to industrial property are as follows:

— real estate used for industrial purposes and not included in any other class is covered by class 5b;

— industrial real estate consisting of newly constructed buildings or substantially rehabilitated building is a class 6b;

— industrial real estate consisting of abandoned or vacant property and has undergone environmental testing and remediation due to contamination is a class C;

— industrial real estate consisting of newly constructed or substantially rehabilitated buildings or abandoned in areas certified as severe blight is a class 8;

— industrial real estate consisting of newly constructed or substantially rehabilitated buildings or abandoned in areas certified as severe blight and is subject to a qualifying sales tax abatement ordinance is a class 8a;

— and industrial property which is a landmark and has undergone substantial rehabilitation is a class L.

(Cook County Real Property Taxation, Sec. 74-63; Cook County Real Property Taxation, Sec. 74-64; Cook County Real Property Taxation, Sec. 74-70) For more details on the Cook County classification system see ¶ 20-105, Classification of Property.

Property taxes may be abated on industrial property. For further discussion see ¶ 20-810.

Industrial property may be subject to tax if it classified as a fixture. Under the integrated industrial doctrine rule to determine whether property is a fixture, all machinery of a factory or plant necessary for its operation as a going concern is considered part of the realty for taxation. Under this doctrine, physical annexation is subordinated to the interrelationship between the piece of property and the use of the real estate.

• *Tools*

Illinois does not tax personal property.

[¶ 20-270] Mining, Oil, and Gas Properties

Oil, gas, coal, and other minerals are taxable property. (Property Tax Code, Sec. 1-130 [35 ILCS 200/1-130]) With the exception of coal, which is subject to special valuation (see below), all minerals are assessed separately from the other part of the land at $33^1/_3\%$ of fair cash value. Mines and quarries are taxable property and assessed at the same rate as most Illinois property—$33^1/_3\%$ of its fair cash value. (Property Tax Code, Sec. 9-145 [35 ILCS 200/9-145])

Mining rights which are conveyed by deed or lease are also taxable property and valued separately from the land to which they relate. (765 ILCS 505/7) Under the Property Tax Code, such rights are valued at $33^1/_3\%$ of fair cash value. (Property Tax Code, Sec. 9-145 [35 ILCS 200/9-145])

A royalty interest, the right of the owner-lessor to receive a part of the production under the lease, is assessed with the land at its fair cash value when owned by the owner-lessor of the land.

Lessees of oil and natural gas rights are required by rule to file a property tax return with the Department. (86 Ill. Admin. Code 110.120)

• *Valuation of coal*

Coal is assessed on the basis of its "reserve economic value." (Property Tax Code, Sec. 9-145 [35 ILCS 200/9-145]) This special valuation depends on whether the coal is undeveloped or developed. (Property Tax Code, Sec. 10-175 [35 ILCS 200/10-175]) If undeveloped on property where there has been no mining during the year immediately preceding the assessment date, the undeveloped coal reserve economic value is set at a maximum $75 per acre. There is no per acre value for persons not in the business of mining who have not severed the coal from the land by deed or lease. Unmined coal remaining on acreage mined during the year immediately preceding the assessment date but no longer mined on the assessment date is valued as undeveloped coal. (Property Tax Code, Sec. 10-190 [35 ILCS 200/10-190])

Developed coal is assessed at $33^1/_3\%$ of the current value of the anticipated net income, known as the "developed coal reserve economic value". The developed coal reserve economic value is calculated by a formula which considers three-year averages of spot market prices paid for coal and interest rates charged by the four largest

United States banks. The law limits annual changes in the per acre assessed valuations of coal to 10%, except when acreage classification changes. (Property Tax Code, Sec. 10-180 [35 ILCS 200/10-180]) The term "developed coal" means acreage containing coal for which a permit has been issued under the Surface Coal Mining Land Conservation and Reclamation Act in anticipation of mining during the lesser of (1) five years following the current assessment date, (2) the term of the permit, or (3) the life of the mine. (Property Tax Code, Sec. 1-45 [35 ILCS 200/1-45]) Initial extraction of coal must begin the year following the assessment year.

When coal is separated from the land, the owner or lessee of the coal is liable for the taxes on the coal in the year of first production and each year thereafter until production ceases. (Property Tax Code, Sec. 9-175 [35 ILCS 200/9-175]) Proportional assessments of developed coal may be made for mining starting after the assessment date or ceasing prior to the end of the calendar year. (Property Tax Code, Sec. 10-185 [35 ILCS 200/10-185]) However, proportional assessments do not apply to coal acreage that, due to a mining plan change, was not included in the anticipated five-year mine acreage and is to be mined during the current year.

Developed coal is added to the tax roll. (Property Tax Code, Sec. 10-195 [35 ILCS 200/10-195])

State-calculated county equalization factors or multipliers are not applicable to coal assessments. Local equalization multipliers may be used to achieve the assessments required by law. (Property Tax Code, Sec. 10-200 [35 ILCS 200/10-200])

The Department of Revenue is charged with the responsibility for reviewing coal assessments and may order reassessments. (Property Tax Code, Sec. 16-200 [35 ILCS 200/16-200])

• *Oil and gas machinery and equipment*

Tangible personal property is not subject to tax in Illinois. (Property Tax Code, Sec. 24-5 [35 ILCS 200/24-5]) For more information on personal property, see ¶ 20-295, Personal Property. For information on the valuation of personal property, see ¶ 20-645, Personal Property Valuation.

[¶20-275] Motor Vehicles

Illinois has no specific statutory or regulatory provisions regarding motor vehicles.

[¶20-285] Nonprofit, Religious, Charitable, Scientific, and Educational Organizations

Illinois law provides for special treatment of the property of schools and health service plans, property used for religious purposes, and parking areas owned by nonprofit organizations.

The property of the following entities is exempt from taxation when it is used exclusively for charitable or beneficent purposes, and not leased or used with a view to profit (Property Tax Code, Sec. 15-65 [35 ILCS 200/15-65]):

— institutions of public charity;

— beneficent and charitable organizations;

— old people's homes;

— facilities for developmentally disabled;

— facilities for educational, social, and physical development;

— health maintenance organizations;

— facilities used to distribute, sell, or resell donated goods;

— free public libraries;

— certain historical societies.

The exemption for property used exclusively for charitable purposes is authorized by the Illinois Constitution. (Ill. Const., Art. IX, Sec. 6)

• *Non-profit hospital charitable exemption*

The property tax charitable exemption was amended as it relates to non-profit hospitals. A set of criteria to be applied on a case-by-case basis for exemption applicants. Any hospital property parcel or portion thereof that is owned, leased, licensed, or operated by a for-profit entity cannot qualify for an exemption. (Property Tax Code, Sec. 15-86 [35 ILCS 200/15-86])

Generally, a qualifying hospital applicant will be issued a charitable exemption if the value of services or activities for the year at issue (hospital year) equals or exceeds the relevant hospital entity's estimated property tax liability for the year for which the exemption is sought. Services or activities that will be considered in determining that value are:

— charity care;

— health services to low-income or underserved individuals;

— subsidy of state or local governments;

— support for state health care programs for low-income individuals;

— subsidy of dual-eligible Medicare/Medicaid patients;

— relief of the burden of government related to health care of low-income individuals; and

— any other activity by the hospital entity that the Department of Revenue determines relieves the burden of government or addresses the health of low-income or underserved individuals.

(Property Tax Code, Sec. 15-86(e) [35 ILCS 200/15-86(e)])

• *Ownership factor*

Property that qualifies for this exemption will not lose its exemption if legal title is held by one of the following:

— an entity organized to hold title that qualifies as a charitable organization;

— a partnership or limited liability company (LLC) in which the charitable organization or an affiliate is a general partner of the partnership or managing member of the LLC for purposes of owning low income housing; or

— a qualified LLC.

A qualified LLC, as referenced directly above:

(1) is one whose sole member or members are institutions of public charity that use the property exclusively for charitable purposes;

(2) is a disregarded entity for federal and Illinois income tax purposes; and

(3) does not lease the property or otherwise use it with a view to profit.

(Property Tax Code, Sec. 15-65 [35 ILCS 200/15-65])

• *Leased property*

If a not-for-profit organization leases property to an organization that conducts activity on the leased premises that would entitle the lessee to an exemption from taxes if the lessee were the owner of the property, the leased property is exempt from taxation. (Property Tax Code, Sec. 15-65 [35 ILCS 200/15-65])

• *Exclusive use factor*

A charitable use is one:

(1) that benefits an indefinite number of persons;

(2) that is carried out by an organization that has no capital, capital stock, or shareholders and does not profit from the enterprise;

(3) in which the funds are derived mainly from private and public charity, and the funds are held in trust for the purposes expressed in the charter;

(4) in which the charity is dispensed to all who need and apply for it;

(5) in which no obstacles are placed in the way of those seeking the benefits; and

(6) in which the exclusive (primary) use means the primary purpose for which the property is used.

EXAMPLE: If property is owned by two organizations and only one organization qualifies as a charitable organization, the property will still be eligible for this exemption in proportion to the qualified organization's ownership in the property. For instance, if two organization hold a equal interest in property and only one organization qualifies as a charitable organization the property will be entitled to a 50% exemption to reflect the 50% ownership by the charitable organization.

• *Charging of fees*

A charitable purposes exemption recipient that provides a waiver or reduction of an entrance fee, assignment of assets, or fee for services based on an individual's ability to pay may be periodically reviewed by the Department of Revenue to determine whether the waiver or reduction was a past policy or is a current policy. The Department may revoke the exemption if it finds that the policy for waiver or reduction is no longer current. (Property Tax Code, Sec. 15-65 [35 ILCS 200/15-65])

• *Educational, social, and physical development facilities*

Statutory amendments enacted in 1987 make property of nonprofit organizations that provide service or facilities related to educational, social, and physical development exempt from property tax. The amendments applied retroactively to the assessment year 1982 and following years. (Property Tax Code, Sec. 15-65 [35 ILCS 200/15-65])

Because constitutional limits on property tax exemptions do not include use of property for educational, social, and physical development, the 1987 amendments may be construed to require use of property for such purposes to be charitable as well. (Ill. Const., Art. IX, Sec. 6)

CCH COMMENT: *Criteria outlined for exemption.*—Two elements are required to entitle property to an exemption: exclusive use for charitable purposes and ownership by a charitable organization. The term "exclusive use" refers to the primary purpose for which the property is used, and not to the secondary or incidental purpose. In *Methodist Old Peoples Home v. Korzen*, 39 IllApp2d 149, 233 NE2d 537 (IL SCt. 1968), the Illinois Supreme Court outlined the following criteria in evaluating whether property is exempt from taxation based on a charitable use:

(1) the benefits derived are for an indefinite number of persons [for their general welfare or in some way reducing the burdens of government];

(2) the organization has no capital, capital stock, or shareholders, and does not profit from the enterprise;

(3) funds are derived mainly from private and public charity, and the funds are held in trust for the objects and purposes expressed in the charter;

(4) the charity is dispensed to all who need and apply for it;

(5) no obstacles appear to be placed in the way of those seeking the benefits;

(6) the exclusive (primary) use of the property is for charitable purposes.

These factors are guidelines, and not definitive requirements. *See generally, Institute of Gas Technology v. Illinois Department of Revenue*, 289 IllApp3d 779, 683 NE2d 484, (1st Dist. 1997); *Lutheran General Health Care System and Health Care Medical Foundation v. Illinois Department of Revenue*, 231 IllApp3d 652, 595 NE2d 1214, (2nd Dist. 1992).

In *Midwest Physician Group, Ltd., f/k/a Chicago Osteopathic Academic Medical Practice Plan, Ltd. v. Department of Revenue*, the First District Appellate Court, (April 28, 1999), applied these factors to conclude that the taxpayer was not entitled to the "charitable institutions" exemption from taxation because its three-story office building and adjacent parking lot housed a for-profit medical group's executive and staff personnel. The staff in the building exclusively provided billing and collection services, and administered the physicians' benefits package, but neither patient care nor instructional classes took place on the property, thus, the activities conducted on the property could not be viewed as charitable in nature. Further, the taxpayer did not use its property for charitable purposes and it was not owned by a charitable organization.

• *Schools*

Educational institutions are generally exempt from Illinois property taxes. The Illinois Constitution authorizes the legislature to exempt the property of school districts. (Ill. Const. Art. IX, Sec. 6) The Constitution also exempts property used exclusively for school purposes. Pursuant to this authorization, the legislature has implemented the constitutionally created exemptions in several statutory provisions, as discussed below.

Statutory exemptions.—The following are exempt from property taxation by the statutes:

— all property donated, granted, received, or used for public school, college, theological seminary, university, or other educational purposes (Property Tax Code, Sec. 15-35 [35 ILCS 200/15-35]);

— all property of schools used exclusively for school purposes (Property Tax Code, Sec. 15-35 [35 ILCS 200/15-35]);

— property of schools leased to a municipality for municipal purposes on a not-for-profit basis (Property Tax Code, Sec. 15-35 [35 ILCS 200/15-35]);

— —all property donated by the United States for school purposes that is not sold or leased (Property Tax Code, Sec. 15-35 [35 ILCS 200/15-35]);

— student residences, dormitories, and other housing for students, their spouses and children (Property Tax Code, Sec. 15-35 [35 ILCS 200/15-35]);

— school-owned-and-operated dormitories or residence halls occupied by students belonging to fraternities, sororities, or other campus organizations (Property Tax Code, Sec. 15-35 [35 ILCS 200/15-35]);

— staff housing facilities (Property Tax Code, Sec. 15-35 [35 ILCS 200/15-35]);

— property on or adjacent to school grounds that is used by research, academic, or professional organizations to advance the field of study taught by the school. (Property Tax Code, Sec. 15-35 [35 ILCS 200/15-35]) (The exemption is applicable only in counties of more than 200,000 population that classify real property (Cook County; see ¶ 20-105 Classification of Property). A public street, alley, sidewalk, parkway or other public way can separate the property);

— property owned by a school district. (Property Tax Code, Sec. 15-35 [35 ILCS 200/15-35]) (The exemption is not affected by leasebacks or other agreements entered into by the district for the purpose of financing. If the district conveys property, the district must retain an option to purchase the property at a later date or the property must revert back to the school district. Conveyed property is no longer exempt as of the date when (1) the district's right to use, control, and possess the property is terminated; (2) the district no longer has an option to purchase or otherwise acquire the property; or (3) there is no provision for a reverter of the property to the district within the limitations period for reverters);

— property of public school districts and community college districts that is not leased or otherwise used by the districts with a view to profit (Property Tax Code, Sec. 15-135 [35 ILCS 200/15-135]);

— property of military schools and academies, including buildings, equipment and lands, not exceeding ten acres. (Property Tax Code, Sec. 15-90 [35 ILCS 200/15-90]) (Property must be used exclusively for school purposes. Military science and instruction must be a part of the area of study and regularly taught. There are other requirements as to teachers and graduates); and

— property of a corporation that is an exempt entity under IRC Sec. 501(c) or its successor law used by the corporation to conduct continuing education for professional development of personnel in energy-related industries, to maintain a library of energy technology information available to students and the public free of charge, and to conduct research in energy and environment the results of which could be ultimately accessible to persons involved in education. (Property Tax Code, Sec. 15-35 [35 ILCS 200/15-35]) The exemption is available only in counties with more than 200,000 population that classify property.

School property is exempt whether owned by a resident or nonresident of Illinois or by a corporation whether incorporated in the state or another state. (Property Tax Code, Sec. 15-35 [35 ILCS 200/15-35])

Property used exclusively for both school and religious purposes is also exempt under the religious exemption statute. (Property Tax Code, Sec. 15-40 [35 ILCS 200/15-40]) See the discussion below.

• *Religious use of property*

The Illinois Constitution authorizes the exemption of property used for religious purposes. (Ill. Const. Art. IX, Sec. 6) An exemption under the corollary statute extends to property that is:

(a) owned by a church or religious institution;

(b) used by a church and school;

(c) used as housing facilities for ministers of such churches or institutions; or

(d) used as orphanages.

(Property Tax Code, Sec. 15-40 [35 ILCS 200/15-40])

The exempt property cannot be leased or otherwise used with a view to profit. However, the Illinois Supreme Court has held that if the primary use of leased property is not for the production of income, but to serve a tax-exempt purpose, the tax-exempt status continues, though the leased use may involve an incidental production of income. (*Childrens Development Center, Inc. v. Olson* (IL SCt 1972) 52 IllApp2d 332, 288 NE2d 388)

Housing facilities.—Property owned by religious institutions that is used as housing facilities for ministers performing the duties of their vocation as well as their spouses, children, and domestic workers, is exempt from taxation. (Property Tax Code, Sec. 15-40 [35 ILCS 200/15-40]) Convents and monasteries are included within the exemption. Bishops, district superintendents, and similar church officials whose ministerial duties are not limited to a single congregation are included in the definition of "ministers."

A parsonage, convent, monastery or other housing facility is exclusively used for religious purposes when the religious institution requires that the persons who perform religious activities reside in the quarters as a condition of their employment. (Property Tax Code, Sec. 15-40 [35 ILCS 200/15-40]) In passing on the constitutionality of this exemption, the Illinois Supreme Court held that a parsonage qualified for an exemption if it reasonably and substantially facilitates the aims of religious worship or religious instruction because the pastor's religious duties require him to live in close proximity to the church or because the parsonage has unique facilities for religious worship and instruction or is primarily used for such purpose. (*McKenzie v. Johnson* (IL SCt 1983) 98 IllApp2d 87, 456 NE2d 73)

• *Health maintenance organizations*

To qualify under the charitable institution exemption, health maintenance organizations must be certified by the Director of the Department of Insurance under the provisions of the Health Maintenance Organization Act. Property remains exempt even though there is a provision of services to members at prepaid rates approved by the Department of Insurance. However, membership in the organization must be sufficiently large or of indefinite classes to benefit the community. Any HMO adjudicated by a court to have denied admission because of race, color, creed, sex, or national origin is not exempt. (Ill. Const. Art. IX, Sec. 6)

• *Historical societies*

A historical society is deemed to be a charitable organization eligible for a charitable purpose property tax exemption only if all the taxing districts within which its property is situated have adopted a resolution finding that the society is a charitable organization using the property exclusively for charitable purposes. (Property Tax Code, Sec. 15-40 [35 ILCS 200/15-40])

• *Nonprofit parking areas*

Parking areas owned by a school district, nonprofit hospital or school, or religious or charitable institution that meet the requirements for property tax exemption are exempt. (Property Tax Code, Sec. 15-125 [35 ILCS 200/15-125(a)]) In order to qualify, the parking areas generally cannot be leased or used for profit. However, parking areas owned by a religious institution may remain exempt if they are leased or rented to (1) a mass transportation entity for the limited free parking of the commuters or (2) (beginning August 28, 2017) a municipality to provide free public parking. Municipal leases or rentals cannot be for more than "nominal consideration," which means maintenance and insurance of the parking areas. (Property Tax Code, Sec. 15-125 [35 ILCS 200/15-125(a)])

• *Health services plans*

Health services plan organizations organized under the Voluntary Health Services Plans Act are deemed by the statute to be charitable and benevolent corporations and their property is thereby exempt from state, county, district, municipal, and school tax or assessment. (Voluntary Health Services Act, Sec. 27 [215 ILCS 165/27]) Notwithstanding these provisions, the Illinois Supreme Court found that these corporations must comply with the constitutional requirement of "charitable purposes" as found in Article IX, Sec. 6. (*Illinois Hospital & Health Service, Inc. v. Aurand* (IL App Ct 1978) 58 IllApp3d 79, 373 NE2d 1021) The legislature had no authority to exempt a not-for-profit corporation organized under the Voluntary Health Services Plans Act, unless the same is an operation for charitable purposes as required in the state constitution.

[¶20-295] Personal Property

Personal property is exempt from property tax in Illinois.

[¶20-310] Real Property

Real property is land and things permanently affixed to the land, such as trees, buildings, and bridges.

The term "real property" or "real estate" includes:

— land;

— buildings and structures;

— improvements;

— permanent fixtures on the land;

— oil, gas, coal, and other minerals in the land and the right to remove the oil, gas, and other minerals, excluding coal, from the land;

— mobile homes and manufactured homes installed on private property outside of mobile home parks; and

— all rights and privileges belonging or pertaining to the land.

(Property Tax Code, Sec. 1-130 [35 ILCS 200/1-130])

Low-income housing federal tax credits authorized by IRC Sec. 42 are not included in the definition of "property" or "real property". ([35 ILCS 200/1-130(a)])

Other types of real estate are discussed at ¶20-305 Railroads and Rolling Stock and ¶20-290 Nurseries and Florists.

[¶20-330] Utilities

Utilities in Illinois are subject to several taxes determined on the basis of gross receipts and invested capital as discussed in a separate division beginning at ¶80-002. Utility property owned by the U.S. Government may not be taxed by Illinois unless the federal government permits taxation of such property. This exemption is included in the discussion of government property at ¶20-190 Governmental and Public Property.

[¶20-400]
RATES

[¶20-405] Rates of Tax

The establishment of property tax rates is, for the most part, entirely within the province of the local government. There are no state property taxes, although the Department of Revenue assesses certain kinds of property that are then included in the local tax base.

The county clerk computes a tax rate for each taxing district. The actual calculation of the several tax rates by the county clerk begins with the locally assessed values of all property (with the exception of farmland) to which is applied the Department of Revenue's final equalization factor. (Property Tax Code, Sec. 18-40 [35 ILCS 200/18-40])

The county clerk next divides each taxing district's tax levy by the total equalized assessed value of all taxable property within the district's jurisdiction to determine the tax rate, which is expressed in terms of a percentage or in dollars and cents per $100 of assessed value. The computed rate cannot exceed statutory maximums (see below). (Property Tax Code, Sec. 18-45 [35 ILCS 200/18-45])

A county clerk can begin the process of extending taxes only after a board of review or the Board of Appeals has completed its work, state assessments and a final equalization factor have been certified to the county, and all taxing units have levied. Unless the county is using the estimated billing method, its county clerk must also wait for surrounding counties to complete their assessment process, or make estimates as to the assessed values for portions of taxing districts overlapping into surrounding counties. The tax rates applicable to each parcel of property and the total tax due for each taxing district are recorded in the collector's books by the county clerk and turned over to the county or town collectors on or before December 31 each year. Therefore, extension of taxes does not begin until the year following the assessment year. (Property Tax Code, Sec. 18-45 [35 ILCS 200/18-45]; Property Tax Code, Sec. 18-150 [35 ILCS 200/18-150]; Property Tax Code, Sec. 18-270 [35 ILCS 200/18-270])

• *Rates*

The Illinois Department of Revenue provides average property tax rates on its website at https://www2.illinois.gov/rev/localgovernments/property/Pages/General-Information.aspx.

• *Property Tax Extension Limitation Law (PTELL)*

Illinois has a law designed to limit the increases in property tax extensions for non-home rule districts when property values and assessments are increasing faster than the rate of inflation. However, the Property Tax Extension Limitation Law (PTELL) (Property Tax Code, Sec. 18-185 [35 ILCS 200/18-185] —Property Tax Code, Sec. 18-245 [35 ILCS 200/18-245]) is not a "tax cap" and does not cap either individual property tax bills or individual property assessments. (*PIO-62, An Overview of the Property Tax Extension Limitation Law by Referendum*, Illinois Department of Revenue, February 2012) The extension limitation generally is equal to:

— the lesser of 5% or the percentage increase in the Consumer Price Index during the 12-month calendar year preceding the levy year or

— the rate of increase approved by voters.

(Property Tax Code, Sec. 18-185 [35 ILCS 200/18-185])

• *Home rule units*

Home rule units are not subject to statutory tax rate limits. Tax rates for these units may be set at the level necessary to raise the amount of the levy. Cities with a population over 25,000, any cities that pass a home rule referendum, and counties with an elected chief executive are home rule units. Cook County is the only home rule county. (Ill. Const., Art. VII, Sec. 6)

[¶20-500]
EXEMPTIONS

[¶20-505] Exemptions in General

The provisions regarding application for an exemption, continued exempt status, and loss of exempt status are described below.

• *Application for exemption*

An original application for an exemption, other than homestead exemptions, must be filed with the county board of review. (Property Tax Code, Sec. 15-5 [35 ILCS 200/15-5]; Property Tax Code, Sec. 16-70 [35 ILCS 200/16-70]; Property Tax Code, Sec.

16-95 [35 ILCS 200/16-95]) The initial application for exempt status is usually made on the forms prescribed by the Department of Revenue. If an application for an exemption is filed that would reduce the assessed valuation of real property by more than $100,000, other than a homestead exemption, the owner shall give notice to any municipality, fire protection district, school district, or community college district in which the property is situated. (Property Tax Code, Sec. 16-70 [35 ILCS 200/16-70]; Property Tax Code, Sec. 16-130 [35 ILCS 200/16-130])

Department of Revenue review.—Whenever the board of review determines the exempt or taxable status of property, other than homestead property, and the question as to the liability of such property to taxation has not previously been judicially determined, the decision of the board is not final until approved by the Department of Revenue. (Property Tax Code, Sec. 16-70 [35 ILCS 200/16-70]; Property Tax Code, Sec. 16-130 [35 ILCS 200/16-130]) In other words, with the exception homestead exemptions, final approval of an exemption claim lies with the Department of Revenue, not with the local board.

In making its review, the Department of Revenue considers the information forwarded to it by the applicable board. It is the duty of the clerk of the board to supply the Department with all the facts in the case. Supporting documents, such as a photographic or certified copy of the deed, a copy of the application for exemption, the charter or articles of incorporation, and a financial statement, if necessary, must be sent by a board to the Department.The decision of the Department is forwarded to the appropriate board. (Property Tax Code, Sec. 16-70 [35 ILCS 200/16-70]; Property Tax Code, Sec. 16-130 [35 ILCS 200/16-130]; 86 Ill. Admin. Code Sec. 110.115)

The Department of Revenue must send property tax exemption decisions to the applicant by certified mail. A party who feels aggrieved by the decision may file a written application for hearing within 60 days after notice of the decision has been given by certified mail. After reconsideration and hearing, the Illinois Department of Revenue must issue a notice of decision by certified mail. Within 30 days after notice of the decision, any party may file a written request for rehearing. The action of the Illinois Department of Revenue on a petition for hearing will become final the later of 30 days after the issuance of a notice of decision, if no request for rehearing is made, or upon the issuance of the denial of the request for rehearing or the issuance of a notice of a final decision. (Property Tax Code, Sec. 8-35 [35 ILCS 200/8-35])

If the property is determined to be exempt, the appropriate board corrects the assessment list. If the property is taxable, the property remains on the assessment list. If the property has been unlawfully exempt or is no longer exempt, the Department must direct the chief county assessment officer, before January 1, to assess the property and return it to the assessment roll. The decision is subject to review and hearing upon application by the owner. Applications for review of exemption determinations must be filed within 10 days after publication of the assessment list in the "official newspaper". (Property Tax Code, Sec. 15-25 [35 ILCS 200/15-25]; 86 Ill. Admin. Code Sec. 110.145)

Effect on extension of taxes.—While the board of review or board of appeals examines exemption applications and while that decision is being reviewed by the Department, the extension of taxes of any assessment of the property is not delayed. (Property Tax Code, Sec. 16-70 [35 ILCS 200/16-70]; Property Tax Code, Sec. 16-130 [35 ILCS 200/16-130]) If subsequently the property is found exempt, any taxes extended are abated or, if already paid, refunded.

Final decisions of the Department on exemption claims are reviewable in the courts under the Administrative Review Law. (Property Tax Code, Sec. 16-70 [35 ILCS 200/16-70]; Property Tax Code, Sec. 16-130 [35 ILCS 200/16-130]) An application for review of an exemption determination must first be filed with the Department of Revenue as a prerequisite to judicial review. (Property Tax Code, Sec. 15-25 [35 ILCS 200/15-25])

Exceptions to Department of Revenue screening.—Department of Revenue approval of property tax exemption claims does not apply to homestead exemption claims for:

— disabled veterans; (Property Tax Code, Sec. 15-165 [35 ILCS 200/15-165];

— returning veterans; (Property Tax Code, Sec. 15-167 [35 ILCS 200/15-167];

— disabled persons; (Property Tax Code, Sec. 15-168 [35 ILCS 200/15-168];

— disabled veterans standard; (Property Tax Code, Sec. 15-169 [35 ILCS 200/15-169];

— senior citizens; (Property Tax Code, Sec. 15-170 [35 ILCS 200/15-170];

— senior citizens assessment freeze; (Property Tax Code, Sec. 15-172 [35 ILCS 200/15-172];

— natural disasters; (Property Tax Code, Sec. 15-173 [35 ILCS 200/15-173];

— general homestead; (Property Tax Code, Sec. 15-175 [35 ILCS 200/15-175];

— alternative general homestead; (Property Tax Code, Sec. 15-176 [35 ILCS 200/15-176];

— long-time occupant; and (Property Tax Code, Sec. 15-177 [35 ILCS 200/15-177];

— homestead improvements. (Property Tax Code, Sec. 15-180 [35 ILCS 200/15-180];

(Property Tax Code, Sec. 16-70 [35 ILCS 200/16-70]; Property Tax Code, Sec. 16-130 [35 ILCS 200/16-130])

• *Requirements for continued exempt status*

Once the initial tax exemption application has been granted, it is not necessary to make a new application in each subsequent year or quadrennium. Instead, an affidavit of exempt status generally is filed annually with the chief county assessment officer by the titleholder or owner of the exempt property. (Property Tax Code, Sec. 15-10 [35 ILCS 200/15-10])

The titleholder or owner of a beneficial interest in property exempt under the religious purposes, orphanages, or school and religious purposes, burial grounds (in counties with a population of less than 3 million), or U.S. property exemption is not required to file an affidavit. (Property Tax Code, Sec. 15-10 [35 ILCS 200/15-10])

The annual affidavit of exempt status, other than the homestead exemption, must be filed by January 31 of each year. Affidavits for the homestead exemption for the elderly must be filed by May 31. (Property Tax Code, Sec. 15-10 [35 ILCS 200/15-10])

The affidavit must state whether there has been a change in the ownership or use of the property or in the status of the owner/resident or whether a disabled veteran now owns and uses the property as of January 1. (Property Tax Code, Sec. 15-10 [35 ILCS 200/15-10]) With respect to property of the state of Illinois, a copy of any written lease or agreement with respect to parcels of land of one acre or more in effect on March 30 of the assessment year or, if none, an explanation of the terms of any oral agreement under which the property is leased, subleased, or rented in parcels of one or more acres must accompany the affidavit. (Property Tax Code, Sec. 15-55 [35 ILCS 200/15-55])

¶20-505

The failure to properly file a certificate of status may, in the discretion of the assessment officer, be cause to terminate the exemption from taxation. (Property Tax Code, Sec. 15-10 [35 ILCS 200/15-10])

Owners of five or more exempt parcels within a county may file a single annual affidavit in lieu of an affidavit for each parcel. When requested, the assessment officer will furnish an affidavit form to such owners. The owner then lists all the properties, giving the same information for each parcel as required of owners of individual certificates. (Property Tax Code, Sec. 15-10 [35 ILCS 200/15-10])

An additional notice must be given to the chief county assessment officer, in writing, by the owner or titleholder when there is a change in the exempt status or the property is leased, loaned, or otherwise made available for profit. (Property Tax Code, Sec. 15-20 [35 ILCS 200/15-20]) The owner must file a copy of the leases or agreements together with a complete description of the premises. Failure to file the lease or agreements is, in the chief county assessment officer's discretion, cause to terminate the exemption. (Property Tax Code, Sec. 15-15 [35 ILCS 200/15-15])

Owners of exempt property may enter into agreements with taxing districts for payment by the owner of direct and indirect costs of services provided by the district. Agreements may be up to five years in duration and are renewable for no more than five years. (Property Tax Code, Sec. 15-30 [35 ILCS 200/15-30])

The owner's failure to enter such an agreement may not be used by a district to defer or delay zoning changes, site exceptions from zoning, or other administrative measures as a means to coerce the owner into entering into an agreement. Any zoning change, site exception from zoning, or other variance or special use granted by a municipality will be reversed and returned to its prior status if the property is acquired by a taxable entity or used for taxable purposes within 10 years after a zoning change, site exception, variance, or special use is granted.

• *Loss of exempt status*

The Department of Revenue has the power to return property to the assessment rolls when it determines that the property has been unlawfully exempted from taxation or is no longer entitled to exemption. (Property Tax Code, Sec. 15-25 [35 ILCS 200/15-25]) Property that is found to be no longer exempt is assessed for the current year and subsequent years. Property previously exempt cannot be returned to the assessment rolls, however, until the taxpayer affected has been notified and given an opportunity for a hearing. (Property Tax Code, Sec. 15-25 [35 ILCS 200/15-25])

If property is listed as exempt and there is a change in use, leasehold interest, or ownership, the transferee has the obligation to notify the county assessor or supervisor of assessments, in writing, within 90 days of the change. (Property Tax Code, Sec. 15-20 [35 ILCS 200/15-20]) If the required notice is not given, resulting in the assessing official continuing to list the property as exempt, the property is considered "omitted property" and subject to back taxes.

Property that is transferred from an exempt use to a taxable use is taxable from the date of purchase or conveyance. (Property Tax Code, Sec. 9-200 [35 ILCS 200/9-200]) The county collector will send a tax bill to the person holding title for the portion of the year for which the property is taxable.

• *Charter exemptions*

Prior to the adoption of the 1870 Constitution, a large number of corporate charters issued by the legislature to private educational and charitable institutions granted property tax exemptions. The exemptions were challenged, but the Illinois Supreme Court held that a university's charter did not violate the equal protection clause of the fourteenth amendment by arbitrarily discriminating against other educational institutions whose exemptions from taxation are not so broad. The court found that the contract with the state affords a rational distinction between the university and other institutions and that the different tax exemption accorded institutions organized after the adoption of the constitution of 1870 does not alter the situation. (*People ex rel. the County Collector of Cook County v. Northwestern University* (IL SCt 1972) 51 IllApp2d 131, 281 NE2d 334) The purpose of the tax exemption was to stimulate donations of money or property to the institution.

Leasehold interests in property granted a charter exemption, however, are taxable. Northwestern University's charter tax exemption does not proscribe the taxing of taxpayer's leasehold estates under Sec. 26, Revenue Act of 1939. (now Property Tax Code, Sec. 9-195 [35 ILCS 200/9-195]) The lessees were subject to property tax on the value of their leasehold estates. (*Nabisco, Inc. v. Korzen* (IL SCt 1977) 68 IllApp2d 451, 369 NE2d 829)

[¶ 20-600]

VALUATION, ASSESSMENT, AND EQUALIZATION

[¶ 20-610] Valuation Procedures

The county clerk in the quadrennial or other assessment year must deliver to the assessors by January 1 a complete assessment listing of all property within the county. (Property Tax Code, Sec. 9-100 [35 ILCS 200/9-100]) The arrangement and content of the list are controlled by statute. (Property Tax Code, Sec. 9-100 [35 ILCS 200/9-100]; Property Tax Code, Sec. 9-125 [35 ILCS 200/9-125]) Generally the property listing must show the name of the owner, legal description, and other vital facts. A mistake in the name of the owner is not sufficient to invalidate an assessment. (Property Tax Code, Sec. 9-95 [35 ILCS 200/9-95])

Property must be listed according to its proper legal description. (Property Tax Code, Sec. 9-95 [35 ILCS 200/9-95]) A permanent real estate index numbering system may be set up in the county as an adjunct or in lieu of a legal description of the property. (Property Tax Code, Sec. 9-45 [35 ILCS 200/9-45]) The system describes the property by township, section, block, parcel, street or post office address, and street code number. An explanation of the component parts of the property index system is described in the *Real Property Appraisal Manual*. In cases where property cannot be described without a metes and bounds description, it is the owner's duty to have the land surveyed and platted and to have the plat certified and recorded. (Property Tax Code, Sec. 9-55 [35 ILCS 200/9-55])

Owners of whole sections, half sections, quarter sections, or half-quarter sections may request consolidation provided there are no outstanding forfeited or delinquent taxes against the property. (Property Tax Code, Sec. 9-120 [35 ILCS 200/9-120])

The assessment books are organized to correspond with organized townships in counties having township organization and by congressional townships for those counties not under township organization. (Property Tax Code, Sec. 9-105 [35 ILCS 200/9-105]) In all counties separate books are prescribed for all property within the corporate limits of cities, villages, and incorporated towns, if ordered by the county board.

• *Dates of assessment*

After the books are turned over to the assessing official, the assessing officer or the deputy must "actually view and determine as near as practicable" the value of each parcel of real property according to its condition on January 1. (Property Tax Code, Sec. 9-155 [35 ILCS 200/9-155]) The assessment must be complete by June 1 in all counties having a population of less than 3,000,000 inhabitants, and as soon as the assessor reasonably can in Cook County or in counties that have been divided into assessment districts.

Assessments done locally by township and multi-township assessors in counties of less than 600,000 people must be completed by June 15 (April 15, prior to 2010) of the assessment year and delivered to the supervisor of assessments with an affidavit, stating that the books contain a full and complete list of all real property in the township or multi-township or assessment district. (Property Tax Code, Sec. 9-230 [35 ILCS 200/9-230])

Assessments done locally by township and multi-township assessors in counties of 600,000 or more, but no more than 700,000 people, must return their assessment books or workbooks to the supervisor of assessments by July 15 of the assessment year. Assessments done locally by township and multi-townships in counties with less than 3 million must return their assessment books or workbooks to the supervisor of assessments by November 15 of the assessment year. (Property Tax Code, Sec. 9-230 [35 ILCS 200/9-230])

The review process by county assessment officials then begins.

Assessments are not rendered invalid by informality in making the assessment or the tax lists or by failure to complete the process within the statutory period of time. (Property Tax Code, Sec. 26-5 [35 ILCS 200/26-5]; Property Tax Code, Sec. 26-10 [35 ILCS 200/26-10])

• *Improvements*

The construction of new or added buildings, structures, or other improvements on property after January 1 causes the property owner to be liable for an increased assessment on a proportionate basis from the date on which the occupancy permit was issued or on which the improvement was inhabitable and fit for occupancy or for intended customary use. The owner must notify the assessor within 30 days of the issuance of an occupancy permit or within 30 days of completion of the improvement and must request reassessment. (Property Tax Code, Sec. 9-180 [35 ILCS 200/9-180]; Property Tax Code, Sec. 9-160 [35 ILCS 200/9-160])

• *Destroyed property*

When any buildings, structures, or other improvements are destroyed and rendered uninhabitable or unfit for occupancy or for customary use by "accidental means," the owner must notify the assessor within 90 days after the destruction or in counties with fewer than three million inhabitants, 90 days after mailing of an application form by the township assessor. (Property Tax Code, Sec. 9-180 [35 ILCS 200/9-180]) The owner is entitled to a diminution of assessed valuation on a proportionate basis for the period during which the improvements were uninhabitable or unfit. Failure to notify the assessor during this time period results in disallowance of a reduced assessment.

Taxing districts in counties with fewer than 1 million inhabitants that are involved in litigation over the assessed valuation of real property that is used for a power-generating facility are permitted to enter into property tax assessment settlement agreements with persons responsible for taxes on the property. (Property Tax Code, Sec. 9-45 [35 ILCS 200/9-45])

• *Individual notice of assessment changes*

In counties other than Cook County, taxpayers must receive individual notices of changes in assessments caused by:

    (1) reassessment;

    (2) the action of the local board of review; or

    (3) equalization by the chief county assessment officer or board of review.

In Cook County, individual notices must be provided on any proposed changes in valuation. (see below)

Personal notice is in addition to newspaper publication.

Notice of assessment or reassessment.—Except in Cook County, notice of qualifying changed assessment is required unless the changes are caused by a change in the county equalization factor by the Department of Revenue or in the case of qualifying changes resulting from equalization by the chief county assessor. Each notice of changed assessment must contain the following:

— the previous year's assessed value after equalization;

— the current assessed value and the date of the valuation;

— the percentage of change from the previous value to the current value;

— the qualifying full fair market value;

— a statement that assessments of property, other than farmland and coal, are required to be assessed at 33 $1/3$% of fair market value;

— the name, address, phone number, and (if one exists) Web site address of the assessor;

— information related to the newspaper in which the list of assessments will be published;

— information on steps to follow if the taxpayer wishes to challenge either the full fair market value or the uniformity of the assessment;

— the deadline date for filing an appeal with the board;

— an explanation of the relationship between the assessment and the tax bill; and

— a notice of possible eligibility for various homestead exemptions.

In counties in which the chief assessment officer maintains and controls a qualifying electronic database, the notice should include the physical characteristics of the taxpayer's property that are available in that database as well as the URL address of the website. If the county chief assessment officer does not have a qualifying electronic database, the notice should include township databases, if any, that have that information and a URL address of that database. (Property Tax Code, Sec. 12-30 [35 ILCS 200/12-30])

The notice is mailed to the assessee at the address shown on the assessor's records. (Property Tax Code, Sec. 12-30 [35 ILCS 200/12-30]) The notice may go to the institution holding the mortgage, which must mail a copy of the notice to the taxpayer within 15 days of receipt. (Property Tax Code, Sec. 12-35 [35 ILCS 200/12-35])

Notice after board of review action.—Generally, the board of review must publish notice in a newspaper of general circulation prior to increasing assessments. (Property Tax Code, Sec. 12-40 [35 ILCS 200/12-40]) The board must mail notices to the taxpayer or, if the taxpayer is represented by an attorney, to the taxpayer's attorney if final board of review action changes the taxpayer's assessment. In Cook County, the notices can be sent to the taxpayer by e-mail if the taxpayer's e-mail address is in the hearing records or the complaint to the board; if the taxpayer is represented by an attorney, the notice in Cook County can be sent by e-mail to the attorney. (Property Tax Code, Sec. 12-50 [35 ILCS 200/12-50]) The notice must include the assessed value prior to board of review action, the assessed value after final board of review action but prior to any equalization, and the assessed value as equalized by the board of review. The notice must state that the value as certified to the county clerk will be the locally assessed value of the property for that year and each succeeding year until revised. The notice must set forth specifically the facts upon which the board's decision is based and a statement that the decision may be appealed within 30 days after mailing. Finally, written notice must also be given to any taxpayer who filed a complaint to the board of review and whose assessment was not changed.

Notice after intracounty equalization.—Individual mailed notices of local equalization must be provided by the board of review. (Property Tax Code, Sec. 12-50 [35 ILCS 200/12-50]) The notice sent by a board of review must contain the assessed valuation prior to and after application of the equalization factor. Equalization by chief county assessment officers or township assessors is authorized (Property Tax Code, Sec. 9-205 [35 ILCS 200/9-205]), but notice to individual taxpayers is not required. (Property Tax Code, Sec. 12-10 [35 ILCS 200/12-10]) Instead, a general statement indicating that assessments have been changed because of the application of the equalization factor is included in the published assessment list. (Property Tax Code, Sec. 12-10 [35 ILCS 200/12-10])

Cook County.—Although a Property Tax Code provision (Property Tax Code, Sec. 12-20 [35 ILCS 200/12-20]) authorizing the assessment of property in Cook County requires only publication of quadrennial assessment lists and assessment change lists in nonquadrennial years, another provision of the Property Tax Code (Property Tax Code, Sec. 12-55 [35 ILCS 200/12-55]) requires the county assessor to give individual notice of any proposed assessment increases.

[¶ 20-620] Income Method of Valuation

The income approach to property valuation is a means of estimating the present value of future benefits of real property ownership. The approach converts net income produced by such property into an indication of the amount of investment required to produce an equally desirable net income. This approach is widely applied in appraising property that is bought and sold on its ability to generate net income. (*e.g.*, commercial real estate)

> *EXAMPLE:* Assume that a small bookstore is leased for $425 per month or $5,100 annually and that the prevailing rate of interest for borrowing business funds is 9%. Under a simple application of the income method, the bookstore would be valued at $56,666 ($5,100 divided by 9%). In practice, this simple example would be complicated by such issues as (1) whether the actual rent is representative of the property's income potential; (2) how much of an offset for operating expenses would be allowed against the rental income; and (3) what is the appropriate capitalization rate.

The conversion is accomplished by capitalizing the income. The capitalization process is based on the concept that an investor in buildings is entitled to a return of his investment capital in addition to interest for the use of money. The mathematical formula for the capitalization process is expressed as:

Market value = net income ÷ capitalization rate

The appraiser, in using the income approach, estimates the present value of property by his selection of the capitalization rate and the net income. Net income is derived through the collection, examination, and analysis of income and expense data on property that best typifies market activity. It refers to the residue of the potential gross income remaining after all operating expenses including maintenance, taxes, and insurance are paid.

The capitalization rate consists of the rate of return of depreciable items of a real estate investment (recapture) and the annual rate of return on a real estate investment (interest). The capitalization rate is derived from an analysis of market data. The three methods of capitalization most frequently used are direct capitalization, straight capitalization, and annuity capitalization. Of these three methods, the straight-line and direct methods are most commonly used for property tax purposes. The direct method is the simplest. The appraiser, after analyzing comparable properties and employing a formula (income value ÷ rate), develops a range from which he or she selects the rate most applicable to the property. The straight capitalization method with straight-line or sinking fund recapture assumes that the income-producing capacity of the property will decline as the building gets older. The annuity capitalization method is used when the property is under a long-term lease or when the income is guaranteed; it requires reference to annuity tables to arrive at a factor that will provide for a return on the investment as well as a return of the investment over the anticipated life of the property.

The basic difference in the methods is in the treatment of recapture. The recapture rate provides for a return of the real estate investment over the economic life of the improvement. This rate is calculated with the assumption that the improvement will have no value at the end of its economic life. Straight capitalization with either straight-line or sinking fund recapture is the most frequently used method.

[¶20-625] Sales Method of Valuation

The market data approach (also called the market approach) is based on the economic principle that the justifiable price of a property is no more than the cost of acquiring an equally desirable substitute property. Using price as an indicator of value, the appraiser compares the property of unknown value—the one being appraised—with one or more similar properties that have recently sold on the open market. The selling prices of comparable properties set the upper and lower limits of value, or the range, within which the value of the property will fall.

This comparable-sales approach is dependent on the availability of comparable properties and the validity of the judgments made in regard to their similarities and dissimilarities. Since no two properties are identical, value adjustments must be made to account for differences between the properties being compared. Some of the tangible and intangible factors influencing value involve differences in location, construction, age, condition, desirability, and usefulness.

The significance of the market-data approach lies in its ability to produce estimates of value that directly reflect the attitude of the market. Its widest application is in the appraisal of vacant land and residential properties where there are sales from which to select comparable properties.

[¶20-630] Cost Method of Valuation

The cost approach can be used on all types of construction. Its widest application is in the appraisal of properties where reliable and adequate market sales and income data are not available.

The cost approach values property by estimating the value of the land as if it were vacant and the depreciated cost of reproducing the improvements to the land. The land value estimation is obtained by use of the market data or the income approaches. The market data approach is applied by comparing the subject property with known sales of comparable properties. The income approach is applied by capitalizing the residual income that is imputable to the land after the other costs of ownership have been paid.

Replacement or reproduction cost of the improvement is then calculated. Replacement cost is the cost of replacing an existing structure with a contemporary building having equal utility to the subject property; it includes the total cost of construction incurred by the builder whether preliminary to, during the course of, or after completion of the construction of a particular building. Examples of this category include labor, material, all subcontracts, builders' overhead and profit, architectural and engineering fees, consultation fees, survey and permit fees, legal fees, taxes, insurance, and the cost of financing. The concept of replacement cost evolves from the appraisal principle that value of property is no more than the cost of acquiring an equally desirable substitute. Replacement cost is the upper limit of building value. Reproduction cost refers to the cost of constructing an exact replica of the building with the same design, materials, and quality of workmanship.

There are various methods to estimate replacement cost new. The most widely spread and accepted methods are the unit-in-place or component-part method and the model method. The unit-in-place method establishes in-place prices for the various individual components of a building on the basis of unit measures, such as the cost per pound of steel, the cost per cubic foot of concrete, and the like. The unit prices are then multiplied by the respective quantities of each as found in the composition of the building, the sum of which is equal to the replacement cost. The model method establishes unit prices for the entire structure on a square-foot or cubic-foot basis.

Functional/economic depreciation is generally a loss of value due to forces other than physical which result in a limitation on economic life. It is the difference between physical value (replacement cost new less physical depreciation) and present value. Functional depreciation refers to a loss in value due to conditions of the building which cause a failure of the building to serve the purpose for which it was intended. Inadequacy may result from poor construction features, architectural treatment, design, or arrangement. Functional inadequacy causes a loss in desirability and usefulness.

Economic depreciation is an obsolescence caused by influences outside the property, such as physical, economic, social, and governmental changes which have an adverse effect on the stability and quality of the neighborhood in general. Economic obsolescence causes loss in desirability and utility.

In actual practice, appraisers often use "remaining economic life" (REL) charts to determine depreciation. The use of the chart requires the age of the structure to be known as that chart gives a percentage expression for the remaining life of the structure.

[¶20-635] Unit Method of Valuation

Illinois has no statutory or regulatory provisions regarding the unit method of valuation used for property that crosses taxing jurisdictions because there is no personal property tax in Illinois.

[¶20-640] Real Property Valuation

Various techniques are used for the valuation of land (residential, commercial, and industrial) and of residences.

• *Valuation of land*

With the exception of Cook County, real estate is valued at $33^1/3$% of its fair cash value. (Property Tax Code, Sec. 9-145 [35 ILCS 200/9-145]) In Cook County, unimproved real estate is assessed at 10%. (see ¶20-105)

The overall appraisal of land is accomplished through the development of land value maps which provide a visual representation of the market for vacant land and are a basis for further analysis of that market. The aerial base tax map or recorded plats of subdivisions and plat books can be used. Once the maps have been developed, the assessing official obtains a record of sales of vacant land. These sales should be arm's-length transactions and cover a period of time that is sufficient to accurately reflect the market. The sale price and date of sale along with special factors or features which affect value are entered onto the map. These maps are then taken into the field for a physical inspection of the parcels that were sold. Notations of any special features are made directly on the land valuation maps.

Residential land.—With residential property, a unit of comparison is determined by the market. The most commonly used units are site, front foot, and square foot. The proper unit is generally the one used in the market. The assessor then develops base values for those units. This is done by an analysis of the sales which have been listed on the land value map applicable to the area. The different property characteristics, such as location, topography, access, and site work, must be considered to determine a standard lot for the area and the base unit value to be applied to that standard.

The base unit values are adjusted to reflect physical features that add to or subtract from value as supported by market analysis. The modifier may be based on tables, percentage adjustments, or dollar amounts as indicated by the market.

Commercial land.—The principles applicable to the valuation of residential land generally govern the valuation of commercial land. However, since commercial land is purchased principally for its income-producing capability, the income approach to value is also used.

As with residential land, the unit of comparison is determined by and abstracted from the market. The units most commonly used for commercial land are square foot and front foot. Square foot is an appropriate unit where area rather than frontage is of prime consideration, such as in a shopping center or parking lot. Front-foot unit is best utilized in areas, such as downtown retail districts, where the amount of frontage is important. Other units of comparison include the number of units that can be constructed on a site in the case of apartment projects or number of parking spaces.

The procedure for developing the base values for residential property is utilized for commercial land. Adjustments reflecting physical factors (size, shape, elevation), socio-economic factors (population, rent capability), and legal factors (city planning, zoning, taxation) must be made in the base values provided they are clearly identifiable in the market for commercial land.

In areas where sales of vacant commercial land are limited or nonexistent, the capitalization of rent rather than direct market comparison is used to establish base unit values. The capitalization of rent into value indications is divided into two methods: the capitalization of ground rents, and the capitalization of land residual income developed from rents on an improved property.

Industrial land.—The valuation of industrial land follows the same procedures for residential and commercial lands. Although the units of comparison differ, usually square feet and acres, the establishment of base unit values and the methods of adjusting those values are similar.

Other methods.—Three other methods can be used when sales of comparable vacant land do not exist or when reliable sales data are not available: the land residual capitalization technique (analyzing the income stream of a real or hypothetical income-producing property that is improved to its highest and best use); the allocation method (based on the appraisal principle of balance, which states there is a sense of proportion between the value of the land and the value of the improvements); and the development method (used primarily to value land in transition from agricultural use to residential or commercial use).

• *Residential property*

Single family residences, condominiums, and cooperative apartment buildings are assessed in Cook County at 10% of fair market value; all other residential real estate generally is assessed at 25% of market value. (Cook County Real Property Taxation, Sec. 74-63; Cook County Real Property Taxation, Sec. 74-64) In all other Illinois counties, residential real estate is assessed at $33^1/3$%. (Property Tax Code, Sec. 9-145 [35 ILCS 200/9-145])

¶20-640

Cost approach.—The appraiser estimates the value of the subject tract of land, with the land value allocated to each unit according to the declared ownership percentage as set forth in a declaration recorded by the developer. Replacement cost of the condominium building, excluding specific amenities that are owned absolutely by each unit owner, is then calculated. This cost estimate is converted to an average square foot cost that is used in estimating the base cost of each unit.

A depreciated value is computed for each air lot unit using the base cost estimate and making adjustments for individual amenities. The average square foot cost is also used to allocate the common elements to each owner.

The sum of the land value, the depreciated unit value, and common element values is the unit market value.

Sales approach.—The procedure for valuing the site under the cost approach applies to the sales approach. The appraiser then analyzes sales data to support a value estimate for each unit of the condominium. The sum of the values for all of the units, minus land value, is then divided by the total square floor area to derive an average value per square foot.

The average value per square foot is multiplied by the number of square feet of common elements to derive their total value. The total value is then allocated to each air lot unit according to the ownership percentage.

Income approach.—The income approach has limited application to a condominium since most condominium properties are not exchanged in the market for investment purposes.

Since unit ownership of condominium property is similar to ownership of single family residences, the use of the gross rent multiplier is used. The gross rent multiplier expresses the ratio between the sales price of a property and its monthly income. The multiplier is established for condominium property by analyzing the rental market. Sales prices of the units selling can be related to the gross rent of comparable units that are occupied by tenants.

To capitalize net income is difficult since most expenses are attributable to the whole property rather than to a particular air lot.

Maintenance and repair of residential property.—Maintenance and repairs of residential property do not increase the assessed value of the property. To qualify as maintenance or repair, the work must not increase the square footage of the property, alter its existing character, or add materials of greater value than the materials being replaced and can only prolong the life or keep well maintained existing improvements. (Property Tax Code, Sec. 10-20 [35 ILCS 200/10-20])

Apartment buildings.—Except for Cook County, apartment buildings are assessed at $33^1/_3$% of fair cash value. (Cook County Real Property Assessment Classification Ordinance, Sec. 2)

The appraisal of apartments by the income approach follows the procedures applicable to commercial valuation. The basic procedure involves:

(1) the collection and analysis of income and expense data in order to determine the net income and

(2) the capitalization of the net income into an indication of value.

Low-income housing.—In determining the fair cash value of property receiving benefits from the low-income housing federal tax credits authorized by IRC Sec. 42, emphasis must be given to the income approach, except in circumstances where another valuation method is clearly more appropriate. (Property Tax Code, Sec. 10-235 [35 ILCS 200/10-235])

[¶20-645] Personal Property Valuation

There is no personal property tax in Illinois.

[¶20-750]
PAYMENT, COLLECTION OF TAXES

[¶20-752] Interest

In all counties delinquent property taxes are charged interest at the rate of 1.5% per month or a portion of a month. (Property Tax Code, Sec. 21-15 [35 ILCS 200/21-15]; Property Tax Code, Sec. 21-20 [35 ILCS 200/21-20]; Property Tax Code, Sec. 21-25 [35 ILCS 200/21-25])

Interest at the rate of 10% is charged on any late payment of omitted property taxes after a 2-year deferral period. (Property Tax Code, Sec. 9-265 [35 ILCS 200/9-265])

Under certain circumstances, if a delinquency is the fault of a mortgage lender, the mortgage lender, not the borrower, is assessed the interest. If the mortgage lender is at fault the lender will be assessed the interest on the delinquent amount and must pay the delinquent taxes, redeem the property, and take steps to remove all liens against the property. However, there are no specific provisions authorizing the waiver of penalties, *i.e.*, for reasonable cause, etc. (Property Tax Code, Sec. 21-15 [35 ILCS 200/21-15])

New Developments: Illinois legislation allows counties to waive interest penalties on late property tax payments due during 2020 (except for the final installment payment). The legislation applies to all counties except Cook County, which already provided similar relief. The waiver can be for a period of: (i) 120 days; or (ii) until the first day of the first month during which there is no longer a statewide COVID-19 public health emergency as declared by the Governor. (P.A. 101-0635 (S.B. 685), Laws 2020)

• *Waiver for senior citizens and disabled persons*

An interest penalty on a delinquent tax payment will be waived if the taxpayer:

(1) qualifies for a grant under the Senior Citizens and Disabled Persons Property Tax Relief Act for the year in issue;

(2) requests the waiver in writing by filing the proper form with the county treasurer on or before the first day of the month that a tax installment is due;

(3) pays the tax installment in full on or before the third day of the month that the installment is due; and

(4) the county treasurer approves the waiver.

(Property Tax Code, Sec. 21-27 [35 ILCS 200/21-27])

• *Disaster areas*

Any county that has been designated in whole or in part a disaster area by the President of the United States or the Governor of Illinois may allow interest assessed on delinquent installments of real property taxes not to accrue until a court enters an order for sale of the property. A person may pay a delinquent installment without interest being assessed until the last working day before the court enters the order. A county may also postpone the date of an installment, exempt any specified installment, and order the county collector not to give notice of application for judgment of sale and not to apply for judgment and order of sale until after the postponed delinquency date for the final installment. (Property Tax Code, Sec. 21-40 [35 ILCS 200/21-40])

• *Omitted assessments*

Omitted property assessments are subject to interest at the annual rate of 10% beginning two years after the date the correct tax bill should have been received. Interest is waived when:

(1) the omission was caused by an incorrect survey or other ministerial assessor error; and

(2) the owner has paid the omitted assessment.

(Property Tax Code, Sec. 9-265 [35 ILCS 200/9-265])

When the interest has been waived, the owner is not charged with any penalty for nonpayment of taxes until he or she receives actual notice of, and is billed for, the principal amount of back taxes. (Property Tax Code, Sec. 21-15 [35 ILCS 200/21-15])

• *Tax sales and forfeited property*

If a purchaser at a tax sale fails to pay the back taxes, the purchase is void, but the purchaser does not receive a refund of the amount paid at the time of the initial sale. Instead the amount is treated as a payment and a lien remains on the property in favor of the purchaser until paid with interest at 5% per year. No redemption can be made without payment of the amount, and no future sale of the property can be made except subject to the lien of the purchaser. (Property Tax Code, Sec. 21-250 [35 ILCS 200/21-250])

If there are no bids on property at a tax sale, the property is automatically forfeited to the state. (Property Tax Code, Sec. 21-225 [35 ILCS 200/21-225]) Forfeitures remain a lien on the property until paid or sold. Interest at 12% is added each year until the forfeiture is paid or the property is sold, and the addition of each year's interest is considered a separate forfeiture. (Property Tax Code, Sec. 18-250 [35 ILCS 200/18-250])

• *Payment under protest*

If a taxpayer is successful in a court or board hearing, interest is paid on the refund amount from the date of payment or from the date payment is due, whichever is later, to the date of refund at the rate of the lesser of 5% per year or the percentage increase in the Consumer Price Index for All Urban Consumers during the 12-month calendar year preceding the levy year for which the refund was made. (Property Tax Code, Sec. 23-20 [35 ILCS 200/23-20])

• *Certificate of error*

If a certificate of error results in the allowance of a homestead exemption not previously allowed, the county collector must pay the taxpayer 6% interest on the amount of exemption. (Property Tax Code, Sec. 20-175 [35 ILCS 200/20-175]) When the county collector makes any refunds due on certificates of error, the county collector shall pay the taxpayer interest on the amount of the refund at the rate of 0.5% per month. (Property Tax Code, Sec. 20-178 [35 ILCS 200/20-178])

[¶20-756] Payment of Tax

With certain exceptions discussed below, real estate taxes are payable in two equal installments. (Property Tax Code, Sec. 20-210 [35 ILCS 200/20-210]) The first installment is due on the later of June 1 or the day after the date specified on the real estate tax bill as the first installment due date. The second installment is due on the later of September 1 or the day after the date specified on the real estate tax bill as the second installment due date. (Property Tax Code, Sec. 21-15 [35 ILCS 200/21-15]) These dates may be modified by ordinance. If either due date falls on a Sunday or legal holiday, the due date is extended to the succeeding business day. (Property Tax Code, Sec. 21-40 [35 ILCS 200/21-40])

Cook County accelerates its tax payment procedure. Under this system, the first installment, billed January 31, is equal to 55% of the preceding year's tax bill and is due by March 1 (or no later than June 1, by ordinance). The second installment is mailed June 30 and covers the balance of taxes due, computed by subtracting the first billing from the total taxes for the present year; it is due August 1. This accelerated billing system may also be adopted by counties with fewer than 3,000,000 inhabitants. (Property Tax Code, Sec. 21-20 [35 ILCS 200/21-20]; Property Tax Code, Sec. 21-25 [35 ILCS 200/21-25]; Property Tax Code, Sec. 21-30 [35 ILCS 200/21-30])

A third billing method has been authorized in counties with a population of less than three million. The county board may defer the delinquency date for half of each installment of real estate taxes for 60 days by adopting an ordinance. (Property Tax Code, Sec. 21-40 [35 ILCS 200/21-40])

There is no extension of time for payment and discounts are not given for early payment.

The county tax collector is permitted to accept payments of the property tax on an undivided share of property when a particular specification of the part is furnished. Interest is then computed only on the unpaid balance. (Property Tax Code, Sec. 20-210 [35 ILCS 200/20-210])

Installment payments are applied first to any interest or costs due to previous delinquencies, with the remainder applied to the current tax. (Property Tax Code, Sec. 20-215[35 ILCS 200/20-215])

Arrearage due to administrative error.—If a taxpayer owes an arrearage of taxes due to an administrative error and the county collector sends a separate bill for that arrearage, any part of the arrearage that remains unpaid on the day after the due date specified on that tax bill shall be deemed delinquent and shall bear interest after that date at the rate of 1.5% per month. (Property Tax Code, Sec. 21-20 [35 ILCS 200/21-20]; Property Tax Code, Sec. 21-25 [35 ILCS 200/21-25])

Senior citizen deferral.—Taxpayers over the age of 65 are permitted to defer property taxes plus interest on their residential dwellings if certain conditions are met. Under the Senior Citizens Real Estate Tax Deferral Act, the deferred taxes become a lien that is recorded and continues in effect until the deferred taxes are paid. (Senior Citizens Real Estate Tax Deferral Act, Sec. 1 [320 ILCS 30/1]) The terms of the agreement set forth in the statute provide:

(1) the deferred taxes, plus interest, for the year of deferral does not exceed 80% of the taxpayer's equity interest in the property;

(2) the deferred taxes, plus interest at the rate of 6% annually, are a lien on the real estate until paid;

(3) upon death of the taxpayer, the heirs, assignees or legatees have first priority to the real estate upon payment of the lien, plus interest. If the heir, assignee or legatee is the surviving spouse, the tax deferred status of the property may continue if the survivor is 55 years of age or older within 6 months of the death of the taxpayer, and enters into a tax deferral and recovery agreement;

(4) the deferred taxes and interest are recoverable from the state within one year of the taxpayer's death, provided there is no continued deferment by the spouse. The lien is also payable within 90 days after the tax deferred property is disqualified;

(5) the agreement must have the prior written approval of a joint owner;

(6) a guardian may act for a qualified taxpayer; and

(7) the qualifying property has fire and casualty insurance in the amount of at least the deferred taxes.

• *Bill preparation, notice, and statement.*

Tax bills are mailed by the county or town collector the year following the year the assessments are made. The tax bills can be e-mailed to taxpayers who have asked the collector in writing to do so. (Property Tax Code, Sec. 20-5 [35 ILCS 200/20-5]) Tax bills are prepared in triplicate for each installment and mailed at least 30 days before the due date. Where tax bills are mailed to a mortgage lender, a copy of the bill must be sent by the lender to the borrower within 15 days of the receipt of the bill. (Property Tax Code, Sec. 20-10 [35 ILCS 200/20-10]) If the county uses the accelerated billing method, the copy is mailed to the borrower with the final installment. Failure to mail a bill or to receive one, however, does not affect the validity of the tax or relieve the taxpayer of the tax liability. (Property Tax Code, Sec. 20-15 [35 ILCS 200/20-15])

The county tax bill or a separate statement accompanying the bill must show the following:

(1) a statement itemizing the rate at which taxes were extended for each taxing district in the county, including, in counties using electronic data processing equipment, the dollar amounts allocated to each of the taxing districts and a separate statement of amounts allocated for public library purposes;

(2) a separate rate statement for each taxing district showing amounts allocated for public pension and retirement purposes;

(3) the total tax rate;

(4) the total amount of tax due;

(5) the amount by which the total tax and allocated amounts differ from the prior tax bill;

(6) the property index number;

(7) the assessment of the property;

(8) the equalization factors;

(9) the equalized assessment;

(10) information that certain taxpayers may be eligible for tax exemptions, abatements, and other assistance; and

(11) information that certain taxpayers may be eligible for the Senior Citizens and Disabled Persons Property Tax Relief Act.

(Property Tax Code, Sec. 20-15 35 ILCS 200/20-15)

A county collector must send a notice by certified mail to a taxpayer who owes arrearage due to an administrative error. If the notice is mailed on or before October 1 in any year, then either:

— the county collector may send a separate bill for the arrearage, which may be due no sooner than 30 days after the due date for the next installment of taxes, or

— the arrearage is to be added to the tax bill for the second year after the notice, and payment is due in two equal installments on June 1 and September 1 in the second year, unless the county has adopted an accelerated method of billing, in which case the arrearage may be billed separately and shall be due in equal installments on the dates on which each installment of tax is due in the following year.

(Property Tax Code, Sec. 14-41 [35 ILCS 200/14-41])

A county may not bill, collect, claim a lien for, or sell an arrearage of taxes caused by an administrative error for tax years earlier than the two most recent tax years, including the current tax year. An "administrative error" includes, but is not limited to, a failure to include an extension for a taxing district on the tax bill, an error in the calculations of tax rates or extensions or any other mathematical error by the county clerk, or a defective coding by the county. It does not include a failure by the county to send a tax bill to the taxpayer, a failure by the taxpayer to notify the assessor of a change in the tax-exempt status of property, or any error concerning the assessment of the property. (Property Tax Code, Sec. 14-41 [35 ILCS 200/14-41])

• *Payment methods*

Property taxes are payable in legal tender of the United States, cashier's check, certified check, post office or bank money order, or personal or corporate check drawn on a state or national bank insured by the Federal Deposit Insurance Corporation. Payments may be made by credit card in accordance with the Local Governmental Acceptance of Credit Cards Act. County collectors may refuse to take a personal or corporate check within 45 days before a tax sale. In addition, the county collectors may refuse to accept a check at any time if a previous payment by the same payer was returned by a bank for any reason. (Property Tax Code, Sec. 20-25(a) [35 ILCS 200/20-25(a)]) A receipt is given at the time of payment. (Property Tax Code, Sec. 20-45 [35 ILCS 200/20-45])

Cook County generally is required to accept payment by credit card for each installment of property taxes, although the taxpayers must also pay any credit card service charges or fees. However, the county need not accept payment by credit card for delinquent payments or for purposes of any tax sale or scavenger sale. (Property Tax Code, Sec. 20-25(b) [35 ILCS 200/20-25(b)])

[¶20-758] Assessment of Delinquent Tax

All real estate taxes are payable in two installments. In most counties, the first installment is delinquent if not paid on or before June 1. The second installment is delinquent if not paid on or before September 1. In Cook County, the first installment is delinquent if not paid on or before March 1, or no later than June 1 by ordinance. The second installment is delinquent if not paid on or before August 1. The lien may be foreclosed and the property sold whenever the taxes for two or more years have been forfeited to the state. (Property Tax Code, Sec. 21-30 [35 ILCS 200/21-30])

Delinquent taxes are a lien upon the property until the taxes are paid or until the property is sold. A lien may be foreclosed whenever the taxes for two or more years on the property have been forfeited to the State. The lien may be enforced at any time after six months from the day the tax becomes delinquent out of the rents and profits of the land accruing, or accrued and under the control or jurisdiction of a court. (Property Tax Code, Sec. 21-75 [35 ILCS 200/21-75])

[¶20-762] Agreements in Compromise of Tax Due

Following the filing of a tax objection in a circuit court, the court may hold a conference with the objector and the State's Attorney. Compromise agreements on tax objections reached by conference shall be filed with the court. (Property Tax Code, Sec. 23-30 [35 ILCS 200/23-30]) Similarly, in actions before the Property Tax Appeal Board, the parties are permitted to engage in settlement discussions and negotiations outside of the presence of the PTAB provided that the board is advised in writing of the disposition of the appeal at any time during the pendency of the appeal. (86 Ill. Adm. Code 1910.72)

[¶20-768] Audits

Applicants for either the senior citizens assessment freeze homestead exemption and the long-time occupant homestead exemption can be audited by the chief county assessment officer to verify that the taxpayer is eligible to receive the exemption. Applications for the exemptions must contain a notice that any taxpayer who receives the exemption is subject to an audit. (Property Tax Code, Sec. 15-172 [35 ILCS 200/15-172]; Property Tax Code, Sec. 15-177 [35 ILCS 200/15-177])

Similarly, a county clerk may audit applications for the housing opportunity area abatement program to determine that the properties subject to the tax abatement meet the requirements of the abatement law provisions. (Property Tax Code, Sec. 18-173(c) [35 ILCS 200/18-173(c)]

[¶20-770] Penalties

In all Illinois counties delinquent property taxes are charged interest at the rate of $1^1/2\%$ per month or portion of a month, which is considered a penalty. (see ¶20-815 Interest) (Property Tax Code, Sec. 21-15 [35 ILCS 200/21-15])

Railroad penalties.—The failure to file required statements or schedules results in assessment by the Department on the basis of its available information and in the imposition of a penalty in an amount equal to 50% of the valuation. (Property Tax Code, Sec. 11-115 [35 ILCS 200/11-115])

Redemption penalties.—For property that is redeemed, the amount of the penalty levied increases at six-month intervals from the date of the tax sale until redemption. (Property Tax Code, Sec. 21-355 [35 ILCS 200/21-355]) The percentage varies with the time of redemption, the type of tax sale, and the type of property that was sold. The penalty schedule for annual tax sales differs from that prepared for scavenger sales and forfeiture foreclosure sales.

[¶20-800]
CREDITS, ABATEMENTS, REFUNDS, INCENTIVES

[¶20-805] Credits

Illinois counties may adopt an deadline postponement ordinance or resolution that, among other things, directs the county assessor to give a credit against the general corporate levy of the county for the year following the year in which a qualifying disaster was declared to the owner of property approved for relief in an amount equal to any interest penalty paid by that owner on any installment of tax due on the property in the year the disaster was declared. The interest penalty must have been paid before the ordinance or resolution was adopted or before the postponed delinquency dates. (Property Tax Code, Sec. 21-40 [35 ILCS 200/21-40])

[¶20-810] Abatement

Some property, while not exempt, is given preferred treatment either through special methods of valuation or in the form of property tax abatements. Enterprise zone property and property of a commercial or, under certain circumstances, industrial firm are examples of the latter category. The purpose of such program is to encourage businesses to locate or rehabilitate property within a taxing district by offering financial incentives in the form of property tax abatements. As a practical matter, the effect of an abatement is to reduce or eliminate property taxes on a specific parcel of property.

If property taxes paid were higher than required by law because of an error in the calculation of tax rates or extension of taxes by the county clerk, the clerk is required to abate any excess taxes paid. (Property Tax Code, Sec. 18-145 [35 ILCS 200/18-145])

• *General authority—any taxing district*

On approval of its governing authority, any Illinois taxing district may order abatement of any portion of its taxes on designated property types. (Property Tax Code, Sec. 18-165(a) [35 ILCS 200/18-165(a)])

Upon a majority vote of its governing authority, any municipality may, after the determination of the assessed valuation of its property, order the county clerk to abate any portion of its taxes on any property that is located within the corporate limits of the municipality in accordance with Section 8-3-18 of the Illinois Municipal Code. (Property Tax Code, Sec. 18-165 [35 ILCS 200/18-165(b)]) Similarly, any taxing district may, upon a majority vote of its governing body, abate a portion of the Illinois property taxes on a property if:

(1) a new business first occupies a facility located on the property during the taxable year and

(2) the facility was vacant for at least 24 continuous months prior to being occupied by the business.

The abatement may not exceed two years and the aggregate amount of abated taxes for all taxing districts combined may not exceed $4 million. (Property Tax Code, Sec. 18-184.5 [35 ILCS 200/18-184.5])

Counties are permitted, under the County Historic Preservation Act, to abate property taxes on any landmark or property within a preservation district. (Counties Code, Sec. 5-30004 [55 ILCS 5/5-30004(14)])

• *Governmental unit acquisitions*

Acquisitions of property by certain Illinois governmental units will result in abatement of all due or unpaid taxes and the voiding of existing liens for unpaid property taxes. For counties, municipalities, school districts, park district, and forest preserve districts, the abatements are effected:

— through foreclosure of a lien;

— through a judicial deed;

— through foreclosure of receivership certificate lien; or

— by acceptance of a deed of conveyance in lieu of foreclosing any lien against the property.

Also, among other items, the abatements occur when a government unit acquires property under either the Abandoned Housing Rehabilitation Act or a blight reduction or abandoned property program administered by the Illinois Housing Development Authority. (Property Tax Code, Sec. 21-95 [35 ILCS 200/21-95])

• *Business corridors*

Illinois property that is not otherwise exempt from property tax and is situated in a qualifying business corridor created by an intergovernmental agreement is entitled to a property tax abatement. (Property Tax Code, Sec. 18-165(a)(10) [35 ILCS 200/18-165(a)(10)]) A qualifying "business corridor" is property that encompasses territory along the common border of two disadvantaged municipalities and is:

(1) undeveloped or underdeveloped and

(2) not likely to be developed without the creation of the business corridor.

(Property Tax Code, Sec. 18-184.10(a) [35 ILCS 200/18-184.10(a)])

A "disadvantaged municipality" is one with:

(1) a per capita equalized assessed valuation less than 60% of the state average and

(2) more than 15% of its population below the national poverty level.

(Property Tax Code, Sec. 18-184.10(d) [35 ILCS 200/18-184.10(d)])

¶20-810

A corridor agreement can only be adopted after each of the municipalities holds a public hearing on the issue. (Property Tax Code, Sec. 18-184.10(c) [35 ILCS 200/18-184.10(c)]) The abatement under any such agreement cannot exceed 10 years in duration. (Property Tax Code, Sec. 18-184.10(a) [35 ILCS 200/18-184.10(a)])

• *Surviving spouse of fallen police officer, soldier, rescue worker*

A county or municipality may abate any percentage of its taxes levied on a parcel of qualified property owned by the surviving spouse of a fallen police officer, soldier, or rescue worker. (Property Tax Code, Sec. 18-178(a) [35 ILCS 200/18-178(a)]) An ordinance enacting the abatement can specify its percentage amount and duration. (Property Tax Code, Sec. 18-178(b) [35 ILCS 200/18-178(b)])

A "fallen police officer, soldier, or rescue worker" is an individual who dies:

(1) as a result of or in the course of employment as a police officer;

(2) while in the active service of a fire, rescue, or emergency medical service; or

(3) while on active duty as a member of the United States Armed Services, including the National Guard, serving in Iraq or Afghanistan.

However, that definition does not include a police officer, soldier, or rescue worker whose death was a result of that individual's own willful misconduct or abuse of alcohol or drugs. "Qualified property" is a parcel of real property occupied by not more than two families, that is used by a surviving spouse, and that was:

(1) owned by the fallen police officer, soldier, or rescue worker at the time of death;

(2) acquired by the surviving spouse within two years of the death if the spouse was domiciled in the state at the time of the death; or

(3) acquired more than two years after the death if the surviving spouse qualified for an abatement for a former qualified property within the jurisdiction.

A "surviving spouse" is a spouse, who has not remarried, of a fallen police officer, soldier, or rescue worker. (Property Tax Code, Sec. 18-178(c) [35 ILCS 200/18-178(c)])

• *Enterprise zone property*

Local property tax abatement is authorized for real property, or any class thereof, located within an enterprise zone created under the Illinois Enterprise Zone Act. The amount of taxes that may be abated cannot exceed the amount attributable to new construction, renovation, or rehabilitation. In the case of property within a redevelopment area created under the Real Property Tax Increment Allocation Redevelopment Act, or the County Economic Development Project Area Property Tax Allocation Act, abatement cannot exceed the amount of taxes allocable to the taxing district. (Property Tax Code, Sec. 181-70 [35 ILCS 200/18-170]; Illinois Municipal Code, Sec. 11-74.4-1 [65 ILCS 5/11-74.4-1]; 20 ILCS 3505/7.80)

CCH COMMENT: *Assessment reduction available in Cook County only.*—Cook County offers special property tax incentives for industrial property located anywhere within the county. However, property in enterprise zones receives special consideration under the Class 6b-Industrial Program. Industrial property in Cook County is generally assessed at 36% of market value. Under the special incentives, improvements to enterprise zone property are assessed at 16% of market value for eight years. The tax rate remains the same, but a company's tax liability drops because the rate is being multiplied by a much smaller property value. This program also applies to the purchase of existing buildings in enterprise zones, provided that the buildings have been vacant for 24 continuous months. (Cook County Real Property Taxation, Sec. 74-63)

• *Human resource and job programs*

Municipalities may abate their taxes in an amount not to exceed 50% of a taxpayer's donation of not less than $10,000 to a qualified program that provides for the creation or expansion of job-training and counseling programs, youth day-care centers, congregate housing programs for senior adults, youth recreation programs, alcohol and drug abuse prevention programs, mental health counseling programs, and domestic violence shelters. The facilities or programs must be located in a designated target area. (Municipal Code, Sec. 8-3-18 [65 ILCS 5/8-3-18])

• *Leaseholds on Department of Natural Resources property*

Real property taxes are abated on interests in a parcel of real property of the Department of Natural Resources on which there is a restaurant and overnight lodging facilities that were constructed from at least 50% private nonstate funding and that were opened for business after January 1, 1992. (Property Tax Code, Sec. 18-175 35 ILCS 200/18-175)

• *Leaseholds by state housing authorities*

Qualifying properties containing multi-family dwellings or certain multi-building developments that are leased for a minimum of 20 years to a state housing authority for use as low-rent housing are eligible for abatement from Illinois property taxes in the form of a reduction in payments due under the lease. The properties must be located in municipalities with populations of one million or more and counties with populations of three million or more. Properties that are used for commercial purposes are not eligible for the abatement. (Property Tax Code, Sec. 18-177(a)(2) [35 ILCS 200/18-177(a)(2)])

The housing authority must annually file a certificate of the property's use during the previous year with the city clerk to ensure that the property meets abatement requirements, eligible residential units have been inspected within the previous 90 days, and the units meet all housing quality standards. If only a portion of the property is eligible for abatement, the certificate must identify the eligible portion as a percentage of the total equalized and assessed value of the property. Additionally, if the dwellings or units on the property are individually assessed, no more than 40% of the units are certifiable. If the dwellings or units are not individually assessed, the portion of the certifiable property may not be more than 40% of the residential units. Abatement is wholly unavailable if the owner of an otherwise eligible property has outstanding and overdue debts to the municipality in which the property is located. (Property Tax Code, Sec. 18-177(a)(3) [35 ILCS 200/18-177(a)(3)])

The percentage limitation on the certification of residential units is deemed satisfied for developments described in qualifying resolutions adopted by the Board of Commissioners of the Chicago Housing Authority. (Property Tax Code, Sec. 18-177(b) [35 ILCS 200/18-177(b)])

• *Housing Opportunity Area Abatement Program*

For tax years 2004 through 2024, an owner of property located within a housing opportunity area who has a housing choice voucher contract with a housing authority may apply to the housing authority for an annual abatement of Illinois property tax. "Housing opportunity area" means a census tract where less than 10% of the residents live below the poverty level and that is located within a qualified township, except for a census tract located within a township that is located wholly within a municipality with 1 million or more inhabitants is considered a housing opportunity area if less than 12% of the residents of the census tract live below the poverty level. A "qualified township" means a township located within a county with 200,000 or more inhabitants whose tax capacity exceeds 80% of the average tax capacity of the county in which it is located, with certain exceptions. (Property Tax Code, Sec. 18-173 [35 ILCS 200/18-173])

The property's value may be reduced by a percentage calculated as follows: 19% of the equalized assessed value of the property multiplied by a fraction, the numerator of which is the number of qualified units and the denominator of which is the total number of dwelling units located within the property. (Property Tax Code, Sec. 18-173(e) [35 ILCS 200/18-173(e)]) A qualified unit must meet certain housing quality standards and must be rented to and occupied by a tenant who is participating in a housing choice voucher program. No more than 2 units or 20% of the total units contained within the property, whichever is greater, may be considered qualified units. No property may receive an abatement for more than 10 tax years. (Property Tax Code, Sec. 18-173 [35 ILCS 200/18-173(b)])

[¶20-815] Refunds

Property tax refunds are authorized for taxes:

(1) paid on property assessed twice in the same year,

(2) assessed before the property becomes taxable, or

(3) overpaid by the same claimant or by different claimants.

Refund claims are filed with the county collector who issues a refund to the proper claimant. If the county collector is unable to determine the proper claimant, a petition must be filed for refund directly with the circuit court in accordance with the provisions of the Civil Practice Law. The final judgment of the circuit court may be appealed by either party. No claim for refund is allowed unless a petition is filed within five years from the date the right to a refund arose. (Property Tax Code, Sec. 20-175(a) [35 ILCS 200/20-175(a)])

Payment under protest is not a statutory requirement to a refund action. Overpayments of an estimated tax bill as compared with the actual tax bill prepared by a county using the accelerated method of property tax billing are refunded. The county collector refunds the overpayment amount to the person who paid the estimated installments. (Property Tax Code, Sec. 21-60 [35 ILCS 200/21-60])

The courts have permitted county treasurers to offset refunds against taxes owed. (*Lake County Board of Review v. Property Tax Appeal Board* (Marriott Corp.), IL SCt, 519 NE2d 459 (1988))

Annexed property.—If property is annexed to an Illinois municipality at any time during a taxable year, taxpayers owning annexed property may be entitled to a property tax refund from the municipality. Specifically, the municipality would have to refund an amount of property tax:

(1) paid by the taxpayer,

(2) distributed to the municipality, and

(3) attributable to the annexed property for the portion of the taxable year during which the property was not included in the municipality.

The refund should be made within 60 days after the application is received. This law applies to home rule units. (Property Tax Code, Sec. 20-27 [35 ILCS 200/20-27])

[¶20-820] Incentives

Many states take positive action to lure new business and industry. Even states that do not aggressively seek to entice new firms are often receptive to bargaining efforts by business principals who offer to locate factories or administrative facilities in the state. The types of incentives that a state can provide are wide-ranging and can involve many taxes in addition to the property tax. In the simplest example, states can reduce property tax, or waive it for a given number of years. Credits can be given, based upon the number of new employees to be hired in an area. Favorable valuation of properties, both real and personal, can be negotiated. In some cases, grants by the state have enabled new business to add the infrastructure—roads, drainage, overpasses, and utilities—needed to serve the business.

Most often these incentives are not statutory, or, often, even publicized, but rather are negotiated by state or county officials and the principals of the business, including corporate counsel. Meetings are most effective when the corporate representatives bring factual detail to the table: expected investment, number of employees, anticipated gross receipts, etc., together with a suggested package of the incentives sought by the business.

[¶20-900]
TAXPAYER RIGHTS AND REMEDIES

[¶20-904] Overview of Appeal Process

Illinois taxpayers who want to appeal an assessment of property tax have a variety of options. However, there are time limits for appeals at each stage of the process. Taxpayers are entitled to representationin their appeals. Appeals can be made locally to, in turn, the local assessor and then the county board of review, except that in Cook County, the local review is to the board of appeal. If still dissatisfied, the taxpayer may appeal to the state Property Tax Appeal Board or to the local circuit court.

CCH Planning Note: Preliminary steps to formal protests.—Prior to instituting the formal protest process, a good first step in most cases is to review the assessor's valuation records, which are public records, for neighboring and/or comparable properties to confirm whether any glaring inconsistencies are evident. For example, if the other properties have been assigned relatively higher values, that may caution against proceeding with a protest to avoid the risk of having an appraised value increased or otherwise alerting the assessor to what may essentially be a favorable appraisal. It also may be useful to directly contact the assessor to discuss what factors the assessor considered in valuing the property, as this may alert the parties to obvious valuation errors that the assessor may be willing to correct without requiring the property owner to pursue a formal protest.

[¶20-906] Protest and Appeal of Assessments

Discussed here in relation to the assessment appeals are:

— representation of taxpayers;
— limitations periods for appeals;
— informal conferences;
— local administrative hearings;
— state administrative hearings; and
— judicial appeals and remedies.

A comprehensive set of administrative and legal remedies is afforded under the Property Tax Code for taxpayers aggrieved by the assessment placed on their property. In all but a limited number of circumstances, it is necessary for the taxpayer to seek review of a property tax assessment at the appropriate administrative tribunal prior to appealing to the courts or to the Property Tax Appeal Board. Generally, the appeal mechanism differs between Cook County and the rest of the Illinois counties.

• *Representation of taxpayer*

In counties with under 3 million in habitants, in actions before a county board of review to contest property tax assessments in which an attorney has filed on behalf of a complainant, all notices and correspondence from the board relating to the appeal are directed to the attorney. If the attorney fails to file proof of authority to represent the complainant when asked to do so by the board, the complaint may be dismissed. (Property Tax Code, Sec. 16-55 [35 ILCS 200/16-55(c)]) Attorneys also may file complaints before the Cook County Board of Review. (Property Tax Code, Sec. 16-115 [35 ILCS 200/16-115])

Parties to actions before the Property Tax Appeal Board (PTAB) have the right to be represented by an attorney. Accountants, tax representatives, tax advisers, real estate appraisers, real estate consultants, and others not qualified to practice law in Illinois cannot either appear in a representative capacity or conduct questioning, cross-examination, or other investigation at the hearing. However, they may testify at hearings and may assist parties and attorneys in preparation of cases for presentation at hearings. While parties generally may represent themselves at hearings, corporations, LLCs, partnerships, and other similar entities must be represented by a licensed attorney. Attorneys generally cannot appear before the PTAB as both an advocate and a witness. (86 Ill. Adm. Code 1910.70)

• *Limitations periods for appeals*

Listed below are the limitation periods of interest to Illinois property taxpayers who seek an abatement, reduction in tax liability, or other ameliorating change:

— Administrative review, local board of review (except Cook County), 30 calendar days after the date of publication of the assessment list; (Property Tax Code, Sec. 16-55(d) [35 ILCS 200/16-55(d)])

— Appeal to Board of Appeal (Cook County), at least 20 days after publication of notice of the date and place at which complaints can be filed; (Property Tax Code, Sec. 16-110 [35 ILCS 200/16-110])

— Appeal to Property Tax Appeal Board (except in Cook County), 30 days after the date of written notice of the decision of the board of review; (Property Tax Code, Sec. 16-160 [35 ILCS 200/16-160])

— Appeal to Property Tax Appeal Board (Cook County), the later of 30 days after the date of the board of review notice or within 30 after the date of the board transmits its final action to the county assessor; (Property Tax Code, Sec. 16-160 [35 ILCS 200/16-160])

— Tax objection complaints before a county circuit court (except in Cook County), within 75 days after the first penalty date of the final installment of taxes for the year; (Property Tax Code, Sec. 23-10 [35 ILCS 200/23-10])

— Tax objection complaints before Cook County Circuit Court, within 165 days after the first penalty date of the final installment of taxes for the year; (Property Tax Code, Sec. 23-10 [35 ILCS 200/23-10])

— Certificate of error, three years after the date on which the annual judgment and order of sale for that tax year was first entered. (Property Tax Code, Sec. 14-15 [35 ILCS 200/14-15])

• *Informal conferences*

Taxpayers in counties other than Cook County may complain to the supervisor of assessments of an alleged overvaluation of an original initial assessment at any time during the year. (Property Tax Code, Sec. 9-10 [35 ILCS 200/9-10]) To obtain an assessment adjustment for the immediate tax year, the taxpayer should complain at the time he or she receives the mailed notice of assessment change from the assessor. This personal notice alerts the taxpayer to a proposed change in assessment that, if erroneous, can be corrected by the assessor without using the formal appeals process. However, there is no statutory requirement that the taxpayer must request an informal review before the assessing official or that the assessing official must provide a hearing for the taxpayer.

In tax objection actions before a local circuit court and in actions before the PTAB, the parties can engage in settlement discussions and negotiations. See generally ¶20-762.

A Cook County taxpayer begins the appeal process by filing a complaint with the Cook County assessor, who has the authority to revise assessments each year on his own initiative or upon the written complaint of the taxpayer. (Property Tax Code, Sec. 9-85 [35 ILCS 200/9-85]; Property Tax Code, Sec. 14-35 [35 ILCS 200/14-35]; 86 Ill. Admin. Code Sec. 110.135)

• *Local administrative hearings*

In discussing property tax appeals in general, Illinois law distinguishes between counties with populations under three million and over three million. Cook County is the only county in the state with a population greater than three million.

County Board of Review—all counties except Cook County.—In counties other than Cook County, taxpayers may bypass the assessor and file a complaint before the local board of review, which is an administrative agency in each county that decides appeals from property owners on the assessed value of their properties. (Property Tax Code, Sec. 16-20 [35 ILCS 200/16-20]) Failure to file a proper protest with a board of review will bar a suit in circuit court to revise an assessment. (Property Tax Code, Sec. 23-10 [35 ILCS 200/23-10])

After receiving a written complaint, the board shall review the assessment, but in no case shall the property be assessed at a higher percentage of fair cash value than other property in the assessment district prior to equalization by the board or the Department. A complaint to affect the assessment for the current year must be filed on or before 30 calendar days after the date of publication of the assessment list. (Property Tax Code, Sec. 16-55 [35 ILCS 200/16-55]) Complaints are classified by townships or taxing districts by the clerk of the board, except that if a taxpayer has two or more complaints pending and the township books are available, such complaints must be consolidated for hearing. (Property Tax Code, Sec. 16-45 [35 ILCS 200/16-45])

The board may summon the assessor to appear before it to give testimony regarding the accuracy of any valuation. (Property Tax Code, Sec. 12-50 [35 ILCS 200/12-50]) The board must mail notices to the taxpayer or, if the taxpayer is represented by an attorney, to the taxpayer's attorney if final board of review action changes the taxpayer's assessment. (Property Tax Code, Sec. 16-10 [35 ILCS 200/16-10])

Taxpayers dissatisfied with a board of review's decision have the choice of filing a complaint in circuit court or appealing to the state Property Tax Appeal Board within 30 days of the notice of the board's written decision. The taxpayer cannot initiate both procedures. (Property Tax Code, Sec. 12-50 [35 ILCS 200/12-50])

Cook County Board of Review.—In Cook County, if a taxpayer does not accept the assessor's ruling on a complaint, then the taxpayer may take the case to the Cook

County Board of Review. (Property Tax Code, Sec. 16-115 [35 ILCS 200/16-115]) Taxpayers also may file their complaints with the board without filing with the assessor. (Property Tax Code, Sec. 23-15 [35 ILCS 200/23-15])

The board of review reviews the taxpayer's complaints. (Property Tax Code, Sec. 16-95 [35 ILCS 200/16-95]) The board convenes its session for each tax year annually on or before the second Monday in September. (Property Tax Code, Sec. 16-105 [35 ILCS 200/16-105]) The actual time and date for filing assessment complaints and for hearings for the various towns or taxing districts is published in the newspaper, after which taxpayers have at least 20 days to file complaints. (Property Tax Code, Sec. 16-110 [35 ILCS 200/16-110])

Complaints that property is underassessed, overassessed, or exempt may be filed by any taxpayer or any affected taxing body. Complaints must identify the particular piece of property, and at least two copies must be filed. Complaints regarding property in Cook County may be filed electronically. (Property Tax Code, Sec. 16-115 [35 ILCS 200/16-115]) No hearing may be held on any complaint until the owner of the property affected and the assessor have been given notice and an opportunity to be heard. (Property Tax Code, Sec. 16-120 [35 ILCS 200/16-120]; Property Tax Code, Sec. 16-125 [35 ILCS 200/16-125]) In Cook County, the notices can be sent to the taxpayer by e-mail if the taxpayer's e-mail address is in the hearing records or the complaint to the board; if the taxpayer is represented by an attorney, the notice in Cook County can be sent by e-mail to the attorney. (Property Tax Code, Sec. 12-50 [35 ILCS 200/12-50])

Assessment appeal hearings are open and public. Board files are available for public inspection during regular office hours. (Property Tax Code, Sec. 16-105 [35 ILCS 200/16-105]) The board may also summon any assessor to appear to give testimony regarding the accuracy of any valuation. (Property Tax Code, Sec. 16-10 [35 ILCS 200/16-10]) If there is a change to an assessment, the Board directs the assessor to correct any mistake or error; the Board makes no changes on its own. (Property Tax Code, Sec. 16-145 [35 ILCS 200/16-145])

Certificates of error.—Certificates of error are issued to correct mistakes or errors that are discovered before judgment or order for sale. In counties other than Cook County, the chief county assessment officer and the board of review may draw up and issue a certificate for mistakes, other than errors of judgment as to valuation. A certificate must set forth the nature of the error and the causes that produced it. A certificate must be endorsed by both the board of review and the chief county assessment officer. The certificate of error may be used as evidence in any proceeding to collect delinquent taxes. (Property Tax Code, Sec. 14-20 [35 ILCS 200/14-20]; Property Tax Code, Sec. 16-75 [35 ILCS 200/16-75])

Certificates of error may be issued on court or Department of Revenue exemption approvals if:

(1) the property became tax exempt at an earlier time, limited to certificates for the three preceding assessment years;

(2) the owner failed to file an application for exemption; or

(3) the property was erroneously assessed after the exemption claim is approved.

(Property Tax Code, Sec. 14-25 [35 ILCS 200/14-25])

The certificate of error must be executed no more than three years after the date on which the annual judgment and order of sale for that tax year was first entered. (Property Tax Code, Sec. 14-15 [35 ILCS 200/14-15])

In counties with a population of less than 3 million, if an owner fails to file an application for any homestead exemption provided under Article 15 of the Property Tax Code during the previous year and qualifies for it, the chief county assessor may issue a certificate of error providing the correct taxable value of the property. (Property Tax Code, Sec. 14-20 [35 ILCS 200/14-20])

In Cook County, certificates of error originate with the county assessor upon discovery of assessment errors or mistakes. There is no language prohibiting issuance on the basis of errors of judgment, a restriction that applies to the rest of the Illinois counties. The certificate needs to be endorsed only by the county assessor unless the assessment has been appealed to the Board of Review, in which case both must endorse the certificate. The certificate may be received in evidence in any court of competent jurisdiction. A certificate of error proceeding is separate and distinct from the procedures available to a taxpayer under complaint provisions. (Property Tax Code, Sec. 14-15 [35 ILCS 200/14-15]; *Chicago Sheraton Corp. v. Zaban*, IL SCt, 71 IllApp2d 85, 373 NE2d 1318 (1977), *cert. denied* US SCt, 439 US 888, 99 SCt 242 (1978))

A certificate of error may be executed, endorsed, issued, or adjudicated if:

(1) the annual judgment and order of sale for the tax year in question was reopened for further proceedings upon consent of the county collector and county assessor, represented by the State's Attorney; and

(2) a new final judgment was subsequently entered.

Generally, a certificate of error will not be executed for any tax year more than three years after the date on which the annual judgment and order of sale for that tax year was first entered. However, certificates that establish a property tax exemption approved by the Department of Revenue or certificates correcting an assessment to $1, on a parcel of land that a subdivision or planned development has acquired by adverse possession and used as a common area and that the application was filed prior to December 31, 1997, are exceptions to the three year limitation period. (Property Tax Code, Sec. 14-15 [35 ILCS 200/14-15])

In Cook County, the county assessor may certify to the Board of Review that a mistake or error, other than a mistake or error of judgment, has been made as to the valuation or assessment of property. Upon making of the certification, the Board, after notice to the taxpayer and an opportunity to be heard, has the power to order the county assessor to correct the mistake. Both commissioners must endorse their signatures on the certificate of correction. (Property Tax Code, Sec. 14-10 [35 ILCS 200/14-10])

• *State administrative hearings*

Taxpayers dissatisfied with a board of review's decision have the choice of filing a complaint in circuit court (see below) or appealing to the state Property Tax Appeal Board (PTAB) within 30 days of the notice of the board's written decision. (Property Tax Code, Sec. 12-50 [35 ILCS 200/12-50])

The State Property Tax Appeal Board is the final administrative review agency to which assessment appeals from the decisions of the local boards of review are taken. Cook County taxpayers may appeal assessments to the PTAB or file a tax objection complaint in the circuit court of Cook County. (Property Tax Code, Sec. 16-160 [35 ILCS 200/16-160]; 86 Ill. Admin. Code Sec. 1910.10)

There is no statutory or judicial requirement that taxpayers must exhaust this final step in the appeal process as a precondition to judicial review.

General matters of PTAB procedure are covered by rule. (86 Ill. Admin. Code Sec 1910.5) To begin an appeal before the PTAB, the taxpayer or taxing body must file a petition for appeal within 30 days after the date and/or postmark of the written decision of the local board of review. In Cook County, the petition must be filed either by that date or 30 days after the board of review transmits to the county assessor its final action on the township in which the property is located, whichever is later. (86 Ill. Admin. Code Sec. 1910.30(a)) The board of review has 90 days within which to submit evidence in support of its assessment. (86 Ill. Admin. Code Sec. 1910.40)

Each appeal will be limited to the grounds listed in the petition filed with the Property Tax Appeal Board. All appeals to the PTAB are considered *de novo*. (Property Tax Code, Sec. 16-180 [35 ILCS 200/16-180])

An appeal before the PTAB does not delay the extension of taxes. If the PTAB reduces the assessment, any overpaid taxes are refunded with interest. (Property Tax Code, Sec. 16-185 [35 ILCS 200/16-185])

The local board of review has 30 days from the date of notice to submit its response. A hearing is granted on request. (Property Tax Code, Sec. 16-170 [35 ILCS 200/16-170]) At least 20 days prior to the scheduled date of the hearing, all parties must be given notice of the time and place scheduled for the hearing. (86 Ill. Admin. Code Sec. 1910.67)

Hearing officers have the right to require the taxpayer to produce any books, records, papers, or documents that may be necessary to make a just decision. The chairman may also issue subpoenas. (Property Tax Code, Sec. 16-175 [35 ILCS 200/16-175])

A concurrence of the majority of the PTAB members is sufficient for a decision to be made. The decision is then certified to each of the parties and to other proper authorities within 10 days after being made and entered. (Property Tax Code, Sec. 16-185 [35 ILCS 200/16-185])

Decisions of the PTAB are based on equity and weight of the evidence, not on constructive fraud, which is the ground in a civil action. By rule, a three-year assessment level to be based on relevant sales during the previous three years will be considered when sufficient probative evidence is presented that indicates the estimate of full market value of the subject property on the relevant real property assessment date of January 1. PTAB decisions are binding upon the taxpayer and government officials in absence of fraud or appeal. (Property Tax Code, Sec. 16-185 [35 ILCS 200/16-185])

In cases of an appeal of the effect of the equalizing factor assigned by the board of review to all property or classes of property within the county, a reduction of an assessment is limited to the amount that was added as the result of the application of the factor where the taxpayer had filed no initial complaint with the board of review. (Property Tax Code, Sec. 16-180 [35 ILCS 200/16-180])

The PTAB may grant relief from disparity in levels of assessment within a county. The PTAB has no jurisdiction to determine the tax rate, the amount of a tax bill, or property exemptions.

If a PTAB decision lowering the assessed value of the property is made after the deadline for filing complaints with the board of review for the following year, the taxpayer may directly appeal the assessment for such year to the PTAB within 30 days of its written notice. (Property Tax Code, Sec. 16-185 [35 ILCS 200/16-185])

If the PTAB lowers the assessment of owner-occupied property, the reduced assessment, subject to equalization, remains in effect for the remainder of the general assessment period unless the parcel is subsequently sold in an arms's-length transaction establishing a fair cash value on which the PTAB's assessment is based or the decision of the PTAB is overruled. (Property Tax Code, Sec. 16-185 [35 ILCS 200/16-185])

Court review of the final decisions of the PTAB is governed by the provisions of the Administrative Review Law, except that every case in which a change in assessed valuation of $300,000 or more was sought shall be appealed directly to the appropriate Appellate Court. (Property Tax Code, Sec. 16-195 [35 ILCS 200/16-195])

Centrally-assessed property appeals.—The procedure for review of property value assessments made by the Illinois Department of Revenue is similar to that applicable to locally assessed property owners. The Department publishes a complete list of all state assessed property in the state "official newspaper". Any person or corporation seeking to challenge the assessment may, within 10 days of the publication, apply to the department for review and correction. All applications for review of assessments must be written and contain a brief of the points and authorities relied upon. (Property Tax Code, Sec. 8-35 [35 ILCS 200/8-35]; 86 Ill. Admin. Code Sec. 110.145)

Appeal from an adverse decision of the department must be filed with the Department within 20 days after its decision. No action for the judicial review of any assessment of the Department is allowed unless the party has first filed an application for a hearing and the Department has acted upon such application. An action for review of an assessment does not delay the extension of taxes. (Property Tax Code, Sec. 8-35 [35 ILCS 200/8-35])

Judicial review of a department assessment is taken under the Administrative Review Law. (Property Tax Code, Sec. 8-40 [35 ILCS 200/8-40]) However, no action for judicial review will stay or suspend the assessment or the extension of taxes. (Property Tax Code, Sec. 8-45 [35 ILCS 200/8-45]) The taxpayer is entitled to a refund if the court sets aside or reduces its assessment.

CCH COMMENT: Where a change in assessed valuation involves valuation in excess $300,000 or more, then review is directly in the Illinois Appellate Court for the district in which the property is located. An action to review a final board decision, when the change in assessed valuation was less than $300,000 is begun by filing a complaint and summons in the circuit court within 35 days from the date that a copy of the decision sought to be reviewed was served upon the party affected by the decision. It is important to note that failure to join the board of review or any intervenor or other party of record before the board may lead to dismissal of the action. (Property Tax Code, Sec. 16-195 35 ILCS 200/16-195)

• *Judicial appeals and remedies*

Taxpayers can appeal assessment decisions to the local county circuit court, and appeals may be taken from the circuit courts' final judgments as in other civil cases. In addition, some final decisions of the Property Tax Appeal Board may be made directly to the state appellate courts.

Circuit courts.—Taxpayers who seek judicial relief of an alleged overvaluation must pay the taxes under protest and file a tax objection complaint in the circuit court in the county in which the property is located. Taxpayers must pay the tax due within 60 days from the first penalty date of the final installment of taxes for that year. In Cook County, a tax objection complaint must be filed within 165 days after the first penalty date of the final installment of taxes for the year in question. A 75-day deadline applies to tax objection complaints filed in all other counties. (Property Tax Code, Sec. 23-5 [35 ILCS 200/23-5]; Property Tax Code, Sec. 23-15 [35 ILCS 200/23-15]) The court may enter judgment for a refund of any excess amount paid or for payment of taxes, special assessments, interest and penalties that are due. (Property Tax Code, Sec. 21-175 [35 ILCS 200/21-175])

A court may not hear an objection to an assessment if an administrative remedy was available by complaint to the board of review unless that remedy was exhausted prior to the filing of the tax objection complaint. (Property Tax Code, Sec. 23-10 [35 ILCS 200/23-10]) Class action complaints are not permitted, but joinder of plaintiffs is permissible. (Property Tax Code, Sec. 23-15 [35 ILCS 200/23-15])

Within 10 days after the filing of a complaint, the court clerk must deliver one copy to the State's Attorney and one copy to the county clerk. The county clerk must notify the affected taxing districts within 30 days from the last day for the filing of complaints. (Property Tax Code, Sec. 23-10 [35 ILCS 200/23-10])

Following the filing of an objection complaint, the court may hold a conference with the taxpayer objector and the state's attorney. Compromise agreements reached at the conference are filed with the court. (Property Tax Code, Sec. 23-30 [35 ILCS 200/23-30])

When the error in levy, certification, filing, or publication can be corrected by amendment, then no error or informality of an officer in making the tax levy or in certifying or filing can defeat the levy or affect the tax in judicial tax proceedings. (Property Tax Code, Sec. 23-40 [35 ILCS 200/23-40])

The court sits without a jury and hears all objections to assessments *de novo*. Taxes, assessments, and levies are presumed correct and legal, but the presumption is rebuttable. (Property Tax Code, Sec. 23-15 [35 ILCS 200/23-15])

In counties other than Cook County, if a court renders a decision lowering the assessment of a particular parcel on which a residence occupied by the owner is situated, the reduced assessment, subject to equalization, remains in effect for the remainder of the general assessment period, with certain exceptions. (Property Tax Code, Sec. 23-15 [35 ILCS 200/23-15])

Estimated or accelerated first installment objection.—In Cook County, which has adopted an accelerated method of property tax collection, any taxpayer may protest the estimated first installment on the grounds that the estimate is based on

(1) a tax bill pertaining to any property that was divided after preparation of the collector's books for the previous year, or

(2) such property is no longer located within the corporate limits of the taxing district.

If the protest is correct, the estimated tax bill will be canceled. There is no prepayment requirement for the filing of this type of objection. (Property Tax Code, Sec. 21-55 [35 ILCS 200/21-55])

Interest: If a taxpayer is successful in a court or board hearing, interest is paid on the refund amount from the date of payment or from the date payment is due, whichever is later, to the date of refund at the rate of the lesser of 5% per year or the percentage increase in the Consumer Price Index for All Urban Consumers during the 12-month calendar year preceding the levy year for which the refund was made. (Property Tax Code, Sec. 23-20 [35 ILCS 200/23-20])

Appellate court.—For a final PTAB ruling that results in a change in assessed valuation of at least $300,000, an appeal is directly to the appropriate Court of Appeal, not to the local circuit court. (Property Tax Code, Sec. 16-195 [35 ILCS 200/16-195])

For circuit court final judgments, appeals may be taken as in other civil cases. (Property Tax Code, Sec. 23-15 [35 ILCS 200/23-15])

MISCELLANEOUS TAXES AND FEES

[¶35-000]
GAMBLING TAXES

[¶35-001] Gambling Taxes

New Developments: Enacted legislation changes the gaming privilege tax structure in Illinois, as well as providing other relief. Specifically, the legislation establishes new privilege tax schedules for a city of Chicago casino and provides tax relief for existing casinos by extending the payment period for reconciliation payments and waiving interest on those payments. Existing casinos also find relief from the accelerated privilege tax rate structure and the one-year extension of the sports wagering license fee due date.

Slot machines. The new Chicago tax schedule for slot machines is as follows:

- Total rate of 22.5% (12% state and 10.5% city) for adjusted gross receipts of $0-$25 million;
- Total rate of 30% (16% sate and 14% city) for adjusted gross receipts of $25-$50 million;
- Total rate of 37.5% (20.1% state and 17.4% city) for adjusted gross receipts of $50-$75 million;
- Total rate of 40% (21.4% state and 18.6% city) for adjusted gross receipts of $75-$100 million;
- Total rate of 42.5% (22.7% state and 19.8% city) for adjusted gross receipts of $100-$150 million;
- Total rate of 45% (24.1% state and 20.9% city) for adjusted gross receipts of $150-$225 million;
- Total rate of 50% (26.8% state and 23.2% city) for adjusted gross receipts of $225 million-$1 billion; and
- Total rate of 74.7% (40% state and 34.7% city) for adjusted gross receipts of over $1 billion.

Table games. The new Chicago tax schedule for table games is as follows:

- Total rate of 15% (8.1% state and 6.9% city) for adjusted gross receipts of $0 to $25 million;
- Total rate of 19.1% (10.7% state and 8.4% city) for adjusted gross receipts of $25-$75 million;
- Total rate of 21% (11.2% state and 9.8% city) for adjusted gross receipts of $75-$175 million;
- Total rate of 25% (13.5% state and 11.5% city) for adjusted gross receipts of $175-$225 million;
- Total rate of 28% (15.1% state and 12.9% city) for adjusted gross receipts of $225-$275 million;
- Total rate of 30% (16.2% state and 13.8% city) for adjusted gross receipts of $275-$375 million; and
- Total rate of 35% (18.9% state and 16.1% city) for adjusted gross receipts of over $375 million.

Additional relief provisions. The legislation also does the following:

¶35-001

- Provides that the new, lower privilege (wagering) tax schedule enacted by P.A. 101-0031 takes effect on July 1, 2020 instead of the first day that one of the newly authorized casinos begins operations, either in a temporary or permanent facility. This acceleration of the implementation of the lower privilege tax schedule applies to all existing Illinois casinos;

- Delays the deadline for payment of the initial sports wagering license fee by an organization licensee (i.e., owner of a racetrack) or an owner's license (for a casino) from July 1, 2020, to July 1, 2021;

- Requires the Illinois Gaming Board to reopen the license application process for new casino owners' licenses if, at any point after June 1, 2020, there are no pending applications for one of the new owners' licenses and not all of the new owners' licenses have been issued (rather than if the Illinois Gaming Board does not issue all owners licenses for newly authorized casinos within the specified time period). It also requires, as a part of this process, the applicant for a license make a public presentation to the local corporate authority and post a summary of its casino proposal on a public website;

- Increases, from 2 years to 6 years, the payment period for the reconciliation payments owed by new casinos and new organization gaming licensees ("racinos") as well as new gaming positions purchased by existing casinos. It also waives interest on the reconciliation payments. The reconciliation payments equal 75% of the adjusted gross receipts earned by the casinos during the most lucrative 12-month period in their first three years of operations. Adjusted gross receipts are gaming receipts minus amounts paid to winners;

- Provides that amounts paid by organization gaming licensees ("racinos") to their purse accounts will not be counted as part of their adjusted gross receipts for tax purposes; and

- Allows the Illinois Department of Agriculture to operate video gaming terminals at the Springfield and Du Quoin State Fairs.

(P.A. 101-0648 (S.B. 516), Laws 2020, effective June 30, 2020, except as noted; *Press Release*, Illinois Gov. JB Pritzker and City of Chicago Mayor Lori Lightfoot, June 30, 2020)

Nature of Tax.—Illinois imposes tax on a variety of gambling businesses. Discussed here are the bingo license and tax, the charitable games tax, the pull tabs and jar games tax, and the riverboat gambling taxes and fees.

- *Bingo license and tax*

The Bingo License and Tax Act restricts the conducting of bingo games to licensees that are determined by the Department of Revenue to be a bona fide religious, charitable, labor, fraternal, youth athletic, senior citizen, educational, or veterans' organization organized in Illinois, operating without profit to its members, and in existence in Illinois for a period of five continuous years immediately preceding application for a license. A license authorizes the licensee to conduct the game of "bingo," in which prizes are awarded on the basis of designated numbers or symbols on a card conforming to numbers or symbols selected at random. (Bingo License and Tax Act, Sec. 1 [230 ILCS 25/1])

Administration.—The Bingo License and Tax Act is administered by the Department of Revenue. (Bingo License and Tax Act, Sec. 5.1 [230 ILCS 25/5.1]) Various enforcement provisions of the Retailers' Occupation Tax Act are made applicable to the bingo license and tax. The Uniform Penalty and Interest Act applies to the Bingo License and Tax Act. (Bingo License and Tax Act, Sec. 3 [230 ILCS 25/3])

¶35-001

Basis and rate of tax.—The bingo tax is imposed at the rate of 5% of the gross proceeds of any game of bingo conducted by the licensee. (Bingo License and Tax Act, Sec. 3 [230 ILCS 25/3])

License fees.—The annual fee for a bingo license is $200; however, a restricted license may be authorized to senior citizen organizations for an annual fee of $10. Any person, firm, or corporation selling, leasing, supplying, or distributing bingo game equipment to any organization licensed to conduct bingo games is required to be licensed and pay a fee of $200. (Bingo License and Tax Act, Sec. 1 [230 ILCS 25/1])

Returns and payment.—The bingo tax must be paid quarterly, by the 20th day of April, July, October, and January, and must be accompanied by reports on forms prescribed by the Department. Payment must be made by money order or certified check. (Bingo License and Tax Act, Sec. 3 [230 ILCS 25/3])

• *Charitable games tax*

The Charitable Games Tax Act restricts the conducting of charitable games to licensees that are determined by the Department of Revenue to be qualified charitable, religious, fraternal, veterans, labor, or educational organizations, operating without profit, and exempt from federal income taxation under Secs. 501(c)(3), 501(c)(4), 501(c)(5), 501(c)(8), 501(c)(10), or 501(c)(19) of the Internal Revenue Code. (Charitable Games Tax Act, Sec. 2 [230 ILCS 30/2]) Qualified organizations must have been in existence in Illinois for a period of five years immediately before making application for a license. (Charitable Games Tax Act, Sec. 3 [230 ILCS 30/3])

Administration.—The Charitable Games Tax Act is administered by the Department of Revenue. (Charitable Games Tax Act, Sec. 13 [230 ILCS 30/13]) Various enforcement provisions of the Retailers' Occupation Tax Act are made applicable to the charitable games tax. Beginning January 1, 1994, the Uniform Penalty and Interest Act applies to the Charitable Games Tax Act. (Charitable Games Tax Act, Sec. 9 [230 ILCS 30/9])

Basis and rate of tax.—The charitable games tax is imposed at the rate of 3% of the gross proceeds of any charitable game conducted by the licensee. (Charitable Games Tax Act, Sec. 9 [230 ILCS 30/9])

License fees.—The annual fee for a charitable games license is $200. Any person, firm, or corporation selling, leasing, supplying, or distributing game equipment to any organization licensed to conduct games is required to be licensed and pay a fee of $200. (Charitable Games Tax Act, Sec. 3 [230 ILCS 30/3]) An Illinois person, firm, or corporation renting or providing premises for the conducting of charitable games is required to secure a providers' license and pay an annual license fee of $50. (Charitable Games Tax Act, Sec. 5 [230 ILCS 30/5]) Any Illinois person, firm, or corporation selling, leasing, lending, distributing or supplying supplies and devices for use in playing charitable games is required to obtain a supplier's license and pay a license fee of $500. (Charitable Games Tax Act, Sec. 6 [230 ILCS 30/6])

Returns and payment.—The charitable games tax must be paid within 30 days after completion of the games, and the payment must be accompanied by reports on forms prescribed by the Department. Payment must be made by money order or certified check. (Charitable Games Tax Act, Sec. 9 [230 ILCS 30/9])

• *Pull tabs and jar games tax*

The Illinois Pull Tabs and Jar Games Act, enacted by P.A. 85-1012, Laws 1988, went into effect July 1, 1988. (Pull Tabs and Jar Games Act, Sec. 1 [230 ILCS 20/1]) The Act imposes a gross receipts tax on nonprofit charitable, religious, and educational organizations that conduct pull tabs and jar games (Pull Tabs and Jar Games Act, Sec. 5 [230 ILCS 20/5]), as well as imposing license fees on suppliers and operators of such games. (Pull Tabs and Jar Games Act, Sec. 2 [230 ILCS 20/2])

Administration.—The pull tabs and jar games tax is administered by the Department of Revenue. (Pull Tabs and Jar Games Act, Sec. 2 [230 ILCS 20/2]) Various enforcement provisions of the Retailers' Occupation Tax Act are made applicable to pull tabs and jar games. (Pull Tabs and Jar Games Act, Sec. 5 [230 ILCS 20/5]; 86 Ill. Adm. Code 432.160) Beginning January 1, 1994, the Uniform Penalty and Interest Act applies to the Pull Tabs and Jar Games Tax. (Pull Tabs and Jar Games Act, Sec. 5 [230 ILCS 20/5])

Basis and rate of tax.—The tax is imposed at a rate of 5% of gross receipts from pull tabs and jar games. (Pull Tabs and Jar Games Act, Sec. 5 [230 ILCS 20/5]) "Gross receipts" includes total receipts and is not limited to "net proceeds," the amount left after winning tickets are paid. (86 Ill. Adm. Code 432.170)

"Pull tabs" and "jar games" are defined as games using single-folded or banded tickets or a card, the face of which is initially covered or otherwise hidden from view in order to conceal numbers or symbols, some of which are winners. (Pull Tabs and Jar Games Act, Sec. 1.1 [230 ILCS 20/1.1]) Players with winning tickets receive a prize stated on a promotional display. "Pull tabs" also means a game in which prizes are won by pulling a tab from a board, thereby revealing a number that corresponds to the number for a given prize.

License fees.—Licenses for conducting pull tabs and jar games are available to any local fraternal mutual benefit organization that was chartered at least 40 years before it applies for a license, as well as to any other eligible nonprofit religious, charitable, labor, fraternal, youth athletic, senior citizen, educational, or veterans' organization, for the following fees:

Group No. (license expiration date)	Fee
1 (December 31, 1990)	$250
2 (March 31, 1991)	375
3 (June 30, 1991)	500
4 (September 30, 1991)	625

(Pull Tabs and Jar Games Act, Sec. 2 [230 ILCS 20/2])

Licenses expire on June 30 following the date of issuance; however, beginning June 30, 1990, licenses are staggered into four groups, as noted above. Each game location must be separately licensed. Eligible suppliers and manufacturers of pull tabs and jar games may be licensed for a $5,000 fee. (Pull Tabs and Jar Games Act, Sec. 5 [230 ILCS 20/5])

Returns and payment.—The tax must be paid quarterly together with a report describing the games conducted. (Pull Tabs and Jar Games Act, Sec. 5 [230 ILCS 20/5]) Payment must be received within 20 days after the end of each quarter (April 20, July 20, October 20, and January 20) on forms prescribed by the Department. (86 Ill. Adm. Code 432.170)

• *Riverboat gambling taxes and fees*

The Illinois Riverboat Gambling Act, enacted by P.A. 86-1029, Laws 1990, went into effect February 7, 1990, and was amended effective June 25, 1999, to authorize riverboat gambling operating upon any water other than Lake Michigan, that constitutes a boundary of Illinois. (Riverboat Gambling Act, Sec. 1 [230 ILCS 10/1]; Riverboat Gambling Act, Sec. 3 [230 ILCS 10/3]) The Act imposes a tax upon admissions to riverboat gambling operations (Riverboat Gambling Act, Sec. 12 [230 ILCS 10/12]) and imposes license fees on owners and suppliers of riverboat gambling authorized under the act regardless of whether it conducts excursion cruises. (Riverboat Gambling Act, Sec. 3 [230 ILCS 10/3]) Each holder of an owner's license must maintain an account at a designated financial institution, to handle electronic fund transfers, and maintain a minimum account balance, sufficient to cover all tax liabilities due under and required by both the admission tax and the wagering tax. (86 Ill. Adm. Code 3000.1071)

Regulations provide that riverboat casinos in Illinois may conduct table game tournaments and slot machine tournaments, using specially designed poker chips and microprocessor components, known as Tournament EPROM, with a payout of more than 100%. (86 Ill. Adm. Code 3000.100) These regulations further provide that the cost of cash or noncash prizes and entry fees for such tournaments may not be subtracted from the gross receipts in determining the adjusted gross receipts, as required for Illinois wagering tax and tax schedule forms. (86 Ill. Adm. Code 3000.614(a)(2))

Administration.—The riverboat gambling tax is administered by the Illinois Gaming Board. (Riverboat Gambling Act, Sec. 5 [230 ILCS 10/5]) The Uniform Penalty and Interest Act applies to the Riverboat Gambling Tax. (Riverboat Gambling Act, Sec. 12 [230 ILCS 10/12])

The following gambling tax rates are imposed on the annual adjusted gross receipts of riverboat casino operators:

— 15% (from $0 up to $25 million);

— 27.5% (over $25 million up to $37.5 million);

— 32.5% (over $37.5 million up to $50 million);

— 37.5% (over $50 million up to $75 million);

— 45% (over $75 million up to $100 million);

— 50% (over $100 million up to $250 million); and

— 70% (over $250 million).

(230 ILCS 10/13)

The gambling tax rates will return to the pre-July 1, 2003, rates above upon the earlier of (1) July 1, 2005, or (2) the date any additional riverboat casino begins to conduct gambling operations in the state under a dormant or newly authorized license.

"Riverboat" means a self-propelled excursion boat or a permanently moored barge on which lawful gambling is authorized and licensed. "Gambling game" includes, but is not limited to, baccarat, twenty-one, poker, craps, slot machine, video game of chance, roulette wheel, klondike table, punchboard, faro layout, keno layout, numbers ticket push card, jar ticket, or pull tab that is authorized by the Board as a wagering device. "Gross receipts" means the total amount of money exchanged for the purchase of chips, tokens, or electronic cards by riverboat patrons. "Adjusted gross receipts" means the gross receipts less winnings paid to wagerers. (230 ILCS 10/4)

The riverboat casino admission tax is

— $2 per person admitted for licensees that admitted at most 1 million persons in calendar year 2004 and

— $3 per person admitted for all other licensees.

However, a person who exits and then reenters a riverboat gambling facility within the same gaming day is subject only to the initial admission fee. (230 ILCS 10/12)

License fees.—A $50,000 application fee for an owner's license to conduct riverboat gambling is imposed to defray costs of investigation (unused portion is refundable). (Riverboat Gambling Act, Sec. 6 [230 ILCS 10/6]) A $25,000 license fee is imposed on riverboat owners for the first year of operation, and a $5,000 renewal license fee is imposed for each succeeding year. (Riverboat Gambling Act, Sec. 7 [230

ILCS 10/7]) Suppliers of gambling equipment and supplies are required to pay a $5,000 annual license fee. (Riverboat Gambling Act, Sec. 8 [230 ILCS 10/8])

Returns and payment.—Licensed owners are required to keep books and records (Riverboat Gambling Act, Sec. 14 [230 ILCS 10/14]) and, within 90 days after the end of each quarter of each fiscal year, file an audit of all financial transactions with the Gaming Board. (Riverboat Gambling Act, Sec. 15 [230 ILCS 10/15]) The Board must file an annual report for each calendar year with the Governor. (Riverboat Gambling Act, Sec. 16 [230 ILCS 10/16])

• *Video gaming taxes*

Under the terms of the Video Gaming Act, a tax of 30% is imposed on net terminal income. The term "net terminal income" means money put into a video gaming terminal minus credits paid out to players. (Video Gaming Act, Sec. 1[230 ILCS 40/60(a)]) Non-home rule units of government may not impose any annual fee in excess of $25 for the operation of a video gaming terminal. Effective January 1, 2020, the city of Rockford may not impose any annual fee in excess of $250 for the operation of a video gaming terminal. (Video Gaming Act, Sec. 1[230 ILCS 40/65])

Nonrefundable applications for video gaming licenses are set at

    — $5,000 for manufacturers, distributors, and terminal operators;

    — $2,500 for suppliers;

    — $100 for technicians; and

    — $50 for terminal handlers.

(Video Gaming Act, Sec. 1[230 ILCS 40/45(f)]) The maximum annual fee for each license is

    — $10,000 for each manufacturer and distributor;

    — $5,000 for each terminal operator;

    — $2,000 for each supplier;

    — $100 for each technician, licensed establishment, and video gaming terminal; and

    — $50 for each terminal handler.

(Video Gaming Act, Sec. 1[230 ILCS 40/45(g)])

[¶35-050]
MEDICAL SERVICE PROVIDER ASSESSMENT

[¶35-051] Medical Service Provider Assessment

Illinois imposes an annual assessment on hospital providers' inpatient and outpatient services and on nursing home providers. The assessments are administered by the Illinois Department of Healthcare and Family Services. (305 ILCS 5/2-12(3))

• *Hospital provider assessment*

For state fiscal years 2019 and 2020, an annual assessment on inpatient services is imposed on each hospital provider in an amount equal to $197.19 multiplied by the difference of the hospital's occupied bed days less the hospital's Medicare bed days. For the period of July 1, 2020 through December 31, 2020, and calendar years 2021 and 2022, the annual assessment on inpatient services is imposed on each hospital provider in an amount equal to $221.50 multiplied by the difference of the hospital's occupied bed days less the hospital's Medicare bed days, provided however, for the period of July 1, 2020 through December 31, 2020, (i) the assessment is equal to 50% of the annual amount; and (ii) the amount of $221.50 will be retroactively adjusted by a uniform percentage to generate an amount equal to 50% of the Assessment Adjustment. (305 ILCS 5/5A-2)

For state fiscal years 2019 and 2020, an annual assessment on outpatient services is imposed on each hospital provider in an amount equal to .01358 multiplied by the hospital's outpatient gross revenue. For the period of July 1, 2020 through December 31, 2020 and calendar years 2021 and 2022, the annual assessment on outpatient services is imposed on each hospital provider in an amount equal to .01525 multiplied by the hospital's outpatient gross revenue, provided however: (i) for the period of July 1, 2020 through December 31, 2020, the assessment is equal to 50% of the annual amount; and (ii) the amount of .01525 will be retroactively adjusted by a uniform percentage to generate an amount equal to 50% of the Assessment Adjustment. (305 ILCS 5/5A-2)

There is an exemption from the hospital provider fund assessment for any hospital provider, as described in Sec. 1903(w)(3)(F) of the federal Social Security Act, that is:

- a state agency,

- a state university,

- a county, or

- a county with less than 3 million in population or an other local government unit.

(305 ILCS 5/5A-3(b) and (b-2))

Payment of the fees is due on the 14th day of each month and each payment should equal $1/12$ of the annual assessment. (305 ILCS 5/5A-4(a))

• *Nursing home bed fees*

Every nursing home provider must pay a quarterly fee for each licensed nursing bed day. The fee is $1.50 per licensed bed, and the payments are due each quarter on or before September 10, December 10, March 10, and June 10. (305 ILCS 5/5E-10)

The Illinois Supreme Court has determined that the nursing home bed fee does not violate the state's constitutional uniformity clause. (*Grand Chapter, Order of the Eastern Star of the State of Illinois v. Topinka*, Illinois Supreme Court, 2015 IL 117083, January 23, 2015)

[¶37-000]

ALCOHOLIC BEVERAGES

[¶37-001] Alcoholic Beverages

The Illinois alcoholic beverage tax is covered in Liquor Control Act of 1934 Sec. 8-1 [235 ILCS 5/8-1]). Current tax rates per gallon are:

— beer and cider containing not less than 0.5% nor more than 7% alcohol by volume $0.231

— alcoholic liquor other than beer with an alcohol content of up to 14%; alcoholic liquor with an alcohol content of more than 14% and less than 20% $1.39

— alcoholic liquor with an alcohol content of 20% or more $8.55

(https://www2.illinois.gov/rev/research/taxrates/Pages/excise.aspx)

Comprehensive coverage of taxation of alcohol, as well as licensing and distribution information is provided in Wolters Kluwer, CCH Liquor Control Law Reporter. For more information go to CCHGroup.com or contact an account representative at 888-CCH-REPS (888-224-7377).

[¶37-050]
DOCUMENT RECORDING TAX

[¶37-051] Document Recording Tax

For real property located in Illinois, a transaction tax is imposed on transfers of:

- titles to real estate;
- beneficial interests in real property; and
- controlling interests in real estate entities owning property.

(Property Tax Code, Sec. 31-10 [35 ILCS 200/31-10])

CCH Comment: New online system initial launch.—In June 2014, the Illinois Department of Revenue (DOR) launched a new electronic system—MyDec—for handling real property transfer tax transactions. Cook County and the city of Chicago will be part of a pilot program for users to begin submitting, accepting, verifying, and closing declarations through MyDec. After the initial rollout, all counties in the state will be eligible to participate in the program. Individuals, law firms, settlement agencies, and government officials can use the program. While continued use of prepaid stamp meters will be allowed, the DOR plans to phase out the stamp meters as enrollment in MyDec increases. *Informational Bulletin FY 2014-15*, Illinois Department of Revenue, June 2014.

For real estate located within an Illinois county, the county also can impose a tax on a transfer of:

- title to real estate;
- a beneficial interest in a land trust holding legal title to real estate; and
- a qualifying beneficial interest in real estate.

(Counties Code, Sec. 5-1031 [55 ILCS 5/5-1031])

• *Rate of tax*

The Illinois real estate transfer tax is imposed at the rate of tax is 50¢ per $500 of the price stated in the transfer declaration. If the transferring document indicates that the real estate is transferred subject to a mortgage, the amount of the mortgage that remains outstanding at the time of the transfer will not be included in the basis for computing the tax. (Property Tax Code, Sec. 31-10 [35 ILCS 200/31-10]) Generally, the county real estate transfer tax rate is 25¢ per $500 of the transfer price. (Counties Code, Sec. 5-1031 [55 ILCS 5/5-1031(a)]) The Chicago real property transfer tax is imposed at the rate of $5.25 per $500 of the transfer price. (Chicago Municipal Code Sec. 3-33-030.A)

• *Payment*

Payment of the real estate transfer tax is evidenced by a revenue stamp affixed to the deed or trust document. The recorder or registrar of titles who affixes the stamp to the deed will cancel it by mark it with his or her initials with the day, month, and year the affixing occurs to render it unfit for reuse. (Property Tax Code, Sec. 31-20 [35 ILCS 200/31-20])

The Illinois Department of Revenue sells the stamps to county recorders or registrars of titles. The Department must establish a system to allow each country recorder or registrar of titles to purchase the stamps electronically and must deliver the stamps to the recorder or registrar of titles. Recorders and registrars who use electronic stamps or alternative indicia must file a qualifying return and electronically remit the tax to the Department of Revenue on or before the 10th day of the month following the month in which the tax was required to be collected. If a return is not filed or the tax is not fully paid as required within 15 days of the required time period, the department may eliminate the recorder's or registrar's ability to electronically file its returns and electronically remit the tax until such time as the recorder or registrar fully remits the return and tax amount due. (Property Tax Code, Sec. 31-15 [35 ILCS 200/31-15])

Chicago.—In Chicago, primary incidence of the first $3.75 per $500 and the obligation to pay it are on the purchaser, grantee, assignee, or other transferee. However, if the transferee is exempt by operation of state law, then the incidence and obligation shift to the transferor. (Chicago Municipal Code, Sec. 3-33-030.C)

However, the next $1.50 per $500 of the tax (CTA portion) generally shall be paid by the transferor, and a transferee cannot accept a deed or other instrument of transfer if the CTA portion has not been paid. However, if the transferor is exempt, the obligation to pay the tax falls on the transferee. If the CTA portion is not paid when due, both parties are jointly and severally liable for the tax, plus interest and penalties, and the real property will be subject to a lien under Chicago Municipal Code, Sec. 3-33-120. Only one Real Property Transfer Tax Declaration Form (Form 7551) should be filled out for both the buyer and sellers. (*Release*, Chicago Department of Revenue, March 2008)

Title insurance companies will be assessed tax, penalties, and interest where they have collected the tax but have failed to acquire the tax stamps and to affix them to the transfer documents. (*Notice*, Chicago Department of Revenue, March 2008)

• *Exemptions*

The following deeds or trust documents are exempt from the state and county real property transfer taxes:

- deeds representing transfers made prior to January 1, 1968;
- trust documents executed before January 1, 1986;
- deeds to or trust documents relating to property acquired by a governmental body, between governmental bodies, or by or from any corporation, society, association, foundation, or institution organized and operated for charity, religious, or educational purposes;
- deeds or trust documents that secure debt;
- deeds or trust documents that confirm, correct, modify, or supplement a previously recorded document;
- deeds or trust documents where consideration is less than $100;
- tax deeds;
- deeds or trust documents that release property that is security for a debt or other obligation;
- deeds of partition;
- deeds or trust documents made pursuant to mergers, consolidations, or transfers or sales of substantially all of the assets of corporations under a federal reorganization or bankruptcy plan;
- deeds or trust documents made by a subsidiary to a parent corporation for no consideration;
- deeds when there is an actual exchange of real estate and trust documents when there is an actual exchange of beneficial interests;
- deeds issued to a holder of a mortgage; and
- a deed or trust document related to the purchase of a principal residence by a participant in the Home Ownership Made Easy program.

(Property Tax Code, Sec. 31-45 [35 ILCS 200/31-45])

Chicago tax.—For the Chicago tax, the exemptions relate to qualifying transfers:

- of property made prior to January 1, 1974;

- involving governmental or charitable organizations;

- to secured creditors;

- in which the otherwise instrument of transfer relates to a deed, assignment or other instrument of transfer previously recorded or delivered;

- for less than $500;

- of tax deeds;

- in which the instrument of transfer releases property that secures debt or other obligation;

- involving deeds of partition;

- between a subsidiary corporation and its parent or between subsidiary corporations of a common parent;

- between a subsidiary corporation and its parent that involve the cancellation, surrender, issuance or delivery of stock as consideration;

- made pursuant to a confirmed bankruptcy reorganization plan;

- of title to, or beneficial interest in, qualifying real property located in a business enterprise zone;

- to lenders pursuant to a mortgage or security interest foreclosure proceeding or made in lieu of foreclosure; and

- in which the transferee is a participant in the Illinois Home Ownership Made Easy Program.

(Chicago Municipal Code Sec. 3-33-060; *Release*, Chicago Department of Revenue, March 21, 2008)

In addition, the $1.50 increase (CTA portion), which generally applies to transfers taking place after March 2008, does not apply to transfers in which

(1) the transfer price is less than $250,000, and

(2) the transferee is a person at least 65 years old who will occupy the property as a principal dwelling for at least one year following the transfer.

However, that exemption is in the form of a refund, which must be applied for within three years of the transfer. (Chicago Municipal Code Sec. 3-33-060.O)

[¶37-100]

MOTOR VEHICLES

[¶37-101] Motor Vehicles

Illinois has a variety of taxes related to second division motor vehicles. Discussed here are flat weight taxes and the mileage weight taxes for motor vehicles of the second division and the vehicle use tax. Owners of vehicles of the second division may elect to pay a mileage weight tax in lieu of a flat weight tax.

Property taxation of motor vehicles is discussed at ¶20-275 Motor Vehicles and ¶20-325 Transportation Equipment. Sales taxation of motor vehicles is discussed at ¶60-570 Motor Vehicles. The Illinois Commerce Commission tax on common carriers is discussed at ¶80-031 Taxpayer Subject to State Tax.

• *Flat weight taxes*

Second division motor vehicles (motor trucks, trailers, and buses designed for carrying more than ten persons) not opting to pay a flat mileage weight tax must pay a $10 registration fee plus a mileage weight tax. Other second division vehicles include recreational vehicles, trailers, farm trucks, and farm trailers.

The following fees include the $10 registration fee and the general flat weight tax: ([625 ILCS 5/3-815]; [625 ILCS 5/3-818]; [625 ILCS 5/3-819])

Vehicle weight and class	Annual fee
8,000 lbs. and less (B)	$98
8,001 lbs. to 12,000 lbs. (D)	138
12,001 lbs. to 16,000 lbs. (F)	242
16,001 lbs. to 26,000 lbs. (H)	490
26,001 lbs. to 28,000 lbs. (J)	630
28,001 lbs. to 32,000 lbs. (K)	842
32,001 lbs. to 36,000 lbs. (L)	982
36,001 lbs. to 40,000 lbs. (N)	1,202
40,001 lbs. to 45,000 lbs. (P)	1,390
45,001 lbs. to 50,000 lbs. (Q)	1,538
50,001 lbs. to 54,999 lbs. (R)	1,698
55,000 lbs. to 59,500 lbs. (S)	1,830
59,501 lbs. to 64,000 lbs. (T)	1,970
64,001 lbs. to 73,280 lbs. (V)	2,294
73,281 lbs. to 77,000 lbs. (X)	2,622
77,001 lbs. to 80,000 lbs. (Z)	2,790

(Illinois Vehicle Code Sec. 3-815 [625 ILCS 5/3-815])

Flat weight taxes for farm trucks are as follows:

Vehicle weight and class	Annual fee
16,000 lbs. or less (VF)	$150
16,001 to 20,000 lbs. (VG)	269
20,001 to 24,000 lbs. (VH)	290
24,001 to 28,000 lbs. (VJ)	378
28,001 to 32,000 lbs. (VK)	506
32,001 to 36,000 lbs. (VL)	610
36,001 to 45,000 lbs. (VP)	810
45,001 to 54,999 lbs. (VR)	1,026
55,000 to 64,000 lbs. (VT)	1,202
64,001 to 73,280 lbs. (VV)	1,290
73,281 to 77,000 lbs. (VX)	1,350
77,001 to 80,000 lbs. (VZ)	1,490

([625 ILCS 5/3-815])

Flat weight taxes for nonfarm trailers are as follows:

Vehicle weight and class	Annual fee
3,000 lbs. and less (TA)	$18

5,000 lbs. and more than 3,000 (TB) 54
8,000 lbs. and more than 5,000 (TC) 58
10,000 lbs. and more than 8,000 (TD) 106
14,000 lbs. and more than 10,000 (TE) 170
20,000 lbs. and more than 14,000 (TG) 258
32,000 lbs. and more than 20,000 (TK) 722
36,000 lbs. and more than 32,000 (TL) 1,082
40,000 lbs. and more than 36,000 (TN) 1,502

([625 ILCS 5/3-819])

Flat weight taxes for farm trailers are as follows:

Vehicle weight and class . . . . **Annual fee**
10,000 lbs. and less (VDD) $60
10,001 to 14,000 lbs. (VDE) 106
14,001 to 20,000 lbs. (VDG) 166
20,001 to 28,000 lbs. (VDJ) 378
28,001 to 36,000 lbs. (VDL) 650

(Illinois Vehicle Code Sec. 3-815 [625 ILCS 5/3-815]; Illinois Vehicle Code Sec. 3-819 [625 ILCS 5/3-819])

Flat weight taxes for motor homes, mini-motor homes, truck campers, and van camper are as follows:

Vehicle weight . . . . **Annual fee**
8,000 lbs. and less $78
8,001 to 10,000 lbs. 90
10,000 lbs. and over 102

Flat weight taxes for camping trailers or travel trailers are as follows:

Vehicle weight . . . . **Annual fee**
3,000 lbs. and less $18
3,001 to 8,000 lbs. 30
8,001 to 10,000 lbs. 38
10,001 lbs. and over 50

(Illinois Vehicle Code Sec. 3-815 [625 ILCS 5/3-815])

Flat weight taxes for vehicles with permanently mounted equipment are as follows:

Vehicle weight . . . . **Annual fee**
10,000 lbs. and less $45
10,001 lbs. to 20,000 lbs. 90
20,001 lbs. to 30,000 lbs. 135
30,001 lbs. to 40,000 lbs. 180
40,001 lbs. to 50,000 lbs. 225
350,001 lbs. to 60,000 lbs. 270
60,001 lbs. to 70,000 lbs. 315
70,001 lbs. to 73,280 lbs. 340
73,281 lbs. to 80,000 lbs. 385

(Illinois Vehicle Code Sec. 3-812 [625 ILCS 5/3-812])

¶37-101

• *Mileage weight taxes*

Owners of vehicles of the second division can opt to pay a mileage weight tax instead of a flat weight tax.

A mileage weight tax may be paid in lieu of the flat weight tax for vehicles operating inside the state. The mileage weight taxes for buses, trucks, and truck tractors are as follows:

Bus, Truck or Truck Tractor

Gross Weight Vehicle and Load	Class	Minimum Guaranteed Mileage Weight Tax	Maximum Mileage Permitted Under Guaranteed Tax	Mileage Weight Tax for Mileage in Excess of Guaranteed Mileage
12,000 lbs. or less	MD	$73	5,000	26 Mills
12,001 lbs. to 16,000 lbs.	MF	120	6,000	34 Mills
16,001 lbs. to 20,000 lbs.	MG	180	6,000	46 Mills
20,001 lbs. to 24,000 lbs.	MH	235	6,000	63 Mills
24,001 lbs. to 28,000 lbs.	MJ	315	7,000	63 Mills
28,001 lbs. to 32,000 lbs.	MK	385	7,000	83 Mills
32,001 lbs. to 36,000 lbs.	ML	485	7,000	99 Mills
36,001 lbs. to 40,000 lbs.	MN	615	7,000	128 Mills
40,001 lbs. to 45,000 lbs.	MP	695	7,000	139 Mills
45,001 lbs. to 54,999 lbs.	MR	853	7,000	156 Mills
55,000 lbs. to 59,500 lbs.	MS	920	7,000	178 Mills
59,501 lbs. to 64,000 lbs.	MT	985	7,000	195 Mills
64,001 lbs. to 73,280 lbs.	MV	1,173	7,000	225 Mills
73,281 lbs. to 77,000 lbs.	MX	1,328	7,000	258 Mills
77,001 lbs. to 80,000 lbs.	MZ	1,415	7,000	275 Mills

The mileage weight taxes for trailers are as follows:

Trailers

Gross Weight Vehicle and Load	Class	Minimum Guaranteed Mileage Weight Tax	Maximum Mileage Permitted Under Guaranteed Tax	Mileage Weight Tax for Mileage in Excess of Guaranteed Mileage
14,000 lbs. or less	ME	75	5,000	31 Mills
14,001 lbs. to 20,000 lbs.	MF	135	6,000	36 Mills
20,001 lbs. to 36,000 lbs.	ML	540	7,000	103 Mills
36,001 lbs. to 40,000 lbs.	MM	750	7,000	150 Mills

([625 ILCS 5/3-818])

• *Apportioned rates, reciprocity, exemptions, penalties*

Apportioned rates.—Annual fees and taxes paid on a calendar year basis for second division vehicles (trucks, trailers, and buses) are reduced quarterly if the vehicle becomes subject to registration on or after March 31, June 30, or September 30. If the fees and taxes are payable on a fiscal year basis they are reduced quarterly on and after September 30, December 31, and March 31. Two-year fees prescribed for government and charitable vehicles may not be reduced. However, fees for two-year registration of other vehicles may be reduced as follows:

— by 25% on and after June 15;

— by 50% on and after December 15; and

— by 75% on and after the next ensuing June 15.

Reductions do not apply to econd division vehicles registered on a staggered registration basis. (625 ILCS 5/3-803)

Reciprocity.—Any motor vehicle, trailer, semitrailer, or pole trailer operated in interstate commerce does not need to register if it is:

— properly registered in another state pursuant to law or a reciprocity agreement;

— part of a fleet of vehicles owned or operated by the same person who registers the fleet pro rata among the various states;

— part of a fleet of vehicles, a portion of which are registered in Illinois in accordance with an agreement; and

— the vehicle has a reciprocity permit on board.

(625 ILCS 5/3-402)

Exemptions.—The following motor vehicles, trailers, semitrailers, and pole trailers are exempt from registration fees and taxes:

— any vehicle driven or moved on a highway in conformance with the provisions of the Illinois Vehicle Code relating to manufacturers, transporters, dealers, lienholders, nonresidents, or under a temporary registration permit issued by the Secretary of State;

— any implement of husbandry, whether or not of a type otherwise subject to registration, that is only incidentally operated on a highway, including not-for-hire movement for the purpose of delivering farm commodities to a place of first processing or sale or to a place of storage;

— any special mobile equipment;

— any vehicle propelled by electric power from overhead trolley wires, but not operated on rails;

— any emergency vehicle used as a pumper, ladder truck, rescue vehicle, search-light truck, or other fire apparatus, but not a vehicle that is subject to registration as a vehicle of the first division;

— any vehicle owned and operated by the federal government;

— any tow dolly that merely serves as substitute wheels for another legally licensed vehicle.

(625 ILCS 5/3-402)

Penalties.—When a deficiency is found and any fees or taxes required to be paid under the Vehicle Code have not been paid, the Secretary of State may impose an audit fee of $50 per day, $25 per half day. Interest on such deficiency, if it is greater than $100 for all registration years examined, is imposed at the rate of $1/2$ of 1% per month up to 6% per year. When a deficiency is determined to be caused by the willful neglect or negligence of the person audited, an additional 10% penalty of the amount of the deficiency or assessment will be imposed, and the 10% penalty will bear interest at the rate of $1/2$ of 1% on and after the 30th day after the penalty is imposed until it is paid in full. An additional 20% penalty is imposed when a deficiency is caused by fraud or willful evasion. (625 ILCS 5/2-124)

Upon notice from the Secretary of State that the registrant has failed to pay the excess mileage fees, the surety shall immediately pay the fees together with any penalties and interest, in an amount not to exceed the limits of the bond. (625 ILCS 5/3-818(a-1))

¶37-101

• *Vehicle use tax*

A Vehicle Use Tax is imposed on the privilege of using in Illinois any motor vehicle that is purchased from a private party rather than a dealer. The rate of tax is dependent on the model year and selling price of the vehicle. ([625 ILCS 5/3-1001])

[¶37-150]

ENVIRONMENTAL TAXES AND FEES

[¶37-151] Environmental Taxes and Fees

Illinois imposes a number of taxes and fees related to environmental issues.

Included here are discussions of the

— hazardous waste disposal fee;

— environmental impact fee;

— air pollution fees;

— dry cleaning solvent tax; and

— retail tire fees.

•*Hazardous waste disposal site fees*

The Environmental Protection Agency will collect from the owner or operator of each hazardous waste disposal site the following fees:

— 9¢ per gallon or $18.18 per cubic yard of hazardous waste disposed at a hazardous waste disposal site if the disposal site is located off the site where the waste was produced, up to a maximum amount of $30,000 with respect to waste generated by a single generator and deposited in monofills;

— 9¢ per gallon or $18.18 per cubic yard of hazardous waste disposed if the disposal site is located on the site where the waste was produced, up to a maximum fee of $30,000 per year for each such disposal site;

— if the hazardous waste disposal site is an underground injection well, $6,000 per year if not more than 10 million gallons per year are injected, $15,000 per year if more than 10 million gallons but not more than 50 million gallons per year are injected, and $27,000 per year if more than 50 million gallons per year are injected; and

— 3¢ per gallon or $6.06 per cubic yard of hazardous waste received for treatment at a hazardous waste treatment site if the treatment site is located off the site where the waste was produced and if the treatment site is owned, controlled, and operated by a person other than the generator of the waste.

(Environmental Protection Act, Sec. 1022.2 [415 ILCS 5/22.2])

Whenever the unobligated balance of the Hazardous Waste Fund exceeds $10 million, the Agency will suspend the collection of the fees until the unobligated balance of the Fund falls below $8 million.

The owner or operator of a hazardous waste disposal site or management facility must pay an annual fee, to be deposited in the Environmental Protection Permit and Inspection Fund, as follows:

— Hazardous waste disposal site receiving waste produced off site, $70,000;

— Hazardous waste disposal site receiving waste produced on site, $18,000;

— Hazardous waste disposal site that is an underground injection well, $14,000;

— Hazardous waste management facility treating hazardous waste by incineration, $4,000;

— Hazardous waste management facility treating hazardous waste by process other than incineration, $2,000;

— Hazardous waste management facility storing hazardous waste in a surface impoundment or pile, $2,000;

— Hazardous waste management facility storing hazardous waste other than in a surface impoundment or pile, $500.

— hazardous waste generator required to submit an annual or biennial report for hazardous waste generation, $500.

(Environmental Protection Act, Sec. 1022.8 [415 ILCS 5/22.8])

• *Environmental impact fee*

All Illinois receivers of fuel are subject to an environmental impact fee of $60 per 7,500 gallons of fuel, or an equivalent amount per fraction thereof, that is sold or used in Illinois. The fee is paid by the receiver in this State who first sells or uses the fuel. Beginning January 1, 2021 no fee shall be imposed under this Section on receivers of aviation fuel for sale or use for so long as the revenue use requirements of 49 U.S.C. 47107(b) and 49 U.S.C. 47133 are binding on the State. (Environmental Impact Fee, Sec. 310 [415 ILCS 125/310]) The fee is repealed effective January 1, 2025. (Environmental Impact Fee, Sec. 310 [415 ILCS 125/390])

See ¶ 40-001 Gasoline Taxes for a discussion of claims for a credit.

• *Air pollution fees*

For each 12-month period after the date on which the U.S. Environmental Protection Agency approves or conditionally approves Illinois' Clean Air Act Permit Program (CAAPP), developed pursuant to Title V of the Clean Air Act (42 U.S.C. Sec. 7401), but not prior to January 1, 1994, a stationary source of air pollutants must pay an air pollution fee as follows:

— A source allowed to emit less than 100 tons of all regulated air pollutants, or less than 100 tons of a regulated air pollutant that is subject to any standard under Sec. 112 of the Clean Air Act (42 U.S.C. 7412), must pay a fee of $1,800 per year.

— A source allowed to emit 100 tons or more per year of all regulated air pollutants will be assessed by the Illinois Environmental Protection Agency an annual fee of $18.00 per ton for the allowable emissions of all regulated air pollutants at that source during the term of the permit. The maximum fee is $294,000. Except for the first year of the CAAPP, the applicant or permittee may pay the fee annually or semiannually for fees greater than $5,000.

(Environmental Protection Act, Sec. 1039.5(18) [415 ILCS 5/39.5])

• *Dry-Cleaning Solvent Tax*

An annually adjusted tax is imposed on the purchase of dry-cleaning solvents by persons who operate dry-cleaning facilities in Illinois. (415 ILCS 135/65; 415 ILCS 135/75)

Dry-cleaning solvents include chlorine-based, hydrocarbon-based, and green solvents that are used as a primary cleaning agent in dry-cleaning operations. (415 ILCS 135/5(h))

The tax on chlorine-based solvents is $3.50 per gallon; the tax on petroleum-based solvents is $2 per gallon; and the tax on green solvents is $1.75 per gallon, unless the green solvent is used at a virgin facility, in which case the rate is $0.35 per gallon. (415 ILCS 135/65; 415 ILCS 135/75) A "virgin facility" is a dry-cleaning facility that has never had chlorine-based or petroleum-based solvents stored or used at the property prior to becoming a green solvent dry-cleaning facility. (415 ILCS 135/5(w)) The tax rate is set annually by the Dry-Cleaner Environmental Response Trust Fund Council. All dry-cleaning solvents are considered chlorine-based solvents unless the Council determines that the solvents are petroleum-based or green solvents. (415 ILCS 135/75)

The tax is due on or before the 25th day of the month following the calendar quarter for which the return is filed. A seller of drycleaning solvents may, at the time of filing an Illinois drycleaning solvent tax return, deduct from the amount of tax due 1.75% of that amount or $5 per calendar year, whichever is greater. Failure to timely file returns and to provide data requested by the Department of Revenue will result in disallowance of the reimbursement discount. (415 ILCS 135/65(f)) The tax is scheduled to be repealed on January 1, 2020. (415 ILCS 135/85)

The following facilities are not considered dry-cleaning facilities for purposes of this tax: a facility located on a United State military base; an industrial laundry, commercial laundry, or linen supply facility; a penal institution that is engaged in dry-cleaning only as part of a correctional industries program; a not-for-profit health care facility; or a facility located or previously located on state or federal property. (415 ILCS 135/5(f))

• *Used tire fee*

Any person offering or selling tires at retail in Illinois must collect from retail customers a fee of $2.50 per new or used tire sold and delivered in the state. The $2.50 tire fee includes a 50 cents fee for the Emergency Public Health Fund. The fee is collected from the purchaser and is added to the selling price of the tire and must be listed separately on the bill of sale. The fee is not included in gross receipts for purposes of the state or local retailers' occupation tax or the state use tax. The fee applies to tires for highway vehicles, special mobile equipment, and farm equipment and to aircraft tires. (415 ILCS 5/55.8; 415 ILCS 5/55.9)

The fee applies to tires for highway vehicles, special mobile equipment, and farm equipment and to aircraft tires. Imposition of a fee does not apply to mail order sales of tires nor to tires that are included in the retail sale of a motor vehicle. Also, the fee does not apply to the sale of reprocessed tires. (415 ILCS 5/55.8)

The fee is reported and paid to the Department of Revenue by the retail seller on a quarterly basis with the due dates falling on April 30, July 31, October 31, and January 31. However, calendar quarter returns due after January 31, 2010, are due on April 20, July 20, October 20, and January 20, except that the return for October 2009-December 2009 is due on February 20, 2010. Instead of filing returns, a retailer of tires may pay the fee to its supplier of tires at the time of purchase if the supplier is a registered retailer and arranges to collect and remit the fee to the Department. (415 ILCS 5/55.8; 415 ILCS 5/55.10)

A credit of 10¢ per tire is allowed either the retail seller or the tire supplier for incurred expenses, but the credit will only be allowed if the return is timely filed and only for the amount that is timely paid. Retail sellers choosing to pay the fee to their suppliers are not entitled to the credit. (415 ILCS 5/55.8)

Chicago tire fee.—Persons selling new tires at retail or offering new tires for retail sale in the City of Chicago must collect from purchasers a Chicago tire fee of $1 per new tire. A collection allowance of 4 cents per tire may be retained by the seller. The fee applies exclusively to tires to be used for vehicles, aircraft, special mobile equipment, and implements of husbandry. The fee is applicable in instances where tires are sold separately and not in conjunction with the sale of a motor vehicle. (*Release*, Chicago Department of Revenue, August 2005)

The Chicago tire fee does not apply to

— used tires,

— reprocessed tires, or

— mail order sales.

A reprocessed tire is a tire that has been recapped, retreaded, or regrooved and that has not been placed on a wheel rim. If a tire is 100% replaced under a manufacture warranty or road hazard warranty, no fee is applied because such an exchange is not a sale at retail. However, a full $1 fee applies in the case of a pro-rata replacement, because the customer pays something, making the transaction a sale at retail. Sales tax does not apply to the tire fee. (*Informational Bulletin*, Chicago Department of Revenue, August 2005)

The Chicago tire fee must be remitted monthly and is due by the last day of the month following collection. An annual fee return for the period commencing July 1 and ending June 30 of the subsequent year is due by August 15 of each year.

SEVERANCE TAXES

[¶37-300]

SEVERANCE TAXES

[¶37-301] Severance Taxes

Beginning July 1, 2013, oil and gas severed from production units in Illinois are subject to tax. After an initial period, during which the rate of tax on oil and gas will be set at one rate, the rate of tax on severed oil will be graduated, the rate on gas will be set at one rate, and both rates will be subject to reduction based on the nature of the work force on well sites. (Illinois Hydraulic Fracturing Tax Act, Sec. 2-15 [35 ILCS 450/2-15])

The Illinois hydraulic fracturing tax is imposed on the severance and production of oil or gas from a well on a production unit required to be permitted under the Illinois Hydraulic Fracturing Regulatory Act, which was enacted as part of the law that included the fracturing tax. The tax applies equally to all portions of the value of each barrel of oil severed and the value of gas severed. (Illinois Hydraulic Fracturing Tax Act, Sec. 2-15(a) [35 ILCS 450/2-15(a)]) Liability for the tax accrues at the time the oil or gas is removed from the production unit. (Illinois Hydraulic Fracturing Tax Act, Sec. 2-15(f) [35 ILCS 450/2-15(f)])

Generally, the tax is upon the producers of such oil or gas in the proportion to their respective beneficial interests at the time of severance.

- *Rates*

For a period of 24 months from the month in which oil or gas was first produced from a well, the rate of tax will be 3% of the value of the oil or gas severed from the earth or water in the state. Thereafter, the rate will be 6% of the value of gas severed, and the rate on oil severed will be based on each well's average daily production (ADP) each month, as follows:

— where the ADP is less than 25 barrels, the rate is 3% of the oil's value;

— where the ADP is at least 25 barrels but less than 50 barrels, the rate is 4% of the oil's value;

— where the ADP at least 50 barrels but less than 100 barrels, the rate is 5% of the oil's value; and

— where the ADP is at least 100 barrels, the rate is 6% of the oil's value.

Oil produced from a well whose ADP is 15 barrels or less for the 12-month period immediately preceding the production is exempt from the tax imposed by this Act. (Illinois Hydraulic Fracturing Tax Act, Sec. 2-15(a) [35 ILCS 450/2-15(a)])

- *Withholding*

Any purchaser who makes a monetary payment to a producer for his or her portion of the value of products from a production unit shall withhold from such payment the amount of tax due from the producer. Any purchaser who pays any tax due from a producer shall be entitled to reimbursement from the producer for the tax so paid and may take credit for such amount from any monetary payment to the producer for the value of products. To the extent that a purchaser required to collect the tax has actually done so, that tax is held in trust for the benefit of the state. (Illinois Hydraulic Fracturing Tax Act, Sec. 2-25 [35 ILCS 450/2-25])

• *Local work force tax rate reduction*

The rate of tax imposed on working interest owners of a well will be reduced by 0.25% for the life of the well when a minimum of 50% of the total work force hours on the well site are performed by Illinois construction workers being paid wages equal to or exceeding the general prevailing rate of hourly wages. (Illinois Hydraulic Fracturing Tax Act, Sec. 2-17(a)) When more than one well is drilled on a well site, total work force hours shall be determined on a well-by-well basis. (Illinois Hydraulic Fracturing Tax Act, Sec. 2-17(b) [35 ILCS 450/2-17(b)])

The operator shall obtain and retain any other records the department determines are necessary to verify a claim for a reduction in the tax. The operator shall make the records available to the department upon request. (Illinois Hydraulic Fracturing Tax Act, Sec. 2-17(c) [35 ILCS 450/2-17(c)])

• *Other exemptions*

Severance and production of gas will be exempt for gas

— injected into the earth for the purpose of lifting oil, recycling, or repressing;

— used for fuel in connection with the operation and development for, or production of, oil or gas in the production unit where severed;

— lawfully vented or flared; or

— inadvertently lost on the production unit by reason of leaks, blowouts, or other accidental losses. (Illinois Hydraulic Fracturing Tax Act, Sec. 2-15(d) [35 ILCS 450/2-15(d)])

• *Purchaser returns*

Each purchaser must make a return to the department showing the quantity of oil or gas purchased during the month for which the return is filed, the price paid therefore, total value, the name and address of the operator or other person from whom the same was purchased, a description of the production unit in the manner prescribed by the department from which such oil or gas was severed and the amount of tax due from each production unit for each calendar month. All taxes due, or to be remitted, by the purchaser shall accompany the return, which shall be filed on or before the last day of the month after the calendar month for which the return is required. (Illinois Hydraulic Fracturing Tax Act, Sec. 2-45 [35 ILCS 450/2-45)])

• *Operator returns*

The operator is responsible for remitting the tax on or before the last day of the month following the end of the calendar month in which the oil and gas is removed from the production unit where oil or gas is

(1) transported off the production unit where severed by the operator,

(2) used on the production unit where severed, or

(3) is manufactured and converted into refined products on the production unit where severed.

The payment must be accompanied by a return to the Department showing the gross quantity of oil or gas removed during the month for which the return is filed, the price paid therefore, and if no price is paid therefore, the value of the oil and gas, a description of the production unit from which such oil or gas was severed, and the amount of tax. (Illinois Hydraulic Fracturing Tax Act, Sec. 2-50 [35 ILCS 450/2-50)])

• *Filing, payment*

Generally, purchasers and operators must file all returns electronically and make payment by electronic funds transfer (EFT). Returns must be accompanied by appropriate computer-generated magnetic media supporting schedule data in a format prescribed by the department. (Illinois Hydraulic Fracturing Tax Act, Sec. 2-45 [35 ILCS 450/2-45]; Illinois Hydraulic Fracturing Tax Act, Sec. 2-50(b) [35 ILCS 450/2-50(b))])

UNCLAIMED PROPERTY

[¶37-350]

UNCLAIMED PROPERTY

[¶37-351] Unclaimed Property

Generally, property that is unclaimed by its rightful owner is presumed abandoned after a specified period of years following the date upon which the owner may demand the property or the date upon which the obligation to pay or distribute the property arises, whichever comes first.

> *Compliance Alert: Revised Uniform Unclaimed Property Act adopted beginning in 2018.*—Effective January 1, 2018, the Revised Uniform Unclaimed Property Act replaced the uniform unclaimed property law. New types of property were specified, generally with a three-year dormancy period from some event related to the property. Examples include tax-deferred retirement accounts and custodial accounts for minors. In addition, from the time a property is presumed abandoned, any other property right or interest accrued or accruing from the property and not previously presumed abandoned is also presumed to be abandoned.
>
> (P.A. 100-22 (S.B. 9), Laws 2017, effective January 1, 2018)

What is unclaimed property?

Generally, property is certain intangible property or a fixed and certain interest in intangible property held, issued, or owed in the course of a holder's business or by a government body. This property is presumed abandoned when it is unclaimed by the apparent owner for a specified period of time (dormancy period).

> *Comment:* Escheat is an area of potential federal/state conflict. A federal statute may preempt state escheat provisions, as for instance Sec. 514(a) of the Employee Retirement Income Security Act of 1974 (ERISA). Pursuant to this provision, the Department of Labor and Workforce Development has been of the opinion that funds of missing participants in a qualified employee benefit plan must stay in the plan despite a state escheat provision because ERISA preempts application of the state escheat laws with respect to such funds (Advisory Opinion 94-41A, Department of Labor, Pension and Welfare Benefit Administration, Dec. 7, 1994). Some states have challenged the federal position on this and similar narrowly delineated situations. In the case of federal tax refunds, IRC Sec. 6408 disallows refunds if the refund would escheat to a state.
>
> Practitioners are thus advised that a specific situation where federal and state policy cross on the issue of escheat may, at this time, be an area of unsettled law.

What are the dormancy periods for unclaimed property?

General rule. Property not specified is considered abandoned the earlier of three years after the owner first has a right to demand the property or the obligation to pay or distribute the property arises. Where an owner is deceased and the abandonment period for the property is greater than two years, then the property (with certain exceptions related to insurance) is considered abandoned two years from the date of the owner's last indication of interest in the property.

Checks and drafts. Any instrument on which a financial organization or business association is directly liable, is presumed abandoned three years after issuance.

Bank accounts. A demand, savings, or time deposit, is presumed abandoned three years after the later of maturity or the date of the last indication of interest in the property by the apparent owner.

Property distributable in the course of demutualization or related reorganization of an insurance company. Property not specified is considered abandoned the earlier of three years after the owner first has a right to demand the property or the obligation to pay or distribute the property arises. Where an owner is deceased and the abandonment period for the property is greater than two years, then the property (with certain exceptions related to insurance) is considered abandoned two years from the date of the owner's last indication of interest in the property.

Gift certificates, gift cards and credit memos. Gift cards and loyalty cards are not included in the definition of "property" for unclaimed property purposes. A three-year dormancy period applies to stored-value cards.

Securities are presumed abandoned the earlier of:

> three years after a communication by the holder is returned undelivered or

> five years after the date of the apparent owner's las indication of interest.

Other dormancy periods. Most states also have specified dormancy periods for:

> Business association dissolutions/refunds,

> Insurance policies,

> IRAs/retirement funds,

> Money orders,

> Proceeds from class action suits,

> Property held by fiduciaries,

> Safe deposit boxes,

> Shares in a financial institution,

> Traveler's checks,

> Utilities,

> Wages/salaries, and

> Property held by courts/public agencies.

Is there a business-to-business exemption for unclaimed property?

Under the revised uniform unclaimed property law, Illinois no longer has a business-to-business exemption.

What are the notice requirements for unclaimed property?

For property with a value of at least $50, the notice period is not more than one year nor less than 60 days before filing the report.

What are the reporting requirements for unclaimed property?

General requirements. The report generally is due November 1 of each year and must cover the 12 months preceding July 1 of that year. Reports for business associations, utilities, and life insurance companies must be filed before May 1 of each year for the immediately preceding calendar year.

Negative reporting. Negative reporting is required in Illinois.

¶37-351

Minimum reporting. There are no minimum amount requirements for reporting.

Aggregate reporting. Unclaimed property with a value of less than $5 may be reported in the aggregate.

Electronic reporting. Holders must report via the Internet in a form approved by the administrator.

Recordkeeping. Holders are required to retain records for 10 years after the later of the date the report was filed or the last date a timely report was due.

[¶40-000]

MOTOR FUELS

[¶40-001] Gasoline Taxes

Illinois taxes several types of motor fuels. Discussed here are motor fuel taxes. The state also taxes diesel fuel, aviation fuel, and miscellaneous fuels. In addition, Illinois is a member of the International Fuel Tax Agreement.

Specific topics discussed below are:

— products subject to tax,

— point of taxation,

— license requirements,

— basis of tax,

— rate of tax,

— exemptions,

— reports and payments,

— credits, refunds, and reimbursements, and

— local taxes.

Illinois imposes a tax on the privilege of operating motor vehicles on public highways and recreational-type watercraft upon the waters of the state (distributors' tax). (Motor Fuel Tax Law, Sec. 2 [35 ILCS 505/2]) In addition, until 2025 a tax is imposed on the privilege of being a receiver of motor fuel in the state for sale or use (receivers' tax, also referred to as the underground storage tank tax). Beginning January 1, 2021, this tax is not imposed on sales of aviation fuel for so long as the revenue use requirements of 49 U.S.C. 47107(b) and 49 U.S.C. 47133 are binding on the state. (Motor Fuel Tax Law, Sec. 2a [35 ILCS 505/2a]) An environmental impact fee also is imposed on certain fuels. (See discussion at ¶37-151.) Discussed here are the taxes as they relate to fuels commonly or commercially referred to as gasoline (including casing-head and absorption or natural gasoline) and gasohol.

• *Products subject to tax*

As defined, the term "motor fuels" applies to the distributors' tax and, with an exception for fuel used for aviation purposes (see generally ¶40-005), the receivers' tax. Generally, the term refers to all volatile and inflammable liquids produced for, or which are suitable for, operating motor vehicles.

The term "motor fuels" also includes special fuels, which are discussed at ¶40-003.

• *Point of taxation*

The distributor's tax must be collected at the time the fuel is sold or distributed. (Motor Fuel Tax Law, Sec. 6 [35 ILCS 505/6]) Aside from its ordinary meaning, "sale" means any exchange, gift, or other disposition. (Motor Fuel Tax Law, Sec. 1.9 [35 ILCS 505/1.9]) Aside from its ordinary meaning, "distribute" means any disposition of possession, whether by bailment, consignment, or other manner or means whereby physical control or possession is relinquished. (Motor Fuel Tax Law, Sec. 1.10 [35 ILCS 505/1.10])

Any person not licensed as a receiver or a distributor who purchases gasoline as to which there has been no charge of the taxes imposed on distributors or receivers must pay the tax for the privilege of being a receiver and, if the gasoline is used in the operation of a motor vehicle upon the public highways, pay the distributors' tax. (Motor Fuel Tax Law, Sec. 7 [35 ILCS 505/7])

• *License requirements*

Distributors and receivers must be licensed by the Department of Revenue in order to distribute or receive motor fuel in the state.

Applicants for a distributor's license must file a bond with the department. No applicant who is in default for motor fuel taxes due the state will be granted a license to act as a distributor. In addition a license will not be granted to anyone whose principal place of business is in a state other than Illinois unless that person is licensed for motor fuel distribution or export in that other state and is not in default to that state for any monies due for the sale, distribution, export, or use of motor fuel. (Motor Fuel Tax Law, Sec. 3 [35 ILCS 505/3])

Applicants for a receiver's license must file a bond with the department. No applicant who is in default for motor fuel taxes due the state will be granted a license to act as a receiver. (Motor Fuel Tax Law, Sec. 3a [35 ILCS 505/3a])

Requirements for a special fuels supplier's license are discussed at ¶40-003.

• *Basis of tax*

The distributors' tax rate applies to each gallon of motor fuel used to operate motor vehicles and recreational watercraft upon Illinois public highways and waters. (Motor Fuel Tax Law, Sec. 2 [35 ILCS 505/2]; 86 Ill. Adm. Code 500.200)

Receivers are charged at a per-gallon rate for gasoline received for sale or use in the state. (Motor Fuel Tax Law, Sec. 2a [35 ILCS 505/2a])

• *Rate of tax*

The per/gallon rates for gasoline in Illinois are as follows:

gasoline	$0.38 ($0.387 from July 1, 2020, through June 30, 2021)
receiver's tax	$0.003
environmental impact fee	$0.008

(Motor Fuel Tax Rates and Fees) (Motor Fuel Tax Law, Sec. 2 [35 ILCS 505/2]; Motor Fuel Tax Law, Sec. 2a [35 ILCS 505/2a]; Environmental Impact Fee, Sec. 310[415 ILCS 125/310])

In addition to state taxes, Chicago and other county per/gallon rates are as follows:

Chicago	$0.05
Cook County	$0.06
Lake County	$0.08

DuPage, Kane, McHenry, and Will counties . $0.041 (effective for the period July 1, 2020, through June 30, 2021)

(Chicago Municipal Code, Sec. 3-52-020; Cook County Gas Tax, Sec. 74-472; County Motor Fuel Tax Law, Sec. 5-1035.1 [55 ILCS 5/5-1035.1])

For a list of all municipalities in Cook County that imposed a municipal motor fuel tax effective July 1, 2020, see *Information Bulletin FY 2020-35*.

• *Exemptions*

Exemptions from of the motor fuel tax, as it applies to sales of gasoline, include sales:

¶40-001

- to a valid licensed distributor or supplier,
- in which delivery is made to a purchaser outside the state,
- made to the federal government or its instrumentalities,
- made to a municipal corporation owning a local transportation system (certificates of exemption are required for this exemption),
- to privately-owned public utilities owning and operating vehicles used for transporting seven or more passengers, and
- of gasoline to be used by aircraft.

(Motor Fuel Tax Law, Sec. 2 [35 ILCS 505/2]; Motor Fuel Tax Law, Sec. 2a [35 ILCS 505/2a]; Motor Fuel Tax Law, Sec. 6 [35 ILCS 505/6])

Rules provide sample certificates of exemption. (86 Ill. Adm. Code 500.285; 86 Ill. Adm. Code 500.280)

Any exemption that became law after September 16, 1994, is limited by a sunset date. If the date is not specified in the public act enacting the exemption, the taxpayer is not entitled to take it for tax years beginning on or after five years from the effective date of the enacting public law. (Motor Fuel Tax Law, Sec. 2c [35 ILCS 505/2c])

Chicago vehicle fuel tax.—The following sales are exempt from the Chicago fuel tax:

(1) sales by a distributor to another distributor holding a valid registration certificate,

(2) sales by a distributor to a distributor or retailer of vehicle fuel whose place of business is outside Chicago,

(3) sales or use for purposes other than for propulsion or operation of a vehicle,

(4) the sale to or use by any "transportation agency" that is subsidized or operated by the Regional Transportation Authority or its Service Boards,

(5) the sale or use to the extent that the tax imposed would violate the Illinois or United States Constitution, or

(6) sales to a common carrier, certified by the carrier to be used for consumption, shipment, or storage in the conduct of its business, for a flight destined outside the United States.

• *Reports and payments*

Generally, a distributor files a return between the first and 20th days of each calendar month for motor fuel transactions that occurred the preceding month. A person whose distributor's license has been revoked must file a return covering the period from the date of the last return to the date of the revocation, not later than 10 days from the revocation or termination of the license. (Motor Fuel Tax Law, Sec. 5 [35 ILCS 505/5]) Payment of the tax must accompany the return. (Motor Fuel Tax Law, Sec. 6 [35 ILCS 505/6]; 86 Ill. Adm. Code 500.203(a))

The Department of Revenue accepts electronic payments using the ACH credit method from taxpayers filing either Form RMFT-5, Motor Fuel Distributor/Supplier Tax Return or Form RMFT-5-US, Underground Storage Tank Tax and Environmental Impact Fee Receiver Return. (*Informational Bulletin FY 2015-01*, Illinois Department of Revenue)

If the return is timely, the seller may take a discount of 1.75% to reimburse the seller for expenses. The discount for timely filing is applicable only to the amount of payment that accompanies the return. Claims for refund on exempt purchases must be filed within two years after the date the tax was paid. (Motor Fuel Tax Law, Sec. 13 [35 ILCS 505/13])

Distributors are not permitted to deduct a discount for collection costs from the tax paid on motor fuel they used themselves or if their returns are not timely filed. Distributors are required to keep books and records showing the calculations used in determining their collection costs. (Motor Fuel Tax Law, Sec. 6 [35 ILCS 505/6]; 86 Ill. Adm. Code 500.230; 86 Ill. Adm. Code 500.345)

Any person who is not a licensed distributor or supplier and who purchases motor fuel thereafter used in the operation of a motor vehicle upon the public highways must make a payment of the motor fuel tax to the Department no later than the 20th day of the month following the month in which the motor fuel was used. The statute does not apply in cases in which motor fuel was obtained tax-free under an official certificate of exemption. (Motor Fuel Tax Law, Sec. 7 [35 ILCS 505/7])

The Department of Revenue is authorized to adopt rules to require the electronic payment of tax or fees under the Motor Fuel Tax Law. All returns, applications, and other forms required by the Motor Fuel Tax Law must be in a form required by the Department of Revenue. (Motor Fuel Tax Law, Sec. 17a [35 ILCS 505/17a])

Certain details and items must be included on the distributor's timely filed monthly return. Another rule provides rules for timely filing. (86 Ill. Adm. Code 500.203; 86 Ill. Adm. Code 500.400)

Fuel losses.—All licensed suppliers, distributors, and receivers are required to report all motor fuel losses when filing the return for the period during which the loss occurred. Failure to report such loss could result in the disallowance for a credit against tax liability with respect to such loss.

Motor fuel transporters.—Persons transporting gasoline to a point within the state from a point outside the state, and every railroad company, street, suburban or interurban railroad company, pipeline company, motor truck or motor tank company, and water transportation company transporting reportable motor fuel either in intrastate or interstate commerce to points within Illinois must file a return covering deliveries occurring during the month within 30 days after the close of the month. (Motor Fuel Tax Law, Sec. 7b [35 ILCS 505/7b])

Chicago returns.—Returns are filed on an annual basis. Taxpayers or tax collectors must pay or remit the actual amount of tax due on or before the last day of the month following the monthly (or quarterly, if applicable) tax period in which the tax liability was incurred. Certain taxpayers and tax collectors may make estimated payments in lieu of paying or remitting actual amounts due. (Chicago Munic. Code Sec. 3-52-040; Chicago Munic. Code Sec. 3-52-050)

• *Credits, refunds, and reimbursements*

A distributor or supplier may claim a credit or refund, and other persons may claim reimbursement, for Illinois tax paid on motor fuel lost through any cause or used for off-highway use. Any person that purchases motor fuel in Illinois and uses it in another state may be reimbursed for the amount of use tax paid to the other state. The claim must include:

(1) a certified copy of the tax return filed with the other state;

(2) a copy of either the cancelled check paying the tax due or a receipt acknowledging payment; or

(3) such other information the Department may require.

(Motor Fuel Tax Law, Sec. 13 [35 ILCS 505/13]; Motor Fuel Tax Law, Sec. 21 [35 ILCS 505/21]; 86 Ill. Adm. Code 500.230)

A distributor or supplier may also claim a refund for the amount of tax paid on motor fuel used by the taxpayer for nontaxable purposes. Claims for refund on exempt purchases must be filed within two years after the date the tax was paid.

Claims for reimbursement based on idle time are not allowed. (Motor Fuel Tax Law, Sec. 13 [35 ILCS 505/13])

Distributors are required to report immediately all losses of motor fuel sustained by them. Failure to file the report may result in disallowance of credit for tax liability related to the loss. A rule defines the term "loss." For purposes of claims for refund, "loss" means the reduction of motor fuel resulting from fire, theft, spillage, spoilage, leakage, or any other provable cause, but does not include a reduction resulting from evaporation or shrinkage due to temperature variations. In the case of losses due to fire or theft, the claimant must include fire department or police department reports and any other documentation the Department may require. (Motor Fuel Tax Law, Sec. 13 [35 ILCS 505/13]; 86 Ill. Adm. Code 500.204; 86 Ill. Adm. Code 500.100)

Credits and refunds bear interest at the rate and in the manner prescribed by the Uniform Penalty and Interest Act (see ¶89-202). (Motor Fuel Tax Law, Sec. 13 [35 ILCS 505/13]; Motor Fuel Tax Law, Sec. 21 [35 ILCS 505/21])

Claims for credit, refund, or reimbursement must be made on forms provided by the Department. A rule details the general procedure that a distributor or supplier follows in filing claims. Credit or refund claims must be filed no later than one year after the date the tax was paid by the claimant. A person claiming reimbursement for taxes paid to another state that files a claim more than one year, but less than two years, after the date of payment is reimbursed 80% of the amount he would have been entitled had the claim been timely filed. In the case of losses due to fire or theft, the claimant must include fire department or police department reports and any other documentation the Department may require. (Motor Fuel Tax Law, Sec. 13 [35 ILCS 505/13]; 86 Ill. Adm. Code 500.230; 86 Ill. Adm. Code 500.340)

Claims for refund must be supported by purchase documentation such as invoices, sales slips, statements of account, or monthly statements. Purchase documentation may be electronically generated by the claimant's fuel supplier, but manifests will not be treated as purchase documentation. Refund claims may not be supported by estimates of the amount of motor fuel used for a nontaxable purpose. Only claims supported by positive proof of the exact amount of motor fuel used for a nontaxable purpose are accepted. Failure to keep or provide records documentation will result in the denial of claims and recovery of any claims paid. In addition, the Department may recover any claims erroneously paid. (86 Ill. Adm. Code 500.235)

A special procedure is provided in cases in which a customer returns tax-paid motor fuel to a distributor or supplier for credit. (86 Ill. Adm. Code 500.275)

A notice of tax liability for an erroneous refund of tax paid on motor fuel lost through any cause or used for off-highway use may be issued at any time within three years from the making of that refund, or within five years from the making of that refund if it appears that any part of the refund was induced by fraud or the misrepresentation of material fact. (Motor Fuel Tax Law, Sec. 13 [35 ILCS 505/13])

Environmental impact fee, receiver's (underground storage tank) tax.—There are no provisions for a refund of either the environmental impact fee or the receiver's tax, also known as the underground storage tank tax. However, there are provisions for claiming a credit. (Motor Fuel Tax Law, Sec. 13a.8 [35 ILCS 505/13a.8]; Environmental Impact Fee Law, Sec. 320 [415 ILCS 125/13a.8]; 86 Ill. Adm. Code 500.270; RMFT-5-US-X Amended Return/Claim for Credit Underground Storage Tank Tax and Environmental Impact Fee)

• *Local taxes*

Local taxes are authorized both under provisions of the Municipal Code (Ill. Municipal Code Sec. 8-11-15 [65 ILCS 5/8-11-15]) and under home-rule powers granted under the 1970 Illinois Constitution. (Ill. Const. Art. VII, Sec. 6(a)) Under the Municipal Code, municipalities with a population greater than 100,000 may impose a tax of one cent per gallon on gasoline sold in the municipality in addition to any other taxes on motor fuel. Approval of the voters in the municipality is required to impose such a tax. Under the home rule provisions of the constitution, municipalities may tax the sale of motor fuel (Ill. Const. Art. VII, Sec. 6(a)), but since constitutionally authorized taxes may not be levied on occupations, such taxes are levied on the consumer and not the retailer. (Ill. Const. Art. VII, Sec. 6(e))

Cook County imposes a tax on the retail sale of gasoline at the rate of $0.06 per gallon. (Cook County Gas Tax, Sec. 74-472) Beginning July 1, 2020, municipalities located in Cook County are authorized to impose a municipal motor fuel tax at a rate not to exceed 3 cents per gallon (the tax must be imposed in one cent increments) (*Informational Bulletin FY 2020-21*)

A tax is imposed by Chicago on the privilege of purchasing or using in Chicago vehicle fuel purchased at retail at the rate of $0.05 per gallon. The vehicle fuel tax is imposed upon the purchaser or user of vehicle fuel and is collected by each vehicle fuel distributor or dealer doing business in Chicago. (Chicago Municipal Code, Sec. 3-52-020) The tax is collected from retailers by distributors, who are entitled to a 1% commission for the collection and payment of the tax. Sales of domestic fuel used on international flights are exempt from the Chicago vehicle fuel tax. The tax has been held constitutional. (*Illinois Gasoline Dealers Assn. et al. v. City of Chicago*, Nos. 86 L 51112, 86 CH 9396, 86 L 51160, November 18, 1986 (1986 Cir Ct), aff'd (1988, Ill SCt), 519 NE2d 417; *United Airlines, Inc. v. City of Chicago; Midway Airlines, Inc. v. City of Chicago*, Ill. Supreme Ct., 116 Ill. 2d 311, 507 N.E. 2d 858, April 16, 1987)

Every vehicle fuel distributor doing business in Chicago is required to register with the Chicago Department of Revenue within 30 days of starting business. Any retail dealer, purchaser, or user who is required to remit the tax directly to the city on a frequently recurring basis shall register with the Department. (Chicago Munic. Code Sec. 3-52-050)

DuPage, Lake, Kane, McHenry, and Will counties are authorized to impose a tax on motor fuel used to operate motor vehicles and recreational watercraft at a rate up to 8¢ per gallon by the County Motor Fuel Tax Law. (County Motor Fuel Tax Law, Sec. 5-1035.1 [55 ILCS 5/5-1035.1]) The constitutionality of this tax was upheld by the Illinois Supreme Court. (*Cutinello v. Whitley*, Illinois Supreme Court, 161 Ill. 2d 409, 641 N.E. 2d 360, May 19, 1994)

[¶40-003] Diesel Fuel Taxes

Illinois imposes a tax on diesel fuel used to operate motor vehicles upon the public highways and recreational-type watercraft upon the waters of the state. Diesel fuel is included within a class of "special fuels," as defined by the state. (Motor Fuel Tax Law, Sec. 2 [35 ILCS 505/2])

Specific topics discussed here are:

— products subject to tax,

— point of taxation,

— license requirements,

— basis of tax,

— rate of tax,

— exemptions,

— reports and payments, and

— credits, refunds, and reimbursements.

In addition, until 2025 a tax is imposed on the privilege of being a receiver of motor fuel in the state for sale or use (receivers' tax, also referred to as the underground storage tank tax). Beginning January 1, 2021, this tax is not imposed on sales of aviation fuel for so long as the revenue use requirements of 49 U.S.C. 47107(b) and 49 U.S.C. 47133 are binding on the state. (Motor Fuel Tax Law, Sec. 2a [35 ILCS 505/2a]) An environmental impact fee also is imposed on certain fuels. (See discussion at ¶ 37-151.)

• *Products subject to tax*

Special fuels are all volatile and inflammable liquids capable of generating power in an internal combustion engine, except that it does not include gasoline or certain combustible gases. It specifically includes diesel fuel. (Motor Fuel Tax Law, Sec. 1.13 [35 ILCS 505/1.13]) Diesel fuel is separately defined as any product intended for use or offered for sale as a fuel for engines in which the fuel is injected into the combustion chamber and ignited by pressure without electric spark. (Motor Fuel Tax Law, Sec. 2 [35 ILCS 505/2])

• *Point of taxation*

A licensed distributor or a licensed supplier who sells or distributes special fuel must collect the tax on special fuel at the time of the sale or distribution. (Motor Fuel Tax Law, Sec. 6a [35 ILCS 505/6a]; 86 Ill. Adm. Code 500.200)

• *License requirements*

A person may not act as a distributor or a supplier without first securing an appropriate license from the Illinois Department of Revenue. Distributor license requirements are discussed at ¶ 40-001.

Applicants for a supplier's license must file a bond with the department. No applicant who is in default for motor fuel taxes due the state will be granted a license to act as a supplier. In addition a license will not be granted to anyone whose principal place of business is in a state other than Illinois unless that person is licensed for motor fuel distribution or export in that other state and is not in default to that state for any monies due for the sale, distribution, export, or use of motor fuel. (Motor Fuel Tax Law, Sec. 3a [35 ILCS 505/3a]) The main differences between a distributor and a supplier is that a supplier, unlike a distributor, cannot produce, refine or otherwise manufacture fuel, and a supplier's fuel import, export, and distribution activities are restricted to special fuels. (Motor Fuel Tax Law, Sec. 1.2 [35 ILCS 505/1.2]; Motor Fuel Tax Law, Sec. 1.14 [35 ILCS 505/1.14])

A distributor or supplier may not transfer its license or permit if the taxpayer's business is taken over or continued by another person. (86 Ill. Adm. Code 500.500)

• *Basis of tax*

The special fuel tax applies to each gallon of special fuel used to operate motor vehicles and recreational watercraft upon Illinois public highways and waters. (Motor Fuel Tax Law, Sec. 2 [35 ILCS 505/2]; 86 Ill. Adm. Code 500.200)

• *Rate of tax*

The per-gallon rates in Illinois for diesel fuel are as follows:

diesel fuel tax . . . . . $0.455 ($0.462 from July 1, 2020, through June 30, 2021)

receiver's tax. $0.003

environmental impact fee $0.008

¶40-003

(Motor Fuel Tax Rates and Fees) (Motor Fuel Tax Law, Sec. 2 [35 ILCS 505/2]; Motor Fuel Tax Law, Sec. 2a [35 ILCS 505/2a]; Environmental Impact Fee, Sec. 310[415 ILCS 125/310])

• *Exemptions*

Exemptions from of the motor fuel tax apply also to the sale of special fuel. (See ¶ 40-001) However, the special fuel tax also does not apply to sales of dyed diesel fuel made to someone other than a licensed distributor or supplier. (Motor Fuel Tax Law, Sec. 6a [35 ILCS 505/6a])

The rules provide sample certificates of exemption. (86 Ill. Adm. Code 500.285; 86 Ill. Adm. Code 500.280)

The tax on receivers is not imposed on the importation or receipt of diesel fuel sold to or used by a rail carrier to the extent the diesel fuel is used directly in railroad operations. That tax also is not imposed on diesel fuel consumed or used in the operation of ships, barges, or vessels that are used primarily in or for the transportation of property in interstate commerce for hire on rivers bordering the state. Finally, the tax is not imposed on the sale of diesel with delivery to a purchaser outside the state or to a person with a valid receiver's license. (Motor Fuel Tax Law, Sec. 2a [35 ILCS 505/2a])

• *Reports and payments*

Distributors must file returns for special fuel sales as they are required to so do for all motor fuel sales. In addition, motor fuel transporters are subject to the same reporting requirements for special fuel as they are for motor fuel. (See ¶ 40-001) Persons holding an unrevoked supplier's license must, between the 1st and the 20th of each month submit a return to the Department of Revenue for the preceding month disclosing:

- the number of gallons of invoiced special fuels, acquired, received, purchased, sold, exported, and used;

- the amount of special fuel sold, distributed, exported, and used by the supplier;

- the amount of special fuel lost or destroyed;

- the amount of special fuel on hand at the end of the preceding month; and

- other reasonable information the Department of Revenue may require.

(Motor Fuel Tax Law, Sec. 5 [35 ILCS 505/5]; Motor Fuel Tax Law, Sec. 5a [35 ILCS 505/5a])

The Department of Revenue accepts electronic payments using the ACH credit method from taxpayers filing either Form RMFT-5, Motor Fuel Distributor/Supplier Tax Return or Form RMFT-5-US, Underground Storage Tank Tax and Environmental Impact Fee Receiver Return. (*Informational Bulletin FY 2015-01*, Illinois Department of Revenue, July 2014)

Payment of the tax to the Department of Revenue must accompany the monthly return. (Motor Fuel Tax Law, Sec. 6 [35 ILCS 505/6]; Motor Fuel Tax Law, Sec. 6a [35 ILCS 505/6a]; 86 Ill. Adm. Code 500.203(a)) A person whose supplier's license has been revoked must, within 10 days of the revocation, make a return to the department covering the period from the date of the last return to the date of the revocation. (Motor Fuel Tax Law, Sec. 5a [35 ILCS 505/5a])

Suppliers are permitted to subtract a discount from their payment amount in the same manner as distributors are permitted to do so. (See ¶ 40-001)

Any person who is not a licensed distributor or supplier and who purchases special fuel thereafter used in the operation of a motor vehicle upon the public highways must make a payment of the motor fuel tax to the Department no later than

¶ 40-003

the 20th day of the month following the month in which the motor fuel was used. The statute does not apply in cases in which motor fuel was obtained tax-free under an official certificate of exemption. (Motor Fuel Tax Law, Sec. 7 [35 ILCS 505/7])

Fuel losses.—All licensed suppliers, distributors, and receivers are required to report all motor fuel losses when filing the return for the period during which the loss occurred. Failure to report such loss could result in the disallowance for a credit against tax liability with respect to such loss.

Losses of fuel as the result of evaporation or shrinkage due to temperature variations must also be reported; any loss reported that is in excess of 1% of the total gallons in storage at the beginning of the month, plus the receipts of gallonage during the month, minus the gallonage remaining in storage at the end of the month, is subject to tax. For the six-month period from January to June or the six-month period from July to December, the net losses of fuel as the result of evaporation or shrinkage due to temperature variations may not exceed 1% of (total gallons in storage at the beginning of each period) + (the receipts of gallonage for the period) - (gallonage remaining in storage at the end of each period). Any loss in excess of 1% is subject to tax. (Motor Fuel Tax Law, Sec. 5a [35 ILCS 505/5a])

• *Credits, refunds, and reimbursements*

The credit, refund, and reimbursement provisions that apply to distributors for activities that relate to motor fuel in general (See ¶40-001), there are other such provisions for tax refunds that relate to the sale of undyed diesel fuel used:

- in a qualifying "manufacturing process";
- by a manufacturer on private property in research and development;
- by a single unit, self-propelled agricultural fertilizer implement;
- by a commercial motor vehicle for any purpose other than operating the vehicle upon public highways;
- by a unit of local government in its operation of an airport;
- by refrigeration units permanently mounted to a semitrailer;
- by power take-off equipment; or
- by tugs and spotter equipment to shift vehicles or parcels on both private and airport property.

(Motor Fuel Tax Law, Sec. 13a [35 ILCS 505/13a])

Claims for reimbursement based on idle time are not allowed. (Motor Fuel Tax Law, Sec. 13 [35 ILCS 505/13])

Environmental impact fee, receiver's (underground storage tank) tax.—There are no provisions for a refund of either the environmental impact fee or the receiver's tax, also known as the underground storage tank tax. However, there are provisions for claiming a credit. (Motor Fuel Tax Law, Sec. 13a.8 [35 ILCS 505/13a.8]; Environmental Impact Fee Law, Sec. 320 [415 ILCS 125/13a.8]; 86 Ill. Adm. Code 500.270; RMFT-5-US-X Amended Return/Claim for Credit Underground Storage Tank Tax and Environmental Impact Fee)

[¶40-005] Aviation Fuel Taxes

The Illinois motor fuel distributors' tax does not apply to aviation fuel. (Motor Fuel Tax Law, Sec. 2 [35 ILCS 505/2]) However, some aviation fuel is subject to the tax on receivers. (Motor Fuel Tax Law, Sec. 2a [35 ILCS 505/2a])

Specific topics discussed below are:

— products subject to tax,
— point of taxation,

- license requirements,
- basis of tax,
- rate of tax,
- exemptions,
- reports and payments, and
- credits, refunds, and reimbursements.

- *Products subject to tax*

Products subject to the receivers' tax are discussed at ¶40-001.

- *Point of taxation*

The point of taxation for the receivers' tax is discussed at ¶40-001.

- *License requirements*

License requirements for receivers are discussed at ¶40-001.

- *Basis of tax*

The receiver's tax is paid by the receiver in the state who first sells or uses the fuel. (Motor Fuel Tax Law, Sec. 2a [35 ILCS 505/2a])

- *Rate of tax*

The receiver's tax is applied at a rate of $0.003/gallon. (Motor Fuel Tax Law, Sec. 2a [35 ILCS 505/2a])

- *Exemptions*

The receivers' tax does not apply to the importation or receipt of aviation fuels at airports with over 170,000 operations per year located in a city of more than 1 million inhabitants for sale to or use by holders of qualifying certificates of public convenience and necessity or foreign air carrier permits. (Motor Fuel Tax Law, Sec. 2a [35 ILCS 505/2a])

- *Reports and payments*

Reporting requirements for the receivers' tax parallel those for distributors who must make reports for the motor fuel tax. (See generally, ¶40-001) Payment of the tax must accompany the report. Beginning on January 1, 2020 and ending with returns due on January 20, 2021, each person who is required to pay tax on aviation fuel sold or used in Illinois during the preceding calendar month must, instead of reporting and paying tax on aviation fuel as otherwise required, report and pay such tax on a separate aviation fuel tax return or a separate line on the return. (Motor Fuel Tax Law, Sec. 2b [35 ILCS 505/2b])

- *Credits, refunds, and reimbursements*

There are no separate refund provisions for the tax on receivers.

[¶55-000]

CIGARETTES, TOBACCO PRODUCTS

[¶55-001] Cigarettes

The Cigarette Tax Act imposes a tax on the occupation of selling cigarettes at retail. Payment of the tax or responsibility to pay the tax is evidenced by stamps or imprints on cigarette packages. The state also imposes a complementary cigarette use tax. When the cigarette tax is paid, the cigarette use tax, a privilege tax imposed on the user, is not applicable. The Cigarette Use Tax Act largely duplicates the Cigarette Tax Act, and its purpose is to prevent tax evasion by means of interstate purchases of cigarettes for personal use. The Cigarette Machine Operators' Occupation Tax is imposed on cigarette machine operators.

> *CCH Caution: Retailer licenses.*—A license from the Illinois Department of Revenue is required by anyone who engages in business as a retailer of cigarettes or tobacco products, pursuant to amendments of the cigarette tax act, the cigarette use tax act, and the tobacco products tax act. Each applicant for a license will be required to file an application electronically and to pay a fee of $75 for each place of business at which the applicant proposes to sell cigarettes or tobacco products at retail. Anyone seeking a retailer's license under the cigarette tax act and the tobacco products tax act also must be registered under the terms of the state retailers' occupation tax act. Licensed retailers may purchase only:
>
> — cigarettes for sale from a licensed distributor, secondary distributor, or manufacturer representative; and
>
> — tobacco products for sale only from a licensed distributor or secondary distributor.
>
> Certain original invoices must be preserved on the licensed premises for a period of 90 days after a purchase. Criminal penalties also are specified for certain violations. (P.A. 98-1055 (H.B. 2494), Laws 2014, effective January 1, 2016

Cigarettes also are subject to sales tax in the state.

For a discussion of the tax on tobacco products other than cigarettes, see Tobacco Products. Administrative and procedural provisions are discussed at Cigarette, Tobacco Products Tax Practice and Procedure.

Discussed here in relation to the cigarette tax are:

— Persons and products subject to tax,

— Exemptions,

— Basis of tax,

— Rate of tax,

— Reports,

— Payment,

— Credits, refunds, discounts,

— Licenses and permits, and

— Local taxes.

Cigarette taxes are authorized under a constitutional provision granting the legislature exclusive power to raise revenue. (Ill. Const. Art. IX, Sec. 1) Both the sales tax and the use tax have been held constitutional and have survived charges that they are discriminatory. The cigarette tax does not provide uniformity in taxation, but such equality is neither practicable nor required by the Equal Protection Clause of the U.S. Constitution. (*Mutual Tobacco Co., Inc. v. Halpin* (1953 Ill.) 414 Ill 226, 111 N.E.2d 155) The cigarette use tax has a reasonable basis, does not violate the Commerce Clause of the federal Constitution, and is fair to those who buy cigarettes outside the state. (*Johnson v. Halpin* (1952, SCt) 413 Ill 257, 108 NE2d 429, cert. den., 345 US 923, 73 SCt 781; *Galesburg Eby-Brown v. Dept. of Revenue* (1986, App Ct) 497 NE2d 874)

• *Persons and products subject to tax*

The cigarette tax is imposed on the retail sale of cigarettes. However, the tax is prepaid before the cigarettes reach the retailer. (Cigarette Tax Act Sec. 2 [35 ILCS 130/2]; Cigarette Use Tax Act Sec. 3 [35 ILCS 130/3]; 86 Ill. Adm. Code 440.10(j)) There are specific rules for different classes of market participants.

"Cigarette" means any roll for smoking made wholly or in part of tobacco irrespective of size or shape and whether or not such tobacco is flavored, adulterated or mixed with any other ingredient, and the wrapper or cover of which is made with paper or any other substance or material except tobacco. (Cigarette Tax Act Sec. 1 [35 ILCS 130/1]; Cigarette Use Tax Act Sec. 3 [35 ILCS 135/3])

Electronic cigarettes.—A 15% tobacco products tax applies to e-cigarettes. It applies to the wholesale price of e-cigarettes sold or disposed of to Illinois retailers or consumers. It is in addition to any state or local occupation or privilege taxes. (35 ILCS 143/10-10)

Little cigars.—"Little cigar" means and includes any roll, made wholly or in part of tobacco, where such roll has an integrated cellulose acetate filter and weighs less than four pounds per 1,000 and the wrapper or cover of which is made in whole or in part of tobacco. In addition, little cigars are included within the definition of "tobacco products." Further, little cigars in packages of 20 or 25 little cigars are taxed at the same rate as cigarettes and are required to be stamped in the same manner as cigarettes. (Sec. 10-5, Tobacco Products Tax of 1995, [35 ILCS 143/10-5]) Little cigars sold in other quantities do not require stamps. Instead, a stamping distributor must pay the tax due using Form RC-55, Unstamped Little Cigar Sticks Tax Return.

Distributors.—A licensed distributor prepays the tax by purchasing stamps from the Department of Revenue to affix to cigarette packages as evidence that the tax has been paid. The distributor then adds the price of stamp to the selling price of the cigarettes. (Sec. 2, Cigarette Tax Act [35 ILCS 130/2]; Cigarette Use Tax Act Sec. 3 [35 ILCS 135/3]) If the distributor does not collect and pay the tax from the retailer, the distributor becomes liable for the tax. (86 Ill. Adm. Code 440.10(j))

The licensed distributor can sell stamped cigarettes to other licensed distributors, secondary distributors, qualifying manufacturer representatives, or retailers. (Sec. 4e, Cigarette Tax Act [35 ILCS 130/4e]; Sec. 4f, Cigarette Tax Act [35 ILCS 130/4f]; *Informational Bulletin 2012-09*, Illinois Department of Revenue, June 2012) In order to sell cigarettes in Illinois, a distributor must be licensed by the state. In making sales to retailers, distributors also are required to prepay local cigarette taxes.

Manufacturers representatives.—Distributors can sell up to 600 stamped original packages of cigarettes in a calendar year to a qualified manufacturer representative for the purpose of promoting the manufacturer's brands of cigarettes. The representative also may sell cigarettes to retailers on behalf of licensed distributors. (Cigarette Tax Act Sec. 4f [35 ILCS 130/4f])

In-state manufacturers.—Generally, in-state makers, manufacturers, or fabricators (manufacturers) are "distributors" within the meaning of the Cigarette Tax

Act. Rather than purchasing and affixing stamps to indicate that taxes were paid, however, manufacturers may imprint language on the bottom of cigarette packages, which are contained inside a sealed transparent wrapper, that constitutes evidence of the manufacturers' payment of or liability for the taxes due. (Sec. 3, Cigarette Tax Act [35 ILCS 130/3])

Out-of-state manufacturers.—Qualifying out-of-state cigarette manufacturers can obtain permits from the state to pay tax on cigarettes delivered into the state in the same manner as in-state manufacturers. Out-of-state manufacturers who do not want to pay the tax can, instead, apply for permits to deliver unstamped original packages of cigarettes to licensed distributors within the state. (Sec. 4b, Cigarette Use Tax Act [35 ILCS 135/4b])

Users of unstamped cigarettes.—Any person who acquired cigarettes for use in Illinois and did not pay a cigarette tax must submit a return and tax to the Department of Revenue within 30 days. (Sec. 4b, Cigarette Tax Act [35 ILCS 130/4b])

Nonparticipating manufacturer.—A cigarette distributor must not affix any stamp or imprint any package of cigarettes if the tobacco products manufacturer that made or sold the cigarettes failed to become a participating manufacturer, as defined by the Tobacco Product Manufacturers' Escrow Act, or failed to create a qualified escrow fund for any cigarettes manufactured and sold in Illinois. The Department of Revenue may revoke, cancel, or suspend the license of a distributor for a violation of the Tobacco Product Manufacturers' Escrow Enforcement Act. (Cigarette Tax Act Sec. 3 [35 ILCS 130/3])

Cigarette Machine Operators' Occupation Tax Act.—The cigarette machine operators' tax is imposed on persons engaged in the business of operating a cigarette machine. However, the operators may reimburse themselves for their tax liability by separately stating such tax, less any credit claimed by the operator, as an additional charge to users of the cigarettes. (Sec. 1-10, Cigarette Machine Operators' Occupation Tax Act, P.A. 97-688 (S.B. 2194), effective June 24, 2012; *Informational Bulletin FY 2013-01*, Illinois Department of Revenue, July 2012)

• *Exemptions*

Sales in interstate commerce and other sales which, under the U.S. Constitution and laws, may not be taxed by states are exempt from the cigarette tax. (Cigarette Tax Act Sec. 2 [35 ILCS 130/2]) While sales to governmental bodies generally are taxable, direct sales to U.S. Veterans' Hospitals and qualifying sales to military personnel are not. (86 Ill. Adm. Code 440.180)

Distributors' sales of cigarettes and tobacco products made as part of a correctional industries program and sold to prisoners or patients in state-operated mental institutions are not subject to tax. (Cigarette Tax Act, Sec. 2 35 ILCS 130/2])

A person is not a "retailer" if the person transfers cigarettes to a not-for-profit research institution that

(1) conducts tests concerning the health effects of tobacco products and

(2) does not offer the cigarettes for resale.

(Cigarette Tax Act Sec. 1 [35 ILCS 130/1])

A person making the same type of transfer to a qualifying institution is not a "distributor" under the terms of the Cigarette Use Tax Act. (Cigarette Use Tax Act Sec. 1 [35 ILCS 135/1])

The tax does not apply to cigarettes that are shipped by the selling distributor from within Illinois to a point outside the state, not to be returned to a point within the state. (86 Ill. Adm. Code 440.170)

Any exemption against the cigarette or the cigarette use taxes that became law after September 16, 1994, is limited by a five-year sunset date. (Cigarette Tax Act Sec. 3-5 [35 ILCS 130/3-5]; Cigarette Use Tax Act Sec. 3-5 [35 ILCS 135/3-5])

For purposes of the cigarette machine operators' occupation tax, persons renting, leasing, and selling machines, but not operating them, are exempt from the tax. (Sec. 1-165, Cigarette Machine Operators' Occupation Tax Act, P.A. 97-688 (S.B. 2194), effective June 24, 2012) However, they must notify potential machine lessees, lessors, or purchasers of licensure, tax collection and remittance, and packaging and labeling requirements imposed by the machine operators' occupation tax law. (Sec. 1-170, Cigarette Machine Operators' Occupation Tax Act, P.A. 97-688 (S.B. 2194), effective June 24, 2012)

• *Basis of tax*

The basis of the tax for the cigarette tax and the cigarette use tax is each cigarette that a retailer sells in Illinois (Cigarette Tax Act Sec. 2 [35 ILCS 130/2]86 Ill. Adm. Code Sec. 440.10) and a purchaser uses in Illinois. (Cigarette Use Tax Act Sec. 2 [35 ILCS 135/2]) The basis of the tax on cigarette machine operator tax is every cigarette made or fabricated in a cigarette machine owned by a licensed operator. (Sec. 1-10, Cigarette Machine Operators' Occupation Tax Act, P.A. 97-688 (S.B. 2194), effective June 24, 2012; *Informational Bulletin FY 2013-01*, Illinois Department of Revenue, July 2012)

• *Rate of tax*

The rates for the cigarette tax and the cigarette use tax are 149 mills per cigarette ($2.98 per pack of 20). (Cigarette Tax Act Sec. 2 [35 ILCS 130/2]; Cigarette Use Tax Act Sec. 2 [35 ILCS 135/2]; *Informational Bulletin FY 2012-10*, Illinois Department of Revenue, June 2012)

Retailers are not required to pay the tax increase on stamped cigarette packages in their possession as of June 24, 2012. Distributors who have either cigarette packages with tax stamps affixed to them or unaffixed stamps in their possession on that date must pay the tax increase to the extent the calendar year 2012 average monthly volume of cigarette stamps in the distributor's possession exceeds the average monthly volume of cigarette stamps purchased by the distributor in calendar year 2011. Generally, the payment amount, less the distributor's discount, is due on the increased tax by the earlier of June 24, 2012, or the first due date of a cigarette or cigarette use tax return occurring on or after that date. However, distributors may elect to make the payments over a 12-month period, although they will not be entitled to the discount on those payments. (Cigarette Tax Act Sec. 2 [35 ILCS 130/2]; Cigarette Use Tax Act Sec. 2 [35 ILCS 135/2]; *Informational Bulletin FY 2012-10*, Illinois Department of Revenue, June 2012)

A tax is imposed at the rate of 149 mills (previously, 99 mills) per cigarette made or fabricated in a cigarette machine owned by a licensed cigarette machine operator. (Sec. 1-10, Cigarette Machine Operators' Occupation Tax Act, P.A. 97-688 (S.B. 2194); *Informational Bulletin FY 2013-01*, Illinois Department of Revenue, July 2012)

Cook County adds a sales or use tax of $3.00 per package. (Cook County Tobacco Tax Ordinance, Sec. 74-433)

The per-cigarette tax rate in Chicago is $0.059 ($1.18 per 20-pack). (Chicago Municipal Code, Sec. 3-42-020(a))

• *Reports*

Licensed cigarette distributors who are not manufacturers and cigarette machine operators must file a report on or before the 15th of each month. Cigarette manufacturers qualifying as distributors file reports on or before the 5th of the month. (Cigarette Tax Act Sec. 9 [35 ILCS 135/9]; Cigarette Use Tax Act Sec. 11 [35 ILCS

135/11]; 86 Ill. Adm. Code 440.100; Sec. 1-10, Cigarette Machine Operators' Occupation Tax Act, P.A. 97-688 (S.B. 2194), effective June 24, 2012) Out-of-state cigarette distributors must file a similar form by the 15th day of each month.

Little cigars.—Packages of little cigars containing any quantity other than 20 or 25 sticks on which the Illinois cigarette tax has not been paid are not required to have a tax stamp affixed, but they are subject to other reporting and payment requirements. Distributors must report monthly sales of little cigars in qualifying unstamped packages and calculate any tax due on Form RC-55. For reporting periods of July 2012 through October 2012, all returns are due by December 1, 2012, and no penalties or interest for those periods will be assessed. Starting with the November 2012 reporting period, Form RC-55 is due before the 15th day of each month to report transactions made during the preceding month. (*Informational Bulletin FY 2012-12*, Illinois Department of Revenue, June 2012, as superseded in part by *Informational Bulletin FY 2013-06*, Illinois Department of Revenue, November 2012)

Other filing deadlines.—Manufacturers who place their cigarettes in original packages inside sealed, transparent wrappers and, instead of affixing stamps, imprint language as evidence of obligation to pay the tax make occupation (Cigarette Tax Act Sec. 3 [35 ILCS 130/3]; Cigarette Use Tax Act Sec. 11 [35 ILCS 135/11]) and use (Cigarette Use Tax Act Sec. 12 [35 ILCS 135/12]; Cigarette Use Tax Act Sec. 3 [35 ILCS 135/3]) tax payments by the fifth of each month covering the preceding calendar month. (Cigarette Use Tax Act Sec. 3 [35 ILCS 135/3]; 86 Ill. Adm. Code 450.40) Distributors who have permits also file by the fifth for the preceding calendar month. (Cigarette Use Tax Act Sec. 7 [35 ILCS 135/7])

When anyone, including a distributor who acquires cigarettes for personal use, acquires cigarettes on which the use tax has not been paid, he must file Form RC-44, Illinois Cigarette Use Tax Return within 30 days. (Cigarette Use Tax Act Sec. 12 [35 ILCS 135/12])

Manufacturer representatives must file a report electronically on or before the 15th of each month showing the quantity of cigarettes purchased from licensed distributors during the preceding calendar month and the quantity of cigarettes sold to retailers or otherwise disposed of. (Cigarette Tax Act Sec. 9f [35 ILCS 130/9f])

Jenkins Act registration and reporting.—The federal Jenkins Act (15 U.S.C. §§ 375-378), as amended in 2010 by the Prevent All Cigarette Trafficking Act of 2009 (PACT Act), Pub. L. No. 111-154, imposes certain registration and reporting requirements on those who sell, transfer, or ship (or who advertise or offer to do so) cigarettes, roll-your-own tobacco, and smokeless tobacco for profit in interstate commerce to a state, locality, or Indian country of an Indian tribe that taxes the sale or use of such products.

Registration requirement: A statement must be filed with the U.S. Attorney General and with the tobacco tax administrators of the state and place into which the products are shipped (or where advertisements or offers are directed). The statement must provide the name and trade name (if any) of the seller, transferor, or shipper, and the address of its principal place of business and of any other place of business. (15 U.S.C. § 376(a)) Additionally, the statement must include telephone numbers for each place of business, a principal e-mail address, any website addresses, and the name, address, and telephone number of an agent in the state authorized to accept service on behalf of the seller, transferor, or shipper. (15 U.S.C. § 376(a))

As an alternative to filing a statement with the U.S. Attorney General, Form 5070.1 can be filed with the Bureau of Alcohol, Tobacco, Firearms and Explosives (ATF). This federal form is available on the ATF's website at http://www.atf.gov/.

Reporting requirement: The Jenkins Act also imposes a duty to file on the 10th of each month with the relevant state tobacco tax administrator a report of the names and addresses of all of the seller's in-state cigarette and smokeless tobacco purchasers, the brand and quantity of cigarettes or smokeless tobacco, and the name, address, and phone number of the person delivering the shipment. (15 U.S.C. §376(a)) A copy of the report must be filed with the chief law enforcement officer of the local government and any Indian tribe that applies its own local or tribal taxes on the cigarettes or smokeless tobacco purchased. (15 U.S.C. §376(a)) These reports can be used by the state tobacco tax administrators and the local chief law enforcement officers that receive them to enforce the collection of any taxes owed on the sales. (15 U.S.C. §376(c))

• *Payment*

Cigarette distributors who file IL Form RC-1-A, Cigarette Tax Stamp Order Invoice must pay the tax by means of electronic funds transfer (EFT). (Cigarette Tax Act Sec. 3 [35 ILCS 130/3]; Cigarette Use Tax Act Sec. 3 [35 ILCS 135/3])

Stamps are provided by the Department and indicate payment of the tax. (Cigarette Tax Act Sec. 5 [35 ILCS 130/5]; Cigarette Use Tax Act Sec. 3 [35 ILCS 135/3]; 86 Ill. Adm. Code 440.40) Payment for tax stamps must be made by electronic funds transfer. (Cigarette Tax Act Sec. 3 [35 ILCS 130/3]; Cigarette Use Tax Act Sec. 3 [35 ILCS 135/3]) A licensed distributor who buys cigarettes outside Illinois and sells them within the state may affix the stamps before the cigarettes enter the state. (86 Ill. Adm. Code 440.70; 86 Ill. Adm. Code 450.20)

Cigarette machine operators.—Cigarette machine operators must remit the tax imposed by the 15th day of each month covering the preceding calendar month. (Sec. 1-40, Cigarette Machine Operators' Occupation Tax Act, P.A. 97-688 (S.B. 2194), effective June 24, 2012; *Informational Bulletin FY 2013-01*, Illinois Department of Revenue, July 2012)

Discount.—A cigarette distributor may take the following discounts during any fiscal year beginning July 1: 1.75% of the tax up to $3,000,000 and 1.5% of any additional tax. (Cigarette Tax Act Sec. 2 [35 ILCS 130/2]; Cigarette Use Tax Act Sec. 3 [35 ILCS 135/3])

• *Credits, refunds, discounts*

If it is decided that a tax should no longer be collected, distributors who have already paid it by purchasing stamps and can show that they sold the cigarettes to which the stamps were affixed after the tax ended and did not recover the tax from its customers may take credit for this absorbed tax against subsequent tax stamp purchases. (Cigarette Tax Act Sec. 2 [35 ILCS 130/2]; Cigarette Use Tax Act Sec. 2 [35 ILCS 135/2])

If a taxpayer pays a tax or penalty as the result of a mistake of fact, or an error of law, and files a claim on or after January 1 or July 1, the taxpayer should receive a credit memorandum or a refund, unless the amount was erroneously paid more than three years prior to that January 1 or July 1. The credit or refund bears interest in the manner set forth by the Uniform Penalty and Interest Act. (Cigarette Tax Act Sec. 9d [35 ILCS 130/9d]; Cigarette Use Tax Act Sec. 14a [35 ILCS 135/14a]; 86 Ill. Adm. Code 440.230; 86 Ill. Adm. Code 450.120)

There is no provision for refunds for unused cigarette revenue stamps, but a distributor, upon terminating his business, may sell or transfer them to another distributor, provided that at least 24 hours beforehand he has reported to the Department in writing his intention to do so and the name and address of the distributor who will acquire the stamps, together with the total of each of the denominations. (Cigarette Tax Act Sec. 28 [35 ILCS 130/28]; Cigarette Use Tax Act Sec. 33 [35 ILCS 135/33])

If unused stamps become mutilated or are affixed to unusable packages, the Department will issue a credit for the stamps, but it may charge an amount against the credit for any amount due to the Department as a result of the proceedings. (86 Ill.

Adm. Code 440.200) If the Department sends a representative to witness destruction of stamps, it may charge for any costs as a result of doing so. (86 Ill. Adm. Code 440.200; 86 Ill. Adm. Code 440.230) Holders of permits and distributors licensed under the Cigarette Use Tax Act should follow the same procedure to file a claim for replacement. (86 Ill. Adm. Code 450.90)

While stamps may be affixed by tax meters (86 Ill. Adm. Code 440.60), unused meter units are not subject to refund. A distributor who is going out of business should follow the same procedure for selling or transferring them as he would for stamps, indicating in writing to the Department the number of meter units in question. (86 Ill. Adm. Code 440.120)

Cigarette machine operators.—Cigarette machine operators can take a credit against their tax liability for taxes imposed and paid on tobacco products sold to a customer and used in a rolling machine. (Sec. 1-40, Cigarette Machine Operators' Occupation Tax Act, P.A. 97-688 (S.B. 2194), effective June 24, 2012; *Informational Bulletin FY 2013-01*, Illinois Department of Revenue, July 2012)

• *Licenses and permits*

Only distributors licensed under the Cigarette Tax Act or distributors and transporters licensed under the Cigarette Use Tax Act may possess unstamped original packs of cigarettes. (Cigarette Tax Act Sec. 3 [35 ILCS 130/3]; Cigarette Use Tax Act Sec. 3 [35 ILCS 135/3])

The annual fee for a nontransferable distributor license, which is valid for one year, is $250, and applicants must file a bond in the amount of $2,500. (Cigarette Tax Act Sec. 4 [35 ILCS 130/4]; Cigarette Use Tax Act Sec. 4 [35 ILCS 135/4]; 86 Ill. Adm. Code Sec. 440.50; 86 Ill. Adm. Code 450.30) Once revoked, a license cannot be reissued within six months. (Cigarette Tax Act Sec. 6 [35 ILCS 130/6]; Cigarette Use Tax Act Sec. 6 [35 ILCS 135/6])

Out-of-state manufacturers who, if they choose to qualify as distributors, may obtain a free, nontransferable permit authorizing payment of the tax. (Cigarette Tax Act Sec. 4b [35 ILCS 130/4b]; Cigarette Use Tax Act Sec. 7 [35 ILCS 135/7; 86 Ill. Adm. Code Sec. 450.40) It may be revoked at any time and is to be valid for no more than a year. (Cigarette Tax Act Sec. 4b [35 ILCS 130/4b]; Cigarette Use Tax Act Sec. 7 [35 ILCS 135/7]) Transporters also must obtain a permit to move more than 2,000 cigarettes not contained in original packages with Illinois stamps. (Cigarette Tax Act Sec. 9c [35 ILCS 130/9c]; 86 Ill. Adm. Code 440.100)

The following are ineligible for a cigarette distributor's license and permit:

— persons who have bad reputations in their communities,

— unrehabilitated felons,

— corporations if any officer, manager, or director or stockholders owning in the aggregate more than 5% of the stock are ineligible for a license, and

— a person who owns more than 15% of the ownership interests in a person or a related who:

(1) owes any delinquent cigarette taxes;

(2) had a license issued under the cigarette tax laws revoked within two years for certain conduct;

(3) manufactures cigarettes and does not participate in the tobacco master settlement agreement;

(4) imported cigarettes into the country without complying with applicable federal law; or

(5) made a material false statement in an application or failed to produce records, as required.

(Cigarette Tax Act Sec. 4 [35 ILCS 130/4]; 86 Ill. Adm. Code Sec. 450.40; Cigarette Tax Act Sec. 4b [35 ILCS 130/4b]; Cigarette Use Tax Act Sec. 7 [35 ILCS 135/7]; 86 Ill. Adm. Code 450.30)

If a distributor has obtained a license or permit under the Cigarette Tax Act, he does not need to procure another under the Cigarette Use Tax Act. A distributor maintaining a place of business in Illinois who is neither required to have a license nor allowed to obtain a permit under the Cigarette Tax Act must make a verified application to act as a distributor under the Use Tax Act. (Cigarette Use Tax Act Sec. 4 [35 ILCS 135/4])

Additional bond requirements: A distributor or permittee may take 30 days to make the final payment for cigarette stamps, provided he has filed an approved bond, in addition to the bond required of every licensee, payable to the Department in an amount equal to 150% of his average monthly tax liability during the preceding year or $750,000, whichever is less. Bonds filed on or after January 1, 1987, will equal 100% of the average monthly tax liability or $750,000, whichever is less. However, "prior continuous compliance taxpayers," taxpayers who have been licensed for a continuous period of five years, have been neither delinquent nor deficient in paying the cigarette tax, and have complied with the bond requirements for five consecutive years, are exempt from this additional bond requirement. (Cigarette Tax Act Sec. 4b [35 ILCS 130/4b]; Cigarette Tax Act Sec. 3 [35 ILCS 130/3]; Cigarette Use Tax Act Sec. 3 [35 ILCS 135/3])

Cigarette machine users.—Operators must be licensed before engaging in the business of operating a cigarette machine. Each place of business at which a person wants to procure a cigarette machine operator license requires a license application, payment of a $250 annual license fee, and filing of a joint and several surety bond in an amount of $2,500. Applicants also must meet several eligibility requirements. Taxpayers licensed and bonded for five years and who have not been delinquent or deficient in payment of the tax will not be required to furnish a bond to renew their license. (Sec. 1-15, Cigarette Machine Operators' Occupation Tax Act, P.A. 97-688 (S.B. 2194), effective June 24, 2012; *Informational Bulletin FY 2013-01*, Illinois Department of Revenue, July 2012)

• *Local taxes*

Local taxes are authorized both under provisions of the Municipal Code (65 ILCS 5/8-11-3) and under home-rule powers granted under the 1970 Illinois Constitution. (Ill. Const. Art. VII, Sec. 6(a)) Under the Municipal Code, cities may tax retailers at a rate not to exceed one cent per package of 20 cigarettes, provided a municipal retailer's occupation tax is not in force. (65 ILCS 5/8-11-3) Under the home-rule provisions of the constitution, municipalities may tax the sale of cigarettes. (*S. Bloom, Inc. et al. v. Korshak et al.* 284 NE2d 213 (Ill. 1972)) Tax under constitutional authorization is not subject to the one-cent-per-package limitation (65 ILCS 5/8-11-3); however, constitutionally authorized taxes may not be levied on occupations. (Ill. Const. Art. VII, Sec. 6(a)) As a result, such taxes are imposed on the consumer rather than the retailer. If a home-rule unit imposes a tax based on the selling price of cigarettes, that price must include charges added by the Cigarette Tax Act or the Cigarette Use Tax Act, as well as the home-rule unit. (Home Rule Cigarette Tax Restriction Act, Sec. 1 [35 ILCS 140/1])

Cook County and Chicago.—Not all Illinois counties and cities have additional cigarette taxes, but Cook County adds a sales or use tax of $2.00 per package. (Cook County Tobacco Tax Ordinance, Sec. 74-432) Chicago, the only Illinois city that has a population over 2,000,000 and imposes a tax, charges $.034 per cigarette ($0.68 per pack of 20). (Chicago Municipal Code, Sec. 3-42-020(a))

[¶55-005] Tobacco Products

Illinois imposes a tax on tobacco products. For purposes of that tax, cigarettes are not included under the definition of "tobacco products."

Tobacco products also are subject to sales tax in the state.

For a discussion of the cigarette tax, see Cigarettes.

CCH Caution: Retailer licenses.—A license from the Illinois Department of Revenue is required by anyone who engages in business as a retailer of cigarettes or tobacco products, pursuant to amendments of the cigarette tax act, the cigarette use tax act, and the tobacco products tax act. Each applicant for a license will be required to file an application electronically and to pay a fee of $75 for each place of business at which the applicant proposes to sell cigarettes or tobacco products at retail. Anyone seeking a retailer's license under the cigarette tax act and the tobacco products tax act also must be registered under the terms of the state retailers' occupation tax act. Licensed retailers may purchase only:

　　— cigarettes for sale from a licensed distributor, secondary distributor, or manufacturer representative; and

　　— tobacco products for sale only from a licensed distributor or secondary distributor.

Certain original invoices must be preserved on the licensed premises for a period of 90 days after a purchase. Criminal penalties also are specified for certain violations. (P.A. 98-1055 (H.B. 2494), Laws 2014, effective January 1, 2016

Discussed here in relation to the tobacco products tax are:

— Persons and products subject to tax,

— Exemptions,

— Basis of tax,

— Rate of tax,

— Reports,

— Payment,

— Credits, refunds, discounts,

— Licenses and permits, and

— Local taxes,

The current Tobacco Products Tax Act was enacted in 1995. The Illinois Supreme Court upheld the constitutionality of the Act against a claim that the enacting legislation violated the single-subject rule of the Illinois Constitution. (*Arangold Corp. v. Zehnder et al.*, 718 N.E. 2d 191 (Ill. 1999)) Four years later, the court also upheld the Act against claims that it violated the Illinois due process and uniformity clauses. (*Arangold Corp. v. Zehnder*, 787 N.E.2d 786 (Ill. 2003)) Two prior versions of a tobacco products tax were declared unconstitutional. (*S. Bloom, Inc., et al. v. Mahin et al. and Midway Tobacco Co. et al. v. Mahin et al.*, Circuit Court of Cook County, Illinois County Department, July 28, 1969;*Arangold Corp. dba Arango Cigars v. Illinois Dept. of Revenue*, Circuit Court, Cook County Judicial Circuit (Illinois), No. 93-L-51285, January 3, 1995)

• *Persons and products subject to tax*

The tobacco products tax is imposed on the last distributor who sells or disposes of tobacco products to retailers or consumers located in the state. (Tobacco Products Tax Act of 1995 Sec. 10-10 [35 ILCS 143/10-10]; 86 Ill. Adm. Code 660.05)

Compliance Alert: Vapor device capsules—2017.—Capsules containing granulated tobacco for use in a battery-operated device that produced a vapor for users to inhale was not a "tobacco product" subject to the Illinois tobacco products tax. The capsules were imported into the United States and Illinois as a completed product, were made of plastic, and were not suitable for chewing or smoking. This ruling supplements and modifies a prior ruling on the subject. (*Private Letter Ruling, ST 17-0012-PLR*, Illinois Department of Revenue, December 27, 2017)

That ruling supplemented and modified a prior ruling. (*Private Letter Ruling, ST 17-0010-PLR*, Illinois Department of Revenue, September 22, 2017)

For tobacco products tax purposes, "distributors" are defined as:

(1) manufacturers or wholesalers who sell, exchange, or distribute tobacco products in Illinois;

(2) manufacturers engaged in the business of selling tobacco products from without Illinois who sell, exchange, distribute, ship, or transport tobacco products to retailers or consumers located in Illinois and who maintain a place of business or agent in Illinois;

(3) retailers who receive tobacco products on which the tax has not been or will not be paid.

A "stamping distributor" is a distributor licensed under the tobacco products tax act and either the cigarette tax act or the cigarette use tax act. (Tobacco Products Tax Act of 1995 Sec. 10-5 [35 ILCS 143/10-5])

Little cigars are subject to the tobacco products tax. However, packages of little cigars in quantities of 20 or 25 are taxed in the same manner as are cigarettes. For discussions of taxation of little cigars, see ¶55-001 and *Informational Bulletin FY 2014-01*, Illinois Department of Revenue, July 2013.

• *Exemptions*

Sales in interstate commerce and other sales which, under the U.S. Constitution and laws, may not be taxed by states are exempt from the tobacco products tax. (Tobacco Products Tax Act of 1995 Sec. 10-10 [35 ILCS 143/10-10]) Purchases of tobacco products other than little cigars by wholesalers who will not sell the product at retail are exempt from the tobacco products tax, as are purchases of tobacco products by wholesalers and retailers for delivery outside Illinois. The tax also will not be imposed on sales to the U.S. government or its instrumentalities, such as U.S. Veterans' Hospitals or U.S. Military personnel through qualifying officially recognized agencies. (86 Ill. Adm. Code 660.35)

Distributors' and manufacturers' sales of tobacco products made as part of a correctional industries program and sold to prisoners or patients in state-operated mental institutions are not subject to tax. (Tobacco Products Tax Act of 1995 Sec. 10-5 [35 ILCS 143/10-5])

• *Basis of tax*

The tax is imposed on the wholesale sale or other disposition of tobacco products to retailers or consumers. (Tobacco Products Tax Act of 1995 Sec. 10-10 [35 ILCS 143/10-10]) "Tobacco products" include cigars, cheroots, stogies, periques, snuff or snuff flour, plug and twist tobacco, and any other tobacco suitable for chewing or smoking in a pipe or otherwise. (Tobacco Products Tax Act of 1995 Sec. 10-5 [35 ILCS 143/10-5])

¶55-005

• *Rate of tax*

The tax is imposed at the rate 36% of the wholesale price of the tobacco product. Moist snuff is taxed at the rate of $0.30 per ounce, and the tax rate on moist snuff may not exceed 15% of the tax imposed on a package of 20 cigarettes pursuant to the Cigarette Tax Act. (Tobacco Products Tax Act of 1995, Sec. 10-10 [35 ILCS 143/10-10]; *Informational Bulletin FY 2012-11*, Illinois Department of Revenue, June 2012; *Informational Bulletin FY 2013-07*, Illinois Department of Revenue, November 2012)

Cook County.—Cook County imposes tax on tobacco at the following rates:

  (1) smoking tobacco: $0.60 per ounce or fraction thereof,

  (2) smokeless tobacco: $0.60 per ounce or fraction thereof,

  (3) little cigars: $0.05 per unit or cigar, and

  (4) large cigars: $0.30 per unit or cigar.

(Sec. 74-433, Cook County Ord)

• *Reports*

Form TP-1, Tobacco Products Tax Return, is due by the 15th day of the month following the month in which the tobacco products were sold or otherwise disposed. In addition, on or before the 15th day of each month, each stamping distributor must report the quantity of little cigars sold or otherwise disposed of in the preceding month. The Department of Revenue may adopt rules to require the electronic filing of any return or document required to be filed. (Tobacco Products Tax Act of 1995 Sec. 10-30 [35 ILCS 143/10-30]; Tobacco Products Tax, Illinois Department of Revenue)

• *Payment*

The tax liability must be remitted when the return is due to be filed. (Tobacco Products Tax Act of 1995 Sec. 10-30 [35 ILCS 143/10-30]) If the taxpayer had an annual liability of $20,000 or more in the preceding calendar year, the taxpayer must remit any tax payment by Electronic Funds Transfer. (Tobacco Products Tax, Illinois Department of Revenue)

• *Credits, refunds, discounts*

If an amount of the tobacco products tax or penalty has been paid in error, the Department of Revenue will issue a credit memorandum or refund to the person who made the erroneous payment. The department will apply the credit or refund first to any amount of tax or penalty actually due from the taxpayer. As to any claims filed on or after each January 1 or July 1, no amount of tax or penalty erroneously paid more than three years prior to such January 1 and July 1 will be credited or refunded. (86 Ill. Adm. Code 660.35) In addition, a wholesaler who is a stamping distributor making sales of little cigars for use outside the state may file a claim for credit for those sales with the department. (Tobacco Products Tax Act of 1995, Sec. 10-28 [35 ILCS 143/10-28])

• *Licenses and permits*

Distributors of tobacco products must obtain an annual license, but no fee is charged. Any distributor aggrieved by a decision of the Department of Revenue denying a license may protest and request a hearing within 20 days after notice of the decision. The decision of the Department becomes final in absence of such protest and request. (Tobacco Products Tax Act of 1995 Sec. 10-20 [35 ILCS 143/10-20])

• *Local taxes*

Illinois home-rule counties and certain home-rule municipalities can assess local taxes on tobacco products. (55 ILCS 5/5-1009; 65 ILCS 5/8-11-6a)

Cook County.—Cook County imposes a tax on other tobacco products at the rates discussed above. (Sec. 74-433, Cook County Ord)

SALES AND USE
(Retailers' Occupation Tax and Use Tax, Including Service Occupation Tax and Service Use Tax)

[¶60-000]

INTRODUCTION

[¶60-020] Application of Sales and Use Taxes

Illinois has four sales and use taxes for transactions involving tangible personal property: the retailers' occupation tax (ROT), the service occupation tax (SOT), the use tax, and the service use tax (SUT). Illinois imposes sales tax on persons in the business of selling tangible personal property at retail and SOT on persons in the business of selling services in Illinois. (35 ILCS 115/1; 35 ILCS 120/2) Use tax is imposed on persons who use tangible personal property in Illinois, while SUT is imposed when certain property is received while purchasing services. (35 ILCS 105/2; 35 ILCS 110/2) Services are generally not subject to sales and use tax.

The statutes for each of the four taxes contain many identical rules of application. In addition, retailers' occupation (sales) tax regulations that are compatible with the use tax and service occupation tax (SOT) apply to the imposition of use tax and SOT, and SOT regulations that are compatible with the service use tax (SUT) apply to the imposition of SUT. (86 Ill. Adm. Code 140.430; 86 Ill. Adm. Code 150.1201; 86 Ill. Adm. Code 150.1320; 86 Ill. Adm. Code 160.145)

Which transactions are generally subject to sales tax in Illinois?

Illinois imposes retailers' occupation (sales) tax (ROT) on retailers of tangible personal property and service occupation tax (SOT) on persons who transfer tangible personal property incidental to a service. (35 ILCS 115/3-40; 86 Ill. Adm. Code 140.101; 86 Ill. Adm. Code 140.120; 86 Ill. Adm. Code 140.201(f))

Retailers' occupation tax (ROT). Sales tax is imposed on persons who make retail sales of tangible personal property. (35 ILCS 120/2; 86 Ill. Adm. Code 130.101) Sellers are liable for sales tax and generally reimburse themselves by collecting use tax from customers. (86 Ill. Adm. Code 130.101(d)) The amount of tax collected is determined by applying the tax rate to the gross receipts received from sales. (86 Ill. Adm. Code 130.101)

Service occupation tax (SOT). The service occupation tax (SOT) taxes revenue from transfers of property during the performance of a service, not revenue from the actual service performed. Persons who transfer or sell tangible personal property as an incident to a sale of a service, called servicemen, are liable for SOT. (35 ILCS 110/3-55; 86 Ill. Adm. Code 160.101(g); 86 Ill. Adm. Code 140.120; 86 Ill. Adm. Code 140.201(f))Servicemen generally reimburse themselves by collecting service use tax from customers. (35 ILCS 110/3-55; 86 Ill. Adm. Code 160.101(g)) The SOT collected is determined by applying the tax rate to the selling price of tangible personal property transferred as part of the service. (35 ILCS 110/3-55; 86 Ill. Adm. Code 160.101(g))

Local service occupation tax. A serviceman who remits Illinois SOT on a transaction is also liable for local SOT if the serviceman's place of business is in a taxing jurisdiction. (86 Ill. Adm. Code Sec. 230.115; 86 Ill. Adm. Code Sec. 280.115; 86 Ill. Adm. Code Sec. 330.115; 86 Ill. Adm. Code Sec. 380.115; 86 Ill. Adm. Code Sec. 640.120)

Presumption of taxability. All sales of tangible personal property are presumed subject to sales tax and SOT. The person required to remit the tax has the burden of proving that a transaction is not taxable. (35 ILCS 120/7; 35 ILCS 115/4)

Retailers' occupation (sales) tax and service occupation tax (SOT) definitions.

Retailer. A "retailer" is every person engaged in the business of making sales at retail. A person who holds itself out as making retail sales or who habitually makes such sales is considered to be a retailer. (35 ILCS 105/2; 35 ILCS 120/1; 86 Ill. Adm. Code 130.115)

Sale at retail. A "sale at retail" includes:

— the transfer of tangible personal property to a buyer for use or consumption in exchange for consideration (35 ILCS 120/1; 86 Ill. Adm. Code 130.201);

— the transfer of tangible personal property to a buyer when the buyer will transfer the property for no charge (35 ILCS 120/1; 86 Ill. Adm. Code 130.201); and

— the transfer of possession of tangible personal property to a buyer where the seller retains title to the property. (35 ILCS 120/1; 86 Ill. Adm. Code 130.201)

Purchaser. For sales and use tax purposes, a "purchaser" is anyone who acquires tangible personal property in a retail sale. (35 ILCS 105/2; 35 ILCS 120/1; 86 Ill. Adm. Code 150.201) For purposes of SOT and SUT, a "purchaser" is anyone who acquires property through a purchase of services. (35 ILCS 110/2; 86 Ill. Adm. Code 160.105)

Serviceman. A serviceman is a person who sells tangible personal property as an incident to a sale of service.

Which transactions are generally subject to use tax in Illinois?

Illinois imposes use tax on persons who use tangible personal property in Illinois, and service use tax (SUT) on persons who transfer tangible personal property in connection with a service.

Use tax. Illinois use tax is imposed on the use in Illinois of tangible personal property purchased anywhere from a retailer. (35 ILCS 105/3; 86 Ill. Adm. Code 150.101; 86 Ill. Adm. Code 150.125) Purchasers are liable for use tax and remit it to the seller or directly to the state. (86 Ill. Adm. Code 150.130) A buyer is not liable for use tax on a purchase if the seller of the property would not be liable for Illinois sales tax. (35 ILCS 105/3-65; 86 Ill. Adm. Code 150.101; 86 Ill. Adm. Code 150.301)

Example: A purchaser is not liable for use tax when it buys tangible personal property from a seller that is not liable for sales tax on the sale because the seller qualifies as an isolated or occasional seller.

Service use tax (SUT). Service use tax (SUT) is imposed on the use in Illinois of real or tangible personal property received as an incident to a purchase of a service from a serviceman. (35 ILCS 110/3; 86 Ill. Adm. Code 160.101) Purchasers are liable for SUT and remit it to the seller or directly to the state. (35 ILCS 110/3-55; 86 Ill. Adm. Code 160.101(g)) A buyer is not liable for SUT on a purchase if the seller of the service would not be liable for the SOT. (35 ILCS 110/3-55)

Presumption of taxability. The sale of property for delivery to a person residing or engaged in business in Illinois is presumed to be subject to use tax and SUT. (35 ILCS 105/4; 35 ILCS 110/4)

Use tax and service use tax (SUT) definitions.

Use. "Use" is the exercise of any right or power over tangible personal property incident to the ownership of that property. Use does not include the sale of property in the regular course of business. (35 ILCS 105/2; 35 ILCS 110/2; 86 Ill. Adm. Code 150.201; 86 Ill. Adm. Code 160.105) Use also does not include incorporating property into a product as an ingredient, such as during manufacturing, when the other property will be sold outside Illinois. (35 ILCS 105/2; 35 ILCS 110/2)

Purchased from a serviceman. "Purchased from a serviceman" means the acquisition of the ownership of, or title to, tangible personal property through a sale of service.

Retailer. "Retailer" means and includes every person engaged in the business of making sales at retail.

Sale at retail. A "sale at retail" includes the transfer of tangible personal property to a buyer for use in exchange for consideration. (35 ILCS 105/2; 86 Ill. Adm. Code 150.201)

Does Illinois follow destination or origin based sourcing for general retail sales?

In general, Illinois uses destination sourcing for interstate sales and origin sourcing for intrastate sales. (86 Ill. Adm. Code Sec. 130.605(a); 86 Ill. Adm. Code Sec. 140.501(a)) Illinois also provides rules for determining the location of a sale.

Sourcing rules. Illinois specifies the locations of numerous types of sales transactions in order to determine which jurisdiction has authority to tax the transaction for sales tax, use tax, service occupation tax (SOT), service use tax (SUT), and local sales tax purposes. Under the rules, a seller's liability for tax is based on where the seller's predominant and most important selling activities take place. In some instances, Illinois provides presumptions and factors to help determine the jurisdiction where those selling activities take place. If the location cannot be determined based on presumptive rules or sales activities factors, location is either the location of inventory or the seller's headquarters.

Locations presumed by rule. Business locations for the following types of sales are presumed based on selling activities common to those businesses.

Over-the-counter sales. Over-the-counter sales occur at the business location where the buyer is present and pays for the property. The buyer may take possession of the property at the location or the retailer may deliver the property to the buyer.

Vending machine sales. Vending machine sales occur at the vending machine's location. (35 ILCS 120/2-12)

Sales from vehicles carrying an uncommitted stock of goods. The business location for a sale of goods from a vehicle carrying the stock of goods is the place at which the sale and delivery is made.

Sales into Illinois. The business location for an out-of-state seller that has inventory in Illinois is the place where the property is located at the time it is sold.

Sales over the phone, in writing or via the Internet. Sales of property over the phone, in writing or via the Internet occur at the business location where the buyer takes possession of the property.

Leases with an option to purchase. The business location for sellers of tangible personal property to a nominal lessee or bailee for use or consumption under a conditional sales agreement is the physical location of the property at the time the parties enter into the conditional sales agreement.

Sales of coal or other minerals. A producer of minerals mined in Illinois is engaged in the business of selling at the place where the coal or other mineral is extracted. "Minerals" include coal, oil, sand, stone taken from a quarry, gravel, and any other thing commonly regarded as a mineral and extracted from the earth.

(86 Ill. Adm. Code Sec. 220.115; 86 Ill. Adm. Code Sec. 270.115; 86 Ill. Adm. Code Sec. 320.115; 86 Ill. Adm. Code Sec. 370.115; 86 Ill. Adm. Code Sec. 395.115; 86 Ill. Adm. Code Sec. 630.120; 86 Ill. Adm. Code Sec. 670.115; 86 Ill. Adm. Code Sec. 690.115; 86 Ill. Adm. Code Sec. 693.115; 86 Ill. Adm. Code Sec. 695.115)

Location based on "selling activities" and other factors. When none of the transaction specific presumptions apply, "primary selling activities" factors are used to determine location. If a seller engages in three or more primary selling activities in one location for a sale, the seller is liable for tax in that location. "Secondary selling activities" factors are provided to help determine the business location when no more than two primary selling activities occur in any one jurisdiction. When location cannot be determined applying both primary and secondary factors, the sale is deemed to take place where the seller's inventory or its headquarters is located, depending on where more selling activities occur. If the location cannot be determined with the selling activities factors at all, the business location of the sale is the seller's headquarters. (86 Ill. Adm. Code Sec. 220.115; 86 Ill. Adm. Code Sec. 270.115; 86 Ill. Adm. Code Sec. 320.115; 86 Ill. Adm. Code Sec. 370.115; 86 Ill. Adm. Code Sec. 395.115; 86 Ill. Adm. Code Sec. 630.120; 86 Ill. Adm. Code Sec. 670.115; 86 Ill. Adm. Code Sec. 690.115; 86 Ill. Adm. Code Sec. 693.115; 86 Ill. Adm. Code Sec. 695.115)

"Primary selling" activities. "Primary selling" activities factors include the location: 1) of sales personnel, 2) where the seller obligates itself to make the sale, 3) where payment is tendered and received or from which invoices are issued, 4) of inventory, and 5) of the retailer's headquarters.

"Secondary selling" activities. "Secondary selling" activities factors include the location of marketing and solicitation and the location of title passage.

(86 Ill. Adm. Code Sec. 220.115; 86 Ill. Adm. Code Sec. 270.115; 86 Ill. Adm. Code Sec. 320.115; 86 Ill. Adm. Code Sec. 370.115; 86 Ill. Adm. Code Sec. 395.115; 86 Ill. Adm. Code Sec. 630.120; 86 Ill. Adm. Code Sec. 670.115; 86 Ill. Adm. Code Sec. 690.115; 86 Ill. Adm. Code Sec. 693.115; 86 Ill. Adm. Code Sec. 695.115)

Sourcing of local taxes. Sourcing rules are provided for specific local taxes, including:

Home Rule County Retailers' Occupation Tax

Home Rule Municipal Retailers' Occupation Tax Regulations

Regional Transportation Authority Retailers' Occupation Tax

Metro East Mass Transit District Retailers' Occupation Tax

County Water Commission Retailers' Occupation Tax

Special County Retailers' Occupation Tax for Public Safety

Salem Civic Center Retailers' Occupation Tax

Non-Home Rule Municipal Retailers' Occupation Tax

County Motor Fuel Tax

Interstate commerce. Sales of property or services in Illinois where the property or services are delivered outside Illinois generally are not taxable. (86 Ill. Adm. Code Sec. 130.605(c); 86 Ill. Adm. Code Sec. 140.501(b)) To support an exemption for sales made in interstate commerce, the seller or serviceman must keep records showing that it was obligated to make delivery out-of-state and that an out-of-state delivery occurred. (86 Ill. Adm. Code Sec. 130.605(f); 86 Ill. Adm. Code Sec. 140.501(c))

Aspects of a sale that are not relevant when sourcing sales made in interstate commerce include:

— where title to the property passes,

— where the contract of sale or contract to sell is negotiated and executed, and

— the purchaser's residence.

(86 Ill. Adm. Code Sec. 130.605(e); 86 Ill. Adm. Code Sec. 140.501(b)

Does Illinois provide any other information concerning the general applicability of sales and use taxes?

Yes. Illinois provides information on various aspects of sales and use tax.

Rates. Illinois has a general sales tax rate, as well as various local sales and use tax rates.

Due dates. For a discussion of due dates, see Returns, Payments, and Due Dates.

Filing and payment requirements. For a discussion of filing and payment requirements, see Returns, Payments, and Due Dates.

Services. Services are exempt from sales and use tax unless specifically identified as taxable.

Tax holidays. Illinois does not currently have any tax holidays.

Credits. Illinois provides various credits, including a credit for tax paid to out-of-state jurisdictions.

Local taxes. Counties, cities, and certain school districts may impose local sales and use taxes. For a discussion of local taxes and rates, see Local Tax Rates.

[¶60-025] Nexus--Doing Business in State

Whether an obligation to collect Illinois sales or use tax attaches to a sale by an out-of-seller is determined by a combination of federal and state restrictions. At the federal level, the determination revolves around whether a nexus (or connection) between the sale and Illinois can be established. If there is sufficient nexus, it then must be determined whether the seller qualifies as a "retailer engaged in business" in the state.

What is sales and use tax nexus?

In the state tax area, nexus is an important concern for companies that have a multistate presence because it is a threshold issue that must be evaluated to determine whether a business has tax registration, filing, collection, and remittance obligations in a particular jurisdiction. "Sales and use tax nexus" refers to the amount and type of business activity that must be present before the business is subject to the state's taxing authority.

State tax nexus considerations differ by tax type and jurisdiction, and there has been limited guidance from tax authorities as to when nexus conclusively exists. State nexus statutes are subject to federal constitutional restrictions.

In a series of cases, the U.S. Supreme Court established a general rule of "substantial nexus" which required an out-of-state seller to have a physical presence in a state before that state could require the seller to register and collect and remit sales or use taxes. Physical presence can be created by employees or other agents, property owned or leased in the state, or other factors. There are many gray areas when it comes to determining whether nexus conclusively exists, particularly for e-commerce.

However, in *South Dakota v. Wayfair, Inc.*, 585 U.S. ___ (2018), the U.S. Supreme Court held that physical presence is no longer required to establish substantial nexus. Rather, economic and virtual contacts in a state and minimum in-state sales thresholds can establish sales and use tax nexus.

Planning Note: Nexus determinations are based on a taxpayer's specific set of facts. Taxpayers must carefully evaluate whether specific activities or types of contact create/establish nexus in each state in which they do business, as well as how frequently such contacts must occur in order to create tax nexus. A certain combination of business activities or a specific aspect of an activity may result in a different conclusion. To have a complete picture of all tax reporting requirements, multistate businesses should conduct a nexus review. A nexus review helps businesses understand their exposure and avoid audit situations.

South Dakota v. Wayfair. In a 5 to 4 decision, the U.S. Supreme Court held that *Quill Corp. v. North Dakota*, 504 U.S. 298 (1992), and *National Bellas Hess, Inc. v. Department of Revenue of Ill.*, 386 U.S. 753 (1967), are overruled because *Quill's* physical presence rule is unsound and incorrect. As a result, physical presence is no longer required to establish sales and use tax nexus.

The Court held that the *Complete Auto* (*Complete Auto Transit v. Brady*, 430 U.S. 274 (1977)) substantial nexus requirement with the taxing state is satisfied based on both the economic and virtual contacts the respondents have with the state. As a result of this decision, states are now free to levy taxes on sales of goods and services regardless of whether the seller has a physical presence in the state. Due process requirements, unrelated to those required by the "Commerce Clause" of the Constitution still apply, as do other nexus tests of the Commerce Clause. Since the *Wayfair* decision was issued, many states have enacted economic nexus and/or marketplace nexus thresholds. (*South Dakota v. Wayfair, Inc.*, 585 U.S. ___ (2018))

How is nexus established in Illinois?

Any "retailer" or "retailer maintaining a place of business" in Illinois is engaged in making a "sale at retail", has nexus with Illinois, and must collect use tax. (35 ILCS 105/3-45)

Compliance Alert: Illinois has economic nexus and marketplace nexus provisions for sales tax collection.

New Developments: Trade show activities can create sales tax nexus with Illinois. Sales made at a trade show by an out-of-state retailer are subject to both state and local tax. The Illinois Department of Revenue has issued a regulation discussing sales tax registration and collection requirements for remote sellers who make sales at Illinois trade shows. (86 Ill. Adm. Code 150.802)

A "retailer maintaining a place of business in this state" is a retailer:

• having or maintaining within Illinois, directly or by a subsidiary, an office, distribution house, sales house, warehouse or other place of business, or any agent or other representative operating within Illinois under the authority of the retailer or its subsidiary, irrespective of whether such place of business or "agent" or other representative is located here permanently or temporarily, or whether such retailer or subsidiary is licensed to do business in Illinois. However, the ownership of property that is located at the premises of a printer with which the retailer has contracted for printing and that consists of the final printed product, property that becomes a part of the final printed product, or copy from which the printed product is produced shall not result in the retailer being deemed to have or maintain an office, distribution house, sales house, warehouse, or other place of business Illinois;

- having a contract with a person located in Illinois under which the person, for a commission or other consideration based upon the sale of 1 property by the retailer, directly or indirectly refers customers to the retailer by providing a promotional code or other mechanism that allows the retailer to track purchases referred by the person. Examples of mechanisms that allow the retailer to track purchases include the use of a link on the person's website, promotional codes distributed through the person's hand-delivered or mailed material, and promotional codes distributed by the person through radio or other broadcast media;

- soliciting orders for tangible personal property by means of a telecommunication or television shopping system (which utilizes toll free numbers) which is intended by the retailer to be broadcast by cable television or other means of broadcasting, to consumers located in Illinois;

- soliciting orders for tangible personal property by means of advertising which is disseminated primarily to consumers located in Illinois and only secondarily to bordering jurisdictions, pursuant to a contract with a broadcaster or publisher located in Illinois;

- soliciting orders for tangible personal property by mail if the solicitations are substantial and recurring and if the retailer benefits from any banking, financing, debt collection, telecommunication, or marketing activities occurring in Illinois or benefits from the location in Illinois of authorized installation, servicing, or repair facilities;

- that is owned or controlled by the same interests that own or control any retailer engaging in business in the same or similar line of business in Illinois;

- having a franchisee or licensee operating under its trade name if the franchisee or licensee is required to collect tax;

- soliciting orders for tangible personal property by means of advertising which is transmitted or distributed over a cable television system in Illinois, pursuant to a contract with a cable television operator located in Illinois; or

- engaging in activities in Illinois, which activities in the state in which the retail business engaging in such activities is located would constitute maintaining a place of business in that state.

(35 ILCS 105/2; 86 Ill. Adm. Code 150.201)

An "agent" includes anyone acting under a principal's authority in an agency capacity. (86 Ill. Adm. Code 150.201)

Service use tax. Rules similar to the use tax rules exist for collecting service use tax (SUT) by servicemen "maintaining a place of business in the state." (35 ILCS 110/2; 86 Ill. Adm. Code 160.130)

Transient merchants. A transient merchant may be required to make a daily report of the amount of its Illinois sales to the Illinois Department of Revenue and make daily payments of the amount of sales and use tax due. A transient merchant, for tax reporting and paying purposes, includes:

- any person engaged in the business of selling tangible personal property at retail as a concessionaire, or

- any other type of seller at any fair, art show, flea market, or similar exhibition.

(35 ILCS 120/3)

Does Illinois have economic nexus?

Yes. Illinois has economic nexus provisions. Illinois requires remote retailers to collect tax when they meet certain sales thresholds in Illinois. (35 ILCS 105/2; 35 ILCS 110/2; 35 ILCS 120/2; 86 Ill. Adm. Code 150.803) Effective January 1, 2020, marketplace facilitators also have nexus if they meet similar economic thresholds (discussed below). (*Informational Bulletin FY 2020-18*)

Remote Retailer Threshold Requirements. Remote retailers will be liable for collecting use and service use tax if one of two sales thresholds are met for 12 months. They meet the threshold for a given period if:

- their sales of property to customers in Illinois were $100,000 or more; or

- they enter into 200 or more sales transactions in Illinois.

The legislature has added the sales thresholds to other activities that establish sales tax nexus in Illinois, such as maintaining a warehouse or advertising directly to Illinois residents. (35 ILCS 105/2; 35 ILCS 110/2)

Effective July 1, 2020, the economic nexus thresholds trigger a retailers' occupation tax collection requirement for remote retailers in place of the use tax collection requirement. (35 ILCS 120/2; 35 ILCS 105/2)

When the Thresholds Apply. Each quarter, remote retailers must determine whether they meet either threshold. If a retailer meets a threshold for a 12-month period, it are required to collect tax and submit returns for one year. If the retailer meets one of the thresholds for that year, the retailer:

- continues to collect tax; and

- reviews its Illinois sales each year to see whether it meets one of the thresholds.

If, after one year, the retailer does not meet a threshold for that year, it returns to reviewing its sales on a quarterly basis. (35 ILCS 105/2; 35 ILCS 110/2)

Sourcing. Effective January 1, 2021, remote retailers that satisfy an economic nexus threshold are required to use destination sourcing rather than origin sourcing for local retailers' occupation tax rate purposes.

Marketplace Facilitators. In general, a marketplace facilitator that meets one of two economic thresholds for nexus in Illinois is retailer under sales and use tax law. The thresholds are similar to existing thresholds for out-of-state sellers:

- the cumulative gross receipts from sales of tangible personal property to purchasers in Illinois by the marketplace facilitator and by marketplace sellers selling through the marketplace are $100,000 or more; or

- the marketplace facilitator and marketplace sellers selling through the marketplace cumulatively enter into 200 or more separate transactions for the sale of tangible personal property to purchasers in Illinois.

(35 ILCS 105/2d; 35 ILCS 110/2d) (86 Ill. Adm. Code 150.804) (*Informational Bulletin FY 2020-18*)

Compliance Alert: The IDOR issued a compliance alert to clarify the tax obligations of marketplace sellers making sales through a marketplace that are subject to the retailers' occupation tax (ROT).

Background. Effective January 1, 2020, legislation generally shifted the obligation to collect and remit Illinois use tax (UT) from the marketplace seller to the marketplace facilitator. When the tax required to be remitted to the Illinois Department of Revenue (IDOR) for a marketplace sale is UT, a marketplace facilitator that has economic nexus is now the retailer for that sale and the marketplace seller is not the retailer for that sale. The marketplace facilitator, not the marketplace seller, is required to collect and remit UT.

When the tax required to be remitted for a marketplace sale is ROT, the marketplace seller is the retailer for that sale, not the marketplace facilitator. The marketplace seller is required to be registered, file a return, and remit ROT for that sale (including all applicable local taxes). The marketplace facilitator is not the retailer and has no legal authority to remit ROT for that sale. Most often, marketplace sellers incur ROT when purchases are filled from inventory in Illinois.

Some marketplace facilitators have notified their marketplace sellers that they will collect and remit UT on all marketplace sales, but they will not calculate and collect tax on any ROT sales made by marketplace sellers. The tax calculation systems used by many marketplace facilitators cannot calculate both the ROT and UT at the time of sale. Consequently, when ROT is due, the marketplace facilitator is unable to collect the correct amount of tax from the purchaser at the time of sale and transmit it to the marketplace seller, so that they can remit it to the IDOR. Despite these limitations, the marketplace seller remains liable for all ROT.

IDOR solution. Marketplace facilitators report that they are working to correct the limitations in their tax calculation systems. In the meantime, however, IDOR advises the following:

- If the tax required to be remitted for a marketplace sale is ROT, marketplace sellers, not the marketplace facilitator, are the retailer for this sale. The marketplace seller must register or remain registered to remit this tax to IDOR.

- IDOR has no authority to provide marketplace sellers with a credit against their ROT liability for the tax that was remitted to IDOR by the marketplace facilitator.

- Consequently, marketplace sellers remain liable for the entire ROT liability, including applicable local taxes.

(Compliance Alert - CA-2020-3 (N-02/20), Illinois Department of Revenue, February 2020)

A "marketplace" is a physical or electronic place, forum, platform, application, or other method by which a marketplace seller sells or offers to sell items tangible personal property. (35 ILCS 120/1; 86 Ill. Adm. Code 150.804) (*Informational Bulletin FY 2020-18*)

Example: Examples of marketplaces include, but are not limited to, auctions, Internet marketplace platforms on which tangible personal property is offered for sale; antique malls, home shopping networks selling tangible personal property over television, cable or satellite networks; or consignment shops selling tangible personal property on behalf of numerous persons.

A "marketplace facilitator" means a person who, pursuant to an agreement with an unrelated third-party marketplace seller, directly or indirectly through one or more affiliates, facilitates a sale by an unrelated third-party marketplace seller by doing both of the following:

- listing or advertising tangible personal property for sale by the marketplace seller in a marketplace; and

- either directly or indirectly, through agreements or arrangements with third parties, collecting payment from the customer and transmitting that payment to the marketplace seller regardless of whether the marketplace facilitator receives compensation or other consideration in exchange for its services.

(35 ILCS 120/1; 86 Ill. Adm. Code 150.804) (*Informational Bulletin FY 2020-18*)

A "marketplace seller" is a person who sells or offers to sell tangible personal property through a marketplace operated by an unrelated third-party marketplace facilitator. (35 ILCS 120/1; 35 ILCS 105/2d; 86 Ill. Adm. Code 150.804) (*Informational Bulletin FY 2020-18*)

The thresholds apply to marketplace facilitators that facilitate sales:

- directly; or

- indirectly through affiliates.

Each quarter, a marketplace facilitator must determine if it meets either threshold for the prior 12 month period. If it does meet a threshold, the marketplace facilitator must collect tax and file returns for one year. At the end of that year, the marketplace facilitator will review sales revenues and transactions from the prior 12 months to see if it is still required to collect tax. (86 Ill. Adm. Code 150.804)

A marketplace facilitator that meets a threshold will be a retailer in Illinois subject to all the sales and use tax requirements of a retailer registered in Illinois.

A marketplace facilitator required to collect Illinois tax must certify to each marketplace seller that it is a retailer required to collect sales and use tax in Illinois. The marketplace seller must give the facilitator the information it needs to correctly collect and remit taxers for each sale. If tax is not collected on a sale because one party failed to meet the requirements for sharing information with each other, the other party will be liable for the tax due.

Calculating the thresholds. All sales of tangible personal property, even if they are exempt from tax, must be included for purposes of calculating the thresholds, except:

- sales for resale;

- sales of property that are required to be registered with an Illinois agency, including motor vehicles, watercraft, aircraft, and trailers, when these sales are made from locations outside Illinois to Illinois purchasers; and

- sales made through the marketplace on behalf of a marketplace seller or by a marketplace facilitator that are subject to retailers' occupation tax.

(86 Ill. Adm. Code 150.804) (*Informational Bulletin FY 2020-18*)

A regulation provides a list of obligations of marketplace facilitators and obligations of marketplace sellers.

Registering in Illinois. Additional guidance advises taxpayers on whether the thresholds are met. It discusses:

- what types of sales are not included in the thresholds;

- how to register;

- the use tax rate; and

- how to file returns to report use tax.

Does Illinois have click-through nexus?

Yes. Illinois has click-through nexus provisions. Out-of-state retailers and servicemen that satisfy the following criteria are presumed to be maintaining a place of business in Illinois and are required to register, collect, and remit tax on all of their sales to Illinois customers:

- the out-of-state retailer has a contract with a person located in Illinois;

- under the contract, the person in Illinois directly or indirectly refers potential customers to the retailer and the retailer pays to the person in Illinois a commission or other consideration based on the sale of tangible personal property by the retailer;

- the person in Illinois provides to the potential customers a promotional code or other mechanism that allows the retailer to track the purchases made by these customers. Examples of mechanisms that allow the retailer to track purchases referred by such persons include but are not limited to the use of a link on the person's Internet website, promotional codes distributed through the person's hand-delivered or mailed material, and promotional codes distributed by the person through radio or other broadcast media; and

- the cumulative gross receipts from sales of tangible personal property by the retailer to customers who are referred to the retailer by all persons in Illinois under such contracts exceed $10,000 during the preceding 4 quarterly periods ending on the last day of March, June, September, and December.

(35 ILCS 105/2; 35 ILCS 110/2)

A retailer meeting these requirements is presumed to be maintaining a place of business in Illinois but may rebut this presumption by submitting proof that the referrals or other activities pursued within Illinois by such persons were not sufficient to meet the nexus standards of the U.S. Constitution during the preceding four quarterly periods. (35 ILCS 105/2; 35 ILCS 110/2)

Does Illinois have affiliate nexus?

Yes. A retailer maintains a place of business in Illinois when the retailer:

- sells the same or substantially similar line of products as the person located in Illinois and does so using an identical or substantially similar name, trade name, or trademark as the person located in Illinois; and

- provides a commission or other consideration to the person located in Illinois based on the sale of property by the retailer.

This rules applies only if the cumulative gross receipts from sales of tangible personal property by the retailer to customers in Illinois under all such contracts exceed $10,000 during the preceding 4 quarterly periods ending on the last day of March, June, September, and December.

[¶60-100]

RATES

[¶60-110] Rate of Tax

The retailers' occupation (sales) tax, use tax, service occupation tax, and service use tax are imposed at the state rate of 6.25%, except as noted below. (35 ILCS 105/3-10; 35 ILCS 110/3-10; 35 ILCS 115/3-10; 35 ILCS 120/2-10; 86 Ill. Adm. Code 130.101(b); 86 Ill. Adm. Code 140.101(b); 86 Ill. Adm. Code 150.105; 86 Ill. Adm. Code 160.101(c))

A regulation details the methods used for calculating tax on sales of items subject to different tax rates. (86 Ill. Adm. Code 150.525)

For county, municipal, and other local tax rates that are imposed in addition to the state rate, see ¶61-735 Local Rates.

• *Food, medicine, and medical equipment*

The rate of tax imposed on food for human consumption off the premises where it is sold is 1%, except for alcoholic beverages, food consisting of or infused with adult use cannabis, soft drinks, and food prepared for immediate consumption. Medicines, drugs, and medical appliances for human use and insulin, urine testing materials, syringes, and needles used by diabetics are also taxed at the rate of 1%. Modifications to a motor vehicle for the purpose of rendering it usable by a disabled person are subject to the 1% sales and use tax rate. (35 ILCS 105/3-10; 35 ILCS 110/3-10; 35 ILCS 115/3-10; 35 ILCS 120/2-10; 86 Ill. Adm. Code 130.310(a); 86 Ill. Adm. Code 130.311; 86 Ill. Adm. Code 140.101(c); 86 Ill. Adm. Code 140.126)

The service occupation tax and the service use tax are imposed at the rate of 1% on food prepared for immediate consumption and transferred incident to a sale of service by an entity licensed under the Hospital Licensing Act, the Nursing Home Care Act, the MR/DD Community Care Act, or the Child Care Act of 1993. (35 ILCS 110/3-10; 35 ILCS 115/3-10)

For information on food items that qualify for the reduced tax rate, see ¶60-390 Food and Grocery Items.

For information on medicines, drugs, and medical appliances that qualify for the reduced tax rate, see ¶60-520 Medical, Dental, and Optical Supplies and Drugs.

• *Illinois rental purchase agreement occupation and use taxes*

The rental purchase agreement occupation tax (rental sales tax) and the rental purchase agreement use tax (rental use tax) are each imposed on a consumer's use of rented merchandise at a rate of 6.25%. (35 ILCS 180/10; 35 ILCS 180/15)

For further discussion, see ¶60-460 Leases and Rentals.

• *Illinois hotel operators' occupation tax*

The Illinois hotel operators' occupation tax is imposed at a rate of 5% of 94% of the gross rental receipts, plus an additional tax of 1% of 94% of gross rental receipts. (35 ILCS 145/3)

For further discussion, see ¶60-480 Lodging.

• *Illinois automobile renting occupation and use tax*

A 5% tax is imposed on persons or companies engaged in the business of renting automobiles in Illinois when the rental is for a period of a year or less. A 5% tax is also imposed on the privilege of using in the state an automobile that is rented from an auto rental business for a period of a year or less. (35 ILCS 155/2; 35 ILCS 155/3; 35 ILCS 155/4)

For further discussion of the tax, see ¶ 60-570 Motor Vehicles.

• *Parking excise tax*

A parking excise tax is imposed at the rate of: (1) 6% of the purchase price for a parking space paid for on an hourly, daily, or weekly basis; and (2) 9% of the purchase price for a parking space paid for on a monthly or annual basis. (Uncodified Sec. 10-10, P.A. 101-31 (S.B. 690)) (86 Ill. Adm. Code 195.110) (*Informational Bulletin FY 2020-07*)

• *Determination of tax rate when rate changes*

The applicable tax rate is that rate in effect at the time tangible personal property is delivered, unless receipts were received by the seller before the rate change and tax paid on those receipts at the rate in effect at that time. (86 Ill. Adm. Code 130.101(a)(1); 86 Ill. Adm. Code 150.115(a))

Construction contracts.—Property delivered to a construction contractor after the effective date of a rate increase for use in performing a binding construction contract entered into before the effective date of the rate increase is taxed at the rate in effect before the increase, provided the contractor is legally unable to shift the burden of the rate increase to the customer. (86 Ill. Adm. Code 130.101(a)(2); 86 Ill. Adm. Code 150.115(b))

[¶60-200]

TAXABILITY OF PERSONS AND TRANSACTIONS

[¶60-230] Admissions, Entertainment, and Dues

Admission charges to places of public entertainment or amusement such as movie theaters, operas, baseball parks, golf courses, bowling alleys, amusement parks, and carnivals are not taxable. However, persons selling refreshments, beverages, and other property to purchasers at such places of amusement must remit ROT on such sales to the Department of Revenue. (86 Ill. Adm. Code Sec. 130.2030)

• *Cover charges and minimum charges*

Cover charges are not subject to the ROT and UT if made exclusively for the privilege of occupying space in an eating place and if payment of the charge does not entitle a patron to use or consume any food or beverage. However, minimum charges imposed by eating establishments that entitle patrons to be served food or beverages are subject to tax. (86 Ill. Adm. Code Sec. 130.2145(c); 86 Ill. Adm. Code Sec. 150.1201)

• *State and county fairs*

Sales of tangible personal property by Illinois state or county fair concessionaires are subject to the ROT and UT. A concessionaire may be required to make a daily report and payment of tax to the Department of Revenue. (35 ILCS 120/3; 86 Ill. Adm. Code Sec. 150.1201; 86 Ill. Adm. Code Sec. 130.2045)

Property purchased by a nonprofit Illinois county fair association and utilized to conduct, operate, or promote the fair is not subject to tax. (35 ILCS 105/3-5; 35 ILCS 110/3-5; 35 ILCS 115/3-5; 35 ILCS 120/2-5; 86 Ill. Adm. Code Sec. 130.120(z))

• *Cook County amusement tax*

Cook County amusement tax.—Pursuant to its home rule powers, Cook County enacted the Cook County Amusement Tax Ordinance. The tax is levied upon the privilege of participating in or witnessing an amusement in addition to all other taxes imposed by Cook County, the state, or by any other municipal tax. (Cook County Amusement Tax Ordinance Sec. 74-393) The ordinance made it the duty of "every owner, manager, or operator of an amusement or of a place where an amusement is being held" to act as a trustee for the County, to register to collect the tax, and then to collect and remit the tax to the Cook County Department of Revenue. (Cook County Amusement Tax Ordinance Sec. 74-394; Cook County Amusement Tax Ordinance Sec. 74-395)

The tax is imposed on patrons of certain amusements taking place within the county for the privilege to enter, witness, or view such amusements. "Amusement" is defined to include any exhibition, performance, or show for entertainment purposes, including any theatrical, dramatic, musical, or spectacular performance; promotional, motion picture, flower, poultry, or animal show; animal act; circus; rodeo; athletic contest; sport; game; or similar exhibition. (Cook County Amusement Tax Ordinance Sec. 74-391)

CCH Comment: An Illinois Appellate Court held that Cook County could impose amusement tax on additional, separate fees charged with purchases of tickets for club seats or luxury suites to watch Bears home football games in Soldier Field. For the provision of special amenities, the Bears football club charged mandatory club privilege fees with the purchase of a club seat ticket and annual license fees with the licensing of luxury suites, which include seating. The amenities associated with club seats and luxury suites, for which the ticket holders are willing to pay and that are not sold separately from the seats to which the amenities apply, are included in the admission fees or other charges paid by these ticket holders for the privilege of entering, witnessing or viewing a Bears home game. (*Chicago Bears Football Club v. The Cook County Department of Revenue, Appellate Court of Illinois*, First District, 2014 IL App (1st) 122892, August 6, 2014)

Rate of Cook County tax.—The Cook County amusement tax rate is 3% of the admission fees or other charges paid. (Cook County Amusement Tax Ordinance Sec. 74-392)

Exemptions.—For purposes of the tax, the term "amusement" does not include raffles, intertrack wagering facilities, automatic amusement devices, or participatory activities offered for public or member participation such as amusement park rides and games, carnivals, bowling, billiards and pool games, dancing, tennis, golf, racquetball, swimming, weightlifting, and body building. (Cook County Amusement Tax Ordinance Sec. 74-392)

The following amusements are exempt from the tax:

(1) amusements conducted by certain nonprofit organizations and not benefiting any person such as religious, educational, and charitable institutions, societies for the prevention of cruelty to children or animals, societies for maintaining symphony orchestras, opera performances, and artistic presentations, and societies for civic improvement;

(2) amusements sponsored by nonprofit fraternal organizations not more than twice yearly;

(3) amusements conducted by organizations or persons in the United States armed services, National Guard, reserve officers' associations, war veterans' organizations, etc., that are organized in Illinois;

(4) amusements conducted by organizations for the purpose of benefiting police or fire department members, dependents, or heirs of members; and

(5) live performances of professional theater organizations. (Cook County Amusement Tax Ordinance Sec. 74-393)

The Cook County amusement tax has withstood a taxpayer's a challenge under the Equal Protection Clauses of the U.S. and Illinois Constitutions and the provision of the Illinois Constitution prohibiting home rule units from imposing an occupation tax, but failed to withstand the Uniformity Clause challenge.

CCH COMMENT: In *DeWoskin v. County of Cook*, the First District Appellate Court concluded that Cook County had failed to support its burden of proof that certain exemptions from the amusement tax did not violate the Uniformity Clause of the Illinois Constitution, for example, the exemptions for activities sponsored by nonprofit fraternal organizations and the U.S. armed services and similar organizations and the exemption for live professional theater performances. The case was remanded to the Illinois Circuit Court of Cook County for further proceedings regarding the Uniformity Clause challenge.

Although the county ordinance creates a tax to be collected and remitted by owners and operators of amusement places, the Village of Rosemont, which owns and operates amusement places (including the Rosemont Horizon, the Rosemont Theatre, and the Rosemont Convention Center), enacted Ordinance 97-1-8, pursuant to its home rule power, that exempted Village patrons from paying the county tax and that prohibited the Village's employees from collecting the county tax. In 1997, in *County of Cook v. Village of Rosemont and Jam Productions*, the First District Appellate Court vacated a temporary injunction granted by the trial court at the request of the Village of Rosemont as "improvidently granted" and remanded the matter to the trial court with instructions to consider whether the ordinance survived Illinois Constitution Section 6(a) analysis and to determine, by examination of Illinois Constitution Section 6(c), whether the Village of Rosemont ordinance "trumps" the County tax at the Village amusement facilities.

Subsequently, in 1999, in *County of Cook v. Village of Rosemont*, the First District Appellate Court concluded that the Village of Rosemont exceeded its home-rule powers when it enacted the ordinance. The court determined that the Village of Rosemont ordinance was unconstitutional.

• *Chicago amusement tax*

Chicago amusement tax.—The city of Chicago imposes an amusement tax upon the patrons of any amusements within the city on the admission fees or other charges to witness, to view, or to participate in such amusement, where separate fees and charges are imposed for each witnessing, viewing, or participation. The tax includes any paid television programming, whether transmitted by wire, cable, fiber optics, laser, microwave, radio, satellite or similar means. (Chicago Munic. Code Sec. 4-156-010) The basis of the tax excludes federal and state taxes. (Chicago Munic. Code Sec. 4-156-020)

Prior to January 1, 2015, the tax was imposed on persons who sell tickets for theatrics, shows, exhibitions, athletic events and other amusements within Chicago at a place other than the theater or location where the amusement is given or exhibited. (Chicago Munic. Code Sec. 4-156-033)

"Amusement" defined.—The amusement tax ordinance definition of "amusement" includes live theatrical, live musical, or other live cultural performances, but excludes amusements such as athletic events, races, or performances conducted at adult entertainment cabarets. (Chicago Munic. Code Sec. 4-156-010)

Taxable amusements.—Patrons of amusements are liable for tax on (1) any exhibition, performance, presentation or show for public entertainment, including but not limited to, any theatrical, dramatic, musical or spectacular performance, promotional show, motion picture show, flower, poultry or animal show, animal act, circus, rodeo, athletic contest, sport, game or similar exhibition such as boxing, wrestling, skating, dancing, swimming, racing or riding on animals or vehicles, baseball, basketball, softball, football, tennis, golf, hockey, track and field games, bowling, or billiard and pool games; (2) any entertainment or recreational activity offered for public participation or on a membership or other basis including but not limited to, carnivals, amusement park rides and games, bowling, billiards and pool games, dancing, tennis, racquetball, swimming, weight lifting, body building, or similar activities; or (3) any paid television programming, whether transmitted by wire, cable, fiber optics, laser, microwave, radio, satellite or similar means. (Chicago Munic. Code Sec. 4-156-010)

Amusement devices.—The city of Chicago also imposes an annual tax on automatic amusement devices. The rate of tax is $150 for nongambling-type automatic amusement devices, and $225 for gambling-type amusement devices. (Chicago Munic. Code Sec. 4-156-060)

Cable companies.—The Chicago Department of Revenue has issued a chart that lists various categories of cable company charges that are subject to or exempt from Chicago amusement tax and franchise fee. The tax and fee should be calculated net of bad debt, and the chart may not be inclusive of all categories of revenue. (*Informational Bulletin, Vol. 2008, No. 1*, Chicago Department of Revenue, January 2008)

Electronic delivery.—Rental charges paid for the privilege to witness, view or participate in amusements that are delivered electronically to a customer in Chicago are subject to the Chicago amusement tax, including:

- television shows, movies or videos;
- music; and
- games, online or otherwise.

(*Amusement Tax Ruling #5*, Chicago Department of Finance, June 9, 2015)

Payment of Chicago tax.—Every owner, manager or operator of an amusement or place of amusement and every reseller of tickets to an amusement are jointly responsible for collecting amusement tax from patrons and remitting the tax to the Chicago Department of Revenue not later than the last day of the following calendar month. (Chicago Munic. Code Sec. 4-156-030)

Reseller of tickets.—A reseller of tickets is required to collect and remit tax only on the portion of the ticket price that exceeds the amount that the reseller paid for of the tickets. It shall be presumed that the amount that the reseller paid for the tickets is the face amount of the tickets, unless the taxpayer or tax collector proves otherwise. (Chicago Munic. Code Sec. 4-156-030)

"Reseller's agent."—"The term "reseller's agent", as defined in the Chicago amusement tax ordinance, is repealed. (Chicago Munic. Code Sec. 4-156-010) The term includes an auctioneer, broker, or seller of tickets for amusements and applies whether the ticket is resold by bidding, consignment, or other means and whether the ticket is resold in person, at a site on the Internet, or otherwise. (Notice of Amendment, Chicago Department of Revenue, August 25, 2006)

Operator.—The term "operator" includes any person who sells or resells a ticket or other license to an amusement or who, receives or collects charged paid for the sale or resale of such a ticket or license, whether online or not. An operator may be engaged int eh business of selling tickets or in the business of facilitating the sale of tickets. (Chicago Munic. Code Sec. 4-156-010)

Online auction and consignment websites.—An ordinance was passed by the Chicago City Council that required collection and remittance of the Chicago amusement tax by online auction and consignment websites and similar businesses for tickets sold online for Chicago events. The tax is charged based on the difference between the original face value appearing on the ticket and the actual marked up sale price for which the ticket is sold. (*Notice*, Chicago Department of Revenue, May 24, 2006)

CCH Comment: The U.S. Court of Appeals for the Seventh Circuit affirmed the judgments of a federal district court that Chicago may not require Internet auction sites to collect the city's amusement tax on the difference between the original price of tickets resold on the sites and the resale price. The federal appeals court had certified Chicago's appeal to the Illinois Supreme Court for a resolution of the state law issues. The Supreme Court of Illinois agreed that Illinois law does not allow Chicago to collect its tax from the auction sites. (*City of Chicago v. StubHub, Inc.*, U.S. Court of Appeals, 7th Cir., No. 19-3432, November 23, 2011; *City of Chicago v. eBay, Inc.*, U.S. Court of Appeals, 7th Cir., No. 10-1144, November 23, 2011; *City of Chicago v. StubHub, Inc.*, Illinois Supreme Court, No. 111127, November 26, 2012)

Estimated tax payment option: A taxpayer or tax collector may pay or remit estimated tax amounts for any annual tax return equal to $1/12$th ($1/4$th where applicable) of the taxpayer's or tax collector's total liability for the 12-month period immediately preceding the current annual tax year, and the amount paid needs to be accompanied by a payment or remittance coupon. However, a taxpayer or tax collector may make estimated tax payments only if: (1) coupons or returns have been filed and amounts due for the annual return tax have been paid or remitted for the entire 12-month period immediately preceding the applicable annual tax year, (2) the total tax liability for the immediately preceding annual tax year was less than or equal to $2 million, and (3) actual liability during any three consecutive calendar months for the 12-month period immediately preceding the annual tax year was less than or equal to 50% of the total annual liability for the entire 12-month period. (Chicago Munic. Code Sec. 3-4-186)

Annual returns.—Returns are filed on an annual basis, on or before August 15 of each year to the Chicago Department of Revenue. (Chicago Munic. Code Sec. 3-4-186)

Exemptions.—The Chicago amusement tax does not apply to the following patrons and activities:

(1) patrons of automatic amusement machines;

(2) witnessing or participating in a stock show or business show not open to the general public;

(3) hiring a horse-drawn carriage;

(4) witnessing or participating in an amateur production or activity conducted by a not-for-profit organization operated exclusively for charitable, educational, or religious purposes;

(4a) participating in an amateur event where (a) the event takes place primarily on public property, (b) any required permits are obtained, (c) the event, or the organization conducting the event, is open to the public, (d) at least 100 individuals pay to participate in the event, and (e) the event will promote or celebrate the City, its civic institutions, or public activities or events in the City;

(5) witnessing or participating in any amusement that is sponsored or conducted by, and the proceeds of which inure exclusively to the benefit of (a) religious, educational, and charitable organizations, (b) organizations for the prevention of cruelty to children or animals, (c) civic improvement organizations, (d) fraternal organizations, legion posts, social, and political groups that conduct amusements,

sponsored not more often than twice yearly, (e) organizations or persons in the armed services of the United States, or National Guard organizations, reserve officers' associations, or organizations or posts of war veterans, or auxiliary units or societies of such posts or organizations, (f) organizations created to benefit the members, dependents, or heirs of members of the police or fire departments of any political subdivision of the state of Illinois, and (g) societies or organizations conducted solely to maintain symphony orchestras, opera performances, or artistic presentations, if certain conditions are met. (Chicago Munic. Code Sec. 4-156-020)

Generally, applications for exemption from the amusement tax must be filed with the Chicago Department of Finance at least 15 days prior to the holding of such amusement. (Chicago Munic. Code Sec. 4-156-020)

• *Peoria amusement tax*

Peoria amusement tax.—A tax is levied upon the privilege of participating in or witnessing an amusement within the city of Peoria at the rate of 2% of the admission fee charged, exclusive of other state or federal taxes. However the tax does not apply to any consumer attending or participating in an amusement owned by schools located in the city, to governmental units, or to nonprofit religious, educational, or charitable institutions and organizations. (Peoria Munic. Code Sec. 27-202)

Returns and payment.—Owners of each amusement must file tax returns and pay the Peoria amusement tax due on or before the 30th day of each month. (Peoria Munic. Code Sec. 27-204)

[¶60-240] Advertising

Sales of thermometers, pencils, pens, mirrors, silverware, notebooks, diaries, baby books, guest registers, brief cases, wallets, toys, paper weights, pins, watches, rulers, match books, playing cards, blotters, calendars, greeting cards, bags, napkins, dishes, handkerchiefs, and other merchandise bearing the name, monogram, trademark, or advertising inscriptions of the purchaser or of other persons are subject to the ROT and UT. (86 Ill. Adm. Code Sec. 130.1995)

• *Signs*

A sale of a sign is subject to the ROT and UT unless the sign is produced on special order and has value only to the particular purchaser who made the order. For example, signs that spell out "real estate" or "insurance" are subject to tax, while signs that spell out the purchaser's name or the name of the purchaser's product are not. (86 Ill. Adm. Code Sec. 130.2155) However, purchases of property by sign makers that are retransferred in the rendering of the sign production service are subject to the SOT and SUT, even if exempt from the ROT. (86 Ill. Adm. Code Sec. 140.140(q); 86 Ill. Adm. Code Sec. 160.145)

[¶60-250] Agriculture

Sales directly to the public of such items as milk and other dairy products, livestock, meats, hay, grain, vegetables, fruits, plants, flowers, eggs, and young trees are subject to the ROT and UT. Taxable sales include those by farmers from roadside stands or vending vehicles. However, agricultural products sold for purposes of resale are exempt. For example, sales by farmers of eggs to a grocer who purchases the eggs for resale are not subject to tax. (86 Ill. Adm. Code 130.1905)

Also, sales of bulls, stallions, and other breeding livestock for breeding purposes are not subject to tax. (86 Ill. Adm. Code 130.2100)

Association of agriculturists.—An association of agriculturists that conducts a market, "sales barn," or other place at which agricultural produce is sold on behalf of unknown principals must remit ROT on the sales. (86 Ill. Adm. Code 130.1905(c))

• *Machinery*

Sales of new or used farm machinery and equipment certified by the purchaser to be used primarily for production agriculture or state or federal agricultural programs, and replacement parts for such machinery and equipment, are exempt from the ROT, SOT, UT, and SUT. Equipment purchased for lease is included in the exemption. Motor vehicles required to be registered under the Illinois Vehicle Code are not exempt. (35 ILCS 105/3-5; 35 ILCS 110/3-5; 35 ILCS 115/3-5; 35 ILCS 120/2-5; 86 Ill. Adm. Code 130.120(t); 86 Ill. Adm. Code 130.305; 86 Ill. Adm. Code 140.125(n))

An exemption certificate stating that the property will be used primarily in production agriculture or state or federal agricultural programs must be presented to the retailer. (86 Ill. Adm. Code 130.305(m)) Farm machinery and equipment initially used in production agriculture for less than half of its useful life and then converted to nonexempt uses is subject to tax when converted.

"Farm machinery" includes tractors, combines, balers, irrigation equipment, and cattle and poultry feeders, but not improvements to real estate such as fences, barns, roads, grain bins, silos, and confinement buildings. (86 Ill. Adm. Code 130.305(i)) However, the exemption applies to certain machines purchased by farmers from retailers and installed as realty improvements, such as augers, grain dryers, automated livestock feeder bunks, automatic stock waterers, water pumps, specialty heating or lighting equipment, and special heaters. "Farm machinery" also includes husbandry tools and instruments, registered nurse wagons, and farm machinery and agricultural chemical and fertilizer spreaders. (35 ILCS 105/3-5; 35 ILCS 110/3-5; 35 ILCS 115/3-5; 35 ILCS 120/2-5) Agricultural chemical tender tanks and dry boxes includes any units sold separately from licensed motor vehicles and also units that are mounted on licensed motor vehicles when the sales price of the tender is separately stated.

Further included are computers, sensors, software, and related equipment used primarily in the computer-assisted operation of production agriculture facilities, equipment, and activities such as the collection, monitoring, and correlation of animal crop data for purposes of formulating animal diets and agricultural chemicals. Also included is precision farming equipment that is installed or purchased for installation on farm machinery and equipment including tractors, harvesters, sprayers, planters, seeders, or spreaders. Precision farming equipment includes soil testing sensors, computers, monitors, software, global positioning and mapping systems, and other such equipment.

"Equipment" is an independent device or apparatus separate from machinery and essential to production agriculture. Ordinary building materials that are to be permanently affixed to real estate are not exempt. However, some equipment installed as realty improvements are exempt, such as farrowing crates, gestation stalls, poultry cages, portable panels for confinement facilities, and flooring used in conjunction with waste disposal machinery. Equipment used in farm management, repair and servicing of equipment, security and fire protection, farm maintenance, administration, selling, marketing, or the exhibition of products is not exempt. (86 Ill. Adm. Code 130.305(K))

"Production agriculture" defined: "Production agriculture" includes the raising or propagation of livestock; crops for sale for human or livestock consumption; the production seed stock grown for the propagation of feed grains and the husbandry of animals or for the purpose of providing a food product. Aquaculture is considered production agriculture. (35 ILCS 105/3-35; 35 ILCS 110/3-35; 35 ILCS 115/3-35; 35 ILCS 120/2-35; 86 Ill. Adm. Code 130.305(b))

Production agriculture regarding crops is limited to activities necessary in tilling the soil, planting, irrigating, cultivating, applying herbicide, insecticide, or fertilizer, and harvesting and drying of crops. Clearing land, mowing of fence rows, creation of ponds and drainage facilities, and storing or transporting crops and produce are not exempt activities. Processing crops into food is not production agriculture. (86 Ill. Adm. Code 130.305(f))

"Livestock" refers to domestic farm animals raised for profit. The raising of wild animals, game birds, or house pets, and the transport, slaughter, and processing of animals are not production agriculture. (86 Ill. Adm. Code 130.305(f); 86 Ill. Adm. Code 130.305(g))

• *Farm chemicals*

Proceeds from the sale of farm chemicals are exempt from the ROT and UT. (35 ILCS 105/3-5; 35 ILCS 120/2-5; 86 Ill. Adm. Code 130.120(P)) "Farm chemicals" are chemical products used in production agriculture, the products of which are to be sold, or in the production or care of animals or their byproducts that are to be sold, such as stock sprays, disinfectants, stock tonics, serums, vaccines, poultry remedies and other medicinal preparations and conditioners, water-purifying products, insecticides, and weed killers. (86 Ill. Adm. Code 130.1955) The farm chemicals exemption applies to animals only if the chemical's label indicates that it is usable exclusively on farm animals. Also, "crops" has been held to include garden plants.

Persons who spray crops or apply farm chemicals for others are exempt from the SOT on sales of the sprays and chemicals as an incident to the service.

Transfers of pesticides and lawn care chemicals incident to service provided under contracts to maintain lawns, trees, shrubs, and other plants are subject to the SOT. (86 Ill. Adm. Code 140.140(S))

• *Seeds and fertilizer*

Sales of seeds to farmers and other persons who use the seeds to raise vegetables, crops, or plants for sale are deemed sales for resale not subject to the ROT and UT. (86 Ill. Adm. Code 130.2110) See ¶ 60-650 for a discussion of the resale exemption. However, sales of seeds to purchasers who use the seeds in raising lawn grass, vegetables, crops, or other plants for their own use are subject to the tax.

Sales of fertilizer to purchasers who use the fertilizer on lawns, home or private gardens, parks, or boulevards are also subject to the tax, but sales to purchasers engaged in the business of producing agricultural products for sale are exempt. (86 Ill. Adm. Code 130.2110)

Transfers of fertilizers incident to service provided under contracts to maintain lawns, trees, shrubs, and other plants are subject to the SOT. (86 Ill. Adm. Code 140.140(S))

• *Feed*

Feed sold to prepare livestock or poultry for market or to produce eggs or dairy products for sale is not subject to the ROT and UT. (86 Ill. Adm. Code 130.2100; 86 Ill. Adm. Code 150.1201) Sales of feed for purposes other than sales at market are subject to tax.

"Feed" is salt, grains, tankage, oyster shells, mineral supplements, vitamins, limestone, and other generally recognized animal feeds. (86 Ill. Adm. Code 130.2100)

• *Hatcheries*

Sales of baby chicks for consumption by the purchaser are subject to the ROT and UT. (86 Ill. Adm. Code 150.1201; 86 Ill. Adm. Code 130.1970) Proceeds from the sale of baby chicks purchased for resale or for the production of eggs for sale are exempt. See ¶ 60-650 for a general discussion of the resale exemption.

Persons who hatch baby chicks for others from eggs belonging to those other persons are rendering a service and are not subject to ROT. (86 Ill. Adm. Code 130.1970)

Poultry-raising equipment: Sales of brooders, water troughs, and other poultry-raising equipment are subject to the ROT and UT unless used or leased for use primarily in production agriculture. (86 Ill. Adm. Code 130.1970)

• *Veterinarians*

Veterinarians may incur liability for service occupation tax, retailers' occupation (sales) tax, or use tax, depending upon the nature of the transaction. (86 Ill. Adm. Code 130.2165) For further details, see ¶ 60-520 Medical, Dental, and Optical Supplies and Drugs.

The SOT and SUT are not imposed on sales of stock tonics, serums, and other medicinal products to veterinarians for retransfer as an incident to caring of farm animals. (86 Ill. Adm. Code 140.125(l); 86 Ill. Adm. Code 160.145)

• *Semen*

Sales and use of semen for artificial insemination of livestock for direct agricultural production are exempt from ROT, SOT, UT, and SUT. (35 ILCS 105/3-5; 35 ILCS 110/3-5; 35 ILCS 115/3-5; 35 ILCS 120/2-5)

• *Breeding or racing horses*

Horses, or interests in horses, registered with and meeting requirements of the Arabian Horse Club Registry of America, Appaloosa Horse Club, American Quarter Horse Association, United States Trotting Association, or Jockey Club, and used for breeding or racing for prizes, are exempt from ROT, SOT, UT, and SUT. These exemptions are not subject to the five-year sunset provision normally applicable to exemptions. (35 ILCS 105/3-5; 35 ILCS 110/3-5; 35 ILCS 115/3-5; 35 ILCS 120/2-5)

• *Horticultural polyhouses or hoop houses*

Horticultural polyhouses or hoop houses used for propagating, growing, or overwintering plants are considered farm machinery and equipment and are exempt. (35 ILCS 105/3-5; 35 ILCS 110/3-5; 35 ILCS 115/3-5; 35 ILCS 120/2-5)

• *Game and game birds*

Game and game birds purchased at a game breeding and hunting preserve area, an exotic game hunting area, or a hunting enclosure are not subject to the ROT, SOT, UT, and SUT. (35 ILCS 105/3-5; 35 ILCS 110/3-5; 35 ILCS 115/3-5; 35 ILCS 120/2-5)

[¶60-260] Alcoholic Beverages

Sales of alcoholic beverages are subject to ROT and UT. (86 Ill. Adm. Code 130.2060(a); 86 Ill. Adm. Code 150.1201)

[¶60-290] Clothing

Sales of clothing by retailers are subject to the ROT and UT. Also taxable are sales of clothing made on special order. The cost of labor involved in producing custom-made clothing sold at retail is not deductible from the sales price in computing the sales tax basis. (86 Ill. Adm. Code 130.2040; 86 Ill. Adm. Code 150.1201)

[¶60-310] Computers, Software, and Services

In general, computer hardware and canned or prewritten computer software are subject to sales and use tax, but custom computer software and certain computer services are exempt.

Is computer hardware subject to sales tax in Illinois?

Yes. In general, computer hardware is subject to sales tax as tangible personal property. Sales of certain computers used for hospital purposes are exempt

Is computer software subject to sales tax in Illinois?

In general, canned or prewritten computer software is subject to the retailers' occupation tax (sales) tax, service occupation tax (SOT), use tax and service use tax (SUT), while sales of custom software are exempt.

Sales of both canned and custom computer software that are used to operate exempt machinery and equipment used in the process of manufacturing or assembling property for sale or lease are exempt from sales tax, SOT, use tax, and SUT.

Purchases of computer software for resale are not taxable. (35 ILCS 120/1; 35 ILCS 105/2) Software acquired to sell or license aftermodification or adaptation may also be an exempt purchase for resale.

Canned or prewritten software. Canned or prewritten computer software is taxable as tangible personal property. (35 ILCS 105/3; 35 ILCS 110/3; 35 ILCS 115/335 ILCS 120/2) Sales of canned software are taxable regardless of the form in which the software is transferred or transmitted. Retail sales of canned software, including software subject to manufacturer licenses, are taxable. Taxable software includes software used to operate machinery and equipment used in:

— the generation of electricity for wholesale or retail sale;

— the generation or treatment of natural or artificial gas for wholesale or retail sale that is delivered to customers through pipes, pipelines or mains; or

— the treatment of water for wholesale or retail sale that is delivered to customers through pipes, pipelines or mains.

(35 ILCS 105/3-25; 35 ILCS 110/3-25; 35 ILCS 115/3-25; 35 ILCS 120/2-25)

Charges for updating canned software are taxable.

Custom software. Custom software is exempt from sales tax and SOT. Custom software is software:

— prepared or selected after an analysis by the vendor of the customer's requirement, and

— adapted by the vendor for the use in a specific work environment.

Modification of an existing prewritten program to meet a customer's needs is custom software. A charge for modifying prewritten software is exempt if the modification is done to meet the customer's specific requirements and results in real and substantial changes to the software's coding. Modified software held for general or repeated sale or lease is taxable.

Example: A programmer buys canned software with a resale certificate. the programmer modifies the software to meet a customer's specific needs. The transfer of the modified software to the customer is exempt. However, if the modified program is sold to other customers without further modification it is taxable. Also, copies or repeat orders of such modified software are taxable.

Software licenses. A license of canned software is not taxable if:

(1) the parties enter a written license agreement,

(2) the license agreement restricts the customer's duplication and use of the software,

(3) the license agreement prohibits the customer from licensing, sublicensing, or transferring the software,

(4) the licensor's policy of providing replacement copies for little or no charge if the customer loses or damages the software, or of permitting a customer to make and keep an archival copy, is stated in the license agreement, and

(5) the customer must destroy or return all copies of the software to the licensor at the end of the license period.

Example: A retailer sells a shrink-wrapped software package to a customer. The package contains a "license agreement" which becomes effective when the package is opened and is not signed by the customer. This agreement states that the customer does not receive title to the software but may make a back up or archival copy of the software. It also does not prohibit the customer from selling the software. If the customer loses or damages the software, the retailer will not replace it. Since the sale of the software does not meet all the requirements of an exempt licensee of software, the sale is taxable.

Are computer services taxable?

No. Computer services generally are not taxable. Charges for training, telephone support, installation, and consultation related to sales of canned software are specifically exempt if they are separately stated from the selling price.

Hardware maintenance agreements. Sales of maintenance agreements for computer hardware owned by the customer generally are not taxable.

Software maintenance agreements. Sales of software maintenance agreements are generally not taxable. However, sellers of maintenance agreements must pay sales tax on materials they purchase to complete a maintenance agreement.

Is cloud computing taxable?

The taxability of cloud computing depends on the category under which the activity is classified. Cloud computing is a term used to describe the delivery of computing resources, including software applications, development tools, storage, and servers over the Internet. Rather than purchasing hardware or software, a consumer may purchase access to a cloud computing provider's hardware or software. Cloud computing offerings are generally divided into three categories: software as a service, platform as a service, and infrastructure as a service.

Software as a service. Under the SaaS model, a consumer purchases access to a software application that is owned, operated, and maintained by a SaaS provider. The consumer accesses the application over the Internet. The software is located on a server that is owned or leased by the SaaS provider. The software is not transferred to the customer, and the customer does not have the right to download, copy, or modify the software.

Sales tax authority on SaaS transactions is still evolving. Some states have taken the position that SaaS transactions are a sale of software, reasoning that using software by electronically accessing it is no different than downloading it. Other states have deemed it a service based on the fact that no software is transferred. In some states, the taxability may depend on the specific facts and whether the object of the transaction is the use of software or some other purpose.

Illinois has no specific authority on the taxability of SaaS.

Platform as a service. Under the PaaS model, the provider sells access to a platform and software development tools that a consumer uses to create its own applications. A consumer deploys the applications it creates onto the provider's infrastructure. The consumer has control over its deployed applications but does not control the underlying infrastructure.

Illinois has no authority or guidance on the taxability of PaaS.

Infrastructure as a service. IaaS providers sell access to storage, networks, equipment, and other computing resources that the provider operates and maintains. A consumer purchases the ability to store data or deploy and run software using the provider's equipment. The consumer does not manage or control the cloud infrastructure but has control over its applications and data.

Illinois has no authority or guidance on the taxability of IaaS.

Does a sales tax holiday apply to computer items in Illinois?

No, Illinois does not currently have any sales tax holidays.

[¶60-330] Construction

In general, a contractor's purchases aretaxable, but construction-related services are exempt.

Are construction materials and supplies taxable in Illinois?

Yes, purchases of construction materials and supplies are subject to retailer's occupation (sales) tax and use tax unless they are purchased 1) for resale; 2) to fulfill a contract with an exempt organization; 3) to fulfill a contract that includes the integration of certain systems into real estate; or 4) for use in a real estate project outside Illinois.

Purchases in Illinois by construction contractors, as well as real estate developers and speculative builders, for use or consumption or for incorporation into real estate are subject to sales tax. However, when purchases are made outside Illinois for use in Illinois, use tax applies. Taxable items for consumption or use include tools, equipment, fuel, and supplies. Taxable items that are incorporated or converted into real estate include building materials, fixtures, and plants.

Resales. A contractor's purchases are not taxable if the contractor purchases the property for resale. A contractor that is unsure at the time of purchase whether the property will be incorporated into real estate or resold to customers may purchase all the property for resale. The contractor will beliable for state and local sales tax on any of the items that are incorporated into real estate rather than resold.

Example: A contractor who also sells items "over the counter" purchases drywall from a supplier in Springfield, Illinois and provides a resale certificate. Later, the contractor incorporates some of the drywall into real estate on a job. The contractor is liable for state sales tax and Springfield home rule municipal retailers' occupation tax which the supplier would have charged on the sale of the drywall.

Exempt organizations and government bodies. Sales of materials to construction contractors are exempt when:

— the contract covers real estate owned by:

exclusively charitable, religious, or educational organizations,

a nonprofit organization that has no compensated officers or employees and was organized for the recreation of persons 55 years of age or older, or

government bodies; and

— the supplier claiming exemption receives an exemption certificate from the contractor.

Out-of-state construction. Purchases of building materials and fixtures either inside or outside Illinois by a combination retailer and construction contractor are not taxable if they are stored temporarily in Illinois and later incorporated into real property outside Illinois. (35 ILCS 105/3-55; 86 Ill. Adm. Code 150.310(5))

Materials installed under construction contracts. A contractor's transfer of construction materials by incorporating them into real estate during construction is not subject to service occupation tax (SOT), unlike general transfers of property in connection with services. In addition, receipts from labor and materials integrally incorporated into a structure are not subject to sales or use tax when the materials are installed under a construction contract.

Example: Items that are exempt from sales tax when installed under a construction contract include:

— screen doors and windows,

— storm doors and windows,

— weather stripping,

— insulation material,

— Venetian blinds,

— window shades,

— awnings,

— cabinets built into the structure,

— floor coverings cemented or otherwise permanently affixed to the structure by use of tacks, staples, or wood striping filled with nails that protrude upward, called tacking strips or tack-down strips,

— plumbing systems or parts thereof, such as bathtubs, lavatories, sinks, faucets, water pumps, water heaters, water softeners, water pipes, etc.,

— heating systems, such as furnaces, stokers, boilers, heating pipes, etc. and heating systems parts,

— ventilation systems and parts,

— commercial refrigeration systems and parts,

— electrical systems and parts,

— brick,

— lumber,

— sheet metal, and

— roofing materials.

Example: Floor coverings or area rugs or that are attached to the structure using only two-sided tape are subject to sales tax, even though they are installed under a construction contract.

Rate increase during construction contract. If a tax rate increases after a construction contract has been entered into, but before property is delivered to a construction contractor, the sale of the property is taxed at the new sales or use tax rate, unless the contractor can legally shift the burden of the rate increase to the customer under the contract. If the contractor cannot legally shift the burden of a sales or use tax rate increase to its customer, the contractor must provide the supplier with a written, signed certification describing the contract and indicating its ability to do so.

Definitions. A "construction contractor" includes general contractors, subcontractors and specialized contractors, such as alandscape contractor. A "contractor" is any person in the business of entering construction contracts.

A "real estate developer" is any person engaged in the business of transferring legal or equitable title to real estate. The term does not include the occasional sale of real estate by a person not engaged in the real estate business or a sale by a real estate agent who does not take title to the property.

How does Illinois tax construction related services?

In Illinois, services, including construction related services, are generally not subject to the retailers' occupation (sales) tax and use tax.

Are labor charges taxable in Illinois?

No. Labor charges are not subject to the retailers' occupation (sales) tax and use tax.

What incentives or credits are available for contractors in Illinois?

Purchases of building materials for use in a South Suburban Airport remodeling, rehabilitating, or new construction project are exempt. To document the exemption, the retailer must obtain from the purchaser:

— a Certificate of Eligibility for Sales Tax Exemption issued by the Department of Transportation (DOT); and

— a certificate prepared by the purchaser.

The certificate prepared by the purchaser must include:

— a statement that the building materials are being purchased for incorporation in the South Suburban Airport in accordance with the Public-Private Agreements for the South Suburban Airport Act;

— the location or address of the project into which the building materials will be incorporated;

— the name of the project;

— a description of the building materials being purchased; and

— the purchaser's signature and date of purchase.

Sales tax exemptions and incentives are available for items used to equip data centers, and for items used in construction projects located in enterprise zones.

What certificate or form must a contractor use to claim an exemption in Illinois?

In general, purchases made by contractors in Illinois are taxable. However, Illinois provides an exemption certificate for contractors involved in special projects where an exemption for building materials is available.

Does Illinois have special rules concerning subcontractors?

No. The rules that apply to general contractors apply to subcontractors.

Does Illinois have other provisions related to construction?

Yes, Illinois provides additional guidance on contractors and developers acting as retailers and on fabrication.

Construction contractors and real estate developers as retailers. Sales tax is imposed on retailers. While a construction contractor or real estate developer may not be a retailer, the contractor or developer is liable for sales tax or use tax when it sells property to customers in the form in which it is purchased. If the contractor or developer sells property at retail while fulfilling a lump sum contract, the contractor or developer must collect tax from the customer based on the contractor's or developer's cost of the property. If the contract charges separately for the property, the contractor or developer must collect sales tax or use tax on the greater of the amount charged under the contract or the contractor's or developer's cost of the property.

Construction contracts for integrated systems. Construction contractors who contract for the engineering, installation, and maintenance of voice, data, video, security, and all telecommunication systems in real estate are liable for use tax on those items if they are sold at one specified contract price. Sales tax does not apply to such contracts.

Fabrication. A contractor who purchases materials and manufactures them into an item to be incorporated into real estate is liable for tax on the cost of materials used to fabricate and install the item.

[¶60-340] Drop Shipments

A drop shipment is a shipment of tangible personal property from a seller directly to the purchaser's customer, at the direction of the purchaser. These sales are also known as third-party sales because they require that there be, at arm's length, three parties and two separate sales transactions. Generally, a retailer accepts an order from an end purchaser/consumer, places this order with a third party, usually a manufacturer or wholesale distributor, and directs the third party to ship the goods directly to the end purchaser/consumer. Drop shipments are examined as two transactions: (1) the sale from the primary seller to the purchaser and (2) the sale from the purchaser to the purchaser's customer.

• *Illinois treatment of drop-shipment sales*

When all the parties are located in the state, the retailer furnishes a resale certificate to the primary seller, rendering the first sale a nontaxable transaction. The retailer then collects sales tax on behalf of the state on the secondary sale to its customer. However, different considerations arise when one or more of the parties are not within the state.

Illinois exempts the primary sale, that to an out-of-state retailer by an Illinois manufacturer who drop ships the product to the retailer's customer, if the retailer furnishes a resale number issued by Illinois or other evidence that the sale is for resale. The out-of-state retailer would then be responsible for collecting the tax from its Illinois customer if the out-of-state retailer has nexus with Illinois. If, however, the out-of-state vendor has no nexus with Illinois and cannot be required to collect the tax because of constitutional limitations, the ultimate customer is subject to use tax inasmuch as the sales tax has not been paid. (35 ILCS 105/3-45; 86 Ill. Adm. Code 130.225)

For a discussion on certificates of resale, see ¶60-650 Resales.

For a discussion of nexus, see ¶60-025 Nexus—Doing Business in Illinois.

[¶60-360] Enterprise Zones and Similar Tax Incentives

Illinois offers exemptions from ROT, SOT, UT, and SUT for enterprise zone businesses under the Illinois Enterprise Zone Act. (20 ILCS 655/1)

Enterprise zones scheduled to expire in 2016, 2017 or 2018, including zones that are extended until July 1, 2016, must submit applications to the Department of Commerce and Economic Opportunity to retain designation as an enterprise zone after the expiration date. (20 ILCS 655/5.3)

• *Enterprise zone eligibility requirements*

An area is qualified to become an enterprise area if it:

   (1) is a contiguous area;

   (2) comprises a minimum of one-half square miles and not more than 12 square miles, or 15 square miles if the zone is located within the jurisdiction of four or more counties or municipalities, exclusive of lakes and waterways;

(3) is entirely within a municipality or the unincorporated areas of a county or comprises all or part of a municipality and an unincorporated area of a county; and

(4) meets three out of 10 criteria set forth in the statute.

(20 ILCS 655/4)

A "depressed area" is one in which pervasive poverty, unemployment, and economic distress exist.

A designated area qualifies as an enterprise zone for 30 years. Enterprise zones that are designated on or after August 7, 2012, are effective for 15 years, but are subject to review by the enterprise zone board after 13 years for an additional 10-year designation as an enterprise zone. (20 ILCS 655/5.3)

If property is purchased under an exemption and later converted to a nonexempt use, it becomes subject to tax based on its fair market value at the time of conversion. (86 Ill. Adm. Code 130.1951(b); 86 Ill. Adm. Code 130.1951(c); 86 Ill. Adm. Code 130.1951(d))

Exemptions apply only to high impact businesses and to business enterprises that meet the following criteria (35 ILCS 105/12; 35 ILCS 110/12; 35 ILCS 115/12; 35 ILCS 120/1f; 86 Ill. Adm. Code 130.1951(d)):

(1) they make investments that cause the creation of at least 200 full-time Illinois jobs, make investments that cause the retention of at least 2,000 full-time Illinois jobs, or make investments of a minimum of $40 million and retain at least 90% of the jobs in place on the date on which the exemption is granted and for the duration of the exemption;

(2) they are located in an enterprise zone established under the Enterprise Zone Act; and

(3) they are certified by the Department of Commerce and Economic Opportunity as complying with the foregoing requirements.

(35 ILCS 120/1f; 86 Ill. Adm. Code 130.1951(g))

A "high impact business" is one that intends to invest at least $12 million in placing qualified property in service and to create 500 full-time equivalent jobs or one that intends to invest at least $30 million in placing qualified property in service and to retain 1,500 full-time jobs as defined by statute. (20 ILCS 655/5.5)

For a discussion of the South Suburban Airport building and materials exemption, see ¶60-330 Construction.

• *Enterprise zones and building materials*

An exemption from ROT, SOT, UT, and SUT is provided for "qualified sales" of building materials sold by a retailer to be incorporated into real estate in an enterprise zone established by a county or municipality under the Illinois Enterprise Zone Act. The exemption may be limited by the municipality or county that created the enterprise zone into which the building materials will be incorporated. However, the neither the municipality or county may require or prohibit the purchase of building materials from any retailer in order to qualify for the exemption. Thus, materials used for remodeling, rehabilitation, or new construction may be exempt when calculating the tax imposed under the Retailers' Occupation (sales) Tax Act. (20 ILCS 655/5.5; 35 ILCS 120/5k) The proceeds from the sale are also deductible from the tax bases of SOT, UT, and SUT. (35 ILCS 120/12; 35 ILCS 110/12; 35 ILCS 115/12)

Qualified sales.—On and after July 1, 2013, "qualified sale" means a sale of building materials that will be incorporated into real estate as part of a building project for which an Enterprise Zone Building Materials Exemption Certificate has been issued to the purchaser by the Department of Revenue. A construction contractor or other entity shall not make tax-free purchases unless it has an active exemption certificate issued by the Department at the time of the purchase. Before July 1, 2013, "qualified sale" means a sale of building materials that will be incorporated into real estate as part of a building project for which a Certificate of Eligibility for Sales Tax Exemption has been issued by the administrator of the enterprise zone in which the building project is located. (35 ILCS 120/5k)

For a discussion of enterprise zone building materials exemption certificates, see ¶ 61-020 Exemption Certificates.

CCH Planning Note: Local ordinance limitations and requirements must be complied with to qualify for sales tax exemption.—Any retailer in Illinois who makes a sale of building materials that are to be physically incorporated into real estate in an enterprise zone established by a county or municipality under the Illinois Enterprise Zone Act may deduct the receipts from such sales when calculating the state's portion of the sales tax, though the municipality or county that created the enterprise zone in which the retailer's place of business is located may limit the tax exemption based on specific ordinance requirements. (35 ILCS 120/5k)

The Illinois Department of Revenue has provided administrative guidance on what materials are considered "building materials" in the following releases:

Illinois Private Letter Ruling, ST 00-0026-PLR, Illinois Department of Revenue.

Illinois Private Letter Ruling, ST 00-0025-PLR, Illinois Department of Revenue.

Illinois Private Letter Ruling, ST 00-0013-PLR, Illinois Department of Revenue.

Illinois Private Letter Ruling, ST 01-0001-PLR, Illinois Department of Revenue.

Illinois General Information Letter, ST 01-0046-GIL, Illinois Department of Revenue.

A copy of the ordinance or resolution changing the deduction must be sent to the Department of Revenue within five days of publication. (35 ILCS 105/12; 35 ILCS 110/12; 35 ILCS 115/12; 35 ILCS 120/5k)

A regulation details the requirements for establishing that a retailer is located within a county or municipality containing an enterprise zone, that the retailer purchased qualifying materials, and the supporting documentation necessary. It also gives examples of excludable property. (86 Ill. Adm. Code 130.1951(a))

Each retailer who sells building materials that will be incorporated into a high impact business location may deduct receipts from those sales when calculating only the ROT. A retailer may also deduct receipts from these sales when calculating any applicable local taxes. However, a retailer is not eligible for the credit or deduction if it is eligible for the enterprise zone exclusion discussed in the preceding paragraph. A Department regulation provides eligibility guidelines for the deduction. (35 ILCS 120/5l; 86 Ill. Adm. Code 130.1952)

• *Certificates of eligibility for exemption*

Approval of a designated enterprise zone will be made by the Department through certification. (20 ILCS 655/5.3)

A qualifying high impact business may apply to the Department for a certificate of eligibility. The certificate must be presented by the business to its supplier when it makes an initial exempt purchase, along with a certification by the business enterprise that the property is exempt from tax. Subsequent purchases may be made without payment of tax if the buyer indicates on the face of the purchase order that the transaction is exempt by referencing the certificate and the buyer's certification. (35 ILCS 120/1f; 86 Ill. Adm. Code 130.1951(d))

For a discussion of building materials exemption certificates and exemption certificates in general, see ¶61-020 Exemption Certificates.

• *Data centers*

The Illinois DOR will issue qualifying Illinois data centers certificates of exemption through June 30, 2029, that are valid for up to 20 years, from the:

- Retailers' Occupation Tax Act,
- Use Tax Act,
- Service Use Tax Act,
- Service Occupation Tax Act,
- all locally-imposed retailers' occupation taxes administered and collected by the DOR, and
- the Chicago non-titled use tax, and

(20 ILCS 605/605-1025(a)-(b), (d); 86 Ill. Adm. Code 130.1957)

Additionally, for taxable years beginning on or after January 1, 2019, the DOR will issue a credit certification against income taxes imposed on the net income of individuals, corporations, trusts, and estates under the Illinois Income Tax Act. (20 ILCS 605/605-1025(a)-(b))

Available exemptions.—An exemption certificate holder is allowed to purchase qualified tangible personal property exempt from sales and use tax. "Qualified tangible personal property" is all tangible personal property that is essential to the operations of a computer data center. Qualified tangible personal property includes building materials physically incorporated into the qualifying Illinois data center. (*Informational Bulletin FY 2020-04*, Illinois Department of Revenue)

Qualified tangible personal property also includes: electrical systems and equipment; climate control and chilling equipment and systems; mechanical systems and equipment; monitoring and secure systems; emergency generators; hardware; computers; servers; data storage devices; network connectivity equipment; racks; cabinets; telecommunications cabling infrastructure; raised floor systems; peripheral components or systems; software; mechanical, electrical, or plumbing systems; battery systems; cooling systems and towers; temperature control systems; other cabling; and other data center infrastructure equipment and systems necessary to operate qualified tangible personal property, including fixtures; and component parts of any of the foregoing, including installation, maintenance, repair, refurbishment, and replacement of qualified tangible personal property to generate, transform, transmit, distribute, or manage electricity necessary to operate qualified tangible personal property; and all other tangible personal property that is essential to the operations of a computer data center. (20 ILCS 605/605-1025(c); 86 Ill. Adm. Code 130.1957) (*Informational Bulletin FY 2020-04*, Illinois Department of Revenue)

Definitions.—A "data center" is a facility:

- whose primary services are the storage, management, and processing of digital data; and
- that is used to house (a) computer and network systems, such as associated components like servers, network equipment and appliances, telecommunications, and data storage systems, (b) systems for monitoring and managing infrastructure performance, (c) Internet-related equipment and services, (d) data

communications connections, (e) environmental controls, (f) fire protection systems, and (g) security systems and services.

(20 ILCS 605/605-1025(c)) (*Informational Bulletin FY 2020-04*, Illinois Department of Revenue)

In general, the data center must be located in Illinois and must be carbon neutral or have attained certification under certain green building standards. The data center must also meet certain statutory capital investment thresholds and certain job creation thresholds. (*Informational Bulletin FY 2020-04*, Illinois Department of Revenue)

A "qualifying Illinois data center" is a new or existing data center that:

- is located in Illinois;

- if an existing data center, made a capital investment of at least $250 million collectively by the data center operator and the tenants of the data center over the 60-month period immediately before January 1, 2020, or committed to make a capital investment of at least $250 million over a 60-month period beginning before January 1, 2020, and ending after January 1, 2020;

- if a new data center, or an existing data center making an upgrade, makes a capital investment of at least $250 million over a 60-month period;

- if an existing or new data center, results in the creation of at least 20 full-time or full-time equivalent new jobs over a period of 60 months by the data center operator and the tenants of the data center, collectively, associated with the operation or maintenance of the data center. The jobs must have a total compensation equal to or greater than 120% of the average wage paid to full-time employees in the county where the data center is located, as determined by the U.S. Bureau of Labor Statistics; and

- within 90 days after being placed in service, certifies to the Department that it is carbon-neutral or has attained certification under one or more of the following green building standards: (a) BREEAM for New Construction or BREEAM In-Use; (b) ENERGY STAR; (c) Envision; (d) ISO 50001-energy management; (e) LEED for Building Design and Construction or LEED for Operations and Maintenance; (f) Green Globes for New Construction or Green Globes for Existing Buildings; (g) UL 3223; or (h) an equivalent program approved by the Department of Commerce and Economic Opportunity.

(20 ILCS 605/605-1025(c))

A "full-time equivalent job" is a job in which the new employee works for the owner, operator, contractor, or tenant of a data center or for a corporation under contract with the owner, operator or tenant of a data center for at least 35 hours per week. An owner, operator or tenant who employs labor or services at a specific site or facility under contract with another can declare one full-time, permanent job for every 1,820 man hours worked per year under the contract. Vacations, paid holidays, and sick time are included in this computation. Overtime is not considered part of regular hours. (20 ILCS 605/605-1025(c))

Claiming the exemption.—To document the exemption, the retailer must obtain from the purchaser a copy of the certificate of eligibility issued by the DOR. (20 ILCS 605/605-1025(c))

Applying for the exemption.—The DOR will determine the application process. A memorandum of understanding must be entered into between the DOR and a data center seeking the exemption (including a data center operator on behalf of itself and its tenants). (20 ILCS 605/605-1025(d))

Contractors and subcontractors.—New and existing data centers seeking a certificate of exemption related to the rehabilitation or construction of a data center in Illinois must:

- require the contractor and all subcontractors to comply with the requirements of the Illinois Procurement Code concerning responsible bidders,

- require the contractor to present satisfactory evidence of this compliance to the DOR, and

- require the contractor to enter into a project labor agreement approved by the DOR.

(20 ILCS 605/605-1025(f)-(g))

Annual reports.—A qualifying data center issued a certificate of exemption must file an annual report with the DOR detailing the total data center tax benefits it received. Reports are due by May 31 each year and cover the previous calendar year. The first report for calendar year 2019 is due May 31, 2020. Failure to file the report can result in suspension or revocation of the certificate of exemption. (20 ILCS 605/605-1025(h))

A qualifying data center issued a certificate of exemption is not required to additionally report building materials for which it has obtained:

- an Enterprise Zone Building Materials Exemption Certificate, or

- a High Impact Business Building Materials Exemption Certificate.

(20 ILCS 605/605-1025(h))

- *Developmental assistance agreements and applications*

The Corporate Accountability for Tax Expenditures Act, establishes a definition of "development assistance" that encompasses Illinois enterprise zone incentives, provides for developmental assistance agreements between state bodies granting incentives and incentive recipients, and establishes standardized application requirements for developmental assistance. (20 ILCS 715/5)

- *Recapture or "claw back"*

The Corporate Accountability for Tax Expenditures Act requires that all development assistance agreements for ROT, SOT, UT, and SUT enterprise zone business exemptions and other forms of development assistance must contain several recapture provisions, including:

- incentive recipients must make the level of capital investment in the economic development project specified in the development assistance agreement, create and/or retain the requisite number of jobs, paying at least the wages specified for the jobs, for the duration of time specified in the authorizing legislation or the implementing administrative rules;

- incentive recipients that fail to create or retain the requisite number of jobs for the specified time period will no longer qualify for the economic assistance and the applicable recapture provisions will take effect; and

- taxpayers operating in Illinois enterprise zones that qualify for the Illinois retailers' occupation (sales) tax exemption for building materials incorporated into a high impact business location that fail to create or retain the requisite number of jobs within the requisite period of time must pay to Illinois the full amount of the exemption they received as a result of the high impact business designation.

(20 ILCS 715/25)

The Director of Revenue may waive enforcement of any contractual provision of a development assistance agreement if the waiver is necessary to avert a hardship to a recipient that may result in the recipient's insolvency or in the discharge of workers. If the Director grants a waiver, the recipient must agree to contractual modifications, including recapture provisions, to the development assistance agreement. (20 ILCS 715/25)

- *Aircraft maintenance facilities and certified aircraft support centers*

An exemption from ROT, SOT, UT, and SUT is provided for machinery and equipment primarily used to maintain, repair, or rebuild aircraft in an aircraft maintenance facility within an enterprise zone and for tangible personal property used or consumed by such a facility in the process of maintaining, repairing, or rebuilding aircraft. Also exempt are repair and replacement parts for exempt machinery and equipment, and equipment, fuels, material, and supplies for the maintenance, repair, or operation of exempt machinery and equipment. (35 ILCS 105/12; 35 ILCS 110/12; 35 ILCS 115/12; 35 ILCS 120/1m; 35 ILCS 120/1n)

An "aircraft maintenance facility" means a facility operated by an interstate carrier for hire that is used primarily for the maintenance, rebuilding, or repair of aircraft, aircraft parts, and auxiliary equipment owned or leased by the carrier and used as rolling stock moving in interstate commerce and that (1) will invest at least $400 million in an enterprise zone; (2) will create at least 5,000 full-time jobs in the enterprise zone; (3) is located in a county with a population of not less than 150,000 and not more than 200,000 that contains three enterprise zones as of December 31, 1990; (4) enters into a legally binding agreement with the Department of Commerce and Economic Opportunity; and (5) is certified by the Department of Commerce and Economic Opportunity to be in compliance with the foregoing requirements. (35 ILCS 120/1k)

A business enterprise may apply to the Department of Commerce and Economic Opportunity for a certificate of eligibility for exemption. The certificate must be presented by the business to its supplier when making an initial purchase, along with a certification by the business that the machinery and equipment are exempt. Subsequent purchases may then be made by indicating the exempt status on the face of the purchase orders. (35 ILCS 120/1k)

Qualified sales.—An exemption from ROT, SOT, UT, and SUT is also provided for purchases of jet fuel and petroleum products used or consumed directly in the process of maintaining, rebuilding, or repairing aircraft in a qualifying aircraft support center. (35 ILCS 120/1o; 35 ILCS 115/12; 35 ILCS 105/12; 35 ILCS 110/12)

An "aircraft support center" means a support center operated by a carrier for hire that is used primarily for the maintenance, rebuilding, or repair of aircraft, aircraft parts, and auxiliary equipment and which carrier (1) will invest at least $30 million in a federal Air Force base in Illinois; (2) will create at least 750 full-time jobs at an airport located on the base that is used by military and civilian personnel; (3) enters into a legally binding agreement with the Department of Commerce and Economic Opportunity; and (5) is certified by the Department of Commerce and Economic Opportunity to be in compliance with the foregoing requirements. (35 ILCS 120/1o)

A business enterprise may apply to the Department of Commerce and Economic Opportunity for a certificate of eligibility for exemption. The certificate must be presented by the carrier to its supplier when making an initial purchase, along with a certification by the business that the items are exempt. Subsequent purchases may then be made by indicating the exempt status on the face of the purchase orders. (35 ILCS 120/1o)

- *Disaster areas*

For the time period determined by statute, personal property that is donated for disaster relief and is to be used in a state or federally declared disaster area in Illinois or bordering Illinois is exempt from sales and use tax. The personal property must be donated by a manufacturer or retailer that is registered in Illinois. The recipient of the donation must be a corporation, society, association, foundation, or institution that assists victims of the disaster who reside within the declared disaster area and that has been issued a sales tax exemption identification number by the Department of Revenue. (35 ILCS 105/3-5; 35 ILCS 110/3-5; 35 ILCS 115/3-5; 35 ILCS 120/2-5)

During the same time period, personal property that is used in the performance of infrastructure repairs in Illinois made necessary by a state or federally declared disaster in Illinois or bordering Illinois is exempt from sales and use tax when the repairs are initiated on facilities located in the declared disaster area within six months after the disaster. The exemption includes personal property used in the repair of municipal roads and streets, access roads, bridges, sidewalks, waste disposal systems, water and sewer line extensions, water distribution and purification facilities, storm water drainage and retention facilities, and sewage treatment facilities. (35 ILCS 105/3-5; 35 ILCS 110/3-5; 35 ILCS 115/3-5; 35 ILCS 120/2-5)

• *Energy facilities and natural resources*

Electric generation facility and related industries.—Illinois businesses that encourage the establishment of new coal-powered electric generation facilities and certain related industries that would also encourage the creation of new jobs are eligible for the high impact business credit for qualified investments against Illinois corporate income tax and personal income tax, property tax abatements, and the exemption from electricity excise tax and gas revenue tax. Qualifying businesses are also eligible for retailers' occupation (sales) tax exemptions on purchases of building materials and equipment. (35 ILCS 105/12; 35 ILCS 120/5l)

Eligible businesses include those businesses intended to establish new electric generating facilities through newly constructed generation plants or expansions to generation plants; businesses intended to establish new coal mines, re-establish coal production at a closed coal mine, or expand production at an existing coal mine; businesses intended to establish new gasification facilities; and businesses intended to establish new transmission facilities or upgrade existing transmission facilities that transfer electricity from supply points to delivery points. However, certain credits and exemptions are not available until the new or expanded facility or mine is operational. (20 ILCS 655/5.5)

To be eligible for the high impact business credit, abatement, or exemption, each business industry must fulfill certain requirements. All businesses must certify to the Department of Commerce and Economic Opportunity that the creation or expansion of facilities would not be possible without the credits or exemptions. (20 ILCS 655/5.5)

Electric generating facilities.—A new or expanded electric generation facility must be designed to provide baseload electric generation and must operate continuously throughout the year. It must have an aggregate rate generating capacity of at least 1,000 megawatts for all new units if it uses natural gas as its primary fuel, or have an aggregate rated generating capacity of at least 400 megawatts for all new units if it uses coal or gases derived from coal as its primary source of fuel. If coal is the primary source of fuel, then the expansion must include the creation of at least 150 new coal mining jobs in Illinois. An electric generation facility may also qualified for the above tax benefits if it is funded through a federal Department of Energy grant before December 31, 2010, or if it uses coal gasification or integrated gasification-combined cycle units that generate electricity or chemicals, or both. (20 ILCS 655/5.5)

Gasification facilities.—A new gasification facility must generate chemical feedstocks or transportation fuels derived from coal (including methane, methanol, and nitrogen fertilizer) and must qualify for financial assistance from the Department before December 31, 2010. (20 ILCS 655/5.5)

Coal mines.—A new, reopened, or expanded coal mine operation must result in the creation of 150 new jobs and the coal extracted must be the predominant source used for a new electric generating facility. The expansion must begin no sooner than July 1, 2001. (20 ILCS 655/5.5)

Transmission facilities.—A newly constructed or expanded transmission facility must have transmission lines with a voltage rating of 115 kilovolts and transmit a majority of the electricity generated by a new electric generation facility. Construction for new or expanded facilities must begin no sooner than July 1, 2001. (20 ILCS 655/5.5)

Wind power facilities.—A business that intends to establish a new wind power facility in Illinois may apply to be designated as a high impact business under the Illinois Enterprise Zone Act and may qualify for the retailers' occupation (sales) tax exemption for building materials that will be incorporated into a high impact business location. (20 ILCS 655/5.5)

"New wind power facility" means a newly constructed electric generation facility, or a newly constructed expansion of an existing electric generation facility, placed in service on or after July 1, 2009, that generates electricity using wind energy devices. The facility will be deemed to include all associated transmission lines, substations, and other equipment related to the generation of electricity from wind energy devices. "Wind energy device" means any device, with a nameplate capacity of at least 0.5 megawatts, that is used in the process of converting kinetic energy from the wind to generate electricity. An eligible wind energy business will not be subject to certain administrative and penalty provisions that are applicable to other high impact businesses under the Act. (20 ILCS 655/5.5)

• *High impact service facility machinery and equipment exemption*

Machinery and equipment used in the operation of a high impact service facility within an enterprise zone are exempt from ROT, SOT, UT, and SUT. "Machinery and equipment" includes (1) motor-driven heavy equipment, other than rolling stock, that is used to transport parcels, machinery, or equipment; (2) trailers used to ship parcels; (3) equipment used to maintain and provide in-house services; and (4) automated machinery and equipment used to transport parcels within the facility and all components, parts, pieces, and computer software or hardware contained in the related electronic control system. (35 ILCS 105/12; 35 ILCS 110/12; 35 ILCS 115/12; 35 ILCS 120/1j)

A business enterprise may apply to the Department of Commerce and Economic Opportunity for a certificate of eligibility for exemption. The certificate must be presented by the business to its supplier when making an initial purchase, along with a certification by the business that the machinery and equipment are exempt. Subsequent purchases may then be made by indicating the exempt status on the face of the purchase orders. (35 ILCS 120/1i)

"High impact service facility," defined.—A "high impact service facility" is a facility used primarily for sorting, handling and redistribution of mail, freight, cargo, or other parcels for delivery to an ultimate destination on an item-by-item basis and which will

    (1) make an investment by a business enterprise project of $100 million or more;

    (2) cause the creation of at least 750 jobs in an enterprise zone; and

    (3) be certified by the Department of Commerce and Economic Opportunity as contractually obligated to meet the foregoing two requirements (35 ILCS 120/1i)

Jet fuel and petroleum products used by high impact service facilities.—Jet fuel and petroleum products sold to and used by a high impact service facility located in an enterprise zone will be exempt from sales and use tax. However, the business enterprise must have waived its right to exemption for charges imposed under the Public Utilities Act.

The minimum period for which an exemption may be granted is ten years regardless of the duration of the enterprise zone in which the project is located. (35 ILCS 120/1j.1)

A high impact service facility seeking this exemption will be ineligible for the exemption of taxes imposed by the Public Utilities Act. Also, a high impact service facility that qualifies under this section and seeks an exemption under the Public Utilities Act will be ineligible for the exemption of taxes on machinery and equipment used in the operation of a high impact service facility. (35 ILCS 120/1j.2)

• *Intermodal terminal facility projects*

An Illinois sales, use, service use, and service occupation tax exemption is allowed for qualified sales of building materials to be incorporated into real estate in a redevelopment project area within an intermodal terminal facility area by remodeling, rehabilitating, or new construction. To document the exemption, the retailer must obtain from the purchaser a copy of a Certificate of Eligibility for Sales Tax Exemption that has been issued by the municipality in which the building project is located. (35 ILCS 105/12; 35 ILCS 110/12; 35 ILCS 115/12; 35 ILCS 120/2-6)

In addition, the retailer must obtain a certificate from the purchaser that contains a statement that the building materials qualify for exemption, the location or address of the real estate, the name of the intermodal terminal facility area, and other specified information. (35 ILCS 120/2-6)

A regulation has been adopted to implement the exemption for building materials to be incorporated into a redevelopment project area within an intermodal terminal facility area. (86 Ill. Adm. Code 130.1953)

• *Manufacture, assembly and graphic arts exemption*

Sales of tangible personal property to be used or consumed in an enterprise zone or by a high-impact business in the process of the manufacture or assembly of tangible personal property for wholesale or retail sale or lease or in the process of graphic arts production, if used or consumed at a facility certified by the Department are exempt from ROT, SOT, UT and SUT. The exemptions include repair and replacement parts for equipment and machinery used in manufacturing or assembling or in graphic arts production, and equipment, fuels, material, and supplies for the maintenance, repair, or operation of the machinery and equipment. The exemption does not apply to 1) the generation of electricity for wholesale or retail sale, 2) the generation or treatment of natural or artificial gas for wholesale or retail sale that is delivered to customers through pipes, pipelines or mains, or 3) the treatment of water for wholesale or retail sale that is delivered to customers through pipes, pipelines or mains, although the enacting legislation states that the amendments are declaratory of existing law. (35 ILCS 105/12; 35 ILCS 110/12; 35 ILCS 115/12; 35 ILCS 120/1d; 86 Ill. Adm. Code 130.1951(g), (h))

• *Pollution control facility exemption*

Exempt from the ROT, SOT, UT, and SUT is tangible personal property used or consumed in the operation of pollution control facilities within an enterprise zone. A regulation gives examples of property qualifying for the exemption. (35 ILCS 105/12; 35 ILCS 110/12; 35 ILCS 115/12; 35 ILCS 120/1e; 86 Ill. Adm. Code 130.1951(d))

• *River Edge Redevelopment Project*

An Illinois sales, use, service use, and service occupation tax exemption is provided for qualified sales of building materials to be incorporated into real estate within a River Edge Redevelopment Zone by remodeling, rehabilitating, or new construction. "Qualified sale" means a sale of building materials that will be incorporated into real estate as part of an industrial or commercial project for which a Certificate of Eligibility for Sales Tax Exemption has been issued by the corporate authorities of the municipality in which the building project is located. (35 ILCS 105/12; 35 ILCS 110/12; 35 ILCS 115/12; 35 ILCS 120/2-54; 86 Ill. Adm. Code 130.1954)

Beginning July 1, 2013, the retailer must obtain the purchaser's River Edge Building Materials Exemption Certificate to document the exemption. A construction contractor or other entity must not make tax-free purchases unless it has an active exemption certificate at the time of purchase. Before July 1, 2013, to document the exemption, the retailer must obtain a copy of the certificate of eligibility from the purchaser. In addition, before July 1, 2013, the retailer must obtain from the purchaser a certificate that contains a statement that the building materials are being purchased for incorporation into real estate located in a River Edge Redevelopment Zone, the address of such real estate, and other prescribed information. (35 ILCS 120/2-54; 86 Ill. Adm. Code 130.1954)

Corporate and personal income tax incentives and property tax abatements under the River Edge Redevelopment Zone Act are also available.

[¶60-390] Food and Grocery Items

Food for human consumption is taxable either at the full (high) state rate of tax or at a reduced (low) state rate, plus any applicable local tax. Generally, food for human consumption that is to be consumed off the premises where sold, except for alcoholic beverages, food consisting of or infused with adult use cannabis, soft drinks, candy, and food prepared for immediate consumption, is subject to retailer's occupation tax (sales) (ROT), service occupation tax (SOT), use tax (UT), and service use tax (SUT) at the low state rate. The high state rate of tax applies to food prepared for immediate consumption (such as hot food), and to soft drinks, candy, and alcoholic beverages. (35 ILCS 105/3-10; 35 ILCS 110/3-10; 35 ILCS 115/3-10; 35 ILCS 120/2-10; 86 Ill. Adm. Code 140.126(a))

For tax rates, see ¶60-110 Rate of Tax.

Two distinct factors must be considered in determining whether food is taxed at the high rate or the low rate. The first factor is whether the retailer provides premises for the consumption of food. If so, a rebuttable presumption is created that all food sales by that retailer are taxable at the high rate. The second factor is the nature of the food item being sold. Some foods, such as hot foods, soft drinks, candy, and alcoholic beverages, are always taxed at the high rate. (86 Ill. Adm. Code 130.310)

Test to determine high or low rate of tax.—The Department has created the following test for determining whether food is taxed at the high rate as "food prepared for immediate consumption" or the low rate as "food prepared for consumption off the premises where sold". (86 Ill. Adm. Code 130.310)

• If the retailer provides seating or facilities for on-premises consumption of food, all food sales by that retailer are presumed to be taxable at the high rate. However, this presumption can be rebutted if (1) the area for on-premises consumption is physically separated or otherwise distinguishable from the area where food not for immediate consumption is sold and (2) the retailer has a separate means of recording and accounting for collection of receipts from both high-rate and low-rate food sales.

If the retailer does not provide seating or facilities for on-premises consumption of food, then the low rate of tax will be applied to all food items except for "food prepared for immediate consumption" (see definition below) and except for soft drinks, candy, and alcoholic beverages. In order for the low rate of tax to apply, a retailer that sells both high and low rate foods must separately record and account for collection of receipts from both types of food sales.

The phrase "separate means of recording and accounting for collection of receipts" includes cash registers that separately identify high-rate and low-rate sales, separate cash registers, and other methods by which the tax on high-rate and low-rate sales is recorded at the time of collection.

Definitions; flow chart: A Department regulation provides a food flow chart to help retailers ascertain whether to apply the high or low rate of tax on particular food items. The regulation also provides definitions for "food," "food prepared for immediate consumption," and "premises." (86 Ill. Adm. Code 130.310)

"Food prepared for immediate consumption".—is subject to tax at the high rate and is defined as food that is prepared or made ready by a retailer to be eaten without substantial delay after the final stage of preparation by the retailer. (86 Ill. Adm. Code 130.310)

Included items: Food prepared for immediate consumption includes, but is not limited to, the following:

(1) all hot foods sold at any location ("hot" meaning any temperature greater than room temperature);

(2) sandwiches, either hot or cold, prepared by a retailer to the individual order of a customer;

(3) salad, olive, or sushi bars offered by a retailer at which individuals prepare their own salads (hot or cold);

(4) all coffee, tea, cappuccino, and other drinks prepared by a retailer for individual consumption, whether hot or cold;

(5) all food sold for consumption on the premises where sold. (86 Ill. Adm. Code 130.310)

Excluded items: Food prepared for immediate consumption does not include:

(1) bakery items (e.g., donuts, cookies, bagels) prepared by a retailer and sold either individually or in another quantity selected by the customer, provided they are for consumption off the premises where sold;

(2) whole breads, pies, and cakes prepared by a retailer, even when prepared to the individual order of a customer;

(3) sandwiches prepared by a retailer and placed in a deli case or other storage unit;

(4) cold salads, jellos, stuffed vegetables, or fruits sold by weight or by quart, pint, or other quantity by a retailer;

(5) cheese, fruit, vegetable, or meat trays prepared by a retailer, either to the individual order of a customer or premade and set out for sale;

(6) food items sold by a retailer that are not prepared or otherwise manufactured by that retailer, such as pre-packaged snacks or chips, unless these items will be consumed on the premises where sold (e.g., in a sandwich shop). (86 Ill. Adm. Code 130.310)

Additional examples of food items that are or are not considered food prepared for immediate consumption are provided in a department regulation. (86 Ill. Adm. Code 130.310)

Food establishments.—A Department regulation discusses the tax treatment of food sales by (1) grocery stores with on-premises facilities for consumption of food, (2) grocery stores without such premises, (3) restaurants and cafeterias, (4) bakeries, (5) delicatessens, (6) ice cream stores, (7) food courts, (8) convenience stores, and (9) coffee shops. (86 Ill. Adm. Code 130.310)

Exemption for persons receiving medical assistance in licensed facility.—Until June 30, 2016, food as described above is exempt from tax when purchased for use by persons receiving medical assistance under the Illinois Public Aid Code and residing in a licensed long-term care facility as defined in the Nursing Home Care Act or in a licensed facility as defined in the ID/DD Community Care Act, the MC/DD Act, or the Specialized Mental Health Rehabilitation Act of 2013. (35 ILCS 105/3-5; 35 ILCS 110/3-5; 35 ILCS 115/3-5; 35 ILCS 120/2-5) A regulation details the exemption for purchases of food, drugs, medicines, medical appliances, insulin, and other items for use by persons residing in a licensed long-term care facility and receiving medical assistance. (86 Ill. Adm. Code 150.337)

Certain hospital and child care meals are subject to tax at a reduced rate; see discussion on "Meals" below.

Certain food sales by nonprofit organizations are not taxable. See the discussion at ¶60-580 Nonprofit Organizations, Private Schools, and Churches.

Candy.—Candy does not qualify as "food for human consumption that is to be consumed off the premises where it is sold." As a result, candy is subject to the full state tax rate. "Candy" is a preparation of sugar, honey, or other natural or artificial sweeteners in combination with chocolate, fruits, nuts, or other ingredients or flavorings in the form of bars, drops, or pieces. However, "candy" does not include any preparation that contains flour or requires refrigeration. (35 ILCS 105/3-10; 35 ILCS 110/3-10; 35 ILCS 115/3-10; 35 ILCS 120/2-10)

For examples of candy and non-candy items, see *Informational Bulletin FY 2010-01*, Illinois Department of Revenue, July 2009.

Vending machine sales.—All food sold through a vending machine, except soft drinks, candy, and hot food products, will be taxed at the 1% sales and use tax rate for "food for human consumption that is to be consumed off the premises where it is sold," regardless of the location of the vending machine. (35 ILCS 105/3-10; 35 ILCS 110/3-10; 35 ILCS 115/3-10; 35 ILCS 120/2-10; 86 Ill. Adm. Code 130.310)

Sales tax does not apply to sales from automatic vending machines that prepare and serve hot foods or beverages, such as soup, coffee, or cocoa. (86 Ill. Adm. Code 130.332)

The use of vending machines in any other activity will not qualify for the exemption, including service or dispensing unheated food or beverage products. (86 Ill. Adm. Code 130.332)

"Food" and "soft drinks" defined.—"Food" is any solid, liquid, powder, or item intended primarily for human internal consumption, including condiments, spices, seasonings, vitamins, bottled water, and ice.

Soft drinks, as specially defined by statute, do not qualify for the reduced tax rate for food and therefore are subject to the full state tax rate. "Soft drinks" are defined as non-alcoholic beverages that contain natural or artificial sweeteners. However, "soft drinks" do not include beverages that contain milk or milk products, soy, rice or similar milk substitutes, or greater than 50% of vegetable or fruit juice by volume. (35 ILCS 105/3-10; 35 ILCS 110/3-10; 35 ILCS 115/3-10; 35 ILCS 120/2-10; 86 Ill. Adm. Code 130.310)

For examples of soft drinks, see *Informational Bulletin FY 2010-01*, Illinois Department of Revenue, July 2009.

Chicago soft drink tax: Soft drinks that are subject to the full state tax rate are subject to the Chicago soft drink tax, while soft drinks that qualify for the reduced state tax rate are exempt from the Chicago soft drink tax. Chicago soft drink taxes are discussed at ¶61-710 Local Taxes. Local tax rates are discussed at ¶61-735 Local Rates.

"Premises" defined.—"Premises" means the area over which a retailer exercises control and the area in which facilities for eating are provided. They include areas provided by employers to employees and common or shared eating areas in shopping centers or public buildings if customers of food vendors adjacent to such areas may use them for consumption of food. (86 Ill. Adm. Code 130.310)

Local taxes on food and beverages are discussed at ¶ 61-710. Tax rates are given at ¶ 61-735.

• *Cooperative associations*

All sales by cooperative associations and by agricultural cooperative associations organized under "The Agricultural Co-operative Act" are subject to the ROT and UT. (86 Ill. Adm. Code 130.1945; 86 Ill. Adm. Code 150.1201)

A "cooperative association" is a group of persons organized for the purpose of purchasing or producing and selling such items as groceries, provisions, or other articles at retail for reasonable prices. (86 Ill. Adm. Code 130.1945)

To the extent that an agricultural co-operative association engages in selling services, those receipts are subject to the Service Occupation Tax Act. (86 Ill. Adm. Code 130.1945(b)(2))

• *Meals*

Persons in the business of selling meals, such as hotels, restaurants, caterers, boarding houses, and concessionaires are generally taxable on receipts from those sales. (86 Ill. Adm. Code 130.2145) It makes no difference whether a profit is realized from sales of meals, as long as the seller is engaged in a commercial enterprise. Other sales of meals are discussed below.

Hospital and child care meals.—Food prepared for immediate consumption and transferred incident to sales of services by an entity licensed under the Hospital Licensing Act, the Nursing Home Care Act, the MR/DD Community Care Act, or the Child Care Act of 1969 is subject to the SOT and SUT at a reduced rate. (35 ILCS 110/3-10; 35 ILCS 115/3-10; *Informational Bulletin FY 2000-4,* Department of Revenue, October 1999) See ¶ 60-110 for the applicable rate of tax. For a general discussion of sales made by nonprofit hospitals and nursing homes, see ¶ 60-580.

Meals for elderly.—Meals served to participants in the federal Nutrition Program for the Elderly pursuant to grants or contracts under Title VII of the Older American Act of 1965 are exempt from the sales and use tax if served in return for contributions by the participants that correspond to federal guidelines. (35 ILCS 105/2; 35 ILCS 120/1; 86 Ill. Adm. Code 150.1201; 86 Ill. Adm. Code 130.120(o); 86 Ill. Adm. Code 150.201(h))

Meals sold by charitable or religious organizations.—Meals sold to the public by charitable or religious organizations are taxable unless done not more than twice in one year and the profits used for charitable or religious purposes. A church or religious organization is not taxable on receipts from frequent sales of meals if (1) the profits are used for religious purposes, (2) the meals are sold only to church members or guests and not to the public, and (3) the meals are served in connection with a religious service or function. (86 Ill. Adm. Code 130.2005(b))

School meals.—Sales of meals by schools to students and employees from a cafeteria or dining facility on school premises are not subject to tax. However, all sales are taxable if the facility is open to other persons. Also subject to tax are sales of soft drinks, candy, peanuts, popcorn, chewing gum, and similar items to students or the public from a book store, through vending machines, or from other places other than a restricted school cafeteria. (86 Ill. Adm. Code 130.2005(b))

See ¶ 60-580 for a discussion of the UT, SUT, SOT, and ROT exemptions for personal property, including food, purchased through school fund-raising events.

Airlines.—Sales of food and beverages to airlines for use in serving passengers without a separate charge for the meal by the airlines are taxable. Sales of meals to airlines for their crews are nontaxable sales for resale where the cost is deducted from a food allowance, but the airline is subject to ROT on its receipts from reselling the meals to the crews. (86 Ill. Adm. Code 130.2145(a))

Employer provided meals.—Sales of meals from an employer-operated cafeteria are taxable. However, the furnishing of meals to employees at no charge is not subject to tax. Employers who do furnish free meals to employees are liable for use tax on the cost price of the meals, which is presumed to be 75 cents per meal in the absence of evidence showing a lower figure. (86 Ill. Adm. Code 130.2050)

Food in connection with room rental.—A regulation explains the application of the true-object test in determining the taxability of charges made by hotels and similar establishments for the rental of a meeting, conference, banquet, or similar type of room when food and beverages are provided. Examples of these situations include wedding receptions, conferences, and business luncheons. If only snacks or non-alcoholic beverages are transferred incidental to the renting of a room, the true object of the transaction will be deemed to be the rental of the room, and the charges for the room rental will not be subject to tax. If, however, any food other than snacks is provided or alcohol is served, the true object of the transaction will be deemed to be the sale of food or beverages, and the charges for the room rental will be considered part of the seller's taxable gross receipts. Numerous examples applying these provisions are provided. (86 Ill. Adm. Code 130.2145)

Food-related charges.—The regulation also provides examples of other types of charges related to the provision of food and beverages that are considered taxable (e.g., food serving or carving and corkage fees) and examples of charges that are not related to the provision of food and beverages that are considered nontaxable (e.g., security, valet, coat check, and entertainment). (86 Ill. Adm. Code 130.2145)

• *Mandatory service charges*

A mandatory service charge that is separately stated on a customer's food or beverage bill is exempt from the ROT, SOT, UT, and SUT to the extent that the proceeds are turned over as tips or as a substitute for tips to employees who participate directly in preparing, serving, hosting, or cleaning up the food or beverage function with respect to which the service charge is imposed. The entire service charge is taxable if any part of it is used to fund or pay wages, labor costs, employee benefits, or employer costs of doing business. (35 ILCS 105/3-5; 35 ILCS 110/3-5; 35 ILCS 115/3-5; 35 ILCS 120/2-5; 86 Ill. Adm. Code 130.120(r); 86 Ill. Adm. Code 130.2145(d))

• *Packaging*

Sales to and use by food and beverage vendors, such as restaurants and cafeterias, of nonreusable tangible personal property are exempt from tax if the items are transferred to customers in connection with the delivery, packaging, or consumption of food or beverages. (35 ILCS 105/2; 35 ILCS 120/1; 86 Ill. Adm. Code 130.2070(c)(3)) Examples of items that may qualify for the exemption include paper and plastic cups, plates, baskets, boxes, sleeves, buckets or other containers, utensils, straws, placemats, doggie bags, and wrapping or packaging materials that cannot be reused by the vendors and that are transferred to customers. Paper products, servings trays and dishes, utensils, condiment bottles, and other items that are not transferred to customers do not qualify for the exemption. (86 Ill. Adm. Code 130.2070(c)(3)) Vendors may rely on their own experience in determining what portion of their nonreusable items qualify for exemption. (86 Ill. Adm. Code 130.2070(c)(5))

• *Food service companies*

Generally, persons engaged in the business of selling meals to purchasers for use or consumption incur sales tax liability on their receipts from such sales. (86 Ill. Adm. Code 130.2145(a)) The Department of Revenue has issued the following rulings regarding the tax treatment of food service companies and food management companies, i.e., businesses that contract with corporations, schools, universities, hospitals, nursing homes, and other entities to provide meals.

Agent for exempt entity.—A food service company that acts as an agent for a school district can use the district's tax exemption identification number when it purchases tangible personal property on behalf of the district pursuant to their contract provided the district pays for the property and title to the property passes directly from the vendors to the district and remains at all times in the district. (*Private Letter Ruling ST 88-0541-PLR*, Illinois Dept. of Revenue, August 02, 1988)

Employee meals.—Where an employer itself or through an agent operates a restaurant that provides meals to its own employees, the sales tax consequences depend upon whether such meals are sold or provided free of charge. Where the employer sells meals to the employees, the sales are subject to sales tax at the full tax rate because the food is being sold for immediate consumption. (*Private Letter Ruling ST 97-0004-PLR*, Illinois Dept. of Revenue, January 27, 1997)

Gross receipts.—A catering company that contracts with a university to utilize the university's kitchen facilities to prepare catered meals for sale to an outside entity is subject to Illinois sales tax on the catered sales because it is selling tangible personal property to users or consumers. The entire receipts from such transactions would be taxable without any deduction for service costs or other overhead expenses. A commission based on a percentage of the catered sales that is paid to the university would not be subject to sales tax because it is not a tangible transaction. The commission would be a portion of the costs of doing business and may not be deducted from the catering gross receipts subject to sales tax. The activities may affect the university's sales and property tax exempt status. (*Private Letter Ruling ST 91-0664-PLR*, Illinois Dept. of Revenue, August 22, 1991)

Taxable charges.—A caterer's charges to clients for food preparation and waiting services are costs of doing business which must be included in the sales tax calculation. If consumable products are purchased with a resale certificate and subsequently transferred to the customer, tax would be measured on the separately listed selling price. If nonconsumable items are purchased with a view to rent to customers (e.g., tables, chairs), use tax should be paid at the time of purchase. (*Private Letter Ruling ST 90-0377-PLR*, Illinois Dept. of Revenue, July 2, 1990)

Meal coupon book.—A food service retailer that contracts with schools and colleges to provide dining services and that sells coupon books used by students, faculty, and staff members to purchase meals does not incur sales tax liability on the sale of coupon books because the coupon book is an intangible. Rather, the business incurs sales tax liability when the coupons are redeemed. The tax liability is based upon the value of the coupons received. (*Private Letter Ruling ST 90-0601-PLR*, Illinois Dept. of Revenue, September 14, 1990)

• *Local taxes*

Certain localities may impose a food tax that is administered and collected by the local government rather than the state Department of Revenue. The rates listed and administered by the Department can be found with the Tax Rate Finder on the Department's website at http://www.revenue.state.il.us/Publications/taxratefinder.htm

Chicago.—

Restaurant tax.—Chicago imposes a tax on the selling price of food and beverages sold at retail by places for eating located in Chicago. (Chicago Munic. Code Sec.

3-30-020; Chicago Munic. Code Sec. 3-30-030) A "place for eating" means any restaurant or other business, by whatever name, that is engaged in the sale of food prepared for immediate consumption and provides for on-premises consumption of the food it sells.

"Food prepared for immediate consumption" has the same meaning as set forth in 35 ILCS 120/2-10, and generally means food made by the retailer to be eaten without substantial delay after the final stage of preparation. "On-premises consumption" has the same meaning as set forth in 86 Ill. Adm. Code 130.310, and generally means the area over which the business exercises control. (Chicago Department of Revenue, Addendum to Notice Published May 13, 2004)

Chicago exempts all sales of food and beverage that are exempt from the Illinois ROT as set forth in 35 ILCS 120/1 et seq. (Chicago Munic. Code Sec. 3-30-040)

Occasional or de minimis sales.—A place for eating with an annual tax liability of $200 or less is not required to file a return or pay the restaurant tax. However, this exception is not available to places for eating that separately state and charge tax to customers during the tax year. (Chicago Munic. Code Sec. 3-30-050)

Returns and payment.—Places for eating subject to the restaurant tax must pay or remit the actual amount of tax due on or before the last day of the month following the monthly (or quarterly, if applicable) tax period in which the tax liability was incurred. Certain taxpayers and tax collectors may make estimated payments in lieu of paying or remitting actual amounts due. Returns must be filed on an annual basis on or before August 15 of each year. (Chicago Munic. Code Sec. 3-30-060)

Soft drink tax.—Businesses that sell soft drinks at retail in Chicago must collect and pay the Chicago Soft Drink Tax. (Chicago Munic. Code Sec. 3-45-040) This tax replaced the Chicago Department of Revenue's soft drink tax on distributors. The tax is imposed at the rate of 3% of the gross receipts from sales of soft drinks other than fountain soft drinks. The tax is administered by the Illinois Department of Revenue. (Chicago Munic. Code Sec. 3-45-050)

"Soft drink" is defined as any complete, finished, ready-to-use nonalcoholic drink, whether carbonated or not, including soda water, cola, fruit juice, vegetable juice, and carbonated water. (Chicago Munic. Code Sec. 3-45-020(E) and 35 ILCS 120/2-10) The soft drink does not have to be contained in a closed or sealed bottle, can, carton, or container to be taxable. "Soft drinks" do not include coffee, tea, noncarbonated water, infant formula, or milk.

Returns and payment.—Retailers who are subject to the tax must file Form ST-14, Chicago Soft Drink Tax Return, and pay taxes due at the time they file.

All taxes returns shall be filed with the Chicago department of revenue on an annual basis on or before August 15 of each year. (Chicago Munic. Code Sec. 3-45-090) Taxpayers or tax collectors must pay or remit the actual amount of tax due on or before the last day of the month following the monthly (or quarterly, if applicable) tax period in which the tax liability was incurred. Certain taxpayers and tax collectors may make estimated payments in lieu of paying or remitting actual amounts due.

Fountain soft drink tax.—A tax is imposed on all persons engaged in the business of selling fountain soft drinks at retail in the city of Chicago at the rate of 9% of the cost price of the fountain soft drinks. The tax is administered by the Chicago Department of Revenue. (Chicago Munic. Code Sec. 3-45-060)

"Cost price" is defined as the consideration paid by a retail seller for the purchase of soft drink syrup or concentrate that is designed to be further mixed with water before it is consumed as a soft drink, valued in money, whether paid in money or otherwise, including cash, credits and services, determined without any deduction on account of any of the soft drink supplier's costs or other expenses. (Chicago Munic. Code Sec. 3-45-060) "Fountain soft drink" is defined as any soft drink that is prepared by a retail seller by mixing soft drink syrup or concentrate with water, by hand or through a soft drink dispensing machine, at or near the point and time of sale to retail purchasers. (Chicago Munic. Code Sec. 3-45-020(D))

Returns and payment.—Soft drink suppliers must collect the tax from retailers to whom they sell soft drink syrup or concentrate and remit the tax to the Chicago Department of Revenue. The supplier collects the tax by adding the tax to the selling price of soft drink syrup or concentrate to be used to prepare fountain soft drinks for sale in the city (Chicago Munic. Code Sec. 3-45-080)

Returns are filed on an annual basis, on or before August 15 of each year. Taxpayers or tax collectors must pay or remit the actual amount of tax due on or before the last day of the month following the monthly (or quarterly, if applicable) tax period in which the tax liability was incurred. Certain taxpayers and tax collectors may make estimated payments in lieu of paying or remitting actual amounts due. Soft drink supplier must file a sworn report of soft drink syrup and concentrate sales made to retailers during the immediately preceding month. (Chicago Munic. Code Sec. 3-45-090) Payment must accompany the return. Suppliers may retain 1.75% of the tax collected as reimbursement for expenses incurred in collecting and remitting the tax. (Chicago Munic. Code Sec. 3-45-100) Further, soft drink suppliers must register with the Chicago Department of Revenue within 30 days after commencing business. (Chicago Munic. Code Sec. 3-45-120)

Bottled Water Tax.—Chicago imposes a per bottle tax on the retail sale of bottled water in the city. (Chicago Munic. Code Sec. 3-43-030)

Collection of tax: The tax shall be collected and remitted by each wholesale bottled water dealer who sells bottles of water to a retail bottled water dealer located in the city, who in turn shall collect the tax from the retail purchaser. If a retailer obtains or receives bottled water upon which tax has not been collected by the wholesale bottled water dealer, the retailer must collect and remit the tax directly to the Chicago Department of Revenue. (Chicago Munic. Code Sec. 3-43-050) The ultimate liability for payment of the tax is to be bourne by the purchaser. (Chicago Munic. Code Sec. 3-43-040)

A wholesale or retail bottled water dealer that timely remits the tax to the Chicago Department of Revenue may retain a percentage of the tax remitted as reimbursement for the expenses incurred in collecting and remitting the tax, keeping records, and filing returns. (Chicago Munic. Code Sec. 3-43-100)

Exemptions: The tax does not apply to purchases of bottled water by passengers on an interstate carrier. (Chicago Munic. Code Sec. 3-43-110)

Tax payment and return: Tax payments and remittances must be made in accordance with Chicago Munic. Code Sec. 3-4-187, (i.e., generally, due on or before the last day of the month following the monthly tax period in which the liability was incurred.) Provisions for annual and estimated payments may apply. Tax returns are due on an annual basis on or before August 15 of each year. (Chicago Munic. Code Sec. 3-43-060)

Registration: Every wholesale bottled water dealer in existence on January 1, 2008, must register with the Department before February 1, 2008. Every wholesale bottled water dealer commencing business after January 1, 2008, must register with the Department within 30 days after commencing such business. (Chicago Munic. Code Sec. 3-43-120)

[¶60-420] Government Transactions

Generally, sales to the government of the United States are exempt from retailers occupation (sales) tax (ROT) and use tax (UT) both by Illinois statute and by constitutional constraints discussed below. Also, sales to state or local governmental units are not subject to tax. (35 ILCS 105/3-5; 35 ILCS 120/2-5)

The sale or transfer of tangible personal property as an incident to the rendering of service for the United States government is not subject to service occupation tax (SOT) and service use tax (SUT). (35 ILCS 110/2; 35 ILCS 115/2)

Personal property purchased by a lessor who leases the property for one year or longer to a governmental body that has been issued an active sales tax exemption identification number is exempt from sales and use tax. (35 ILCS 105/3-5(32); 35 ILCS 110/3-5(16); 35 ILCS 115/3-5(17); 35 ILCS 120/2-5(29))

CCH COMMENT: Tax applies upon expiration of lease.—The sales and use tax exemption for personal property purchased by a lessor who leased the property for a year or longer, to a governmental body that has been issued an active sales tax exemption identification number expired on January 1, 2001, but was restored and is available beginning on August 2, 2001. Once the property that qualified for the exemptions comes off the lease, the lessor incurs either Illinois use tax or Illinois service use tax on the fair market value of the property. However, for use tax purposes, any lease agreements entered into between January 1, 1996, and December 31, 2000, continue to be exempt after January 1, 2001, until the items are no longer leased in a qualifying manner or used in a qualifying manner. (86 Ill. Adm. Code 130.120(mm) and (nn); 86 Ill. Adm. Code 150.332; 86 Ill. Adm. Code 140.125; 86 Ill. Adm. Code 130.2011; 86 Ill. Adm. Code 130.2012)

The discussion below is separated into U.S. government transactions, state and local transactions, foreign government transactions, and public school transactions.

• *United States government transactions*

Sales to and by the U.S. government are exempt by statute and regulation. (35 ILCS 105/3-5; 35 ILCS 120/2-5; 35 ILCS 110/2; 35 ILCS 115/2; 86 Ill. Adm. Code 130.120(i); 86 Ill. Adm. Code 130.2055; 86 Ill. Adm. Code 130.2080; 86 Ill. Adm. Code 150.330)

A sale or transfer of tangible personal property as an incident to the rendering of service by the government is also exempt. (35 ILCS 110/2; 35 ILCS 115/2; 86 Ill. Adm. Code 140.125(h)(3); 86 Ill. Adm. Code 140.201(e)(3))

In addition, the Supremacy Clause (Article VI) of the U.S. Constitution declares that the U.S. Constitution and laws are the supreme law of the land, and the U.S. Supreme Court held early that this clause invalidated a state tax imposed directly on a federal instrumentality. (*McCulloch v. Maryland* (1819, US SCt) 17 US 316)

Tax-free purchases may be made only if the government has an exemption identification number issued by the Department of Revenue. The exemption identification number or renewal is valid for five years after the first day of the month following the month of issuance. However, no exemption number is required if a purchase is made with a U.S. Government Bank Card. (35 ILCS 105/3-5; 35 ILCS 120/2-5; 35 ILCS 110/2; 35 ILCS 115/2; 35 ILCS 120/1g; 86 Ill. Adm. Code 130.2080; 86 Ill. Adm. Code 150.330; 86 Ill. Adm. Code 130.2007)

Government contractors.—Materials sold for incorporation into real estate owned by governmental bodies are not subject to the ROT and UT. A supplier that claims exemption must have a certification from the contractor stating that the purchases are for conversion into real estate under a contract with a governmental body. The person claiming exemption has the burden of proving that the contractor's customer qualifies as a governmental body. (86 Ill. Adm. Code 130.2075(d))

Tangible personal property purchased by a government contractor where the contract with the government unit explicitly requires the contractor to sell the items purchased to the government unit is exempt from ROT. The contract must state that the government unit requires the contractor to provide the tangible personal property to the government unit but does not have to be item specific. For example, within the contract a statement that title to all tangible personal property must be transferred to the government unit is sufficient to allow for the exemption. (86 Ill. Adm. Code 130.2076)

The supplier of the tangible personal property must keep a certificate of resale in his/her records. (86 Ill. Adm. Code 130.2076)

Federal areas.—The federal Buck Act provides that state sales tax can be collected in federal areas, such as military reservations, although not from the government itself. Motor fuel sold on military or other federal reservations is also subject to state tax. (4 U.S.C. § 104; 4 U.S.C. §§ 105–110; 86 Ill. Adm. Code 130.1101; 86 Ill. Adm. Code 130.1105; 86 Ill. Adm. Code 130.1110)

• *State and local transactions*

Sales to any state or local governmental body are exempt from ROT and UT. (35 ILCS 105/3-5; 35 ILCS 120/2-5; 86 Ill. Adm. Code 130.120(i); 86 Ill. Adm. Code 130.2080; 86 Ill. Adm. Code 150.330)

Also, a sale or transfer of tangible personal property as an incident to the rendering of service for or by any governmental body is exempt from SOT and SUT. (35 ILCS 110/2; 35 ILCS 115/2; 86 Ill. Adm. Code 140.125(h)(3); 86 Ill. Adm. Code 140.201(e)(3))

The state of Illinois and its local governments are subject to ROT if they are engaged in the selling of tangible personal property at retail other than in the performance of a governmental function. The furnishing of utility services to the public is exempt. (86 Ill. Adm. Code 130.2055)

Tax-free purchases may be made only if the governmental body has an exemption identification number issued by the Department of Revenue. The exemption identification number or renewal is valid for five years. (35 ILCS 105/3-5; 35 ILCS 120/2-5; 35 ILCS 110/2; 35 ILCS 115/2; 35 ILCS 120/1g; 86 Ill. Adm. Code 130.2080; 86 Ill. Adm. Code 150.330; 86 Ill. Adm. Code 130.2007)

The rental or lease of tangible personal property by a lessor who leases the property to a governmental body, with an active sales tax exemption number, under a lease of one year or longer is exempt from UT, SUT, SOT, and ROT. (35 ILCS 105/3-5; 35 ILCS 120/2-5; 35 ILCS 110/2; 35 ILCS 115/2)

Contractors.—Materials sold for incorporation into real estate owned by governmental bodies are not subject to the ROT and UT. Materials sold to construction contractors for incorporation into public improvements to be transferred to local government units upon completion are also not subject to tax. (86 Ill. Adm. Code 130.2075(d); 86 Ill. Adm. Code 130.2075(e))

A supplier that claims exemption must have a certification from the contractor stating that the purchases are for conversion into real estate under a contract with a governmental body. The person claiming exemption has the burden of proving that the contractor's customer qualifies as a governmental body. (86 Ill. Adm. Code 130.2075(d))

Tangible personal property purchased by a government contractor where the contract with the government unit explicitly requires the contractor to sell the items purchased to the government unit is exempt from ROT. The contract must state that the government unit requires the contractor to provide the tangible personal property to the government unit but does not have to be item specific. For example, within the contract a statement that title to all tangible personal property must be transferred to the government unit is sufficient to allow for the exemption. (86 Ill. Adm. Code 130.2076)

The supplier of the tangible personal property must keep a certificate of resale in his/her records. (86 Ill. Adm. Code 130.2076)

Municipal convention hall.—Tangible personal property purchased by a public-facilities corporation for purposes of constructing or furnishing a municipal convention hall is exempt from ROT, UT, SOT, and SUT. The exemption is allowed only if legal title to the municipal convention hall is transferred to the municipality without any further consideration at the time of completion of the hall or upon the retirement or redemption of any bonds or other debt instruments issued in connection with the development of the hall. The exemption is not subject to the automatic sunset provision. (35 ILCS 105/3-5(35); 35 ILCS 110/3-5(27); 35 ILCS 115/3-5(28); 35 ILCS 120/2-5(40))

• *Foreign government transactions*

Sales to a foreign governmental body are exempt from ROT and UT. (35 ILCS 105/3-5; 35 ILCS 120/2-5; 86 Ill. Adm. Code 130.120(i); 86 Ill. Adm. Code 130.2080; 86 Ill. Adm. Code 150.330)

Also exempt are sales or transfers of property as an incident to the rendering of service for or by a foreign governmental body. (35 ILCS 110/2; 35 ILCS 115/2; 86 Ill. Adm. Code 140.125(h)(3); 86 Ill. Adm. Code 140.201(e)(3))

Sales by a foreign government are not subject to ROT. (86 Ill. Adm. Code 130.2055)

The purchase of property by corporations whose stock is owned by foreign governments is taxable. (86 Ill. Adm. Code 130.2080)

Tax-free purchases may be made only if the foreign governmental body has an exemption identification number issued by the Department of Revenue. The exemption identification number or renewal is valid for five years. (35 ILCS 105/3-5; 35 ILCS 120/2-5; 35 ILCS 110/2; 35 ILCS 115/2; 35 ILCS 120/1g; 86 Ill. Adm. Code 130.2080; 86 Ill. Adm. Code 150.330; 86 Ill. Adm. Code 130.2007)

CCH COMMENT: *Classification system violated constitution.*—In *Japan Air Lines Co. v. Zehnder*, consolidated with *Scandinavian Airlines Systems et al. v. Zehnder*, Nos. 1-99-1826 and 1-99-1827 (unpublished order pursuant to Sup. Ct. Rule 23), December 28, 2000, the Illinois Appellate Court, First Judicial District held that airline companies owned in part by foreign governments were entitled to a credit against Illinois retailers' occupation (sales) tax and use tax on purchases of fuel, in-flight meals, and other tangible personal property because the airlines were exempt from such taxes under the most-favored-nation status clause of the federal Treaty of Friendship, Commerce, and Navigation. The commercial activities of the airline companies, rather than percentage of governmental ownership of company stock, determined if these companies should be treated the same as another foreign government-owned airline company that was exempt from tax due to most-favored-nation status under the Treaty. All three airlines engaged in similar commercial activity and, thus, by exempting one government-owned airline from tax, the Department was required to exempt other government-owned airlines from tax.

Further, the Illinois Department of Revenue lacked the authority to amend 86 Ill. Adm. Code 130.2080 in 1984 to provide that the purchase of meals, fuels, and other tangible personal property by corporations were taxable sales at retail notwithstanding the fact that the stock of such corporations may be owned exclusively or in part by foreign governments because the Department had previously determined that the airlines were exempt and, therefore, could only change the exemption determination by legislative sanction.

Finally, whether the Uniformity Clause of the Illinois Constitution was violated was not addressed as the taxable status of the companies was already determined.

Diplomatic personnel.—The U.S. State Department issues tax exemption identification cards to foreign diplomatic and consular officials. (86 Ill. Adm. Code 130.2080)

• *Public school transactions*

Public and private school transactions are discussed at ¶ 60-580 Nonprofit Organizations, Private Schools, and Churches. School meals are discussed at ¶ 60-390 Food and Grocery Items.

[¶ 60-445] Internet/Electronic Commerce

Sales or use tax may apply to a variety of transactions in an electronic commerce environment. Such transactions include (1) purchases over the Internet of taxable services and property that are delivered in a nonelectronic form and (2) purchases of services or property that are delivered electronically and that may or may not be the equivalent of services or property that also can be delivered by nonelectronic means. General principles concerning the taxability of such transactions are discussed below.

Taxes on sales of computer software and services are discussed at ¶ 60-310 Computer Software and Services.

If a transaction in an electronic commerce environment is taxable, the seller may or may not have a sufficient taxable connection, or nexus, with the taxing jurisdiction to be required to collect and remit tax on that transaction. Nexus issues in an electronic commerce environment are discussed below.

Under the federal Internet Tax Freedom Act (ITFA) (P.L. 105-277, 112 Stat. 2681, 47 U.S.C. Sec. 151 note, amended by P.L. 107-75, P.L. 108-435, P.L. 110-108, P.L. 113-164; P.L. 113-235; P.L. 114-113; and P.L.114-125) and its amendments, state and local governments are barred from imposing multiple or discriminatory taxes on electronic commerce and taxes on Internet access, except for Internet access taxes allowed under grandfather clauses. The moratorium is permanent effective February 24, 2016. The Internet Tax Freedom Act and its amendments are discussed below.

CCH COMMENT: *Sale of Tangible Personal Property.*—Tangible personal property sold at retail over the Internet is taxed in the same manner as any other retail sale. If the sale of tangible personal property is made from an Illinois location or filled from an inventory at an Illinois location and delivered to an Illinois location, Illinois sales tax is due (35 ILCS 120/1 et seq.) unless the purchaser documents a valid exemption from tax. (35 ILCS 120/2-5) If the sale of tangible personal property is made from an out-of-state location to an Illinois location, the Illinois use tax is due (35 ILCS 105/1 et seq.) unless the purchaser documents a valid exemption from tax. (35 ILCS 105/3-5)

• *Taxability of transactions in electronic commerce*

The federal Internet Tax Freedom Act (ITFA) defines "electronic commerce" as any transaction conducted over the Internet or through Internet access, comprising the sale, lease, license, offer, or delivery of property, goods, services, or information, whether or not for consideration, and includes the provision of Internet access.

Transactions involving nonelectronic delivery.—Sales over the Internet may include the purchase of services that are delivered in a nonelectronic form, tangible personal property that is commonly delivered by mail or common carrier, or property in an electronic form capable of being processed by a computer ("digital property") that is stored on tangible storage media that is commonly delivered by mail or common carrier.

The taxability of such sales over the Internet generally is governed by the same rules as the purchase of such services or property in a traditional Main Street environment. However, the obligation of the seller to collect tax on such remote sales depends on whether the seller has nexus with the taxing jurisdiction, which is discussed below. If a sale is taxable and the seller does not collect tax, then the buyer generally is responsible for remitting use tax on the transaction.

A state may consider digital property stored on tangible storage media to be included in the definition of "tangible personal property" and, therefore, subject to the same taxability standard. Many states have special rules concerning the taxability of software and these are discussed at ¶ 60-310 Computers, Software, and Services.

Transactions involving electronic delivery.—Sales over the Internet may also include the purchase of digital property, services, or information delivered electronically.

While most states impose sales and use tax generally on all sales of tangible personal property, the taxability of sales of digital property delivered electronically varies among the states. In some states, a sale of certain types of digital property delivered electronically is considered a taxable sale of tangible personal property. In other states, such a sale is treated as not involving the transfer of tangible personal property and, therefore, is nontaxable. In yet other states, sales of some software delivered electronically are taxable while sales of other items delivered electronically are nontaxable.

Some states may also draw a distinction based on whether the digital property delivered electronically would be considered tangible personal property if the same content were transferred on tangible storage media. That is, some states may only tax sales involving the electronic delivery of property if the property is the digital equivalent of tangible personal property.

Most states apply a true object of the transaction test in making taxability determinations. For example, if a state does not tax legal services, the delivery of a will electronically would not be taxable even if the state taxes the digital equivalent of tangible personal property, just as delivery of a will prepared on paper would not be taxable as the sale of tangible personal property.

The taxability of services varies among the states. Illinois imposes a Service Occupation Tax (SOT) on persons engaged in the business of making sales of services (35 ILCS 115/1 et seq.; 86 Ill. Adm. Code 140.101; 35 ILCS 120/2-5), as well as a Service Use Tax (SUT) (35 ILCS 110/1 et seq.; 86 Ill. Adm. Code 160.101) Generally, technical support services are exempt if they are separately stated from the selling price of canned computer software, for example. See ¶ 60-665 Services and ¶ 60-310 Computers, Software, and Services.

For example, a retail sale of canned computer software transmitted over the Internet would be subject to the Illinois Retailers' (Sales) Occupation Tax Act (ROT). (35 ILCS 120/1 et seq.; 86 Ill. Adm. Code 130.1935(a)) However, custom computer programs, prepared to the special order of the customer, would not be subject to tax according to an Illinois Department of Revenue regulation. (86 Ill. Adm. Code 130.1935(c)(1))

Neither the licenses of computer software, whether canned or custom, nor the transfer of the subsequent software updates related to that software that meet all of the criteria provided in Section 130.1935(a)(1) will be subject to sales tax.

Thus, a license of software is not a taxable retail sale if:

—it is evidenced by a written agreement signed by the licensor and the customer;

—it restricts the customer's duplication and use of the software;

—it prohibits the customer from licensing, sublicensing, or transferring the software to a third party (except to a related party);

—the vendor will provide another copy at minimal or no charge if the customer loses or damages the software;

—the customer must destroy or return all copies of the software to the vendor at the end of the license period. (86 Ill. Adm. Code 130.1935(a))

For a discussion of software and software licenses, see ¶60-310 Computers, Software, and Services

Electronic downloads of intangible personal property such as books, musical recordings, newspapers, and magazines are not subject to retailers' occupation tax and use tax. (86 Ill. Adm. Code 130.2105)

For a discussion of the application of Chicago's amusement tax to certain electronically delivered amusements, see ¶60-230 Admissions, Entertainment, and Dues.

• *Nexus and collection responsibility*

Once it is determined that a taxable transaction is involved, it must be determined whether nexus is sufficient to trigger tax liability and on whom tax collection responsibility rests.

In the absence of specific statutes or other defined policy governing taxation of sales of personal property that are made over the Internet, the law and issues applicable to mail order sales may provide a basis for determining sales and use tax treatment of sales made by electronic commerce.

As with mail order sales, a transaction involving an electronic sale to a purchaser by a vendor that has no physical presence in the purchaser's state raises nexus issues. Under *Quill Corp. v. North Dakota*, 504 US 298 (1992), unless a vendor has substantial nexus with the purchaser's state, the state has no constitutional basis for the imposition of sales and use tax collection responsibility on that vendor. Sales and use tax nexus and other constitutional issues are discussed at ¶60-025 Nexus-Doing Business in Illinois and ¶60-075 U.S. Constitution.

Among the factors specific to an electronic commerce environment that may be taken into account in determining whether nexus exists is the maintenance of a web page on a computer server located in the taxing state and the nature and extent of in-state services performed for a vendor by a company maintaining the vendor's website.

As with mail order sales, transactions involving electronic sales of tangible personal property to Illinois purchasers by vendors that have no physical presence in Illinois may raise nexus issues. Unless a vendor has substantial nexus with the purchaser's state, the state has no constitutional basis for the imposition of sales or use tax collection responsibility.

Nexus is not established if an out-of-state retailer makes sales to Illinois customers via the Internet, where the out-of-state retailer's only presence in Illinois is through advertising over the Internet even if the Internet provider maintains servers in Illinois. An out-of-state retailer that does not have sufficient nexus with Illinois to be required to submit to Illinois tax laws does not incur Illinois Retailers' Occupation (sales) tax on sales into Illinois and is not required to collect use tax on behalf of its Illinois customers. However, the retailer's Illinois customers will still incur use tax on the purchase of the out-of-state goods and have a duty to self-assess their use tax liability and remit the amount directly to the state. See *Brown's Furniture, Inc. v. Wagner*, Illinois Supreme Court, No. 78195 (1996).

CCH COMMENT: *Telecommuting employee creates nexus.*—An out-of-state Internet seller with a single employee located in Illinois who telecommuted to work via the Internet would have nexus with Illinois for tax purposes and would not be protected from such taxation under the Internet Tax Freedom Act, according to an Illinois Department of Revenue release. (*General Information Letter IT 99-0058-GIL*, Illinois Department of Revenue, May 24, 1999)

Affiliate nexus.—Certain out-of-state sellers will be treated as retailers or servicemen maintaining a place of business in Illinois, thus requiring them to collect use or service use tax on items or services sold for use in Illinois. A retailer or service man will be considered "a retailer maintaining a place of business in this state" for use tax purposes if the retailer or serviceman has a contract with a person located in Illinois under which the retailer or serviceman sells the same or substantially similar line of products or services as the person located in Illinois and does so using an identical or substantially similar name, trade name, or trademark as the person located in Illinois, and the retailer or serviceman provides a commission or other consideration to the person located in Illinois based upon the sale of tangible personal property or services. (35 ILCS 105/2; 35 ILCS 110/2)

For a discussion of nexus, see ¶ 60-025 Nexus—Doing Business in Illinois.

• *Federal Internet Tax Freedom Act*

The federal Internet Tax Freedom Act (ITFA) (P.L. 105-277, 112 Stat. 2681, 47 U.S.C. Sec. 151 note, amended by P.L. 107-75, P.L. 108-435, P.L. 110-108, P.L. 113-164; P.L. 113-235; P.L. 114-113; and P.L.114-125) bars state and local governments from imposing multiple or discriminatory taxes on electronic commerce and taxes on Internet access. The moratorium is permanent effective February 24, 2016.

Tax on Internet access.—The term "tax on Internet access" applies regardless of whether such a tax is imposed on a provider of Internet access or a buyer of Internet access and regardless of the terminology used to describe the tax. However, the term "tax on Internet access" does not include taxes on or measured by net income, capital stock, net worth, or property value, or other state general business taxes, such as gross receipts taxes, that are structured in such a way as to be a substitute for or supplement the state corporate income tax.

Grandfather provision.—A state or local government may continue to tax Internet access if the tax was generally imposed and actually enforced prior to October 1, 1998. However, this grandfather clause does not apply to any state that, prior to November 1, 2005, repealed its tax on Internet access or issued a rule that it no longer applies such a tax.

Internet access definition.—"Internet access" means a service that enables users to connect to the Internet to access content, information, or other services. The definition includes the purchase, use, or sale of telecommunications by an Internet service provider to provide the service or otherwise enable users to access content, information, or other services offered over the Internet. It also includes incidental services such as home pages, electronic mail, instant messaging, video clips, and personal electronic storage capacity, whether or not packaged with service to access the Internet. However, "Internet access" does not include voice, audio or video programming, or other products and services using Internet protocol for which there is a charge, regardless of whether the charge is bundled with charges for "Internet access."

Telecommunications services.—Under the latest amendments to the Act in 2007, state and local governments that continue to impose tax on telecommunications service purchased, used, or sold by a provider of Internet access have until June 30, 2008, to end these disputed taxes. However, this provision only operates if a public ruling applying such a tax was issued prior to July 1, 2007, or such a tax is the subject of litigation that was begun prior to July 1, 2007.

CCH COMMENT: Disputed taxes on telecommunications.—Some states dispute the assertion that taxes they impose on telecommunications service purchased by Internet service providers to connect their customers to the Internet (so-called "backbone" services) were prohibited by Congress in the 2004 renewal of the moratorium. The 2007 amendment and the revised definition of "Internet access" (discussed above) are intended to resolve this issue and end state and local taxation of Internet "backbone" service. According to the Congressional Budget Office, as many as eight states (Alabama, Florida, Illinois, Minnesota, Missouri, New Hampshire, Pennsylvania, and Washington) and several local governments in those states were collecting such taxes in 2007.

Bundled services.—The Act allows the taxation of otherwise exempt Internet access service charges that are aggregated (i.e. bundled) with and not separately stated from charges for telecommunications or other taxable services, unless the Internet access provider can reasonably identify the charges for Internet access from its books and records kept in the regular course of business.

Discriminatory taxes.—Under the Act, prohibited discriminatory taxes are defined as:

—taxes imposed on electronic commerce transactions that are not generally imposed and legally collectible on other transactions that involve similar property, goods, services or information;

—taxes imposed on electronic commerce transactions at a different rate from that imposed on other transactions involving similar property, goods, services or information, unless the rate is lower as part of a phase-out of the tax over a five-year or lesser period;

—collection or payment obligations imposed upon a different person or entity than would apply if the transaction were not transacted via electronic commerce;

—classification of Internet access service providers or online service providers for purposes of imposing on such providers a higher rate of tax than is imposed on providers of similar information delivered through other means;

—collection obligations imposed on a remote seller on the basis of the in-state accessibility of the seller's out-of-state computer server; and

—collection obligations imposed on a remote seller solely because the Internet access service or online service provider is deemed to be the remote seller's agent on the basis of the remote seller's display of information or content on the out-of-state server or because orders are processed through the out-of-state server.

Multiple taxes.—Prohibited multiple taxes are taxes imposed by a state or local government on the same, or essentially the same, transactions in electronic commerce that are also subject to a tax imposed by another state or local government without a corresponding credit or resale exemption certificate for taxes paid in other jurisdictions.

The moratorium against multiple taxes does not include taxes imposed within a state by the state or by one or more local governments within the state on the same electronic commerce.

The moratorium against multiple taxes does not prohibit other taxes from being imposed on persons who are engaged in electronic commerce even though that commerce has been subject to a sales or use tax.

State Internet access taxes.—Digital service line (DSL) services purchased, used, or sold by a provider of Internet access to provide Internet access are not subject to sales and use tax or telecommunications tax. However, DSL services purchased, used, or sold by a *nonprovider* of Internet access are subject to Illinois telecommunications tax. (*Informational Bulletin FY 2008-18*, Illinois Department of Revenue, June 2008)

The Illinois Telecommunications Excise Tax Act is discussed at ¶60-720, and the telecommunications tax local governments are authorized to impose on intrastate and interstate telecommunications is discussed at ¶80-008. Telecommunications do not include charges for the storage of data or information for subsequent retrieval, or the processing of data or information intended to change its form or content. Persons that provide subscribers access to the Internet, but that do not charge customers for the line or other transmission charges used to obtain access to the Internet, are not considered to be telecommunications retailers. However, persons providing customers with Internet access and thato do charge customers for line or other transmission charges must provide telecommunications providers with certificates for resale and collect telecommunications excise tax for the other charges. For example, persons that provide customers the use of 1-800 service and separately assess customers with per-minute charges are considered to be telecommunications retailers, and will incur the excise tax on charges made for such 1-800 services. (86 Ill. Adm. Code 495.100)

CCH COMMENT: *Internet access service providers.*—If Internet access service providers provide both transmission and data processing services, the charges for each must be disaggregated and separately identified (86 Ill. Adm. Code 495.100). If the access charges are not disaggregated from the telecommunications charges, the telecommunications excise tax is incurred on the entire amount. (*General Information Letter ST 99-0429-GIL*, Illinois Department of Revenue, December 30, 1999)

[¶60-460] Leases and Rentals

Leases and rentals of tangible personal property are not subject to retailer's occupation (sales) tax or use tax in Illinois. (86 Ill. Adm. Code 130.2010; 86 Ill. Adm. Code 150.1201; 86 Ill. Adm. Code 150.305(e))

However, Illinois imposes two taxes on transactions involving merchandise rented to or by consumers:

- the rental purchase agreement occupation tax; and
- the rental purchase agreement use tax.

Are leases and rentals taxable in Illinois?

Yes. While leases and rentals of tangible personal property are not subject to sales and use tax, they may be subject to the rental purchase agreement occupation tax or rental purchase agreement use tax. (86 Ill. Adm. Code 150.2010; 86 Ill. Adm. Code 150.1201; 86 Ill. Adm. Code 150.305(e)) Lessors who rent or lease tangible personal property to others are not engaged in the business of selling property for use or consumption and are not required to remit sales tax on their receipts from such transactions.

Tax on consumer rentals. The rental purchase agreement occupation tax (rental sales tax) is imposed on transactions where a consumer rents merchandise. And the rental purchase agreement use tax (rental use tax) is imposed on a consumer's use of rented merchandise. Both taxes go into effect on January 1, 2018. In addition, a one-time use tax credit will be available for taxpayers that liable for the new taxes.

Transactions subject to rental taxes. The rental sales tax is imposed on persons engaged in the business of renting merchandise under a "rental purchase agreement". The rental use tax is imposed on the privilege of using merchandise which was rented from a merchant under a "rental purchase agreement". A "rental purchase agreement" includes rental agreements between merchants and consumers where:

— the consumer may become the owner of the merchandise;

— the merchandise will be used by the consumer for personal, family, or household purposes; and

— the agreement has an initial period of 4 months or less, but is automatically renewable with each payment after the initial period.

The taxes do not apply to vehicles or other tangible personal property that must be titled and registered by a state agency.

Registering for the taxes. Businesses that rent merchandise must register with the Department of Revenue and collect both the rental sales and rental use tax. Business are liable for the rental sales tax. However, if a consumer does not pay tax to a merchant, the consumer owes the tax. Tax returns for the rental sales and rental use taxes must be filed electronically.

Purchaser certification. When buying merchandise, the purchaser must certify that the item is being purchased for rental under a "rental purchase agreement".

Reporting and paying the taxes. Business must report and pay rental sales tax electronically, using Form ST-201, Rental Purchase Agreement Occupation Tax Return.

Purchases for subsequent lease or rental. Sales to lessors of property that the lessors then rent or lease to others are subject to sales and use tax. (86 Ill. Adm. Code 130.220; 86 Ill. Adm. Code 130.2010; 86 Ill. Adm. Code 130.2013) A purchased item placed in "rental inventory" is taxable on purchase. "Rental inventory" means that the owner has recorded the property in its books and records as rental property using generally accepted accounting principles.

When a lessor both leases and sells property but does not maintain separate rental and sales inventories, the Department of Revenue will look to the lessor's gross receipts to determine whether the lessor is primarily engaged in the business of renting or selling. If the gross receipts from Illinois locations are primarily from leases or rentals, the lessor is a lessor who incurs a use tax liability on items purchased for rental purposes and a sales tax liability on items sold at retail.

A lease of property purchased under a resale exemption by a person primarily engaged in selling can be leased prior to its resale without becoming subject to the use tax. If the leased property is carried as inventory on the retailer's books or is otherwise available for sale during the lease period, the lease is considered to be an interim use and is exempt from tax. The purchase of property by a person who intends to engage in the business of leasing the property is taxable if it is sold as an incident to the leasing activity. In addition, use tax is not imposed on property purchased for resale that is leased to a prospective buyer for the purpose of allowing the buyer to ascertain whether to purchase the property. Such a lease is considered to be a use for demonstration purposes exempt from tax. (86 Ill. Adm. Code 150.306(a)(2); 86 Ill. Adm. Code 150.306(b)(2))

The purchase of property by a person who intends to engage in the business of leasing the property is subject to tax even if it is sold as an incident to the leasing activity. In addition, use tax is not imposed on property purchased for resale that is leased to a prospective buyer for the purpose of allowing the buyer to ascertain whether to purchase the property; the lease is considered to be a use for demonstration purposes and is exempt from tax. (86 Ill. Adm. Code 150.306(a)(2); 86 Ill. Adm. Code 150.306(b)(2))

When a lessor sells items that it is no longer leasing, the lessor does not incur tax on those sales, unless the lessor is engaged in the business of selling the same type of property. A lessor that incurs sales tax on the sale of an item can take a credit against that liability for any sales or use tax it paid when it purchased that particular item.

Property purchased out of state. Lessors owe use tax on their cost of leased property located in Illinois, whether they purchase the property in Illinois and do not pay sales tax or purchase the property outside Illinois and pay taxes to another state. (86 Ill. Adm. Code 130.2013; 86 Ill. Adm. Code 150.305(e)) If the lessorpaid taxes in another state, the lessor is exempt from the use tax to the extent of tax paid in that other state.

Lease to interstate carrier. A lessor must pay use tax when the property reverts to the lessor's use if the lessor purchased the property:

— for lease to an interstate carrier for one year or more, and

— did not pay use tax to the retailer.

Tax is due by the last day of the month following the month of the reversion. The tax due is based on the "fair market value" of the property on the reversion date. The"fair market value" will not exceed the original purchase price of the property paid by the lessor at the time of purchase.

Leases or rentals with option to purchase. A purported lease to a nominal lessee that is actually a sale is subject to the sales tax. (86 Ill. Adm. Code 130.2010; 86 Ill. Adm. Code 150.1201; 86 Ill. Adm. Code 150.305(e))

Example: A five-year lease of tangible personal property that can be purchased for $1 at the conclusion of the lease is a taxable sale.

Local taxes.

Chicago personal property lease transaction tax. Chicago imposes a transaction tax on the lease or rental of personal property or on the privilege of using personal property that is leased or rented outside the city. The obligation to pay the tax is on the lessee of the personal property. The tax rate is 9% of the lease or rental price. Tax must be paid at the time of each lease or rental payment.

The tax rate imposed on a nonpossessory computer lease of a computer primarily allowing the customer to use the provider's computer and software to input, modify or retrieve data or information that is supplied by the customer is 5.25%. In the case of a nonpossessory computer lease, where the user accesses the provider's computer from a mobile device, the sourcing rules under the Illinois Mobile Telecommunications Sourcing Conformity Act apply.

Exemptions from Chicago personal property lease transaction tax. The following are exempt from the transaction tax:

— governmental bodies,

— organizations organized and operated exclusively for charitable, educational, or religious purposes;

— the use in the city of personal property leased or rented outside the city if primarily used (more than 50%) outside the city;

— the lease or rental from a person subject to Chicago occupation taxes provided that the tax is imposed on the receipts attributable to leases or rentals to the lessee and the tax is passed on to the lessee as a separate charge;

— the lease, rental, or use by aninterstate carrier for hire of rolling stock actually moving in interstate commerce;

— the lease, rental, or use paid for by inserting money into a mechanism attached to the personal property;

— the lease, rental, or use of medical appliances or equipment by a person who intends to use the personal property for correcting or treating themselves;

— the lease, rental, or use of a ground transportation vehicle if the lessor is subject to the Chicago ground transportation tax;

— the lease, rental, or use of personal property if the lessor and lessee are members of the same related group;

— leases by a membership organization to its members;

— a nonpossessory lease of a computer to effectuate the trade of securities, futures contracts and certain other instruments;

— a nonpossessory lease of a computer to effectuate the deposit, withdrawal, transfer or loan of money or securities;

— a nonpossessory lease of a computer in which the customer's use or control of the computer is *de minimis*, such as price quotation and news services;

— the nonpossessory lease of a computer, where the lessor or lessee is a "small new business"; and

— the lease, rental, or use of a motion picture film by an owner, manager, or operator of an amusement that exhibits the film to patrons who are subject to the amusement tax.

Returns for Chicago personal property lease transaction tax. Returns are filed on an annual basis and are due on or before August 15. Taxpayers or tax collectors must pay or remit tax due on or before the last day of the month following the monthly (or quarterly, if applicable) tax period in which the tax liability was incurred. Certain taxpayers and tax collectors may make estimated payments in lieu of paying or remitting actual amounts due.

Definitions for Chicago personal property lease transaction tax. The terms "lease" or "rental" include any transfer of the possession or use or personal property, but not title or ownership, to a user for consideration, whether or not designated as a lease, rental license or by some other term. "Lease" or "rental" includes a "nonpossessory lease".

The term "nonpossessory lease" includes a lease or rental that transfers the use, but not the possession, of personal property. It includes leased time on or use of personal property not otherwise rented itself, such as:

— addressing machines,

— billboards,

— calculators,

— computers,

— computer software,

— copying equipment, or

— data processing equipment.

Are there any special exemptions for leases or rentals in Illinois?

No. Leases and rentals arenot subject to sales and use tax in Illinois. However, purchases made under rent-to-own agreements that are subject to rental sales and use taxes will be exempt from Illinois sales and use tax. To claim the exemption, businesses may use Form ST-261, Exemption Certificate for Property Subject to Rental Purchase Agreement Tax.

One-time use tax credit. A merchant may apply for a credit for use tax paid on purchases of rental merchandise during the six months before January 1, 2018. Merchants must file an application with the department to receive the one-time credit within three months after January 1, 2018. The department will issue a credit which the merchant may apply against the rental sales tax or rental use tax.

[¶60-480] Lodging

A state hotel operators' occupation tax is imposed on individuals or companies engaged in the business of renting, leasing or letting rooms in a hotel, motel, inn, tourist home (or court), lodging house, rooming house or apartment house. In general, the tax is in addition to all other state or local occupation or privilege taxes. (35 ILCS 145/2; 35 ILCS 145/3; 35 ILCS 145/1)

A local tax may also be imposed on hotel occupancies (see "Local taxes" below).

• *Basis and rate of tax*

The state hotel operators' occupation tax is imposed at a rate of 6% of 94% of the gross rental receipts. (35 ILCS 145/3) The 6% state rate consists of a 5% general rate plus a 1% additional rate. All consideration received for a room, including non-money compensation, is included in calculating the tax. (35 ILCS 145/2(6); 86 Ill. Adm. Code 480.101)

Operators subject to the occupation tax can pass the tax along to their customers in the form of a separately stated, additional charge. (35 ILCS 145/3)

Gross rental receipts.—The tax is based on gross rental receipts, which is the consideration received for occupancy, valued in money, and includes all receipts, cash, credits and property or services of any kind. (35 ILCS 145/2; 35 ILCS 145/3)

"Occupancy" is the use or possession or the right to the use or possession of any room or rooms for any purposes, or the right to the use or possession of the furnishings or accommodations to the room or rooms. (35 ILCS 145/2(3)) "Room" means any living quarters, sleeping or housekeeping accommodation. (35 ILCS 145/2(4)) Definitions of "hotel" and other key terms are also provided. (86 Ill. Adm. Code 480.105)

Food in connection with room rental.—A regulation explains the application of the true-object test in determining the taxability of charges made by hotels and similar establishments for the rental of a meeting, conference, banquet, or similar type of room when food and beverages are provided. Examples of these situations include wedding receptions, conferences, and business luncheons. If only snacks or non-alcoholic beverages are transferred incidental to the renting of a room, the true object of the transaction will be deemed to be the rental of the room, and the charges for the room rental will not be subject to tax. If, however, any food other than snacks is provided or alcohol is served, the true object of the transaction will be deemed to be the sale of food or beverages, and the charges for the room rental will be considered part of the seller's taxable gross receipts. Numerous examples applying these provisions are provided. (86 Ill. Adm. Code 130.2145)

• *Exemptions*

Persons engaged in renting, leasing or letting rooms in a hotel only to permanent residents are exempt from the tax. (35 ILCS 145/9) Any proceeds from renting a room to a permanent resident are exempt. (86 Ill. Adm. Code 480.101) A "permanent resident" is any occupant who has or will have a right to the occupancy of any room or rooms, regardless of whether it is the same room or rooms, in a hotel for at least 30 consecutive days. (35 ILCS 145/2(5); 86 Ill. Adm. Code 480.105)

Tax also does not apply to gross rental receipts for which the hotel operator is prohibited from obtaining reimbursement of the tax from the customer because of a federal treaty. (35 ILCS 145/3; 35 ILCS 145/9)

A nonprofit organization receives no exemption as a lessor, and nonprofit and governmental organizations are subject to paying the tax. (86 Ill. Adm. Code 480.101)

List of hotel tax deductions.—A publication lists the deductions that are allowed against the hotel taxes collected by the Department of Revenue. The publication relates to the Illinois Hotel Operators' Occupation Tax, the Metropolitan Pier and Exposition Authority Hotel Tax, the Chicago Municipal Hotel Tax, and the Illinois Sports Facilities Tax. (*Publication 106, Allowable Deductions for IDOR-Collected Hotel Taxes*, Illinois Department of Revenue, January 2008)

Receipts from permanent residents, foreign diplomats, student housing, food and beverage sales, and telephone use are deductible. Deductions are also allowed for (1) bad debts and uncollectables, (2) intracompany sales, (3) refunds, (4) room adjustment charges, allowances, and discounts, (5) local hotel taxes paid directly to local jurisdictions and not collected by the Department of Revenue, (6) receipts associated with display rooms, public rooms, sampler rooms, meeting rooms, dressing rooms for swimming pools, offices, and private dining rooms, and (7) receipts associated with barber shops, laundry and vending services, ticket sales, valet parking, garage rent, promotions, photos, magazines, and sundries. (*Publication 106, Allowable Deductions for IDOR-Collected Hotel Taxes*, Illinois Department of Revenue, January 2008)

Receipts from "no-show" guests and from rentals to government employees and persons affiliated with schools or charitable, religious, or other not-for-profit organizations are subject to tax. Receipts from in-room movies are exempt if certain conditions are met.

• *Reports and payments*

No later than the last day of each month, every operator who was engaged in the business of renting, leasing or letting rooms during the preceding month must file a return and send a payment to the Department of Revenue. (35 ILCS 145/6; 86 Ill. Adm. Code 480.110)

If the operator's average monthly tax liability does not exceed $200, the Department may authorize the operator's returns to be filed on a quarterly basis, with the returns being due on the last day of April, July, October and January. If the operator's average monthly tax liability does not exceed $50, the Department may authorize the returns to be filed on an annual basis, with the return for a given year being due by January 31 of the following year. (35 ILCS 145/6)

If the operator goes out of business or ceases to have a tax liability, then the operator must file a final return not more than one month after discontinuance. Where the same individual or company has more than one business registered with the Department of Revenue, that individual or company cannot file a consolidated return but must file separate returns for each of the registered businesses. (35 ILCS 145/6)

An annual information return may be required to be filed by operators upon receipt of a written notice from the Department of Revenue. The return is due within not less than 60 days after receipt of the notice. (35 ILCS 145/6)

• *Administration of tax*

The hotel occupation tax is administered by the Department of Revenue and is subject to the Administrative Procedures Act. (35 ILCS 145/10) Administrative provisions under the retailers' occupation (sales) tax are made applicable to this tax. (35 ILCS 145/6)

Refund and credit claim procedures are explained in a regulation. (86 Ill. Adm. Code 480.125)

Collection discount.—In addition, taxpayers may take an annual cost-of-collection discount of 2.1% or $25, whichever is greater, of the total state and municipal tax due as reimbursement for expenses incurred in complying with the requirements of the tax. (35 ILCS 145/6)

Records.—Every hotel operator must keep separate books or records to show the taxable rents and occupancies. (35 ILCS 145/4; 86 Ill. Adm. Code 480.115)

Penalties.—All civil penalties and provisions concerning interest, procedures, and the statutes of limitation under the Retailers' Occupation (Sales) Tax Act are applicable to the Hotel Operators' Occupation Tax Act. (86 Ill. Adm. Code 480.120)

Registration requirement.—All persons and companies engaged in the business of renting, leasing or letting rooms in an accommodation in Illinois must apply for and receive a certificate of registration from the Department of Revenue. (35 ILCS 145/5; 86 Ill. Adm. Code 480.110)

• *Local taxes*

County lodging tax.—A county may impose a tax of up to 5% on the gross rental receipts of persons engaged in business of renting leasing or letting rooms in a hotel which is not located within a city, village or incorporated town that already imposes a local hotel operator's occupation tax. "Gross rental receipts" includes receipts from renting, leasing or letting, but excludes proceeds from renting or letting to permanent residents of the hotel. (55 ILCS 5/5-1030)

Winnebago County.—Winnebago County may impose an additional 2% hotel operators' occupation tax above the allowable county rate of 5%. The Winnebago County board may impose the tax by ordinance if the consent of municipalities representing at least 67% of the county's population has been given, as expressed by resolution of those municipalities' corporate authorities. The ordinance will provide for the tax's administration, enforcement, and collection as the county board determines to be necessary or practicable for the effective administration of the tax. (55 ILCS 5/5-1030)

Municipal hotel operators' occupation tax and use tax.—Any municipality may impose a hotel operators' occupation tax or a hotel use tax on gross rental receipts upon all persons engaged in the business of renting, leasing, or letting rooms in a hotel. Such tax may not exceed 5%, with the exception that a hotel operators' occupation tax may not exceed 6% in the City of East Peoria and in the Village of Morton. Rentals to permanent residents are exempt. (65 ILCS 5/8-3-14; 65 ILCS 5/8-3-14a)

A federal district court has twice addressed the application of local hotel operators' occupation tax to room reservations sales by online travel companies (OTCs).

CCH Comment: In June 2016, the U.S. District Court for the Northern District of Illinois held that various online travel companies (OTCs) owed the village of Lombard hotel occupancy taxes, but did not owe hotel occupancy taxes to 12 other Illinois municipalities. The OTCs sell hotel rooms using the "merchant business model," contracting with hotels to purchase hotel rooms at wholesale rates, then selling room reservations to customers at retail rates. Numerous municipalities sought to collect tax from the OTCs' on their receipts attributable to the difference between the wholesale rate paid by the OTCs and the retail rate charged by the OTCs. The OTCs were liable for the Lombard tax because the Lombard tax ordinance provides for a tax on "all persons engaged in the business of renting, leasing or letting rooms in a hotel." Lombard's tax is imposed with proper statutory authorization as the Illinois statute allows municipalities to" impose a tax upon all persons engaged in such municipality in the business of renting, leasing or letting rooms in a hotel." In addition, Lombard's tax does not violate the uniformity clause of the Illinois Constitution. The ordinance language reasonably taxes all persons involved in the hotel business even if they do not own, operate, or manage hotels themselves, and does not broaden Lombard's tax authority. Finally, the ordinance does not violate the U.S. Constitution's commerce clause because both paying to rent a room in Lombard and engaging in the business of renting a room in Lombard are activities with a substantial nexus to Illinois. The ordinances in several other municipalities place the duty to collect tax on the" owner and operator of each hotel." The OTCs, however, were not owners and operators. The words "owner" and "operator" are undefined by the municipalities' ordinances The court noted that operation of a hotel involves more than taking reservations, ensuring reservations are honored, handling complaints, and serving as the primary contact for customers before they stay in rented hotel rooms. Also, hotel owners have the right to possess, use, and convey their hotels, while the OTCs had no such rights with regard to the hotels. The remaining municipalities' ordinances imposed the tax on rental receipts. The OTCs' receipts attributable to the difference between the wholesale rate and the retail rate are not rental receipts. The retail rate includes both the cost of the room rental and the cost of other services provided by the OTCs as evidenced by OTCs' terms of service. (*The Village of Bedford Park v. Expedia, Inc.*, U.S. District Court, N.D. Illinois, No. 13 C 5633, June 20, 2016)

CCH Comment: In October 2011, the U.S. District Court for the Northern District of Illinois held that a 7% hotel tax imposed by the village of Rosemont, Illinois, on the full room rental fees charged by online travel companies (OTCs) is a valid use tax, and it does not violate the dormant Commerce Clause of the U.S. Constitution. The court then held that the full rental fees paid by the customers to the OTCs, not just the charges paid by the OTCs to the hotels, were taxable. OTCs charged Rosemont customers a room rental fee that included (1) the amounts that the hotels charged the OTCs, and (2) the OTCs' markup on the hotels' charges. The ordinance intended to tax the amount paid by customers to occupy a hotel room in Rosemont. OTCs' customers paid the OTCs' charges for the right to occupy hotel rooms in Rosemont. The court held that the OTCs' facilitation of travel-related services was incidental to the rental of hotel rooms, and that the hotel tax was a use tax. In response to an argument made by the OTCs, the court found that the hotel tax did not violate the dormant Commerce Clause. First, the OTCs had nexus with Illinois because (1) the tax was levied for the right to use a hotel room in Illinois, (2) the tax was paid by the person who uses the room, and (3) the OTCs entered into contracts with hotels in Illinois for the right to market, facilitate, and book reservations and they profit from such reservations. Second, the tax was fairly apportioned because it is imposed on a use that can occur in only one place. Third, the tax does not discriminate against interstate commerce as it is applied at the same rate to every hotel reservation in Rosemont. Finally, the tax is related to Illinois services because the renting person has the advantage of the state's police and fire protection, for example, while staying in Illinois. (*The Village of Rosemont v. Priceline.com, Inc.*, U.S. District Court, N.D. Illinois, No. 09 C 4438, October 14, 2011)

Chicago.—

Hotel accommodations tax: A tax of 4.5% is imposed on gross rental or lease charges made by a guest to a hotel, motel, inn, apartment hotel, lodging house, or dormitory for accommodations in the city of Chicago. The tax is collected by the operator and paid over to the Chicago Department of Revenue on a monthly basis on forms to be provided by the city. The tax is due on the last day of the calendar month following the month in which receipts are received. While the tax is in addition to the state and local hotel occupation taxes, it does not apply to accommodations that provide fewer than 10 rooms. Chicago will impose the 4.5% tax on "shared housing units,". (Chicago Munic. Code Sec. 3-24-030) An "operator" includes any person who has the right to rent or lease hotel accommodations or who receives or collects the price paid for the rental or lease of hotel accommodations, and persons engaged in the business of facilitating hotel rentals either online or in person. (Chicago Munic. Code Sec. 3-24-020)

Returns are filed on an annual basis due on or before August 15. (Chicago Munic. Code Sec. 3-24-060)

An exemption is allowed for hotel accommodations that are a tenant's domicile and permanent residence. (Chicago Munic. Code Sec. 3-24-030) Chicago Hotel Accommodations Tax Ruling No. 1 provides guidelines for documenting the exemption.

Shared housing unit surcharge: The city of Chicago will impose a 4% surcharge on sales of hotel accommodations at "vacation rentals" and "shared housing units,". The new surcharge will not apply to:

• an accommodation a lessee or tenant occupies a his or her domicile or permanent residence;

• temporary accommodations in nonprofit medical institutions, hospitals, or accredited medical education institutions; or

• rooms rented by a bed-and-breakfast.

(Chicago Munic. Code Sec. 3-24-020; Chicago Munic. Code Sec. 3-24-030; Chicago Munic. Code Sec. 3-24-035)

"Vacation rental" will mean a dwelling unit that contains 6 or fewer sleeping rooms that are available for rent or for hire for transient occupancy by guests. "Shared housing" will mean a dwelling unit containing 6 or fewer sleeping rooms any portion of which is rented, for transient occupancy by guests, but will not include:

— single-room occupancy buildings;

— hotels;

— corporate housing;

— bed-and-breakfast establishments,

— guest suites; or

— vacation rentals.

(Chicago Munic. Code Sec. 4-14-010)

Illinois Sports Facilities Authority: The Illinois Sports Facilities Authority, created by the Illinois Sports Facilities Authority Act, P.A. 84-1470, Laws 1986 (70 ILCS 3205/19), imposes a 2% gross receipts tax on 98% of the receipts received by persons engaged in renting hotel rooms located within the city of Chicago, except for receipts from renting to permanent residents and proceeds from the Metropolitan Pier and Exposition Tax on hotel operators. (http://tax.illinois.gov/TaxRates/Excise.htm) The tax is collected and enforced by the Department of Revenue, under the provisions of the Hotel Operators' Occupation Tax Act. (35 ILCS 145/1)

Metropolitan Pier and Exposition Authority: The Metropolitan Pier and Exposition Authority is authorized to levy a hotel occupation tax upon all persons engaged in the corporate limits of the city of Chicago in the business of renting, leasing, or letting rooms in a hotel at the rate of 2.5% of gross rental receipts. "Gross rental receipts" do not include charges from any state or local occupation tax on hotels, nor do they include receipts from permanent residents. (70 ILCS 210/13)

Peoria.—

Peoria imposes a tax upon the use and privilege of renting a hotel or motel room within the city at the rate of 5% of the rental or leasing charge for each room rented for each 24-hour period or portion thereof. However, the tax does not apply to any person renting a hotel or motel room for more than seven consecutive days or to a person who works and lives in the same hotel or motel. (Peoria Munic. Code Sec. 27-147)

Owners of hotels and motels within the city must file a tax return showing tax receipts received during each monthly period on the first day of every monthly period. The return is due on or before the 30th day of the calendar month succeeding the end of the monthly filing period. (Peoria Munic. Code Sec. 27-151)

[¶60-510] Manufacturing, Processing, Assembling, or Refining

In general, a manufacturer's purchases of machinery and equipment, as well as items incorporated as a part of other property are exempt from retailers' occupation (sales) tax, use tax, service occupation tax (SOT) or service use tax (SUT), but its sales of tangible personal property are subject to sales tax.

Are purchases by manufacturers, processors, assemblers, or refiners taxable in Illinois?

Certain machinery and equipment and property used and consumed during the manufacturing, processing, assembling, or refining of property is exempt.

Manufacturing exemption. Purchases of machinery and equipment are exempt from sales and use tax when the machinery and equipment are "used primarily" in the process of manufacturing or assembling tangible personal property for wholesale, retail sale or lease. (35 ILCS 105/3-5(18); 35 ILCS 120/2-5(14); 86 Ill. Adm. Code 130.120(q); 86 Ill. Adm. Code 130.330(a)) Service occupation tax (SOT) and service use tax (SUT) do not apply to sales of machinery and equipment. (35 ILCS 110/2; 35 ILCS 115/2; 86 Ill. Adm. Code 140.125(o); 86 Ill. Adm. Code 140.201(e)(7))

The manufacturing exemption applies to machinery and equipment that: (1) replaces machinery and equipment in an existing manufacturing facility; or (2) are for use in an expanded or new manufacturing facility. (35 ILCS 105/3-50; 35 ILCS 120/2-45) The exemption applies even when a manufacturer uses a small portion of the manufactured products as sample articles or for quality control testing.

Supplies and consumables used in manufacturing are exempt from Illinois sales and use tax beginning July 1, 2019. The manufacturing exemption to again includes production related tangible personal property.

Primary use of machinery and equipment. Machinery and equipment are "used primarily" in manufacturing or assembling when the machinery or equipment is used more than 50% of the time in manufacturing or assembling. Machinery and equipment that are essential to manufacturing because they are required by law or are practically necessary does not mean they used primarily for manufacturing or assembling.

Exempt uses generally include:

— effecting a direct and immediate physical change on the property to be sold;

— guiding or measuring a direct and immediate physical change on the property to be sold;

— inspecting, testing or measuring the property to be sold;

— conveying, handling or transporting the property to be sold within production stations on the production line or directly between such production stations or buildings within the same plant;

— placing the property to be sold into the container, package, or wrapping in which such property is normally sold;

— crushing, washing, sizing and blending if the process results in the assembling of an article of tangible personal property with a different form than the material extracted, which possesses new qualities or combination;

— producing or processing food, such as baking bread, by a central bakery or a retail grocery store; and

— using buffers, builders, or vulcanizing equipment to retread tires.

Nonexempt uses include:

— the construction, reconstruction, alteration, remodeling, servicing, repairing, maintenance, or improvement of real estate;

— the research and development of new products or production techniques, machinery, or equipment;

— storing, conveying, handling or transporting materials or parts or sub-assemblies before they become a part of the production process;

— storing, conveying, handling or transporting finished articles of tangible personal property to be sold or leased after the production process has ended;

— transporting work in process, or semifinished goods, between plants;

— using machinery or equipment in managerial, sales, or other nonproduction, nonoperational activities;

— using machinery or equipment to prevent or fight fires or to protect employees

— general ventilation, heating, cooling, climate control or general illumination, not required by the manufacturing process;

— a retailer's preparation of food and beverages for retail sale; and

— using machinery or equipment used in the last step of the retail sale.

Chemicals acting as catalysts. Chemicals acting as catalysts are exempt if the chemicals effect a direct or immediate change upon the product being manufactured or assembled for sale or lease. Exempt chemicals include:

— a chemical acid used to etch copper off the surface of a printed circuit board; or

— an aluminum oxide catalyst used in a cracking process to refine heavy gas into gasoline.

Purchases of machinery and equipment by fabrication services providers. The manufacturing exemption is available to fabrication services providers if the goods produced for others will be sold or leased to customers for use or consumption.

Machinery and equipment ceasing to qualify for exemption. Machinery or equipment used primarily in manufacturing or assembling becomestaxable when: (1) it has been used for less than one-half of its useful life; and (2) is converted to a nonexempt use. At that point, the purchaser will owe tax in an amount equal to the previously exempt tax.

Electricity, natural or artificial gas and water. The machinery and equipment exemption does not apply to machinery and equipment, repair and replacement parts or in-house manufactured machinery and equipment used in:

— the generation of electricity for wholesale or retail sale;

— the generation or treatment of natural or artificial gas for wholesale or retail sale that is delivered to customers through pipes, pipelines or mains; or

— the treatment of water for wholesale or retail sale that is delivered to customers through pipes, pipelines or mains.

(35 ILCS 105/3-5; 35 ILCS 105/3-50; 35 ILCS 110/2; 35 ILCS 115/2; 35 ILCS 120/2-5; 86 Ill. Adm. Code 130.330)

Foundation for equipment. Foundations for, or special purpose buildings to house or support, machinery and equipment are not exempt.

Property incorporated as a part of other property. Purchases of property that goes into and forms a part of a manufactured product are exempt as resales when the product will be sold at retail. The property purchased may be an ingredient or a constituent of the manufactured product. Purchases of property that become part of intentionally produced byproducts of manufacturing are also exempt. Slag produced during the manufacturing of pig iron or steel is an intentionally produced byproduct of manufacturing. (35 ILCS 120/1; 35 ILCS 105/2; 86 Ill. Adm. Code 130.210; 86 Ill. Adm. Code 150.201)

Property may be purchased partly for becoming part of the product and partly for general use. The property that forms a part of the product qualifies for exemption.

Example: A steel manufacturer buys and uses coal and coke to produce both: 1) heat in its manufacturing operation; and 2) carbon as an ingredient of steel and by-products to sell. The coal and coke used for heat is taxable. The coal and coke bought to provide carbon is exempt.

Exemption certificates. To obtain the exemption when making a purchase of qualified property, the manufacturer must give the seller an active registration or resale number or an exemption certificate. This requirement applies to purchases of machinery and equipment and to purchases of property to be used as an ingredient or constituent part of a manufactured product. (35 ILCS 105/3-50; 35 ILCS 120/2-45; 35 ILCS 110/2; 35 ILCS 115/2; 86 Ill. Adm. Code 130.210; 86 Ill. Adm. Code 130.330(g))

Items consumed in production. Purchases of property by manufacturers are taxable when the manufacturer uses or consumes the property in the manufacturing process but does not physically incorporate the property into a manufactured product. (86 Ill. Adm. Code 130.210; 86 Ill. Adm. Code 130.215)

Products added to plating baths. Chemical compounds and addition agents added to plating baths may be exempt, depending on their purpose. Purchases of chemical compounds and addition agents added to modify a physical characteristic of the plating deposit are exempt if a measurable part of the compound or agent becomes part of the end product. A characteristic includes brightness, grain size, hardness, ductility, smoothness or tensile strength. However, purchases of chemical compounds and addition agents added primarily to improve the plating function are taxable. Function improvements include altering the surface tension, suppressing fumes, controlling pH, buffering the solution, acting as a catalyst, acting as a purifier, improving anode efficiency, or acting as a complexing agent.

Leased property. Purchases of machinery and equipment are exempt if the purchaser leases the purchased property to a manufacturer that uses the property in an exempt manner. If the purchaser later leases the machinery or equipment to a lessee that does not use it in an exempt manner, the purchaser becomes liable for an amount equal to the previously exempt tax. (35 ILCS 105/3-50; 35 ILCS 120/2-45) Also exempt is the sale of materials to a manufacturer that manufactures the materials into exempted types of machinery or equipment or tools which it then leases to another manufacturer. However, if the manufacturer uses any significant portion of machinery or equipment for internal consumption, any leased machinery or equipment is not exempt.

Graphic arts machinery and equipment. As of July 1, 2017, the exemption for machinery and equipment includes machinery and equipment used in graphic arts. The exemption applies to:

— machinery;

— equipment;

— repair and replacement parts;

— manufactured on special order, certified for use in for graphic arts production; and

— machinery and equipment purchased for lease

Equipment includes chemicals or chemicals acting as catalysts. However, the chemicals or chemicals acting as catalysts must have a direct and immediate change on a graphic arts product.

Graphic arts machinery, equipment and repair and replacement parts may be either new or used under the exemption.

Centralized purchasing of exempt manufacturing property. Until June 30, 2016, purchases of property made as part of centralized purchasing are exempt from sales tax, use tax, service occupation tax and service use tax even if the property is stored in Illinois after the purchase. The exemption applies if:

— the property is stored in Illinois temporarily while it is being processed, fabricated, or manufactured into, attached to or incorporated into other property;

— the manufactured property is shipped outside Illinois; and

— the manufactured property is used or consumed solely outside Illinois.

(35 ILCS 120/2-5(26);35 ILCS 105/3-55(j); 35 ILCS 110/3-45(f); 35 ILCS 115/3-5(26))

Definitions. The following definitions are used when discussing manufacturing machinery and equipment:

"Manufacturing process." The "manufacturing process" is the production of tangible personal property by procedures commonly regarded as manufacturing, processing, fabricating, or refining. The procedures must substantially or significantly change existing material into a material with a different form, use, or name. The property produced may be a finished product or one used in the manufacture or assembly of another product. The extractive processes of mining or quarrying may constitute manufacturing. Manufacturing does not include, logging, oil or gas drilling, printing, agricultural or horticultural activities, or the preparation of food and beverages. The manufacturing process begins with the first operation or stage of production in a series of manufacturing operations. It ends when the final product is completed in the last operation or stage of production in the series. (35 ILCS 105/3-50; 35 ILCS 120/2-45; 35 ILCS 110/2; 35 ILCS 115/2; 86 Ill. Adm. Code 130.330)

Photoprocessing is considered to be a manufacturing process of tangible personal property for wholesale or retail sale.

"Assembling process." The "assembling process" is the production of tangible personal property by combining existing materials in a way that is commonly regarded as assembling to produce a material in a different form, use, or name. (35 ILCS 105/3-50; 35 ILCS 120/2-45; 35 ILCS 110/2; 35 ILCS 115/2; 86 Ill. Adm. Code 130.330(b))

"Machinery" "Machinery" includes major mechanical machines, or major components of such machines, that contribute to a manufacturing or assembling process. (35 ILCS 105/3-50; 35 ILCS 120/2-45; 35 ILCS 110/2; 35 ILCS 115/2; 86 Ill. Adm. Code 130.330(c))

"Equipment" "Equipment" is an independent device or tool separate from machinery but essential to an integrated manufacturing or assembling process. Chemicals or chemicals acting as catalysts are "equipment" when the chemicals effect a direct and immediate change on a product being manufactured or assembled. (35 ILCS 105/3-50; 35 ILCS 120/2-45; 35 ILCS 110/2; 35 ILCS 115/2)

Examples of "equipment" include:

— a subunit or assembly that is a component of:

machinery,

auxiliary, adjunct, or attachment parts of machinery, such as tools, dies, jigs, fixtures, patterns and molds, and

parts that must be periodically replaced during normal operations; and

— computers used primarily in operating exempt machinery and equipment in a manufacturer's computer-assisted design, computer-assisted manufacturing system (CAD/CAM).

"Equipment" does not include hand tools, supplies, personal apparel, coolants, lubricants, adhesives, coal, fuel oil, electricity, natural or artificial gas, water, refrigerants, or steam.

Are sales by manufacturers, processors, assemblers, or refiners taxable in Illinois?

Yes, sales of tangible personal property by a manufacturer are generally subject to tax. The retailer's occupation (sales) tax is imposed on persons engaged in the business of selling tangible personal property at retail. Since Illinois does not have any specific provisions for sales by manufacturers, processors, assemblers, or refiners, manufacturers would be taxable on sales of tangible personal property under the general taxability statute.

Special orders. Sales of machinery, tools, dies, jigs, patterns, gauges, or other similar equipment that are made on special order may be exempt from sales tax. An exemption for special orders applies when:

— the purchaser employs the manufacturer to design and produce the property primarily for the manufacturer's skill,

— the property has use or value only for the specific purpose for which it is produced,

— the property has commercial value only to the purchaser, and

— orders are for less than 50 of the same item; and

— the order is not a repeat order.

Repeat orders of the same item are taxable because the skill involved in making the item is production skill and not specialized engineering and design skill. A repeat order is an order for the same item without material change that is placed by:

— the same purchaser on a date after the date that the original order was placed

— another purchaser at any time after the original order.

While sales of special-order machinery, tools and similar items are exempt from sales tax, manufacturers offering these special-order items are engaged in a service occupation and are liable for service occupation tax (SOT).

Are self-produced goods used in manufacturing, processing, assembling or refining taxable in Illinois?

No, self-produced goods used for an exempt manufacturing purpose are generally exempt.

The manufacturing machinery and equipment exemption applies to a manufacturer's purchases of materials that are manufactured into an exempted type of machinery, equipment, or tools that the manufacturer uses itself. (35 ILCS 105/3-50; 35 ILCS 120/2-45)

A manufacturer or assembler that uses any significant portion of its machinery or equipment's output for internal consumption or any other nonexempt use may not claim the exemption on that machinery and equipment. A partial exemption for machinery and equipment that is also used for nonexempt purposes is not available.

Are labor and services related to manufacturing, processing, assembling or refining taxable in Illinois?

Illinois does not currently have sales and use tax provisions specifically concerning labor and services used in manufacturing, processing, assembling, or refining. For a general discussion of the taxability of sales of services, see ¶ 60-665 Services.

Are there refund and/or credit provisions for manufacturing, processing, assembling or refining in Illinois?

Illinois does not currently have sales and use tax provisions specifically concerning refunds and credits for manufacturing, processing, assembling, or refining.

For a general discussion of refunds and credits, see ¶ 61-270 Credits and ¶ 61-610 Application for Refund.

[¶60-520] Medical, Dental, and Optical Supplies and Drugs

Sales for human use of prescription and nonprescription medicines, drugs, medical appliances, and insulin, urine testing materials, syringes, and needles used by diabetics are subject to retailers' occupation (sales) tax (ROT), service occupation tax (SOT), use tax (UT), and service use tax (SUT) at a reduced state tax rate of 1%. (35 ILCS 105/3-10; 35 ILCS 110/3-10; 35 ILCS 115/3-10; 35 ILCS 120/2-10)

• *Reduced Rate for Medicines, Drugs, Medical Appliances*

For purposes of the reduced rate of tax, a medicine or drug is any pill, powder, potion, salve, or other preparation intended for human use that purports on the label to have medicinal qualities. A "medical appliance" is an item that is used to directly substitute for a malfunctioning part of the human body (e.g., restorative breast implants, heart pacemakers, artificial limbs, dental prosthetics, crutches and orthopedic braces, dialysis machines, wheelchairs, sleep apnea devices, and hearing aids).

Items that do not directly substitute for a malfunctioning part of the human body (e.g., cosmetic breast implants, nebulizers) do not qualify as medical appliances. (86 Ill. Adm. Code 130.311)

Diagnostic equipment generally is not considered to be a medical appliance. Other medical tools, devices, and equipment, such as x-ray machines, laboratory equipment, and surgical instruments that may be used in the treatment of patients but do not directly substitute for a malfunctioning human body part, do not qualify as medical appliances. (86 Ill. Adm. Code 130.311)

Supplies, such as nonsterile cotton swabs, disposable diapers, toilet paper, tissues and towelettes, and cosmetics do not qualify for the reduced rate. However, sterile dressings, bandages, and gauze do qualify. (86 Ill. Adm. Code 130.311)

Medical appliances qualifying for the reduced rate are those prescribed by licensed health care professionals for use by a patient, purchased by health care professionals for the use of patients, or purchased directly by individuals. Previously, the regulation provided that medical appliances used by health care professionals in providing medical services were not eligible for the reduced rate; however, the regulation was ruled to be invalid and was thus revised. (86 Ill. Adm. Code 130.311)

Modifications to a motor vehicle for the purpose of rendering it usable by a disabled person are subject to the 1% sales and use tax rate. Such modifications include special steering, braking, shifting, and acceleration equipment, and chair lifts. (35 ILCS 105/3-10; 35 ILCS 110/3-10; 35 ILCS 115/3-10;35 ILCS 120/2-10; 86 Ill. Adm. Code 130.311)

Illinois imposes the 1% tax rate on sales of prescribed cancer treatment devices that are classified as Class III medical devices by the U.S. Food and Drug Administration (FDA), as well as any accessories and components related to those devices. (35 ILCS 120/2-10)

Medical cannabis.—"Prescription and nonprescription drugs" includes medical cannabis purchased from a registered dispensing organization under the Compassionate Use of Medical Cannabis Program Act for purposes of the sales, use, retailers' occupation and service occupation taxes. (35 ILCS 105/3-10; 35 ILCS 110/3-10; 35 ILCS 115/3-10; 35 ILCS 120/2-10; 86 Ill. Adm. Code 130.311)

Exemption for feminine hygiene products.—Menstrual pads, tampons, and menstrual cups are exempt. (35 ILCS 105/3-5;35 ILCS 110/3-5; 35 ILCS 115/3-5; 35 ILCS 120/2-5)

Exemption for persons receiving medical assistance in licensed facility.—Prescription and nonprescription medicines, drugs, medical appliances, and insulin, urine testing materials, syringes, and needles used by diabetics, for human use, are not exempt from tax when purchased for use by persons receiving medical assistance under the Illinois Public Aid Code and residing in a licensed long-term care facility as defined in the Nursing Home Care Act or in the ID/DD Community Care Act, the MC/DD Act, or the Specialized Mental Health Rehabilitation Act of 2013. (35 ILCS 105/3-5; 35 ILCS 110/3-5; 35 ILCS 115/3-5; 35 ILCS 120/2-5) A regulation explains this exemption. (86 Ill. Adm. Code 150.337)

Personal grooming and hygiene products.—Grooming and hygiene products for humans do not qualify as "nonprescription medicines and drugs" and, therefore, do not qualify for the reduced tax rate. They are subject to the full state sales tax rate. The term "grooming and hygiene products" includes soaps and cleaning solutions, shampoo, toothpaste, mouthwash, antiperspirants, and sun tan lotions and screens, unless those products are available by prescription only. (35 ILCS 105/3-10; 35 ILCS 110/3-10; 35 ILCS 115/3-10; 35 ILCS 120/2-10; 86 Ill. Adm. Code 130.311)

- *Taxes on cannabis sales*

  The following taxes are due on sales of cannabis in Illinois:
  - cannabis cultivation privilege tax;
  - medical cannabis cultivation privilege tax;
  - cannabis purchaser excise tax; and
  - sales tax.

(*Informational Bulletin FY 2020-12*)

Cannabis cultivation privilege tax. The cannabis cultivation privilege tax is a tax imposed upon the privilege of cultivating cannabis at the rate of 7% of the gross receipts from the first sale of adult use cannabis by a cultivator or craft grower. The Tax is imposed upon cultivation centers and craft growers growing cannabis for sale to cannabis business establishments. (86 Ill. Adm. Code 422.100) (*Informational Bulletin FY 2020-12*) The sale of any product by a cultivator that contains any amount of cannabis or any derivative thereof is subject to the Tax on the full selling price of the product. It is presumed that all sales of cannabis are subject to tax until the contrary is established, and the burden of proving that a transaction is not taxable is upon the cultivator. (86 Ill. Adm. Code 422.110)

Definitions related to the tax can be found at 86 Ill. Adm. Code 422.105.

Medical cannabis cultivation privilege tax. The medical cannabis cultivation privilege tax is a tax imposed upon the privilege of cultivating medical cannabis at the rate of 7% of the sales price per ounce. The privilege tax is paid by a cultivation center, not a dispensing organization or a qualifying patient, and is imposed in addition to all other Illinois state and local occupation and privilege taxes. (410 ILCS 130/200; 410 ILCS 130/220; 86 Ill. Adm. Code 429.110) (*Informational Bulletin FY 2020-12*)

For purposes of computing the tax on medical cannabis infused products, the sales price is the cultivation center's average sales price per gram of high grade cannabis flowers as determined on a monthly basis. The tax on medical cannabis concentrate or extract is calculated based on the sales price of the quantity of concentrate or extract sold. The quantity is the actual weight, in ounces or partial ounces, of the concentrate or extract contained in the package. (86 Ill. Adm. Code 429.110)

Persons subject to the tax must apply to the Department of Revenue for a certificate of registration. The department will prescribe and furnish application forms. A retailer that holds a certificate of registration for the collection of retailers' occupation (sales) taxes does not need to register separately to do business to sell medical cannabis. (410 ILCS 130/205; 86 Ill. Adm. Code 429.115; 86 Ill. Adm. Code 429.120)

A "cultivation center" is a facility operated by an organization or business that is registered by the Department of Agriculture to perform necessary activities to provide only registered medical cannabis dispensing organizations with usable medical cannabis. (410 ILCS 130/10; 86 Ill. Adm. Code 429.105)

Definitions related to the tax can be found at 86 Ill. Adm. Code 429.105.

Cannabis purchaser excise tax. The cannabis purchaser excise tax is a tax imposed on purchasers for the privilege of using cannabis, cannabis concentrate, and cannabis-infused products. Cannabis dispensaries must collect and remit excise tax on all retail sales of adult use cannabis. (86 Ill. Adm. Code 423.100) (*Informational Bulletin FY 2020-12*) The tax is imposed at the following rates:

- 10% of taxable receipts from the sale of adult use cannabis, other than cannabis-infused products, sold with 35% THC or less,

- 25% of taxable receipts from the sale of adult use cannabis, other than cannabis-infused products, sold with greater than 35% THC, and

- 20% of taxable receipts from the sale of adult use cannabis-infused products.

(86 Ill. Adm. Code 423.110) (*Informational Bulletin FY 2020-12*)

The purchase of any product that contains any amount of cannabis or any derivative thereof is subject to the tax on the full purchase price of the product. (86 Ill. Adm. Code 423.110)

Definitions related to the tax can be found at 86 Ill. Adm. Code 423.105.

Sales tax. Both medical cannabis and adult use cannabis are subject to the retailers' occupation tax (receipts for each must be calculated separately). (*Informational Bulletin FY 2020-12*)

Medical cannabis: Medical cannabis is subject to state and local retailers' occupation taxes at the same rate as other qualifying drugs, i.e., 1% state rate and is generally exempt from locally imposed retailers' occupation taxes (except for Regional Transportation Authority and Metro-East Transit District retailers' occupation taxes). (*Informational Bulletin FY 2020-12*)

Adult use cannabis: Adult use cannabis is subject to the 6.25% state retailers' occupation tax as well as local retailers' occupation taxes in the same manner as other general merchandise. In addition, counties and municipalities are authorized to impose, by ordinance, a local retailers' occupation tax on all persons engaged in the business of selling adult use cannabis at retail in the municipality or county on the gross receipts from sales of adult use cannabis (medical cannabis is excluded from these local cannabis-specific taxes). (*Informational Bulletin FY 2020-12*)

The rate imposed under

- the municipal cannabis retailers' occupation tax may not exceed 3%, and

- the county cannabis retailers' occupation tax may not exceed: (i) 3.75% in unincorporated areas of the county, and (ii) 3% in a municipality located in the county

Difference between "adult use" cannabis and "medical" cannabis. "Adult use" cannabis is cannabis intended for recreational adult use without a prescription. (*Informational Bulletin FY 2020-12*)

"Medical" cannabis is cannabis intended for medicinal use to treat or alleviate a registered qualifying patient's debilitating medical condition or symptoms associated with the patient's debilitating medical condition. Adult use or medical cannabis may be

- dried in its physical form to smoke;

- in another physical form after extraction from the cannabis plant, such as hash, ice wax, bubble hash, oil, wax, budder, pie crust, taffy, shatter, nectar, caviar, and kief, regardless of how it is packaged or intended to be used; or

- infused or combined with another product.

THC defined. THC, or tetrahydrocannabinol, is the active chemical in cannabis that produces its psychological effects. With the exception of canabis-infused products, cannabis purchaser excise tax rates are determined by the percent of THC in the product. (*Informational Bulletin FY 2020-12*)

What to include when calculating "total receipts." When totalling receipts for the purpose of calculating taxes, include the following from the reporting period:

- the "selling price" (for cultivators or craft growers) or the customer's "purchase price" (for dispensaries) of all cannabis sold;

- taxes or reimbursement of taxes collected; and
- any charge payment or time sale payment received.

(*Informational Bulletin FY 2020-12*)

"Selling price" means the consideration for a sale of cannabis, valued in money, whether received in money or otherwise (including cash, credits, property, and services), and shall be determined without any deduction on account of the cost of the property sold, the cost of materials used, labor or service cost, or any other expense whatsoever. It does not include separately stated charges identified on the invoice by cultivators to reimburse themselves for their tax liability. (*Informational Bulletin FY 2020-12*)

"Purchase price" means the consideration paid for a purchase of cannabis, valued in money, whether received in money or otherwise (including cash, credits, property, and services), and shall be determined without any deduction on account of the cost of materials used, labor or service costs, or any other expense whatsoever. It does not include consideration paid for: any charge for a payment that is not honored by a financial institution; any finance or credit charge, penalty or charge for delayed payment, or discount for prompt payment; and any amounts added to a purchaser's bill because of charges made for the cannabis purchaser excise tax, the municipal cannabis retailers' occupation tax, the county cannabis retailers' occupation tax, the retailers' occupation tax, the use tax, the service occupation tax, the service use tax, or any locally imposed occupation or use tax. (*Informational Bulletin FY 2020-12*)

Cannabis-infused products. Cannabis-infused products are products containing cannabis, whether medicinal or not, including

- food and beverage products prepared for consumption;
- cooking oils;
- tinctures or tonics, such as sprays or drops;
- topicals, such as ointments, balms, oils, lotions, gels, or patches;
- bath salts or oils; and
- aromatherapy sprays or essences.

(*Informational Bulletin FY 2020-12*)

CBD products, such as CBD oils, derived from industrial hemp that contain 0.3% or less of THC are not subject to the medical or adult use Cannabis Cultivation Privilege Taxes, the Cannabis Purchaser Excise Tax, or the cannabis-specific local retailers' occupation taxes. (*Informational Bulletin FY 2020-12*)

Tax returns for cannabis sales. All returns and tax payments for the cannabis taxes:

- are due monthly on the 20th; and
- must be filed and paid electronically.

(86 Ill. Adm. Code 422.115; 86 Ill. Adm. Code 423.130; 86 Ill. Adm. Code 429.125)

Local cannabis retailers' occupation tax authorized for municipalities and counties. Beginning July 1, 2020, municipalities and counties may impose a local cannabis retailers' occupation tax. (*Informational Bulletin FY 2020-16*)

Municipalities may impose a tax on retail sales of cannabis, other than medical cannabis, at a rate that may not exceed 3%, imposed in 0.25% increments. (86 Ill. Adm. Code 425.110) (*Informational Bulletin FY 2020-16*) Counties may impose a tax (also in 0.25% increments) on retail sales of cannabis, other than medical cannabis, at the following rates:

- In unincorporated areas of the county, the rate may not exceed 3.75%.
- In a municipality located in the county, the rate may not exceed 3%.

(86 Ill. Adm. Code 424.110) (*Informational Bulletin FY 2020-16*)

If a proper ordinance is adopted and filed with the Illinois Department of Revenue on or before April 1, 2020, then the IDOR will administer and enforce the tax beginning on July 1, 2020. Ordinances filed on or after April 2, 2020, but on or before October 1, 2020, will be implemented by the IDOR on January 1, 2021. Municipalities and counties should submit their ordinances to the following address: LOCAL TAX ALLOCATION DIVISION (3-500), ILLINOIS DEPARTMENT OF REVENUE, 101 W JEFFERSON, SPRINGFIELD, IL 62702. (86 Ill. Adm. Code 424.150; 86 Ill. Adm. Code 425.150) (*Informational Bulletin FY 2020-16*)

- *Hospital leases of computers and equipment*

A lessor's purchase of computers and communications equipment utilized for any hospital purpose and equipment used in the diagnosis, analysis, or treatment of hospital patients is exempt from sales and use tax if the equipment is leased for one year or longer by a hospital with an active tax exemption identification number. (35 ILCS 105/3-5; 35 ILCS 110/3-5; 35 ILCS 115/3-5; 35 ILCS 120/2-5)

- *Veterinarians*

A veterinarian may be liable for Illinois service occupation tax, retailers' occupation (sales) tax, or use tax, depending upon the nature of the transaction.

Service occupation tax.—When a licensed veterinarian transfers tangible personal property to a client as a result of the practice of veterinary medicine, a service transaction occurs that results in a service occupation tax liability. (86 Ill. Adm. Code 130.2165)

In order for a transaction to be considered a service transaction, the veterinarian must have established a valid veterinarian-client patient relationship (VCPR) with the service client, must have physically examined the animal, and must maintain medical records demonstrating that the animal was physically examined no more than one year prior to the date on which the tangible personal property was transferred. (86 Ill. Adm. Code 130.2165)

For example, a service transaction occurs when medicines, drugs, and other products are directly applied or administered by a licensed veterinarian during a veterinary examination. A service transaction also occurs when a licensed veterinarian sells medicines, drugs, and other products having a medicinal purpose as part of a continuing plan for the health of an animal under his or her care.

A veterinarian generally remits service occupation tax based on the selling price of the tangible personal property transferred incident to service. However, if the annual aggregate cost price of all items transferred incident to service transactions is less than 35% of annual aggregate gross receipts from service, the veterinarian may elect to pay tax as a "de minimis" serviceman.

The service occupation tax and service use tax are not imposed on sales of stock tonics, serums, and other medicinal products to veterinarians for retransfer as an incident to caring of farm animals. (86 Ill. Adm. Code 140.125(l); 86 Ill. Adm. Code 160.145)

Medicines prescribed by veterinarians for animals are not eligible for the reduced rate and instead are subject to the high rate of tax. (86 Ill. Adm. Code 130.311) The term "medicine, drug or other product having a medicinal purpose" is defined by regulation. (86 Ill. Adm. Code 130.2165)

Sales tax.—Veterinarians are considered retailers and incur ROT liability when they (1) sell items to persons with whom they have not established a valid VCPR or (2) sell items outside the scope of a service transaction. (86 Ill. Adm. Code 130.2165)

The following items are considered to be transferred outside the scope of a service transaction and therefore are subject to sales tax, regardless of whether a VCPR has been established: combs, brushes, shears, nail clippers, name tags, nonmedicated shampoos, leashes, collars, toys, clothing, odor eliminators, and waste handling products.

Use tax.—Veterinarians incur use tax on those items that are consumed by them in the course of performing veterinary services and are not transferred to the service customer. Examples of these items include disposable pads, dryers, combs, towels, cleaning supplies, tables or chairs, thermometers, and hand soap. Veterinarians may not use Certificates of Resale on their purchases of these items. Instead, they must either pay use tax to the suppliers or self-assess and remit use tax to the Department of Revenue. (86 Ill. Adm. Code 130.2165)

[¶60-560] Motor Fuels

Sales of motor fuel and gasohol are subject to retailers' occupation tax, service occupation tax, use tax, and service use tax. (35 ILCS 105/3-10; 35 ILCS 110/3-10; 35 ILCS 115/3-10; 35 ILCS 120/2-10; 86 Ill. Adm. Code 130.2060(b))

For tax rates, see ¶60-110 Rate of Tax.

An exemption applies to petroleum that is certified by the carrier to be used for consumption, shipment, or storage in the conduct of its business as an air common carrier, for a flight that is engaged in foreign trade or is engaged in trade between the United States and any of its possessions, and transports at least one individual or package for hire from the city of origination to the city of final destination on the same aircraft, without regard to a change in the flight number of that aircraft. This exemption will terminate by sunset on August 16, 2018. (35 ILCS 105/3-5; 35 ILCS 110/3-5; 35 ILCS 115/3-5; 35 ILCS 120/2-5; 86 Ill. Adm. Code 130.120(gg); 86 Ill. Adm. Code 130.321)

In addition, sales of fuel used to operate ships, barges, or vessels that transport property or convey passengers on rivers bordering Illinois are not subject to ROT when such fuel is delivered to the purchaser's vessel while afloat. (35 ILCS 120/2-5; 86 Ill. Adm. Code 130.120(k); 86 Ill. Adm. Code 130.315)

An "air common carrier" is a commercial air common carrier certified and authorized to conduct international flights involving passengers or cargo on a regularly scheduled basis. (86 Ill. Adm. Code 130.321)

Flights destined for outside the U.S. include flights that originate in or have a stopover in Illinois and that may have intermediate stops at other locations in the U.S. before arriving at the destination outside the U.S. Fuel is taxable if an intended international flight stops in the U.S. and does not continue to the foreign destination. (86 Ill. Adm. Code 130.321)

The sale of petroleum products to a purchaser is not subject to ROT if the seller is prohibited by federal law from charging tax to that purchaser. (35 ILCS 120/2-5; 86 Ill. Adm. Code 130.120(s))

Assessment of Oil and Gas Production.—To fund the activities of the Illinois Petroleum Resources Board, an assessment shall be deducted from the proceeds of oil and gas production and collected by the first purchaser. A levy in the amount of 1/10th of 1% of gross revenues of oil and gas produced from each well in Illinois shall be assessed. (225 ILCS 728/30)

The assessment, imposed on the producer of oil and gas, shall be remitted to the Department of Revenue by the first purchaser on a tax return filed no later than the 15th of each month following the end of the month in which the assessment was collected. (225 ILCS 728/30)

See ¶60-510 Manufacturing, Processing, Assembling, or Refining.

350

Guidebook to Illinois Taxes

Definitions.—"Producer" means a person who produces oil and gas or who derives a majority of his or her oil and gas income from working interest. (225 ILCS 728/5)

• *Gasohol*

ROT, SOT, UT, and SUT is imposed on 80% of the sale proceeds, cost price, or selling price (depending on the tax involved) of gasohol sold (or transferred incident to the sale of service) for the period July 1, 2003, through December 31, 2018, and on 100% of the proceeds thereafter. However, if the tax rate of any of the above taxes falls to 1.25% at any time during the exemption period, the fuel will be subject to full taxation during that time. (35 ILCS 105/3-10; 35 ILCS 110/3-10; 35 ILCS 115/3-10; 35 ILCS 120/2-10) (*Informational Bulletin FY 2000-4*)

"Gasohol" is motor fuel that is a blend of denatured ethanol and gasoline that contains no more than 1.25% water by weight. The blend must contain 90% gasoline and 10% denatured ethanol. A maximum of 1% error factor in the amount of denatured ethanol used in the blend is allowable to compensate for blending equipment variations. (35 ILCS 105/3-40; 86 Ill. Adm. Code 130.320)

• *Blended ethanol and fuels*

For the period July 1, 2003, through December 31, 2018, a full exemption from ROT, SOT, UT, and SUT is allowed for sales of (1) majority blended ethanol fuel, (2) 100% biodiesel, and (3) biodiesel blends with more than 10% but no more than 99% biodiesel. For the same period, the taxes will apply to 80% of the proceeds of sales of biodiesel blends with no less than 1% and no more than 10% biodiesel. If the tax rate of any of the above taxes falls to 1.25% at any time during the exemption period, the exemption will be suspended and the fuel will be subject to full taxation during that time. After 2013, the above fuels will be fully taxed. (35 ILCS 105/3-10; 35 ILCS 110/3-10; 35 ILCS 115/3-10; 35 ILCS 120/2-10)

Definitions.—"Majority blended ethanol fuel" means motor fuel that contains not less than 70% and no more than 90% denatured ethanol and no less than 10% and no more than 30% gasoline. (35 ILCS 105/3-44) "Biodiesel" means a renewable diesel fuel derived from biomass that is intended for use in diesel engines. (35 ILCS 105/3-41) "Biomass" means non-fossil organic materials that have an intrinsic chemical energy content and includes soybean oil, other vegetable oils, and ethanol. (35 ILCS 105/3-43) "Biodiesel blend" means a blend of biodiesel with petroleum-based diesel fuel in which the resultant product contains no less than 1% and no more than 99% biodiesel. (35 ILCS 105/3-42)

• *Aviation fuel for retailers*

In order to comply with Federal Aviation Administration guidelines, retailers of aviation fuel (i.e., jet fuel and aviation gasoline) are required to report and pay sales and use tax on aviation fuel on Form ST-70, Aviation Fuel Sales and Use Tax Return. Additional requirements identified by the Federal Aviation Administration are applicable. (*Informational Bulletin FY 2020-08*)

Form ST-70. Retailers that sell aviation fuel at more than one location (site) must collect and remit the tax according to the rates at each particular location. The retailer must complete Form ST-71, Multiple Site Form, to show the breakdown of taxes collected and paid from each site and combine the liability on a single Form ST-70. Illinois law requires that you file Form ST-70 and pay the tax electronically. Form ST-70 is due on or before the 20th day of the month following the end of the reporting period. (*Informational Bulletin FY 2020-08*)

Rate. The sales tax rate on aviation fuel might change with the new requirements. The state sales tax rate of 6.25% will remain the same. However, the rate

¶60-560

imposed by the local government where the aviation fuel is sold might change, depending on the certification filed with the Illinois Department of Transportation (IDOT) by the unit of local government. The Illinois Department of Revenue (IDOR) will notify retailers if there is a rate change. In addition, when you file electronically using MyTax Illinois your rates will be populated for you. (*Informational Bulletin FY 2020-08*) For the local rate changes effective July 1, 2020, see *Informational Bulletin FY 2020-30*.

Discount for sales of aviation fuel. On or after December 1, 2019, the discount is removed on the 1.25% local portion of the 6.25% state tax and the locally imposed tax, if any. The discount is still allowed on the 5% state portion of the tax for timely filing and paying sales and use tax on aviation fuel. (*Informational Bulletin FY 2020-08*)

[¶60-570] Motor Vehicles

Sales of motor vehicles by a dealer, lending institution, leasing agency, or retailer are generally subject to the ROT and UT. (35 ILCS 105/10; 35 ILCS 120/3)

See also ¶61-220 Returns, Payments, and Due Dates.

• *Exemptions*

Exemptions are provided for the following:

(1) sales to certain nonresidents (see Nonresident Exemption below);

(2) motor vehicles that are donated to a corporation, limited liability company, society, association, foundation, or institution that is organized and operated exclusively for educational purposes; and

(3) prior to January 1, 2014, motor vehicles of the first division, a motor vehicle of the second division that is a self-contained motor vehicle designed or converted to provide living quarters for recreational, camping, or travel use with direct walk through access to the living quarters from the driver's seat, or a motor vehicle of the second division that is of the van configuration designed to transport at least 7 but not more than 16 passengers, if used for automobile renting. Effective January 1, 2014, the exemption for rented automobiles will apply only to automobiles as defined for purposes of the automobile renting occupation tax.

(35 ILCS 105/3-5; 35 ILCS 110/2(4a-5); 35 ILCS 115/2(d-1.1); 35 ILCS 120/2-5; 86 Ill. Adm. Code 130.120(w))

An exemption is also allowed for certain motor vehicles used as rolling stock moving in interstate commerce; see ¶60-740 Transportation.

• *Purchase from an individual*

The purchase of motor vehicles from an individual is subject to the vehicle use tax rather than the ROT/UT.

See ¶37-101 Motor Vehicles.

• *Automobile renting occupation and use tax*

A tax is imposed on persons or companies engaged in the business of renting automobiles in Illinois when the rental is for a period of a year or less. A tax is also imposed on the privilege of using in the state an automobile that is rented from an auto rental business for a period of a year or less. (35 ILCS 155/2; 35 ILCS 155/3)

See ¶60-110 Rate of Tax.

"Automobile" means a motor vehicle carrying not more than 10 passengers, recreational vehicles and vans used to transport not less than 7 or more than 10 passengers. It also includes a motor vehicle of the second division which has a gross vehicle weight rating of 8,000 pounds or less. (35 ILCS 155/2)

The occupation tax is based on the gross receipts received from automobile rentals. "Gross receipts" do not include receipts received by an automobile dealer from a manufacturer or service contract provider as reimbursement for the use of an automobile by a person while that person's automobile is being repaired by the automobile dealer, provided that the repair is made pursuant to a manufacturer's warranty or service contract and the reimbursement is made merely for the dealer to recover the costs of operating the automobile as a loaner vehicle. The use tax is based on the rental price of the automobile paid to the renter under a rental agreement. "Rental price" does not include any special fee charged by the business for possible damage, a separately stated charge for insurance or the cost of refueling, or other separately stated charges that are not for the use of the property. (35 ILCS 155/2; 35 ILCS 155/3; 35 ILCS 155/4; 86 Ill. Adm. Code 180.125)

Renters are required to collect the use tax from automobile rentees as a separately stated, additional charge. The Department of Revenue has the authority to prescribe bracket systems to aid rental businesses in collecting the use tax. (35 ILCS 155/4)

No tax, occupation or use, is imposed on the rental of automobiles to the following (35 ILCS 155/3; 35 ILCS 155/4):

1. Any governmental body.

2. Any charitable, religious or educational corporation, society, association, foundation or institution.

3. Any nonprofit corporation, society, association, foundation, institution or organization that is operated primarily for the recreation of persons 55 years of age or older.

Every person or company engaged in the business of renting automobiles must obtain a certificate of registration from the Department unless a retailers' occupation (sales) tax certificate has already been issued to them. (35 ILCS 155/3)

The automobile renting occupation tax and the automobile renting use tax imposed by the Metropolitan Pier and Exposition Authority are discussed at ¶ 61-710 Local Power to Tax.

See ¶ 61-735 Local Rates

Reports and payments.—In general, both taxes are administered and collected by the Department under provisions of the state retailers' occupation (sales) tax and use tax laws (except for provisions relating to transaction returns and quarter-monthly payments). (35 ILCS 155/3; 35 ILCS 155/4)

Payment of the use tax is made by the renter to the auto rental business which, in turn, remits the tax to the Department. If for some reason the use tax is not paid to the business, then the renter must pay the tax directly to the Department. (35 ILCS 155/4)

• *Leases*

The sale of an automobile to an automobile lessor for use as a rental automobile under lease terms of one year or less is exempt from ROT and UT. (86 Ill. Adm. Code 130.220; 86 Ill. Adm. Code 130.2010(c)) The sale of used rental vehicles by a person engaged in the business of leasing them to others is subject to ROT and UT. (35 ILCS 105/1a; 35 ILCS 120/1c; 86 Ill. Adm. Code 130.111; 86 Ill. Adm. Code 180.135)

A lessor who purchases tangible personal property, including but not limited to motor vehicles and aircraft, for lease to an interstate carrier under a lease for at least one year, in effect or executed at the time of purchase, and who did not pay use tax to the retailer must, by the last day of the month following the month the property reverts to the lessor's use, file a return and pay the use tax on the "fair market value" of the property on the date of reversion. (35 ILCS 105/10; *Informational Bulletin FY 2000-4*, October 1999)

> **CCH COMMENT:** *Definition of "Fair Market Value" Restricted.*—In determining the fair market value at the time of reversion, the fair market value of the property will not exceed the original purchase price of the property paid by the lessor at the time of purchase. (35 ILCS 105/10)

See ¶ 60-460 Leases and Rentals.

Vehicles leased for more than a year.—For certain motor vehicles sold on or after January 1, 2015, for the purpose of leasing the vehicle for a defined period that is longer than one year, "selling price" or "amount of sale" means the consideration received by a lessor under a lease contract, including amounts due at lease signing and all monthly or other regular payments charged over the term of the lease. Such motor vehicles include a motor vehicle of the first division or a motor vehicle of the second division that:

- is a self-contained motor vehicle designed or permanently converted to provide living quarters for recreational, camping, or travel use, with direct walk-through access to the living quarters from the driver's seat;

- is of the van configuration designed for the transportation of not less than seven or more than 16 passengers; or

- has a gross vehicle weight rating of 8,000 pounds or less.

(35 ILCS 105/2; 35 ILCS 120/1; *Information Bulletin FY 2015-03*)

Also included in the "selling price" is any amount received by the lessor from the lessee for the leased vehicle that is not calculated at the time the lease is executed, including, but not limited to, excess mileage charges and charges for excess wear and tear. (35 ILCS 105/2; 35 ILCS 120/1)

Reporting and paying tax due.—For sales that occur in Illinois, with respect to any amount received by the lessor from the lessee for the leased vehicle that is not calculated at the time the lease is executed, the lessor does not incur use tax on those amounts, and the retailer that makes the retail sale of the motor vehicle to the lessor is not required to collect the use tax or pay the sales tax on those amounts. However, the lessor must report and pay to the Department of Revenue sales and use taxes on those amounts received in the same form in which the retailer would have reported and paid such amounts if the retailer had accounted for the tax to the department. For amounts received by the lessor that are not calculated at the time the lease is executed, the lessor must file the return and pay tax by the due date otherwise required for returns other than transaction returns. If the retailer is entitled to a collection allowance for reporting and paying the tax, then the lessor will also be entitled to a collection allowance with respect to the tax paid by the lessor for any amount received by the lessor from the lessee for the leased vehicle that is not calculated at the time the lease is executed. (35 ILCS 105/2; 35 ILCS 120/1)

Traded-in property.—The "selling price" of a motor vehicle that is sold on or after July 1, 2014, for the purpose of leasing for a defined period of longer than one year will not be reduced by the value of or credit given for traded-in tangible personal property owned by the lessor. The "selling price" also will not be reduced by the value of or credit given for traded-in tangible personal property owned by the lessee, regardless of whether the trade-in value thereof is assigned by the lessee to the lessor. (35 ILCS 105/2; 35 ILCS 120/1)

Vehicle sales after lease contract ends.—In the case of a motor vehicle that is sold for the purpose of leasing for a defined period of longer than one year, the sale occurs at the time of the delivery of the vehicle, regardless of the lease payment due dates. A lessor who incurs a sales tax liability on the sale of a motor vehicle coming off-lease may not take a credit against that liability for use tax paid on the lessor's purchase of the motor vehicle if the "selling price" was calculated using the definition of "selling price" as described above. A credit also is not available for any tax the lessor paid with respect to any amount received by the lessor that was not calculated at the time the lease was executed. (35 ILCS 105/2; 35 ILCS 120/1)

Electronic filing required.—All lessors must electronically file and pay the tax due under these provisions. This rule does not apply to leases of motor vehicles for which, at the time the lease is entered into, the term of the lease is not a defined period, including leases with a defined initial period with the option to continue the lease on a month-to-month or other basis beyond the initial defined period. (35 ILCS 105/2; 35 ILCS 120/1)

Interim use permits.—A leased motor vehicle is eligible for the interim use exemption on use tax if the leased vehicle remains in the vehicle dealer's inventory and is available for sale during the lease period. For example, if a dealer enters into a lease of a vehicle with a lessee and simultaneously sells the vehicle to a third party, then the lease of the vehicle does not subject the dealer to use tax liability. However, the dealer's sale of the vehicle, with or without the lease, to third party is taxable and the third party incurs use tax liability. (86 Ill. Adm. Code 150.306(a))

This exemption also applies to vehicles leased by a vehicle manufacturer to its employees. (86 Ill. Adm. Code 150.306(a))

• *Demonstrators*

A person who purchases tangible personal property for resale may use it for demonstration purposes without being subject to use tax. (86 Ill. Adm. Code 150.306(b)) However, the sale of an automobile by a dealer to a salesman for use in demonstration is subject to ROT. (86 Ill. Adm. Code 130.2065) A salesman's sale of his own demonstrator is an isolated or occasional sale not subject to tax.

• *Refunds on returned vehicles*

A retailer of a motor vehicle is entitled to a ROT refund or credit memorandum when the manufacturer of a motor vehicle sold by the retailer accepts the return of that automobile and refunds to the purchaser the selling price as provided in the New Vehicle Buyer Protection Act. The amount of the refund or credit is equal to the amount of tax paid by the retailer on the initial sale of the vehicle. (35 ILCS 120/6)

• *Nonresident exemption*

Reciprocal "out-of-state buyer" exemption.—Nonresidents may not claim an "out-of-state buyer" exemption from Illinois sales tax on purchases of motor vehicles or trailers that will be titled in a state that does not give Illinois residents a reciprocal exemption on their purchases in that state of motor vehicles or trailers that will be titled in Illinois. (35 ILCS 105/3-55(h); 86 Ill. Adm. Code 130.605)

Illinois sales tax on the sale of a motor vehicle in Illinois to a resident of another state that does not allow a reciprocal exemption shall be imposed at a rate equal to the state's rate of tax on taxable property in the state in which the purchaser is a resident, except that the tax may not exceed the tax that would otherwise be imposed under Illinois law. (86 Ill. Adm. Code 130.605)

The Department of Revenue has released a chart that (1) lists whether each state does or does not provide a reciprocal exemption to Illinois residents and (2) for states that do not, specifies the tax rate to be used to compute tax due on vehicles/trailers purchased in Illinois by residents of such states. The chart can be found at http://www.revenue.state.il.us/Publications/OtherPub.htm.

Vehicles ineligible for exemption.—The exemption for purchases of motor vehicles by nonresidents does not apply to (1) a watercraft, personal watercraft, or boat equipped with an inboard motor, (2) all-terrain vehicles, (3) motorcycles or motor driven cycles not properly manufactured or equipped for general highway use, (4) off-highway motorcycles, or (5) snowmobiles. (86 Ill. Adm. Code 130.605)

If a watercraft, personal watercraft, or boat is included with the sale of a trailer, the trailer may qualify for exemption. If the two items are sold together for one non-itemized price, only the gross receipts representing the selling price of the trailer are exempt.

Documentation of nonresidency.—A regulation specifies the documentation of nonresidency that must be retained by the retailer to support a nonresident exemption. A retailer claiming the exemption must keep evidence that the purchaser is not a resident of Illinois, along with the records related to the sale. Different documentation requirements apply to purchasers who are natural persons and purchasers that are not natural persons, such as corporations, partnerships, limited liability companies (LLC's), and trusts. (86 Ill. Adm. Code 130.605)

• *Parking excise tax*

Operators of parking spaces, parking areas, and garages are required to collect and remit a state-level parking excise tax based on the purchase price (rent) paid by the purchaser to park a (1) motor vehicle, (2) recreational vehicle, or (3) other self-propelled vehicle. (Uncodified Sec. 10-10, P.A. 101-31 (S.B. 690)) (86 Ill. Adm. Code 195.100) The "operator" of the parking area or garage must collect the tax from the purchaser. (Uncodified Sec. 10-25, P.A. 101-31 (S.B. 690); Uncodified Sec. 10-5, P.A. 101-31 (S.B. 690)) (*Informational Bulletin FY 2020-07*)

Rates.—The tax is imposed at the rate of: (1) 6% of the purchase price for a parking space paid for on an hourly, daily, or weekly basis; or (2) 9% of the purchase price for a parking space paid for on a monthly or annual basis. (Uncodified Sec. 10-10, P.A. 101-31 (S.B. 690)) (86 Ill. Adm. Code 195.110) (*Informational Bulletin FY 2020-07*)

Operator.—An operator

• engages in the business of renting, for a charge, parking spaces for the purpose of parking or storing motor vehicles, recreational vehicles, or other self-propelled vehicles, even if the charge is to another parking operator,

• provides parking valet services for a charge, or

• collects from the purchaser the charge for parking (i.e., acts as a facilitator or aggregator).

(*Informational Bulletin FY 2020-07*) (86 Ill. Adm. Code 195.105)

An operator is not required to collect the tax in the following circumstances:

• the operator is engaged in the business of renting three or fewer parking spaces throughout Illinois;

• the parking space is owned and operated by the federal government, the State of Illinois, State universities created by statute, and units of local government;

• the parking space is provided for residential off-street parking for home, apartment tenants, or condominium occupants, and is covered by the lease or separate agreement between the landlord and tenant; and

• the parking space is provided for hospital employees and is owned and operated by the hospital for which they work.

(*Informational Bulletin FY 2020-07*)

Valet services.—Persons engaged in the business of providing valet services are subject to the tax on the purchase price received in connection with their valet parking operations. Tips received by persons parking cars for operators providing valet services are not subject to the tax if the tips are retained by the person receiving the tip. If the tips are turned over to the valet business, the tips shall be included in the purchase price. (86 Ill. Adm. Code 195.145)

Invoices.—The tax should be separately stated on the invoice to the customer when possible. If not possible, the Illinois Department of Revenue may waive this requirement if purchasers are notified by language on the invoice or by a sign that the tax is included in the purchase price. (Uncodified Sec. 10-25, P.A. 101-31 (S.B. 690))

Filing and paying tax due.—Form PE-100, Parking Excise Tax Return, is used to report and pay the tax. Form PE-100 must be filed and the tax must be paid electronically. A taxpayer may request a waiver of the electronic filing requirement if it is a hardship to file a return or pay the tax electronically. Form PE-100 is due, along with any payment you owe, on or before the last day of each calendar month following the end of your reporting period. The return is due monthly. However, operators of parking areas for 14 days or less in a calendar year qualify for an annual filing frequency. New registrants will receive a letter informing them of their filing status (i.e., monthly or annual). (Uncodified Sec. 10-5, P.A. 101-31 (S.B. 690)) (86 Ill. Adm. Code 195.125) (*Informational Bulletin FY 2020-07*)

• *Donated motor vehicles*

See ¶ 60-580 Nonprofit Organizations, Private Schools, and Churches.

• *Illinois tire user fee*

Persons subject to tax—Rates.—Any person offering or selling tires at retail in Illinois must collect from retail customers a fee of $2.50 per new or used tire sold and delivered in the state. The $2.50 tire fee includes a 50 cents fee for the Emergency Public Health Fund. The fee is collected from the purchaser and is added to the selling price of the tire and must be listed separately on the bill of sale. The fee is not included in the state or local retailers' occupation tax or the state use tax. (415 ILCS 5/55.8; 415 ILCS 5/55.9)

The fee applies to tires for highway vehicles, special mobile equipment, and farm equipment and to aircraft tires. (415 ILCS 5/55.8)

Exemptions.—Imposition of a fee does not apply to mail order sales of tires nor to tires that are included in the retail sale of a motor vehicle. Also, the fee does not apply to the sale of reprocessed tires. (415 ILCS 5/55.8)

Reports and payments.—The due dates for quarterly returns and payments are April 20, July 20, October 20, and January 20. Instead of filing returns, a retailer of tires may pay the fee to its supplier of tires at the time of purchase if the supplier is a registered retailer and arranges to collect and remit the fee to the Department. (415 ILCS 5/55.8; 415 ILCS 5/55.10)

Collection allowance.—A collection allowance of 10¢ per tire may be retained by the retail seller if the tire user fee return is filed on time and only for the amount that is timely paid. Retail sellers who choose to pay the tire user fee to their suppliers may not claim the collection allowance. In such cases, the suppliers are entitled to the allowance. A tire retailer is entitled to a collection allowance only if the return is timely filed and only for the amount that is timely paid. (415 ILCS 5/55.8)

The city of Chicago tire fee is discussed under "Local taxes" below.

• *Local taxes*

Chicago motor vehicle lessor tax.—A motor vehicle lessor tax is imposed by Chicago on the privilege of leasing motor vehicles within Chicago on a daily or weekly basis. The tax rate is $2.75 per vehicle, per lease transaction. Payments and returns are due by the last day of the month following the month in which the vehicles are leased, and must be physically received by the Chicago Department of

Revenue by the due date. Although the company leasing the vehicle is liable for the tax, the tax may be passed on to the firm's customers as a separate charge on the rental bill or invoice. (Chicago Munic. Code Sec. 3-48-030)

Returns are filed on an annual basis, on or before August 15 of each year. Taxpayers or tax collectors must pay or remit the actual amount of tax due on or before the last day of the month following the monthly (or quarterly, if applicable) tax period in which the tax liability was incurred. Certain taxpayers and tax collectors may make estimated payments in lieu of paying or remitting actual amounts due. (Chicago Munic. Code Sec. 3-48-030)

Chicago parking lot and garage operations tax.—Chicago imposes a parking lot tax on each motor vehicle parked in a parking lot or garage based on the amount of the daily, weekly, or monthly charge or fee imposed for the privilege of parking. A 22% tax is imposed on daily, weekly or monthly charges or fees. (Chicago Munic. Code Sec. 4-236-020; *Information Bulletin: Chicago Parking Tax*, Chicago Department of Finance, June 2013) The tax is collected by parking lot owners and remitted to the city of Chicago by the 30th day of the month following the quarter for which the tax was collected. Returns are filed on an annual basis, due on or before August 15 of each year. (Chicago Munic. Code Sec. 3-4-186)

Exemptions.—The tax does not apply if the charge or fee imposed for the privilege of parking does not exceed $2 for a 24-hour period or less, or $10 for a weekly period, or $40 for a monthly period. (Chicago Munic. Code Sec. 4-236-020(d)(ii))

Valet parking—A 20% tax is imposed on Chicago valet parking businesses. (Chicago Munic. Code Sec. 4-236-025)

Returns.—Returns are filed on an annual basis due on or before August 15. Taxpayers or tax collectors must pay or remit the actual amount of tax due on or before the last day of the month following the monthly (or quarterly, if applicable) tax period in which the tax liability was incurred. Certain taxpayers and tax collectors may make estimated payments in lieu of paying or remitting actual amounts due. (Chicago Munic. Code Sec. 4-236-070)

Chicago tire fee.—Persons selling new tires at retail or offering new tires for retail sale in the City of Chicago must collect from purchasers a Chicago tire fee of $1 per new tire. A collection allowance of 4 cents per tire may be retained by the seller. The fee applies exclusively to tires to be used for vehicles, aircraft, special mobile equipment, and implements of husbandry. The fee is applicable in instances where tires are sold separately and not in conjunction with the sale of a motor vehicle. (*Release*, Chicago Department of Revenue, August 2005)

Exemptions.—The Chicago tire fee does not apply to (1) used tires, (2) reprocessed tires, or (3) mail order sales. A reprocessed tire is a tire that has been recapped, retreaded, or regrooved and that has not been placed on a wheel rim. If a tire is 100% replaced under a manufacture warranty or road hazard warranty, no fee is applied because such an exchange is not a sale at retail. However, a full $1 fee applies in the case of a pro-rata replacement, because the customer pays something, making the transaction a sale at retail. Sales tax does not apply to the tire fee. (*Informational Bulletin*, Chicago Department of Revenue, August 2005)

Returns.—The Chicago tire fee must be remitted monthly and is due by the last day of the month following collection. An annual fee return for the period commencing July 1 and ending June 30 of the subsequent year is due by August 15 of each year.

[¶60-580] Nonprofit Organizations, Private Schools, and Churches

In general, sales to but not sales by, charitable, educational, and religious institutions and other qualifying nonprofit organizations are exempt from retailers' occupation (sales) tax and use tax, as discussed below.

• *Charitable, educational, and religious institutions*

A sale of tangible personal property to any corporation, limited liability company, society, association, foundation, or institution organized and operated exclusively for charitable, religious, or educational purposes is exempt from retailers' occupation (sales) tax (ROT) and use tax (UT) and a sale or transfer of tangible personal property as an incident to the rendering of service for or by such an entity is exempt from service occupation tax (SOT) and service use tax (SUT). A limited liability company may qualify for these exemptions only if it is organized and operated exclusively for educational purposes. Sales by these organizations are generally taxable, as discussed below. (35 ILCS 105/3-5; 35 ILCS 120/2-5; 35 ILCS 110/2; 35 ILCS 115/2; 86 Ill. Adm. Code 130.120(h); 86 Ill. Adm. Code 130.201(a)(3); 86 Ill. Adm. Code 130.501(b)(2); 86 Ill. Adm. Code 150.325; 86 Ill. Adm. Code 140.125(h)(1); 86 Ill. Adm. Code 140.201(e)(3); 86 Ill. Adm. Code 160.110(e))

To qualify for exemption, the charitable, religious, or educational organization must have an active exemption identification number issued by the Department of Revenue. If the entity is organized and operated exclusively for charitable purposes and has more than 50 subsidiary organizations in Illinois, the Department may issue one exemption identification number. Each number or renewal is valid for five years. (35 ILCS 120/1g; 86 Ill. Adm. Code 150.325; 86 Ill. Adm. Code 130.2007)

Upon request, the Department will furnish any county or municipality a list of each exempt organization that has a valid exemption identification number and that is located within the corporate limits of the municipality or unincorporated territory of a county. (35 ILCS 120/1h)

Sales by organization.—Sales by an exclusively charitable, religious, or educational corporation, society, association, foundation, or institution are generally subject to ROT and UT except for the following (35 ILCS 105/2; 35 ILCS 120/1; 86 Ill. Adm. Code 130.2005(a); 86 Ill. Adm. Code 130.2005(b); 86 Ill. Adm. Code 130.2105(a)):

(1) sales to members, students (but not sales of school supplies, school books, clothing, or furniture by schools to students), patients, or inmates primarily for purposes of the selling organization, such as sales of uniforms and scouting equipment by scout organizations and sales of Bibles or choir robes by a church to its members;

(2) sales of property which is not sold by persons organized for profit, i.e., sales that do not compete with business establishments, such as infrequent sales of cookies or calendars by scout organizations, sales of school annuals by schools, or sales of books containing an organization's own individualized literature; and

(3) conducting occasional (not more than twice in any calendar year) dinners, socials, or similar activities regardless of whether they are open to the public, including fun fairs, carnivals, rummage sales, bake sales, and bazaars.

All other nonprofit service organizations that are not exclusively charitable, religious, or educational organizations are subject to ROT on their sales of tangible personal property to members, guests, or the public. (35 ILCS 105/2; 35 ILCS 120/1; 86 Ill. Adm. Code 130.2005(a); 86 Ill. Adm. Code 150.201(h)) Returns are required to be filed monthly, but may be filed annually if the taxpayer's average monthly liability is $50 or less and the Department grants permission. A church should generally file a return for itself and its organizations, and a board of education should file returns instead of each school or school organization. (86 Ill. Adm. Code 130.2005(c))

Regulations provide guidelines in determining whether an organization is organized and operated exclusively for charitable, religious, or educational purposes. Specifically discussed are nonprofit social, recreational, and athletic organizations and nonprofit fraternal benefit societies; nonprofit fraternities and sororities; lodges; and nonprofit professional and trade associations, labor unions, civic clubs, and patriotic organizations. Examples of exempt entities are provided in a regulation. (86 Ill. Adm. Code 130.2005(e); 86 Ill. Adm. Code 130.2005(f); 86 Ill. Adm. Code 130.2005(g); 86 Ill. Adm. Code 130.2005(k))

"Organized and operated exclusively".—The Department has not defined the term "exclusively," but indicates that if a substantial purpose or activity of the organization includes an activity that is not a charitable, religious, or educational purpose or activity, the entity will not be considered "exclusively" organized and operated for charitable, religious, or educational purposes. (86 Ill. Adm. Code 130.2005(n))

The purpose for which an entity is "organized and operated" is determined by reference to its charter (in the case of a corporation) or to its constitution and bylaws. (86 Ill. Adm. Code 130.2005(j))

"Educational organizations".—A corporation, limited liability company, society, association, foundation, or institution organized and operated exclusively for educational purposes includes all tax-supported public schools; private schools whose course of study compares with that of public schools; vocational and technical schools or institutes organized and operated exclusively to provide a course of study of not less than six weeks; and licensed nonprofit day care centers as defined in Section 2.09 of the Child Care Act of 1969. Organizations operated for the purpose of offering professional, trade, or business seminars; self-improvement or personality development courses; avocational or recreational courses; television or radio courses; correspondence courses; or courses not offering specialized training within a specific vocational or technical field are not organized exclusively for educational purposes. (35 ILCS 105/2c; 35 ILCS 110/3c; 35 ILCS 115/2c; 35 ILCS 120/2h)

"Educational purposes" is construed by the Department to mean "school purposes" as interpreted by the Illinois Supreme Court; a regulation provides additional guidance. Schools are exempt whether nonprofit or business-operated. (86 Ill. Adm. Code 130.2005(l))

"Charitable organizations".—A charitable organization must be organized and conducted on a nonprofit basis with no personal profit inuring to anyone. However, payment of salaries to employees for services rendered is allowed. There can be no capital structure or capital stock, no provisions for disbursing dividends or profits, and no payment of director's fees. Also, the organization must be organized and operated to benefit an indefinite number of the public and relieve the public of a duty it would have to those persons or otherwise provide some benefit on the public. (86 Ill. Adm. Code 130.2005(h); 86 Ill. Adm. Code 130.2005(i))

Examples of exclusively charitable organizations are parent-teacher organizations, American National Red Cross, Community Fund or United Fund organizations, YMCA, YWCA, and Boy and Girl Scout organizations. (86 Ill. Adm. Code 130.2005(a))

Hospital, nursing home, and child care sales.—Sales of food or medicine made by nonprofit hospitals, nursing homes, or sanitaria (that are exclusively charitable institutions) in the course of rendering service to patients are not subject to the ROT and UT. In addition, such hospitals are not taxable on their sales of drugs to anyone. Also, food prepared for immediate consumption and transferred incident to a sale of service by an entity licensed under the Hospital Licensing Act, the Nursing Home

Care Act, the MR/DD Community Care Act, or the Child Care Act of 1969 is subject to the SOT and SUT at a reduced rate. (35 ILCS 110/3-1; 35 ILCS 115/3-10;86 Ill. Adm. Code 130.2005(b))

Sales made by a hospital cafeteria that is open to the public are taxable. In addition, sales by nonprofit hospitals of such items as candy, chewing gum, tobacco products, and razor blades are taxable because these items are not necessary to the rendering of hospital services. (86 Ill. Adm. Code 130.2005(b))

To qualify for exemption, a hospital or sanitaria must not reject patients or doctors on the basis of race, color, creed, or religion and must not reject patients unable to pay. However, it may refuse to admit persons with dangerously contagious diseases. (86 Ill. Adm. Code 130.2005(m))

Sales of food, medicine, and other property by business-operated hospitals, sanitaria, or nursing homes as an incident to rendering services to patients are subject to SOT. However, such sales of food and medicine are taxed at a reduced rate. (86 Ill. Adm. Code 140.126; 86 Ill. Adm. Code 130.2005(p); 86 Ill. Adm. Code 140.140(m))

An exemption is allowed for food, medicine, drugs, and other items purchased for use by persons receiving medical assistance and residing in a licensed facility.

For a discussion of the exemptions for food, medicine, drugs, and other items, see ¶60-390 Food and Grocery Items and ¶60-520 Medical, Dental, and Optical Supplies and Drugs.

Gift shops and rummage stores.—Sales by gift shops or rummage stores operated by charitable or religious organizations are subject to the ROT and UT. (86 Ill. Adm. Code 130.2005(b))

Suppliers; sales to nonprofit organizations.—Suppliers incur ROT liability when selling property to any nonprofit purchaser unless the sale is (1) for resale, (2) made to any purchaser organized exclusively for charitable, religious, or educational purposes, or (3) made to a nonprofit organization with no compensated officers or employees and that is organized primarily for the recreation of persons 55 years of age or older. Adequate books and records must be maintained by the supplier in support of its deductions of exempt sales receipts. (86 Ill. Adm. Code 130.2005(d); 86 Ill. Adm. Code 130.2005(r))

Educational, scientific, and similar institutions.—Persons engaged habitually, for livelihood or gain, in hospital, educational, religious, scientific, social, or cultural enterprises are engaged in a service occupation that is still a business and are liable for ROT on sales of property. ROT is not imposed on property transferred as a part of a service, but SOT is imposed on their purchase of property for retransfer as an incident to the service. Suppliers of these businesses do not incur ROT liability on sales of property for resale or for retransfer incident to a service. (86 Ill. Adm. Code 130.2005(p); 86 Ill. Adm. Code 130.2005(o); 86 Ill. Adm. Code 130.2005(q))

• *Nonprofit organizations for the elderly*

A sale to any nonprofit corporation, society, association, foundation, institution, or organization with no compensated officers or employees and that is organized and operated primarily for the recreation of persons age 55 or older is exempt from ROT and UT (35 ILCS 105/3-5; 35 ILCS 120/2-5; 86 Ill. Adm. Code 130.120(h); 86 Ill. Adm. Code 150.325) and a sale or transfer of property as an incident to the rendering of service for or by any such entity is exempt from SOT and SUT. (35 ILCS 110/2; 35 ILCS 115/2; 86 Ill. Adm. Code 140.125(h))

The exemption is not applicable unless the corporation, society, association, foundation, or institution has, on and after July 1, 1987, an active exemption identification number issued by the Department. (86 Ill. Adm. Code 150.325; 86 Ill. Adm. Code 130.2007) If the entity is organized and operated exclusively for charitable

¶60-580

purposes and has more than 50 subsidiary organizations in Illinois, the Department may issue one exemption identification number. (35 ILCS 120/1g) Each number or renewal is valid for five years.

Upon request, the Department will furnish any county or municipality a list of each exempt organization that has a valid exemption identification number and that is located within the corporate limits of the municipality or unincorporated territory of a county. (35 ILCS 120/1h)

Service organizations.—Sales by a nonprofit corporation, society, association, foundation, institution, or organization that is organized and operated as a service enterprise for the benefit of persons 65 years of age or older are exempt from ROT, UT, SOT, and SUT, provided that the property was not purchased by the enterprise for the purpose of resale. (35 ILCS 105/3-5; 35 ILCS 110/3-5; 35 ILCS 115/3-5; 35 ILCS 120/2-5; 86 Ill. Adm. Code 140.125; 86 Ill. Adm. Code 130.120(bb); 86 Ill. Adm. Code 130.2008)

• *Not-for-profit arts or cultural organizations*

Sales of personal property to, and use of personal property by, any nonprofit arts or cultural organization that is exempt from federal income tax and that is organized and operated for the presentation or support of arts or cultural programming, activities, or services, including but not limited to, music and dramatic arts organizations such as symphony orchestras and theatrical groups, arts and cultural service organizations, local arts councils, visual arts organizations, and media arts organizations, are exempt from ROT, UT, SOT, and SUT. Formerly, the exemption applied only to live public performances of musical or theatrical works on a regular basis. Eligibility and documentation requirements are provided by regulation. (35 ILCS 105/3-5; 35 ILCS 110/3-5; 35 ILCS 115/3-5; 35 ILCS 120/2-5; 86 Ill. Adm. Code 130.2004; 86 Ill. Adm. Code 140.125(h); 86 Ill. Adm. Code 130.120(aa))

• *County fair associations*

The sale of property to an Illinois county fair association for use in conducting, operating, or promoting a county fair are exempt from ROT, UT, SOT, and SUT. (35 ILCS 105/3-5; 35 ILCS 110/3-5; 35 ILCS 115/3-5; 35 ILCS 120/2-5; 86 Ill. Adm. Code 140.125(h); 86 Ill. Adm. Code 130.120(z))

• *Teacher-sponsored student organizations*

Sales of property by a teacher-sponsored student organization affiliated with an Illinois public or private elementary or secondary school are exempt from ROT, UT, SOT, and SUT. Such an organization is defined as an organization that collects and disburses monies as approved by the local board of education. Examples of exempt organizations are student councils, student clubs, and choral and band groups. (35 ILCS 105/3-5; 35 ILCS 110/3-5; 35 ILCS 115/3-5; 35 ILCS 120/2-5; 86 Ill. Adm. Code 130.120(x); 86 Ill. Adm. Code 130.2006; 86 Ill. Adm. Code 140.125(v))

However, an exempt organization's purchases of items for its own use or consumption are taxable; purchases for resale are not subject to tax. Purchases for resale may be made without paying tax only if the school, school district, or treasurer appointed by the Board applies to the Department for a reseller's certificate to be issued in the name of the school, school district, or student activity fund. (86 Ill. Adm. Code 130.2006)

• *School fundraising sales*

Personal property, including food, purchased through fundraising events for the benefit of a public or private elementary or secondary school, a group of those schools, or one or more school districts is exempt from UT, SUT, SOT, and ROT if the events are sponsored by an entity recognized by the school district that consists primarily of volunteers and includes parents and teachers of the school children.

These exemptions do not apply to personal property purchased through fundraising events (1) for the benefit of private home instruction or (2) for which the fundraising entity purchases the personal property sold at the events from another individual or entity that sold the property for the purpose of resale by the fundraising entity and that profits from the sale to the fundraising entity. The exemptions are not subject to any general or specific sunset date provisions and, thus, are available indefinitely. (35 ILCS 105/3-5; 35 ILCS 110/3-5; 35 ILCS 115/3-5; 35 ILCS 120/2-5)

• *Exempt sales of food and drugs*

The Department will not collect from eligible nonprofit organization the ROT, SOT, UT, or SUT imposed on food that is to be consumed off the premises where sold (other than alcoholic beverages, soft drinks, and food that has been prepared for immediate consumption), medicines, drugs, medical appliances, insulin, urine testing materials, syringes, and needles used by diabetics. As a condition of participation in the program, the organizations are required to perform community service in a county or municipality that notifies the Department in writing that the county or municipality does not want the tax to be collected from such organizations. (35 ILCS 105/3-5.5; 35 ILCS 110/3-5.5; 35 ILCS 115/3-5.5; 35 ILCS 120/2-5.5)

• *Donated motor vehicles*

A motor vehicle donated to a corporation, limited liability company (LLC), society, association, foundation, or institution that is determined by the Department to be organized and operated exclusively for educational purposes is exempt from UT, SUT, SOT, and ROT. For purposes of these exemptions, the corporation, LLC, society, association, foundation, or institution may be (1) a tax-supported public school, (2) a private school that offers systematic instruction in useful branches of learning by methods common to public schools and that compares favorably in scope and intensity with the course of study presented in tax-supported schools, or (3) a vocational or technical school or institute organized and operated exclusively to provide a course of study of at least six weeks duration and designed to prepare individuals to follow a trade or pursue a manual, technical, mechanical, industrial, business, or commercial occupation. (35 ILCS 105/3-5; 35 ILCS 110/3-5; 35 ILCS 115/3-5; 35 ILCS 120/2-5; 86 Ill. Adm. Code 130.120(uu); *Informational Bulletin FY 2000-4*, Department of Revenue, October 1999)

Public-facilities corporation's construction of municipal convention hall

Tangible personal property sold to a public-facilities corporation for purposes of constructing or furnishing a municipal convention hall is exempt from sales and use tax. (65 ILCS 5/11-65-15)

A "public-facilities corporation" means an Illinois not-for-profit corporation whose purpose is charitable and civic, organized solely for the purpose of (1) acquiring a site for a municipal convention hall; (2) constructing, building, and equipping thereon a municipal convention hall; and (3) collecting the revenues therefrom, entirely without profit to the public-facilities corporation, its officers, or directors. (65 ILCS 5/11-65-10)

[¶60-650] Resales

A sale of property for purposes of resale is exempt from ROT and UT. This exemption generally applies to the extent the property is not first used prior to its resale. (35 ILCS 105/2; 35 ILCS 120/1; 86 Ill. Adm. Code 130.120(c); 86 Ill. Adm. Code 130.210; 86 Ill. Adm. Code 150.201)

Sales of property to a purchaser who transfers the property to others in connection with the furnishing of services are sales for resale. (86 Ill. Adm. Code 130.205; 86 Ill. Adm. Code 130.2120)

A sale of property for purposes of resale is also exempt from SOT and SUT. (35 ILCS 110/2; 35 ILCS 115/2; 86 Ill. Adm. Code 140.125(g); 86 Ill. Adm. Code 140.201(e)(2))

The sale of property by a supplier for delivery to a person residing or engaged in business in Illinois is prima facie evidence that it was sold for the purpose of resale as an incident to a sale of service. (35 ILCS 115/4)

The use of items such as nonreusable paper plates and cups, napkins, straws, and other packaging materials by persons engaged in the business of operating an eating establishment is considered a sale for resale and is exempt from tax. (35 ILCS 105/2)

A sale is tax free if the purchaser presents a resale certificate to the seller. This certificate is a statement signed by the purchaser that the property is purchased for purposes of resale. The certificate must bear the names and addresses of the seller and purchaser, the date signed by the purchaser, identification of the property, and the registration number or resale number or certification of resale to an out-of-state purchaser. The Department of Revenue provides Form CRT-61 as a resale certificate. The resale certificate has no stated expiration period. (35 ILCS 120/2c; 86 Ill. Adm. Code 130.1405; 86 Ill. Adm. Code 140.1001)

A purchaser not registered with the Department of Revenue must apply for a resale number, unless the purchaser is from out of state and will always resell and deliver the property to customers outside Illinois. A failure to furnish a registration or resale number raises a rebuttable presumption that a sale is not for resale. Agricultural producers not registered with the Department as retailers are given a resale number (0110) as a class (individual applications not required) in order to buy feed, seed, fertilizer, and baby chicks for resale. (35 ILCS 120/2c; 86 Ill. Adm. Code 130.210; 86 Ill. Adm. Code 130.1415)

No certificates of resale are necessary for sales made to a corporation, society, association, foundation, or institution organized and operated exclusively for charitable, religious, or educational purposes, sales made to nonprofit organizations with no compensated officers or employees that are organized primarily for the recreation of persons 55 years of age or older, or sales made to a governmental body. (86 Ill. Adm. Code 130.1401)

See ¶ 61-020 Exemption Certificates.

• *Blanket certificates*

A blanket certificate of resale may be accepted by a seller from a purchaser whose purchases are all for resale. Blanket certificates of resale may also cover purchases of a given type of property or a certain percentage of purchases from a particular seller. The certificates should be updated periodically, and no less frequently than every three years. (86 Ill. Adm. Code 130.1405)

• *Withdrawals from inventory*

The use tax does not apply to tangible personal property produced by the user of the property or acquired in a manner other than a purchase at retail. (86 Ill. Adm. Code 150.305(a)) However, although a user is not taxable on the value of a finished product he produces, the use tax applies to tangible personal property that the user purchases and incorporates into a finished product used in Illinois.

The basis of tax for tangible personal property that a user purchases and incorporates into a finished product is the purchase price. (86 Ill. Adm. Code 150.305(b))

[¶60-665] Services

Services are exempt from sales and use tax in Illinois.

What services are taxable in Illinois?

None. Services are not taxable in Illinois.

What about transactions that also involve tangible personal property?

The sales price of property provided in a service transaction is generally subject to service occupation tax. (SOT). SOT applies when two requirements are met: 1) the seller is in the business of selling services, and 2) the property sold is an incidental addition to the service. (35 ILCS 115/3-10; 86 Ill. Adm. Code 140.101) If the sales price of property provided is not separately shown on the service provider's bill, SOT will be imposed on 50% of the entire billing. Illinois registered service providers with a de minimis amount of property sales subject to SOT are liable for SOT based on the service provider's cost price of the property provided. In no case may the sales price of the property provided be less than the service provider's cost price of the property for SOT purposes.

Sales tax applies to property sold by service providers when the property is not related to the service provided.

How is tangible personal property purchased by the service provider treated?

Purchases of property by a service provider that will retain and use or consume the property are subject to sales tax. If the property will be transferred by the service provider while providing services, the purchase qualifies as an exempt purchase for resale.

Does Illinois provide any detailed guidance on specific services?

Yes, the Illinois Department of Revenue has issued detailed guidance for the service providers listed below.

Property sold separately from services.

Certain property sold by the following service providers is subject to sales tax, not SOT:

Barber and beauty shops

Blacksmiths

Chiropractors and osteopaths

Dentists

Optometrists and opticians

Pharmacists

Physicians

Picture framers

Seminar providers

Veterinarians

[¶60-740] Transportation

Retail sales of transportation equipment and supplies are subject to retailer's occupation (sales) tax, use tax, service occupation tax (SOT) and service use tax (SUT) in Illinois unless a specific exemption applies. Transportation services are exempt.

How does Illinois tax transportation equipment and supplies?

In Illinois, transportation equipment and supplies are taxable unless a exemption applies to the type of property purchased. (35 ILCS 105/3-55; 35 ILCS 110/2; 35 ILCS 115/2; 35 ILCS 120/2-5)

Railroads. Sales of property to railroad companies are subject to sales and use tax unless:

- the property is purchased by a rail common carrier or a motor common carrier; and

- the carrier receives the property in Illinois and transports the property outside the state.

Rolling stock. An exemption is available for certain property sold to be "used as rolling stock moving in interstate commerce." The exemption applies to motor vehicles and trailers purchased on or after July 1, 2017, when three requirements are met:

(1) the motor vehicle or trailer is used to transport persons or property for hire;

(2) the purchaser certifies that the motor vehicle or trailer will be used by an interstate carrier or carriers for hire who hold an active USDOT Number with certain classifications; and

(3) for motor vehicles, the gross vehicle weight rating exceeds 16,000 pounds.

The exemption is also available for items purchased on or after July 1, 2017, that are to be used as a part in a motor vehicle or trailer. (35 ILCS 105/3-61; 35 ILCS 110/3-51; 35 ILCS 115/2d; 35 ILCS 120/2-51)

If an exempt item no longer meets the three requirements, then tax is imposed on the selling price, allowing for a reasonable depreciation for the period during which the item qualified for the exemption.

In addition, the exemption applies to:

- motor vehicles that have a gross vehicle weight exceeding 16,000 pounds, until June 30, 2017;

- limousines;

- certain aircraft and watercraft; and

- trailers, semitrailers and pole trailers.

(35 ILCS 105/3-61; 35 ILCS 110/3-51; 35 ILCS 115/2d; 35 ILCS 120/2-51)

"Rolling stock" is defined as transportation vehicles of an interstate transportation company for hire. Railroad "rolling stock" includes all railroad cars, passenger and freight, and locomotives or mobile power units of every nature for moving railroad cars that operate on railroad tracks. The exemption covers sales of property attached to the cars or locomotives, as well as equipment loaded on the cars to transport property (e.g. trailers) that are not attached to the cars. (86 Ill. Adm. Code 130.340)

Sales for use. Rules for sales to interstate carriers were repealed effective July 1, 2017. Prior to July 1, 2017, an exemption was available for sales of property to interstate carriers for hire when the property is used as rolling stock moving in interstate commerce. (35 ILCS 105/3-55; 35 ILCS 110/2; 35 ILCS 115/2; 35 ILCS 120/2-5; 86 Ill. Adm. Code 130.120(l); 86 Ill. Adm. Code 130.340; 86 Ill. Adm. Code 140.125(s); 86 Ill. Adm. Code 140.201(e); 86 Ill. Adm. Code 150.310)

The exemption is available for sales of property to owners, lessors or shippers of tangible personal property which is used by interstate carriers for hire as rolling stock moving in interstate commerce. (86 Ill. Adm. Code 140.125(t))

Sales for lease. Rules for sales to lessors were repealed effective July 1, 2017. Prior to July 1, 2017, sales to lessors of property used as rolling stock moving in interstate commerce were exempt if the leases with interstate carriers will be for at least one year or are in effect at the time of purchase. (35 ILCS 105/3-55; 35 ILCS 110/2; 35 ILCS 115/2; 35 ILCS 120/2-5; 86 Ill. Adm. Code 130.120(l); 86 Ill. Adm. Code 130.340; 86 Ill. Adm. Code 140.125(s); 86 Ill. Adm. Code 140.201(e); 86 Ill. Adm. Code 150.310)

Telecommunications equipment. Sales of equipment are exempt if the equipment is permanently installed in aircraft moving in interstate commerce and is operated by a telecommunications provider. The telecommunications provider must be licensed as a common carrier by the Federal Communications Commission (FCC) for the exemption to apply. (35 ILCS 105/3-55; 35 ILCS 110/2; 35 ILCS 115/2; 35 ILCS 120/2-5; 86 Ill. Adm. Code 130.120(l); 86 Ill. Adm. Code 130.340; 86 Ill. Adm. Code 140.125(s); 86 Ill. Adm. Code 140.201(e); 86 Ill. Adm. Code 150.310)

Also exempt are sales to owners, lessors or shippers of equipment operated by a telecommunications provider which is permanently installed in or affixed to aircraft moving in interstate commerce. The telecommunications provider must be licensed as a common carrier by the FCC for the exemption to apply. (86 Ill. Adm. Code 140.125(t))

Purchases outside Illinois. An exemption from SUT is available for the use of property acquired outside the state and moved into Illinois for use as rolling stock moving in interstate commerce. (35 ILCS 110/3-45)

Short-term use in Illinois. Purchases of rolling stock used by an interstate carrier for hire between points in Illinois are exempt if the property is used to transport persons whose journeys, or property whose shipments, originate or terminate outside Illinois. (35 ILCS 105/3-60; 35 ILCS 110/3-50; 35 ILCS 120/2-50; 86 Ill. Adm. Code 130.340)

Trips or mileage method. When claiming the rolling stock exemption, the purchaser elects a method to determine whether the purchase qualifies for the exemption. The purchaser may choose either:

- the trips method (more than 50% of total trips taken), or
- the mileage method (more than 50% of total miles driven).

(35 ILCS 105/3-61; 35 ILCS 110/3-51; 35 ILCS 115/2d; 35 ILCS 120/2-51)

The purchaser cannot later change the method. If no election is made, the person is deemed to have chosen the mileage method. (35 ILCS 105/3-61; 35 ILCS 110/3-51; 35 ILCS 115/2d; 35 ILCS 120/2-51)

In addition, property purchased for the purpose of being attached as a part of aircraft or watercraft also qualifies for the exemption if the aircraft or watercraft itself qualifies as rolling stock. Taxpayers who purchased aircraft or watercraft before January 1, 2014, must make an election to use either the trips or mileage method for the aircraft or watercraft, and document that election in their books and records for purposes of qualifying for the election. (35 ILCS 105/3-61; 35 ILCS 110/3-51; 35 ILCS 115/2d; 35 ILCS 120/2-51)

Aircraft. Aircraft are taxable in Illinois under general sales and use tax provisions or under the aircraft use tax provision, unless an exemption applies. Only qualifying taxpayers may take an exemption.

Aircraft use tax. An Illinois aircraft use tax is imposed on the use in Illinois of aircraft acquired by gift, transfer or purchase. The tax is equal to 6.25% of the selling price or fair market value of the aircraft. The aircraft use tax will not apply if: (35 ILCS 157/10-15; 35 ILCS 157/10-20)

- the use of the aircraft is subject to Illinois use tax;
- the aircraft is bought and used by a governmental agency or by a charitable, religious, or educational entity;
- the use of the aircraft is exempt from use tax under the rolling stock exemption; or
- the aircraft is transferred as gift to a surviving spouse in the administration of an estate.

Aircraft leaving Illinois after sale. An exemption is available for an aircraft that leaves Illinois within 15 days after the later of:

- the issuance of the final billing for the sale or purchase of the aircraft; or
- the authorized approval for return to service, completion of the maintenance record entry, and completion of the test flight and ground test for inspection.

(35 ILCS 105/3-55; 35 ILCS 120/2-5; 86 Ill. Adm. Code 130.605)

The aircraft must not be based or registered in Illinois after the sale or purchase. (35 ILCS 105/3-55; 35 ILCS 120/2-5; 86 Ill. Adm. Code 130.605)

Aircraft temporarily in Illinois for prepurchase evaluation. An exemption is allowed for an aircraft that is located in Illinois for a prepurchase evaluation if the aircraft will not be based or registered in Illinois after the evaluation. (35 ILCS 105/3-55)

Aircraft repair, maintenance, and replacement items. Through December 31, 2024, materials, parts, equipment, components, and furnishings are exempt if they are incorporated into or upon an aircraft as part of the aircraft's:

- modification,
- refurbishment,
- completion,
- replacement,
- repair, or
- maintenance.

(35 ILCS 105/3-5(35); 35 ILCS 110/3-5(27); 35 ILCS 115/3-5(28); 35 ILCS 120/2-5(40))

However, no claim for credit or refund is allowed for taxes paid as a result of the disallowance of this exemption on or after January 1, 2015 and prior to February 5, 2020. (35 ILCS 105/3-5(35); 35 ILCS 110/3-5(27); 35 ILCS 115/3-5(28); 35 ILCS 120/2-5(40))

The exemption does not include items used in modifying, replacing, repairing, and maintaining aircraft engines or power plants. (35 ILCS 105/3-5(35); 35 ILCS 110/3-5(27); 35 ILCS 115/3-5(28); 35 ILCS 120/2-5(40))

The exemption is available for consumable supplies, such as:

- adhesive,
- tape,
- sandpaper,
- general purpose lubricants,
- cleaning solution,
- latex gloves, and
- protective films.

(35 ILCS 105/3-5(35); 35 ILCS 110/3-5(27); 35 ILCS 115/3-5(28); 35 ILCS 120/2-5(40))

Taxpayer qualification requirements. The exemption for aircraft repair, maintenance, and replacement items is available only to organizations that:

• hold an Air Agency Certificate and are empowered to operate an approved repair station by the Federal Aviation Administration;

• have a Class IV Rating; and

• conduct operations in accordance with Part 145 of the Federal Aviation Regulations.

(35 ILCS 105/3-5(35); 35 ILCS 110/3-5(27); 35 ILCS 115/3-5(28); 35 ILCS 120/2-5(40))

The exemption does not cover aircraft operated by a commercial air carrier providing scheduled passenger air service pursuant to authority issued under Part 121 or Part 129 of the Federal Aviation Regulations. (35 ILCS 105/3-5(35); 35 ILCS 110/3-5(27); 35 ILCS 115/3-5(28); 35 ILCS 120/2-5(40))

Watercraft. Watercraft are taxable in Illinois under general sales and use tax provisions or under the watercraft use tax provision, unless an exemption applies.

Watercraft use tax. A use tax is imposed on any watercraft acquired by gift, transfer, or purchase. (35 ILCS 158/15-10) The watercraft use tax does not apply to a watercraft that is:

— otherwise taxed under the Illinois Use Tax Act;

— bought and used by a governmental agency or a society, association, foundation, or institution organized exclusively for charitable, religious, or educational purposes;

— not subject to tax because imposing the tax would lead to multistate taxation;

— a gift to a surviving spouse in the administration of an estate; or

— exempt from the Boat Registration and Safety Act, Sec. 3-12, unless the watercraft is used upon the waters of Illinois for more than 30 days a year.

(35 ILCS 158/15-10)

The rate of the tax is 6.25% of the purchase price. (35 ILCS 158/15-15) "Purchase price" is the reasonable consideration paid for the watercraft, including cash, credits, property, and services. The purchase price also includes the value of any motor sold with or in conjunction with the watercraft. (35 ILCS 158/15-5)

"Watercraft" means a Class 2, Class 3, or Class 4 watercraft (as defined in Sec. 3-2 of the Boat Registration and Safety Act), or a personal watercraft (as defined in Sec. 1-2 of the Boat Registration and Safety Act.) (35 ILCS 158/15-5)

Demonstrator aircraft and watercraft. In general, watercraft or aircraft purchased for resale may be used by the dealer for demonstration or other interim use purpose without giving rise to use tax liability. However, if the period of such use exceeds 18 months, the retailer must pay use tax calculated on the basis of the retailer's original cost price. (35 ILCS 105/2) No credit is permitted if the watercraft or aircraft is subsequently sold by the retailer. "Watercraft" means a Class 2, Class 3, or Class 4 watercraft (as defined in Sec. 3-2 of the Boat Registration and Safety Act), a personal watercraft, or any boat equipped with an inboard motor.

Fuel used in interstate commerce An exemption from use tax and service use tax is available for fuel purchased outside Illinois and brought into Illinois in the fuel supply tanks of locomotives engaged in freight hauling and passenger service. (35 ILCS 105/3-55; 35 ILCS 110/3-45)

What is the tax treatment of transportation services in Illinois?

In Illinois, transportation services are not subject to sales tax. Service occupation tax (SOT), however, is imposed on property that is transferred incidentally as part of a service transaction.

Railroad repairs. A railroad that, on a nonprofit basis, repairs cars for another railroad at an interchange point in connection with the interchange of traffic is not engaged in rendering services and is not subject to SOT. (86 Ill. Adm. Code 140.120)

Passenger tickets. Federal law prohibits a state and its political subdivisions from collecting or levying a tax, fee, head charge, or other charge on: (1) a passenger traveling in interstate commerce by motor carrier; (2) the transportation of a passenger traveling in interstate commerce by motor carrier; (3) the sale of passenger transportation in interstate commerce by motor carrier; or (4) the gross receipts derived from such transportation. (Sec. 14505, Title 49 U.S.C.)

[¶60-750] Utilities

Sales of coke, fuel oil, briquettes, wood, coal, or other combustibles are expressly subject to the ROT and UT. Sales of steam are also subject to ROT and UT. (86 Ill. Adm. Code 130.2095; 86 Ill. Adm. Code 130.2156)

Electricity and natural gas.—Transactions involving the following are exempt from retailers' occupation (sales) tax, use tax, service occupation tax (SOT) and service use tax (SUT):

- electricity delivered to customers by wire;

- natural or artificial gas that is delivered to customers through pipes, pipelines or mains; and

- water that is delivered to customer's through pipes, pipelines or mains.

(35 ILCS 105/3; 35 ILCS 110/2; 35 ILCS 115/2; 35 ILCS 120/2) The legislation that enacted the exemptions states that the amendments are declaratory of existing law. (35 ILCS 105/3; 35 ILCS 110/2; 35 ILCS 115/2; 35 ILCS 120/2)

In Illinois, an electricity excise tax (EET) is imposed on the privilege of using in the state electricity purchased for use or consumption. The incidence of this state tax is on the consumers of electricity and is collected by the delivering supplier. There are limited exemptions from the EET. (*General Information Letter ST 07-0060-GIL*, Illinois Department of Revenue, June 11, 2007)

- *Transportation services*

See ¶60-740 Transportation.

- *Community water supply*

Exemption is allowed for tangible personal property used in the construction or maintenance of a community water supply that is operated by a not-for-profit corporation that holds a valid water supply permit issued under Title IV of the Environmental Protection Act. This exemption is not subject to the general five-year sunset provision for tax exemptions. (35 ILCS 105/3-5; 35 ILCS 110/3-5; 35 ILCS 115/3-5; 35 ILCS 120/2-5; 86 Ill. Adm. Code 130.1934)

[¶61-000]

EXEMPTIONS

[¶61-020] Exemption Certificates

Purchasers who make tax-exempt purchases must provide retailers with proper documentation showing the purchase is exempt. In some cases, retailers are required to submit their documentation with their tax returns. (*Publication 104, Common Sales Tax Exemptions*)

• *Building materials*

Contractors and other entities participating in a real estate construction, rehabilitation, or renovation project in an Enterprise Zone or a River Edge Redevelopment Zone, or for a state-certified High Impact Business, may purchase building materials for the project exempt from sales tax. (35 ILCS 120/5k; *Information Bulletin FY 2013-16*, Illinois Department of Revenue, June 2013)

For discussions of the various exemptions, see ¶60-360 Enterprise Zones and Similar Tax Incentives.

Beginning July 1, 2013, the building materials exemption is available only to contractors or other entities that have obtained a building materials exemption certificate from the Department of Revenue. (35 ILCS 120/5k; *Information Bulletin FY 2013-16*, Illinois Department of Revenue, June 2013) Prior to July 1, 2013, a "qualified sale" is a sale of building materials that will be incorporated into real estate as part of a building project for which a Certificate of Eligibility for Sales Tax Exemption has been issued by the administrator of the enterprise zone in which the building project is located. (35 ILCS 120/5k)

The following persons are eligible for the certificate:

— each construction contractor or other entity that purchases building materials to be incorporated into real estate in an Enterprise Zone or River Edge Redevelopment Zone by rehabilitation, remodeling or new construction; and

— each construction contractor or other entity that purchases building materials that will be incorporated into a High Impact Business location as designated by the Department of Commerce and Economic Opportunity.

(*Information Bulletin FY 2013-16*, Illinois Department of Revenue, June 2013)

Construction contractors, zone administrators and high impact businesses engage in different certificate application processes and use Form EZ-1. A certificate is valid for two years. A certificate holder who uses the certificate or allows it to be used to improperly avoid tax will be assessed taxes and penalties on the purchase, will be subject to an additional monetary penalty equal to the state and local sales taxes on the purchase, and may be barred from securing certificates for other projects. (*Information Bulletin FY 2013-16*, Illinois Department of Revenue, June 2013)

• *Machinery and equipment*

Machinery and equipment used on a farm (¶60-250) or in graphic arts (¶60-630) may be purchased tax-free only if a resale or exemption certificate is presented to the seller. Retailers may accept blanket exemption certificates but are responsible for maintaining the certificates as part of their records. (86 Ill. Adm. Code 130.305(m); 86 Ill. Adm. Code 130.325 (b)(8))

Machinery and equipment used primarily in manufacturing are not subject to tax if the purchaser provides the seller with an active registration or resale number, or presents an exemption certificate. (¶60-510)

Form ST-587, Equipment Exemption Certificate, is used to claim the exemptions for machinery and equipment used on a farm, in graphic arts, coal and aggregate mining or in manufacturing. The seller must keep the certificate. The purchaser may provide a blanket exemption certificate to any seller from whom all purchases made from the identified seller will be exempt. Qualified exemptions include items used:

- primarily in the manufacturing or assembling of tangible personal property for wholesale or retail sale or lease, including graphic arts production;
- primarily in production agriculture; and
- primarily for coal and aggregate exploration and related mining, off-highway hauling, processing, maintenance, and reclamation, but excluding motor vehicles required to be registered under the Illinois Vehicle Code.

A blanket certificate can also specify that a percentage of the purchases made from the identified seller will be exempt. In either instance, blanket certificates should be kept up-to-date. If a specified percentage changes, a new certificate should be provided. Otherwise, all certificates should be updated at least every three years.

- *Nonprofit organizations and governmental agencies*

Purchases by exclusively charitable, religious, or educational organizations (see ¶60-580) and government entities (see ¶60-420) are exempt only if the purchaser has an active exemption identification number. Each number or renewal is valid for five years after the first day of the month following the month of issuance. (35 ILCS 120/1g; 35 ILCS 105/3-5(3); 35 ILCS 110/3-5(3); 35 ILCS 115/3-5(3); 35 ILCS 120/2-5(9); 86 Ill. Adm. Code 150.710; 86 Ill. Adm. Code 130.2007)

The rental or lease of tangible personal property purchased by a lessor who leases the property to a governmental body, with an active sales tax identification number, under a lease of one year or longer is exempt from UT, SUT, SOT, and ROT. (35 ILCS 105/3-5; 35 ILCS 110/3-5; 35 ILCS 115/3-5; 35 ILCS 120/2-5)

- *Purchases of property by a serviceman*

SOT is not imposed on purchases of property by a serviceman who gives a valid exemption certificate to the supplier. A serviceman who cannot determine at the time it purchases property how the property will be disposed of may give the supplier an exemption certificate which relieves the supplier of liability for collecting SOT. The certificate is not valid unless the serviceman has an active registration or resale number and this number appears on the certificate. (86 Ill. Adm. Code 140.125(e); 86 Ill. Adm. Code 140.1305)

For resale exemption certificate requirements, see ¶60-650 Resales.

- *Railroad rolling stock*

A purchaser who claims the rolling stock exemption (¶60-740) must provide certification that it is an interstate carrier for hire, and that the property is being purchased for use as rolling stock in interstate commerce. If the purchaser is a carrier, it must include its Interstate Commerce Commission Certificate of Authority number or certify that it is a type of interstate carrier for hire that is not required to have such a certificate. (86 Ill. Adm. Code 130.340(e))

- *Recordkeeping*

A taxpayer's books and records must contain detailed information to support deductions arising from nontaxable transactions. (35 ILCS 120/7)

Regulations explain how retailers must maintain exemption certificates in their books and records. Specifically, the certificate must include the seller's name and address, the purchaser's name and address, and a statement that the property purchased will be used primarily in graphic arts production. Further, if a graphic arts producer or lessor purchases at retail from a vendor who is not registered to collect the Illinois use tax, then the purchaser must maintain a copy of the certification in his records to support the deduction on the return. (86 Ill. Adm. Code 130.325 (b)(8))

• *Expiration procedures*

Once a tax exemption certificate expires, for example, on the purchase of leased items at the term of the lease, and the property that qualified for exemption no longer qualifies, the taxpayer then incurs either the use tax or a service use tax on the fair market value of the property. (*Informational Bulletin FY 2001-18*, Illinois Department of Revenue, December 2000)

• *Sunset date for exemptions*

Except as noted below, exemptions are limited by a sunset date. If the sunset date is not specified in the public act enacting the exemption or the sunset date is later amended, the taxpayer is not entitled to take the exemption for tax years beginning on or after five years from the effective date of the enacting public law. (35 ILCS 105/3-90; 35 ILCS 110/3-75; 35 ILCS 115/3-55; 35 ILCS 120/2-70)

The exemptions for personal property, including food, purchased through school fundraising events (see ¶ 60-580) are not subject to the general sunset date provisions or any specific sunset date provisions and, thus, are available indefinitely. (35 ILCS 105/3-5(28); 35 ILCS 110/3-5(21); 35 ILCS 115/3-5(22); 35 ILCS 120/2-5(34))

[¶61-100]
BASIS OF TAX

[¶61-110] Tax Base

The ROT is based on "gross receipts" from retail sales of tangible personal property. (35 ILCS 120/2-10; 86 Ill. Adm. Code 130.101(a))

"Gross receipts" means the total selling price or amount of retail sales. Payments from charge and time sales are included in gross receipts only when received. Receipts from the assignment of accounts receivable to a wholly owned subsidiary are likewise not included in basis until the purchaser makes payment. Amounts received as down payments are included in gross receipts. (35 ILCS 120/1; 86 Ill. Adm. Code 130.401; 86 Ill. Adm. Code 130.430)

"Selling price" or the "amount of sale" is defined as the consideration for a sale valued in money, including cash, credits, property, and services. The selling price is determined without deduction for the cost of the property sold, the cost of materials used, the labor or service cost, the freight or transportation costs, salesmen's commissions, interest paid by the seller, or any other expenses. However, the selling price does not include value given for traded-in property of "like kind and character." (35 ILCS 120/1; 86 Ill. Adm. Code 130.425; 86 Ill. Adm. Code 130.410)

"Selling price" does not include charges added to prices on account of the seller's ROT or UT liability or on account of the seller's duty to collect local taxes. However, there is a rebuttable presumption that taxes were not collected if the seller fails to state the tax as a separate item from the selling price, and no deduction is allowed unless the seller has documentary evidence showing that the tax was collected. Charges added to prices by sellers on account of the seller's liability under the Cigarette Tax Act or the seller's duty to collect tax imposed under the Cigarette Use Tax Act or home rule cigarette tax are included in the selling price. (35 ILCS 120/1; 86 Ill. Adm. Code 130.425; 86 Ill. Adm. Code 130.405)

A retailer whose place of business is within a county or municipality that has established an enterprise zone may deduct from gross receipts its receipts from sales of building materials to be incorporated into real estate in such enterprise zone. (35 ILCS 120/5k)

See ¶ 60-360 Enterprise Zones and Similar Tax Incentives.

• *UT*

The use tax is generally imposed on the selling price of tangible personal property purchased at retail and used in Illinois. If property used or consumed is a by-product or waste product that has been refined, manufactured, or produced from property purchased at retail, the use tax basis is the lower of (1) the fair market value, if any, of the by-product or waste product or (2) the selling price of the purchased property. "Fair market value" is the price at which property would change hands between a willing buyer and a willing seller and is established either by Illinois sales by the taxpayer of the by-product or waste product, or, if there are no such sales, comparable Illinois sales or purchases of property of like kind and character. "Selling price" has the same meaning as provided under the ROT. (35 ILCS 105/3-10; 35 ILCS 105/2; 35 ILCS 105/2b; 86 Ill. Adm. Code 150.135; 86 Ill. Adm. Code 150.201(e); 86 Ill. Adm. Code 150.1101)

The use tax does not apply to a finished product used by the producer of the product. However, the basis of tax for tangible personal property that a user purchases and incorporates into a finished product is the purchase price. (86 Ill. Adm. Code 150.305 (b)) See ¶60-650, Resales.

Deduction from the use tax basis is permitted in an amount representing a reasonable allowance for depreciation for the prior out-of-state use of property that was purchased at retail outside Illinois and used outside Illinois before being brought to Illinois for use. (35 ILCS 105/3-10; 86 Ill. Adm. Code 150.105)

For property other than motor vehicles, a reasonable method of depreciation is deemed to be the amount determined by the straight-line method of depreciation. For motor vehicles, the Department of Revenue presumes that the average life expectancy of the vehicle is 50 months and the depreciation allowance is therefore 2% for each month of prior out-of-state use. (86 Ill. Adm. Code 150.110)

• *SOT and SUT*

The service occupation and service use taxes imposed on service providers are generally based on the "selling price" of tangible personal property transferred incidental to services. (35 ILCS 110/3-10; 35 ILCS 115/3-10; 86 Ill. Adm. Code. 140.101(b))

"Selling price" is the consideration for a sale valued in money including cash, credits, and service, without deduction for the service providers cost of the property sold, cost of materials used, labor or service cost, or any other expense, but not including interest or finance charges separately stated or charges added to prices by sellers by reason of the seller's duty to collect the SUT from the purchaser. (35 ILCS 110/2; 86 Ill. Adm. Code 140.201(h); 86 Ill. Adm. Code 160.105(e))

For purposes of computing the SOT and SUT, the selling price can in no event be less than the cost price of the property to the serviceman. (35 ILCS 110/3-10; 35 ILCS 115/3-10; 86 Ill. Adm. Code 140.101(e))

"Cost price" is the consideration paid by a serviceman for the purchase of tangible personal property from a supplier, without deduction of the supplier's cost of the property sold or any other expense of the supplier. (35 ILCS 110/2; 35 ILCS 115/2; 86 Ill. Adm. Code 140.201(a); 86 Ill. Adm. Code 140.301(a))

There is a presumption that the cost price of property transferred by a subcontractor is equal to 50% of the subcontractor's charges to the serviceman, in the absence of proof of the consideration actually paid.

The SOT and SUT are based on 50% of the service provider's entire billing to the service customer in the event the selling price of each item of property transferred incident to a sale of service is not shown as a separate and distinct item on the service provider's billing. (35 ILCS 115/3-10; 35 ILCS 110/3d; 86 Ill. Adm. Code 140.101(e))

In addition, if a primary service provider purchases property from a secondary service provider, cost price is either the selling price of the property set forth on the invoice from the secondary service provider or, if no selling price is separately stated, 50% of the total invoice including labor and service charges. (86 Ill. Adm. Code 140.145)

The service use tax basis on property acquired and used outside Illinois before being used in this state is reduced by an amount that represents a reasonable allowance for depreciation for the period of prior out-of-state use. A reasonable allowance for depreciation is deemed to be the amount of depreciation determined by using a straight-line method. (35 ILCS 110/3-10; 86 Ill. Adm. Code 160.101(d))

See ¶60-510 Manufacturing, Processing, Assembling, or Refining.

Elections available to service providers.—At the election of any registered service provider made for each fiscal year, sales of service in which the aggregate annual cost price of tangible personal property transferred incident to the sales of service is less than 35% of the aggregate annual total gross receipts from all sales of service (75% in the case of service providers transferring prescription drugs or providers engaged in graphic arts production), the SOT and SUT will be based on the service provider's cost price of the tangible personal property transferred incident to the sale of those services. (35 ILCS 110/3-10; 35 ILCS 115/3-10)

A registered service provider not required to be otherwise registered as a retailer under the ROT may elect not to be subject to the SOT and SUT.

[¶61-200]
RETURNS, PAYMENTS, AND RECORDS

[¶61-220] Returns, Payments, and Due Dates

Persons engaged in the business of selling tangible personal property at retail and servicemen must generally file returns with the Department of Revenue on or before the 20th day of each calendar month covering the preceding calendar month. (35 ILCS 105/9; 35 ILCS 110/9; 35 ILCS 115/9; 35 ILCS 120/3; 86 Ill. Adm. Code 130.501; 86 Ill. Adm. Code 140.401; 86 Ill. Adm. Code 150.901(a); 86 Ill. Adm. Code 160.135) However, special provisions apply with respect to motor vehicles, aircraft, watercraft, trailers, and cigarettes, as discussed below. Also, the Department may require or authorize quarterly returns or annual returns for taxpayers with low average monthly liabilities. It may require concessionaires at flea markets, art shows, and fairs to file daily reports and make daily payments of tax.

New Developments: Retailers must file Illinois returns electronically when reporting and remitting:

- sales tax;
- use tax;
- sales occupation tax; and
- service occupation tax.

(35 ILCS 105/9; 35 ILCS 110/9; 35 ILCS 115/9; 35 ILCS 120/3)

Returns are filed under penalty of perjury on forms prescribed and furnished by the Department. The return must be signed by the owner or, in the case of a corporation, by the president, vice president, secretary, or treasurer, or by an agent whose power of attorney is filed with the Department. (35 ILCS 105/9; 35 ILCS

110/9; 35 ILCS 115/9; 35 ILCS 120/3; 86 Ill. Adm. Code 130.505; 86 Ill. Adm. Code 130.560; 86 Ill. Adm. Code 140.415; 86 Ill. Adm. Code 130.525; 86 Ill. Adm. Code 130.1801; 86 Ill. Adm. Code 130.1805; 86 Ill. Adm. Code 130.1810; 86 Ill. Adm. Code 140.1701)

When the seller is a limited liability company, the return filed on behalf of the company must be signed by a manager, member, or properly accredited agent. Returns must be filed even if the taxpayer has no tax liability for the reporting period. A noncorporate business's first return must show the names and addresses of all owners. (35 ILCS 120/3; 86 Ill. Adm. Code 130.545; 86 Ill. Adm. Code 130.515)

If a taxpayer fails to sign a sales or use tax return within 30 days after proper notice and demand for signature by the Department, the return will be considered valid and any amount shown due on the return will be deemed assessed. (35 ILCS 105/9; 35 ILCS 110/9; 35 ILCS 115/9; 35 ILCS 120/3)

The Department has prescribed and furnished a combination or joint return covering the ROT, SOT, UT, and SUT. (35 ILCS 105/9; 35 ILCS 110/9; 35 ILCS 115/9; 86 Ill. Adm. Code 160.135)

Rounding to whole dollars.—Any amount that is required to be shown or reported on any return or other document must be rounded to a whole dollar amount. If the total amount of ROT payable is less than 50¢, the amount will be disregarded. (35 ILCS 120/3)

• *Electronic filing*

Retailers and servicemen must file sales tax and service occupation tax returns electronically. (35 ILCS 105/9; 35 ILCS 115/9; 86 Ill. Adm. Code 760.100)

Illinois does not require electronic filing for returns for motor vehicles, water-craft, aircraft, and trailers that must be registered in Illinois. (35 ILCS 105/9; 35 ILCS 115/9; 86 Ill. Adm. Code 760.100)

This requirement does not apply to retailers and service providers whose gross receipts average less than $20,000. Further, the Department of Revenue will waive the requirement for taxpayers that show they:

- they do not have access to the Internet; or
- hardship in filing electronically.

(35 ILCS 105/9; 35 ILCS 115/9; 86 Ill. Adm. Code 760.100)

The Department also has voluntary programs for certain returns and other documents. (86 Ill. Adm. Code 760.100) A participant in the voluntary electronic filing program is required by the administrative rules to:

- apply to the Department for permission to participate in the program using the Department's Form EDI-1, Registration for Electronic Data Interchange (86 Ill. Adm. Code 760.210);
- make return payments by electronic means for all returns that are filed electronically (86 Ill. Adm. Code 760.220);
- submit a revised form EDI-1 if changes in the information submitted change (86 Ill. Adm. Code 760.210);
- complete and submit Form EFT-1, Authorization Agreement for Electronic funds Transfer, as part of the registration process for electronic filing, regardless of the type of electronic payment method selected under the rules, unless the taxpayer is already enrolled in the Department's Electronic Funds Transfer Program for the returns or other documents for which the rules authorize electronic filing (86 Ill. Adm. Code 760.220);

- ensure the security and confidentiality of all transmitted data until it has been received directly by the Department or by a value added network (VAN) (86 Ill. Adm. Code 760.300); and

- retain copies of all acknowledgment files received from the Department or third party transmitters, which the Department provides for both electronic filings and electronic payments. (86 Ill. Adm. Code 760.300)

• Quarterly returns

The Department may require the filing of quarterly returns on or before the 20th day of the calendar month following the end of each calendar quarter. In addition, the taxpayer must file a return for each of the first two months of each quarter on or before the 20th day of the following calendar month. (35 ILCS 105/9; 35 ILCS 110/9; 35 ILCS 115/9; 35 ILCS 120/3; 86 Ill. Adm. Code 130.501; 86 Ill. Adm. Code 140.405; 86 Ill. Adm. Code 150.901)

A taxpayer normally required to file a monthly return whose average monthly tax liability does not exceed $200 may be authorized by the Department to file returns on a quarter-annual basis, with the returns being due on April 20, July 20, October 20 of the current year, and January 20 of the following year. The decision to permit quarterly filing will be based upon information obtained by the Department, including registration and audit information regarding the retailer's average monthly liability. (35 ILCS 105/9; 35 ILCS 110/9; 35 ILCS 115/9; 35 ILCS 120/3; 86 Ill. Adm. Code 140.405; 86 Ill. Adm. Code 130.502)

• Annual returns

A taxpayer required to file a monthly or quarterly return whose average monthly tax liability does not exceed $50 may be authorized by the Department to file returns on an annual basis, with the return being due by January 20 of the following year. The decision to permit annual filing will be based upon information obtained by the Department, including registration and audit information regarding the retailer's average monthly liability. (35 ILCS 105/9; 35 ILCS 110/9; 35 ILCS 115/9; 35 ILCS 120/3; 86 Ill. Adm. Code 140.405; 86 Ill. Adm. Code 150.901; 86 Ill. Adm. Code 130.510)

• Payment of tax

Payment of ROT, SOT, UT, and SUT is generally made at the time the return is filed. More frequent payments are required if a taxpayer's average monthly tax liability exceeds specified amounts, as discussed below. In addition, as discussed below, certain taxpayers must make their payments by electronic funds transfer. (35 ILCS 105/9; 35 ILCS 110/9 35 ILCS 115/9; 35 ILCS 120/3; 86 Ill. Adm. Code 130.535)

Quarter-monthly payments.—A taxpayer whose average monthly ROT, UT, SOT, and SUT liability (excluding prepaid tax on motor fuel) was $10,000 or more during the preceding four calendar quarters is required to make quarter-monthly payments. However, such taxpayers continue to make monthly returns. The payments are due on the 7th, 15th, 22nd, and last days of the months during which the liability is incurred. Each payment must equal 22.5% of the taxpayer's actual liability for the month or 25% of the taxpayer's liability for the same calendar month of the preceding year. The amount of such quarter-monthly payments is credited against the taxpayer's final tax liability for the month. The requirement to make quarter-monthly payments continues until the taxpayer's average monthly liability during the preceding four calendar quarters is less than $9,000 or until the average monthly liability for each calendar quarter of the four preceding calendar quarter period is less than $10,000. However, if a taxpayer can demonstrate that a substantial change in its business has caused its reasonably foreseeable average monthly tax liability to fall below $10,000, the Department must change the taxpayer's reporting status unless it finds the change to be seasonal in nature. (35 ILCS 105/9; 35 ILCS 120/3; 86 Ill. Adm. Code 130.535)

A distributor or supplier of motor fuel who is required to collect and remit prepaid taxes and whose average amount of collected tax exceeded $25,000 per month during the preceding two calendar quarters is also required to make payments to the Department on or before the 7th, 15th, 22nd, and last day of the month during which the liability was incurred. Each payment must equal either 22.5% of the taxpayer's actual liability for the month or 26.25% of the taxpayer's liability for the same calendar month of the preceding year. The amount of the payments is credited against the final tax liability for that month. The requirement to continue making quarter-monthly payments continues until the average monthly prepaid tax collections during the preceding two calendar quarters is $25,000 or less. (35 ILCS 120/3; 86 Ill. Adm. Code 130.535)

A distributor, supplier, or reseller of motor fuel must make quarter monthly payments if the average monthly prepaid taxes are in excess of $20,000. (35 ILCS 120/3)

Electronic funds transfer.—Payment by electronic funds transfer is required for all taxpayers whose annual combined retailers' occupation, service occupation and service use tax liability for the preceding calendar year was $20,000 or more. (*Informational Bulletin FY 2011-01*) "Average monthly tax liability" means the sum of a taxpayer's liabilities under all state and local occupation and use tax laws administered by the Department for the immediately preceding calendar year divided by 12. Before August 1 of each year, the Department will notify all taxpayers required to make payments by electronic funds transfer. Such taxpayers must make electronic funds transfer payments for a minimum of one year, beginning on October 1. Any taxpayer not required to make payments by electronic funds transfer may make such payments with the permission of the Department. (35 ILCS 105/9; 35 ILCS 110/9; 35 ILCS 115/9; 35 ILCS 120/3; 86 Ill. Adm. Code 750.300)

Taxpayers who elect to file returns or other documents electronically must make any required payments relating to those returns or documents through electronic means, and those means include funds transfers under the Electronic Funds Transfer Program. (86 Ill. Adm. Code 760.220)

A holder of a direct pay permit who is required to pay retailers' occupation tax or use tax directly to the Department of Revenue must make all such tax payments through the use of electronic funds transfer. (35 ILCS 120/2-10.5(g); 35 ILCS 105/3-10.5)

• *Returns and payment by purchaser*

A purchaser who does not pay use tax to a retailer and who does not file returns as a retailer generally must file returns and pay the use tax by the last day of the month following a month in which any payment was made on the selling price. (35 ILCS 105/10; 86 Ill. Adm. Code 150.701) However, certain purchasers may file an annual return (see "Annual returns," below). A retailer who files returns must also include in its tax payment the tax on the selling price of property that it purchased from another retailer but on which UT was not paid to such other retailer. (35 ILCS 105/9; 86 Ill. Adm. Code 150.730; 86 Ill. Adm. Code 150.901(c))

A person who did not pay SUT to a service provider upon the acquisition of property as an incident to the purchase of a service and who does not file returns as a service provider must file returns and pay the SUT by the last day of the month following the month in which any payment on the selling price is made. (35 ILCS 110/10; 86 Ill. Adm. Code 160.135)

A service provider filing a return must include and pay the tax upon the selling price of property it purchased for use as an incident to a sale of service. (35 ILCS 105/9)

Individuals.—In lieu of filing monthly use tax returns, individuals may elect to report their use tax liability on their standard individual income tax return if their annual individual use tax liability does not exceed $600. If an individual chooses to report use tax owed on the income tax return, the use tax may be: (1) treated as being due at the same time as the income tax obligation, (2) assessed, collected, and deposited in the same manner as income taxes, and (3) treated as an income tax liability for all purposes. The income tax return instructions must explain the imposition of the use tax and how to pay and report use tax when filing the income tax return. (35 ILCS 5/502.1)

Lessors.—A lessor who purchases property, including but not limited to motor vehicles and aircraft, for lease to an interstate carrier under a lease for at least one year, in effect at the time of purchase, and who did not pay use tax to the retailer must, by the last day of the month following the month the property reverts to the lessor's use, file a return and pay the tax on the fair market value on the date of reversion. (35 ILCS 105/10; 86 Ill. Adm. Code 150.701; 86 Ill. Adm. Code 150.310)

CCH COMMENT: *Definition of "Fair Market Value" Restricted.*—When determining the fair market value at the time of reversion, the fair market value of the property will not exceed the original purchase price of the property paid by the lessor at the time of purchase. (35 ILCS 105/10; *Informational Bulletin FY 2000-4, Illinois Department of Revenue*)

Annual returns.—Except regarding motor vehicles, aircraft, and cigarettes, if a purchaser's annual use tax liability does not exceed $600, the purchaser may file a return on an annual basis on or before April 15th of the year following the year use tax liability is incurred. (35 ILCS 105/10)

• *Payment of tax by manufacturers and wholesalers*

Manufacturers, importers, and wholesalers whose products are sold by numerous retailers or servicemen in Illinois may assume the responsibility for accounting and paying all taxes with respect to such sales if the retailers or servicemen do not object. (35 ILCS 105/9; 35 ILCS 115/9; 35 ILCS 120/3; 86 Ill. Adm. Code 130.550; 86 Ill. Adm. Code 140.425)

• *Timely filing*

A mailed return or payment is deemed to be filed with and received by the Department of Revenue on the postmark date. If not received or if the postmark is illegible, erroneous, or omitted, the return or payment is deemed filed on the date it was mailed as long as the sender shows it was deposited on or before the due date. (86 Ill. Adm. Code 130.1201; 86 Ill. Adm. Code 140.1101)

If a due date falls on a weekend or holiday, the due date is considered to be the next business day. (86 Ill. Adm. Code 140.1101; 86 Ill. Adm. Code 130.1205)

For electronic filers of returns or other documents, the receipt date of the electronic transmission constitutes the receipt date of the electronic return or other document if the transmission is acknowledged as accepted, or accepted with error, with a detailed acknowledgment from the Department. However, any return acknowledged as rejected with a functional or detailed acknowledgment is considered not filed. For taxpayers transmitting directly to the Department, the receipt date of the electronic transmission is when the telephone transmission ends. (86 Ill. Adm. Code 760.240)

• *Final business returns*

A service provider or retailer that ceases to engage in a business must file a final return with the Department not more than one month after discontinuing its business. A taxpayer is not considered to have discontinued business as long as it continues to collect taxable receipts. Returns must be filed regularly and tax paid with the returns with respect to receipts accruing on taxable transactions made before discontinuing business. (35 ILCS 105/9; 35 ILCS 110/9; 35 ILCS 115/9; 35 ILCS 120/3; 86 Ill. Adm. Code 130.520; 86 Ill. Adm. Code 140.410; 86 Ill. Adm. Code 150.901(h); 86 Ill. Adm. Code 130.1601; 86 Ill. Adm. Code 140.1501)

However, a retailer that has used gross sales as the method for computing liability does not have to file returns after selling out or discontinuing business, except for the final return. (86 Ill. Adm. Code 130.1605)

• *Multiple businesses*

A taxpayer with separately registered businesses must file separate returns for each business. A taxpayer who conducts business at more than one location and who has not obtained separate certificates of registration must file consolidated returns covering business operations at all of the locations and not separate returns for each location. (35 ILCS 105/9; 35 ILCS 110/9; 35 ILCS 115/9; 35 ILCS 120/3; 86 Ill. Adm. Code 130.530)

• *Leased departments*

A lessee selling property or services under its own trade name from a location leased from a lessor who also is engaged in the business of selling property or services may file its own returns. (86 Ill. Adm. Code 130.1301; 86 Ill. Adm. Code 140.1201)

If the lessee operates under the identity of the lessor, the lessee's tax should be accounted for on the lessor's return and the Department may proceed against either party if the lessee files its own returns and does not properly discharge its ROT or SOT liability. (86 Ill. Adm. Code 130.1305; 86 Ill. Adm. Code 140.1205)

"Lessor" includes concessioners and licensors, and "lessee" includes concessionaires and licensees. (86 Ill. Adm. Code 130.1310; 86 Ill. Adm. Code 140.1210)

• *Motor vehicle, watercraft, aircraft, and trailer returns*

A retailer selling motor vehicles, watercraft, trailers, or aircraft that are required to be registered with an Illinois agency must file a separate return for each transaction within 20 days after delivery of the property sold. The transfer by a retailer of more than one motor vehicle, watercraft, trailer, or aircraft to another retailer for resale may be reported by the latter. Retailers who sell only motor vehicles, watercraft, aircraft, or trailers, and who are not otherwise required to file monthly or quarterly returns, need not file monthly or quarterly returns. However, these retailers must file returns on an annual basis. (35 ILCS 105/9; 35 ILCS 120/3; 86 Ill. Adm. Code 130.540)

The term "watercraft" is defined as a Class 2, Class 3, or Class 4 watercraft (as defined in Sec. 3-2 of the Boat Registration and Safety Act), a personal watercraft, or any boat equipped with an inboard motor. Sellers are not required to report sales of the following vessels on a transaction-by-transaction basis: canoes, kayaks, and vessels less than 16 feet in length that do not have inboard motors. Instead, sales of these items may be reported on Form ST-1 (Sales and Use Tax Return). Sellers must continue to report sales of other vessels on a transaction-by-transaction basis using Form ST-556. (35 ILCS 105/9; 35 ILCS 120/3; *Informational Bulletin FY 95-5*)

Purchasers of motor vehicles and aircraft who purchase such items from an out-of-state retailer must file a return for each such purchase not later than 30 days after the property is brought into Illinois for use. (35 ILCS 105/10)

The transaction returns must show the name and address of the purchaser and seller, selling price, amount allowed for traded-in property, balance payable after the amount of the trade-in is deducted, amount of tax due from the retailer, amount of tax collected from the purchaser or evidence that tax is not due, place and date of sale, and identification of the property sold. The motor vehicle return is the same document as the Uniform Invoice referred to in Sec. 5-402 of the Illinois Vehicle Code. (35 ILCS 105/9; 35 ILCS 120/3; 35 ILCS 105/10; 86 Ill. Adm. Code 130.540(b))

Each return filed with the Department of Revenue must be accompanied by the tax due or evidence that the sale was not taxable. The Department will issue in the purchaser's name a use tax receipt (or certificate of exemption) that the purchaser may submit to the agency responsible for registering or titling the property. No certificate of title or registration will be issued unless such receipt or certificate of exemption is issued. The return and remittance of tax or proof of exemption may be transmitted to the Department by way of the state agency with which the property must be titled or registered if the Department and agency determine that this will expedite the processing of title or registration applications. (35 ILCS 105/9; 35 ILCS 120/3; 35 ILCS 105/10; 86 Ill. Adm. Code 130.540(e); 86 Ill. Adm. Code 150.715; 86 Ill. Adm. Code 130.540(d))

A purchaser who has paid the tax to a retailer that fails or refuses to remit the tax may obtain a title or registration by satisfying the Department that it paid the tax to the retailer. A purchaser who wants the retailer to file the return and remit the tax sooner than the retailer is willing to do so may, upon certification to the Department of the retailer's delay, transmit the information required by the return and remit the tax directly to the Department. (35 ILCS 105/9; 35 ILCS 120/3; 86 Ill. Adm. Code 130.540(f); 86 Ill. Adm. Code 150.720; 86 Ill. Adm. Code 130.540(g); 86 Ill. Adm. Code 150.705; 86 Ill. Adm. Code 150.725)

One purchase, one return policy.—In regards to any purchases of tangible personal property for use in Illinois with respect to motor vehicles, aircraft, water-craft, and trailers, a separate return must be filed for each item purchased, unless otherwise provided. Returns that report purchases of more than one item of tangible personal property are allowed for purchases made for resale, used as qualifying rolling stock, or of multiple purchases of like items. (86 Ill. Adm. Code 150.705)

Annual returns.—The provision that allows a purchaser to file a use tax return on an annual basis if the purchaser's annual use tax liability does not exceed $600 does not apply with respect to motor vehicles and aircraft. (35 ILCS 105/10)

• *Cigarettes*

Use tax return and payment for cigarettes.—If cigarettes are purchased from a retailer for use in Illinois by a purchaser who did not pay Illinois use tax to the retailer and who does not file returns as a retailer, the purchaser must file a use tax return and pay the tax due within 30 days after acquiring the cigarettes. (35 ILCS 105/10)

The provision that allows a purchaser to file a use tax return on an annual basis if the purchaser's annual use tax liability does not exceed $600 does not apply with respect to cigarettes. (35 ILCS 105/10)

• *Resellers of motor fuel*

A reseller of motor fuel must file a return by the 20th of the month following the month in which a transaction occurred showing the amount of fuel sold, distributed, and used by the reseller; the purchaser's name; the purchaser's tax registration number; amount of tax collected from the purchaser or delivery point if delivered to an unregistered purchaser outside the state; and the name and address and quantity of fuel sold or transferred to each purchaser in the preceding month. (35 ILCS 120/2f; 35 ILCS 120/2g)

"Reseller of motor fuel" is defined at ¶61-230 Prepayment of Taxes.

• *Alcohol distributors, manufacturers, and retailers*

Alcohol retailers.—Any retailer of alcoholic liquor who is not a distributor or manufacturer must file a statement with the Department of Revenue, at a time prescribed by the Department, showing the total amount paid for alcoholic liquor purchased during the preceding month. (35 ILCS 120/3; 86 Ill Adm. Code 130.552)

Alcohol distributors and manufacturers.—Every distributor, importing distributor, and manufacturer of alcoholic liquor must file a statement, by electronic means, no later than the 10th day of the month for the preceding month, showing the total gross receipts from alcoholic liquor sold or distributed during the preceding month to purchasers. The statement must identify the purchaser, the purchaser's tax registration number, and other information reasonably required by the Department. A copy of the monthly statement must be sent to the retailer no later than the 10th day of the month for the preceding month. (35 ILCS 120/3; 86 Ill Adm. Code 130.552)

In addition, the distributor, importing distributor, and manufacturer must provide each retailer listed on the monthly statement a report, by personal delivery, mail, or electronic means, containing a cumulative total of the total sales of alcoholic liquor to that retailer no later than the 10th day of the month for the preceding month. Distributors and manufacturers must notify retailers as to the method by which the sales information will be provided and must provide the information by personal delivery or mail if the retailer is unable to receive it by electronic means. (35 ILCS 120/3)

"Electronic means" includes the use of a secure Internet website, e-mail, or facsimile. (35 ILCS 120/3)

• *Vending machines*

A person selling property at retail through vending machines must file an annual information return by January 31 showing the number of machines used in its business on the preceding December 31. (35 ILCS 110/8; 86 Ill. Adm. Code 130.555)

• *Fair, art show, and flea market reports*

A person who promotes, organizes, or provides retail selling space for concessionaires or other types of sellers at fairs, art shows, flea markets, and similar exhibitions, including any transit merchant, must file a report with the Department of Revenue providing information about the merchant's business not later than the 20th day of the month next following the month during which the sale event was held. The fine for failure to file such reports is $250. (35 ILCS 120/3)

• *Annual information returns*

The Department of Revenue may require a taxpayer to file an annual information return for a specific tax year. The return is due within 60 days of notice by the Department. The return must include a statement of gross receipts for the year specified. If the amount of receipts reported in the statement does not agree with the amount reported on the taxpayer's income tax return, the retailer must attach a schedule to the information return reconciling the difference. The return must disclose the cost of goods sold, opening and closing inventories, costs of goods used from stock, payroll information, and other information required by the Department. (35 ILCS 115/9; 35 ILCS 120/3; 86 Ill. Adm. Code 150.725)

• *Collection discount*

An allowance of 1.75% of tax liability or $5 per calendar year, whichever is greater, is provided to offset recordkeeping and preparation costs of the taxpayer. The discount is not available if the tax is paid late. If electronic filing is required, retailers and service providers are allowed a discount for collecting applicable taxes only if the tax returns are properly filed.The discount does not apply to the amount of prepaid tax on motor fuel that is remitted by distributors, suppliers, or resellers to the Department. However, any prepayment of motor fuel taxes by a retail seller is included in the amount on which its discount is computed. In addition, no discount is allowed when use tax is remitted directly to the Department by a user. (35 ILCS 105/9; 35 ILCS 110/9; 35 ILCS 115/9; 35 ILCS 120/3; 35 ILCS 120/2d; 86 Ill. Adm. Code 130.501; 86 Ill. Adm. Code 140.401; 86 Ill. Adm. Code 140.105; 86 Ill. Adm. Code 160.135(e), 86 Ill. Adm. Code 150.905; 86 Ill. Adm. Code 130.551)

A retailer who reports and pays the tax on a transaction basis (see "motor vehicles and aircraft returns," above) takes the discount with each remittance instead of when the periodic return is filed. (35 ILCS 105/9; 35 ILCS 120/3)

The vendor's discount will be reduced if any required quarter-monthly payment of ROT or UT is not timely made or if a credit taken was not actually due the taxpayer. (35 ILCS 105/9; 35 ILCS 120/3)

The collection allowance for the tire user fee is discussed at ¶60-570 Motor Vehicles.

• *Confidentiality*

Information contained in returns or derived from an investigation is confidential and any person improperly divulging such information is guilty of a class B misdemeanor, and, such person is subject to a fine not to exceed $7,500. However, the names and addresses of taxpayers may be disclosed, and tax information may be disclosed to the federal government or any state government for official purposes. "Official purposes" include the furnishing of information to a surety, the Liquor Control Commission, the Auditor General, the taxpayer's attorney, or a home rule unit imposing a similar tax. (35 ILCS 120/11)

Information sharing.—The Director of the Department of Revenue is authorized to make available to the Secretary of State information about a limited liability company that has filed articles of organization with the Secretary pertaining to failure to file returns; failure to pay the tax, penalty, and interest; and failure to pay final assessments of tax. (35 ILCS 120/11)

For the limited purpose of enforcing bidder and contractor certifications, the Department may make available to state agencies information regarding whether a person bidding on or entering into a contract for goods or services with a state or local governmental agency has failed to pay, collect, or remit Illinois sales or use taxes. (35 ILCS 120/11)

The Director may divulge information pursuant to a request or authorization from the taxpayer or an authorized agent or a spouse if a joint return is filed. (35 ILCS 120/11)

• *Itemizing receipts subject to UT but not ROT*

A seller making sales into the state from more than one state other than Illinois must, in reporting receipts that are subject to UT but not ROT, file a supplemental schedule showing an itemization of such receipts and the tax for each state from which the seller makes the sales that result in property being delivered into Illinois. (86 Ill. Adm. Code 150.915)

[¶61-240] Vendor Registration

A person making retail sales of property or maintaining a place of business in the state must obtain a certificate of registration from the Department of Revenue. An applicant for a certificate must furnish a bond or an irrevocable bank letter of credit not to exceed the lesser of three times the applicant's average monthly tax liability or $50,000. (35 ILCS 105/6; 35 ILCS 110/6; 35 ILCS 115/6; 35 ILCS 120/2a; 86 Ill. Adm. Code Sec. 130.701; 86 Ill. Adm. Code Sec. 140.105; 86 Ill. Adm. Code Sec. 140.601; 86 Ill. Adm. Code Sec. 160.130)

A certificate must be conspicuously displayed at the person's principal place of business in the state. Sub-certificates of registration bearing the same registration number as the certificate to which it relates are issued for display in a person's other places of business in the state, including each truck, wagon, or other vehicle from which a person conducts business. A person who sells property through vending machines is given sub-certificates for each vending machine that must be attached to a conspicuous part of each machine. A duplicate copy of a certificate may be issued when the original is destroyed or defaced. Also, a certificate is not transferable and should be destroyed if a place of business is discontinued. (35 ILCS 105/6; 35 ILCS 110/6; 35 ILCS 115/6; 35 ILCS 120/2a; 86 Ill. Adm. Code Sec. 130.725; 86 Ill. Adm. Code Sec. 130.715; 86 Ill. Adm. Code Sec. 130.740; 86 Ill. Adm. Code Sec. 130.730; 86 Ill. Adm. Code Sec. 130.735)

When a person has two or more businesses that are substantially different, operated under different trade names, or operated under other substantially dissimilar circumstances, the Department may issue separate certificates of registration for each business. (35 ILCS 105/6; 35 ILCS 110/6; 35 ILCS 115/6; 35 ILCS 120/2a; 86 Ill. Adm. Code Sec. 130.720)

A certificate of registration of a taxpayer required to file monthly returns is valid for five years and will be automatically renewed for an additional year unless the taxpayer receives a notice from the Department. The Department must notify the taxpayer not less than 60 days before the certificate expires of the amount of a default. The Department may approve renewal by an applicant who is in default if the applicant enters into a payment agreement with the Department. (35 ILCS 120/2a)

A certificate may be denied if the owner, or any partner or corporate officer of the applicant, is or has been the owner, or a partner or corporate officer, of another retailer that is in default for moneys due. (35 ILCS 120/2a)

A surety is discharged or security returned within 30 days after a taxpayer becomes a "prior continuous compliance taxpayer" (see below) or if the taxpayer stops collecting receipts subject to tax and has filed a final business return. Procedures for the forfeiture of security are provided in the law and regulations. (35 ILCS 120/2a; 86 Ill. Adm. Code Sec. 130.710)

A person aggrieved by any decision of the Department may protest and request a hearing within 20 days after notice of the decision. (35 ILCS 120/2a; 86 Ill. Adm. Code Sec. 130.705)

Out-of-state taxpayers: The Department may authorize a retailer, serviceman, or supplier not maintaining an Illinois place of business to collect use tax, service occupation tax, or service use tax if the out-of-state taxpayer furnishes adequate security to insure collection and payment. If so authorized, the taxpayer will be issued a permit. The permit may be revoked by the Department after notice and hearing if (1) the out-of-state taxpayer fails to comply with sales and use tax law, rules, or regulations; (2) the security furnished by the person is deemed inadequate; or (3) the Department determines that the tax can be collected more effectively from a person maintaining a place of business within Illinois. (35 ILCS 105/6; 35 ILCS 115/6; 35 ILCS 110/7; 35 ILCS 105/13; 35 ILCS 110/14; 86 Ill. Adm. Code Sec. 160.130; 86 Ill. Adm. Code Sec. 150.805)

Users: A user who is only occasionally liable to pay use tax or service use tax directly to the Department and not on a frequently occurring basis and who is not required to file returns as a retailer or serviceman does not have to register with the Department. However, if the user has a frequently recurring direct use or service use tax liability to the Department, it must obtain a certificate of registration. (35 ILCS 105/10; 35 ILCS 110/10; 86 Ill. Adm. Code Sec. 150.701(b))

• *Continuous compliance taxpayers*

A taxpayer that is verified by the Department of Revenue as having faithfully and continuously complied with the condition of its bond or other security for a period of three consecutive years is classified as a "prior continuous compliance taxpayer" and is exempt from the furnishing of security requirements. The exemption continues until the taxpayer becomes delinquent in filing returns or paying taxes. (35 ILCS 120/2a; 86 Ill. Adm. Code Sec. 130.701(f)(3))

The law also provides that any person required to file a bond and who has continuously complied with all provisions of the law for 24 consecutive months is not required to comply with the bonding provisions so long as the person continues to comply with the law. (35 ILCS 105/10a; 35 ILCS 110/10a; 35 ILCS 115/10a; 35 ILCS 120/2i)

• *Certificate revocation*

The Department may revoke, after notice and hearing, the registration certificate of any person who violates any provisions of the sales and use tax law.Notice must be given to the taxpayer within 90 days after the noncompliance and at least seven days prior to the hearing. The Department is not precluded from conducting revocation proceedings after the 90-day period has lapsed. The Department may obtain an injunction in circuit court to restrain any person from selling property at retail or maintaining a place of business without a certificate of registration. (35 ILCS 105/2b; 86 Ill. Adm. Code Sec. 130.745)

It is not a defense in a revocation proceeding that the holder of the certificate is a party to an installment payment agreement (see below) if the liability that is the basis of the revocation proceeding was (1) incurred after the date of the agreement approved by the Department, (2) incurred prior to the date the agreement was approved by the Department but not included in the agreement, or (3) included in the agreement but the taxpayer is in default of the agreement. (35 ILCS 105/2b)

• *Installment payment agreements*

The Department may, in its discretion, approve certificate renewal for an applicant who is in default if the applicant pays a percentage of the defaulted amount and agrees in writing to waive all limitations upon the Department for collection of the remaining defaulted amount over a period not to exceed five years from the date of the certificate's renewal. No such renewal application will be approved, however, if the applicant's immediately preceding renewal was conditioned upon an installment payment agreement. If an installment agreement is executed, the applicant will be subject to both the agreement and the security requirement that is imposed on a taxpayer who is not considered a "prior continuous compliance taxpayer" (see discussion above). The execution of a payment agreement does not toll the accrual of interest. (35 ILCS 120/2a)

[¶61-270] Credits

The use in Illinois of property acquired outside the state (in such a way that there is no ROT or SOT liability) is not subject to use or service use taxes to the extent that a tax has been paid to another state on the sale or use of the property. (35 ILCS 105/3-55; 35 ILCS 110/3-45; 86 Ill. Adm. Code 150.310(3); 86 Ill. Adm. Code 160.110(2))

• *Overpayment of tax*

A taxpayer may request a credit memorandum for excess tax payments within 30 days of the date of payment. If no request is made, the taxpayer may credit the excess payment against tax liability subsequently to be remitted. (35 ILCS 105/9; 35 ILCS 120/3)

See ¶61-610 Application for Refund.

A credit memorandum is issued to a retailer of motor fuel in an amount equal to the excess of the taxpayer's liability for the month that the return is filed. (35 ILCS 120/3)

● *Other credits*

High Impact Business.—Retailers, suppliers, servicepersons, and other taxpayers are allowed to claim a credit or refund for the sales or use tax paid on sales of building materials to a "High Impact Business."

See ¶ 60-360 Enterprise Zones and Similar Tax Incentives.

Taxes paid in error.—A retailer who is required to pay ROT or UT on gross receipts from retail sales may, without filing a formal claim, take credit against the ROT or UT liability to the extent to which the retailer has paid ROT or UT in error to its supplier of the same property bought for resale and not first used before resale. Penalties and interest are not charged on the amount of such credit. If the credit is allowed to the retailer, the supplier may not refund any tax to the retailer and file a claim for credit or refund. (35 ILCS 105/19; 35 ILCS 120/6a)

● *Sunset provisions*

Except as noted below, exemptions are limited by a sunset date. If the sunset date is not specified in the public act enacting the exemption or the sunset date is later amended, the taxpayer is not entitled to take the exemption for tax years beginning on or after five years from the effective date of the enacting public law. (35 ILCS 105/3-90; 35 ILCS 110/3-70; 35 ILCS 115/3-55)

The exemptions for personal property, including food, purchased through school fundraising events are not subject to the general sunset date provisions or any specific sunset date provisions and, thus, are available indefinitely.

See ¶ 60-580 Nonprofit Organizations, Private Schools, and Churches.

[¶61-600]

TAXPAYER REMEDIES

[¶61-610] Application for Refund

Retailers, service persons, suppliers, and purchasers who pay sales and use tax, penalty, or interest erroneously, whether through a mistake of fact or error in law, may file a claim for credit or refund. The Department of Revenue, if requested by the taxpayer, normally issues a credit memorandum or refund to the person who made the erroneous payment. However, if the person has died or is under legal disability the credit memorandum or refund is issued to the person's legal representative. (35 ILCS 120/6; 35 ILCS 110/17; 35 ILCS 115/17; 35 ILCS 105/19; 86 Ill. Adm. Code Sec. 130.1501; 86 Ill. Adm. Code Sec. 140.1401; 86 Ill. Adm. Code Sec. 150.1401; 86 Ill. Adm. Code Sec. 160.150)

A claim for refund or credit filed on or after January 1 and July 1 is not valid unless the erroneous payment was made within three years prior to January 1 and July 1 of the year of the claim. If the taxpayer and the Department agree to extend the period of limitations to issue a notice of tax liability, the claim may be filed at any time prior to the end of the agreed upon extension period. (35 ILCS 120/6; 35 ILCS 105/21; 35 ILCS 115/19)

Refund or credit claims are made on forms furnished by the Department. A claim is considered filed on the date it is received by the Department. The Department examines the claim and issues a tentative determination as soon as practicable after a credit or refund claim is filed. (35 ILCS 110/17; 35 ILCS 115/17; 35 ILCS 105/19; 35 ILCS 120/6a; 35 ILCS 105/20; 35 ILCS 110/18; 35 ILCS 115/18; 35 ILCS 120/6b)

If it determines that a refund or credit memorandum should issue, the Department may first apply the amount against any tax, penalty, or interest due under the Retailers' Occupation, Use Tax, Service Occupation, or Service Use Tax Acts, as well as under other local taxes. If the amount of the credit is less than $10 and one year or more has passed since the date of issuance of the credit memorandum, the Department may cancel the credit and issue a refund to the taxpayer for the remaining balance. (35 ILCS 120/6; 35 ILCS 105/22; 35 ILCS 110/20; 35 ILCS 115/20; 86 Ill. Adm. Code Sec. 130.1501)

• *Notice of protest and request for hearing*

After an audit but prior to the issuance of a denial of refund, the Department will issue a proposed denial of refund that the taxpayer can appeal to the Informal Conference Board. (86 Ill. Adm. Code Sec. 215.100)

See ¶ 89-230 Taxpayer Conferences.

With regard to the UT, SOT, and SUT, a taxpayer may file a protest and request a hearing within 60 days after notice of the Department's tentative determination. With regard to the ROT, a taxpayer may file a protest and request a hearing within 60 days after notice of the determination. After such a hearing, the Department will issue a final determination that is subject to circuit court review. (35 ILCS 105/20; 35 ILCS 110/18; 35 ILCS 115/18; 35 ILCS 120/6b)

If a protest to the Department's tentative determination is not timely filed and a request for a hearing is not made as provided above, the tentative determination will become a final determination. Upon issuance of a credit memorandum or refund for the amount found by the Department to be due, the taxpayer's claim will be closed to further review before the Department or in any court of the state. The taxpayer's claim will also be closed to further review if the Department's tentative determination, upon becoming a final determination, indicates no amount due to the claimant. (35 ILCS 105/20; 35 ILCS 110/18; 35 ILCS 115/18; 35 ILCS 120/6c)

No credit or refund is allowed unless the claimant (1) bore the burden of such amount, has not been relieved or reimbursed therefore, and has not shifted the burden; or (2) has unconditionally repaid the amount to the vendee who (a) bore the burden and has not shifted the burden, (b) who has repaid the amount to its own vendee if the burden was shifted, the burden, and (c) who is not entitled to reimbursement from any other source except from its vendor. (35 ILCS 120/6; 35 ILCS 110/17; 35 ILCS 115/17; 35 ILCS 105/19)

Unconditional repayment.—The purpose of requiring the claimant to make an unconditional repayment is to prevent unjust enrichment. To establish that the claimant was not unjustly enriched, it must demonstrate that it gave unconditional payment to the purchaser. The claimant satisfies the unconditional repayment requirement when it provides the purchaser with an unconditional promissory note, irrevocable credit memoranda, or other instrument upon which the purchaser can make demand upon the claimant for payment of the tax made in error and recovered if the claim for credit is allowed. (86 Ill. Code Sec. 130.1501; 86 Ill. Code Sec. 140.1401; 86 Ill. Code Sec. 160.150)

No credit or refund is allowed unless the claimant has repaid any tax collected from the purchaser. Also, no claim is allowed for any amount paid to the Department in total or partial liquidation of an assessment that became final before the claim for credit or refund is filed with the Department or if paid in total or partial liquidation of a court order or judgment. (35 ILCS 120/6; 35 ILCS 105/21; 35 ILCS 115/19)

A refund is made only from an appropriation that is available for that purpose, and if it appears that there is not an amount appropriated to permit everyone to receive a cash refund, refunds will be made only in hardship cases, that is, cases in which the taxpayer could not use a credit memorandum. Credit memoranda are issued which the taxpayer could not use a credit memorandum. Credit memoranda are issued to all others. (35 ILCS 120/6; 35 ILCS 110/17; 35 ILCS 115/17; 35 ILCS 105/19; 86 Ill. Adm. Code Sec. 130.1510; 86 Ill. Adm. Code Sec. 140.1410; 86 Ill. Adm. Code Sec. 150.1410; 86 Ill. Adm. Code Sec. 160.160)

Credit memoranda may be assigned to others subject to sales and use taxes. (35 ILCS 120/6; 35 ILCS 105/22; 35 ILCS 110/20; 35 ILCS 115/20; 86 Ill. Adm. Code Sec. 130.1505; 86 Ill. Adm. Code Sec. 140.1405; 86 Ill. Adm. Code Sec. 150.1405; 86 Ill. Adm. Code Sec. 160.155)

Erroneous refunds.—In any case in which there has been an erroneous refund of tax, the Department may issue a notice of tax liability at any time within three years from the making of the refund or, if it appears that any part of the refund was induced by fraud or the misrepresentation of a material fact, within five years from the making of the refund. The amount of any proposed assessment stated in the notice is limited to the amount of the erroneous refund. (35 ILCS 120/6b; 35 ILCS 105/22; 35 ILCS 110/20; 35 ILCS 115/20)

• *Interest*

Credits or refunds bear interest in the rate and manner specified in the Uniform Penalty and Interest Act.

See ¶ 89-202 (Interest and Penalties In General) and ¶ 89-204 (Interest Rates).

[¶61-620] Administrative Remedies

A taxpayer who receives a notice of tax liability may file a protest and request a hearing

• *Administrative hearings*

All administrative hearings are held at the Departments's office closest to the taxpayer's principal place of business except for a taxpayer whose principal place of business is in Cook County, in which case the hearing is held in Cook County. Hearings are conducted in Sangamon county for a taxpayer not having its principal place of business in Illinois. (35 ILCS 120/12)

A hearing is initiated with the filing of a protest. An administrative law judge presides over a hearing and makes a report to the Director of Revenue at the conclusion of the hearing. A party may represent itself or may be represented by an attorney. (86 Ill. Adm. Code Sec. 200.120; 86 Ill. Adm. Code Sec. 200.101; 86 Ill. Adm. Code Sec. 200.165; 86 Ill. Adm. Code Sec. 200.110)

Regulations also provide for notice of the time and place for the hearing, continuances, discovery, prehearing conference, attendance of witnesses, stipulations, procedure at the hearing, and notice of the final decision. The Department may designate an impartial employee to recommend a solution before the hearing if requested by the taxpayer within 30 days after the filing of a timely protest. (86 Ill. Adm. Code Sec. 200.115; 86 Ill. Adm. Code Sec. 200.160; 86 Ill. Adm. Code Sec. 200.125; 86 Ill. Adm. Code Sec. 200.130; 86 Ill. Adm. Code Sec. 200.145; 86 Ill. Adm. Code Sec. 200.150; 86 Ill. Adm. Code Sec. 200.155; 86 Ill. Adm. Code Sec. 200.170; 86 Ill. Adm. Code Sec. 200.135)

Disclosure of administrative decisions.—The Director of Revenue is required to make administrative decisions available for public inspection and publication. (35 ILCS 120/11)

An administrative decision must be made available under this provision within 180 days after the decision is issued and in a manner that prevents the following taxpayer information from being disclosed:

(1) the names, addresses, and identification numbers of the taxpayer, related entities, and employees; and

(2) at the Director's discretion, trade secrets or other confidential information identified as such by the taxpayer no later than 30 days after receiving the administrative decision.

The Director will determine the extent of the deletions allowed under (2), above. If the taxpayer does not submit deletions, the Director will make only the deletions specified in (1). (35 ILCS 120/11)

• *Taxpayer rights*

The "Taxpayers' Bill of Rights Act" ensures that taxpayer rights, privacy, and property are adequately protected during the process of the assessment and collection of tax. (20 ILCS 2520/1; 20 ILCS 2520/2)

Department duties.—The Department must (1) furnish each taxpayer with a written statement of rights when a notice of liability is sent, (2) explain tax liabilities and penalties on notices, (3) abate taxes and penalties if based on its erroneous written advice, (4) not cancel an installment contract unless the taxpayer fails to provide requested information or fails to pay tax, (5) place nonperishable property or bank accounts seized for taxes in escrow for 20 days, (6) allow taxpayer recording of interviews, (7) pay interest on overpayments, (8) grant automatic extensions to taxpayers that received federal extensions, (9) identify areas of recurrent taxpayer noncompliance, and (10) provide a closing letter to an audited taxpayer if no violations are found. (20 ILCS 2520/4; 86 Ill. Adm. Code Sec. 205.20)

Interviews.—Interviews are conducted at the taxpayer's place of business or at another place mutually agreed upon. (86 Ill. Adm. Code Sec. 205.30)

Costs.—A taxpayer may recover attorney's or accountant's fees against the Department if it prevails in an action under the Administrative Review Law and the Department made an assessment or denied a claim without reasonable cause. (20 ILCS 2520/7)

[¶61-700]

LOCAL TAXES

[¶61-735] Local Tax Rates

For specific rates imposed by home rule cities, non-home rule cities, and counties in Illinois, refer to the Tax Rate Finder website below.

Retailers subject to any local tax may use the bracket schedules at ¶60-130 or may multiply the transaction amount by the combined rate of tax and round up to the nearest unit. (86 Ill. Adm. Code 150.405)

• *Local sales tax rates*

An online Tax Rate Finder is provided by the Illinois Department of Revenue for obtaining local tax rates. The Tax Rate Finder can be found on the Department's website at https://mytax.illinois.gov/_/.

For a list of locally imposed sales taxes administered by the Illinois Department of Revenue, see ST-62.

[¶80-030]

STATE TAXPAYERS BASIS AND RATE

[¶80-031] Taxpayers Subject to State Tax

The burdens of the individual utility taxes falls on different taxpayers, depending on the tax.

• *Public Utilities Act*

Generally, the gross revenue tax on utilities applies to utilities except that it does not apply to gross revenues derived from the production, transmission, distribution, sale, delivery, or furnishing of electricity or from amounts paid by telecommunications retailers under the Telecommunications Infrastructure Maintenance Act. (Public Utilities Act, Sec. 2-201 [220 ILCS 5/2-202])

• *Electricity*

Generally, the burdens of the electricity excise tax and the public utilities tax fall on distributors of electricity. However, there are exceptions and exclusions, and other taxes apply to the distribution, use or consumption of electricity.

Electricity excise tax.—The electricity excise tax is imposed on the privilege of using electricity in the state purchased for use or consumption and not for resale. The tax does not apply to municipal corporations owning and operating a local transportation system for public service. (Electricity Excise Tax, Sec. 2-4(a) [35 ILCS 640/2-4])

There are two types of persons who remit the tax to the state. The first type is a "delivering supplier," which is any person engaged in the business of delivering electricity for use or consumption and not for resale; if more than one person participates in the delivery of electricity to a specific purchaser, the last supplier engaged in the delivery prior to its receipt by the purchaser is the delivering supplier. A "self-assessing purchaser" is any purchaser for non-residential electric use who elects to register with and to pay the electricity excise tax directly to the Department of Revenue. (Electricity Excise Tax, Sec. 2-3 [35 ILCS 640/2-3]; 86 Ill. Adm. Code 511.110)

Public utilities revenue tax.—Generally, the public utilities revenue tax is imposed on the distribution of electricity and is assessed on a graduated basis according to the number of kilowatt-hours distributed. However, that tax does not apply to electric cooperatives, school districts, or units of local government that distribute electricity. However, the Public Utilities Revenue Act does impose a tax on some electric cooperative's invested capital. (Public Utilities Revenue Act, Sec. 2a.1 [35 ILCS 620/2a.1])

Retailer's Occupation Tax Act.—Selected provisions of the Retailer's Occupation Tax Act apply, as far as practicable, to the sale and distribution of electricity. References in incorporated provisions of that law to "taxpayers" and to "persons engaged in the business of selling tangible personal property at retail" mean both "purchasers" and "delivering suppliers", as required by context, when used under the Electricity Excise Tax Law. Similarly, references in the incorporated provisions to "gross receipts" or "gross receipts received" mean "purchase price" or "kilowatt-hours used or consumed", as used in the electricity tax law. (Electricity Excise Tax, Sec. 2-12 [35 ILCS 640/2-12])

Similarly, the same incorporated provisions of the Retailer's Occupation Tax Act apply to the Public Utilities Revenue Act, as follows: when the Retailer's Occupation Tax Act uses the terms "retailers," "sellers," or "persons engaged in the business of selling tangible personal property," it means "persons engaged in the business of distributing electricity" as that term is used in the Public Utilities Revenue Act. References in the Retailer's Occupation Tax to "sales of tangible personal property" mean "the distributing of electricity," as used in the Public Utilities Revenue Act. (Public Utilities Revenue Act, Sec. 5 [35 ILCS 620/5])

• *Telecommunications*

Beginning January 1, 2016, the statewide surcharge will be imposed on customers of telecommunications carriers and wireless carriers. ([50 ILCS 750/20])

The excise telecommunications tax and the telecommunications infrastructure maintenance fee are discussed at ¶ 60-720 Telecommunications.

• *Gas*

The gas revenue tax and the gas use tax are imposed on different taxpayers.

Gas revenue tax: The per-therm tax assessed under the Gas Revenue Tax Act is imposed on persons engaged in the business of distributing, supplying, furnishing, or selling gas to persons for use or consumption and not for resale. After October 1, 2003, no tax is imposed under the Gas Revenue Tax Act on transactions with customers who incur a tax liability under the Gas Use Tax Law. (Gas Revenue Tax, Sec. 2 [35 ILCS 615/2])

The tax on invested capital assessed under the Gas Revenue Tax Act generally is imposed on persons who are subject to Illinois income tax and who are engaged in the business of distributing, supplying, furnishing, or selling gas. However, the tax does not apply to school districts or units of local governments or to persons who are not regulated by the Illinois Commerce Commission. (Gas Revenue Tax, Sec. 2a.1 [35 ILCS 615/2a.1])

Gas use tax.—Gas purchasers are liable for gas use tax on the use in Illinois of gas obtained in an out-of-state purchase. (35 ILCS 173/5-10) "Gas" is defined as any gaseous fuel distributed through a pipeline system. (35 ILCS 173/5-5)

• *Water*

The invested capital tax on water companies applies generally to water companies that are subject to the Illinois income tax. However, it does not apply to persons who are not regulated by the Illinois Commerce Commission and who are subject to the tax only with respect to transactions between the seller and tenants of buildings owned or operated by the seller. (35 ILCS 625/3) Further, the definition of "water company" does not include water companies owned by any political subdivision or municipal corporation or purely mutual concerns having no rates or charges for services. (35 ILCS 625/2)

[¶80-035] Credits

Some utility taxes are subject to credits.

• *Public Utilities Act*

Public utilities required to enter into long-term contracts to purchase electricity from qualified solid waste energy facilities are entitled to credits applied against their obligations to pay the electricity excise tax. The credits are equal to the amount by which payments for the electricity exceed:

— the then current rate at which the utility must purchase electricity, minus

— any costs, expenses, losses, damages, or other amounts incurred by the utility, or for which it becomes liable, arising out of its failure to obtain electricity from other sources.

A delivering supplier who is required or authorized to collect the electricity excise tax must make a return on or before the 15th day of each month stating the preceding month's amount of credits to which the taxpayer is entitled on account of purchases of electricity from a qualified solid waste energy facility. (220 ILCS 5/8-403.1)

Each qualified solid waste energy facility must file a form with the Department of Revenue before the 15th of each month regardless of whether the facility received any payment in the previous month. A qualified solid waste energy facility that fails to file timely will be subject to penalties and interest. The Department of Revenue may impose and enforce a tax lien against a solid waste energy facility that fails to file the form and make payment. (220 ILCS 5/8-403.1)

• *Electricity*

Both the electricity excise tax and the public utilities revenue tax provide for at least the possibility of credits.

Electricity excise tax: A public utility is allowed the same credit against its obligation to remit electric excise tax as other utilities are allowed under the Public Utilities Act whenever a utility is required to purchase electricity from qualified solid waste energy facilities. (Electricity Excise Tax Law, Sec. 2-7, [35 ILCS 640/2-7]) Generally, when a utility is required to make such a purchase, it is entitled to a credit against remitted taxes in an amount equal to:

— the then current rate at which the utility must purchase electricity, minus

— any costs, expenses, losses, damages, or other amounts incurred by the tactility, or for which it becomes liable, arising out of its failure to obtain electricity from other sources.

(Public Utilities Act, Sec. 8-403.1 [220 ILCS 5/8-403.1])

Public utilities revenue tax: The Department of Revenue will issue credit memoranda to qualifying taxpayers for any taxable period in which its receipts from the public utilities revenue tax are in excess of an amount equalling $145,279,553 plus one of two alternative increments of the tax received during the immediately preceding taxable period. The increment would be the lesser of 5% or the percentage increase in the Consumer Price Index for the immediately preceding taxable period. This subsection is not subject to the terms of the Uniform Penalties and Interest Act. (Public Utilities Revenue Act, Sec. 2a.1(c) [35 ILCS 620/2a.1(c)])

• *Telecommunications*

For purposes of the telecommunications excise tax, as it applies to interstate telecommunications, taxpayers who can show a tax paid to another state on a communication subject to the Illinois tax will be allowed a credit to the extent of the out-of-state payment. (Telecommunications Excise Tax, Sec. 4 [35 ILCS 630/4])

• *Gas*

Purchasers of gas that can prove payment of tax to another state on purchases of gas are entitled to a credit against the gas use tax. (35 ILCS 173/5-45)

[¶80-040] Exemptions

Each act concerning utilities specifies exempt customers and sales for the tax or taxes it imposes.

• *Enterprise and foreign trade zones*

A certified business that makes eligible investments in an enterprise zone or high-impact foreign trade zone or subzone may be exempt from additional charges added to its utility bills as a pass-on of municipal and state utility taxes on electricity, gas, and telecommunications. The business must be certified by the Department of Commerce and Economic Opportunity (DCEO) to have made investments

(1) that cause the creation of a minimum of 200 full-time jobs in Illinois,

(2) of at least $175,000,000 that cause the creation of a minimum of 150 full-time jobs in Illinois,

(3) that cause the retention of a minimum of 300 full-time equivalent jobs in the manufacturing sector in an area in Illinois in which the unemployment rate is above 9% and makes an application to the Department within three months after January 21, 2010, and certifies relocation of the 300 full-time equivalent jobs within 48 months after the application;

(4) that cause the retention of a minimum of 1,000 full-time jobs in Illinois; or

(5) (after making an application to the Department by March 21, 2010) that cause the retention of a minimum of 500 full-time equivalent jobs in 2009 and 2010, 675 full-time jobs in Illinois in 2011, 850 full-time jobs in 2012, and 750 full-time jobs per year in 2013 through 2017, in the manufacturing sector as defined by the North American Industry Classification System.

The exemption period cannot exceed of 20 years, except in the case of the Whiteside County/Carroll County enterprise zone, where, solely with respect to industrial purposes and uses, the exemption period cannot exceed 30 years. The exemption of a percentage of gross receipts requires adoption by municipal ordinance for municipal taxes. The percentage of exemption from state taxes is specified by the DCEO. (35 ILCS 620/1; 35 ILCS 615/1; 35 ILCS 630/2(a); 220 ILCS 5/9-222.1(1))

• *High impact businesses*

An exemption from electricity excise tax and gas revenue tax is available for business enterprises certified as high impact businesses with the Department of Commerce and Economic Opportunity. To qualify as a High Impact Business, a business must intend to:

— invest at least $12 million which will be placed in service in qualified property in Illinois, and create 500 full-time-equivalent jobs;

— invest at least $30 million which will be placed in service in qualified property and intend to retain 1,500 full-time jobs;

— establish a qualifying new electric generating facility in the state, with funding from the federal Department of Energy granted before July 1, 2006;

— establish a new gasification facility in the state that qualifies for financial assistance from the Illinois Department of Commerce and Economic Opportunity before December 31, 2006;

— establish production operations at a new coal mine, re-establish production operations at a closed coal mine, or expand production at an existing coal mine; or

— construct new transmission facilities or upgrade existing transmission facilities in the state.

(20 ILCS 655/5.5(a)(3); 220 ILCS 5/9-222; 220 ILCS 5/9-222.1A)

¶80-040

• *Public Utilities Act*

Generally, the gross revenue tax on utilities does not apply to gross revenues derived from the production, transmission, distribution, sale, delivery, or furnishing of electricity or from amounts paid by telecommunications retailers under the Telecommunications Infrastructure Maintenance Act. (Public Utilities Act, Sec. 2-201 [220 ILCS 5/2-202])

In addition, public utilities subject to the tax do not include:

(1) public utilities that are owned by any political subdivision, public institution or higher education, or municipal corporation of the state and are operated by them or their agent;

(2) water companies that are mutual concerns having no charges but paying operating expenses by assessment on company members only;

(3) electric suppliers subject to the Electric Suppliers Act;

(4) qualifying natural gas cooperatives;

(5) sewage disposal companies that provide the service on a mutual basis and pay the operating expenses by assessment upon the members of the company;

(6) cogeneration, small power-production, and other facilities that qualify under the Public Regulatory Policies Act;

(7) qualifying sales of compressed natural gas at retail for use only as a motor vehicle fuel;

(8) alternative retail electric suppliers; and

(9) subject to certain qualifications, entities that furnish the service of charging electric vehicles.

(Public Utilities Act. Sec. 5/3-105 220 ILCS 5/3-105)

• *Electricity*

The electricity excise tax is not imposed on electricity that is used by

(1) certified businesses within enterprise zones (see Public Utilities Act, Sec. 9-222.1 [220 ILCS 5/9-222.1]) or

(2) businesses certified as high impact businesses (see Public Utilities Act, Sec. 9-222.1A. [220 ILCS 5/9-222.1A])

(Electricity Excise Tax Law, Sec. 2-4(c), [35 ILCS 640/2-4(c)]) In addition, the electricity excise tax does not apply to the extent that a taxpayer has paid taxes to another state for electricity used in Illinois. (Electricity Excise Tax Law, Sec. 2-5, [35 ILCS 640/2-5])

The public utilities revenue tax as applied to distribution of electricity applies to all distributors of electricity except for electric cooperatives, school districts and units of local government. The invested capital tax imposed on electric cooperatives does not apply to electric cooperatives not required to file reports with the Rural Utilities Service. (Public Utilities Revenue Act, Sec. 2a.1 [35 ILCS 620/2a.1])

For purposes of the public utility revenue tax, gross receipts of electric utilities do not include receipts from:

(1) minimum charges where the customer has received no gas or electricity;

(2) bad check charges;

(3) finance or credit charges;

(4) charges for reconnecting services, repairs, or service on customer's premises;

(5) lease or rental of equipment which is not necessary to distribution of gas or electricity; and

(6) sales to taxpayers exempt from tax by state or federal constitution.

(35 ILCS 620/1)

• *Telecommunications*

The telecommunications excise tax, as it applies to interstate telecommunications, does not apply to taxpayers who can show a tax paid to another state on the same communication. (Telecommunications Excise Tax, Sec. 4 [35 ILCS 630/4])

The gross receipts of telecommunications companies do not include receipts from the following:

(1) collect calls received from outside of Illinois;

(2) leased time on equipment such as computers and calculators that store data or information for subsequent retrieval and processing;

(3) equipment charges separately identified from taxable charges;

(4) charges for telecommunications between parent corporations and subsidiaries or between subsidiaries;

(5) bad debts; and

(6) charges paid by inserting coins in a telecommunication device.

Value added services such as computer processing are exempt from the tax and only receipts for the actual message transmission are included. (35 ILCS 630/2)

Federal and state governments and state universities created by statute are exempt from taxation on the telecommunications they purchase for their own use. The entities must collect and remit the tax, however, if they sell telecommunications to others as retailers. (35 ILCS 630/2(k); 86 Ill. Adm. Code 495.105)

• *Gas*

For purposes of the gas revenue tax, gross receipts do not include receipts from:

(1) minimum charges where the customer has received no gas or electricity;

(2) bad check charges;

(3) finance or credit charges;

(4) charges for reconnecting services, repairs, or service on customer's premises;

(5) lease or rental of equipment which is not necessary to distribution of gas or electricity; and

(6) sales to taxpayers exempt from tax by state or federal constitution.

(35 ILCS 615/1)

The invested capital tax in the Gas Revenue Tax Act is not imposed on persons who are not regulated by the Illinois Commerce Commission. (35 ILCS 615/2a.1)

Gas use tax: The gas use tax does not apply to:

(1) gas used by business enterprises located in an enterprise zone;

(2) gas used by governmental bodies or qualified charitable, religious, or educational entities;

(3) gas used in the production of electric energy;

(4) gas used in a petroleum refinery operation;

(5) gas purchased by persons for use in liquefaction and fractionation processes that produce value added natural gas byproducts for resale;

(6) gas used in the production of anhydrous ammonia and downstream nitrogen fertilizer products for resale.

(35 ILCS 173/5-50) In addition, a purchaser may claim a credit against the gas use tax to the extent of any taxes paid to another state on the gas. (35 ILCS 173/5-45)

• *Water*

The invested capital tax on water companies does not apply to persons who are not regulated by the Illinois Commerce Commission and who are subject to the tax only with respect to transactions between the seller and tenants of buildings owned or operated by the seller. (35 ILCS 625/3) Further, the definition of "water company" does not include water companies owned by any political subdivision or municipal corporation or purely mutual concerns having no rates or charges for services. (35 ILCS 625/2)

[¶80-060] Rate of Tax

State rates are applicable to the gross receipts tax, and an administrative services tax discussed below.

• *Public Utilities Act*

The gross revenue tax on public utilities is assessed at the rate of 0.1% of gross revenues. (83 Ill. Adm. Code Sec. 270.5)

• *Electricity*

The rate of tax applied under the electricity excise tax or the public utilities revenue tax depends on what or who is being taxed.

Electricity excise tax. —Generally, the electricity excise tax is applied at a graduated rate based on the number of kilowatt hours used or consumed in a month, as follows:

(i) for the first 2,000 hours, 0.330¢ per kilowatt-hour;

(ii) for the next 48,000 hours, 0.319¢ per kilowatt-hour;

(iii) for the next 50,000 hours, 0.303¢ per kilowatt-hour;

(iv) for the next 400,000 hours, 0.297¢ per kilowatt-hour;

(v) for the next 500,000 hours, 0.286¢ per kilowatt-hour;

(vi) for the next 2,000,000 hours, 0.270¢ per kilowatt-hour;

(vii) for the next 2,000,000 hours, 0.254¢ per kilowatt-hour;

(viii) for the next 5,000,000 hours, 0.233¢ per kilowatt-hour;

(ix) for the next 10,000,000 hours, 0.207¢ per kilowatt-hour; and

(x) for anything in excess of 20,000,000 hours, 0.202¢ per kilowatt-hour.

(Electricity Excise Tax Law, Sec. 2-4(a), [35 ILCS 640/2-4(a)])

Self-assessing purchasers are taxed at the rate of 5.1% of the purchase price for all electricity distributed, supplied, furnished, sold, transmitted, and delivered to them. (Electricity Excise Tax Law, Sec. 2-4(a), [35 ILCS 640/2-4(a)])

The tax on purchases of electricity from qualifying municipal utilities or electric cooperatives is assessed pursuant to whichever one of two alternative methods produces the lower rate in a billing period. The alternative rates are applied to electricity distributed, supplied, furnished, sold, transmitted, and delivered by a municipal utility or electric cooperative, as follows:

— 0.32¢ per kilowatt-hour, or

— 5% of a purchaser's purchase price.

(Electricity Excise Tax Law, Sec. 2-4(b), [35 ILCS 640/2-4(b)])

Public utilities revenue tax. —Generally, the tax on electricity distributed is applied at graduated rates based on the number of kilowatt-hours distributed during a taxable period, as follows:

    (i) for the first 500,000,000 kilowatt-hours, .031¢ per kilowatt-hour;

    (ii) for the next 1,000,000,000 kilowatt-hours, .050¢ per kilowatt;

    (iii) for the next 2,500,000,000 kilowatt-hours, .070¢ per kilowatt;

    (iv) for the next 4,000,000,000 kilowatt-hours, .140¢ per kilowatt;

    (v) for the next 7,000,000,000 kilowatt-hours, .180¢ per kilowatt;

    (vi) for the next 3,000,000,000 kilowatt-hours, .142¢ per kilowatt; and

    (vii) for all kilowatt-hours in excess of 18,000,000,000, .131¢ per kilowatt-hour.

(Public Utilities Revenue Act, Sec. 2a.1 [35 ILCS 620/2a.1(a)]) The invested capital tax on electric cooperatives that are required to file reports with the Rural Utilities Service is assessed at the rate of 0.8%. (Public Utilities Revenue Act, Sec. 2a.1 [35 ILCS 620/2a.1(b)])

• *Telecommunications*

Beginning January 1, 2016, the statewide surcharge is imposed on carriers at the rate of $0.87 per network connection. ([50 ILCS 750/20])

• *Gas*

Each of the taxes imposed under the Gas Revenue Tax Act has alternative rates. Similarly, the Gas Use Tax has optional rates.

Gas revenue tax.—The tax imposed on persons engaged in the business of distributing, supplying, furnishing, or selling gas to persons for use or consumption and not for resale is subject to one of two rates—for each customer, the rate that produces the lower rate as applied to the customer is the rate that is applied. The first alternative is assessed at the rate of 2.4¢ per therm of all gas distributed, supplied, furnished, or sold. The second rate equals 5% of the gross receipts received from each customer. (35 ILCS 615/2)

The invested capital tax generally is assessed at the rate of 0.8% of each qualifying person's invested capital for the taxable period. However, for persons who are subject to both the invested capital tax and the tax on the distribution of electricity imposed under the Public Utilities Revenue Act, the tax is the lesser of:

    (i) an amount equal to 0.8% of the person's invested capital for the taxable period multiplied by a fraction, the numerator of which is the average of the beginning and ending balances of the person's gross gas utility plant in service, and the denominator of which is the of the beginning and ending balances of the person's gross electric and gas utility plant in service, and

(ii) an amount equal to 0.8% of the person's invested capital for the taxable period ended December 31, 1996, multiplied by a fraction, the numerator of which is the average of the beginning and ending balances of the person's gross gas utility plant in service and the denominator of which is the average of the beginning and ending balances of the person's gross electric and gas utility plant in service.

(35 ILCS 615/2a.1)

Gas use tax.—Self-assessing purchasers, that is, purchasers that pay tax directly to the Department of Revenue, must pay a gas use tax rate of 2.4 cents per therm or 5% of the purchase price for the billing period, whichever is the lower rate. Purchasers may elect an alternative tax rate of 2.4 cents per therm to be paid to a delivering supplier that maintains a place of business in Illinois. (35 ILCS 173/5-10)

• *Water*

The water company invested capital tax is assessed at the rate of 0.8% of invested capital for the taxable period. (35 ILCS 625/3)

INSURANCE

[¶88-000]
INSURANCE

[¶88-001] Overview

The insurance tax is administered by the Department of Insurance, which is subject to the administrative rules and procedures of the Administrative Procedure Act. (Insurance Code, Sec. 407.1 [215 ILCS 5/407.1])

The surplus line tax is also a privilege tax on licensed insurers who procure insurance from companies not licensed or authorized to do insurance business in Illinois.

Illinois imposes retaliatory taxes and license requirements on foreign and alien insurers according to the laws of the domicile of such foreign insurer.

The fire marshal's tax is a separate chapter of the Illinois law providing for the maintenance and support of the Division of Fire Prevention of Department of Public Safety. However, the tax administration is also through the Insurance Department, and it reaches all insurance premiums from policies written under Class 2 or Class 3 of the Insurance Code.

All domestic insurance companies (Insurance Code, Sec. 51 [215 ILCS 5/51]) and foreign or alien insurance companies (Insurance Code, Sec. 24 [215 ILCS 5/24]), except surplus line agents (see below), must obtain a certificate of authority to do insurance business in Illinois. Domestic insurance companies must apply to the Department of Insurance and meet minimum financial surplus and other specified requirements to be awarded a certificate of authority. (Insurance Code, Sec. 51 [215 ILCS 5/51]) Foreign or alien insurance companies must also apply to the Department of Insurance, pay the required fees and taxes, list specified information (Insurance Code, Sec. 109 [215 ILCS 5/109]), and conform to the requirements of the law to be awarded a certificate of authority. (Insurance Code, Sec. 111 [215 ILCS 5/111]) Certificates of authority for foreign or alien companies are automatically renewed each year upon payment of the net receipts tax. (Insurance Code, Sec. 114 [215 ILCS 5/114])

Illinois generally follows the federal income tax treatment of insurance companies, as set out in IRC Secs. 801 through 848. For more information on insurance companies subject to the corporate income tax, please see ¶10-335.

• *Surplus line agents*

Surplus line agents must have a license to act in such a capacity. (Insurance Code, Sec. 445(1) [215 ILCS 5/445(1)]) Surplus line agents must pass a written examination and post a surety bond of $20,000. An annual license fee of $400 is required. All licensed surplus line agents are automatically members of the Surplus Line Association of Illinois (Insurance Code, Sec. 445.1 [215 ILCS 5/445.1]), and must submit every insurance contract issued under such license to the Association (Insurance Code, Sec. 445(5) [215 ILCS 5/445(5)]) for recording and a countersignature. (Insurance Code, Sec. 445(6) [215 ILCS 5/445(6)])

[¶88-010] Companies Subject to Tax

Illinois imposes and collects a privilege tax on the net premiums of the following:

— life, accident, and health insurers;

— property and casualty insurers;

— health maintenance organizations;

— voluntary health service plans;

— dental service plans;

— limited health service organizations; and

— risk retention groups. (215 ILCS 5/409(1); 50 Ill. Adm. Code 2510.20(a))

Domestic captive insurance companies are taxed for the privilege of doing business in Illinois to the same extent and in the same manner as any other domestic insurance company. (215 ILCS 5/123C-16) Captive insurance companies include:

— pure captive insurance companies that insure only risks of parent or affiliated companies or both; (215 ILCS 5/123C-1(D), (L))

— association captive insurance companies that insure risks of the member organizations of an association, and their affiliated companies; (215 ILCS 5/123C-1(C), (D))

— industrial insured captive insurance company that insure risks of industrial insureds that are members of the industrial insured group, and their affiliated companies; (215 ILCS 5/123C-1(D), (F))

If a company survives or was formed by a merger, consolidation, reorganization, or reincorporation, the premiums received and the amounts returned or paid by the companies will be regarded as received, returned, or paid by the surviving or new company for purpose of this tax. (215 ILCS 5/409(3); 50 Ill. Adm. Code 2510.80) Tax deductions credits, or offsets cannot be transferred as a result of a merger, consolidation, reorganization or reincorporation if the company that holds the tax deduction, credit, or offset still exists after the merger, consolidation, reorganization or reincorporation. Additionally, tax deductions, credits, or offsets will not be considered transferred or owned by another taxpayer simply as the result of an assumption reinsurance agreement or as a result of a restructuring of a company or companies. (50 Ill. Adm. Code 2510.80)

• *Fire marshal tax*

Every insurance company or business doing any form of fire insurance business in Illinois must pay the annual marshal tax on total taxable premiums. (425 ILCS 25/12; 50 Ill. Adm. Code 2520.20)

• *Retaliatory tax*

A retaliatory tax is imposed on insurance companies incorporated outside of Illinois if the company's state of incorporation imposes any charges, fees, taxes, or penalties on Illinois insurers doing business in that state that are greater than those imposed by Illinois on insurers from that state. (215 ILCS 5/444(1); 50 Ill. Adm. Code 2515.20) The tax does not apply to residual market or special purpose assessments or guaranty fund or guaranty association assessments. Any tax offset or credit for any such assessment will be treated as tax paid. (215 ILCS 5/444(2))

• *Surplus lines tax*

Surplus lines producers that are licensed in Illinois must pay a surplus lines tax on gross premiums from all surplus line insurance submitted to the Surplus Line Association of Illinois (SLAI). (215 ILCS 5/445(3)(a)) Each surplus line producer must also pay the Illinois fire marshal tax on all fire insurance procured from unauthorized insurers and submitted to the SLAI. (215 ILCS 5/445(3)(b))

Surplus lines insurance is property and casualty insurance on a risk:

— that is procured from an unauthorized insurer that meets certain financial standards after the insurance producer representing the insured or the surplus line producer is unable, after diligent effort, to procure the insurance from authorized insurers; and

— where Illinois is the home state of the insured, for policies effective, renewed or extended on July 21, 2011 or later and for multiyear policies upon the policy anniversary that falls on or after July 21, 2011; and

— that is located in Illinois, for policies effective before July 21, 2011. (215 ILCS 5/445(1); *Company Bulletin*, Illinois Department of Insurance, July 13, 2011)

Home state determination.—Illinois is the insured's home state if:

— the insured maintains its principal place of business in Illinois;

— in the case of an individual, the individual's principal residence is located in Illinois; or

— 100% of the insured risk is located outside of Illinois, but the greatest percentage of the insured's taxable premium for that insurance contract is allocated to Illinois. (215 ILCS 5/445(1); *Company Bulletin*, Illinois Department of Insurance, July 13, 2011)

If more than one insured from an affiliate group are named insureds on a single nonadmitted insurance placement, Illinois will be considered the home state for that placement if Illinois is the home state of the member of the affiliated group that has the largest percentage of premium attributed to it under such insurance contract. (215 ILCS 5/445(1); *Company Bulletin*, Illinois Department of Insurance, July 13, 2011)

Illinois also addresses the determination of home state if more than one insured from a group that is not affiliated are named insureds on a single surplus line insurance contract. If the individual insureds pay 100% of the premium for the insurance from their own funds then a home state determination must be made for each insured separately and taxes and filings are made with the individual insured's home state. (215 ILCS 5/445(1); *General Bulletin #43*, Surplus Line Association of Illinois, January 5, 2015) If the group pays any portion of the premium, the group's home state applies to all transactions for the policy, regardless of group member locations, and all taxes and filings go to the group's home state. (*General Bulletin #43*, Surplus Line Association of Illinois, January 5, 2015)

• *Industrial insureds tax*

Policies independently procured from unauthorized insurers by industrial insureds are subject to a premiums tax and the fire marshal tax. (215 ILCS 5/121-2.08(b)*General Bulletin #43*, Surplus Line Association of Illinois, January 5, 2015) An "industrial insured" is an insured that:

— employs or regularly consults with a qualified risk manager to buy insurance;

— buys insurance directly from an unauthorized insurer; and

— is an exempt commercial purchaser whose home state is Illinois. (215 ILCS 5/121-2.08(a))

An exempt commercial purchaser is any insured purchasing commercial insurance that, at the time of placement, meets the following requirements:

— the insured employs or retains a qualified risk manager to negotiate insurance coverage; and

— the insured has paid aggregate nationwide commercial property and casualty insurance premiums in excess of $100,000 in the immediately preceding 12 months. (215 ILCS 5/445(1))

The insured must also meet at least one of the following criteria:

— the insured possesses a net worth of $20 million or more, as adjusted for inflation;

— the insured generates annual revenues in $50 million or more, as adjusted for inflation;

— the insured employs more than 500 full-time or full-time equivalent employees or is a member of an affiliated group employing more than 1,000 employees in the aggregate;

— the insured is a not-for-profit organization or public entity generating annual budgeted expenditures of $30 million or more, as adjusted for inflation; or

— the insured is a municipality with a population 50,000 or more. (215 ILCS 5/445(1))

[¶88-015] Exemptions

Illinois provides exemptions from the insurance privilege tax for:

— fraternal benefit societies;

— farm mutual companies;

— religious charitable risk pooling trusts; and

— residual market and special purpose entities statutorily required to participate in the insurance market. (215 ILCS 5/409(1))

An exemption from Illinois surplus lines premiums tax applies to contracts of insurance with industrial insureds that qualify as safety-net hospitals. (215 ILCS 5/121-2.08(e)) Illinois hospitals that provide a disproportionate share of care to Medicaid and uninsured patients qualify as saftey-net hospitals. (215 ILCS 5/121-2.08(a))

[¶88-020] Basis of Tax

The Illinois insurance privilege tax is based on the gross amount of premiums received on direct business during the calendar year on contracts covering risks in Illinois, except:

— premiums on annuities;

— premiums on which Illinois premium taxes are prohibited by federal law;

— premiums paid by Illinois for health care coverage for Medicaid eligible insureds;

— premiums paid for health care services included as an element of tuition charges at any university or college owned and operated by the state of Illinois;

— premiums on group insurance for state employees; and

— premiums on deferred compensation plans for state and local government or school district employees. (215 ILCS 5/409(1); 50 Ill. Adm. Code 2510.40)

The Illinois retaliatory tax that is imposed on certain insurance companies incorporated outside of Illinois is based on the difference between:

— the sum of Illinois penalties, fees, charges, or taxes paid by the out-of-state insurance company; and

— the sum of penalties, fees, charges, or taxes an Illinois domiciled insurance company would have paid in the domiciliary state or country if it transacted similar operations there as did the out-of-state company did in Illinois. (215 ILCS 5/444(1); 50 Ill. Adm. Code 2515.50)

Effective January 9, 2015, terms "penalties," "fees," "charges," and "taxes" with respect to the retaliatory tax include the penalties, fees, charges, and taxes collected on a cash basis. Further, the term "taxes" means the aggregate Illinois corporate income taxes paid during the calendar year for which the retaliatory tax calculation is being made, less the recapture of any Illinois corporate income tax cash refunds to the extent that the amount of tax refunded was reported as part of the Illinois basis in the calculation of the retaliatory tax for a prior tax year. However, the recaptured refund is limited to the amount necessary to make the Illinois basis equal to the out-of-state insurance company's basis in its state of incorporation for such tax year. (215 ILCS 5/444(3))

[¶88-030] Rates

Illinois imposes a privilege tax on the premiums of insurance companies doing in the state at a rate of:

— 0.5% on life insurance companies;

— 0.4% on accident and health insurance companies;

— 0.4% on health maintenance organizations (HMOs) and limited health service organizations;

— 0.4% on dental service plans; (215 ILCS 5/409(1))

— 3.5% on surplus lines insurers; (215 ILCS 5/445(3))

— 3.5% on industrial insureds for self-procured contacts effective before January 1, 2018; and

— 0.5% on industrial insureds for self-procured contacts effective January 1, 2018 or later. (215 ILCS 5/121-2.08(c))

Insurance companies must also pay a fire marshal tax at a rate of 1%. (425 ILCS 25/12)

[¶88-035] Credits

Credits may be claimed against Illinois insurance privilege tax liability for the following:

— corporate income and replacement tax payments;

— fire department tax payments; and

— new markets equity investments.

• *Corporate income and replacement tax payments*

Insurance companies may claim a credit against Illinois privilege tax liability equal to the amount by which the aggregate income and replacement tax paid by the company for the preceding calendar year exceeds 1.5% of the company's net taxable premium written for that prior calendar year. (215 ILCS 5/409(2); 50 Ill. Adm. Code 2510.60(a)(2)) the aggregate income taxes paid shall be reduced by any corporate and/or replacement income tax cash refunds received in that same calendar year. (50 Ill. Adm. Code 2510.60(a)(2)(B))

If the company is part of a state income tax unitary group, the allocation of the aggregate income taxes paid for the unitary group must be based on each individual company's Illinois premium written, including annuity considerations (excluding annuity deposit funds), as reported in each company's annual statement as a percent-age of the unitary group's total Illinois premium written. Each company's determination of the aggregate income taxes paid is the allocation percent multiplied by the unitary group's amount of the corporate and replacement income taxes paid in the calendar year, less the unitary group's tax cash refunds received in that same calendar. Each company may only use its allocated portion for the determination of the aggregate income tax deduction and may not transfer any allocated aggregate income taxes to another company or carry forward to another year. (50 Ill. Adm. Code 2510.60(b))

The credit for income and replacement tax payments may be claimed on a company's annual Illinois privilege and retaliatory tax return. (Form IL446-0126-H, Privilege and Retaliatory Tax Return for Health Maintenance Organizations, Limited Health Service Organizations, Voluntary Health Service Plans and Dental Service Plans; Form IL446-0126-L, Privilege and Retaliatory Tax Return for Life and Accident and Health Companies; Form IL446-0126-P, Privilege and Retaliatory Tax Return for Property and Casualty Insurers; Form IL446-0126-R, Privilege and Retaliatory Tax Return for Risk Retention Groups (RRG))

• *Fire department tax*

A credit may be claimed on an insurance company's annual Illinois privilege and retaliatory tax return (Form IL446-0126-H, Privilege and Retaliatory Tax Return for Health Maintenance Organizations, Limited Health Service Organizations, Voluntary Health Service Plans and Dental Service Plans; Form IL446-0126-L, Privilege and Retaliatory Tax Return for Life and Accident and Health Companies; Form IL446-0126-P, Privilege and Retaliatory Tax Return for Property and Casualty Insurers; Form IL446-0126-R, Privilege and Retaliatory Tax Return for Risk Retention Groups (RRG)) for the amount of any municipal fire department taxes paid by the company during the preceding calendar year. (215 ILCS 5/409(2); 50 Ill. Adm. Code 2510.60(a)(1))

• *New markets credit*

Insurance companies that invest in long-term debt securities issued by a qualified community development entity (CDE) that participates in the federal new markets tax credit program and provides financing to businesses in Illinois low-income communities may claim a credit against Illinois insurance privilege tax liability. (20 ILCS 663/5; 20 ILCS 663/10; 215 ILCS 5/444)

The Illinois New Markets Development Program (NMDP) credit is equal to 39% of the equity investment made by the taxpayer and may be claimed over the course of 7 years as follows:

— 0% of the equity investment purchase price for each of the first 2 years after the investment is initially made;

— 7% of the equity investment purchase price on the 3 year anniversary date of the investment; and

— 8% of the equity investment purchase price on the anniversary date of the investment for years 4-7. (20 ILCS 663/5; 20 ILCS 663/10)

The Illinois NMDP credit may be claimed on a company's annual Illinois privilege and retaliatory tax return. A schedule of the Tier 2 investor allocation of the credits must be attached to the return. (Form IL446-0126-H, Privilege and Retaliatory Tax Return for Health Maintenance Organizations, Limited Health Service Organizations, Voluntary Health Service Plans and Dental Service Plans; Form IL446-0126-L, Privilege and Retaliatory Tax Return for Life and Accident and Health Companies; Form IL446-0126-P, Privilege and Retaliatory Tax Return for Property and Casualty Insurers; Form IL446-0126-R, Privilege and Retaliatory Tax Return for Risk Retention Groups (RRG))

[¶88-040] Practice and Procedure

• *Annual returns and payments*

Every company doing any form of insurance business in Illinois must file a privilege and retaliatory tax return for the taxable year by March 15 (215 ILCS 5/409(4)) using the following forms:

— Form IL 446-0126-H, for health maintenance organizations (HMOs), limited health service organizations, voluntary health service plans, and dental service plans;

— Form IL 446-0126-L for life, accident and health insurance companies;

— Form IL 446-0126-P, for property and casualty insurers; or

— Form IL 446-0126-R, for risk retention groups.

The surplus line producer's semi-annual tax statement and payment are due twice per year:

— August 1 for all policies filed from January to June; and

— February 1 for policies filed from July to December. (215 ILCS 5/445(3); 86 Ill. Adm. Code 2801.130)

Every fire insurance company must file an Illinois fire marshal tax return or fire marshal tax return for farm mutuals by March 31. (425 ILCS 25/12)

Effective for tax years before 2014, insurers organized under a Lloyds plan of operation were allowed to file composite income and replacement tax returns and pay composite tax on behalf of all the insurer's underwriters, including corporations and residents.

• *Estimated payments*

All companies transacting insurance in Illinois whose annual privilege and retaliatory tax was $5,000 or more for the immediately preceding calendar year must make quarterly installments equal to 25% of the prior year's tax liability or 80% of the estimated current year's tax liability. The installments must be made electronically or using Form PRT 1 by:

— April 15;

— June 15;

— September 15; and

— December 15. (215 ILCS 5/409(4))

[¶88-050] Special Assessments

Illinois statute creates a Life And Health Insurance Guaranty Association for the purpose of assessing member companies to guarantee that benefits are paid and coverages are continued in cases of impairment or insolvency. (215 ILCS 5/531.01. 531.02)

The Illinois Insurance Guaranty Fund provides a mechanism for the payment of covered claims under certain insurance policies, to avoid excessive delay in payment, to avoid financial loss to claimants or policyholders because of the entry of an Order of Liquidation against an insolvent company, and to provide a fund to assess the cost of such protection among member companies. (215 ILCS 5/532)

PRACTICE AND PROCEDURE

[¶89-010]

TAX CALENDARS

[¶89-012] Annual Tax Calendar

Several Illinois taxes are reported or paid once a year or on a periodic basis other than quarterly or monthly. For a calendar of significant property tax dates, see ¶20-034. The following calendar, arranged by month, lists the principal dates concerning tax assessment, declarations, notices, returns, statements, reports, and payments:

January

10th—Estimated annual gross revenue returns for utility administration tax

20th—Retailers' occupation (sales) tax annual return due for annual filers

February

1st—Surplus line producer's semi-annual tax statement and payment due for policies filed from July to December

March

15th—Insurance company reports and payments due if preceding year's taxes were less than $5,000

31st—Insurance company fire marshal tax returns due

April

15th—Annual income tax returns and payments for corporations, individuals, partnerships, and fiduciaries due

June

15th—Motor vehicle registration fees are reduced by one-half for part-year license plates

August

1st—Surplus line producer's semi-annual tax statement and payment due for policies filed from January to June

15th—Annual returns and annualization schedule due in city of Chicago

[¶89-014] Quarterly Tax Calendar

Several Illinois taxes are reported or paid on a quarterly basis. Unless otherwise noted, payments are due in April, June, September, and December for calendar-year taxpayers. For fiscal-year taxpayers, payments are due on the 15th day of the fourth, sixth, and ninth months following the beginning of the tax year and the 15th day of the month following the close of the tax year.

The principal due dates for tax returns, reports, statements, or payments are:

15th (Apr., Jun., Sep., Jan.)—Income tax installments of estimated tax due for individuals

15th (Apr., Jun., Sep., Dec.)—Income tax installments of estimated tax due for corporations

15th (Apr., Jun., Sep., Dec.)—Quarterly installments of estimated tax due for insurers

20th (Apr., Jun., Oct., Jan.)—Quarterly returns of sales and use tax due for quarterly filers with monthly average tax over $200

Last day (Apr., Jun., Oct., Jan.)—Quarterly reports of income tax withheld by employers

[¶89-016] Monthly Tax Calendar

There are deadlines each month for certain Illinois reports and taxes. The following lists the principal monthly dates:

5th—Cigarette manufacturers qualifying as distributors pay cigarette and cigarette use taxes

15th—Alcoholic beverage reports due

Cigarette distributors who are not manufacturers and tobacco product distributors reports due

Oil and gas production assessment due

Utility gross receipts tax returns due

Withholding payment for certain employers due

20th—Motor fuel distributors returns and tax due and unlicensed purchasers of motor fuel taxes due

Special fuel suppliers returns and tax due

Sales and use returns and tax due for monthly filers

30th—Gasoline transporters reports due

Last day—city of Chicago local taxes due

Hotel occupancy returns and tax due

[¶89-050]

ADMINISTRATION OF TAXES

[¶89-060] State Taxing Authority

Most Illinois taxes are administered and collected by the Department of Revenue that is headed by the Director of Revenue.

The list of taxes and credits administered by the Department of Revenue include the following:

• *Excise and utilities taxes*

  — Cigarette and cigarette use tax

  — Dry-cleaning solvent taxes and license fees

  — Gaming taxes

— Hotel operators' occupation tax

— Liquor taxes

— Motor fuel and motor fuel use taxes

— Public utilities revenue tax

— Tobacco product tax

• *Income taxes*

— Income tax

— Personal property replacement tax

— Employers withholding income tax

• *Sales taxes*

— Retailers' occupation tax

— Service occupation tax

— Use tax

— Service use tax

— Automobile renting occupation and use taxes

— Replacement vehicle taxes

— Tire user fee

— Vehicle use tax

• *Other taxes and programs*

— Circuit breaker and pharmaceutical assistance

— Coin-operated amusement device and redemption machine tax

— Taxes collected for local governments

Taxes not administered or collected by the Department of Revenue include

— business license and occupation taxes (Secretary of State),

— corporate franchise tax (Secretary of State),

— motor vehicle fees (Secretary of State),

— gross premiums tax on insurance companies (Director of Insurance),

— estate tax (Attorney General), and

— unemployment compensation tax (Department of Employment Security).

• *Department structure*

The Department is headed by the Director of Revenue who is appointed by the Governor.

In carrying out its responsibilities, the Department is authorized to do the following:

— require the production of books, papers, and documents pertinent to any tax assessment, levy, investigation, inquiry, or hearing. (Civil Administrative Code of Illinois-(Department of Revenue Law), Sec. 2505-315 [20 ILCS 2505/2505-315])

— issue subpoenas, administer oaths, and take testimony. (Civil Administrative Code of Illinois-(Department of Revenue Law), Sec. 2505-315 [20 ILCS 2505/2505-315])

— examine the records and documents in any public office of any taxing district of the state. (Civil Administrative Code of Illinois-(Department of Revenue Law), Sec. 2505-605 [20 ILCS 2505/2505-605])

— exchange tax information with federal and state officials. (Civil Administrative Code of Illinois-(Department of Revenue Law), Sec. 2505-65 [20 ILCS 2505/2505-65])

— exchange tax information with the Illinois Department of Public Aid for the enforcement of a child support order. (Civil Administrative Code of Illinois-(Department of Revenue Law), Sec. 2505-65 [20 ILCS 2505/2505-65])

— recommend tax legislation. (Civil Administrative Code of Illinois-(Department of Revenue Law), Sec. 2505-700 [20 ILCS 2505/2505-700])

— investigate the tax systems of other states. (Civil Administrative Code of Illinois-(Department of Revenue Law), Sec. 2505-705 [20 ILCS 2505/2505-705])

— prosecute public officials or corporations for failure to comply with the tax laws. (Civil Administrative Code of Illinois-(Department of Revenue Law), Sec. 2505-300 [20 ILCS 2505/2505-300])

— hire investigators to conduct searches and seizures. (Civil Administrative Code of Illinois-(Department of Revenue Law), Sec. 2505-300 [20 ILCS 2505/2505-300])

— cancel uncollectible debts after 10 years. (Civil Administrative Code of Illinois-(Department of Revenue Law), Sec. 2505-250 [20 ILCS 2505/2505-250])

— credit overpayments and interest against any final tax liability arising under taxes administered by it. (Civil Administrative Code of Illinois-(Department of Revenue Law), Sec. 2505-275 [20 ILCS 2505/2505-275])

— assist local governments concerning the assessment and equalization of property taxes. (Civil Administrative Code of Illinois-(Department of Revenue Law), Sec. 2505-625 [20 ILCS 2505/2505-625])

— establish an informal assessment review prior to a formal hearing. (Taxpayers' Bill of Rights Act, Sec. 1 [20 ILCS 2520/1])

The functions of the Department are carried out by several offices and bureaus, with most of the units located in both Springfield and Chicago, Illinois. The divisions are as follows: Board of Appeals, Policy and Communications, Legislative, Administrative Services, Information Services Administration, Account Processing Administration, Taxpayer Services Administration, Tax Enforcement Administration, and Audit Bureau. (Civil Administrative Code of Illinois-(Department of Revenue Law), Sec. 2505-500 [20 ILCS 2505/2505-500])

• *Organizational chart*

The following chart depicts the divisions of the Illinois Department of Revenue.

ILLINOIS DEPARTMENT OF REVENUE
DIRECTOR'S OFFICE

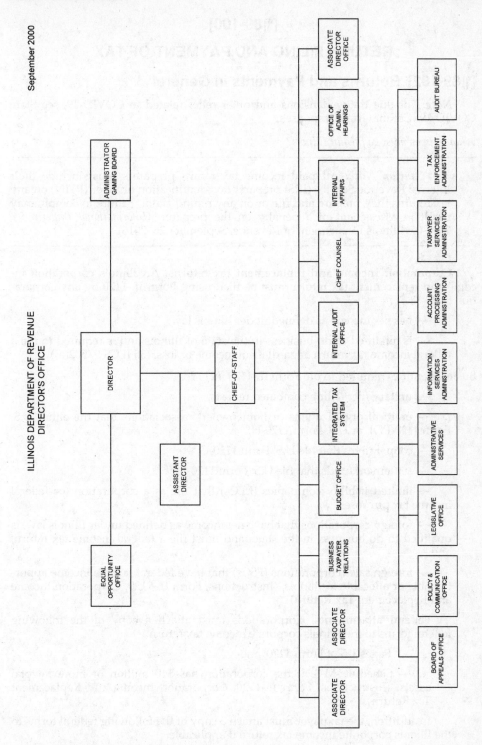

[¶89-100]

RETURN FILING AND PAYMENT OF TAX

[¶89-102] Returns and Payments in General

Note: For due date extensions and other relief related to COVID-19, see State COVID-19 (Coronavirus) Responses.

What returns must be filed in Illinois?

Caution Note: All paid income tax return preparers must include their Internal Revenue Service (IRS) preparer tax identification number (PTIN) on any tax returns they prepare and file or on any refund claim. Failure to comply may result in assessment of a penalty on the preparer. (*Informational Bulletin FY 2017-07*, Illinois Department of Revenue, September 26, 2016)

Corporation income and replacement tax returns. An Illinois corporation income and replacement tax return must be filed using Form IL-1120 by any corporation that:

— has net income as defined under Illinois law;

— is qualified to do business in the state of Illinois and is required to file a federal income tax return, regardless of income or loss. (35 ILCS 5/502(a))

Business entities required to file Form IL-1120 include:

— unitary filers filing combined reports;

— political organizations or homeowners' associations that file either U.S. Form 1120-POL or U.S. Form 1120-H;

— cooperatives that file U.S. Form 1120-C;

— settlement funds that file U.S. Form 1120-SF;

— limited liability companies (LLCs) that file as a corporation for federal income tax purposes;

— foreign corporations that have net income as defined under Illinois law, is qualified to do business in the state, and must file a federal income tax return; and

— foreign sales corporations (FSCs) that have federal taxable income apportionable or allocable to Illinois. (Instructions, Form IL-1120, Corporation Income and Replacement Tax Return)

Federal attachments. Corporations must attach a copy of the following federal forms to the Illinois corporate income tax return:

— Pages 1-5 of Form 1120; and

— Schedule M-3, if the corporation has $10 million or more in total assets. (Instructions, Form IL-1120, Corporation Income and Replacement Tax Return)

In addition, the taxpayer must attach a copy of the following federal forms to the Illinois corporate income tax return if applicable:

— Form 8886, Reportable Transaction Disclosure Statement; and

— Form 982, Reduction of Tax Attributes Due to Discharge of Indebtedness. (Instructions, Form IL-1120, Corporation Income and Replacement Tax Return)

If a corporation does not file a standard federal income tax return, it must attach the following to the Illinois corporate income tax return:

— Form 1120-H, Income Tax return for Homeowners Associations;

— Page 1 (and Schedule A, if filed) of Form 1120-L, Life Insurance Company Income Tax Return;

— Page 1 (and Schedule A, if filed) of Form 1120-PC, Property and Casualty Insurance Company Income Tax Return;

— Form 1120-POL, Income Tax Return for Certain Political Organizations; or

— Form 1120-SF, Income Tax Return for Settlement Funds. (Instructions, Form IL-1120, Corporation Income and Replacement Tax Return)

A corporation that is included in a consolidated federal tax return must provide a pro forma copy of federal Forms 1120, 1120-L, 1120-PC, and all applicable schedules, as if the corporation filed a separate federal return. (Instructions, Form IL-1120, Corporation Income and Replacement Tax Return)

Short period returns. Illinois follows federal law with regard to short period returns. (35 ILCS 5/401)

Signature requirements. An Illinois corporation income tax return must be signed by the president, vice president, treasurer, or any other officer duly authorized to sign the return. (35 ILCS 5/503(b); Instructions, Form IL-1120, Corporation Income and Replacement Tax Return) If the corporation is in bankruptcy proceedings, the receiver, trustee, or assignee must sign any return required to be filed for a corporation. (35 ILCS 5/502(b)(4)) The signature verifies by written declaration and under penalties of perjury that the signing individual has personally examined the return and the return is true, correct, and complete. (35 ILCS 5/504; Instructions, Form IL-1120, Corporation Income and Replacement Tax Return) The fact that an individual's name is signed to a return is prima facie evidence that the individual is authorized to sign the return for the corporation. (35 ILCS 5/503(b); Instructions, Form IL-1120, Corporation Income and Replacement Tax Return)

Any person paid to prepare the return, other than a regular employee of the taxpayer, must provide a signature, date the return, and write the preparer's taxpayer identification number. If the preparer is an employee or partner of a firm or corporation, the preparer must also provide the firm's name, address, and instead of the preparer's taxpayer identification number, the preparer must provide the firm's FEIN. Self-employed preparers must provide their own name, address, and taxpayer identification number. (Instructions, Form IL-1120, Corporation Income and Replacement Tax Return)

CCH Caution: If a taxpayer fails to sign a return within 30 days after notice and demand for signature, the return is considered valid and any amount shown to be due is deemed assessed. If the return is not signed, any overpayment of tax is considered forfeited if, after notice and demand for signature, the taxpayer fails to provide a signature within three years from the date the return was filed. (35 ILCS 5/503(e); Instructions, Form IL-1120, Corporation Income and Replacement Tax Return)

Small business corporation replacement tax returns. An Illinois small business corporation replacement tax return must be filed using Form IL-1120-ST by any S corporation that:

— has net income as defined under Illinois law;

— is qualified to do business in the state of Illinois and is required to file a federal income tax return, regardless of income or loss. (35 ILCS 5/502(a); Instructions, Form IL-1120-ST, Small Business Corporation Replacement Tax Return)

S corporation members of a unitary business group are not eligible to file as part of an Illinois combined return. (Instructions, Form IL-1120-ST, Small Business Corporation Replacement Tax Return; Instructions, Schedule UB, Combined Apportionment for Unitary Business Group) Such members are required to file Illinois separate unitary returns, as well as make separate tentative tax payments, separate estimated tax payments separate claims for refunds and separate amended returns. (Instructions, Schedule UB, Combined Apportionment for Unitary Business Group) However, the unitary business group, including S corporation members, must complete only one Illinois Schedule UB to determine the income of the unitary group that is apportionable to Illinois. (86 Ill. Adm. Code 100.5215; Instructions, Schedule UB, Combined Apportionment for Unitary Business Group) A copy of the apportionment schedule must be included with the S corporation member's Illinois replacement tax return. (Instructions, Schedule UB, Combined Apportionment for Unitary Business Group)

Federal attachments. S corporations are not specifically required to attach any portion of the federal return to the Illinois small business corporation replacement tax return. However, the following federal forms must be attached to the Illinois return if applicable:

— Form 982, Reduction of Tax Attributes Due to Discharge of Indebtedness; and

— Form 8886, Reportable Transaction Disclosure Statement or Schedule M-3, Net Income (Loss) Reconciliation for S Corporations With Total Assets of $10 Million or More.

Schedule K-1s. S corporations that file an Illinois small business corporation replacement tax return must complete and provide a Schedule K-1-P to each shareholder by the original or extended due date of the corporation's Illinois replacement tax return. A copy of Schedule K-1-P(2), instructions for completing Schedule K-1-P, also must be provided to each shareholder. (Instructions, Schedule K-1-P, Partner's or Shareholder's Share of Income, Deductions, Credits, and Recapture)

Signature requirements. An Illinois small business corporation replacement tax return must be signed by the president, vice president, treasurer, or any other officer duly authorized to sign the return. (35 ILCS 5/503(b); Instructions, Form IL-1120-ST, Small Business Corporation Replacement Tax Return) If the corporation is in bankruptcy proceedings, the receiver, trustee, or assignee must sign any return required to be filed for the corporation. (35 ILCS 5/502(b)(4)) The signature verifies by written declaration and under penalties of perjury that the signing individual has personally examined the return and the return is true, correct, and complete. (35 ILCS 5/504; Instructions, Form IL-1120-ST, Small Business Corporation Replacement Tax Return) The fact that an individual's name is signed to a return is prima facie evidence that the individual is authorized to sign the return on behalf of the corporation. (35 ILCS 5/503(b); Instructions, Form IL-1120-ST, Small Business Corporation Replacement Tax Return)

Any person paid to prepare the return, other than a regular employee of the taxpayer, must provide a signature, date the return, and write the preparer's taxpayer identification number. If the preparer is an employee or partner of a firm or corporation, the preparer must also provide the firm's name, address, and instead of the preparer's taxpayer identification number, the preparer must provide the firm's FEIN. Self-employed preparers must provide their own name, address, and taxpayer identification number. (Instructions, Form IL-1120-ST, Small Business Corporation Replacement Tax Return)

CCH Caution: If a taxpayer fails to sign a return within 30 days after notice and demand for signature, the return is considered valid and any amount shown to be due is deemed assessed. If the return is not signed, any overpayment of tax is considered forfeited if, after notice and demand for signature, the taxpayer fails to provide a signature within three years from the date the return was filed. (35 ILCS 5/503(e); Instructions, Form IL-1120-ST, Small Business Corporation Replacement Tax Return)

Partnership replacement tax returns. Any business entity classified as a partnership for federal income tax purposes, including a limited liability partnership (LLP) or limited liability company (LLC), must file an Illinois replacement tax return using Form IL-1065, if it has base income or loss attributable to state sources. (35 ILCS 5/502(d); Instructions, Form IL-1065, Partnership Replacement Tax Return) Partnerships that qualify as an "investment partnership" (35 ILCS 5/1501(a)(11.5)) are not subject to Illinois replacement tax and are not required to file a replacement tax return. However, an investment partnership may elect to file an Illinois replacement tax return by checking the appropriate box on the return. (Instructions, Form IL-1065, Partnership Replacement Tax Return)

A single member limited liability company (SMLLC) that is treated for federal income tax purposes as a disregarded entity and taxed as a sole proprietorship, with all income reported on the single member's federal personal income tax return, must report all profits (or losses) of the LLC on Schedule C and submit it with the sole member's Illinois personal income tax return. If the single member is a partnership, then an Illinois partnership replacement tax return is filed. (86 Ill. Adm. Code 100.9750; *Unofficial Department Guidance*, Illinois Department of Revenue, April 9, 2012)

Federal attachments. Partnerships, LLPs, and LLCs are not specifically required to attach any portion of the federal return to the Illinois partnership replacement tax return. However, the following federal forms must be attached to the Illinois return if applicable:

— Form 4797, Sales of Business Property;

— Form 6252, Installment Income from Sales of Property; and

— Form 8886, Reportable Transaction Disclosure Statement or Schedule M-3, Net Income (Loss) Reconciliation for Certain Partnerships.

Schedule K-1s. Partnerships, LLPs, and LLCs that file an Illinois replacement tax must complete and provide a Schedule K-1-P to each partner or member by the original or extended due date of the partnership's Illinois replacement tax return. A copy of Schedule K-1-P(2), instructions for completing Schedule K-1-P, also must be provided to each partner or member. (Instructions, Schedule K-1-P, Partner's or Shareholder's Share of Income, Deductions, Credits, and Recapture)

Signature requirements. An Illinois partnership replacement tax return must be signed by a partner, an LLC manager or member, or any other officer duly authorized to sign the return. (35 ILCS 5/503(c); Instructions, Form IL-1065, Partnership Replacement Tax Return) If the partnership is in bankruptcy proceedings, the receiver, trustee, or assignee must sign any return required to be filed for the partnership. (Instructions, Form IL-1065, Partnership Replacement Tax Return) The signature verifies by written declaration and under penalties of perjury that the signing individual has personally examined the return and the return is true, correct, and complete. (35 ILCS 5/504; Instructions, Form IL-1065, Partnership Replacement Tax Return) The fact that an individual's name is signed to a return is prima facie evidence that the individual is authorized to sign the return on behalf of the partnership. (35 ILCS 5/503(c); Instructions, Form IL-1065, Partnership Replacement Tax Return)

Any person paid to prepare the return, other than a regular employee of the taxpayer, must provide a signature, date the return, and write the preparer's taxpayer identification number. If the preparer is an employee or partner of a firm or corporation, the preparer must also provide the firm's name, address, and instead of the preparer's taxpayer identification number, the preparer must provide the firm's FEIN. Self-employed preparers must provide their own name, address, and taxpayer identification number. (Instructions, Form IL-1065, Partnership Replacement Tax Return)

CCH Caution: If a taxpayer fails to sign a return within 30 days after notice and demand for signature, the return is considered valid and any amount shown to be due is deemed assessed. If the return is not signed, any overpayment of tax is considered forfeited if, after notice and demand for signature, the taxpayer fails to provide a signature within three years from the date the return was filed. (35 ILCS 5/503(e); Instructions, Form IL-1120, Corporation Income and Replacement Tax Return)

Composite income and replacement tax returns. Effective for tax years before 2014, an Illinois composite income and replacement tax return could be filed and tax paid on behalf of participating nonresident individuals, trusts, and estates who were partners, S corporation shareholders, or underwriters who transacted insurance business under a Lloyd's plan of operation. (35 ILCS 5/502(f); 86 Ill. Admin. Code 100.5100(a); *Informational Bulletin FY 2014-10*, Illinois Department of Revenue, January 2014) Resident individuals, trusts, and estates could be included in a composite return if a petition was filed with the Illinois Department Revenue before the end of the S corporation's or partnership's tax year. (86 Ill. Admin. Code 100.5100(c)) A partnership or S corporation could, but was not required to, make estimated composite payments for its partners or shareholders.

Exempt organization income and replacement tax returns. An Illinois income and replacement tax return, Form IL-990-T, must be filed by exempt organizations that have unrelated business income (UBI) (35 ILCS 5/505(a)(3); Instructions, Form IL-990-T Instructions, Exempt Organization Income and Replacement Tax Return) and that:

— have net income as defined under Illinois law;

— are a resident or qualified to do business in the state of Illinois and are required to file a federal unrelated business income tax return, regardless of income or loss. (Instructions, Form IL-990-T, Exempt Organization Income and Replacement Tax Return)

Federal attachments. A copy of page 1 of the federal unrelated business income tax return must be attached to the Illinois exempt organization income and replacement tax return. If the exempt organization participated in a reportable transaction, including a listed transaction during the tax year, a copy of Form 8886, Reportable Transaction Disclosure Statement, also must be attached to the Illinois return. (Instructions, Form IL-990-T, Exempt Organization Income and Replacement Tax Return)

Signature requirements. If an exempt organization that is a corporation, the Illinois exempt organization income and replacement tax return must be signed by the president, vice president, treasurer, or any other officer duly authorized to sign the return. If the corporation is in bankruptcy proceedings, the receiver, trustee, or assignee must sign any return required to be filed on for the corporation. If the organization is a trust, the return must be signed by a fiduciary of the trust. If there are two or more joint fiduciaries, the signature of one will comply with the signature requirements. (Instructions, Form IL-990-T, Exempt Organization Income and Replacement Tax Return)

The signature verifies by written declaration and under penalties of perjury that the signing individual has personally examined the return and the return is true, correct, and complete. (35 ILCS 5/504; Instructions, Form IL-990-T, Exempt Organization Income and Replacement Tax Return) The fact that a individual's name is signed to a return is prima facie evidence that the individual is authorized to sign the return on behalf of the corporation or trust. (Instructions, Form IL-990-T, Exempt Organization Income and Replacement Tax Return)

Any person paid to prepare the return, other than a regular employee of the taxpayer, must provide a signature, date the return, and write the preparer's taxpayer identification number. If the preparer is an employee or partner of a firm or corporation, the preparer must also provide the firm's name, address, and instead of the preparer's taxpayer identification number, the preparer must provide the firm's FEIN. Self-employed preparers must provide their own name, address, and taxpayer identification number. (Instructions, Form IL-990-T, Exempt Organization Income and Replacement Tax Return)

CCH Caution: If a taxpayer fails to sign a return within 30 days after notice and demand for signature, the return is considered valid and any amount shown to be due is deemed assessed. If the return is not signed, any overpayment of tax is considered forfeited if, after notice and demand for signature, the taxpayer fails to provide a signature within three years from the date the return was filed. (35 ILCS 5/503(e); Instructions, Form IL-990-T, Exempt Organization Income and Replacement Tax Return)

Personal income tax returns. Every resident part-year resident, and nonresident that meets Illinois filing thresholds must file an Illinois personal income tax return (35 ILCS 5/502(a)(2)) using Form IL-1040. (Instructions, Form IL-1040, Individual Income Tax Return) Part-year residents and nonresidents must also file Schedule NR showing the computation of taxable income attributable to state sources. (Instructions, Form IL-1040, Illinois Individual Income Tax Return) Nonresident individuals are not required to file a return (35 ILCS 5/502(a)(2); Instructions, Form IL-1040, Illinois

Individual Income Tax Return) if the only income attributable to Illinois is from one or more partnerships, S corporations, or trusts that satisfied Illinois nonresident income tax withholding requirements.

Federal attachments. Individuals are not specifically required to attach any portion of their federal return to their Illinois personal income tax return. However, the following federal forms must be attached to the Illinois return if applicable:

— Form 1040NR, U.S. Nonresident Alien Income Tax Return, or Form 1040NR-EZ, U.S. Income Tax Return for Certain Nonresident Aliens With No Dependents;

— Form 1040 or 1040A, page 1 and Form W-2, to support any subtraction claimed for retirement income and social security benefits;

— Form 1099-R or Form SSA-1099, if Form 1040, page 1, does not clearly identify reported retirement income and social security benefits;

— Form 1040, Schedule D, for a gain on the sale or exchange of employer securities;

— Form 1040, Schedule B or Schedule 1, for interest and dividend income from U.S. retirement bonds; or

— Form 8886, Reportable Transaction Disclosure Statement. (*Publication 120, Retirement Income*, Illinois Department of Revenue; Instructions, Form IL-1040, Illinois Individual Income Tax Return)

Deceased taxpayers. A taxpayer who is filing a joint return for a deceased spouse should:

— print their name and their spouse's name on the appropriate lines;

— write "deceased" and the date of death above their spouse's name; and

— sign their name in the area provided for the taxpayer's signature, and write "filing as surviving spouse" in place of the decedent's signature. (Instructions, Form IL-1040, Illinois Individual Income Tax Return)

A personal representative filing a return on behalf of a single deceased taxpayer should:

— print the name of the taxpayer on the appropriate line;

— write "deceased" and the date of death above the decedent's name; and

— write "in care of", and the representative's name and address. (Instructions, Form IL-1040, Illinois Individual Income Tax Return)

A personal representative, like an executor or administrator, must sign and date the return. The representative's title and telephone number must be provided. (Instructions, Form IL-1040, Illinois Individual Income Tax Return)

Fiduciary income and replacement tax returns. An Illinois fiduciary income and replacement tax return, IL-Form 1041, must be filed by the fiduciary for an estate or trust that:

— has net income or loss as defined under the Illinois law, regardless of any deduction for distributions to beneficiaries;

— is an Illinois resident that files, or is required to file, a federal income tax return; or

— is a nonresident that received income from Illinois sources. (35 ILCS 5/502(b)(3); Instructions, Form IL-1041, Fiduciary Income and Replacement Tax Return)

A fiduciary income and replacement return is not required for grantor trusts. (Instructions, Form IL-1041, Fiduciary Income and Replacement Tax Return)

Federal attachments. Fiduciaries are not specifically required to attach any portion of the federal return to the Illinois fiduciary income and replacement tax return. However, the following federal forms must be attached to the Illinois return if applicable:

— Form 1041, page 1, and supporting schedules for federally taxed retirement income;

— Form 1041, Schedule D, for a gain on the sale or exchange of property, including employer securities;

— Form 4797, Sales of Business Property;

— Form 6252, Installment Income from Sales of Property; and

— Form 8886, Reportable Transaction Disclosure Statement. (Instructions, Form IL-1041, Fiduciary Income and Replacement Tax Return)

Signature requirements. An Illinois fiduciary income and replacement tax return must be signed by the fiduciary of the trust or estate. If there are two or more joint fiduciaries, the signature of one will comply with the requirements. (35 ILCS 5/503(d); Instructions, Form IL-1041, Fiduciary Income and Replacement Tax Return) The signature verifies by written declaration and under penalties of perjury that the signing fiduciary has personally examined the return and the return is true, correct, and complete. (35 ILCS 5/504; Instructions, Form IL-1041, Fiduciary Income and Replacement Tax Return) The fact that a fiduciary's name is signed to a return is prima facie evidence that the fiduciary is authorized to sign the return on behalf of the trust or estate. (35 ILCS 5/503(d); Instructions, Form IL-1041, Fiduciary Income and Replacement Tax Return)

Any person paid to prepare the return, other than a regular employee of the taxpayer, must provide a signature, date the return, and write the preparer's taxpayer identification number. If the preparer is an employee or partner of a firm or corporation, the preparer must also provide the firm's name, address, and instead of the preparer's taxpayer identification number, the preparer must provide the firm's FEIN. Self-employed preparers must provide their own name, address, and taxpayer identification number. (Instructions, Form IL-1041, Fiduciary Income and Replacement Tax Return)

CCH Caution: If a taxpayer fails to sign a return within 30 days after notice and demand for signature, the return is considered valid and any amount shown to be due is deemed assessed. If the return is not signed, any overpayment of tax is considered forfeited if, after notice and demand for signature, the taxpayer fails to provide a signature within three years from the date the return was filed. (35 ILCS 5/503(e); Instructions, Form IL-1041, Fiduciary Income and Replacement Tax Return)

Withholding income tax returns. Illinois withholding income tax returns, Form IL-941, must be filed by taxpayers who paid:

— wages and other employee compensation reported to a recipient on a Form W-2;

— pensions, annuities, unemployment income, and sick pay reported to a recipient on a Form 1099;

— gambling and lottery winnings reported to a recipient on a Form W-2G; or

— amounts to purchase rights to Illinois lottery winnings reported on a Form 1099-MISC. (35 ILCS 5/704A; 86 Ill. Adm. Code 100.7300; 86 Ill. Adm. Code 100.7325; Publication 131, Withholding Income Tax Payment and Filing Requirements, Illinois Department of RevenueForm IL-941, Information and Instructions)

Employers must maintain employee W-2 records for three years from the due date or payment of the tax, whichever is later. (86 Ill. Adm. Code 100.7300; Publication 110, W-2, W-2G, and 1099 Filing and Storage Requirements for Employers and Payers, Illinois Department of Revenue)

If the W-2 is lost or destroyed, the employer must furnish two substitute copies to the employee and retain one copy to provide to the Illinois Department of Revenue upon written request. All such copies must be clearly marked "Reissued by Employer." (86 Ill. Adm. Code 100.7200(f)) A taxpayer who has lost a W-2 form or was not provided one, and is unable to obtain a duplicate from the employer may obtain a substitute W-2 form from the Internal Revenue Service. (35 ILCS 5/506.5) The Department of Revenue will presume that tax was withheld by the employer in an appropriate amount on the basis of the number of withholding exemptions used to determine the federal income tax withholding for the taxpayer if:

— the substitute W-2 form indicates the appropriate amount of federal taxes withheld;

— the taxpayer files a copy of the substitute W-2 form with his or her Illinois income tax return; and

— the taxpayer provides a mailing address to which any correspondence or refund may be sent. (35 ILCS 5/506.5)

Sales and use tax. Form ST-1 must be filed by anyone making retail sales of:

— general merchandise;

— qualifying foods, drugs, and medical appliances; and/or

— prepaid wireless telecommunications service.

(Instructions, Form ST-1, Sales and Use Tax and E911 Surcharge Return)

Form ST-44, Illinois Use Tax Return, must be filed by anyone who purchases general merchandise taxable in Illinois and did not pay sales tax or an amount of sales tax that would be due in Illinois

Amended returns. Taxpayers that need to correct or change a previously filed income or sales and use tax return must file one of the following returns:

— Form IL-1120-X, Amended Corporation Income and Replacement Tax Return

— Form IL-1065-X, Amended Partnership Replacement Tax Return

— Form IL-990-T-X, Amended Exempt Organization Income and Replacement Tax Return

— Form IL-1040-X, Amended Individual Income Tax Return

— Form IL-1041-X, Amended Fiduciary Income and Replacement Tax Return

— Form ST-1, Amended Sales and Use Tax and E911 Surcharge Return

When are returns due?

Corporation income and replacement tax returns. Illinois corporation income and replacement tax returns must be filed by:

— April 15 (March 15 for taxable years before 2016) for calendar year corporations; or

— the 15th day of the fourth month (15th day of the third month for taxable years before 2016) after the close of a corporation's fiscal year. (35 ILCS 5/505(a)(1); 86 Ill. Adm. Code 100.5000(a)(2); Instructions, Form IL-1120, Corporation Income and Replacement Tax Return

Extensions. An automatic 6-month extension (7-month for taxable years beginning before 2016) will be granted for the filing of an Illinois corporate income tax return. Illinois does not require any paper or electronic filing request to obtain the extension. However, 100% of the outstanding income and replacement tax liability must be paid using Form IL-1120-V or electronically by the original due date of the return (35 ILCS 5/602; 86 Ill. Adm. Code 100.5020(b); Instructions, Form IL-1120-V, Payment Voucher for Corporation Income and Replacement Tax) to avoid interest and penalties.

An additional extension beyond the initial automatic extension period will be granted if a longer federal extension has been granted by the Internal Revenue Service (IRS). The additional Illinois extension will be equal to the federal extension, plus one month. A copy of the federal extension must be attached to the Illinois return when it is filed. (35 ILCS 5/505(b); 86 Ill. Adm. Code 100.5020(c))

Reporting federal changes. An amended Illinois corporate income tax return must be filed within 120 days of any partial agreement or federal finalization notification that changes the taxable income or loss, any item of income or deduction, the income tax liability, or any tax credit reported in an original or amended federal income tax return for any taxable year. (35 ILCS 5/506(b); Instructions, Form IL-1120-X, Amended Corporation Income and Replacement Tax Return) If a federal change decreases Illinois corporate income tax liability and the corporation is entitled to a refund, the amended Illinois return must be filed within two years plus 120 days of the federal finalization. (Instructions, Form IL-1120-X, Amended Corporation Income and Replacement Tax Return)

A copy of the federal finalization or proof of acceptance from the IRS, along with a copy of the amended federal return, must be attached to the amended Illinois corporate income tax return. (Instructions, Form IL-1120-X, Amended Corporation Income and Replacement Tax Return) Examples of federal finalization include a copy of one or more of the following items:

— a federal refund check;

— an audit report from the IRS; or

— a federal transcript verifying federal taxable income. (Instructions, Form IL-1120-X, Amended Corporation Income and Replacement Tax Return)

¶89-102

Small business corporation replacement tax returns. Illinois small business corporation replacement tax returns must be filed by:

— March 15 for calendar year S corporations; or

— the 15th day of the fourth month (15th day of the third month for taxable years before 2016) after the close of an S corporation's fiscal year. (35 ILCS 5/505(a)(1); 86 Ill. Adm. Code 100.5000(a)(2); Instructions, Form IL-1120-ST, Small Business Corporation Replacement Tax Return)

Extensions. S corporations are entitled to an automatic 7-month extension for the filing of an Illinois small business replacement tax return. Illinois does not require any paper or electronic filing request to obtain the extension. However, 100% of the outstanding income and replacement tax liability must be paid using Form IL-1120-ST-V or electronically by the original due date of the return (35 ILCS 5/602(b); 86 Ill. Adm. Code 100.5000(a)(2)) (Instructions, Form IL-1120-ST-V, Payment Voucher for Small Business Corporation Replacement Tax) to avoid interest and penalties.

An additional extension beyond the initial automatic extension period will be granted if a longer federal extension has been granted by the Internal Revenue Service (IRS). The additional Illinois extension will be equal to the federal extension, plus one month. A copy of the federal extension must be attached to the Illinois return when it is filed. (35 ILCS 5/505(b); 86 Ill. Adm. Code 100.5020(c))

Reporting federal changes. An amended Illinois small business replacement tax return must be filed and additional tax paid within 120 days of any partial agreement or federal finalization notification that increases Illinois replacement tax liability for any taxable year. (35 ILCS 5/506(b); Instructions, Form IL-1120-ST-X, Amended Small Business Corporation Replacement Tax Return) If a federal change decreases Illinois replacement tax liability and the corporation is entitled to a refund, the amended Illinois return must be filed within two years plus 120 days of the federal finalization. (Instructions, Form IL-1120-ST-X, Amended Small Business Corporation Replacement Tax Return)

A copy of the federal finalization or proof of acceptance from the IRS, along with a copy of the amended federal return, must be attached to the amended Illinois small business replacement tax return. (Instructions, Form IL-1120-ST-X, Amended Small Business Corporation Replacement Tax Return) Examples of federal finalization include a copy of one or more of the following items:

— a federal refund check;

— an audit report from the IRS; or

— a federal transcript verifying federal taxable income. (Instructions, Form IL-1120-ST-X, Amended Small Business Corporation Replacement Tax Return)

Partnership replacement tax returns. Illinois partnership replacement tax returns must be filed by:

— April 15 for calendar year partnerships; or

— the 15th day of the fourth month following the close of a partnership's fiscal tax year. (35 ILCS 5/505(a)(2); 86 Ill. Admin. Code 100.5000(a)(4); Instructions, Form IL-1065, Partnership Replacement Tax Return)

Extensions. Partnerships and LLCs classified as partnerships for income tax purposes are entitled to an automatic 6-month extension for the filing of an

Illinois partnership replacement tax return. Illinois does not require any paper or electronic filing request to obtain the extension. However, 100% of the outstanding income and replacement tax liability must be paid using Form IL-1065-V or electronically by the original due date of the return (35 ILCS 5/602(a); 86 Ill. Adm. Code 100.5020(b); Instructions, Form IL-1065-V, Payment Voucher for Partnership Replacement Tax) to avoid interest and penalties.

An additional extension beyond the initial automatic extension period will be granted if a longer federal extension has been granted by the Internal Revenue Service (IRS). The additional Illinois extension will be equal to the federal extension. (35 ILCS 5/505(b); 86 Ill. Adm. Code 100.5020(c)) A copy of the federal extension must be attached to the Illinois return when it is filed. (35 ILCS 5/505(b); 86 Ill. Adm. Code 100.5020(c))

Reporting federal changes. An amended Illinois partnership replacement tax return must be filed and additional tax paid within 120 days of any partial agreement or federal finalization notification that increases Illinois replacement tax liability for any taxable year. (35 ILCS 5/506(b); Instructions, Form IL-1065-X, Amended Partnership Replacement Tax Return) If a federal change decreases Illinois replacement tax liability and the partnership is entitled to a refund, the amended Illinois return must be filed within two years plus 120 days of the federal finalization. (Instructions, Form IL-1065-X, Amended Partnership Replacement Tax Return)

A copy of the federal finalization or proof of acceptance from the IRS, along with a copy of the amended federal return, must be attached to the amended Illinois partnership replacement tax return. (Instructions, Form IL-1065-X, Amended Partnership Replacement Tax Return) Examples of federal finalization include a copy of one or more of the following items:

— proof of the federal finalization date, including a signed and dated copy of any federal report of income tax examination changes, if applicable;

— an audit report from the IRS, including copies of preliminary, revised, corrected, and superseding reports, if applicable; and

— a federal record of account verifying ordinary business income. (Instructions, Form IL-1065-X, Amended Partnership Replacement Tax Return)

If an amended federal return decreases Illinois replacement tax liability, a copy of the federal return, including any other related forms, schedules, or attachments, must also be attached to the Illinois amended return. (Instructions, Form IL-1065-X, Amended Partnership Replacement Tax Return)

Exempt organization income and replacement tax returns. Illinois exempt organization income and replacement tax returns must be filed by:

— May 15 for calendar year organizations; or

— the 15th day of 5th month after close of the organization's fiscal year. (35 ILCS 5/505(a)(3); 86 Ill. Adm. Code 100.5000(a)(6); Instructions, Form IL-990-T, Exempt Organization Income and Replacement Tax Return)

Returns for employee trusts under IRC Sec. 401(a) are due by:

— April 15; or

— the 15th day of 4th month after the close of the fiscal year. (Instructions, Form IL-990-T, Exempt Organization Income and Replacement Tax Return)

Extensions. Automatic extensions for filing a return will be granted to exempt organizations equal to:

— 7 months for organizations classified federally as corporations or IRC Sec. 501(c) trusts; and

— 6 months for organizations classified federally as IRC Sec. 401(a) trusts. (35 ILCS 5/602(a); 86 Ill. Adm. Code 100.5020(b); Instructions, Form IL-990-T, Exempt Organization Income and Replacement Tax Return)

Illinois does not require any paper or electronic filing request to obtain the extension. However, 100% of the outstanding unrelated business income and replacement tax liability must be paid using Form IL-990-T-V or electronically by the original due date of the return (35 ILCS 5/602(a); 86 Ill. Adm. Code 100.5020(b); Instructions, Form IL-990-T-V, Payment Voucher for Exempt Organization Income and Replacement Tax) to avoid interest and penalties.

An additional extension beyond the initial automatic extension period will be granted if a longer federal extension has been granted by the Internal Revenue Service (IRS). (86 Ill. Adm. Code 100.5020(c); Instructions, Form IL-990-T, Exempt Organization Income and Replacement Tax Return) The additional Illinois extension will be equal to the federal extension, plus one month in the case of an exempt organization that is a corporation. A copy of the federal extension must be attached to the Illinois return when it is filed. (86 Ill. Adm. Code 100.5020(c); Instructions, Form IL-990-T, Exempt Organization Income and Replacement Tax Return)

Reporting federal changes. An amended Illinois exempt organization income and replacement tax return must be filed and additional tax paid within 120 days of any partial agreement or federal finalization that increases Illinois tax liability for any taxable year. If a federal change decreases Illinois tax liability and the taxpayer is entitled to a refund, the amended Illinois return must be filed within two years plus 120 days of the federal finalization. 35 ILCS 5/506(b); Instructions, (Form IL-990-T-X, Amended Exempt Organization Income and Replacement Tax Return) Proof of the federal finalization date must be attached to the amended Illinois return showing that the change was reported within 120 days of IRS acceptance (Instructions, Form IL-990-T-X, Amended Exempt Organization Income and Replacement Tax Return) to avoid penalties.

Personal income tax returns. Illinois personal income tax returns must be filed by:

— April 15 for calendar year taxpayers; or

— the 15th day of the fourth month following the close of the taxpayer's fiscal tax year. (35 ILCS 5/505(a)(2); 86 Ill. Adm. Code 100.5000(a)(1); Instructions, Form IL-1040, Illinois Individual Income Tax Return)

The final return of a deceased taxpayer must be filed by the decedent's spouse or personal representative at the time, including extensions, it would have been due if the decedent were still alive. (86 Ill. Adm. Code 100.5000)

Extensions. Individuals are entitled to an automatic 6-month extension for the filing of an Illinois personal income tax return. Illinois does not require any paper or electronic filing request to obtain the extension. However, 100% of the outstanding income tax liability must be paid using Form IL-505-I or electronically by the original due date of the return (35 ILCS 5/602(a); 86 Ill. Adm. Code 100.5020(b); Instructions, Form IL-505, Automatic Extension Payment for Individuals) to avoid interest and penalties.

An additional extension beyond the initial automatic extension period will be granted if a longer federal extension has been granted by the Internal

Revenue Service (IRS). The additional Illinois extension will be equal to the federal extension. (35 ILCS 5/505(b); 86 Ill. Adm. Code 100.5020(c); Instructions, Form IL-505, Automatic Extension Payment for Individuals) A copy of the federal extension must be attached to the Illinois return when it is filed. (35 ILCS 5/505(b); 86 Ill. Adm. Code 100.5020(c); Instructions, Form IL-505, Automatic Extension Payment for Individuals)

Taxpayers who are living or traveling outside the U.S. and Puerto Rico on the original due date of the Illinois personal income tax return are allowed an automatic 2-month extension to June 15 or the 15th day of the 6th month following the close of the taxpayer's fiscal year. If married taxpayers are filing a joint return, the extension is available if either spouse is living or traveling outside the U.S. and Puerto Rico on the original due date of the return. (35 ILCS 5/505(c))

Reporting federal changes. An amended Illinois individual income tax return must be filed and additional tax paid within 120 days of any federal finalization date that increases Illinois tax liability for any taxable year. If a federal change decreases Illinois tax liability and the taxpayer is entitled to a refund, the amended Illinois return must be filed within two years plus 120 days of the federal finalization notification. (35 ILCS 5/506(b); Instructions, Form IL-1040-X, Amended Individual Income Tax Return) A copy of the federal amended return and proof of federal finalization must be attached to the return. (Instructions, Form IL-1040-X, Amended Individual Income Tax Return) Proof of federal finalization includes:

— a copy of the refund check or the check for tax payment;

— a federal record of account; or

— a copy of the federal agreement or judgment. (Instructions, Form IL-1040-X, Amended Individual Income Tax Return)

Fiduciary income and replacement tax returns. Illinois fiduciary income and replacement tax returns must be filed by:

— April 15 for calendar year estates or trusts; or

— the 15th day of 4th month after the close of estate's or trust's fiscal year. (35 ILCS 5/505(a)(2); 86 Ill. Adm. Code 100.5000(a)(5); Instructions, Form IL-1041, Fiduciary Income and Replacement Tax Return)

Extensions. Fiduciaries are entitled to an automatic 6-month extension for the filing of an Illinois fiduciary income and replacement tax return. Illinois does not require any paper or electronic filing request to obtain the extension. However, 100% of the outstanding income and replacement tax liability must be paid using Form IL-1041-V or electronically by the original due date of the return (35 ILCS 5/602(a); 86 Ill. Adm. Code 100.5020(b); Instructions, Form IL-1041-V, Payment Voucher for Fiduciary Income and Replacement Tax) to avoid interest and penalties.

An additional extension beyond the initial automatic extension period will be granted if a longer federal extension has been granted by the Internal Revenue Service (IRS). The additional Illinois extension will be equal to the federal extension. A copy of the federal extension must be attached to the Illinois return when it is filed. (35 ILCS 5/505(b); 86 Ill. Adm. Code 100.5020(c))

Reporting federal changes. An amended Illinois fiduciary income and replacement tax return must be filed and additional tax paid within 120 days of any federal finalization date that increases Illinois tax liability for any taxable year. If a federal change decreases Illinois tax liability and the taxpayer is entitled to a refund, the amended Illinois return must be filed within two years plus 120 days of the federal finalization notification. (35 ILCS 5/506(b); Instructions, Form 1041-X, Amended Fiduciary Income and Replacement Tax Return) A copy of the federal amended return and proof of federal finalization must be attached to the return. (Instructions, Form 1041-X, Amended Fiduciary Income and Replacement Tax Return) Proof of federal finalization include:

— proof of the federal finalization date, including a signed and dated copy of any federal report of income tax examination changes, if applicable;

— an audit report from the IRS, including copies of preliminary, revised, corrected, and superseding reports, if applicable; and

— a federal record of account verifying federal taxable income. (Instructions, Form 1041-X, Amended Fiduciary Income and Replacement Tax Return)

Withholding income tax returns. All withholding taxpayers must file quarterly returns by the last day of April, July, and October, of the current calendar year, and January of the following year. (35 ILCS 5/704A(b); 86 Ill. Adm. Code 100.7325(a); Publication 131, Withholding Income Tax Payment and Filing Requirements, Illinois Department of Revenue; *Informational Bulletin FY 2017-07*, Illinois Department of Revenue, September 26, 2016)

Taxpayers who are required to withhold income tax for household domestic employees may elect to report and pay the tax annually when filing their Illinois personal income tax return. (35 ILCS 5/704A(e); 86 Ill. Adm. Code 100.7325(d)(2); 86 Ill. Adm. Code 100.7350; Publication 121, Illinois Income Tax Withholding for Household Employees)

Employers must provide employees, on or before January 31 of the succeeding year, a wage statement, Form W-2, showing the total compensation paid during the preceding year and the amount of tax deducted and withheld. (35 ILCS 5/703; 86 Ill. Adm. Code 100.7200) Payroll providers and employers with 250 or more employees must transmit W-2s electronically using the same format as that required by the Social Security Administration (MMREF format). (86 Ill. Adm. Code 100.7300(b)(2); Publication 110, Form W-2 Requirements, Illinois Department of Revenue) All original W-2s must be accepted as filed by the Illinois Department of Revenue no later than January 31 after the close of the calendar year. (Publication 110, Form W-2 Requirements, Illinois Department of Revenue)

Sales and use tax. Form ST-1 must be filed on or before the 20th day of the month following the reporting period, although a quarterly filing period can be assigned based on average monthly liability. (Instructions, Form ST-1, Sales and Use Tax and E911 Surcharge Return)

Form ST-44 must be filed on or before April 15 if the total tax liability is less than $600. Otherwise, the form must be filed on the last day of the month following the month in which the purchase was made. (Use Tax Information and Instructions for Form ST-44)

How and when are tax payments made?

Tax payments must be made at the same time as the return due date (35 ILCS 5/601(a)) for the following Illinois taxes:

— corporation income and replacement tax;

— small business corporation replacement tax;

— partnership replacement tax;

— exempt organization income and replacement tax;

— personal income tax; and

— fiduciary income and replacement tax.

Withholding income tax payments. Illinois assigns all withholding taxpayers to a monthly or semi-weekly payment schedule. (*Informational Bulletin FY 2017-07*, Illinois Department of Revenue, September 26, 2016)

Semi-weekly payments. Each employer who withheld or was required to withhold more than $12,000 during the one year look-back period ending on June 30 of the immediately preceding calendar year, must pay withholding tax electronically:

— on or before each Friday of the calendar year, for taxes withheld or required to be withheld on the immediately preceding Saturday, Sunday, Monday, or Tuesday; or

— on or before each Wednesday of the calendar year, for taxes withheld or required to be withheld on the immediately preceding Wednesday, Thursday, or Friday. (35 ILCS 5/704A(c); 86 Ill. Adm. Code 100.7300(d)(1); 86 Ill. Adm. Code 100.7310(b)(2); 86 Ill. Adm. Code 100.7325(c); Publication 131, Withholding Income Tax Payment and Filing Requirements, Illinois Department of Revenue)

Monthly payments. Employers that have been registered less than 18 months, or have a compliance problem and reported more than $1,000 but no more than $12,000 in withholding during the look-back period must pay by the 15th of each month for amounts withheld on the previous month. (35 ILCS 5/704A(c)(3); 86 Ill. Adm. Code 100.7300(d)(2); 86 Ill. Adm. Code 100.7325(b); Publication 131, Withholding Income Tax Payment and Filing Requirements, Illinois Department of Revenue)

Sales and use tax. Sales tax must be paid on or before the 20th day of the month following the reporting period, although a quarterly filing period can be assigned based on average monthly liability. (Instructions, Form ST-1, Sales and Use Tax and E911 Surcharge Return)

Use tax must be paid on or before April 15 if the total tax liability is less than $600. Otherwise, the tax must be paid on the last day of the month following the month in which the purchase was made. (Use Tax Information and Instructions for Form ST-44)

Where else can I find further information on returns and payments in Illinois?

Additional information relating to Illinois returns and payments is provided in the discussions of:

— estimated tax returns and payments;

— electronic filing;

— electronic funds transfer (EFT) and other payment methods;

— mailing rules and legal holidays;

— limitations periods for audits and assessments; and

— interest rates and penalties;

¶89-102

[¶89-104] Estimated Payments and Returns

Note: For due date extensions and other relief related to COVID-19, see State COVID-19 (Coronavirus) Responses.

Are payments of estimated tax required?

Corporate income and replacement tax. Corporations, other than S corporations, that reasonably expect to have Illinois income and replacement tax liability exceeding $400, after Illinois tax credits and withholding payments made on the corporation's behalf, must pay estimated tax. (35 ILCS 5/803(a); 86 Ill. Adm. Code Sec. 100.8000(a); Instructions, Form IL-1120-V, Payment Voucher for Corporation Income and Replacement Tax)

A unitary business group filing a combined report is treated as one taxpayer for estimated tax purposes. Accordingly, payments of estimated tax are made on a combined basis. (86 Ill. Adm. Code Sec. 100.5230)

Pass-through entity income and replacement tax. S corporations, partnerships, limited liability companies (LLCs) classified as partnerships for income tax purposes, and fiduciaries may, but are not required, to pay estimated Illinois income and/or replacement tax liability. (35 ILCS 5/803(a); 86 Ill. Adm. Code Sec. 100.8000(a); Instructions, Form IL-1120-ST, Small Business Corporation Replacement Tax Return; Instructions, Form IL-1065, Partnership Replacement Tax Return; Instructions, Form IL-1041, Fiduciary Income and Replacement Tax Return)

Pass-through entity income and replacement tax withholding. Income and replacement tax must be withheld and paid for nonresident partners, shareholders, and beneficiaries that receive Illinois business income from S corporations, partnerships, LLCs, trusts, and estates. (35 ILCS 5/709.5; 86 Ill. Adm. Code Sec. 100.7035; *Informational Bulletin FY 2009-02, Pass-through Entity Payments*, Illinois Department of Revenue)

Exemptions and waivers. Pass-through entity withholding payments are required for all nonresident owners, except:

— publicly traded partnerships or investment partnerships; (35 ILCS 5/709.5(a)) and

— non-individual owners that document to the pass-through entity on Form IL-1000-E that the owner will file an Illinois income tax return and pay the tax. (35 ILCS 5/709.5(c); 86 Ill. Adm. Code Sec. 100.7035(g); *Informational Bulletin FY 2009-02, Pass-through Entity Payments*, Illinois Department of Revenue; Instructions, Form IL-1000-E, Certificate of Exemption for Pass-through Entity Payments)

The exemption certificate must be signed by the owner, officer, fiduciary, or authorized representative (Instructions, Form IL-1000-E, Certificate of Exemption for Pass-through Entity Payments) and retained by the pass-through entity. (Illinois Income Tax Act, Sec. 709.5(c)(4) 35 ILCS 5/709.5(c)(4); 86 Ill. Adm. Code Sec. 100.7035(h)(2)) The exemption certificate must only be completed, signed, and submitted once to the pass-through entity. It does not need to be resubmitted on an annual basis. (Instructions, Form IL-1000-E, Certificate of Exemption for Pass-through Entity Payments)

If an owner that has provided a pass-through entity with an exemption certificate fails to timely file a return that reports its share of the business income apportioned to Illinois by the pass-through entity or to timely pay the tax liability shown on the return, the Illinois Department of Revenue may at any time revoke the certificate by sending a notice to the pass-through entity at its usual place of business or by mail to the entity's last-known address. The revocation is effective for all payments and returns of withholding due more than 60 days after the date of notification. (35 ILCS 5/709.5(c); 86 Ill. Adm. Code Sec. 100.7035(h)(3))

Basis of tax. S corporations, partnerships, and fiduciaries must withhold Illinois income tax on a nonresident shareholder's, partner's, or beneficiary's distributive share, whether distributed or undistributed, of ordinary income, capital gains or losses, rents, dividends, interest, royalties, guaranteed payments, Illinois addition and subtraction modifications, apportionable to the state and reported on Schedule K-1-P for partners and shareholders or Schedule K-1-T for beneficiaries. (35 ILCS 5/709.5(a); 86 Ill. Adm. Code Sec. 100.7035(a); Instructions, Schedule K-1-P(3), Pass-through Withholding Calculation for Nonresident Members; Instructions, Schedule K-1-T(3), Pass-through Withholding Calculation for Nonresident Members)

Rate of tax. The withholding income tax on nonresident corporate owners is imposed at the applicable Illinois corporation income tax rate. The tax on nonresident individuals and estates is imposed at the applicable personal income tax rate. The tax is imposed on owners that are S corporations and partnerships at the applicable replacement tax rate. Finally, the tax on owners that are nonresident trusts consists of the combined personal income and replacement tax rates. (35 ILCS 5/201(b)-(d); 35 ILCS 5/709.5(a); 86 Ill. Adm. Code Sec. 100.7035(a); Schedule K-1-P(3), Pass-through Withholding Calculation for Nonresident Members; Schedule K-1-T(3), Pass-through Withholding Calculation for Nonresident Members)

Exempt organization income and replacement tax. Exempt organizations that reasonably expect Illinois income and replacement tax liability to be more than $400 for the tax year must pay estimated tax. (35 ILCS 5/803(a); 86 Ill. Adm. Code Sec. 100.8000(a); Instructions, Form IL-990-T, Exempt Organization Income and Replacement Tax Return)

Composite income and replacement tax. Effective for tax years before 2014, S corporations, partnerships, and fiduciaries that filed an Illinois composite income and replacement tax return for eligible shareholders, partners, and trusts were allowed to pay estimated composite income and replacement tax. (Instructions, Form IL-516-I and Form IL-516-B, Pass-through Prepayment Voucher)

Personal income tax. Individuals must pay estimated tax if they reasonably expect their Illinois income tax liability to exceed $500 after subtracting withholding, pass-through withholding payments, and tax credits. (35 ILCS 5/803(a); 86 Ill. Adm. Code Sec. 100.8000(a); Instructions, Form IL-1040-ES, Estimated Income Tax Payments for Individuals) The estimated tax requirement does not apply to:

— farmers whose gross income from farming for the taxable year is at least 2/3 of total gross income for that year; or

— individuals who are 65 years of age or older and permanently resident living in a nursing home. (86 Ill. Adm. Code Sec. 100.8000(c))

Sales and use tax. A retail seller of motor fuel who is not a licensed distributor or supplier must, on its fuel purchases, prepay part of the retailers' occupation (sales) tax to its distributor, supplier, or other reseller and claim credit for the amount paid against the tax due. Liquid propane gas is excluded from the prepayment requirement.

How are payments of estimated tax made?

Corporate income and replacement tax. Estimated Illinois corporate and replacement tax liability is generally paid in four equal installments of 25% of the required annual payment. (35 ILCS 5/803(d); 35 ILCS 5/804(c)(1); 86 Ill. Adm. Code Sec. 100.8010(d)(1))

Safe harbor calculation. The "required annual payment" or safer harbor calculation to avoid an underpayment of estimated tax penalty is the lesser of:

— 90% of the tax shown on the return for the taxable year; or

— 100% (150% for installments due after January 31, 2011, and before February 1, 2012) of the tax shown on the return for the preceding taxable year. (35 ILCS 5/804(c); 86 Ill. Adm. Code Sec. 100.8010(d)(1)(A); *Informational Bulletin, FY 2011-09,* Illinois Department of Revenue)

Annualized income installment method. A taxpayer may use an annualized income installment method for purposes of determining the amount of installments due if income was not received evenly throughout the year. The annualized income installment is the excess of an amount equal to the applicable percentage of the tax for the taxable year computed by dividing the net income for months in the taxable year ending before the due date of the installment by the aggregate amount of any prior required installments for the taxable year. (35 ILCS 5/804(c); 86 Ill. Adm. Code Sec. 100.8010(d)(2))

Pass-through entity income and replacement tax. S corporations, partnerships, LLCs classified as partnerships for income tax purposes, and fiduciaries may voluntarily prepay Illinois income and/or replacement tax liability in equal installments or any other method. (Instructions, Form IL-516-I and Form IL-516-B, Pass-through Prepayment Voucher)

Pass-through entity income and replacement tax withholding. Pass-through income and replacement tax withholding payments by S corporations, partnerships, LLCs classified as partnerships for income tax purposes, and fiduciaries for nonresident shareholders, partners, members, or beneficiaries must be reported and paid annually. (35 ILCS 5/709.5(a); 86 Ill. Adm. Code Sec. 100.7035(a)) A partnership, LLC, S corporation or fiduciary may voluntarily prepay Illinois income and replacement tax withholding in installments or any other method. (Instructions, Form IL-516-I and Form IL-516-B, Pass-through Prepayment Voucher)

Exempt organization income and replacement tax. Exempt organizations must make quarterly payments of estimated Illinois income and replacement tax liability. (Instructions, Form IL-990-T, Exempt Organization Income and Replacement Tax Return)

Personal income tax. Estimated Illinois personal income tax liability is generally paid in four equal installments of 25% of the required annual payment. (35 ILCS 5/803(d); 35 ILCS 5/804(c)(1); 86 Ill. Adm. Code Sec. 100.8010(d)(1))

Safe harbor calculation. The "required annual payment" or safer harbor caculation to avoid an underpayment of estimated tax penalty is the lesser of:

— 90% of the tax shown on the return for the taxable year; or

— 100% (150% for installments due after January 31, 2011, and before February 1, 2012) of the tax shown on the return for the preceding taxable year. (35 ILCS 5/804(c); 86 Ill. Adm. Code Sec. 100.8010(d)(1)(A); *Informational Bulletin, FY 2011-09,* Illinois Department of Revenue)

If an individual taxpayer filed a joint return for the preceding taxable year, but does not file a joint return with the same spouse for the current taxable year, the individual's tax shown on the return for the preceding taxable year must be that portion of the tax shown on the joint return that bears the same ratio to the amount of the tax for which the taxpayer would have been liable had a separate return been filed for the preceding taxable year bears to the sum of the taxes for which the taxpayer and his or her spouse would have been liable had each spouse filed a separate return for the preceding taxable year. (86 Ill. Adm. Code Sec. 100.8010(d)(1)(B))

If a married couple files a joint return for the current taxable year, but did not file a joint return with each other for the preceding taxable year, the tax shown on the return for the preceding taxable year must be the sum of the taxes shown on the separate returns of each spouse for that preceding taxable year or the amount determined under 86 Ill. Adm. Code Sec. 100.8010(d)(1)(B) for each spouse that filed a joint return in the preceding taxable year. (86 Ill. Adm. Code Sec. 100.8010(d)(1)(C))

Joint Payment. If they are eligible to do so for federal tax purposes, a husband and wife may pay estimated tax as if they were one taxpayer, in which case the liability with respect to the estimated tax is joint and several. If a joint payment is made but the husband and wife elect to determine their taxes separately, the estimated tax for the year may be treated as the estimated tax of either husband or wife, or may be divided between them, as they may elect. (86 Ill. Adm. Code Sec. 100.8000(e))

If one of the spouses dies during the taxable year and joint estimated tax payments were made, but a joint return is not subsequently filed, estimated tax payments, including any joint payments made after the death of the spouse, may be divided between the decedent and the surviving spouse in the proportion to which the surviving spouse and the legal representative of the decedent may agree. The Illinois Department of Revenue will accept any allocation between the surviving spouse and the decedent, provided only that the total of the amounts allocated equals the total amount paid. In the event the surviving spouse and legal representative fail to agree, the estimated tax must be allocated between the surviving spouse and decedent in the same manner as the estimated tax of husband and wife who fail to agree to an allocation of estimated tax to separate returns. (86 Ill. Adm. Code Sec. 100.8000(e))

Annualized income installment method. A taxpayer may use an annualized income installment method for purposes of determining the amount of installments due if income was not received evenly throughout the year. The annualized income installment is the excess of an amount equal to the applicable percentage of the tax for the taxable year computed by dividing the net income for months in the taxable year ending before the due date of the installment by the aggregate amount of any prior required installments for the taxable year. (35 ILCS 5/804(c); 86 Ill. Adm. Code Sec. 100.8010(d)(2))

Sales and use tax. Every distributor, supplier, or other reseller of motor fuel registered under the Motor Fuel Tax Act must remit the sales tax prepayment collected from motor fuel retailers who are not licensed distributors or suppliers.

What are due dates for estimated tax?

Corporate income and replacement tax. Estimated Illinois income and replacement tax for corporations, other than S corporations, must be paid by:

— April 15 for calendar year taxpayers or the 15th day of the 4th month for fiscal year taxpayers;

— June 15 for calendar year taxpayers or the 15th day of the 6th month for fiscal year taxpayers;

— September 15 for calendar year taxpayers or the 15th day of the 9th month for fiscal year taxpayers; and

— December 15 for calendar year taxpayers or the 15th day of the 12th month for fiscal year taxpayers. (35 ILCS 5/803(d) and (g); 86 Ill. Adm. Code Sec. 100.8010(c)(1))

Pass-through entity income and replacement tax. There are no required due dates for S corporations, partnerships, LLCs classified as partnerships for income tax purposes, and fiduciaries that voluntarily prepay Illinois income and/or replacement tax liability. (Instructions, Form IL-516-I and Form IL-516-B, Pass-through Prepayment Voucher) However, the Illinois Department of Revenue suggests the following prepayment schedule:

— April 15 for calendar year taxpayers or the 15th day of the 4th month for fiscal year taxpayers;

— June 15 for calendar year taxpayers or the 15th day of the 6th month for fiscal year taxpayers;

— September 15 for calendar year taxpayers or the 15th day of the 9th month for fiscal year taxpayers; and

— January 15 of the following year for calendar year taxpayers or the 15th day of the 1st month of the following year for fiscal year taxpayers. (Instructions, Form IL-516-I and Form IL-516-B, Pass-through Prepayment Voucher)

Pass-through entity income and replacement tax withholding. Pass-through income and replacement withholding tax payments for nonresident shareholders, partners, members, or beneficiaries must be reported and paid annually by the original due date of the pass-through entity's Illinois:

— small business corporation replacement tax return;

— partnership replacement tax return; or

— fiduciary income and replacement tax.

There are no required due dates for S corporations, partnerships, LLCs classified as partnerships for income tax purposes, and fiduciaries that voluntarily prepay Illinois income and replacement withholding tax. (Instructions, Form IL-516-I and Form IL-516-B, Pass-through Prepayment Voucher) However, the Illinois Department of Revenue suggests the following prepayment schedule:

— April 15 for calendar year taxpayers or the 15th day of the 4th month for fiscal year taxpayers;

— June 15 for calendar year taxpayers or the 15th day of the 6th month for fiscal year taxpayers;

— September 15 for calendar year taxpayers or the 15th day of the 9th month for fiscal year taxpayers; and

— January 15 of the following year for calendar year taxpayers or the 15th day of the 1st month of the following year for fiscal year taxpayers. (Instructions, Form IL-516-I and Form IL-516-B, Pass-through Prepayment Voucher)

Exempt organization income and replacement tax. Exempt organizations must pay estimated Illinois income and replacement tax according to the same installment schedule as estimated corporate income and replacement tax liability. (Instructions, Form IL-990-T, Exempt Organization Income and Replacement Tax Return)

Personal income tax. Estimated Illinois personal income tax must be paid by:

— April 15 for calendar year taxpayers or the 15th day of the 4th month for fiscal year taxpayers;

— June 15 for calendar year taxpayers or the 15th day of the 6th month for fiscal year taxpayers;

— September 15 for calendar year taxpayers or the 15th day of the 9th month for fiscal year taxpayers; and

— January 15 of the following year for calendar year taxpayers or the 15th day of the 1st month of the following year for fiscal year taxpayers. (35 ILCS 5/803(d) and (g); 86 Ill. Adm. Code Sec. 100.8010(c)(1))

Sales and use tax. A distributor or supplier collecting prepaid tax must deliver a statement of tax paid to each purchaser and remit tax to the Department of Revenue not later than the 20th day of the month following the month the transaction occurred.

What forms are required for filing estimated tax?

Corporate income and replacement tax. Estimated Illinois corporate income and replacement tax must be reported and paid using Form IL-1120-V, (Instructions, Form IL-1120-V, Payment Voucher for Corporation Income and Replacement Tax) except certain taxpayers must pay the tax by electronic funds transfer.

Pass-through entity income and replacement tax. S corporations, partnerships, LLCs classified as partnerships for income tax purposes, and fiduciaries can voluntarily pay estimated Illinois income and/or replacement tax liability using:

— Form IL-1120-ST-V for payments by S corporations; (Instructions, Form IL-1120-ST, Small Business Corporation Replacement Tax Return)

— Form IL-1065-V for payments by partnerships; (Instructions, Form IL-1065, Partnership Replacement Tax Return) and

— Form IL-1041-V for payments by fiduciaries. (Instructions, Form IL-1041, Fiduciary Income and Replacement Tax Return)

Pass-through entity income and replacement tax withholding. Illinois pass-through income and replacement withholding payments for nonresident shareholders, partners, members, and beneficiaries are computed on:

— Schedule K-1-P(3) for withholding by S corporations, partnerships, and LLCs classified as partnerships; (Instructions for Partnerships and S Corporations Completing Schedule K-1-P and Schedule K-1-P(3)) or

— Schedule K-1-T(3) for withholding by fiduciaries. (Instructions for Trusts and Estates Completing Schedule K-1-T and Schedule K-1-T(3))

Pass-through income and replacement withholding payments must be reported to nonresident shareholders, partners, members, and beneficiaries on:

— Schedule K-1-P for nonresident shareholders, partners, and members; (Instructions for Partnerships and S Corporations Completing Schedule K-1-P and Schedule K-1-P(3))

— Schedule K-1-T for nonresident beneficiaries. (Instructions for Trusts and Estates Completing Schedule K-1-T and Schedule K-1-T(3))

Pass-through entity's must:

— keep a copy of the withholding computation and reporting schedules for inspection by Illinois Department of Revenue agents and employees, and

— attach any reporting schedule issued by another partnership, S corporation, trust or estate to the pass-through entity's Illinois return. (Instructions for Partnerships and S Corporations Completing Schedule K-1-P and Schedule K-1-P(3); Instructions for Trusts and Estates Completing Schedule K-1-T and Schedule K-1-T(3))

Pass-through income and replacement withholding payments must be reported to the Department of Revenue with the pass-through entity's Illinois return:

— Form IL-1120-ST; (Instructions, Form IL-1120-ST, Small Business Corporation Replacement Tax Return)

— Form IL-1065; (Instructions, Form IL-1065, Partnership Replacement Tax Return) or

— IL-Form 1041. (Instructions, Form IL-1041, Fiduciary Income and Replacement Tax Return)

Pass-through income and replacement withholding tax must be paid with:

— the pass-through entity's return;

— extension payments; or

— voluntarily prepaid. (Instructions, Form IL-1120-ST, Small Business Corporation Replacement Tax Return; Instructions, Form IL-1065, Partnership Replacement Tax Return; Instructions, Form IL-1041, Fiduciary Income and Replacement Tax Return)

Taxpayers making an extension payment or a voluntary prepayment of their tax liabilities must use:

— Form IL-1120-ST-V for payments by S corporations; (Instructions, Form IL-1120-ST, Small Business Corporation Replacement Tax Return)

— Form IL-1065-V for payments by partnerships; (Instructions, Form IL-1065, Partnership Replacement Tax Return) and

— Form IL-1041-V for payments by fiduciaries. (Instructions, Form IL-1041, Fiduciary Income and Replacement Tax Return)

Exempt organization income and replacement tax. Exempt organizations must report and pay Illinois estimated income and replacement tax using Form IL-990-T-V. (Instructions, Form IL-990-T-V, Payment Voucher for Exempt Organization Income and Replacement Tax)

Personal income tax. Estimated Illinois personal income tax must be reported and paid using Form IL-1040-ES. (Instructions, Form IL-1040-ES, Estimated Income Tax Payments for Individuals)

Sales and use tax. Form PST-1, Prepaid Sales Tax Return, and Form PST-2, Prepaid Sales Tax Statement of Tax Paid, are required for filing the prepayments. (Instructions, Form PST-1, Prepaid Sales Tax Return)

Where can I find other information on estimated tax payments and returns?

Additional information relating to Illinois returns and payments is provided in the discussions of:

— returns and payments in general;

— electronic filing;

— electronic funds transfer (EFT) and other payment methods;

— mailing rules and legal holidays; and

— interest rates and penalties;

[¶89-106] Electronic Filing

The Department of Revenue authorizes the electronic filing of various tax returns. Electronic payment methods are also available or required for a variety of Illinois taxes. (see ¶89-108)

•*General requirements and procedures*

Enrollment.—All participants that file electronically or on magnetic media, except Electronic Return Originators and transmitters approved in the IRS Electronic Filing Program, must complete and submit an enrollment form with the Department. (86 Ill. Adm. Code 760.210)

Electronic signature.—Taxpayers must select an electronic signature, which will be used in lieu of a written signature when filing electronic returns, forms, or other documents. (86 Ill. Adm. Code 760.230)

The Department will normally acknowledge its receipt of an electronically transmitted return or payment within 24 hours. (86 Ill. Adm. Code 760.310; 86 Ill. Adm. Code 760.320)

Electronic payment.—Taxpayers who voluntarily choose to electronically file returns and other documents with the Department must make any required payments relating to those returns or documents through electronic means. (86 Ill. Adm. Code 760.220) Several electronic payment methods are available. (see ¶89-108)

Other requirements.—Electronic filers must comply with various requirements regarding timeliness, confidentiality, and recordkeeping. (86 Ill. Adm. Code 760.300)

•*C and S corporation income tax returns*

Illinois participates in the federal Modernized e-File (MeF) Program. (*Implementation Guide for Business Income Tax Federal/State Electronic Filing Program* Illinois Department of Revenue, January 2013) Participation in the program is open to software developers, transmitters, electronic return originators, and taxpayers using the services of approved electronic filers. (86 Ill. Adm. Code 760.200; *Implementation Guide for Business Income Tax Federal/State Electronic Filing Program* Illinois Department of Revenue, January 2013)

Mandates and options.—Beginning with returns for taxable years ending on or after December 31, 2011, any corporation or S corporation that is required to file its federal income tax return by electronic means is required to file its equivalent Illinois corporation income tax return or small business corporation replacement tax return for the same taxable year by electronic means. (86 Ill. Adm. Code 760.100(c)(4);

Implementation Guide for Business Income Tax Federal/State Electronic Filing Program, Illinois Department of Revenue, January 2013)

Waiver or taxpayer opt-out.—Illinois does not provide procedures for taxpayers to opt-out or request a waiver from the electronic filing mandate. (86 Ill. Adm. Code 760.100(c)(4); *Implementation Guide for Business Income Tax Federal/State Electronic Filing Program,* Illinois Department of Revenue, January 2013)

Forms and Schedules.—Illinois accepts the following forms through the MeF program:

— Form IL-1120, including unitary filings, and supporting schedules;

— Form IL-1120-ST, excluding unitary filings, and supporting schedules.

(*Implementation Guide for Business Income Tax Federal/State Electronic Filing Program,* Illinois Department of Revenue, January 2013)

Penalties.—Illinois does not impose a penalty on taxpayers or tax return preparers that fail or refuse to comply with the electronic filing mandate that is separate from other Illinois tax penalties. (*Implementation Guide for Business Income Tax Federal/State Electronic Filing Program,* Illinois Department of Revenue, January 2013)

Extension requests.—Illinois does not require the filing of either paper or electronic extension requests. (86 Ill. Adm. Code 100.5020(b))

• *Partnership, LLPs and LLC replacement tax returns*

Illinois participates in the federal Modernized e-File Program. (*Implementation Guide for Business Income Tax Federal/State Electronic Filing Program* Illinois Department of Revenue, January 2013) Participation in the program is open to software developers, transmitters, electronic return originators, and taxpayers using the services of approved electronic filers. (86 Ill. Adm. Code 760.200; *Implementation Guide for Business Income Tax Federal/State Electronic Filing Program* Illinois Department of Revenue, January 2013)

Mandates and options.—Beginning with returns for taxable years ending on or after December 31, 2011, any partnership, limited liability partnership(LLP), or limited liability company (LLC) classified as partnership for federal income tax purposes, that is required to file its federal income tax return by electronic means is required to file its equivalent Illinois partnership return for the same taxable year by electronic means. (86 Ill. Adm. Code 760.100(c)(4); *Implementation Guide for Business Income Tax Federal/State Electronic Filing Program,* Illinois Department of Revenue, January 2013)

Waiver or taxpayer opt-out.—Illinois does not provide procedures for taxpayers to opt-out or request a waiver from the electronic filing mandate. (86 Ill. Adm. Code 760.100(c)(4); *Implementation Guide for Business Income Tax Federal/State Electronic Filing Program,* Illinois Department of Revenue, January 2013)

Forms and Schedules.—Illinois accepts Form IL-1065, excluding unitary filings, and supporting schedules through the MeF program. (*Implementation Guide for Business Income Tax Federal/State Electronic Filing Program,* Illinois Department of Revenue, January 2013)

Penalties.—Illinois does not impose a penalty on taxpayers or tax return preparers that fail or refuse to comply with the electronic filing mandate that is separate from other Illinois tax penalties. (*Implementation Guide for Business Income Tax Federal/State Electronic Filing Program,* Illinois Department of Revenue, January 2013)

Extension requests.—Illinois does not require the filing of either paper or electronic extension requests. (86 Ill. Adm. Code 100.5020(b))

• *Individual income tax returns*

The Illinois Department of Revenue (IDOR), in conjunction with the Internal Revenue Service (IRS), accepts electronically filed individual income tax returns as part of the IRS Modernized e-File (MeF) Program. Participation in the program is open to software developers, transmitters, electronic return originators, and taxpayers using the services of approved electronic filers. (86 Ill. Adm. Code 760.200)

Mandates and options.—Beginning with taxable years after 2011, individual income tax return preparers who are required to file a federal income tax return by electronic means (i.e., preparers who file more than 10 returns in a calendar year) are required to file an Illinois individual income tax return by electronic means. This does not require electronic filing of amended returns. (86 Ill. Adm. Code 760.100(c)(4)) The electronic filng mandate for 2011 tax year applied to tax return preparers who were required to file any federal income tax return by electronic means and who prepared more than 100 Illinois income tax returns for individuals during the preceding calendar year. (86 Ill. Adm. Code 760.100(c)(3); 86 Ill. Adm. Code 760.100)

Waiver or taxpayer opt-out.—Illinois taxpayers may opt-out of the individual income tax electronic filing mandate by completing and signing Form IL-8948, Electronic Filing Opt-Out Declaration. Preparers must retain the opt-out form for three years. (Instructions, Form IL-8948, Electronic Filing Opt-Out Declaration)

Forms and Schedules.—Illinois residents, part-year residents, and non residents may e-file Form IL-1040 and supporting schedules through the MeF program. (86 Ill. Adm. Code 105.100)

Extension requests.—Illinois does not require the filing of either paper or electronic extension requests. (86 Ill. Adm. Code 100.5020(b))

Penalties.—Illinois does not impose a penalty on taxpayers or tax return preparers that fail or refuse to comply with the electronic filing mandate that is separate from other Illinois tax penalties.

Online filing.—Illinois no longer allows the option of filing personal income tax returns through TeleFile. However, *MyTax Illinois*, will be available to personal income taxpayers and tax professionals beginning September 30, 2013, which can be used to:

— file and view an individual income tax return, Form IL-1040, and all supporting schedules;

— print a copy of a tax return;

— view correspondence received from the Illinois Department of Revenue; and

— view Illinois 1099-G information, which is the notification sent to taxpayers who have a refund that the taxpayer may be required to report as income to the Internal Revenue Service.

(*Informational Bulletin FY 2014-02*, Illinois Department of Revenue, September 2013)

MyTax Illinois is available for use by nonresidents, part-year residents, and taxpayers who are in a civil union. Individuals who do not have a valid Illinois driver's license or state identification card and who have not previously filed an Illinois income tax return cannot use *MyTax Illinois*. Master users can grant access rights to secondary and third-party users. (*Informational Bulletin FY 2014-02,* Illinois Department of Revenue, September 2013)

Functions such as viewing correspondence will require a MyTax Illinois account user name and password. Access to the Illinois WebFile application for individual income taxpayers will no longer be available. (*Informational Bulletin FY 2014-02,* Illinois Department of Revenue, September 2013)

MyTax Illinois can also be used by employers for electronic return filing of Illinois personal income withholding tax effective July 1, 2013. The current WebFile application for withholding income tax will not be available after June 30, 2013. (*Informational Bulletin FY 2013-14,* Illinois Department of Revenue, May 2013)

• *Fiduciary returns*

Illinois does not allow electronic filing for fiduciary returns through the Modernized e-File (MeF) Program. (86 Ill. Adm. Code 760.100(c)(4)) However, electronic filing of income and replacement tax returns by fiduciaries will be allowed effective July 1, 2013 through *MyTax Illinois,* an online account management program. (*Informational Bulletin FY 2013-14,* Illinois Department of Revenue, May 2013)

• *Other electronic filing programs*

The Department has mandatory and voluntary electronic filing programs for certain tax returns and other documents. (86 Ill. Adm. Code 760.100) Some types of returns and documents are excluded from electronic filing. (86 Ill. Adm. Code 760.110)

Telecommunications excise tax returns.—Beginning January 1, 2003, telecommunications providers who have average monthly tax billings for the preceding calendar year that exceed $1000 must file their tax returns and supporting schedules electronically. (86 Ill. Adm. Code 760.100)

Cigarette distributors.—Beginning January 1, 2003, cigarette distributors with 30 or more invoice transactions per month are required to file supporting schedule data on computer-generated magnetic media in a format prescribed by the Department. (86 Ill. Adm. Code 760.100)

Sales and use tax.—Taxpayers may file forms ST-1 (Sales and Use Tax Return) and ST-2 (Multiple Site Form) electronically on a voluntary basis. (86 Ill. Adm. Code 760.100)

Cigarette taxes.—Beginning January 1, 2003, original or amended cigarette tax returns and schedules may be filed electronically on a voluntary basis. (86 Ill. Adm. Code 760.100)

Alcoholic beverage taxes.—Manufacturers and importing distributors may file liquor taxes electronically on a voluntary basis. The manufacturer and importing distributor will receive a discount of 1.75% or $1,250, whichever is less, on the tax due for the expenses incurred in keeping and maintaining records, preparing and filing the electronic returns, remitting the tax, and supplying data to the Department. (235 ILCS 5/8-2; 86 Ill. Adm. Code 760.100)

• *Chicago tax returns—2016*

Beginning January 1, 2016, the City of Chicago generally requires that tax return filings and payment of taxes be made through the website of the city Department of Finance (department). All transfer tax declarations must be made through MyDec. The electronic filing mandate does not apply to the sale of stamps, stickers, and decals; the automatic amusement device tax; or the cigarette tax. In an ordinance ruling, the department discusses web-based applications for real property transfer declarations and other city taxes; use of city computers; late filing and payment penalties; and waiver of the mandatory web filing requirement. (*Uniform Revenue Procedures Ordinance Ruling #5*, Chicago Department of Finance, December 8, 2015)

[¶89-108] Payment Methods

Tax payments can be made by check or money order, electronic funds transfer, direct debit, or credit card.

For a discussion relating to payment methods for property tax, see ¶20-756.

• *Electronic funds transfer (EFT)*

Payment can be made through electronic funds transfer (EFT, however, the requirements for mandatory EFTs differ for from tax to tax).

Mandatory EFT.—Electronic payments are now required for most Illinois taxpayers who have an annual tax liability of $20,000 or more and more than $12,000 for withholding income tax, beginning January 1, 2011. (*Informational Bulletin FY 2011-01*, Illinois Department of Revenue, July 2010)

Corporate income and personal income taxes: Beginning October 1, 2010, a taxpayer, other than an individual taxpayer, that has an annual tax liability of $20,000 or more and an individual taxpayer who has an annual tax liability of $200,000 or more must make all payments by EFT. The term "annual tax liability" means, for a taxpayer that incurs an Illinois income tax liability, the greater of the amount of the taxpayer's withholding tax liability for the immediately preceding calendar year or the taxpayer's estimated tax payment obligation for the immediately preceding calendar year. (Civil Administrative Code of Illinois-(Department of Revenue Law), Sec. 2505-210 [20 ILCS 2505/2505-210])

Prior to October 1, 2010, a taxpayer who had an annual income tax liability of $200,000 or more was required to make all payments of that tax to the Department by electronic funds transfer (EFT). (Civil Administrative Code of Illinois-(Department of Revenue Law), Sec. 2505-210 [20 ILCS 2505/2505-210]; Illinois Income Tax Act, Sec. 601.1 [35 ILCS 5/601.1]; 86 Ill. Adm. Code 750.300)

Service groups or other agents of taxpayers are allowed to submit on behalf of such taxpayers authorization agreements to make tax payments through the use of EFT. All service groups and agents submitting authorization agreements are required to retain in their books and records a valid Power of Attorney for Electronic Processing for each such taxpayer. (86 Ill. Adm. Code 750.400)

For employer's return and payment of tax withheld, all semi-weekly payments must be made by EFT beginning with calendar year 2011. (Illinois Income Tax Act, Sec. 704A(c)(1)(B) [35 ILCS 5/704A(c)(1)(B)])

Sales and use tax: A taxpayer who has an annual state and local occupation (sales) and use tax liability of $20,000 or more must make all payments of that tax to the Department by electronic funds transfer (EFT). The term "annual tax liability" means the sum of the taxpayer's liability reported on that taxpayer's Form ST-1, Sales and Use Tax Return. (*Informational Bulletin FY 2011-01*, Illinois Department of Revenue; Use Tax Act, Sec. 9 [35 ILCS 105/9]; Service Use Tax Act, Sec. 9 [35 ILCS 110/9]; Service Occupation Tax Act, Sec. 9 [35 ILCS 115/9]; Retailers' Occupation Tax Act, Sec. 120 [35 ILCS 120/3]; 86 Ill. Adm. Code 750.300) Prior to October 2010, the annual liability requirement was $200,000.

Cigarette taxes: A tobacco products distributor who has an annual tobacco products tax liability of $20,000 or more in the preceding calendar year must pay for its cigarette revenue tax stamps by electronic funds transfer (EFT). (*Informational Bulletin FY 2011-01*, Illinois Department of Revenue) Prior to October 2010, the annual liability requirement was $200,000.

Also, each distributor who pays for cigarette tax stamps with a postdated draft must pay for the draft by EFT. (Cigarette Tax Act, Sec. 3 [35 ILCS 130/3]; 86 Ill. Adm. Code 750.300) Distributors who purchase cigarette tax stamps using EFT must pay for their purchases using the ACH debit method rather than the ACH credit method. ACH debits initiated via electronic data transfer (modem-to-modem) must be acknowledged as accepted before 12:00 p.m. (noon-central time) on the last business banking day prior to the due date of the payment. (86 Ill. Adm. Code 750.600)

Liquor taxes: A taxpayer who has an annual alcoholic beverage tax liability of $20,000 or more in the preceding calendar year must make all payments of that tax by electronic funds transfer. (*Informational Bulletin FY 2011-01*, Illinois Department of Revenue; Liquor Control Act of 1934, Sec. 8-2 [235 ILCS 5/8-2]; 86 Ill. Adm. Code 750.300) Prior to October 2010, the annual liability requirement was $200,000.

Telecommunications taxes: A taxpayer who has an average monthly tax liability of $1,000 or more for telecommunications excise tax and simplified municipal telecommunications tax in the preceding calendar year must make all payments of those taxes by electronic funds transfer. (*Informational Bulletin FY 2011-01*, Illinois Department of Revenue; 86 Ill. Adm. Code 750.300)

Other taxes: Payments of Illinois electricity excise tax, hotel operators' occupation tax, and soft drink tax must be made by electronic funds transfer if the taxpayer has an annual tax liability of $20,000 or more for that tax in the preceding calendar year. (86 Ill. Adm. Code 750.300) Prior to October 2010, the annual liability requirement was $200,000.

Voluntary EFT.—Taxpayers who are not required to pay taxes by electronic funds transfer may apply to voluntarily participate in the electronic funds transfer program. A regulation lists the taxes and fees for which the Department accepts voluntary electronic funds transfer payments. (86 Ill. Adm. Code 750.500)

• *MyTax Illinois*

Corporate income and replacement tax.—*MyTax Illinois* will provide taxpayers an online account management program, effective on July 1, 2013, for the following:

— electronic payment of Illinois income and replacement tax for corporations, S corporations, partnerships and limited liability companies (LLCs), fiduciaries, and exempt organizations; and

— electronic payment of Illinois composite income and replacement tax for pass-through entities. (*Informational Bulletin FY 2013-14*, Illinois Department of Revenue, May 2013)

Personal income tax.—Electronic return payment of Illinois personal income withholding tax by employers using the *MyTax Illinois* account management system will be available beginning on July 1, 2013. (*Informational Bulletin FY 2013-14*, Illinois Department of Revenue, May 2013)

The *MyTax Illinois* account management system will be available to personal income taxpayers and tax professionals beginning September 30, 2013 and can be used to:

— schedule, view, and change electronic payments, including estimated payments, extension payments, and balance due payments;

— look up an Illinois Personal Identification Number (IL-PIN);

— view correspondence received from the Illinois Department of Revenue; and

— view account information, including refund information and balances. (*Informational Bulletin FY 2014-02*, Illinois Department of Revenue, September 2013)

MyTax Illinois is available for use by nonresidents, part-year residents, and taxpayers who are in a civil union. Master users can grant access rights to secondary and third-party users. (*Informational Bulletin FY 2014-02*, Illinois Department of Revenue, September 2013)

Functions such as viewing correspondence and making estimated and extension payments will require a MyTax Illinois account user name and password. (*Informational Bulletin FY 2014-02*, Illinois Department of Revenue, September 2013)

• *Credit card*

Taxpayers filing their individual income tax returns electronically may pay any balance due by credit card. (Illinois Income Tax Act, Sec. 605 [35 ILCS 5/605]; 86 Ill. Adm. Code 107.300)

Taxpayers not filing electronically may pay any balance due by credit card by calling 1-800-272-9829 or access www.officialpayments.com on the Internet. (Instructions, Form IL-1040, Illinois Individual Income Tax Return)

MasterCard, American Express, and Discover are the only credit cards accepted. An additional convenience fee will be assessed to the taxpayer's credit card account by the credit card processor. (Illinois Income Tax Act, Sec. 605 [35 ILCS 5/605]; Instructions, Form IL-1040, Illinois Individual Income Tax Return)

Operators of Illinois drycleaning facilities can pay their license application fees with a credit card only if the credit card issuer does not require the Department of Revenue to pay a discount fee. (DryCleaner Environmental Response Trust Fund Act, Sec. 60 [415 ILCS 135/60])

The Department of Revenue may not adopt rules and regulations for payment by credit card of any amount due if the department must pay a discount fee charged by the credit card issuer. (Civil Administrative Code of Illinois-(Department of Revenue Law), Sec. 2505-255 [20 ILCS 2505/2505-255])

• *Checks or money orders*

While taxpayers can pay liabilities by check or money order, a $25 bad check penalty may be assess for checks and other drafts that are not honored by the financial institution from which it was drawn. (35 ILCS 735/3-7.5) Any payment to the Illinois Department of Revenue that is made by check or money order that is not payable to the department must, within 15 days after receipt, be returned to the taxpayer or, if the amount of payment equals the amount owed to Illinois, the department may deposit the check. (35 ILCS 5/604)

• *Direct debit*

Only personal income tax taxpayers with a personal identification number (PIN) can make direct debit payments. PINs can be found above the taxpayer's name located on the pre-printed label in the tax booklet mailed to the taxpayer. In addition, a PIN can be obtained by calling 1-800-732-8866 or by accessing the online IL-PIN inquiry system.

• *City of Chicago*

Business owners may pay city of Chicago taxes online at www.cityofchicago.org, the Department of Finance Electronic Tax Filing and Payment site. Taxpayers will need to enter their account number and PIN number, mailed with their tax return, in order to participate.

[¶89-110] Mailing Rules and Legal Holidays

Returns and payments transmitted by U.S. mail are deemed filed on the date shown by the postmark stamp. If the due date of a return falls on a Saturday, Sunday, or legal holiday, the return is timely if it is filed on the first day following the due date that is not a Saturday, Sunday, or legal holiday. (Statute on Statues, Sec. 1.11 [5 ILCS 70/1.11]; Statute on Statues, Sec. 1.25 [5 ILCS 70/1.25])

[¶89-130]

AUDITS

[¶89-132] Audits in General

The tax laws administered by the Department of Revenue require taxpayers to self-assess the amount of tax they owe. The purpose of the Department audit program is to promote voluntary compliance, educate taxpayers to correctly file required returns, collect deficiencies, and facilitate refunds. Illinois has no general administrative provisions governing audit procedures; rather the audit provisions are distinguished according to tax type.

Illinois became an associate member of the Multistate Tax Compact in 1996. The compact, a document to which states may subscribe in the interest of uniform taxation of multistate corporate income, created the Multistate Tax Commission and established a joint audit program for member states.

[¶89-134] Audits by Tax Type

Illinois has specific audit provisions applicable to income tax (corporate and personal), sales and use tax, and motor fuels tax, as discussed below.

• *Income tax*

Records.—Every corporation, individual, trust, estate, and partnership liable for Illinois income tax are required to keep records, submit returns, and file notices that comply with the rules of the Department of Revenue. (Illinois Income Tax Act, Sec. 501(a) [35 ILCS 5/501(a)]) Books and records must be available for inspection by the Department during regular business hours. (Income Tax Act, Sec. 913 [35 ILCS 5/913]) Failure to keep such books and records as required is a criminal penalty. (Income Tax Act, Sec. 1301 [35 ILCS 5/1301])

Electronic records.—For taxpayers that maintain records electronically, the Department may examine the integrity of the electronic recordkeeping system during an audit. Illinois Department of Revenue Publication 107 provides details concerning the systems and controls the Department will examine during the audit process.

• *Sales and use tax*

The Department of Revenue may hold investigations and hearings in order to administer and enforce the sales and use tax laws that include retailers' occupation (sales) (ROT), service occupation (sales) (SOT), use (UT), and service use tax (SUT). (Use Tax Act, Sec. 11 [35 ILCS 105/11]; Service Use Tax Act, Sec. 11 [35 ILCS 110/11];

Service Occupation Tax Act, Sec. 11 [35 ILCS 115/11]; Retailers' Occupation Tax Act, Sec. 8 [35 ILCS 120/8]) Books, papers, records, or memoranda relating to the sale and use of tangible personal property or services may be examined at such investigations or hearings. Persons with knowledge of a business may be required to attend. The attendance of witnesses and the production of records may be compelled by the issuance of subpoenas or by an attachment for contempt issued by any circuit court. (Retailers' Occupation Tax Act, Sec. 10 [35 ILCS 120/10]) No person may be excused from testimony or the production of records because by doing so, the person will be subject to a criminal penalty; however, such person will not be prosecuted regarding any transaction regarding which the person testifies or produces evidence. (Retailers' Occupation Tax Act, Sec. 9 [35 ILCS 120/9])

Certified Audit Program.—Subject to appropriation, the Illinois Department of Revenue is authorized to initiate a pilot certified audit program for Illinois retailers' occupation (sales) tax, service occupation (sales) tax, service use tax, and use tax purposes to enhance tax compliance reviews by qualified practitioners and to encourage taxpayers to hire qualified practitioners at their own expense to review and report on their compliance. As an incentive for taxpayers to incur the costs of a certified audit, the Department will abate penalties and interest due on any tax liabilities revealed by a certified audit. However, the Department will not abate any liability for taxes collected by the taxpayer but not remitted to the Department. Further, the Department may not abate fraud penalties.

To participate in the Certified Audit program, the qualified practitioner must notify the Department of the engagement to perform a certified audit and confirm that the taxpayer is not already under by the Department. The Department may exclude the taxpayer from a certified audit or may limit the taxes or periods subject to the certified audit on grounds that the Department already conducted an audit, that is in the process of conducting an investigation or other examination of the taxpayer's records, or for just cause.

The Certified Audit Program expired July 1, 2004. (Certified Audit Program Law, [20 ILCS 2510/2510])

[¶89-142] Record Maintenance and Production

Specific provisions regarding record maintenance and production vary by the type of tax imposed.

• *Income tax*

Books and records must be available for inspection at all times during regular business hours if the Department requires such records to determine whether the taxpayer may have an income (corporate and personal) tax liability. (Income Tax Act, Sec. 913 [35 ILCS 5/913])

Employers that are required to withhold Illinois income tax need only provide one Form W-2 for each employee. Employers are not required to send the Department of Revenue copies of Form W-2. However, they must maintain employee W-2 records for three years from the due date or payment of tax, whichever is later. (86 Ill. Adm. Code 100.7300)

• *Sales and use tax*

Illinois retailers, users, service providers, and suppliers are required to keep books and records relating to sales and purchases of tangible personal property for the time period which the Department of Revenue may issue notices of tax liability. (Use Tax Act, Sec. 11 [35 ILCS 105/11]; Service Use Tax Act, Sec. 110 [35 ILCS 110/11];

Service Occupation Tax Act, Sec. 11 [35 ILCS 115/11]; Retailers' Occupation Tax Act, Sec. 7 [35 ILCS 120/7]) Such records include invoices, bills of lading, sales records, copies of bills of sale, inventories, credit memos, debit memos, shipping records, summaries, recapitulations, totals, journal entries, ledger accounts, accounts receivables and payables, statements, and tax returns. (86 Ill. Adm. Code 130.801) Records must be preserved until the expiration of the limitations period for audits by the Department, unless the Department authorizes the destruction of the records prior to such expiration. (86 Ill. Adm. Code 130.815)

[¶89-144] Limitations Period for Audits

Illinois has specific limitations provisions for income and sales and use tax.

• *Income tax*

The Illinois Department of Revenue (IDOR) must issue a notice and demand for payment of an income tax assessment no later than 3 years after the date the return was filed by the taxpayer. (35 ILCS 5/902(a)) A notice of deficiency for Illinois corporate or personal income tax must be issued no later than 3 years after the return was due (35 ILCS 5/905(h); 86 Ill. Adm. Code Sec. 100.9320(h)) or the return was filed by the taxpayer. (35 ILCS 5/905(a); 86 Ill. Adm. Code Sec. 100.9320(a)) A notice of deficiency for withholding tax liability may be issued at any time no later than 3 years after the 15th day of the 4th month following the close of the calendar year in which withholding was required by the taxpayer. (35 ILCS 5/905(j); 86 Ill. Adm. Code Sec. 100.9320(j))

The expiration of the period for issuing a notice of deficiency for a taxable year does not preclude the IDOR from asserting:

— any adjustments to net income or credits reported by a taxpayer, if the adjustments would reduce or eliminate a refund claimed by the taxpayer for that taxable year; or

— any adjustments to the amount of any credit earned, the amount of net loss deduction, or any credit carryforward that is properly taken in that taxable year, in order to compute the amount of net loss deduction or credit carryforward allowable in another taxable year, so that a timely notice of deficiency may be issued for that other taxable year or a claim for refund for that other taxable year may be denied in whole or in part. (86 Ill. Adm. Code Sec. 100.9320(a))

Example: Corporation A and its wholly-owned subsidiary Corporation B are members of a unitary business group, but filed separate returns for calendar years 2005 through 2009. Corporation A reported positive net income every year, and Corporation B reported net losses for every year. For 2010, the corporations filed a combined return, and used losses incurred by Corporation B in 2010 and carryforwards of losses reported by Corporation B in prior years to reduce combined net income to zero. The corporations also filed refund claims for 2007, 2008 and 2009, computing their liability on a combined basis, and reporting net losses carried to 2010. The limitations periods for issuing notices of deficiency have expired for 2005 and 2006, but not for the later years. The IDOR may examine the returns for 2005 and 2006 and may adjust the combined net income or loss of the corporations for those years and for each subsequent year in order to determine the correct amount of any combined net income or loss for each year, and the correct amount of any net loss deduction to be used in each year, so that the correct liabilities for 2007, 2008, 2009 and 2010 can be determined and any deficiency for the later years can be assessed and any excessive refund claim denied. If the limitations period for issuing a notice of deficiency for 2007 expires before the IDOR begins its examination of the corporations' returns, but before any refund is paid, the IDOR may nevertheless make any adjustment to the net income or net loss of either corporation for 2007, as well as to any net loss carryforwards from 2005 and 2006, in order to reduce the allowable refund for that year or to reduce the net losses available to carry to subsequent years.

A notice of additional tax resulting from mathematical errors, which is not considered a notice of deficiency, must be issued no later than 3 years after the date the return was filed. (35 ILCS 5/903(a)) "Mathematical error" means:

— arithmetic errors or incorrect computations on the return or supporting schedules;

— entries on the wrong lines;

— omission of required supporting forms or schedules or of the information required on those forms and schedules; and

— an attempt to claim, exclude, deduct, or improperly report, in a manner directly contrary to Illinois income tax law and related regulations, any item of income, exemption, deduction or credit. (35 ILCS 5/1501(a)(12))

Substantial understatement of tax.—If a taxpayer omits from base income more 25% of the base income stated in the return, a notice of deficiency may be issued up to 6 years after the date the return was due or the return was filed. (35 ILCS 5/905(b); 86 Ill. Adm. Code Sec. 100.9320(b)) If an employer fails to report on a return an amount required to be withheld in excess of 25% of the total amount of withholding required to be reported on that return, a notice of deficiency may be issued no later than 6 years after the return was filed by the taxpayer. (86 Ill. Adm. Code Sec. 100.9320(j))

Reportable transactions.—If a taxpayer fails to include on any return or statement for any taxable year any information on a reportable transaction, a notice of deficiency may be issued up to 6 years after the date the return was due or the return was filed for the taxable year in which the taxpayer participated in the reportable transaction. The deficiency is limited to amount resulting from any correction to item that the taxpayer failed to report. (35 ILCS 5/501(b); 35 ILCS 5/905(b); 86 Ill. Adm. Code Sec. 100.9320(b))

Fraud or failure to file.—A deficiency notice may be issued at any time if the taxpayer:

— fails to file a return; or

— files a fraudulent return to evade tax. (35 ILCS 5/905(c); 86 Ill. Adm. Code Sec. 100.9320(c))

However, if the taxpayer had reasonable cause for failing to file a return, a notice of deficiency may be issued no later than 6 years after the original or extended due date of the return. The issuance of a notice of deficiency does not cause the running of any limitations period to begin. If a fraudulent return is filed, the subsequent filing of a nonfraudulent amended return does not cause the running of any limitations period to begin. (86 Ill. Adm. Code Sec. 100.9320(c))

Any taxpayer who is required to join in the filing of a combined return for a taxable year ending on or after December 31, 2013 (see ¶11-550) and who is not included on that return and does not file its own return for that taxable year is considered to have failed to file a return. The amount of any proposed assessment set forth in a notice of deficiency is limited to the amount of any increase in liabilitythat should have been reported on the combined return for that taxable year resulting from proper inclusion of that taxpayer on that combined return. A taxpayer is included on a combined return if it is identified on that return and its base income and apportionment factors are reported on that return as those of a member of the unitary business group that does not have taxable nexus with Illinois. (86 Ill. Adm. Code Sec. 100.9320(c))

Federal changes.—If a taxpayer notifies the IDOR of a change in a federal tax return by filing an amended return, a deficiency notice must be issued no later than 2 years after the amended return is received. (35 ILCS 5/905(e); 86 Ill. Adm. Code Sec. 100.9320(e)) If the taxpayer fails to report a federal change, a deficiency notice may be issued at any time. 35 ILCS 5/905(d); 86 Ill. Adm. Code Sec. 100.9320(d)) The statute of limitations applies, even if the federal change is made after the statute of limitations has expired for assessing a federal income tax deficiency for that taxable year. (86 Ill. Adm. Code Sec. 100.9320(d) and (e))

The amount of the assessment is limited to the amount of deficiency resulting from recomputing the taxpayer's net income, net loss, or tax credits for the taxable year after accounting for the reported federal changes. (35 ILCS 5/905(e); 86 Ill. Adm. Code Sec. 100.9320(e))

Waiver or reduction of limitation periods.—The period of limitations may be extended by written agreement between the taxpayer and the IDOR. If the taxpayer is a partnership, S corporation, a notice of deficiency may be issued to the partners, shareholders, or beneficiaries of the taxpayer at any time before the expiration of the period agreed upon. Any proposed assessment in the notice is limited to the amount of any deficiency resulting from recomputation of items of income, deduction, credits, or other amounts of the taxpayer that are taken into account by the partner, shareholder, or beneficiary in computing their Illinois income liability. (35 ILCS 5/905(f); 86 Ill. Adm. Code Sec. 100.9320(f))

Corporations may request a prompt determination of liability and reduce the period of limitations to 18 months if:

— the corporation anticipates dissolution and it is completed by the expiration of the 18-month period; and

— the dissolution has in good faith begun; or

— the dissolution has been completed, if it is complete at the time the written request is made. (35 ILCS 5/905(i); 86 Ill. Adm. Code Sec. 100.9320(i))

Transferees.—A notice of deficiency may be issued to an initial transferee up to 2 years after the expiration of the period of limitation for assessment against the transferor. If a court proceeding for judicial review of the assessment, (see ¶89-236) against the transferor has begun, the limitations period is up to 2 years after the return of the certified copy of the judgment in the court proceeding. A notice of deficiency to successive transferees may be issued up to 2 years after the expiration of the period of limitation for assessment against the preceding transferee, but not more than 3 years after the expiration of the period of limitation for assessment against the initial transfer. If, before the expiration of the period of limitation for the assessment of the liability of the transferee, a court proceeding for the collection of the tax or liability has been begun against the initial transferor or the last preceding transferee, the period of limitation expires 2 years after the return of the certified copy of the judgment in the court proceeding. (35 ILCS 5/905(m))

Decrease in net loss.—The IDOR cannot issue a notice of deficiency resulting for a decrease in the net loss incurred by a taxpayer in any taxable year before December 31, 2002, unless the IDOR has notified the taxpayer of the proposed decrease within 3 years after the return reporting the loss was filed or within 1 year after an amended return reporting an increase in the loss was filed. If the taxpayer filed an amended return, a decrease proposed by the IDOR more than 3 years after the original return was filed may not exceed the increase claimed by the taxpayer on the amended return. (35 ILCS 5/905(n); 86 Ill. Adm. Code Sec. 100.9320(l))

The expiration of the limitations period does not preclude the IDOR from:

— decreasing a net loss reported by a taxpayer in order to deny some or all of a refund claimed by a taxpayer as the result of claiming a carryforward deduction of that net loss; or

— adjusting the net income of the taxpayer, before net loss deductions, for any year to which a net loss is carried in order to issue a notice of deficiency for that year or reduce the amount of net loss remaining available to carry to latter years, so that a notice of deficiency may be issued for one or more later years. (86 Ill. Adm. Code Sec. 100.9320(l))

• *Sales and use tax*

All sales and use tax returns are examined by the Department of Revenue. If the Department determines that the tax owed is greater than the amount stated on the return, a deficiency assessment is issued together with a 15% penalty. An additional penalty may be imposed if the deficiency is due to negligence or fraud. A deficiency assessment may also be issued to a taxpayer who files a return and does not pay the tax due. No deficiency notice will be issued on and after each July 1 and January 1 covering gross receipts received during any time period more than three years prior to the July 1 or January 1 when the notice was issued. (Retailers' Occupation Tax Act, Sec. 4 [35 ILCS 120/4])

[¶89-160]

COLLECTION OF TAX

[¶89-164] Assessment of Delinquent Tax

The amount of tax that is shown to be due on an Illinois return is considered to be assessed on the date the return was filed, (35 ILCS 5/903(a); 86 Ill. Adm. Code Sec. 100.9200(a)(1)) including any amended returns showing an increase of tax. (35 ILCS 5/903(a)) Any amount paid as tax, other than withholding or estimated tax, is considered to be assessed on the date payment is received by the Illinois Department of Revenue (IDOR). Estimated tax is considered to be assessed on the filing and payment due date. (86 Ill. Adm. Code Sec. 100.9200(a)(1)) If the taxpayer files a return without the computation of the tax, the tax computed by the IDOR is considered to be assessed on the date when payment is due. (35 ILCS 5/903(a))

If the taxpayer fails to file a tax return, the IDOR must determine the amount of tax due using any reasonable method and according to its best judgment and information. (35 ILCS 5/904(b); 86 Ill. Adm. Code Sec. 100.9300(b)) The term "reasonable method" is any method or combination of methods to reconstruct the taxpayer's Illinois net income established or acceptable under federal law, including methods based in whole or part on cash register receipts, specific items of income or expense, bank deposits, expenditures, net worth, or other acceptable or accepted method. (86 Ill. Adm. Code Sec. 100.9300(b)) The IDOR's determination is considered to be correct and evidence of the correctness of the amount of tax due. (35 ILCS 5/904(b); 86 Ill. Adm. Code Sec. 100.9300(b))

The IDOR may not issue a deficiency assessment for a taxable year, unless a notice of deficiency was issued before the expiration of the statute of limitations period. (35 ILCS 5/903(b); 86 Ill. Adm. Code Sec. 100.9200(a)(1))

• *Notice of deficiency*

If the amount of tax shown on a taxpayer's return is less than the correct amount, the IDOR must issue a notice of deficiency to the taxpayer that sets forth the amount of tax and penalties it proposes to assess. (35 ILCS 5/904(a); 86 Ill. Adm. Code Sec. 100.9300(a)) If the taxpayer does not file a written protest of the notice, the IDOR's final action is not an administrative decision from which the taxpayer may seek judicial review. (86 Ill. Adm. Code Sec. 100.9300(a)) If the tax paid is more than the correct amount, the IDOR must credit or refund the overpayment. (35 ILCS 5/904(a); 86 Ill. Adm. Code Sec. 100.9300(a)) The IDOR's findings are considered to be correct and evidence of the correctness of the amount of tax and penalties due. (35 ILCS 5/904(a); 86 Ill. Adm. Code Sec. 100.9300(a))

If a notice of deficiency has been issued, the amount of the deficiency is considered to be an assessment of the amount of tax and penalties specified in the notice 60 days after the date on which it was issued. If the taxpayer is outside the U.S., the deficiency is considered to be an assessment 150 days after the date the notice of deficiency was issued. (35 ILCS 5/903(a); 35 ILCS 5/904(c)) If the taxpayer files a protest, the date of assessment is considered to be the date when the decision of the IDOR becomes final. (35 ILCS 5/903(a))

A notice of deficiency must set forth the reasons and a basis sufficient to inform the taxpayer of the adjustments underlying the proposed assessment. (86 Ill. Adm. Code Sec. 100.9300(c)) If married taxpayers filed a joint Illinois personal income tax return, the notice of deficiency may be a single joint notice. However, if the IDOR is notified by either spouse that separate residences have been established, joint notices must be issued to each spouse. (35 ILCS 5/904(c); 86 Ill. Adm. Code Sec. 100.9300(c))

If taxpayer is required to file more than one return, a separate notice of deficiency may be issued for each return for the taxable year. For example, if a taxpayer is required to file both an individual income tax return, and an employer's quarterly withholding tax return, the returns may be examined separately at different times and if adjustments result a notice of deficiency may be issued with respect to each return. (86 Ill. Adm. Code Sec. 100.9330(b)) However, the IDOR cannot issue additional notices of deficiency for any taxable year for which a notice of deficiency was previously issued, a protest was filed, and the IDOR's decision on the protest has become final, except in the case of fraud, mathematical error, or federal change. (86 Ill. Adm. Code Sec. 100.9330(a))

• *Mathematical error notices*

If the amount of tax is understated on the taxpayer's return due to a mathematical error, the IDOR must notify the taxpayer before the expiration of the statute of limitations period (see ¶89-144) that the understated amount of tax is due and has been assessed. The notice of additional tax due is not considered a notice of deficiency and the taxpayer does not have any right of protest. (35 ILCS 5/903(a))

Mathematical error notices are distinguishable from notice of deficiency adjustments resulting from an examination (i.e., an audit) of the return after it is accepted and processed. (86 Ill. Adm. Code Sec. 100.9200(a)(2)) It is an informal inquiry that enables the IDOR with a minimum of correspondence and inconvenience to taxpayers to process or to complete the processing of returns containing defects, including:

— arithmetic errors or incorrect computations on the return or supporting schedules;

— entries on the wrong lines;

— omission of required supporting forms or schedules or of the information required on those forms and schedules; and

— an attempt to claim, exclude, deduct, or improperly report, in a manner directly contrary to Illinois income tax law and related regulations, any item of income, exemption, deduction or credit. (86 Ill. Adm. Code Sec. 100.9200(a)(2))

Taxpayers that receive a mathematical error notice of additional tax due should pay the amount due, within the time specified in the notice, to avoid other collection efforts and the assessment of interest, unless the defect(s) can be corrected by the taxpayer's furnishing correct information, including, for example, any supporting forms or schedules that have been omitted from the return. If the IDOR timely receives payment or correcting information that satisfactorily corrects all of the defects indicated in the notice, it must cancel the previously issued notice of additional tax due. If the information received only partially corrects the defects indicated in the notice, the IDOR may issue an amended notice. (86 Ill. Adm. Code Sec. 100.9200(a)(2))

• *Affect of federal changes*

If an amended income tax return or report is filed to report a change on a taxpayer's federal income tax return, any deficiency in tax resulting from the federal change is considered to be assessed on the date the report or amended return was filed. (35 ILCS 5/903(a); 86 Ill. Adm. Code Sec. 100.9200(a)(4)) It is the IDOR's position and practice to rely upon and accept the federal Internal Revenue Service (IRS) final determination on the amount of a taxpayer's adjusted gross or taxable income and the number of exemptions to which the taxpayer is entitled for federal income tax purposes, except in rare circumstances where the IRS for some reason might fail or decline to act, or where the statutory period of limitations for prosecution would expire before action by the IRS. Taxpayers must report federal changes to the IDOR within a specified number of days after the final determination of the federal adjustment. (see ¶89-102) Finality also exists if a taxpayer executes an agreement waiving the restrictions on assessment or pays any asserted tax increase, even if it is the taxpayer's intent afterwards to file a claim for refund. (86 Ill. Adm. Code Sec. 100.9200(a)(4))

• *Waiver of restrictions on assessment and collection*

A taxpayer may waive restrictions on assessment and collection. (35 ILCS 5/907; 86 Ill. Adm. Code Sec. 100.9210(a)) Payment of understated tax for any taxable year (e.g., payment of an additional amount due on an amended return showing an increase of tax) before a deficiency notice has been mailed by the IDOR is also considered to be a waiver of restrictions on assessment and collection. (86 Ill. Adm. Code Sec. 100.9210(a))

If a waiver is submitted without payment and a notice and demand for the tax is not issued by the IDOR within 30 days, interest will not be imposed on the deficiency during the period beginning immediately after the 30th day and ending with the date of the notice and demand. (86 Ill. Adm. Code Sec. 100.9210(a))

Waiver of the restrictions on assessment and collection does not have the effect of a closing agreement and does not prevent the expiration of the statute of limitations period (see ¶89-144) for certain adjustment items and issues. It does preclude a right to judicial review, (see ¶89-236) unless the taxpayer files a claim for refund (see ¶89-224) that is finally denied by the IDOR. (86 Ill. Adm. Code Sec. 100.9210(b))

¶89-164

[¶89-166] Other Liable Parties

A purchaser or transferee of a taxpayer's property or business is liable for any unpaid tax of the seller or transferor to the extent of the value of the property sold or transferred. (Illinois Income Tax Act, Sec. 902 [35 ILCS 5/902])

The term "transferee" includes donee, heir, legatee, distributee, and bulk purchasers. (Illinois Income Tax Act, Sec. 1405 [35 ILCS 5/1405])

Trustees, receivers, executors, or administrators that continue to operate, manage, or control a business are liable for retailers' occupation (sales) tax on retail sales made in the course of liquidation. (86 Ill. Adm. Code 130.105)

If a business is insolvent or a responsible corporate officer willfully fails to remit withholding tax, the responsible officer is held personally liable for the unpaid tax, interest, and penalties. (Illinois Income Tax Act, Sec. 1002 [35 ILCS 5/1002])

[¶89-168] Jeopardy Assessments

The Illinois Department of Revenue may issue a jeopardy assessment to prevent a taxpayer from departing from the state, concealing himself or his property in the state, or otherwise rendering any collection action ineffective. If the collection of income tax will be jeopardized by delay, the Department may give the taxpayer notice of such findings and make demand for immediate return and payment of any amounts due. Upon such demand, the amount due is considered assessed and immediately due and payable. (Illinois Income Tax Act, Sec. 1102 [35 ILCS 5/1102])

If the taxpayer does not comply with the notice or show the Department that such findings are erroneous within five days, the Department may file a notice of jeopardy assessment lien in the office of the county recorder of deeds in any county in which property of the taxpayer is located. The Department is required to notify the taxpayer. When the taxes in jeopardy are those for the current year, the Department closes the taxable year prior to issuing a notice and demand. The tax liability computed is then based on income accrued and deductions incurred for the period prior to the closing of the tax year.

Within 20 days after being notified of the filing of a jeopardy assessment, a taxpayer who protests the amount of the assessment or believes that no jeopardy to the revenue in fact exists may request a hearing. After the hearing, the Department will notify the taxpayer of its decision as to whether or not the lien will be withdrawn. (Illinois Income Tax Act, Sec. 1102 [35 ILCS 5/1102])

[¶89-172] Tax Liens

The Department of Revenue has a lien for tax, interest, and penalties due upon all real and personal property of any person who has been issued a final assessment or has filed a return without payment of tax owed. The lien attaches after the period for judicial review has expired or judicial proceedings have terminated.

Compliance Note: Lien registration system enacted beginning in 2018.— Effective January 1, 2018, for taxes administered by the Department of Revenue (DOR), a state tax lien registration program has been established to provide a uniform statewide system for filing notices of tax liens that are in favor of or enforced by the DOR. The scope of the program is real property and personal property, tangible and intangible, of taxpayers or other persons against whom the DOR has liens pursuant to law for unpaid final tax liabilities. ([35 ILCS 750/1-5])

If any person neglects or refuses to pay any final tax liability, the DOR may file in the registry a notice of tax lien within three years from the date of the final liability. The lien is perfected at the time of the filing and attaches to all after-acquired property of the debtor. The notice of lien is a lien for 20 years from the date of the filing unless the DOR files an earlier release of lien in the registry. ([35 ILCS 750/1-15])

Notice of lien.—A lien expires unless a notice of lien is filed within three years from the termination of judicial proceedings or the expiration of the period for judicial review. If the lien arose from the filing of a return without payment, the lien expires unless a notice of lien is filed within three years from the date the return was filed.

Lien priorities.—The rights of a bona fide purchaser, holder of security interest, mechanics lienholder, mortgagee, or judgment lien creditor that arise before the filing of a notice of lien have priority over the Department of Revenue. Also, the Department's lien is inferior to a lien for general taxes, special assessments, or special taxes levied by a political subdivision.

Release of lien.—The Department will issue a certificate of complete or partial release of lien upon payment by the taxpayer to the Department of any filing fees paid by the Department to file the lien and to file release of the lien to the extent that the fair market value of the attached property exceeds the lien amount plus the amount of prior liens, the lien becomes unenforceable, the lien and interest due are paid, the taxpayer furnishes a bond conditioned on payment of the lien, or if the assessment is reduced pursuant to a rehearing or Department review. (Illinois Income Tax Act, Sec. 911.3 [35 ILCS 5/911.3]; Illinois Income Tax Act, Sec. 1103 [35 ILCS 5/1103]; Retailers' Occupation Tax Act, Sec. 5a [35 ILCS 120/5a])

[¶89-174] Warrants for Collection of Tax

The Department of Revenue may demand payment of any delinquent tax. If the tax remains unpaid for 10 days after such demand, the Department may direct the sheriff or other officer by warrant to levy upon the taxpayer's property and property rights. The property levied upon may be seized and sold. (Illinois Income Tax Act, Sec. 1109 [35 ILCS 5/1109])

No proceedings for a levy may be commenced more than 20 years after the latest date for filing the notice of lien regardless of whether the notice was actually filed. (Retailers' Occupation Tax Act, Sec. 5f [35 ILCS 120/5f])

[89-176] Other Collection Methods

• *Taxpayer disclosure requirements*

A copy of a federal disclosure statement must be filed by any taxpayer for any reportable transaction that must be disclosed for federal income tax purposes. The disclosure statement must be attached to the taxpayer's Illinois income tax return for each year the taxpayer participated in reportable transactions or, if no return is required, by the due date of the first return that the taxpayer would have been required to file. A copy of the federal return also must be sent to the Illinois Department of Revenue (DOR). (35 ILCS 5/501 86 Ill. Adm. Code 100.5060) Protective disclosures may also be made. (86 Ill. Adm. Code 100.5060(e))

The disclosure requirements apply to the same categories of reportable transactions as provided under federal law and includes any listed transaction that is required to be disclosed. (35 ILCS 5/501(b); 86 Ill. Adm. Code 100.5060(a)(2)) A penalty may be imposed on any taxpayer for failure to disclose a reportable transaction.

Exceptions to disclosure requirements. Disclosure is not required for transactions if before disclosure:

— an amended Illinois return has been filed reporting net income and tax liability computed without the tax benefits of the reportable transaction, other than allowable tax benefits as determined by a federal audit;

— a federal application for a change in accounting method has been filed after a determination by the Internal Revenue Service (IRS) that the change is necessary to reflect proper tax treatment of the transaction; (35 ILCS 5/501(b); 86 Ill. Adm. Code 100.5060(d))

— the same or substantially similar transactions have been removed from federal listed transactions; or

— a federal or state determination is made that disclosure is not required. (86 Ill. Adm. Code 100.5060(d))

Combined group members. If a disclosure statement must be made by any member of a combined report that is taken into account in computing the group's combined net income for the group's common taxable year, a copy of the disclosure must be filed for each common taxable year. If a member of a combined group is required to file a disclosure statement for a taxable year during which it was not a member of the combined group, a copy of the disclosure must be filed with the combined return. The designated agent should indicate that the statement relates to a separate return year of the member and indicate the taxable year to which the disclosure relates. (86 Ill. Adm. Code 100.5060(c))

Consolidated group members. If a taxpayer is a member of an affiliated group of corporations filing a federal consolidated income tax return for the taxable year that is required to file a federal disclosure statement, a copy of the disclosure must be filed if, taking into account the rule that the taxpayer must determine its Illinois taxable income on a separate basis, the taxpayer would be considered to have participated in the transaction for federal income tax purposes. (86 Ill. Adm. Code 100.5060(c))

Partners and S corporation shareholders. If a reportable transaction is engaged in during the taxable year by a partnership or S corporation in which the taxpayer is a partner or shareholder, the taxpayer's disclosure obligation is met if the disclosure is made on a timely replacement tax return or, effective for taxable years beginning before 2014, a composite return filed by the partnership or S corporation. (86 Ill. Adm. Code 100.5060(c))

• *Material advisor disclosure requirements*

Any material advisor that is required under IRC Sec. IRC 6111 to file a federal disclosure statement for a reportable transaction or maintain a list of investors in abusive tax shelters or reportable transactions must send a duplicate of the statement or list to the DOR no later than the date that the statement must be filed or the list must be furnished under federal law. (35 ILCS 5/1405.5(a); 35 ILCS 5/1405.6(a); 86 Ill. Adm. Code 100.5070(a); 86 Ill. Adm. Code 100.5080(c)) A list of investors must be furnished to the DOR at an earlier time upon written request. (35 ILCS 5/1405.6(a); 86 Ill. Adm. Code 100.5070(a))

The disclosure requirements apply to transactions or abusive tax shelters that have nexus with Illinois. A reportable transaction has nexus with Illinois if the transaction is entered into by an Illinois taxpayer. A listed transaction has nexus with Illinois if, at the time the transaction is entered into, the transaction has one or more investors that is an Illinois taxpayer. (35 ILCS 5/1405.5(c); 35 ILCS 5/1405.6(c); 86 Ill. Adm. Code 100.5070(a); 86 Ill. Adm. Code 100.5080(c)) A tax shelter has Illinois nexus if it is:

— organized in Illinois;

— doing Business in Illinois, or

— deriving income from sources in Illinois. (86 Ill. Adm. Code 100.5070(a))

Any list that includes a listed transaction having nexus with Illinois must be furnished to the DOR, regardless of whether the list is furnished to the IRS, by the later of 60 days after:

— entering into the transaction; or

— the transaction becomes a listed transaction. (86 Ill. Adm. Code 100.5070(b))

Exceptions to disclosure requirements. A material advisor is not required to furnish a list of investors to the DOR if before furnishing the list:

— the same or substantially similar transactions have been removed from federal listed transactions;

— the DOR makes a determination by published guidance that a list is not required to be furnished for a particular transaction or type of transaction; or

— the same list had previously been furnished to the DOR and the list furnished to the IRS does not contain additional information. (86 Ill. Adm. Code 100.5070(c))

Designation agreements. If a material advisor's disclosure obligations are satisfied under a designation agreement by a person that is not a material advisor for a transaction having nexus with Illinois, the material advisor for the transaction having nexus with Illinois must file a copy of the disclosure statement or furnish a list of investors at the time the information is provided to the IRS. (86 Ill. Adm. Code 100.5070(d); 86 Ill. Adm. Code 100.5080(c)) A list of investors must be furnished to the DOR at an earlier time upon written request. (86 Ill. Adm. Code 100.5070(d)) The disclosure statement or list may be filed for the material advisor by the person designated under the designation agreement. (86 Ill. Adm. Code 100.5070(d); 86 Ill. Adm. Code 100.5080(c))

Protective filings or disclosures. If a material advisor believes in good faith that Illinois does not have jurisdiction to require disclosure of a list of investors in abusive tax shelters or reportable transactions, a statement may be filed with the DOR setting forth the basis for that claim. The advisor is entitled to abatement of any penalty for failure to furnish a list of investors, if the statement:

— contains a detailed description of the transaction that describes both the tax structure and its expected tax treatment;

— discloses the number of investors the person is required to include on the list; and

— includes an explanation of the basis for believing that disclosure is not required. (86 Ill. Adm. Code 100.5070(e))

If the material advisor's reportable disclosure obligation for a transaction having nexus with Illinois is satisfied by the filing of a federal protective disclosure, then the filing of a copy of the protective disclosure with the DOR will satisfy the advisor's Illinois disclosure obligation. (86 Ill. Adm. Code 100.5080(c))

Federal ruling requests. If a material advisor's federal reportable transaction disclosure obligation for a transaction having nexus with Illinois is satisfied by the filing of a federal ruling request, the filing of a copy of the federal submission by the last day of the month following the end of the calendar quarter in which the IRS notified the material advisor that the submission satisfies the federal disclosure requirement will satisfy the advisor's Illinois disclosure obligation. (86 Ill. Adm. Code 100.5080(c))

• *Levy on wages*

Following a demand, any officer or employee of the Department is authorized to serve the process to levy on the accounts or wages of the taxpayer. The wages of employees of other states may not be levied upon. However, the wages of federal officers, employees, or elected officials may be levied upon as authorized by the Government Organization and Employees Act Section 5520a (5 U.S.C. 5520a). Persons other than the defendant who claim to own property being levied upon must, in order to preserve their rights, notify the levying officer of their claim within 10 days. (Illinois Income Tax Act, Sec. 1109 [35 ILCS 5/1109])

• *Foreclosure*

The Department may foreclose in circuit court any lien on real property provided that there are no hearings or review proceedings pending and the time for instituting such hearings or proceedings has expired. Foreclosure proceedings may not be instituted more than five years after the filing of a notice of lien for unpaid income tax and not more than 20 years after the filing of such notice for unpaid sales and use tax. (Illinois Income Tax Act, Sec. 1108 [35 ILCS 5/1108]; Retailers' Occupation Tax Act, Sec. 5e [35 ILCS 120/5e])

• *Offsets*

The Department may credit the amount of any overpayments, including accrued interest, against any income tax liabilities owed, even if the statute of limitations has run for other collection procedures. (Illinois Income Tax Act, Sec. 909 [35 ILCS 5/909]) Overpayments may also be offset against estimated tax due for subsequent years. (Illinois Income Tax Act, Sec. 909 [35 ILCS 5/909])

The Department participates in the IRS federal offset program under which Illinois personal income tax debts may be offset against federal tax refunds.

CCH COMMENT: Effective January 1, 2000, the Illinois Department of Revenue will begin participating in the IRS federal offset program under which Illinois personal income tax debts may be offset against federal tax refunds. The federal Internal Revenue Service Restructuring and Reform Act of 1998 (P.L. 105-206) provided that state income tax debts that have been reduced to judgement may be offset against federal tax overpayments if the taxpayer who makes the overpayment has shown on the federal return for the year of the overpayment an address within the state seeking the offset. Offsets are prioritized in the following order: any federal tax liability; past-due child support; past-due, legally enforceable debt owed to a federal agency; past-due, legally enforceable state income tax debt; future liability for federal tax. *Remarks made by Director Glen L. Bower,* Illinois Department of Revenue, December 6, 1999; Telephone conversation with Legislative Office, December 7, 1999.

• *Delinquent taxpayer postings*

The Department publishes an annual list of delinquent taxpayers that includes the name, address, type of tax, and amount due regarding the delinquent account. (86 Ill. Adm. Code 710.10) Prior to disclosure, the taxpayer's final tax liability must be greater than $10,000, and at least six months must have passed from the time the liability became final. (86 Ill. Adm. Code 710.20)

The taxpayer's final tax liability must be greater than $1,000. (Civil Administrative Code of Illinois-(Department of Revenue Law), Sec. 2505-425 [20 ILCS 2505/2505-425])

• *Denial of license or public contract*

The Department of Revenue may inform an Illinois governmental agency that a person licensed by such agency has failed to file income tax returns or to pay income tax. In addition, for the purpose of enforcing bidder and contractor certifications (see below), the Department may make available to state agencies information regarding whether a person bidding on or entering into a contract for goods or services with a state or local governmental agency has failed to pay, collect, or remit Illinois income, sales, or use taxes. (Illinois Income Tax Act, Sec. 917 [35 ILCS 5/917]; Retailers' Occupation Tax Act, Sec. 11 [35 ILCS 120/11])

Under the Illinois Procurement Code, no person may enter into a contract with a state agency unless the person and all of its affiliates collect and remit Illinois use tax on all sales of tangible personal property into the state of Illinois regardless of whether the person or affiliate is a retailer maintaining a place of business within Illinois. Every bid and contract must contain a certification that the bidder or contractor is in compliance with the above use tax collection and remittance requirement and that the bidder or contractor acknowledges that the contracting state agency may void the contract if the certification is false. ([30 ILCS 500/50-12])

[¶89-178] Requirement to Post Bond or Security

The Department of Revenue will issue a certificate of release of lien to the extent that the taxpayer furnishes a bond that is conditioned upon the payment of the amount of the lien, along with accrued interest. (Illinois Income Tax Act, Sec. 1105 [35 ILCS 5/1105])

Vendors making retail sales of property or maintaining a place of business in Illinois must obtain a certificate of registration and furnish a bond or irrevocable bank letter of credit not to exceed the lesser of three times the vendor's average monthly tax liability or $50,000. (Use Tax Act, Sec. 6 [35 ILCS 105/6]; Service Use Tax Act, Sec. 6 [35 ILCS 110/6]; Service Occupation Tax Act, Sec. 6 [35 ILCS 115/6]; Retailers' Occupation Tax Act, Sec. 2a [35 ILCS 120/2a])

Insurance surplus line agents must obtain a license, pass a written examination, and post a surety bond of $20,000. (Illinois Insurance Code, Sec. 445 [215 ILCS 5/445])

[¶89-180] Civil Action

The Department of Revenue may file a civil action against a taxpayer to recover taxes, interest, and penalties owed within six years after the deficiency assessment becomes final. If a taxpayer dies or becomes legally disabled, the action may be filed against the taxpayer's estate. The statute of limitations for filing suit is suspended during the pendency of a restraining order, an automatic stay imposed as a result of the filing of a bankruptcy petition, or if the taxpayer departs from and remains out of Illinois. (Retailers' Occupation Tax Act, Sec. 5 [35 ILCS 120/5])

[¶89-182] Civil Action in Another Jurisdiction

Illinois courts recognize and enforce on a reciprocal basis the liability for taxes imposed by other states. Under reciprocal tax collection statutes, Illinois has the right to sue in the courts of another state to recover any tax that may be owing to it when a similar right is accorded to the other state. (Tax Collection Suit Act, Sec. 1 [35 ILCS 705/1])

The Illinois Attorney General may bring a civil action in an out-of-state court to collect any tax legally due to Illinois or to any political subdivision on whose behalf Illinois acts to collect tax. (Tax Collection Suit Act, Sec. 1 [35 ILCS 705/1])

The only states that do not grant comity by statute or court decision are Montana, New Mexico, and Utah.

[¶89-184] Intergovernmental Tax Collection Agreements

There are a number of agreements among governmental agencies to provide for assistance in tax collection, both between the Internal Revenue Service and the states, and among the states themselves.

The Illinois Department of Revenue has the authority to exchange information that is necessary for efficient tax administration, except where specifically prohibited, with any state, local subdivision of any state, and the federal government. The Department has the power to exchange information with the Illinois Department of Public Aid any information that may be necessary for the enforcement of child support orders. However, the Department is not liable for any information disclosed by the Department of Public Aid. (Civil Administrative Code of Illinois-(Department of Revenue Law), Sec. 2505-65 [20 ILCS 2505/2505-65]; Senior Citizens and Disabled Persons Property Tax Relief and Pharmaceutical Assistance Act, Sec. 4.1 [320 ILCS 25/4.1])

• *Agreement with IRS*

Abusive Tax Avoidance Transactions (ATAT) Memorandum of Understanding.— The Small Business/Self-Employed Division of the Internal Revenue Service signed ATAT Memorandums of Understanding with 40 states and the District of Columbia on September 16, 2003, that provide for information sharing on abusive tax avoidance transactions. (*Memorandum of Understanding*, Internal Revenue Service) The Memorandum authorizes the IRS and a state to:

— exchange tax returns and return information,

— share audit results from ATAT participant cases,

— exchange information on identified types of ATAT schemes, and

— share audit technique guides.

The IRS will provide states with a list of participants in a particular ATAT scheme on a semi-annual basis on July 31 and January 31. The IRS generally refers to an abusive tax shelter arrangement as the promise of tax benefits with no meaningful change in the taxpayer's control over or benefit from the taxpayer's income or assets.

Illinois has signed the ATAT Memorandum of Understanding with the IRS.

• *Reciprocal collection agreements*

The DOR may enter into reciprocal collection agreements with states that have similar reciprocal agreement laws and have entered into an agreement with Illinois. (Civil Administrative Code of Illinois-(Department of Revenue Law), Sec. 2505-640[20 ILCS 2505/2505-640]) Upon the request and certification by a claimant state, the DOR will collect the tax and deposit the amount collected into the reciprocal tax collection fund. (Reciprocal Tax Collection Act, Sec. 5-5(b)(1) [35 ILCS 717/5-5(b)(1)]) Certification must include:

— the full name and address of the taxpayer;

— the taxpayer's Social Security number or federal employer identification number;

— the amount of tax due and a detailed statement of related tax, interest, and penalties;

— a statement whether a return was filed by the taxpayer and, if so, whether it was filed under protest; and

— a statement that all appropriate administrative and judicial remedies have been exhausted or have lapsed and that the amount requested is legally enforceable under the laws of the claimant state.

(Reciprocal Tax Collection Act, Sec. 5-5(b)(2) [35 ILCS 717/5-5(b)(2)])

Taxpayers have 60 days from receipt of notice of the claim to protest the collection of all or a portion of the taxes by filing a written protest. If a protest is timely filed, the DOR must refrain from collecting the tax and forward the protest to the claimant state for determination of the protest on its merits. (Reciprocal Tax Collection Act, Sec. 5-5 (b)(3) [35 ILCS 717/5-5(b)(3)])

Illinois has reciprocal agreements with Iowa, Kentucky, Michigan, and Wisconsin to exempt from Illinois taxation and withholding the compensation paid to a resident of the other state who is working in Illinois. (Illinois Income Tax Act, Sec. 701(d) [35 ILCS 5/701(d)]; *Publication 130*, Who is Required to Withhold Illinois Income Tax, Illinois Department of Revenue) Employees who are residents of a state with a reciprocal agreement exempting residents of that state from withholding of Illinois tax on compensation paid in Illinois must file a signed statement of nonresidence in Illinois, Form IL-W-5-NR, in order to receive the exemption. (86 Ill. Adm. Code 100.7120)

• *Multistate Agreements*

Multistate Tax Compact.—Illinois is an associate member of the Multistate Tax Compact. The Compact seeks to provide solutions to the problems of state taxation of interstate commerce by state action, rather than by federal restriction of state taxing powers. The Multistate Tax Compact is a document to which states may subscribe in the interest of uniform taxation of multistate corporate income tax and sales and use tax. The Compact created the Multistate Tax Commission and established for member states a joint audit program for multistate taxpayers.

Sales and use.—The Compact provides a use tax credit for sales or use tax paid to another state, provides that when a vendor accepts in good faith a resale or exemption certificate, the vendor is relieved of liability for tax on the transaction and provides for interstate audits, arbitration of apportionment disputes, and continuing study of interstate taxation problems.

Corporate income.—The Compact adopts UDITPA as an optional method of apportionment in member states. The option is not significant in such states as Illinois that have adopted UDITPA as their apportionment law.

Uniform Division of Income for Tax Purposes Act (UDITPA).—Illinois has provisions that substantially follow the Uniform Division of Income for Tax Purposes Act (UDITPA). UDITPA is a model act for the allocation and apportionment of income among states. UDITPA was drafted to remedy the diversity that existed among the states for determining their respective shares of a corporation's income. As of 1986, UDITPA had been adopted, in whole or in part, by the majority of states.

Income tax agreements.—The Director of the Illinois Department of Revenue may enter into an agreement with the taxing authorities of any state which imposes a tax on or measured by income to provide that compensation paid in such state to residents of Illinois shall be exempt from such tax; in such case, any compensation paid in Illinois to residents of such state shall not be allocated to Illinois. (Illinois Income Tax Act, Sec. 302 [35 ILCS 5/302])

[¶89-186] Agreements in Compromise of Tax Due

A petition in the nature of an offer in compromise may be filed by the taxpayer after the tax liability has become final only if there is uncertainty as to collectibility of such liability. (86 Ill. Adm. Code 210.115)

[¶89-188] Installment Payments

Taxpayers can apply to the Illinois Department of Revenue for an installment payment arrangement for corporate and personal income taxes. Forms are available on the DOR website at http://tax.illinois.gov/TaxForms/Misc/Payment/.

• *Sales tax*

The Department may enter into installment payment agreements with registered retail vendors who are delinquent in paying tax if the vendor pays a percentage of delinquent amount and waives in writing all limitations upon the Department for collection of remaining amount owed. The execution of an installment agreement does not toll the accrual of interest. (Retailers' Occupation Tax Act, Sec. 2a [35 ILCS 120/2a])

• *Estate tax*

Illinois estate tax is due and payable when federal estate tax is due and payable. To qualify for deferred or installment payments, the estate must owe and pay federal estate tax and be allowed to pay the federal tax under IRC Sec. 6166. (Illinois Estate and Generation-Skipping Transfer Tax Act, Sec. 6(b) [35 ILCS 405/6(b)])

[¶89-190] Recovery of Erroneous Refunds

The Illinois Department of Revenue (IDOR) may recover erroneous refunds of income and sales and use taxes.

• *Income tax*

If income tax has been erroneously refunded, a notice of deficiency may be issued within 2 years from the date of the refund. The limitations period is 5 years from the date of the refund if it appears that any part of the refund was induced by fraud or misrepresentation of a material fact. (35 ILCS 5/905(g); 86 Ill. Adm. Code Sec. 100.9320(g)) An erroneous refund is a tax deficiency on the date made and is deemed assessed and collectible. (35 ILCS 5/912; 86 Ill. Adm. Code Sec. 100.9420)

Interest will be charged on an erroneous refund from the date of payment of the refund. However, interest will not be charged if the erroneous refund is for an amount less than $500 and is due to a mistake of the IDOR. (86 Ill. Adm. Code Sec. 100.9420)

• *Sales and use tax*

Under circumstances in which there has been an erroneous refund of sales or use tax, the IDOR may issue a notice of tax liability within three years of making the refund or, if the refund was induced by fraud or misrepresentation of a material fact, within five years of making the refund. The proposed assessment amount is limited to the amount of the erroneous refund. (35 ILCS 120/6b; 35 ILCS 105/22; 35 ILCS 110/20; 35 ILCS 115/20)

[¶89-200]

INTEREST AND PENALTIES

[¶89-202] Interest and Penalties in General

Illinois has adopted the Uniform Penalty and Interest Act (UPIA), which contains uniform provisions for assessing penalties and interest. (Uniform Penalty and Interest Act, Sec. 3-1 [35 ILCS 735/3-1], *et seq.*) Unless otherwise specified in another tax act, the UPIA applies to all taxes administered by the Illinois Department of Revenue that are due after 1993, except for taxes imposed by the following statutes:

(1) Racing Privilege Tax Act;

(2) Property Tax Code;

(3) Real Estate Transfer Tax Act; and

(4) Coin Operated Amusement Device Tax

(Uniform Penalty and Interest Act, Sec. 3-1A [35 ILCS 735/3-1A]; Publication 103, Illinois Department of Revenue)

For a discussion on current interest rates on underpayments and overpayments, see ¶89-204. For current civil penalty provisions, see ¶89-206. For criminal penalty provisions, see ¶89-208. Abatement of interest and penalties is discussed at ¶89-210.

[¶89-204] Interest Rates

In 2013 Illinois amended its method of determining interest rates charged to taxpayers on tax underpayments and paid by the Illinois Department of Revenue on tax overpayments. The amendment returned the determination method to its pre-2004 terms.

If a taxpayer files a written notice of a waiver of restrictions on the assessment and collection of all or any part of a proposed assessment and if notice and demand by the Director for the payment of the amount were not made within 30 days after the filing of the waiver, interest will not be imposed on the amount for the period beginning immediately after the 30th day and ending with the date of notice and demand. (Illinois Income Tax Act, Sec. 1003 [35 ILCS 5/1003])

• *Methods of determination*

The method of determining the general interest rate on Illinois tax underpayments and overpayments depends on the tax year involved. The general rate does not apply to taxes imposed under the Racing Privilege Tax Act, Property Tax Code, Real

Estate Transfer Tax Act, and Coin-Operated Amusement Device Tax. (Uniform Penalty and Interest Act, Sec. 3-1A [35 ILCS 735/3-1A])

Calendar years before 2004 and after 2013.—For periods prior to 2004 and after 2013, the underpayment rate under IRC Sec. 6621 was used as the interest rate on Illinois underpayments and overpayments for all periods. (Uniform Penalty and Interest Act, Sec. 3-2 [35 ILCS 735/3-2])

• *Current percentage rates*

For the period January 1, 2020, through June 30, 2020, the interest rate charged on tax underpayments and overpayments is 5%. For the period July 1 through December 31, 2020, the interest rate is 3% on underpayments and overpayments. Interest is calculated on the tax due from the day after the original due date of the return through the date the tax is paid. (*Interest Rates*, Illinois Department of Revenue, https://www2.illinois.gov/rev/individuals/Pages/interestrate.aspx)

Interest rates for prior periods can be found at https://www2.illinois.gov/rev/individuals/Pages/interestrate.aspx.

• *Withholding*

Employers who fail to file a return or pay withholding tax are subject to interest for the delinquent period. The interest and any penalty are paid by the employer and may not be passed through to employees. If a business is not solvent, or if a responsible corporate officer or employee willfully fails to collect or remit withholding tax, the responsible officer is held personally liable for the unpaid tax, plus penalties and interest. (Illinois Income Tax Act, Sec. 1002 [35 ILCS 5/1002])

• *Estate*

Interest on unpaid estate tax is imposed at the rate of 10% per year on any unpaid amount. (Illinois Estate and Generation-Skipping Transfer Tax Act, Sec. 9 [35 ILCS 405/9])

• *Insurance*

Interest on delinquent insurance taxes is imposed at the rate of 12% per annum from the due date unless a higher rate is established under the provisions of IRC Sec. 6621(b). (Illinois Insurance Code, Sec. 412(4) [215 ILCS 5/412(4)])

[¶89-206] Civil Penalties

Under the Uniform Penalties and Interest Act (UPIA), Illinois assesses penalties for several tax issues or violations, including:

— failure to file or pay; (Uniform Penalty and Interest Act, Sec. 3-3 [35 ILCS 735/3-3])

— failure to file correct information returns; (Uniform Penalty and Interest Act, Sec. 3-4 [35 ILCS 735/3-4])

— collection penalty; (Uniform Penalty and Interest Act, Sec. 3-4.5 [35 ILCS 735/3-4.5])

— negligence; (Uniform Penalty and Interest Act, Sec. 3-5 [35 ILCS 735/3-5])

— fraud; (Uniform Penalty and Interest Act, Sec. 3-6 [35 ILCS 735/3-6])

— personal liability; and (Uniform Penalty and Interest Act, Sec. 3-7 [35 ILCS 735/3-7])

— bad checks. (Uniform Penalty and Interest Act, Sec. 3-7.5 [35 ILCS 735/3-7.5])

Some of these penalties are periodically, even annually amended. The UPIA applies to all taxes administered by the Illinois Department of Revenue except for taxes imposed under the following statutes:

(1) Racing Privilege Tax Act;

(2) Property Tax Code;

(3) Real Estate Transfer Tax Act; and

(4) Coin-Operated Amusement Device and Redemption Machine Tax Act.

(Uniform Penalty and Interest Act, Sec. 3-1A [35 ILCS 735/3-1A]; Publication 103, Illinois Department of Revenue)

• *Late filing or nonfiling*

The penalty for late filing or nonfiling of a tax return is equal to 2% of the tax required to be shown due on the return, up to a maximum amount of $250, reduced by any tax paid or allowable credit. If a return is not filed within 30 days after notice of nonfiling is mailed to the last known address of the taxpayer, an additional penalty will be imposed that is equal to the greater of $250 or 2% of the tax shown on the return, but not to exceed $5,000. A $100 penalty is imposed on the failure to timely file an sales and use transaction reporting return only if no tax was due with the return. If any unprocessable return is corrected and filed within 30 days after notice by the Department, the late filing or nonfiling penalty shall not apply. Also, the penalty shall be abated in any case where a tax return is required to be filed more frequently than annually and the late filing is nonfraudulent and has not occurred in the two preceding years. (Uniform Penalty and Interest Act, Sec. 3-3(a-10) [35 ILCS 735/3-3(a-10)])

• *Late payment or nonpayment*

The penalty for late payment or nonpayment of estimated or accelerated taxes is:

(1) 2% of any amount paid no later than 30 days after the due date, and

(2) 10% of any amount paid later than 30 days.

(Uniform Penalty and Interest Act, Sec. 3-3(b-20)(1) [35 ILCS 735/3-3(b-20)(1)])

The penalty for failure to pay by the due date the amount shown as due on a return (except for qualifying amended returns for late payment or nonpayment of income tax) is:

(1) 2% of any amount that is paid no later than 30 days after the due date;

(2) 10% any amount paid later than 30 days and prior to the date the Department of Revenue has initiated an audit or investigation; and

(3) 20% of any amount that is paid after the date the Department has initiated an audit or investigation.

The 20% penalty will be reduced to 15% if the entire amount is paid not later than 30 days after the Department has provided the taxpayer with an amended return (following completion of an occupation, use, or excise tax audit) or a form for waiver of restrictions on assessment (following completion of an income tax audit). However, the 15% reduction will be rescinded in some qualifying instances, such as if the taxpayer makes any claim for refund or credit of the tax penalties or interest determined to be due upon audit. (Uniform Penalty and Interest Act, Sec. 3-3(b-20)(2) [35 ILCS 735/3-3(b-20)(2)])

The late payment or nonpayment penalty is assessed at the time the tax upon which the penalty is computed is assessed. However, if the penalty reduction to 15% is rescinded because a claim for a refund or credit has been filed, the increase in penalty shall be deemed assessed at the time the claim for refund or credit is filed. (Uniform Penalty and Interest Act, Sec. 3-3(b-20)(3) [35 ILCS 735/3-3(b-20)(3)])

The basis of a late payment penalty is the tax shown or required to be shown on a return reduced by any part of the tax that is paid on time and by any allowable credit. (Uniform Penalty and Interest Act, Sec. 3-3(c) [35 ILCS 735/3-3(c)]) In addition, the penalty applies even if the tax required is less than the tax shown on the return. (Uniform Penalty and Interest Act, Sec. 3-3(d) [35 ILCS 735/3-3(d)])

If a taxpayer has a tax liability that is eligible for amnesty under the Tax Delinquency Amnesty Act and fails to satisfy the liability during the amnesty period, the penalty imposed for late payment will be 200% of the amount that would otherwise be imposed. (Uniform Penalty and Interest Act, Sec. 3-3(i) [35 ILCS 735/3-3(i)])

Penalties for 2004.—generally, for tax returns due during calendar year 2004, the penalty for late payment or nonpayment of an admitted liability was:

(1) 2% of any amount that is paid no later than 30 days after the due date;

(2) 10% any amount paid later than 30 days and not later than 90 days after the due date;

(3) 15% of any amount that is paid later than 90 days and not later than 180 days after the due date; and

(4) 20% of any amount that is paid later than 180 days after the due date.

If notice and demand were made for the payment of tax due, and the amount due was paid within 30 days, then the penalty for late payment or nonpayment would not accrue after the date of notice and demand. (Uniform Penalty and Interest Act, Sec. 3-3(b-15) [35 ILCS 735/3-3(b-15)])

Penalties for 2001-2003.—Generally, for returns due after 2000 and before 2004, the penalty for late payment or nonpayment of tax was:

(1) 2% any amount paid no later than 30 days after the due date;

(2) 5% of any amount paid later than 30 days and not later than 90 days after the due date;

(3) 10% of any amount paid later than 90 days and not later than 180 days after the due date; and

(4) 15% of any amount paid later than 180 days after the due date.

If notice and demand are made for the payment of tax due, and the amount due was paid within 30 days, then the penalty for late payment or nonpayment would not accrue after the date of notice and demand. In addition, the penalty was waived if the taxpayer paid the full amount of taxes owed within 30 days after the Department issued a notice of arithmetic error, notice and demand, or a final assessment. (Uniform Penalty and Interest Act, Sec. 3-3(b-10) [35 ILCS 735/3-3(b-10)])

• *Collection penalty*

A collection penalty is imposed if any liability for tax, penalties, or interest is not paid in full and received prior to the 31st day after a notice and demand, a notice of additional tax due, or a request for payment of a final liability is issued. The collection penalty is:

(1) $30 if the unpaid liability is less than $1,000 or

(2) $100 if the unpaid liability is $1,000 or more.

(Uniform Penalty and Interest Act, Sec. 3-4.5 [35 ILCS 735/3-4.5])

• *Business license denial, suspension*

The Illinois Department of Financial and Professional Regulation (DFPR) will deny, refuse to renew, or suspend the business license of any person who has not filed an appropriate return or paid a tax for any tax administered by the state Department of Revenue (DOR). The DFPR will implement the license actions following qualifying notice from the Illinois Department of Revenue that the person has failed to:

— file a return;

— pay a tax, penalty, or interest shown on a filed return; or

— pay an final assessment of tax, penalty, or interest.

In the notice, the DOR also must certify the amount of any unpaid tax liability and/or the years for which a return was not filed. The notice constitutes prima facie evidence of a licensee's or applicant's failure to comply with any tax law administered by the DOR, and no hearing is required before the DFPR acts upon the person's license. However, any order issued under this rule will be immediately stayed for 60 days in order to allow the licensee or applicant to file a request for a hearing with the DOR. The DFPR will restore or renew any person's license that was suspended, refused renewal, or denied if the licensee or applicant, who otherwise qualifies for the license, provides proof of a satisfactory repayment record with the DOR. (Civil Administrative Code of Illinois-(Department Professional Regulation Law), Sec. 2105-15(g) [20 ILCS 2105/2105-15(g)]; 68 Ill. Adm. Code 1100.560)

• *Income tax*

A taxpayer that fails to make a required disclosure statement under Treasury Regulations (see Illinois Income Tax Act, Sec. 501(b) [35 ILCS 5/501(b)]) is subject to a $15,000 penalty for each failure to disclose. (Illinois Income Tax Act, Sec. 1001(b) [35 ILCS 5/1001(b)]) However, a taxpayer that fails to report a "listed transaction" is subject to a $30,000 penalty for each failure to disclose. The total penalty cannot exceed 10% of the increase in net income that would result had the taxpayer not participated in any reportable transaction affecting the taxpayer's net income for the taxable year. (Illinois Income Tax Act, Sec. 1001(c) [35 ILCS 5/1001(c)])

The Department may rescind all or a portion of any penalty for failing to disclose a reportable transaction if:

— the failure to disclose did not jeopardize the best interests of the State and is not due to willful neglect or intent not to comply;

— the taxpayer has a history of complying with the Illinois Income Tax Act;

— the violation is due to an unintentional mistake of fact;

— imposing the penalty would be against equity and good conscience;

— rescinding the penalty would promote compliance with the Illinois Income Tax Act and effective tax administration; or

— the taxpayer can show that there was reasonable cause for the failure to disclose and the taxpayer acted in good faith.

(Illinois Income Tax Act, Sec. 1001(b) [35 ILCS 5/1001(b)])

Abusive Tax Shelter.—llinois Department of Revenue Publication 103 states that taxpayers found to have participated in an abusive tax shelter transaction that did not report and pay any liability associated with that transaction before they were contacted by the IRS or the Department of Revenue, will be assessed interest on that liability at 150% of the rate in effect at that time.

More information regarding reportable transactions is available at ¶89-102, ¶89-134, and ¶89-176.

• *Income tax preparers*

For returns prepared by an income tax preparer for a taxpayer, the preparer is required to sign the return as the preparer. (Illinois Income Tax Act, Sec. 503(a) [35 ILCS 5/503(a)]) Thus, by verifying the return, the preparer is made subject to the penalties of fraud and perjury. (Illinois Income Tax Act, Sec. 504 [35 ILCS 5/504])

An "income tax preparer" is any person who prepares for compensation, or who employs others to prepare, any Illinois tax return or claim for refund. The preparation of a substantial portion of a return is treated as preparing the entire return. Preparers do not include persons who only provide typing or other mechanical assistance, prepare returns for their regular employer, or prepare returns as a fiduciary. (Illinois Income Tax Act, Sec. 1501(a) [35 ILCS 5/1501(a)])

• *Frivolous returns*

A penalty of $500 is imposed on any individual who files a return that does not contain information from which the substantial correctness of the stated tax liability can be determined, who has a desire to delay or impede the administration of the income tax, or who maintains a frivolous position on a return. (Illinois Income Tax Act, Sec. 1006 [35 ILCS 5/1006]) Examples of frivolous positions that will trigger a penalty are listed in a regulation and include the position that an income tax is not allowed by the U.S. or Illinois Constitution and the position that wages and other forms of compensation for personal services are not subject to income tax. (86 Ill. Adm. Code 100.5050)

• *Disclosure of client information*

A penalty of up to $10,000 for each violation may be imposed by the Department of Professional Regulation against an accountant upon proof of misconduct (Illinois Public Accounting Act, Sec. 20.01(a)(7)[225 ILCS 450/20.01(a)(7)]) or for the violation of any rule adopted under the Illinois Public Accounting Act. (Illinois Public Accounting Act, Sec. 20.01(a)(8) [225 ILCS 450/20.01(a)(8)]) Under professional conduct rules pursuant to the Act, registered public accountants are prohibited from the disclosure of any confidential client information without the specific consent of the client. (68 Ill. Adm. Code 1430.3010(a))

• *Franchise tax*

Domestic and foreign corporations are subject to penalties of 10% of the amount of annual franchise tax for a failure to file any annual report or report of cumulative changes in paid-in capital and pay any tax by the due date. (Business Corporation Act of 1983, Sec. 16.05(a) [805 ILCS 5/16.05(a)])

• *Estate tax*

The penalty for failure to file an estate return with the Illinois Attorney General by the due date is 5% of any amount that is paid no later than a month from the due date, with an additional 5% for each additional month until the tax is paid. However, the penalty cannot exceed 25% of the tax. (Illinois Estate and Generation-Skipping Transfer Tax Act, Sec. 8(a) [35 ILCS 405/8(a)])

¶89-206

• *Insurance tax*

The penalty for failure to file an insurance tax return or pay tax is the greater of $400 or 10% of the tax due per month. However, the entire penalty cannot exceed the greater of $2,000 of 50% of the tax due. (Illinois Insurance Code, Sec. 412(2) [215 ILCS 5/412(2)])

In addition, the penalty for failing to pay the full amount of any insurance tax or fee due is 10% of the amount due. If the Director determines after a hearing that the failure to pay the full amount was willful, the penalty is the greater of 50% of the deficiency or 10% of the amount due per month or portion thereof until the deficiency is paid. The penalty for willful nonpayment is in lieu of the penalty for failure to pay. (Illinois Insurance Code, Sec. 412(3) [215 ILCS 5/412(3)])

If an insurance company or domestic affiliated group fails to pay the full amount of any insurance fee of $200 or more, a penalty shall be imposed that is equal to the greater of $100 or 10% of the deficiency for each month the deficiency remains unpaid. (Illinois Insurance Code, Sec. 412(7) [215 ILCS 5/412(7)])

The penalties for failing to file and failing to pay are separate and cumulative.

Interest on any deficiency is 12% per annum from the date due until the date paid, unless a higher rate is established by the Internal Revenue Service under the provisions of IRC Sec. 6621(b). (Illinois Insurance Code, Sec. 412(4) [215 ILCS 5/412(4)])

• *Quarterly payments*

A company that fails to make quarterly payments of its net receipts or retaliatory tax of at least one-fourth of either the total tax paid in the prior year or 80% of the actual tax for the current year is subject to the penalty provisions listed above. (Illinois Insurance Code, Sec. 409 [215 ILCS 5/409]; Illinois Insurance Code, Sec. 444.1(5) [215 ILCS 5/444.1(5)])

• *Petty offenses*

Any violation of the Insurance Code for which a penalty is not provided in the law is considered a petty offense. (Illinois Insurance Code, Sec. 446 [215 ILCS 5/446])

• *Tax amnesty provisions*

If a taxpayer has a tax liability eligible for amnesty but fails to satisfy the liability during the amnesty period above, then the interest with respect to that liability will be imposed at 200% of the normal rate. (Uniform Penalty and Interest Act, Sec. 3-2 [35 ILCS 735/3-2]; 86 Ill. Adm. Code 521.101) In addition, the penalties for failure to file or pay, negligence, fraud, and issuance of a bad check will be imposed at 200% of the normal amount. (Uniform Penalty and Interest Act, Sec. 3-3 [35 ILCS 735/3-3]; Uniform Penalty and Interest Act, Sec. 3-4 [35 ILCS 735/3-4]; Uniform Penalty and Interest Act, Sec. 3-5 [35 ILCS 735/3-5]; Uniform Penalty and Interest Act, Sec. 3-6 [35 ILCS 735/3-6]; Uniform Penalty and Interest Act, Sec. 3-7.5 [35 ILCS 735/3-7.5])

• *Tax Amnesty Program for 2008*

S.B. 1544 (Laws 2007) creates an amnesty program for taxpayers owing any franchise taxes or license fees that will run from February 1, 2008 through March 15, 2008. Participants are only required to pay all taxes that would have been payable during the last four years. All interest and penalties will be abated. (S.B. 1544)

[¶89-208] Criminal Penalties

The following criminal penalties will be assessed for violations of the tax provisions.

• *Income tax*

A person who fails to file a return, files a fraudulent return, or willfully attempts to evade tax, or any agent who knowingly enters false information on a taxpayer's return is guilty of a Class 4 felony for the first offense and a Class 3 felony for each subsequent offense. A taxpayer signing a fraudulent return is guilty of perjury. Failure to keep books and records constitutes a Class A misdemeanor. (Illinois Income Tax Act, Sec. 1301 [35 ILCS 5/1301])

Caution Note: The Illinois Supreme Court has determined that Public Act 88-669 (effective November 29, 1994), which last amended Illinois Income Tax Act, Sec. 1301 [35 ILCS 5/1301], was enacted in violation of the single-subject requirement of the Illinois Constitution and, therefore, is void in its entirety. *(People of the State of Illinois v. Olender,* Illinois Supreme Court, December 15, 2005) That section was reenacted by P.A. 1074 (S.B. 3088), Laws 2006, effective December 26, 2006.

[¶89-210] Abatement of Interest, Penalties, or Additions to Tax

A taxpayer may file a petition for abatement of a penalty or interest imposed due to delinquent tax if the late filing was due to reasonable cause, an unreasonable delay by the Department of Revenue, or a timely payment was made by a person other than the taxpayer liable for the tax. (Uniform Penalty and Interest Act, Sec. 3-8 [35 ILCS 735/3-8]; 86 Ill. Adm. Code 210.120) Other provisions regarding abatement of penalties and interest by the Department of Revenue vary by the type of tax. For a discussion of abatement of property tax, see ¶20-810.

• *Income tax*

Taxpayers, who are members of the United States Armed Forces serving in a combat zone and granted a filing extension, are exempt from penalties and interest. (Illinois Income Tax Act, Sec. 602 [35 ILCS 5/602])

• *Reasonable cause*

Penalties for failure to file or pay tax, failure to file a correct information return, or negligence will not apply if the taxpayer establishes that such failure was due to reasonable cause. (Uniform Penalty and Interest Act, Sec. 3-8 [35 ILCS 735/3-8]) Reasonable cause is determined on a case by case basis. One factor is the extent to which the taxpayer made a good faith effort to determine the proper tax liability and to file and pay tax in a timely fashion. Good faith is shown if the taxpayer exercised ordinary business care and prudence. The taxpayer's filing history is considered when making a good faith determination. Isolated computational or transcriptional errors generally do not indicate a lack of good faith. (86 Ill. Adm. Code 700.400)

[¶89-220]

TAXPAYER RIGHTS AND REMEDIES

[¶89-222] Taxpayers' Bill of Rights

Illinois has a Taxpayers' Bill of Rights and a Local Government Taxpayer's Bill of Rights. Relevant provisions of each are summarized below.

• *Taxpayers' Bill of Rights*

The Taxpayers' Bill of Rights guarantees that Illinois taxpayers' rights are protected during the assessment and collection of taxes. (Taxpayers' Bill of Rights Act, Sec. 1 [20 ILCS 2520/1]) Under the Taxpayers' Bill of Rights, the Department must:

— furnish each taxpayer with a written statement upon the taxpayer's receipt of a protestable notice, bill, claim, denial, or reduction regarding any tax explaining the rights of such person and the obligations of the Department during the audit, appeals, refund and collections processes;

— include on all tax notices an explanation of tax liabilities and penalties;

— abate taxes and penalties assessed based upon erroneous written information or advice given by the Department;

— not cancel any installment contracts unless the taxpayer fails to provide accurate financial information, fails to pay any tax, or does not respond to any Department request for additional financial information;

— place nonperishable property seized for taxes in escrow for safekeeping for a period of 20 days to permit the taxpayer to correct any Department error; if seized property is of a perishable nature and in danger of immediate waste or decay, such property need not be placed in escrow prior to sale;

— place seized taxpayer bank accounts in escrow with the bank for 20 days to permit the taxpayer to correct any Department error;

— adopt regulations setting standards for times and places for taxpayer interviews and to permit any taxpayer to record such interviews;

— pay interest to taxpayers who have made overpayments at the same rate as interest charged on underpayments;

— grant automatic extensions to taxpayers in filing income tax returns when a federal extension has been granted; and

— annually identify areas of recurrent taxpayer noncompliances with rules or guidelines and to report findings and recommendations concerning such noncompliance to the General Assembly in an annual report.

Taxpayer suits.—Taxpayers may sue the Department of Revenue if it intentionally or recklessly disregards tax laws or regulations in collecting taxes. The maximum recovery for damages in such a suit are $100,000. If a taxpayer's suit is determined by the court to be frivolous the court may impose a penalty on the taxpayer not to exceed $10,000 to be collected as a tax.

Review of liens.—The Department of Revenue must establish an internal review process concerning liens against taxpayers and if a lien is determined to be improper the Department must publicly disclose this fact and correct the taxpayer's credit record.

Costs.—Attorneys or accountants fees incurred in aiding a taxpayer in an administrative hearing relating to the tax liability or in court are be recoverable against the Department of Revenue if the taxpayer prevails in an action under the Administrative Review Law and the Department has made an assessment or denied a claim without reasonable cause.

Local Government Taxpayers' Bill of Rights.—The Local Government Taxpayers' Bill of Rights was enacted to provide taxpayers with various rights with regard to the assessment and collection of local taxes within Illinois. Local governments are required to:

— adopt a statute of limitations for the assessment of taxes;

— provide for the application of tax payments; and

— publish local tax ordinances.

Procedures for credit and refund claims, proposed audits, and an appeals process are also required. Further, interest rates for underpayments, late filing penalties, and voluntary disclosure programs must be established. (Local Government Taxpayers, Sec. 1 [50 ILCS 45/1])

[¶89-224] Refunds

In general, taxpayers are entitled to credits or refunds for overpayments of tax, penalties, and interest. Property tax refunds are discussed in the Property Tax Division. (see ¶20-815)

•*Income tax*

A claim for an income tax refund may be filed with the Illinois Department of Revenue (IDOR) only if a return has been filed for the taxable year for which the refund is claimed. An original return is not considered to be a claim for refund, but may qualify as an extension of the limitations period for filing a refund claim. A separate claim must be filed for each taxable year for which an income tax overpayment was made. (86 Ill. Adm. Code Sec. 100.9400(f))

Every refund claim must be in writing on an amended return form and must state the specific grounds upon which it is based. (35 ILCS 5/909(d); 86 Ill. Adm. Code Sec. 100.9400(f)) A personal representative who is claiming a refund for a deceased taxpayer must file Form IL-1310. A surviving spouse filing a joint return with a deceased spouse is not required to complete this form. (Instructions, Form 1310, Statement of Person Claiming Refund Due a Deceased Taxpayer)

Income tax refund claims must be filed with the IDOR before the later of:

— 3 years after the date the return was filed; or

— 1 year after the date the tax was paid. (35 ILCS 5/911(a); 86 Ill. Adm. Code Sec. 100.9410(a))

Refund claims for withholding tax must be filed no later than 3 years after the 15th day of the 4th month following the close of the calendar year in which the withholding was made. (35 ILCS 5/911(a); 86 Ill. Adm. Code Sec. 100.9410(a)) Refund claims based on a credit for estimated or withholding tax payments may not be filed more than 3 years after the due date of the return for the year for which the payments were made. (35 ILCS 5/911(f))

Returns filed before the filing deadline are considered to have been filed on the original or extended due date of the return. (35 ILCS 5/911(e); 86 Ill. Adm. Code Sec. 100.9410(e)) If the claim was filed during the limitations period, the amount of the credit or refund cannot exceed the portion of the tax paid for the taxable period, immediately preceding the filing of the claim, plus the period of any extension of time for filing the return. When a claim is not submitted within the limitations period, the refund is limited to tax paid during the year before filing of the claim. (35 ILCS 5/911(d); 86 Ill. Adm. Code Sec. 100.9410(d))

Failure of a taxpayer to file a refund claim before the expiration of the limitations period for a taxable year precludes the IDOR from granting a credit or refund of any overpayment for that taxable year after the date of expiration. The expiration of the period for filing a refund claim for a taxable year does not preclude the taxpayer from asserting any adjustments to:

— net income or credits that would reduce or eliminate a deficiency for that taxable year;

— the amount of net loss incurred or of any credit earned in that taxable year; or

— the amount of net loss deduction or of any credit carryforward taken in that taxable year, in order to compute the amount of net loss deduction or credit carryforward allowable in another taxable year. (86 Ill. Adm. Code Sec. 100.9410(a))

Federal changes.—A refund claim resulting from a change to a taxpayer's federal income tax return, whether or not the taxpayer notified the IDOR of the change, may be filed no later than 2 years after the date the notification was due. The refund amount is limited to any overpayment resulting from the federal change and any corresponding change in the Illinois taxpayer's net income, net loss, or credits for the taxable year, and any corresponding change in a net loss or credit carryover to a later taxable year. (35 ILCS 5/911(b); 86 Ill. Adm. Code Sec. 100.9410(b))

If a refund claim is based on a federal change, the taxpayer must include a detailed explanation that shows the nature of the items of change or alteration. In addition, the original federal documents or correspondence furnished to the taxpayer or other satisfactory proof of the change must be attached that shows an agreed to or final federal Internal Revenue Service acceptance, recomputation, redetermination, change, tentative carryback adjustment or settlement, and that no contest is pending. A premature or incomplete claim is not considered a refund claim and does not start the limitations period for protesting the denial of a refund claim. If a claim is premature, incomplete, or otherwise defective, the IDOR must, as soon as practicable, notify the taxpayer in writing to enable the timely submission of a mature and perfected claim. (86 Ill. Adm. Code Sec. 100.9400(f))

Extension agreements.—The limitations period for refund claims may be extended by written agreement between the IDOR and the taxpayer any time before the expiration of the original or extended limitations period. If the taxpayer is a partnership, S corporation, or trust, a refund claim may be filed by the partners, shareholders, or beneficiaries of the taxpayer at any time before the expiration of the period agreed upon. Any refund resulting from an extension agreement is limited to the amount of any overpayment of tax from recomputation of items of income, deduction, credits, or other amounts of the taxpayer that are taken into account by the partner, shareholder, or beneficiary in computing its Illinois income tax liability. (35 ILCS 5/911(c); 86 Ill. Adm. Code Sec. 100.9410(c))

Net losses.—Refunds are not allowed if the refund is the result of a net loss incurred before December 31, 2002 that was not reported within the limitations period of the original or extended due date of the taxpayer's loss year return or on an amended return. (35 ILCS 5/911(h); 86 Ill. Adm. Code Sec. 100.9410(g)) However, a taxpayer is not precluded from increasing a net loss in order to carry forward the deduction to reduce or eliminate a deficiency for a later taxable year. (86 Ill. Adm. Code Sec. 100.9410(g))

Example: Corporation A and its wholly-owned subsidiary Corporation B are members of a unitary business group, but filed separate returns for calendar years 2005 through 2009. Corporation A reported positive net income every year, and Corporation B reported net losses for each year. After auditing Corporation A's returns for 2007, 2008 and 2009, the IDOR adjusted various items of income and apportionment, and issued notices of deficiency. The limitations periods for filing claims for refund have expired for 2005 and 2006, but not for the later years. The taxpayer may file amended returns for all of the years in question to combine the corporations so that Corporation B's net losses for the years under audit can offset the income of Corporation A. The taxpayer may loss carry any combined net loss properly determined for any year (including 2005 and 2006) to each later year in order to determine the correct liabilities for the years 2007, 2008 and 2009, and reduce or eliminate the deficiencies determined by the IDOR or to claim refunds for the open years.

Denial of claim.—Taxpayers may file a protest with the IDOR or a petition with the Illinois Independent Tax Tribunal within 60 days after the denial of a refund claim. (35 ILCS 5/909(f); 35 ILCS 5/910(a); 86 Ill. Adm. Code Sec. 100.9400(h) and (i)) Taxpayers may also file a protest if the IDOR has failed to act on the claim within 6 months. (35 ILCS 5/909(e); 86 Ill. Adm. Code Sec. 100.9400(g)) In the absence of a written protest, the Department's final action on a refund claim is not an administrative decision subject to judicial review, (see ¶89-236) except as to jurisdictional questions. (86 Ill. Adm. Code Sec. 100.9400(h))

When a protest is filed, the IDOR is required to reconsider the denial and grant a hearing if one is requested by the taxpayer. A claimant also may elect to protest a refund claim denial by filing a petition with the Illinois Independent Tax Tribunal no later than 30 days after the date on which the protest was filed with the IDOR. (35 ILCS 5/910(a)) After the IDOR has issued a notice of decision, the taxpayer has 30 days in which to request a rehearing. The IDOR may grant a rehearing or review, unless it denies the request by mail within 10 days of the request. If a rehearing is granted, the IDOR must issue a notice of final decision as soon as practicable after the review or rehearing. (35 ILCS 5/910(c))

If the taxpayer fails to file a timely protest or petition with the Illinois Independent Tax Tribunal, then the IDOR's notice of deficiency will become a final assessment 60 days after the date the IDOR issued the notice. (35 ILCS 5/910(d); 86 Ill. Adm. Code Sec. 100.9400(h)) If the taxpayer does not file a petition with the Illinois Independent Tax Tribunal, the IDOR's decision on the protest becomes final:

— 30 days after issuance of a notice of decision;

— on the issuance of a denial of a rehearing request or the issuance of a notice of final decision. (35 ILCS 5/910(d))

Erroneous refunds.—The IDOR may recover erroneous refunds of income tax. (see ¶89-190)

Unsigned returns.—An overpayment of tax shown on the face of an unsigned return is forfeited to Illinois if after notice and demand for signature by the IDOR the taxpayer fails to provide a signature and 3 years have passed from the date the return was filed. An overpayment of tax refunded to a taxpayer whose return was filed electronically is considered an erroneous refund if the taxpayer does not provide a required signature document. (35 ILCS 5/503(e); 35 ILCS 5/909(g))

Interest.—Interest is allowed and paid on any overpayment of income tax at the applicable rate. Interest does not begin to accrue before the original due date for filing a return, (35 ILCS 5/909(c); 86 Ill. Adm. Code Sec. 100.9400(c)) the date the entire tax liability was paid, or the date the return was filed by the taxpayer. (86 Ill. Adm. Code Sec. 100.9400(c))

Amended return forms may also be used by taxpayers to claim additional interest if there is a dispute regarding the amount of interest that is due with a refund. A claim for additional interest must be filed either within the limitations period for protesting a refund claim denial or within the limitations period for filing a refund claim for the taxable year for which the interest is due. An "informal claim," like a letter from the taxpayer, is insufficient to establish or extend the protest limitations period. (86 Ill. Adm. Code Sec. 100.9400(f))

Suspension of limitations period.—The refund limitations period is suspended for any individual who is unable to manage his or her financial affairs due to a medically determined physical or mental impairment that can be expected to result in death, or which has lasted or can be expected to last for a continuous period of 12 months or more. An individual will not be treated as financially disabled during any period if that individual's spouse or any other person is authorized to act for that individual with respect to financial matters. A taxpayer who has been determined to be financially disabled for any period of time for federal income tax purposes is considered to be financially disabled for Illinois income tax purposes for the same period. (35 ILCS 5/911(i); 86 Ill. Adm. Code Sec. 100.9410(h)) The financial disability provision applies only to periods that had not expired before August 15, 2014. (86 Ill. Adm. Code Sec. 100.9410(h))

• *Sales and use tax*

Retailers, servicemen, suppliers, and purchasers who pay sales and use taxes, penalties, or interest erroneously may file a claim for refund or credit. A claim filed on or after January 1 and July 1 is not valid unless the overpayment was made within three years prior to January 1 and July 1 of the year of the claim. Claims are filed with the Department of Revenue which issues a tentative determination with respect to such claim. (Retailers, Sec. 6 [35 ILCS 120/6]; Service Use Tax Act, Sec. 17[35 ILCS 110/17]; Service Occupation Tax Act, Sec. 17 [35 ILCS 115/17]; Use Tax Act, Sec. 19 [35 ILCS 105/19])

A taxpayer may file a protest and request a hearing within 60 days after notice of the determination. (Retailers, Sec. 6c [35 ILCS 120/6c]; Service Use Tax Act, Sec. 18 [35 ILCS 110/18]; Service Occupation Tax Act, Sec. 18 [35 ILCS 115/18]; Use Tax Act, Sec. 20 [35 ILCS 105/20])

• *Insurance tax*

Refunds are authorized for overpayments due to an error in calculation, mistake in fact, or erroneous interpretation of a statute within six years prior to the discovery of the overpayment. Refund claims must be filed with the Director of Insurance in writing and with supporting documentation. Such substantiated refund claims must be granted within 120 days of the receipt of the claim or documentation. (Illinois Insurance Code, Sec. 412(1) [215 ILCS 5/412(1)])

[¶89-230] Taxpayer Conferences

For the purpose of reviewing adjustments to Illinois tax returns prior to the issuance of a notice of tax liability, notice of deficiency, or notice of claim denial, the Informal Conference Board (ICB) has been established by regulation. The ICB allows taxpayers to resolve some disagreements with the Department of Revenue prior to formal protest procedures. The ICB does not have the authority to compromise tax and any final actions by the ICB are not subject to administrative review. (86 Ill. Adm. Code 215.100; 86 Ill. Adm. Code 215.120)

Members of the ICB are:

(1) the General Counsel for the Department;

(2) the Chairman of the Board of Appeals;

(3) the Manager of the Audit Bureau; and

(4) at least three Department employees—other than the ICB Administrator—who have experience in state and local tax and procedure.

Members serve on panels of three members each. Any member can appoint a qualified representative for an informal conference, but the member remains personally responsible for approving final actions by the panel. (86 Ill. Adm. Code 215.105)

The Illinois Department of Revenue has issued information on the Informal Conference Board (ICB). (*PIO-58, Informal Conference Board Reveiw*, Illinois Department of Revenue, March 2014)

• *Requesting Review by ICB*

At the conclusion of an audit, the Department will send to the taxpayer a notice of proposed (1) liability, (2) deficiency, or (3) claim denial (audit adjustments). This notice will state the amount of the proposed audit adjustment along with information regarding the taxpayer's right to an informal review by the ICB. A request for hearing before the ICB must be filed within 60 days, the running of which commences with the date the notice was either:

— hand-delivered to the taxpayer, or

— mailed.

(86 Ill. Adm. Code 215.115(a))

Notices of proposed audit adjustments will not be issued if a taxpayer:

— agrees to an audit by signing EDA-105 or IL-870;

— makes a payment of tax deemed assessed under Illinois Income Tax Act, Sec. 903(a)(4) [35 ILCS 5/903(a)(4)]; or

— refuses to extend the statutes of limitations when those statutes would expire prior to the expiration of the 60-day appeal period.

(86 Ill. Adm. Code 215.115(b))

• *Statute of limitations*

A written request for review must state the taxpayer's specific reasons for disagreeing with the proposed assessment. The request may be supplemented up until 30 days before the in-person conference, if one is requested, or within 30 days after the filing of the request otherwise. (86 Ill. Adm. Code 215.115(e))

The filing of a request for review will waive the applicable statute of limitations that would otherwise prevent the Department from issuing a Notice of Tax Liability, Notice of Deficiency, or Notice of Claim Denial following completion of the audit. In such a case, the statute would be tolled from the date the request for review is accepted up to and including 180 days following the date of a final ICB decision. Further, if the ICB matter impacts future audit periods, the taxpayer must execute all necessary waivers for later audit periods upon request or risk dismissal of the case. An "impact on future audit periods" includes situations in which:

— the same issues are involved in both audit periods;

— the subsequent audit period is a mandatory audit due to the amount of liability proposed in the ICB matter; or

— the amounts shown on a return subject to ICB review may be carried to a subsequent year's return.

(86 Ill. Adm. Code 215.115(f))

• *In-person conferences*

An in-person conference must be requested by the taxpayer at the time the request for review is filed. (86 Ill. Adm. Code 215.115(d)) However, the ICB may also request an in-person conference, and the taxpayer's failure to agree could result in denial of the relief sought due to a lack of sufficient information having been supplied by the taxpayer. (86 Ill. Adm. Code 215.130(a))

An in-person conference will be scheduled within 45 days of receipt of the taxpayer's request. (86 Ill. Adm. Code 215.130(d))

Further, if the taxpayer or his or her representative fails to appear at the conference without good cause, the taxpayer's right to another in-person conference will be waived. (86 Ill. Adm. Code 215.130)

At least two of the three ICB panel members or their representatives must participate in the in-person conference, except that only one member or representative must participate if the amount of the proposed audit adjustment is $5,000 or less. Formal rules of evidence do not apply at an in-person conference. (86 Ill. Adm. Code 215.130)

• *Informal review conference*

Upon filing a timely protest and request for hearing, the Department may designate an employee to conduct an informal review conference with the taxpayer within 30 days after the filing of the protest. A request for an informal review shall include a list of all supporting documentation to be presented at the review conference. The taxpayer may be represented by any person of his choice and such representative need not be an attorney. (86 Ill. Adm. Code 200.135)

However, for any notice of proposed audit adjustment issued after May 2007, when the ICB has issued an action decision that addresses the merits of the audit adjustments, a taxpayer that files a protest of any subsequent Notice of Tax Liability, Notice of Deficiency, or Notice of Claim Denial with the Office of Administrative Hearings cannot request informal review as provided by 86 Ill. Adm. Code 200.135. (86 Ill. Adm. Code 215.135)

[¶89-234] Administrative Appeals

Discussed here are administrative appeal options for Illinois taxpayers. There is a general discussion of notices of deficiency, a separate discussion of property tax appeals, and the Independent Tax Tribunal Act of 2012, which will be implemented in 2014.

• *Notices of deficiency*

After a deficiency notice has been issued, a taxpayer has a 60-day period (150 days for taxpayers outside the U.S.) within which to file a written protest and, if desired, request a hearing. If the taxpayer takes no action, the deficiency is deemed assessed at the end of the 60-day (or 150-day) period. (Illinois Income Tax Act, Sec.

908(a) [35 ILCS 5/908(a)]; Illinois Income Tax Act, Sec. 904(d) [35 ILCS 5/904(d)]; 86 Ill. Adm. Code Sec. 100.9200; 86 Ill. Adm. Code Sec. 100.9000)

A deemed assessment is not an administrative decision entitled to judicial review. (86 Ill. Adm. Code Sec. 100.9300)

After a protest decision is issued by the Department, the taxpayer may, within 30 days, request a rehearing. (Illinois Income Tax Act, Sec. 908(b) [35 ILCS 5/908(b)]; Illinois Income Tax Act, Sec. 908(c) [35 ILCS 5/908(c)]) The Department, at its discretion, will deny the request within 10 days or grant a rehearing. If the request is denied, the original protest decision becomes final 10 days after its date of issue. (Illinois Income Tax Act, Sec. 908(d) [35 ILCS 5/908(d)])

After the protest decision is final, the Department is barred from issuing further deficiencies for that taxable year except in the case of fraud, mathematical error, federal return changes, or returns considered unprocessable under the Uniform Penalty and Interest Act Sec. 3-2. If a rehearing is granted, the decisions made at that proceeding become final when issued following its conclusion. (Illinois Income Tax Act, Sec. 906 [35 ILCS 5/906])

CCH COMMENT: Options Available Upon Receipt of Notice of Deficiency (NOD) or Notice of Tax Liability.—The Department of Revenue has explained the options available to taxpayers if they disagree with the issuance of a Notice of Deficiency or Notice of Tax Liability. (*General Information Letter ST 99-0163-GTI,* Illinois Department of Revenue, May 12, 1999) One option is protest at an administrative hearing. If so, then the taxpayer must request an administrative hearing within 60 days after issuance of either the Notice of Deficiency or Notice of Tax Liability. Another option is to request an informal review. Alternatively, the taxpayer may pay the liability, including penalty and interest "under protest" and proceed to the circuit court to litigate the issues see ¶89-236 for more details. Another option is for the taxpayer to pay the liability without protest, and then file a claim for credit or refund after payment.

• *Independent tax tribunal (2014)*

CCH Caution: Tribunal commencement of jurisdiction.—The Illinois Independent Tax Tribunal will "exercise its jurisdiction" beginning January 1, 2014. The tribunal previously had been scheduled to commence jurisdiction on July 1, 2013. Any protests prior to January 1, 2014, will continue to be filed with the DOR, which shall exercise jurisdiction over those matters. However, administrative law judges may be appointed prior to that date and may prior to that date take action that is necessary to enable the tribunal to properly exercise its jurisdiction. Any administrative proceeding commenced after May 2013 that would otherwise be subject to the jurisdiction of the tribunal may be conducted according to the procedures set forth in the Illinois Independent Tax Tribunal Act of 2012, if the taxpayer so elects. Such an election would be irrevocable and can be made on or after January 1, 2014, but no later than February 1, 2014. (Sec. 1-15(d), Illinois Independent Tax Tribunal Act of 2012, as amended by S.B. 1329, Laws 2013, effective June 19, 2013)

Illinois has established a tax tribunal independent of the state Department of Revenue (DOR) to resolve some tax disputes between the DOR and taxpayers prior to requiring the taxpayer to pay the amounts in issue. Beginning in 2014, the tribunal will provide administrative hearings in all tax matters except those matters reserved to the DOR or another entity by statute. (Sec. 1-2, Illinois Independent Tax Tribunal Act of 2012)

Commencement of jurisdiction.—The tribunal will exercise its jurisdiction beginning on January 1, 2014. However, administrative law judges (ALJs) appointed prior to that date may take any action prior to that date that is necessary to enable the tribunal to properly exercise its jurisdiction on and after that date. Taxpayers involved in an administrative proceeding beginning after May 2013 that otherwise would be within the jurisdiction of the tribunal may make an irrevocable election to have the administrative procedure handled by the tribunal, so long as the election is made on or after January 1, 2014, but no later than February 1, 2014. (Sec. 1-15(d), Illinois Independent Tax Tribunal Act of 2012)

Makeup of the tibunal.—The governor will appoint a Chief ALJ for a five-year term. Up to three other ALJs will be appointed for staggered terms of no more than four years each. After the initial staggered terms are over, ALJs other than the Chief ALJ will be appointed to four-year terms. ALJs are eligible for reappointment. (Sec. 1-25, Illinois Independent Tax Tribunal Act of 2012) An ALJ must be a U.S. citizen; have been licensed to practice law in Illinois for eight years at the time of appointment; have substantial knowledge of state tax laws and the making of a record in a tax case; and with certain exceptions, cannot engage in any other gainful employment or business or hold a position of profit in a government office during the ALJ's term. (Sec. 1-30, Illinois Independent Tax Tribunal Act of 2012)

Scope of jurisdiction.—With certain limitations, the tribunal will have original jurisdiction over all determinations of the DOR reflected on a notice of deficiency, notice of tax liability, notice of claim denial, or notice of penalty liability issued under specified taxes administered by the DOR. However, the jurisdiction is limited to notices where either the amount at issue in a notice or the aggregate amount in multiple notices issued for the same year or audit period exceeds $15,000. Generally, no person can contest any matter within the jurisdiction of the tribunal in any action, suit, or proceeding in court in the state. Taxpayers may be required to post a bond, and there is a $500 filing fee for petitions. (Sec. 1-45, Illinois Independent Tax Tribunal Act of 2012)

Prior to the initiation of a hearing, the parties to an action may jointly petition the tribunal for mediation. (Sec. 1-63, Illinois Independent Tax Tribunal Act of 2012)

The tribunal will not have jurisdiction over:

— property tax issues;

— exemption determinations;

— proposed notices of tax liability or proposed deficiency or any notice of intent to take action;

— any action or determination of the DOR that has become finalized;

— informal administrative appeal functions of the DOR; or

— administrative subpoenas issued by the DOR.

(Sec. 1-45(e), Illinois Independent Tax Tribunal Act of 2012)

It may decide questions regarding the constitutionality of statutes and rules as applied to the taxpayer, but it may not determine that a statute or rule is unconstitutional on its face. (Sec. 1-45(f), Illinois Independent Tax Tribunal Act of 2012)

Illinois tax laws to which the tribunal's jurisdiction applies are:

— the Income Tax Act,

— the Use Tax Act,

— the Service Use Tax Act,

— the Service Occupation Tax Act,

— the Retailers' Occupation Tax Act,

— the Cigarette Tax Act,

— the Cigarette Use Tax Act,

— the Tobacco Products Tax Act of 1995,

— the Hotel Operators' Occupation Tax Act,

— the Motor Fuel Tax Law,

— the Automobile Renting Occupation and Use Tax Act,

— the Coin-Operated Amusement Device and Redemption Machine Tax Act,

— the Gas Revenue Tax Act,

— the Water Company Invested Capital Tax Act,

— the Telecommunications Excise Tax Act,

— the Telecommunications Infrastructure Maintenance Fee Act,

— the Public Utilities Revenue Act,

— the Electricity Excise Tax Law,

— the Aircraft Use Tax Law,

— the Watercraft Use Tax Law,

— the Gas Use Tax Law, and

— the Uniform Penalty and Interest Act.

(Sec. 1-45(a), Illinois Independent Tax Tribunal Act of 2012)

Hearings, decisions, and other matters.—Proceedings before the tribunal are tried de novo, and generally the tribunal will take evidence, conduct hearings, rule on motions, and issue final decisions. Hearings will be open to the public, and rules of evidence and privilege as applied in civil cases in circuit courts will be followed. Taxpayers will have the burden of proof on issues of fact. (Sec. 1-65, Illinois Independent Tax Tribunal Act of 2012)

The tribunal must render a decision in a case in writing no later than 90 days after submission of the last brief filed subsequent to completion of the hearing, with a 30-day extension option for good cause. The decision becomes final 35 days after issuance of notice of a decision. (Sec. 1-70, Illinois Independent Tax Tribunal Act of 2012)

Both the taxpayer and the DOR are entitled to seek judicial review of the tribunal's final decision. (Sec. 1-70, Illinois Independent Tax Tribunal Act of 2012) Taxpayers can represent themselves or have an attorney represent them. (Sec. 1-80, Illinois Independent Tax Tribunal Act of 2012) All information received by the tribunal as a result of a hearing or investigation shall be public except for tax returns and information received either under seal or in relation to any mediation proceedings. (Sec. 1-85, Illinois Independent Tax Tribunal Act of 2012)

[¶89-236] Judicial Appeals and Remedies

Various judicial remedies are available for disputing a tax liability. Taxpayers can either seek direct judicial review by paying the tax under protest or pursue an administrative remedy. However, a taxpayer must elect a remedy and may not pursue both the payment under protest procedure and administrative review.

• *Protest Monies Act*

The Protest Monies Act allows a taxpayer to seek a judicial determination of a disputed tax liability without exhausting administrative remedies. The disputed tax is paid under protest into the protest fund of the state of Illinois. The taxpayer then has 30 days from the date of protest within which to file a complaint and obtain a temporary restraining order or preliminary injunction against the transfer of the protested payment to the appropriate state fund. (Code of Civil Procedure, Sec. 3-102 [735 ILCS 5/3-102])

A taxpayer electing the payment under protest procedure rather than the administrative appeals process has the advantage of a remedy available for all taxes in dispute, an alternative to Departmental hearings, and the review court is not limited to the record made in the administrative review proceedings or to the Department decisions. The review court may try all issues and make an independent factual determination. Moreover, the applicable standard for judicial review is a preponderance of the evidence.

Authorized payments from the protest fund bear interest at the rate of 6% per year from the date of deposit into the fund to the date of disbursement. (State Officers and Employees Money Disposition Act, Sec. 2a [30 ILCS 230/2a])

• *Administrative Review Law*

The Administrative Review Law (ARL) provides the statutory procedure for judicial review of the final decisions of Illinois administrative agencies. The ARL applies only to such final decisions. Rules, regulations, standards, and statements of policy are not administrative decisions. (Code of Civil Procedure, Sec. 3-102 [735 ILCS 5/3-102])

The ARL has been adopted in most of the revenue acts for which the Illinois Department of Revenue is the administrative agency. The ARL has been expressly adopted in the Illinois Income Tax Act, Retailers' Occupation Tax Act, Property Tax Code, Cigarette Use Tax Act, Gas Revenue Act, Water Company Invested Capital Tax Act, Public Utilities Revenue Act, Cigarette Tax Act, Liquor Control Act of 1934, Telecommunications Excise Tax Act, Coin-Operated Amusements Device Tax Act, and Lottery Act. (Illinois Income Tax Act, Sec. 1201 [35 ILCS 5/1201])

The following tax acts have incorporated Section 12 of the Retailers' Occupation Tax Act that expressly adopts the provisions of the ARL: Use Tax Act, Service Use Tax Act, Service Occupation Tax Act, Water Commission Act of 1985, Automobile Renting Occupation and Use Tax Act, Motor Fuel Tax Law, and Hotel Operators Occupation Tax Act.

Proceedings are commenced with the filing of a complaint and issuance of a summons within 35 days from the date that a copy of the decision sought to be reviewed was served upon the taxpayer. Service occurs at the time of personal service or on deposit of the decision in the U.S. mail in an envelope with postage prepaid. Filing suit is barred if a complaint is not filed within the 35-day period. The taxpayer must seek review under the ARL as a prerequisite to filing suit. (Code of Civil Procedure, Sec. 3-103 [735 ILCS 5/3-103])

Circuit courts have jurisdiction to review final administrative decisions. (Code of Civil Procedure, Sec. 3-104 [735 ILCS 5/3-104])

• *Judicial review*

Judicial review of a final administrative decision is confined to the record of the proceedings before the Illinois Department of Revenue. The findings and conclusions of the agency on questions of fact are *prima facie* true and correct. Findings will not be overturned unless they are contrary to the manifest weight of the evidence. A finding is against the manifest weight of the evidence only where an opposite conclusion is clearly evident. (Code of Civil Procedure, Sec. 3-110 [735 ILCS 5/3-110])

Circuit courts.—Circuit courts have jurisdiction to review final administrative decisions. The proper venue for suit is generally prescribed in the individual tax acts. However, in the absence of a venue provision, suit is filed in the circuit court of any county where the administrative hearing was held, any part of the subject matter involved is situated, or any part of the transaction that gave rise to the proceedings occurred. (Code of Civil Procedure, Sec. 3-104 [735 ILCS 5/3-104]) Direct review to the Illinois appellate court is provided for certain administrative actions. (Code of Civil Procedure, Sec. 3-113 [735 ILCS 5/3-113])

The circuit court is given power to affirm or reverse the final decision in whole or in part, or to remand the case for the taking of additional evidence. (Code of Civil Procedure, Sec. 3-111 [735 ILCS 5/3-111]) Appeal from a circuit court decision in administrative review actions is filed in the same manner as other civil cases. (Code of Civil Procedure, Sec. 3-112 [735 ILCS 5/3-112]) (Ill. Const. Art. VI, Sec. 9)

Appellate court.—Circuit court decisions are subject to review in the same manner as other civil cases. Also, administrative decisions can be filed directly to the appellate court as provided by law. (Code of Civil Procedure, Sec. 3-113 [735 ILCS 5/3-113]; Ill. Const., Art. VI, Sec. 6)

Supreme court.—Appellate court decisions are subject to review by the Supreme Court. (Ill. Const., Art. VI, Sec. 4)

• *Injunctions*

In cases challenging the validity of a tax assessment, the judicial remedies of injunction, mandamus, and certiorari are generally unavailable to taxpayers on the basis of the existence of an adequate legal remedy. An action for declaratory relief is generally denied because the statutory remedy of the payment under protest procedure is available.

Injunctive relief against the collection of property taxes is granted only when the tax is unauthorized by law or when the tax is levied on exempt property. Taxpayers must allege in complaints for injunctive relief a basis for equitable jurisdiction, such as fraudulently excessive assessment, and that an adequate remedy at law is not available. There is no requirement that taxes be paid in full before a suit for injunctive relief is instituted.

Mandamus is the remedy to compel a board of review to act and to review a claimed fraudulent assessment, or to assess omitted property.

A writ of certiorari may not be issued when another adequate legal remedy is available. Certiorari is considered necessary upon a showing that an administrative board has exceeded its jurisdiction or proceeded illegally.

• *Federal court actions*

An assessment may be appealed to a federal court if there is a question involving the U.S. Constitution or a federal statute. However, the right to bring a federal suit is limited by the Tax Injunction Act and the fundamental principle of comity. The Tax Injunction Act prohibits injunctions in federal district courts against the assessment, levy, or collection of any state tax when there is a "plain, speedy, and efficient remedy" in state courts. (28 U.S.C. Sec. 1341, 90-068) Because this federal provision has been the subject of considerable litigation, the case law interpreting this provision should be researched if a federal action is contemplated.

In addition, any appeal of a state tax case to a federal court would be subject to established principles of federal jurisdiction and abstention. Federal constitutional provisions are discussed at ¶ 89-052.

[¶ 89-238] Representation of Taxpayer

At hearings and pre-trial conferences before the Department of Revenue, a taxpayer may represent himself or be represented by a licensed attorney. (86 Ill. Adm. Code Sec. 200.110) However, a taxpayer may be represented by an accountant or any other person of his choice at an informal review conference or before the Informal Conference Board. (¶ 89-230) A Power of Attorney (Form IL-2848) must be filed for all non-attorney representatives. (86 Ill. Adm. Code Sec. 200.135; 86 Ill. Adm. Code Sec. 215.110)

[¶ 89-240] Limitations Period for Appeals

For taxpayers seeking review of a tax liability after a notice of deficiency has been issued, the taxpayer must file a written protest and request for a hearing with the Department of Revenue within 60 days after the issuance of the deficiency notice. (Illinois Income Tax Act, Sec. 908(a) [35 ILCS 5/908(a)])

• *Refund claims*

Credit or refund claims must be filed with the Department of Revenue within three years after the date the return was filed, estimated tax payments were paid or tax was withheld, or within one year of the date the tax was paid, whichever is later. (Illinois Income Tax Act, Sec. 911(a) [35 ILCS 5/911(a)])

TOPICAL INDEX

➤➤➤ References are to paragraph (¶) numbers.